Critical acclaim for Kenneth S. Lynn and Hemingway

"Kenneth S. Lynn has much to tell us that is new, provocative, and convincing. His *Hemingway* is . . . an excursion into territory that . . . has never before been examined with such care and insight. . . . A sad story and in many respects a peculiarly American one; he tells it with empathy and compassion, and with great admiration."

Jonathan Yardley
The Washington Post Book World

"Magnificent. . . . Kenneth S. Lynn's biography . . . never denies the ultimate heroism by which Hemingway survived his own debilitating inner conflicts. He never denigrates his genius. He has far too high a respect for the fine fiction that such heroism elicited . . . [An] accomplished, revealing and, all in all, profoundly sympathetic biography."

Times Literary Supplement

"*Hemingway* sets the standard for the art of biography, and if there is to be only one Hemingway biography, Kenneth Lynn's is the unconditional choice."

Seattle Post-Intelligencer

"Kenneth Lynn's *Hemingway* is definitely not just another biography of Papa. Rather, it is a radical interpretation of Hemingway's personal life, public persona, and fiction that breaks new ground on virtually every page. . . . Lynn's rich book is surely one of the major American biographies—and don't be surprised when it wins every award in sight."

Dallas Morning News

"Surely the best biography of Hemingway ever written. Kenneth S. Lynn strips away the false legends that have, for almost half a century, obscured an accurate assessment of Hemingway the artist apart from Hemingway the man. In this powerful psychoanalytical portrait of the greatest American stylist, Lynn not only breaks new ground, but also cultivates that which has been covered before with more insight than any other Hemingway biographer. . . . Lynn's treatise sheds a whole new light on Hemingway's life."

Milwaukee Journal

ALSO BY KENNETH S. LYNN

The Dream of Success
Mark Twain and Southwestern Humor
William Dean Howells: An American Life
Visions of America
A Divided People
The Air-Line to Seattle

HEMINGWAY

BY
KENNETH S. LYNN

FAWCETT COLUMBINE • *New York*

A Fawcett Columbine Book
Published by Ballantine Books
Copyright © 1987 by Kenneth S. Lynn

We have made every effort to trace the ownership of all copyrighted material and to secure permission from copyright holders when required. In the event of any question arising as to the use of any material, we will be pleased to make the necessary corrections in future printings. Thanks are due to the following authors, publishers, photographers, publications, and agents for permission to use the material indicated.

Ezra Pound, "In a Station of the Metro." Quoted from Ezra Pound, *Personae*. Copyright 1926 by Ezra Pound. Reprinted by permission of New Directions Publishing Company.

Ernest Hemingway, "D'Annunzio," "Flat Roofs," "Killed Piave," "Bird of Night" and the first twenty-nine lines of "To a Tragic Poetess." From *88 Poems* by Ernest Hemingway, copyright © 1979 by The Ernest Hemingway Foundation and Nicolas Gerogiannis. Reprinted by permission of Harcourt Brace Jovanovich, Inc.

Letter from Maxwell Perkins to Ernest Hemingway, May 24, 1929. Published with permission of Princeton University Library.

Carlos Baker, letters to Edmund Wilson, November 11, 1923, and to Chard Powers Smith, January 21, 1927, from *Ernest Hemingway: Selected Letters 1917–1961*. Copyright © 1981 by The Ernest Hemingway Foundation Inc. and Carlos Baker. Reprinted with the permission of Charles Scribner's Sons.

Photograph of Ernest Hemingway handling a gun, Teruel, Spain, December 1937, © Robert Capa, courtesy of Magnum Photos, Inc.

Photograph of Ernest Hemingway, Martha Gellhorn, and Hemingway's three sons, Fall 1941, © Robert Capa, courtesy of Magnum Photos, Inc.

Photograph of Ernest Hemingway and his son Gregory, Fall 1941, © Robert Capa, courtesy of Magnum Photos, Inc.

Lloyd R. Arnold photo of Ernest Hemingway at work on *For Whom the Bell Tolls*, December 1939, courtesy of Tillie Arnold.

Lloyd R. Arnold photo of Ernest Hemingway and his wife Mary and Gary Cooper and his wife, November 1946, courtesy of Tillie Arnold.

Cano y Guerra photo of Ernest Hemingway in Spain, Summer 1959, courtesy of Francisco Cano.

Cover photograph of Ernest Hemingway, Ketchum, Idaho, Winter 1959, © John Bryson, courtesy of John Bryson.

Photograph of Ernest Hemingway standing at his writing desk, Ketchum, Idaho, Winter 1959, © John Bryson, courtesy of John Bryson.

Library of Congress Catalog Card Number: 87-91395

ISBN: 0-449-90308-7

This edition published by arrangement with Simon and Schuster.

Cover design by Richard Aquan

Cover photo by John Bryson

Manufactured in the United States of America

First Ballantine Books Edition: June 1988

10 9 8 7 6 5 4 3 2 1

AGAIN, FOR VALERIE

"...that great and unhappy man, whom I both admire and pity..."
(Gibbon on Rousseau)

CONTENTS

PART FIVE: 1936–1945

PART SIX: 1945–1961

PREFACE

ACROSS MORE THAN HALF A CENTURY, the life and work of Ernest Hemingway have been at the center of a critical controversy. For that, Hemingway himself was largely responsible. From the moment he embarked upon his career as a writer, he presented himself to the world as a man's man, and in both his published work and his very public behavior he established a heroic image of himself as an athlete and sportsman, a worldly-wise reporter, a battle-scarred soldier, an aficionado of the Spanish bullfight, and a hard-drinking bon vivant. As his fame grew, his self-dramatizations hardened into myth, for he had tapped into the twentieth century's enormous nostalgia for the manly virtues of earlier times, as defined in America by the pathfinders of Fenimore Cooper, the foretopmen of Herman Melville and the cowboys extolled by Theodore Roosevelt, Owen Wister, and Frederic Remington. So powerful did the Hemingway myth become that his many admiring reviewers were beguiled into the belief that his work could not be understood other than in terms of a correspondence to a supremely masculine life.

Hemingway's debunkers took precisely the opposite view. In the midtwenties a scornful Zelda Fitzgerald informed her husband that his manly friend Ernest was a phony. A decade later, Gertrude Stein and Max Eastman put similar charges into print, and in the wake of these much-talked-about assaults, other critics were emboldened to ridicule what they regarded as his masculine pretensions and to use them as a weapon with which to bludgeon his art. His work was shallow and without genuine feeling. He had no sympathy for women, they said, portraying them either as manhood-destroying bitches or as mere objects of sexual domination, while exalting stoicism and bravery in his heroes in an attempt to prove something about himself that was not true.

In the years since his suicide in 1961, the disagreement over the significance of his life has continued with remarkably little change. Thus, the keepers of the cult of his masculinity have mostly argued that the decision to kill himself was an act of courage, given the irredeemable breakdown in his capacity to write. For the cruelest of his debunkers, by contrast, it constituted the ultimate proof that he had always lived a lie. Such extreme perceptions diminished the stature of his achievement, even in the eyes of some of his idolators. Yet few readers thought to look beyond their prejudices in search of truths that might transcend the controversy.

That search became all the more urgent with the publication, in the spring of 1986, of an abbreviated version of a manuscript on which Hemingway had worked for many years but had never finished. For the transsexual fantasies that inform *The Garden of Eden* have compelled reluctant recognition of the possibility that he was not the writer, or the man, he was thought to be, and that he has been misread and misinterpreted by enthusiasts and detractors alike. Cautious reviewers suggested that the book exposed a new sensibility in the author. In fact, that sensibility had been there all along. From the very first, his best work was infused by more sensitive and complicated feelings about himself and the world than the stereotypes of Hemingway criticism have ever allowed.

In a letter to Scott Fitzgerald in 1934 in which he appeared to be counseling a troubled friend but was actually talking of himself as well, he wrote, "We are all bitched from the start and you especially have to be hurt like hell before you can write seriously. But when you get the damned hurt use it—don't cheat with it. Be as faithful to it as a scientist." Hemingway's hurt began in childhood and expanded until his death like ripples from a hand trailed in a sylvan lake. Uncertain to the point of fear about himself, he was compelled to write stories in which he endeavored to cope with the disorder of his inner world by creating fictional equivalents for it. Perhaps to an extent greater than any of his contemporaries save Thomas Wolfe, he habitually re-created his life through his art, not in unrestrained confessional floods, as Wolfe did, but in the unique stylistic shorthand of his own invention and in the guarded manner of one who, in spite of limited self-understanding, sought to explore, to express, and to find some measure of resolution of agonizing personal conflicts. As he himself said, he wanted to make people feel more than they understood—and yet he also knew that the day would come when his cunningly wrought fiction would be read quite differently than it had been in his lifetime. "Things may not be immediately discernible in what a man writes," he informed the Swedish Academy in 1954 after learning that he had been awarded the Nobel Prize for literature, "and in this sometimes he is fortunate; but eventually they are quite clear and by these and the degree of alchemy that he possesses he will endure or be forgotten."

Things may also not be immediately discernible in what a man does. If a reconsideration of Hemingway's work can be richly rewarding, so a reconsideration of his life can show that while his faults were terrible he was also a more truly heroic figure than even the gaudiest version of his myth would grant him. "If people bring so much courage to this world," he declared through Frederic Henry in *A Farewell to Arms,* "the world has to kill them to break them, so of course it kills them. The world breaks every one and afterward many are strong at the broken places. But those that will not break it kills. It kills the very good and the very gentle and the very brave impartially. If you are none of these you can be sure it will kill you too but there will be no special hurry." A fragment of that passage might serve as the author's own epitaph: "Strong at the broken places." For Ernest Hemingway was a conflicted, haunted man who produced from his torment some of the most memorable fiction of the century.

PART ONE

1899–1919

CHAPTER ONE

"I Had a Wonderful Novel to Write About Oak Park"

SITUATED ONLY NINE MILES WEST OF THE LOOP, suburban Oak Park, Illinois, was connected to the heart of Chicago in the early years of the twentieth century by two public transportation lines, the Chicago and North Western Railroad and the Lake Street elevated. Dr. Clarence Edmonds Hemingway, known to his friends as Ed, was not a man who much cared for cities, but twice a year he liked to take his children to see the Ringling Brothers Circus at the Coliseum, and on weekends he sometimes escorted them to the Field Museum of Natural History, housed in the former Fine Arts building of the World's Columbian Exposition of 1893. Having pushed their way past the templelike building's heavy bronze doors, the children usually paused in awe at the sight of the two elephants in fighting position beneath the dome of the rotunda before scurrying off to examine the exhibits of mastodon bones and other wonders. By the time he was ten, Ernest Hemingway's favorite room was the Hall of African Mammals, with its family groupings in natural settings of cheetahs, lions, warthogs, wildebeests, rhinos, buffaloes, greater kudus, and spotted hyenas. In the soft light of exhibition cases, the animals' glass eyes glistened, making it easy for the young Ernest to imagine—especially when he was wearing a khaki outfit just like the ex-President's—that these creatures were alive and that he was Theodore Roosevelt on safari.

More frequently, the children rode into town with their mother. Over the years, she shepherded all six of them up the grand staircase of the Art Institute, where she held an annual membership in the family's name, to inspect the notable collection of Dutch masters, El Greco's "Assumption of the Virgin"—acquired in 1906 for a controversially high price—and whatever traveling exhibition the Institute was showing at the moment, although it is doubtful that she herself bestowed more than a passing glance upon Marcel Duchamp's "Nude Descending a Staircase" and the other precedent-shattering paintings from the New York Armory Show of 1913. On other occasions, she bought them tickets to concerts at Orchestra Hall by Frederick Stock and the Chicago Symphony, or to performances of grand opera at the huge, elliptically arched Auditorium that Louis Sullivan had designed. For high culture in Chicago was undergoing a remarkable expansion in these years, and in the realms of music and art Grace Hall Hemingway (or Hall-Hemingway, as she sometimes signed her name) was determined to keep her brood abreast of it.

Her ambitions for her children were further served by Oak Park. In addition to its excellent public schools, the hometown of the Hemingways boasted an art center, an opera house, two playhouses, a symphony orchestra, a splendid library, and several extraordinarily good church choirs. Grace took pride in all of these institutions, especially in one of the choirs, which for several years she directed. The community's chief claim to cultural distinction, however, derived from a group of architects whose work she disliked almost as much as she did cubist art and the music of Arnold Schönberg.

2

THE men and women who settled in the tiny village of Oak Park in the two decades following the devastating Chicago fire of 1871 had favored dwellings of historic European design. Typical of their architecturally familiar houses were two that diagonally faced one another on North Oak Park Avenue, the turreted three-story home of the Hemingway children's maternal grandparents, Ernest and Caroline Hall, and the large white clapboard residence of the children's paternal grandparents, Anson and Adelaide Hemingway. So traditional was Oak Park's appearance in this period that when Frank Lloyd Wright and his eighteen-year-old bride arrived in the village in 1889 even he did not choose to build as unconventional a house for himself as he might have.

Until he fled to Europe twenty years later with a prominent local matron, Mamah Borthwick Cheney, Wright continued to live and work in Oak Park, for reasons he found increasingly compelling.

Not only was the community growing in population—in 1902, the number of inhabitants would reach ten thousand, almost three times what it had been fifteen years earlier—but it was changing in character, largely because of the intellectually broader-gauge citizens just coming of age or just moving in.

Wright's male clients in Oak Park were by and large college graduates, no matter whether they were business executives or professional men, while most of his female clients played vigorous roles in community affairs. As home builders, these men and women were anxious to break free of inherited taste, and Wright and his colleagues in the so-called Prairie School of architecture showed them how to do so. For by reducing structural masses and shapes to essential forms—cubes, squares, flat surfaces, straight lines—and by drastically cutting back on the ornamentation of which the Victorian era had been so fond, these men had created a new aesthetic. In time, their work would lead to the revolutionary house designs with which Mies van der Rohe would startle the twenties.

Of all the Prairie School buildings put up in Oak Park between Ernest Hemingway's birth there in 1899 and his departure for a newspaper job in Kansas City in 1917, the ones he was most intimately acquainted with were the house that John S. Bergen did for his uncle, George R. Hemingway, whose habitually sarcastic way of talking would be later recorded in the story called "Indian Camp," and the high school that Robert C. Spencer and Eben E. Roberts designed in 1905, eight years before Ernest entered it as a freshman. The low hipped roof of the George Hemingway house was exactly what Wright had in mind when he called for homes with quiet skylines, while the horizontal courses of brick and stone on the exterior walls of Oak Park and River Forest High School were a persuasive illustration of the Prairie School thesis that horizontal accents symbolized democracy.

The thinking of Wright and his colleagues was distinctly not evident, however, in the home built by Ed and Grace Hemingway. In 1896, the Hemingways had begun their married life in Grace's father's rambling Victorian residence on North Oak Park Avenue. Ever since the death of his wife, Ernest Hall had been exceedingly lonely, so it made sense for his daughter and son-in-law to live with him. But nine years and four grandchildren later, the old man died of Bright's disease, leaving the property to Grace and her brother Leicester. Grace immediately announced that she wanted to sell it and use her half of the proceeds to help finance the construction of a much more capacious abode. Eight bedrooms, a set of medical offices for her husband, and a huge music room for herself were among the features she had in mind. To Ed, her plans sounded alarmingly costly, but Grace rode right over his objections. She had been waiting a long time for her dream house—that was all she cared to think about. While she finally had to call in an architect named Henry George Fiedelke to help her with the blueprints, the oblong-shaped, gray-stucco house that rose on the corner of North Kenilworth Avenue and Iowa Street between the fall of 1905 and the summer of 1906 was very much her work.

From the point of view of the physical needs of a growing and highly active family, the plan of the house was appropriate. Yet the house was also a monument to Grace's ego, not only because the music room was its most expensive feature, but because it asserted a claim—which the results belied—that among her many talents was a sense of good design. The clump of high-standing dormer windows and the badly positioned bay window below were only two of the exterior features which might have caused Frank Lloyd Wright to wince whenever he passed the house, en route to inspecting the residence he himself was building on the opposite side of the street—and if he had ever been invited inside, he would surely not have been at all happy with the odd-shaped floor plan and the variety of decorative "touches" in the principal rooms. The chaste formulas of the Prairie School were simply too subdued for Grace's taste.

The question arises as to whether the achievements of Oak Park's architectural masters meant as little to her gifted son. His pronouncement in *Death in the Afternoon* that "Prose is architecture, not interior decoration, and the Baroque is over," and his recollection in *A Moveable Feast* regarding his early days in Paris that "If I started to write elaborately, I found that I could cut that scrollwork or ornament out and throw it away," are built around metaphors that prompt a more pointed question. The power of rudimentary forms, the fine bare effects that the simplest sentences can achieve—these were conclusions about the art of writing that Hemingway is alleged to have reached via the tutelage of Sherwood Anderson, Gertrude Stein, and Ezra Pound. Was it in fact the Prairie School of architecture which first taught him to see beauty in stripped-down expression?

Apparently, it did not. There is no evidence from his boyhood of his having taken an interest in the Prairie School's ideas, and in later years he never once reminisced with an interviewer about the dramatic alterations in Oak Park's appearance which had taken place when he was growing up there, or about Wright's highly colorful presence in the community. But what makes his silence problematic is his history of reluctance about saying anything complimentary concerning the quality of life in his old hometown.

3

WHETHER or not Hemingway ever said that Oak Park was full of "wide lawns and narrow minds," the wisecrack defined his position. For forty years, he insisted that he had always hated the place and that he had more than once run away from it. The task of convincing the world that the town was just another version of George F. Babbitt's conformitarian Floral Heights was made considerably easier for him by the very availability of such disparaging comparisons. For among the commentators who dominated the discussion of American culture during Hemingway's lifetime, it was more or less taken for granted that suburbia was suffocating. This judgment was a distortion of the truth on the part of the commentators and, as applied to Oak Park, a piece of mythmaking on Hemingway's part. Yet to say so is not to deny that the village in which he grew up was in a number of ways a quite restrictive community.

The sale of alcoholic beverages had been forbidden there since the 1870s. Blue laws kept theaters and movie houses closed on Sundays. Not a single black family lived within the village's ample limits before World War I, and effective efforts were made to discourage the influx of Jews. So numerous were its churches—all but one of which were Protestant—that the community was popularly known as "Saints' Rest." In 1899, the voters rejected with horror an invitation from Chicago to merge with the city. Two years later, the voters further insulated themselves from the pluralism of American life by seceding from the township of Cicero, of which the village had long been a part, because Cicero had been overwhelmed by blue-collar Catholic immigrants who saw nothing wrong with saloons. According to Hemingway's high school contemporary, Robert St. John, who would later make a name for himself as a newspaperman, Oak Park also suffered from intramural snootiness; the "aristocratic" northern section looked down on the predominantly middle-income section south of the "el" tracks.

On Sundays, the houses of God in "Saints' Rest" were usually filled, and some of the faithful engaged as well in devotions at home. During the time when the Hemingways were living with Grandfather Hall, for example, the master of the house not only said grace before meals and prayers before bedtime, but presided over a simple religious service six days a week that the entire household, including

the cook in the kitchen and the girl who made the beds, was required
to attend. He would begin the service by reading a lesson from the
Bible, followed by several passages from a book entitled *Daily
Strength for Daily Needs*. Then all the members of the little congre-
gation would sink to their knees on the thick Belgian carpet and
close their eyes—all, that is, except Abba, as the old man was called
by his grandchildren, from the Biblical word for Father. Raising his
white-haired head toward heaven, his deep blue eyes wide open and
a beaming grin on his shining pink face, the everlastingly genial
Abba would speak to God as if he were talking to a friend, albeit the
words he voiced were from the Book of Common Prayer.

Grandfather Hemingway's religious temperament was much
more somber, and for a time at least his devotion to God encom-
passed much more of his life. Whereas Ernest Hall had come back
from the Civil War with the intention of making money in the
wholesale cutlery business, Anson Hemingway resigned his command of black troops in an infantry division with the idea of working full-time for the Lord. Accordingly, he sought and accepted the
secretaryship of the Chicago YMCA. Friendship with the "drive
wheel" of that institution, Dwight Lyman Moody, who would later
move on to a fabulously successful career as an evangelist, was only
one of the many satisfactions that Anson derived from his work.
Yet with every passing year he found it more and more difficult to
support his growing family on the meager salary he was earning.
Finally, in the mid-1870s, he quit his position and opened a real
estate office on La Salle Street. Eventually he was able to build a
spacious home in the northern section of Oak Park, to send all six
of his children to Oberlin College and to cultivate a certain fastidiousness about the way he dressed and conducted himself; Anson's
manicured fingernails, carefully trimmed gray beard and the dainty
way he held his knife and fork symbolized the distance he had traveled since leaving the "Y." Nevertheless, his Christian rectitude remained uncorrupted. Like his friend Moody, Anson believed that
willpower was everything. Hard work was the foundation of the
moral order; social dancing, card playing, gambling, foul language,
liquor, and smutty books were threats to it.

Fortunately for Anson, his wife Adelaide—six years his senior—
fully shared these views, for in spite of his talk about willpower he
was a most deferential man. Agate-eyed Adelaide, on the other
hand, a graduate in botany from Wheaton College in Illinois—
which Anson also attended—was a woman who knew her own
mind as well as the Latin names of flowers. If she was endlessly
patient about teaching her children all her lore about the natural

world and permissive about letting them romp on the lawn in front of their home ("I am not raising grass; I'm raising boys," she said), she did not tolerate behavior she considered sinful.

A generation later, her son Ed sought to impose Puritanical rules upon his own children, and appealed for support to the forceful Christian woman he had married. Grace Hall, however, had had a comparatively pampered childhood. Her mother had excused her from household duties, so that Grace could concentrate on her music lessons, while her doting father, who had built a remunerative business and retired early, enjoyed indulging her with special treats. As a result, Grace was not as strict a disciplinarian as her husband. While she agreed with him about the iniquity of liquor and cigarettes, she saw nothing wrong with card playing or dancing. Card games were fun, in her opinion, and dancing was good exercise. A certain amount of Dr. Hemingway's unhappiness in his marriage derived from his unshakable belief that his wife was in error about these matters.

Although as a child Grace had honored both her father and mother through simultaneous loyalties to his Episcopalianism and her Congregationalism, by the time of her marriage she had decided she was a Congregationalist. Oak Park's First and Third Congregational churches, both of which she and Dr. Hemingway attended at various times, were bastions of religious liberalism, a doctrine which Grace found congenial because of its insistence that everything in this world can be managed and that evil was explainable as that which must exist in order that virtue might have something to strive against and overcome. Dr. William E. Barton, who took over the First Congregational Church in the fall of 1899 just in time to baptize the Hemingways' baby boy, was of the opinion that even death was a good because it excited sober meditations on heavenly rewards. It was of views like this that church historian H. Richard Niebuhr would be thinking three decades later when he said that liberal Protestantism believed that "a God without wrath brought men without sin into a kingdom without judgment through the ministrations of Christ without a Cross." *

Such a faith was an insult to human suffering, as Hemingway's fiction would ultimately demonstrate. There is absolutely no indication, though, that in his youth he rejected the premises of his parents' religion. Despite his retrospective characterization of himself as a rebel and a runaway, he had no record of absenteeism from

---

* In the twenties, Dr. Barton's son, Bruce, would vulgarize his father's liberalism in an astonishingly successful book, *The Man Nobody Knows,* a portrait of Jesus as a supersalesman and rugged he-man.

church. Inasmuch as his father and mother were firmly agreed that he had to attend, perhaps he felt that resisting their wishes would be futile; in which event there is a kind of poignancy—and perhaps an indication of his powers of repression—in his conformity and eagerness to please. But it is equally possible that the sermons to which he was made to listen were a source of comfort to him, and that it was not simply lip service when he called himself, as he often did, a Christian. For, as his later work revealed, his boyhood was haunted by fears of death, for reasons that he could not bring himself to discuss with anyone. Ministers who were full of assurances that enlightened Christians need not be afraid of the specter of oblivion may have helped him to hold his hobgoblins at bay. In any case, he went to church every Sunday of his boyhood without a peep of protest, so far as can be determined, and his deportment while there was a far cry from Tom Sawyer's. A thirteen-year-old boy's high spirits did get the better of him one Sunday morning in the spring of 1913, but that evening he wrote a formal note of apology to his father. ("My conduct at Church this morning was bad. My conduct tomorrow will be good.") Following which there was no repetition of the occurrence.

That his commitment to the faith of his parents was sincere seems even more likely in the light of his membership in the Plymouth League, a young people's organization which met at the First Church around five o'clock on Sunday afternoons. During his tenure as treasurer of the group, Ernest handled the financing of its charitable activities. In addition, he helped run the program committee and was an occasional speaker at early evening religious services. There was a lighter side to the League that also meant a lot to him. Marie Cole Hunter, the director, knew how important it was for boys and girls to have a good time. To that end, she staged outings on the Des Plaines River and put on plays and arranged social get-togethers at the church. In the words of Marcelline Hemingway, who joined the League at the same time her brother did, "the First Congregational Church became our social center."

The only drawback to Plymouth League parties was that Dr. Barton would not allow dancing. Even when it was pointed out to him that the Unitarian Church across the street had no such rule, his opposition remained adamant. On the other hand, Dr. Hemingway finally lifted his private ban on the practice, following several unpleasant exchanges on the subject with Grace. In the course of their freshman year at Oak Park High, Marcelline and Ernest were both permitted to join Miss Belle Ingram's dancing class at the Colonial Club and to attend dances at school as well. Three years later, Grace sealed the triumph of libertarianism by holding a New Year's Eve ball for Marcelline and Ernest in the Hemingway home. Eighty-one invitations were sent out on pale blue stationery, dance programs were handed out at the door, an orchestra played peppy fox-trots and old-fashioned tunes for square dancing, and the table in the dining room was laden with dishes of tempting food. Ernest may very well have liked the food best of all, for his big feet and awkward coordination made him something of a menace on the dance floor. It had rankled him to be forbidden to dance, but he found that he could take it or leave it, once the prohibition was removed.

4

OAK Park's taste in literature can be easily summarized: Britannia ruled. Only a handful of American writers enjoyed full representation in the unusually well-stocked local library, whereas every standard British writer from Shakespeare onward was available in depth. The library was especially weak in the modern American novel, holding nothing by Frank Norris or Theodore Dreiser and not acquiring a copy of Stephen Crane's *The Red Badge of Courage* until 1916.

At Oak Park High School, the required reading in freshman English in 1913–1914, the year Marcelline and Ernest took the course, consisted of Bible stories, old English ballads, Tennyson's *Idylls of the King,* Coleridge's "Rime of the Ancient Mariner" and Sir Walter Scott's *Ivanhoe,* plus Benjamin Franklin's *Autobiography.* In their sophomore, junior, and senior years, Marcelline and Ernest were assigned several Shakespeare plays; Bunyan's *Pilgrim's Progress;* essays by Addison, Macaulay, and Carlyle; George Eliot's *Silas Marner;* Dickens's *David Copperfield;* extensive selections from the poetry of Chaucer, Milton, Pope, Shelley, Keats, Browning, and Matthew Arnold; but no works at all by American authors. Instruction, moreover, took place in surroundings which made the students even more conscious of England. Although from the outside Oak Park High appeared to be a quintessentially American building, classes in English met in the Oxford Room, which had been specially fitted out with large storied casement windows in stained glass, a fretted beamed ceiling, a tile floor, rows of high-backed oaken chairs, brass sconces on the front wall and a huge oaken bench in front of a fireplace big enough for a yule log. Embossed on one side of the fireplace were Chaucer's words, "And gladly wolde he lerne and gladly teche"; on the other side were two Greek words meaning "the best" that the school had taken for its motto.

The ardently Anglophile Hemingway family saw nothing incongruous about the Oxford Room, nor did they have any quarrel with the courses taught in it. Indeed, as the daughter of parents who had both been born in England, Grace was forever looking for ways to emphasize her heritage. Thus, she named the family's summer cottage in northern Michigan after England's Lake Windermere (eventually the cottage's name was corrupted to Windemere), and she filled the book shelves in their Oak Park home with editions of British authors—Shakespeare, Scott, Dickens, Thackeray, and Stevenson. Marcelline and Ernest, compulsive readers both, went through most of these sets by the time they were out of grammar school. And as an adolescent Ernest and his best friend, Bill Smith, whom he saw every summer in Michigan, loved to talk about modern British fiction. That Ernest was not totally unfamiliar with American literature is evident from the mannerisms of Jack London and O. Henry which crept into the short stories he wrote during his high school years. He also valued Mark Twain's *Huckleberry Finn,* Theodore Roosevelt's *African Game Trails,* and Owen Wister's *The Virginian,* whose cowboy hero had a code of honor which Wister traced back to the chivalric ideals of medieval England. Out of curiosity about a local resident, the boy may have familiarized himself with Edgar Rice Burroughs's novels as well, for the author of *Tarzan of the Apes* (first published in a magazine in 1912) had moved his family to Oak Park in 1914 and wrote several sequels there. For the most part, though, American literature remained terra incognita to Ernest until he was a grown man.

His orientation toward the literature his teachers preferred was emblematic of his larger acceptance of the values of Oak Park High. Its standards of excellence were his, and—eternal competitor that he was—he worked hard to measure up to them. Besides maintaining a grade average of 90, he played cello in the school orchestra, sang in the glee club, belonged to both the boys' debating society and the boys' rifle club, managed the track team for a time and captained the water-polo squad, played in the line on the lightweight football team in his junior year and made the varsity squad—a so-so varsity squad —as a second-string guard in his senior year, earned another varsity letter as a swimmer, contributed short stories to the literary magazine, and reported on athletic and musical events for the school newspaper, in addition to writing a Ring Lardneresque column for it.

While some teachers bored him, he was very fond of Fannie Biggs, a tolerable slim old maid with goggles on, as Huck Finn said of Miss Watson, but who was beautiful when she smiled, so Marcelline remembered. Miss Biggs's courses in the short story and in journalism meant more to Ernest than any others. The salty-tongued Margaret Dixon, who taught senior English, was another teacher whom he respected, and like every other football player in the school, he stood in awe of the varsity coach, Bob Zuppke, whose genius for devising deceptive offenses would soon earn him a call to the University of Illinois, where he would become famous as the mentor of Red Grange.

Among the roughly nine hundred students enrolled at Oak Park High at the time of Ernest's graduation in the spring of 1917, there may well have been some scoffers, but he was not one of them. The well-received speech he gave on Class Day and his serious demeanor at the commencement exercises both bespoke his keen sense of identification with the school. So did the invitation he received the following week from Lloyd E. Harter, the head of the Boys' Department at the First Congregational Church, to speak to an audience of younger boys in regard to the "deeper things" in his high school experience. Although the record of Ernest's remarks at the church has not survived, the significance of his appearance there is clear. If "Huck Hemingstein," as he sometimes called himself, had really been in revolt against being "sivilized" in school, Mr. Harter would have asked someone else to speak.

5

A certain number of Oak Parkers were committed to a conservative, "stand-pat" Republicanism. But a brand of Republican politics that linked old visions with new was far more widely endorsed.

To citizens like Grace and Ed Hemingway, both of whom were proudly conscious of their fathers' war records, it still mattered that it was the GOP that had preserved the Union, and their equation of Republicanism with Americanism acquired new meaning for them when the rough-riding hero of the Spanish-American War succeeded to the Presidency. But while Theodore Roosevelt took his models for the American character from the American past and reaffirmed the importance of manly courage, personal honor, patriotic duty, and other traditional virtues, he also enunciated a Progressive faith that society could not remain strong without the aid of up-to-date intelligence. Progressivism's watchword was expertise, and not unnaturally it attracted experts to it: scientists, engineers, business managers, lawyers, authors, editors—the very kinds of people, in sum, who were the Hemingways' neighbors.

Having reached the White House on a fluke (i.e., the assassin's bullet that struck down President McKinley), T. R. called on the electorate in 1904 to keep him in office, and Oak Park backed him overwhelmingly. When, as ex-President, he came to town in December 1910, lusty young men carried him from the train station through streets packed with cheering admirers, two of whom were white-haired Anson Hemingway—who had never knowingly broken bread with a Democrat—and his eleven-year-old grandson Ernest, who was wearing his Rooseveltian khaki suit for the occasion. And in his run for the Presidency in 1912 on the "Bull Moose" ticket, T. R. again swept Oak Park.

But it wasn't merely a Roosevelt-madness that attested to the town's Progressivism. When Jane Addams came out from Hull House in 1907 to give a series of lectures on such topics as the need for industrial education and the relationship of philanthropy to civic betterment, she spoke to audiences that packed the hall every time. The same year, Oak Park played host to the Illinois Equal Suffrage convention. Two years later, a vigorous campaign was waged by the public-spirited members of the Nineteenth Century Club and other activist women in town to put a member of their sex on the school board. To rally support for women's suffrage on the local and state levels, Oak Parkers of both sexes petitioned the Illinois legislature in Springfield, gave speeches up and down the state, staged fund-raising dinners, and marched in parades. Eight years before female America had its right to vote guaranteed by the Nineteenth Amendment to the U.S. Constitution, the women of Oak Park voted for the first time on local issues. And in the pages of *Oak Leaves,* the local newspaper, a minuscule number of local matrons—three, to be precise—were actually referred to by their own names, rather than their husbands': the suffragist leader Dr. Anna Blount, the Chautauqua lecturer Belle Watson-Melville, and the well-known voice teacher Grace Hall Hemingway.

6

POSSESSED, in the poet Allen Tate's words, of "a mind of great subtlety and enormous powers of selective observation," Hemingway conceivably could have written a novel-length account of his Oak Park boyhood that would have done justice to the town's complexities and contradictions. He tried once and failed. "I had a wonderful novel to write about Oak Park and would never do it because I did not want to hurt liveing [sic] people," he explained in 1952 to a young literary scholar from Yale, Charles Fenton. The explanation was patently false. His fiction had hurt a lot of living people; in some of his early stories, indeed, he had not only portrayed living people to the life, but had identified them by their real names. If he abandoned the idea of writing a novel about his early years in Oak Park, if he largely avoided the community in his short fiction as well, disguising it as a town in Oklahoma in one story and taking flashback glances at it in a couple of others from standpoints far removed, it was because the scene was too hot for him to handle at length, for reasons having to do with the way he had been brought up.

Thanks to the manipulations of his mother, Hemingway did not enjoy a normal childhood. Yet in later years he never mentioned the circumstances of his upbringing to anyone. And whenever he heard that scholars were becoming interested in his formative years, he reacted with alarm. No sooner did Charles Fenton, for instance, inform him of his intention to include a chapter on Oak Park in a book on "the apprenticeship of Ernest Hemingway" than the novelist called on him to "cease and desist." In an irritated tone of voice which failed to conceal an underlying nervousness, he told Fenton that "if I had written about Oak Park you would have a point in studying it. But I did not write about it." On other occasions with other scholars, he announced that he wanted no biography written about him until a hundred years after he was dead, and he left explicit instructions with the executors of his estate that "none of the letters written by me during my lifetime shall be published."

Anyone who was close to him was aware, of course, of his veritable obsession with his mother. "From my earliest days with EH," Hemingway's World War II comrade-in-arms, Major General Charles T. Lanham, has written, "he always referred to his mother as 'that bitch.' He must have told me a thousand times how much he hated her and in how many ways." How much and in how many ways, but except for accusing her of having hounded his father into his grave he never came close to saying why.

~ _____

CHAPTER TWO

A Peculiar Idea

ED HEMINGWAY AND GRACE HALL first met in adolescence. Not long after the Halls settled into their new house across the street from the Hemingways, fifteen-year-old Ed noticed that there were two children in the family, a girl of about his age and a younger boy. The girl was especially noticeable. Five feet eight inches tall and sexually mature, Grace was already endowed with the generous bosom of the diva she hoped to become. Pale blue eyes, fair English skin, rosy cheeks, lovely slim arms, and gleaming masses of chestnut-colored hair completed her eye-catching appearance.

For all her womanliness, Grace was a tomboy. In the Chicago neighborhood where the Halls lived before moving to Oak Park, she was known as the girl who could ride a bicycle. The bike in question belonged to her brother Leicester, and like most such vehicles in the 1880s it had a high front wheel, a small rear wheel and a propensity to tip over. Because of the possibility of physical injury, bike riding was considered inadvisable for the weaker sex. Nevertheless, Grace took Leicester's proudest possession away from him one day and appropriated a pair of his pants as well. As she cycled up the street she looked at first glance rather like a boy. A shopkeeper did a double take, then yelled to a customer, "Come quick and look! It's a *girl* on a bicycle!"

Leicester was two years younger than Grace and a much better student. At Oak Park High School, he did well in all his courses, especially foreign languages, while she barely passed in Latin and science. Following his graduation from Amherst College, Leicester studied law and eventually moved to California, where he became known for his anti-discrimination suits on behalf of Japanese-American and American Indian clients and for his scholarly grasp of ancient Greek. Grace always enjoyed visiting him in his home on the Coast and when she finally produced a second son at the age of forty-two (a few months shy of sixteen years after the birth of Ernest) she was pleased to name him Leicester. As a child, though, her adoration of her brother was shot through with envy. For the appearance of a new baby in the house inevitably ended her monopoly of her parents' attention, and Grace was the sort of person who always wished to sing solo. Moreover, by the time he was eight or nine Leicester was enjoying a greater freedom of action than had been granted to her simply because he was a boy and she was a girl. Tomboyish Grace found society's definitions of masculinity and femininity intolerable; when she grabbed Leicester's bike, it was with the same determination to discredit inequality that would later lead her into the women's suffrage movement.

Ernest Hall was his daughter's idol. Whenever they were alone together, she loved to quiz him about his family background, which was artistically distinguished, or about his early life, which seemed to her romantic. His English great-grandfather on his mother's side, Edward Miller of Doncaster, had been a composer of music, as well as a proficient organist, and held a doctorate in music from Oxford. Edward's son, William Edward, was one of the more accomplished English violinists of his day and the proud owner of a Stradivarius, thanks to the generosity of an Indian prince. William Edward's daughter, Mary, married Charles Hall, who also made an artistic reputation for himself as a silversmith in Sheffield, where their son Ernest was born in 1840.

During his boyhood, Ernest attended St. Saviour's, an artisans' public school in London, and expected his father to send him to Oxford or Cambridge. But when the invention of electroplating drastically reduced his income, Charles pulled up stakes and settled his family on a farm in Dyersville, Iowa, just west of the Mississippi River port of Dubuque. Embittered by the collapse of his educational dreams, Ernest ran away from home at the age of sixteen. (As a parting expression of his feelings about farm life, he drove a team of his father's horses into a stream and left them to drown—like the baggage mules with broken forelegs in the harbor at Smyrna, about which his namesake would write.) For the next four years, he worked as a common laborer in towns along the lower Mississippi and as a deckhand on riverboats. With the coming of the Civil War, he enlisted in the First Iowa Cavalry. Less than a year later, he was mustered out after a Confederate minié ball became permanently lodged in his left thigh, thereby rendering him incapable of riding a horse.

To all his daughter's questions, Ernest gave forthright answers—except to those concerning his military career, for his wound had been suffered in somewhat ambiguous circumstances. In the words of his "Certificate of Disability for Discharge," he had received it "during his term of service, but not in the regular discharge of his duties; though from an enemy in arms against the authority of the United States." His steadfast refusal to explain this statement gave rise to rumors, first in Iowa and later in Illinois, that he had been a deserter, but his daughter took his silence as a further indication of his gallantry. Her son Ernest would grow up with the reminder ringing in his ears that she had named him for "the finest purest noblest man I have ever known, Ernest Hall." It might seem that only by accumulating more bullet wounds than old Ernest could young Ernest ever hope to surpass him in his mother's estimation.

Yet it was not from her supposedly gallant father that Grace learned to be aggressive about taking charge of things and not letting anyone stand in her way. For these lessons she was indebted to two formidable women, the first of whom was her father's mother, Mary Miller Hall. As Grace herself put it, her grandmother "was a woman of great strength of character" whose role in the lives of her husband and children had been "dominating." Throughout the years that her granddaughter knew her, Grandmother Hall was a widow. Even in her lonely old age, though, she remained, in Grace's words, "strong and able, absolutely without fear." With particular vividness Grace recalled seeing her "duck under a train at the railroad tracks, if it did not move fast enough when she wished to cross. She was always darting in front of, or between vehicles on the city streets. She seemed to lead a charmed life." No wonder that Grace would have the boldness to ride her brother's bicycle! She had seen her grandmother in action.

Grace's second instructor in aggressiveness was her mother. Caroline Hancock was the daughter of a venturesome English sea captain who in the wake of his wife's unexpected death had taken his three small children around Cape Horn in a cargo ship, on the chance that he might be able to rebuild his life as a farmer in Australia. When life down under proved not to Captain Hancock's liking, he moved his family to farm-rich Dyersville, Iowa, where his daughter would fall in love with Ernest Hall. Of all the events in her life which proved that Caroline, too, liked to take chances, the most dramatic occurred in the seventh year of her marriage. On the night of the great Chicago fire, the home of Caroline and Ernest Hall was overwhelmed by the flames. Somehow, they managed to get out alive—at which point Caroline, then one month pregnant with Grace, turned around and reentered the house. As a girl in Dyersville, she had been given a portable organ, called a melodeon, and she had brought it with her to Chicago. With utter scorn for her safety, she located the cherished instrument amidst the smoke and flames and dragged it out.

Headstrong Caroline held the reins of power in her marriage to Ernest Hall. Consequently, the decision that their daughter Grace should endeavor to become an opera singer was in all probability primarily hers. Caroline herself had a nice singing voice, but Grace's, she felt, contained intimations of glory. Voice lessons, piano lessons, and violin lessons were duly arranged for the child while she was still in grammar school. Following her graduation from Oak Park High, Grace did not go on to college, as a number of her female classmates did. Instead, she stayed at home, diligently working up foreign languages despite her low aptitude for them, continuing her voice training, giving singing lessons to high school students, and dreaming of the day when she would make her debut. Grace Ernestine Hall, she decided, would be her operatic name, in tribute to her father and his musical forebears—and possibly also to another contralto, the world-famous Ernestine Schumann-Heink.

Apparently Grace had fully absorbed her mother's ambition—but not without some misgivings. According to the story she later told her children, a siege of scarlet fever at the age of seven left her totally blind. For several months she lived in darkness while her parents agonized. Then one day as she was sitting at her mother's melodeon trying to pick out a tune, her sight miraculously returned, although she found that the congenital weakness of her eyes had worsened and that they had become extremely sensitive to bright light. None of her children would doubt this story. Yet scarlet fever has seldom, if ever, been reported as a cause of blindness. What seems more likely is that she suffered a case of hysterical blindness as a result of the conflicted feelings stemming from the realization that she was expected to study music seriously.

When her mother died of cancer in the fall of 1895, Grace reacted with a burst of careerist zeal. A mere three weeks later, she tore herself away from her grieving father, spurned the plea of her fiancé, Ed Hemingway, that they marry immediately, and instead took a train to New York. A chance had arisen to work with a famous voice coach, Louisa Cappianni, and she was not going to allow

anyone to keep her from seizing it. For the next six months she lived
at the Art Students League and practiced her music night and day.
Late in the winter, Madame Cappianni arranged an audition for
Grace with a representative of the Metropolitan Opera Company.
Her voice so impressed him—or so she later said—that he spoke of
putting her under contract. The next step on the ladder to fame was
to participate in a concert one evening at Madison Square Garden.

The concert was not reviewed in the papers, although Grace
would always maintain that it was and that the reviews furthermore
were favorable. Whatever the truth of the matter, the concert ter-
minated her career. In the glare of the high-powered lights at the
Garden her head had pounded and she could barely see. Whether or
not her pain was rooted in an unconscious wish to fail, the ordeal
she went through was very real, and she could not bring herself to
face another. With stunning suddenness, a dream of operatic star-
dom had ended. That summer, she gradually recovered from her
defeat while traveling in Europe with her father. The following
October, in Oak Park's First Congregational Church, she married
Ed Hemingway.

2

IF Ed had a romantic interest in Grace in high school or during his
years at Oberlin College, he had been too shy to express it. Not
until he entered Rush Medical College in Chicago did he begin to
court her. That his attentions did not displease her is evident from a
letter of 1893 in which she kittenishly asked if he were professionally
qualified to prescribe for affections of the heart. Yet when she also
inquired if he regarded going to the theater as morally wrong, she
showed that she was troubled by his Puritanism.

During her mother's final illness, Grace saw her suitor almost
every day. The Halls' physician, Dr. William Lewis, explained to
Mrs. Hall that inasmuch as Ed Hemingway was in his last year at
Rush Medical and lived but a few steps away, he had asked him to
look in on her. Grace was touched by Ed's efforts to alleviate her
mother's suffering. In the presence of imminent death she grew
closer to him than ever. A six-footer with heavily muscled arms and
legs, a chest like a coffer dam and a nose like a hawk, he was certainly an attractive man—although his weak chin was unfortunate.
Would she consider marrying him, he asked, and she said she would.
Would she please abandon the idea of continuing her studies in New
York, he asked, and she angrily turned away from him. Not until

her career hopes had ended did she finally consent to set a wedding date.

Her consent, however, did not mean that she was reverting to a traditional feminine dependency. No sooner were they back from their honeymoon and settled in her father's house than she plunged full-time into giving voice lessons. By the end of the year she had signed up fifty men and women, whose combined payments to her came to a thousand dollars a month, her daughter Marcelline would later claim.

Getting started professionally turned out to be more difficult for the newly fledged Dr. Hemingway. So few patients came to him during the first year of his marriage that there were some months when he earned no more than fifty or sixty dollars. Once she began having children, Grace sharply curtailed her teaching responsibilities, which she could afford to do because of the modest but steady growth in the size of her husband's obstetrical practice.* But at the outset of their life together she was by a wide margin the principal breadwinner—a state of affairs which may not have come as a complete surprise to her; for the weak chin that Ed would soon cover with a Vandyke beard was a symbol of the weaknesses in his personality. After three years as a student at Oberlin, for instance, he had suddenly faltered in his resolve to finish and did not return for his senior year. And then there was the fact that he rarely won a dispute with Grace. In a way, this easily overwhelmed man was exactly the sort of husband she had wanted; at the same time, she was disappointed in him—endlessly disappointed—and out of this feeling there often flowed, in the course of their many years together, contemptuous acts of reprisal, generally in the form of humiliations. To her family and friends, she pretended to be happily married, but on one occasion at least she let the mask slip a little. In the late twenties, she learned by the grapevine that her famous son and his wife had come to a parting of the ways. Having been the recipient over the years of many a moralistic letter from his mother, Ernest must have expected that her reaction to his divorce would be severely disapproving. Instead, she chose to reveal by indirection the emptiness of her own marriage. "I'm sorry to hear that your marriage has gone on the rocks," she wrote to her son on February 20, 1927, "but most marriages ought to. I hold very modern and heretical views on marriage—but keep them under my hat."

---

* In 1900, Dr. Hemingway earned $2,000. Twenty years later, his annual income had increased to $5,000.

The uncertainty of will that Grace discerned in her husband was apparent to some of their neighbors as well, if only because it was so obvious that he was henpecked. But what Oak Park mainly remembered about Ed Hemingway was his incredible energy. He had so much of it to burn that he literally could not sit still for more than a few minutes at a time—and as his family knew, he did not want anyone else to sit still, either. If he came into a room and saw one of his progeny stretched out reading a book or just thinking, he would immediately ask if the child did not have some studying to do or some chore to perform. Being alone was also difficult for him, for he loved to do something and talk about it at the same time. While he chopped wood in the backyard he wanted an audience, and the same rule applied to his trips to the basement, where he canned fruits and vegetables, molded bullets for his guns and made candles for hunting and fishing trips.

According to Ernest's fictional sketch of his father in the brooding story called "Fathers and Sons," Dr. Hemingway wore suits of underwear that stank of his sweat even after they had been freshly laundered. In any event, the real-life doctor was sweatily on the run from early morning until late at night. Besides seeing patients in his office, making house calls and working in the obstetrical section of a local hospital, he did a great deal of charitable work in surrounding communities, donated his professional services to an Oak Park orphanage and served as the medical examiner for a dairy. In his free time he lectured to boys' clubs about nature, ran a Sunday school class and fussed over his collections of coins, stamps, Indian arrowheads, and Indian moccasins, not to mention his stuffed owl, his stuffed squirrel, his two stuffed chipmunks, and the dead snakes he had collected as a boy and preserved in alcohol. For years, he did the food shopping for his family and frequently the cooking as well. In the course of a house call, one patient remembered, Dr. Hemingway phoned home and told whoever answered that it was time to remove a pie from the oven.

When Marcelline and Ernest began to study biology in school, Dr. Hemingway organized their eighth-grade class into an Agassiz Club, which he led on Saturday morning field trips along the Des Plaines River. No matter how swiftly he walked or how volubly he talked, he always saw more than anyone else—the scarlet tanager or rose-breasted grosbeak nesting in the crotch of a tree, the pinkish lavender buds of wild hepatica peeping out from under fallen leaves, the dead-white "Indian pipes" that were such a rarity. For in addition to possessing an unflagging alertness, Dr. Hemingway was blessed with phenomenal eyesight, as his son affirmed in "Fathers and Sons." Standing with young Nick Adams on the shore of a lake in northern Michigan, Dr. Adams could look across to the shore where the family's summer cottage was located and see that the flag was just being put up or that one of his daughters had walked out to the end of the dock, whereas his son could not see any flagpole or any dock, but only the white of the beach and the curve of the shore. His father, Nick swore, "saw as a big-horn ram, or as an eagle sees, literally."

A marvelous marksman with both shotgun and rifle, an accomplished fisherman, a master of every technique for surviving in a wilderness, Dr. Hemingway was the complete woodsman. As the father of two boys born a decade and a half apart, he might have contented himself with passing on his lore to each of them in turn, but he was far too ebullient a teacher not to impart what he knew to his four girls as well, especially to Marcelline, his first child, and to the tomboyish Madelaine, his fourth, whom everyone called Sunny.

Virtually everything that Dr. Hemingway taught his children to kill he taught them to eat. Besides introducing them to such recognized culinary delights as venison, quail, partridge, dove, duck, turtle meat, frogs' legs, and various kinds of fish, he persuaded them that stewed woodchuck was very similar in taste to stewed chicken and that baked opossum with sweet potatoes around it was delicious. Bushwhacking across country with his youthful companions, he showed them which berries and grasses were edible and which were not. Wild onions, he declared, made a wonderful filling for a sandwich, and when Marcelline and Ernest tentatively sampled some, they discovered he was right.

As Marcelline phrased it, "Daddy could make any walk a pleasure." But as she and her siblings learned the hard way, Dr. Hemingway's high spirits could disappear without warning. "My father's dimpled cheeks and charming smile," said Marcelline, "could change in an instant to the stern, taut mouth and piercing look which was his disciplinary self. Sometimes the change from being gay to being stern was so abrupt that we were not prepared for the shock that came, when one minute Daddy would have his arm around one of us or we would be sitting on his lap, laughing and talking, and a minute or so later—because of something we had said or done, or some neglected duty of ours he suddenly thought about—we would be ordered to our rooms and perhaps made to go without supper. Sometimes we were spanked hard, our bodies across his knee. Always after punishment we were told to kneel down and ask God to forgive us." For serious infractions, she added, he went at them with a razor strop that he kept in his closet. Washing their mouths out with bitter-tasting soap and refusing to speak to them for days at a time were other devices he resorted to for making them pay for their transgressions.

Their mother sometimes spanked them too; there were times when she even used her hairbrush instead of her hand. Nevertheless, her chastisements were not nearly as violent as those administered by her husband, and her anger was controlled, whereas his was explosive. That Dr. Hemingway had been a "strict disciplinarian" was the circular explanation for his appalling outbursts that Marcelline would give in the memoir she published in 1962. Thirty-four years after Dr. Hemingway took his father's ancient Smith & Wesson revolver from a drawer of his desk and fired a bullet into his head, his oldest daughter was still unwilling to talk about the possibility that for as long as she had known him he had been struggling with some form of manic-depressive illness—that his convulsive rages, feverish enthusiasms, and sporadic nervous collapses (which twice required "rest cures") were the contrasting parts of a pattern. He was not at ease with himself, this big, burly doctor, and probably never had been. Certainly throughout his married life he was haunted by feelings of inadequacy, first as a husband and then as a parent. Concealed within his savage reactions to juvenile disobedience lay a stricken awareness of his own failures to measure up. In requiring his chastised children to call on God for forgiveness, he could have been begging for it himself.

3

IN certain photographs of Dr. Hemingway in which he is directly staring into the camera, one can see in his eyes the tense expression that was the sign of his inner torment. We all betrayed him in our various ways, Ernest would remorsefully remark through Nick Adams five years after his father's suicide. In his private thoughts, Dr. Hemingway would probably have put it the other way around. Was it not he, after all, who had betrayed his family by not standing up more strongly for principles he knew were right?

He knew, for instance, that the house Grace designed in 1905 was much too grand for them, given the size of their income and the number of mouths they had to feed, and that in 1919 Grace should not have placed a further financial burden on them by building a small cottage across the lake from their summer place just so that she could get away from the family. Yet instead of insisting that they live more modestly, instead of demanding that they save money systematically so that it would not be too much of a strain for them to send their six children to college, he had allowed his wife to bully him into doing what she wanted. (My father, Ernest would say through Nick Adams in "Fathers and Sons," was "both cruel and abused.")

Grace was extravagant about other things besides housing. The gowns, the hats, and the thirty-five pairs of gloves she assembled for her trousseau while traveling with her father in Europe in the summer before her marriage set a standard of sartorial elegance she intended to maintain. Escaping the heat of Oak Park by spending every summer at Walloon Lake in Michigan was agreeable to her in some respects, but many more household tasks devolved upon her there than in Oak Park, where servants were always at her beck and call, so in compensation she expected to be treated at summer's end to a few weeks of carefree vacation on Nantucket Island with one of the children to keep her company. In the wintertime, she occasionally went to visit her brother Leicester on the West Coast or explored some interesting place down South.

In Grace's mind, she not only came from a distinguished family, but was an opera star whose career had been cut off by a quirk of fate, whereas her husband was a suburban obstetrician who worried too much. It was extremely important to her self-image that all during her childbearing years she was invited from time to time to give public concerts—in intimate salons, not in great halls with blinding stage lights—and was in such demand as a voice teacher that she could charge the stiff fee of eight dollars an hour. Sitting down at her piano after the children had gone to bed, she also wrote popular songs, some of which were published by a sheet-music firm in the Loop. Although her royalties never amounted to much, she still could say without exaggeration that she was a composer of music (like her ancestor, Edward Miller), as well as a performer and a teacher. How dare her husband tell such a multitalented woman that she ought to live more modestly!

Dr. Hemingway endured further defeats in their quarrels about moral questions. Mixing stout arguments with dramatic retreats to her bedroom with a sick headache, Grace kept up the pressure until he gave in. Even his adamant opposition to allowing the children to dance was inexorably worn down by her, and when Grace staged a lavish dancing party right in their own home, his humiliation on this issue was complete.

But he had been dealt a much more subtle yet much more devastating defeat soon after the birth of his son Ernest on July 21, 1899, when Grace began to dress and raise their second child as though he and his 1½-year-old sister Marcelline were twins of the same sex. It was, perhaps, no more than the act of a whimsical and doting mother. For her husband, though, it was among the first and deepest humiliations he suffered during their marriage, while for Ernest its consequences would be paradoxical and far-reaching.

4

WHEN her first baby proved to be a girl, Grace was thrilled. Here was another version of herself, through whom she might fulfill the musical ambitions that her own mother had had for her. Given her surging hopes, she may have named the infant not for a saint, as has been suggested, but for Mozart's Marcellina, the aggressive spinster who is finally revealed to be the mother of the hero in *The Marriage of Figaro*.

Eighteen months later, her second child arrived. This time it was a boy and Grace took great satisfaction in naming him Ernest Miller —Ernest for her beloved father, Miller for her father's brother, Miller Hall. Yet no sooner did she pay these tributes to the baby's masculine identity than she began to tamper with it. Among the many photographs of Ernest as a little boy are a number that show him looking exactly like a girl, although none of them seems to have been taken after he was two years old. Others show him in strikingly girlish clothes but with his hair cut boyishly short. Still others show him in boys' clothes with hair of a girlish length.

In dealing with these facts, it cannot be assumed that the dress and hairstyles for little boys were roughly the same at the turn of the century as those of modern times. The illustrations in mail-order and department-store catalogues, the dress-pattern instructions in such monthly periodicals as *The Delineator* and *The Standard Designer,* the illustrations and advertisements in *St. Nicholas, Chatterbox* and other children's magazines of the era, the photographs of little boys which have been reproduced in the biographies of American men who were Hemingway's contemporaries, and the materials on file in the Bettmann Archive and other depositories all attest to the contrary. Eighty or ninety years ago, there was a much greater variety of appearance among little boys than is the case today. In an age of innocence about infantile sexuality, the average mother felt less constrained in making choices about this matter than her modern counterpart would.

Most of the boys who were born in the United States in the final years of the nineteenth century and the first years of the twentieth wore dresses until they were old enough to walk. Only from that point onward did a clear majority wear clothes specially designed for boys. On formal occasions, the typical boy might appear in a navy-blue sailor outfit with white piping, or in a buttoned military tunic that was worn with knickerbockers, leggings, and a campaign hat and was commonly known as a Tommy Atkins or Rough Rider suit, or in an elegant velvet jacket with matching knickers. Striped shirts with broad white collars and either long or short pants were a popular form of informal attire, as were overalls and long-sleeved calico shirts.

Boys who were not taken out of girls' clothes after about a year generally wore blouses and bloomers or ankle-length dresses for another twelve to eighteen months. After the age of 2½, however, most of these boys were also put into boys' clothes. Of the total number of little boys in the United States, no more than 10 or 15 percent were still kept in girls' clothes until they were four or five years old. Their skirts, dresses, and pinafores, moreover, were apt to be more tailored than the comparable outfits worn by little girls; in fact, some of the girlish costumes designed for boys had a distinctly military air. Skirts with a broad box-pleat in front recalled the kilts of Scots Highlanders, while the jackets worn by boys in skirts were often trimmed with officers' straps or braid. Fewer than one out of three of the girlish costumes designed for boys over two were identical in every detail with the costumes worn by girls.

Well over half of the little boys at the turn of the century sported boyish haircuts after they emerged from infancy. Some wore their hair cut short, parted and slicked down, or in a full mop that was trimmed to show the ears. Others were given what would today be called a crew cut. Still others had their hair shaped in a square-cut, above-the-ears style called Dutch-boy. On the other hand, the publication in 1886 of Frances Hodgson Burnett's *Little Lord Fauntleroy* had touched off a fad for shoulder-length hair that was still being imposed upon a fair-sized minority of little boys—Thomas Wolfe among them—in the period when Ernest Hemingway was growing up. Another feminine hairstyle sometimes seen on little boys of that era was the Dutch-dolly, where the hair was cut in bangs across the forehead and squared off on either side well below the ears.

Many different combinations of dress and hairstyle for boys were possible. Yet most of them managed to suggest in one way or another that the child in question was indeed a boy. In the age group between one and two, perhaps as many as twenty boys in a hundred were garbed and coiffed in ways that made them indistinguishable from little girls. The vast majority, however, were sexually identifiable. Boys with long hair were either put into boys' clothes or into girls' clothes marked by distinctively boyish touches, while boys who were attired in altogether girlish clothes had their hair cut short. After the age of two, the number of boys who looked exactly like girls fell off to something like 5 percent, and there is some evidence which suggests that the percentage was considerably smaller. Thus, a sample composed of six hundred illustrative items drawn from widely differing sources contains only one picture of a boy between the ages of two and five whose masculinity is not readily recognizable. An illustration in the July 1897 issue of the dress-pattern magazine, *The Standard Designer,* depicts a child of three or four with shoulder-length locks wearing a pleated dress with puffy sleeves, lace cuffs, and a broad lace collar. Were it not for the legend, "Little Boys' Apron," beneath the picture, one would think that the child was a girl.

In the photographic record of Ernest Hemingway's early childhood, he shows up repeatedly in hair-and-dress combinations that served to set him apart to some degree from the majority of boys of comparable age. Moreover, the photographs reveal a shifting between getups that was most unusual. Not many boys of his generation, it is safe to say, were compelled to alter their appearance as many times as he was. For that oddity too, his mother was responsible. Yet even odder was her elaborate pretense that little Ernest and his sister were twins of the same sex.

In later years, she would account for her treatment of Ernest and Marcelline by saying that she had always wanted to be the mother of twins. Like Marcelline's statement that her father punished his children because he was a strict disciplinarian, it was an explanation which merely restated the problem. Of the many other possible explanations, the most plausible is that Ernest's birth had aroused memories that were painful for her of her brother Leicester's birth. Ernest, after all, had arrived a year and a half after Marcelline, just as Leicester had arrived two years after Grace. Leicester had promptly preempted his parents' attention simply because he was a baby, and later had been given other privileges—such as ownership of a bicycle—simply because he was a boy. How much nicer it would have been for Grace if she and little Leicester had been twins of the same sex. How much nicer, correspondingly, it would be for Marcelline—her mother's surrogate—if she and little Ernest could be turned into twins. Thus, she took early action to assert her authority over even the sexuality of her son.

As she had with Marcelline, Grace began a scrapbook on her second child's development from the day he was born. July 21, 1899, was a warm day, she noted. Baby Ernest weighed 9½ pounds, was "plump and perfect in form" and had a marvelously deep-toned voice, a mahogany-colored complexion, "Grandpa Ernest Hall's nose and mouth," hands and nails "just like Grandpa Ernest's," dark blue eyes and thick black hair—which soon turned blond. Four and a half months later, he seemed to his mother to be "quite as big as his sister, except in length of legs or arms," and when his eyes finally "decided to be brown and not blue-grey," comparisons of his appearance to brown-eyed Marcelline's were even more in order.

In the early weeks of his life, Ernest's principal costume was a baby dress that had been "his Mama's," Grace explained. At five months, he was often seen in a "white lacey dress with Pink bows [and] light blue shoes . . . that Marcelline wore in her year old photograph," and for a formal portrait in a photographic studio his mother dressed him in "the same dress Sister Marcelline at the same age had her picture taken in." A month or so later, Grace began to buy two of everything—although not always in the same size— whenever she went shopping for children's clothes.

Marcelline and Ernest's first look-alike outfits consisted of crocheted bonnets, three-quarter-length coats and ruffled dimity skirts that brushed their ankles. Thereafter, pink gingham gowns with white Battenberg lace hoods were apt to be the order of the day, or fluffy lace-tucked dresses, black patent-leather Mary Janes, high stockings, and picture hats with flowers on them. Beside a photo of Ernest in a picture hat and ankle-length gown that was taken behind Grandfather Hall's house in 1901, Grace wrote, "summer girl." In an accompanying note to a series of group photos dated October 1902, she observed that "these groups [were] taken when Ursula [the Hemingways' third child] was six months old; Ernest Miller, 3½ yrs; Marcelline, 4¾ yrs. The two big children were then always dressed alike, like two little girls." As for their hairstyles, Grace sometimes wanted them to be identical and sometimes not. For a time, she arranged Ernest's hair in a loose, tapered coiffure that was almost as long as Marcelline's. Another of her ideas for him was a crew cut. But the style she apparently liked best featured bangs and a square-cut bob that came well down over the ears, just like Marcelline's latest hairdo. Soon she was referring to each of the children as her "sweet Dutch dolly."

Besides making Marcelline and Ernest look like twins, Grace wanted them, in Marcelline's words, "to feel like twins, by having everything alike." They slept in the same bedroom in twin white cribs; they had dolls that were just alike; they played with small china tea sets that had the same pattern. Later, the children were encouraged to fish together, hike together and visit friends together, and after Grace deliberately held Marcelline back, they entered grade school together. In kindergarten, however, Ernest had worn trousers with suspenders, and thereafter he and Marcelline no longer dressed alike, except for similar winter coats and knitted caps.

Through all the changes in their appearances, Grace kept telling the "twins" that they were beautiful. The only way in which they disappointed her was in the color of their hair. For a time she cherished the hope that Ernest's hair would remain blond, since that would have meant that he favored her family, the Halls, but after his hair turned as dark as Marcelline's she had to admit that both children took after their father's family. Yet her repeated extollings of the beauties of blondness had a lasting influence on both children, particularly on Ernest. Several blondes were destined to figure in his life, but it would remain for his fourth wife, Mary, to provide the most suggestive indication of how powerfully he had been affected by his mother's views. Some months before their marriage, Mary relates in her autobiography, Ernest persuaded her to ask a hairdresser in Havana to change the color of her hair from peanut butter to platinum. "I submitted to the bleaching, and Ernest was entranced by the result. Deeply rooted in his field of esthetics was some mystical devotion to blondness, the blonder the lovelier, I never learned why."

The issue of length also figured in the erotic responsiveness to hair that Grace imparted to her children. In the summer of 1906, for instance, when Ernest was seven years old and Marcelline 8½, she decreed that both children must have their hair cut "boy-fashion" for the duration of their stay in Michigan. When the family returned to Oak Park in the fall, Marcelline's partially grown-out locks were of distressingly different lengths. An older girl in the neighborhood offered to trim off the wisps hanging down in front of her ears. In spite of her misgivings that "Mother might be mad," Marcelline handed the girl a pair of scissors. Not until the job was finished did Marcelline realize that the girl had cut off her hair almost to the top of her ears. "I want you to remember this as long as you live," her mother hissed at her that evening. Instead of spanking Marcelline, Grace made her put on a baby bonnet to conceal the damage. For two painfully embarrassing weeks, the child was compelled to wear the bonnet to school. Finally, Marcelline's second-grade teacher got up the courage to confront Grace and ask her to discontinue the punishment, which she did. One week later, a bonnet-free Marcelline was promoted to the third grade, where "my new classmates knew little about my humiliating experience."

For the next five years, Marcelline and Ernest were in different grades. But between the seventh and eighth grades Marcelline was held out of school for a year so that she could concentrate on the piano, violin, and voice lessons she was taking in a vain effort to fulfill her mother's ambitions for her. When she resumed school, she and Ernest were classmates once again. Even so, their school friends no longer thought of them as twins. In their mother's mind, however, the fantasy of their twinhood was still a fact (which was another reason why she held Marcelline out for a year), and she continued to put pressure on them to act it out for her. If she could no longer make them look as though they had come out of the same egg, she could still insist that they behave as if they were two parts of a whole. During their high school years, she did everything she could think of to throw them together, giving them pairs of season tickets to the opera and often not allowing Marcelline to go to parties with other boys, so that she could ask Ernest to escort his sister. And then, of course, there were her cherished scrapbooks about her children, the vitality of which Grace kept replenishing by continuing to augment them. Ernest and Marcelline's memories of their twinhood might have gradually sunk beneath the surface of their conscious minds had not Grace's fond anecdotes about it been backed by the impact of old photographs and their accompanying captions.

5

WITH his first breath of life, Grace had drawn baby Ernest into a deliciously intimate dependency. For six months he slept in her bed, where she allowed him to pat her face, squeeze up close to her and feed at will from her pillowy breasts. "He is contented to sleep with Mama and lunches all night," she happily recorded in her scrapbook. When he learned to talk, he lispingly called her Fweetee. When he learned his prayers, he knelt at her knee to say them. Sitting beside this gifted, charming, physically impressive woman as she leafed through the bound volumes of a magazine about birds and taught him the names of the different species was his idea of happiness.

At some point, though, in his edenic infancy he awakened to an understanding of the situation in which his mother had placed him. A quarter of a century later, Ernest Hemingway would become known for his habit of beguiling friends and acquaintances into believing that he was well disposed toward them, at the very moment that he was pillorying their habits in fictional works-in-progress. Some of his victims would work off their outrage by denouncing him either in print or to his face as the most treacherous man they had ever known. If he was, perhaps it was because he thought of himself as a victim of treachery long before he knew what to call it.

There were many moments, to be sure, when he acted as though he rather liked the role that had been imposed on him. Among the photographs of his childhood he can be seen smiling at the camera with self-conscious delight as it catches him and Marcelline out for a stroll in their best dresses and fanciest hats, or contentedly at play with her in a let's-pretend tea for two. There were even occasions when he may have taken the lead in expanding his feminine repertoire. In Grace's sewing room one day, he took an interest in what she was doing. "He loves to sew," she soon was able to report. "He delights in mending Daddy's pants, an old pair of which Mama keeps for him to sew on."

The willingness with which the little boy played the part of his sister's sister was more than matched, though, by the vehemency with which he fought it. Even minor frustrations of his will to be a boy could cause him to slap his mother, and one day he symbolically shot her. She called him her Dutch dolly, as was her wont, but this time the feminine epithet triggered an outburst of sexual rage. "I not a Dutch dolly, I Pawnee Bill. Bang, I shoot Fweetee." He also was much given to shooting Marcelline, who was supposed to "fall down dead" every time.

That his mother was delighted to hear him say he was Pawnee Bill was typical of the baffling inconsistency of her behavior. Could it be that she really wanted him to be a boy after all? By sometimes dressing him in pants and a shirt, she tantalized him into thinking so. To a lesser degree, Marcelline was similarly confused by the sexual signals emanating from her mother. For if Grace gave her "twins" identical tea sets, she also bought them identical air rifles. And in their first full summers together in northern Michigan she largely reversed the sartorial drill that obtained in Oak Park and not only dressed Ernest as a boy but Marcelline as well;* in fact, Grace sometimes referred to the two of them as "lads" or "chaps." A picture of Marcelline and Ernest taken at Walloon Lake in August 1900 bears the admiring description, "Two sturdy little chaps in overhauls." Two years later, she further confused their minds by devising for the two of them "a sort of compromise boy-girl costume," as Marcelline described it, consisting of a belted tunic worn over either bloomers or leggings. One of the pictures taken at Walloon Lake in August 1902 shows them wearing this alternative outfit. Both children are sitting down and they are looking at one another. Marcelline has shoulder-length hair. Ernest's hair is short,

---

* The only exception to this generalization is that in the summer of Ernest's first birthday Grace occasionally dressed him in a bonnet and long skirt. For the most part, though, the one-year-old Ernest wore overalls in Michigan—or nothing at all.

and he is holding his air rifle pointed straight up in the air with the butt resting in his crotch.

Dr. Hemingway, meanwhile, seemed to be constantly on the lookout for ways to strengthen his son's sense of himself as a boy. One way was to start taking him along on hunting and fishing trips, even though Ernest was not even three years old. Yet instead of resisting her husband's stratagems by saying that the child was too young to handle a fishing rod, let alone a gun, Grace encouraged these expeditions as opportunities for him to demonstrate what a "little man" he was. In June 1902 she was pleased to record in her scrapbook that "Ernest Miller at 2 years 11 months went fishing with two men—his father and Mr. Glotfelty. He caught the biggest fish of the crowd. He knows when he gets a bite and lands them all himself. He shoots well with his gun and loads and cocks it himself; walks a mile and a half easily to dinner at Jo McConnells."

At the age of two years and four months, Ernest enjoyed his first visit to a barber shop. Grace reacted to the sight of her shorn lamb by exclaiming, "Such a man," even though most of the clothes in her son's closet were dresses. Alongside a series of photographs of Ernest in which he is dressed like a little girl in her Sunday best, she placed the quotation, "A boy's a boy for ah-that." On an envelope containing hair shearings she wrote, "Ernest Miller Hemingway, hair cut off Feb 15th 1906, he can never wear long hair again as he is 6½ yrs and in school. My precious boy, a 'real' boy."

Caught between his mother's wish to conceal his masculinity and her eagerness to encourage it, was it any wonder that he was anxious and insecure? "When asked what he is afraid of," Grace wrote in 1901, "he shouts out *fraid a nothing* with great gusto." Yet the vehemence of his reply suggests that his fears were huge—and his mother's frequent restatements of that challenging question probably had the effect of enlarging them still further. As he marched down the sidewalk carrying half of an old musket on his shoulder and singing "John Brown's Body" in as deep a voice as he could summon up, he sought to convince Oak Park that despite the dress he was wearing he was really a boy. But when he came to his mother shortly before Christmas 1902 and confessed to her that "he was quite fearful . . . as to whether Santa Claus would know he was a boy, because he wore just the same kind of clothes as [his] sister," he revealed how uncertain he was that anyone believed him. Instinctively feeling that male allies would be of help to him, he prayed hard for a baby brother, only to be informed in April 1902 that he now had a sister named Ursula. "I think maybe Jesus will send my baby brother tomorrow," he said wistfully. Two years later, his hopes for a baby brother were rekindled. "My darling [Ernest] was *so* delighted," Grace recalled, "when he came into my bed one morning . . . and I told him the happy secret that God was going to give us another little baby." In November 1904 God sent the Hemingways their third baby girl.

Another symptom of his inner turmoil was the difficulty he experienced in getting to sleep. Years later he worked hard to create the impression that his insomnia had been brought on by battlefield memories, but as Scott Fitzgerald guessed, Hemingway's nocturnal struggles with frightening thoughts had begun in childhood. "As to Ernest as a boy," Fitzgerald observed in his Notebooks, "it is undeniable that the dark was peopled for him."

A passage in "Indian Camp" which Hemingway excised from the manuscript before publication demonstrates how very right Fitzgerald's intuition was. After supper one night, Nick Adams's father and his Uncle George row away into the dark of a Michigan lake to do some fishing by jack light, leaving the ten-year-old Nick to walk back through the woods to their tent by himself. By the end of the passage, the reader is aware of how terrifically vulnerable he is to the siren call of death, although not of the underlying reasons why.

> He was always a little frightened of the woods at night. He opened the flap of the tent and undressed and lay very quietly between the blankets in the dark. The fire was burned down to a bed of coals outside. Nick lay still and tried to go to sleep. There was no noise anywhere. Nick felt if he could hear a fox bark or an owl or anything he would be all right. He was not afraid of anything definite as yet. But he was getting very afraid. Then suddenly he was afraid of dying. Just a few weeks before at home, in church, they had sung a hymn, "Some day the silver cord will break." While they were singing the hymn Nick had realized that some day he must die. It made him feel quite sick. . . . That night he sat out in the hall under the night light trying to read *Robinson Crusoe* to keep his mind off the fact that some day the silver cord must break. The nurse found him there and threatened to tell his father on him if he did not go to bed. He went into bed and as soon as the nurse was in her room came out again and read under the hall light until morning.

That Hemingway's black sweats and waking nightmares were a legacy of what his mother did to him can be extrapolated more easily from the story called "Now I Lay Me," even though the hero's sleeplessness is attributed to war experiences. For the mother of the sleepless hero looms up in his symbol-searching imagination as a destroyer of male sexuality.

As the story begins, a young American lieutenant named Nick is lying on the floor of a silk factory in northern Italy, seven kilometers behind the battle lines. All around him he can hear the sound of silkworms eating the bitter leaves of mulberry plants. The worms' incessant chewing parallels the deliberately induced activity of the lieutenant's mind. Deliberately induced, because ever since being wounded he has been afraid that if he shuts his eyes at night his soul will go out of his body, and the best way to keep awake, he finds, is by recalling incidents of his childhood. His very earliest recollection is of the time when he was still living in his grandfather's house. In the attic of that house his mother and father's wedding cake had hung in a tin box from one of the rafters. There had also been jars of snakes up there that his father had collected as a boy and preserved in alcohol, but unfortunately some of the alcohol had evaporated and the exposed backs of the snakes had turned white. The lieutenant further remembers that after his grandfather's death

> we moved away from that house to a new house designed and built by my mother. Many things that were not to be moved were burned in the back-yard and I remember those jars from the attic being thrown in the fire, and how they popped in the heat and the fire flamed up from the alcohol. I remember the snakes burning in the fire in the back-yard.

The lieutenant does not say who burned the snakes, but his very next recollection implies that it was his mother, for in their new house, he remembers, "my mother was always cleaning things out and making a good clearance." One time while his father was away on a hunting trip, she cleaned out the basement and burned "everything that should not have been there," and the fire was still burning in the road when his father came home.

> "What's this?" he asked.
> "I've been cleaning out the basement, dear," my mother said from the porch. She was standing there smiling, to meet him. My father looked at the fire and kicked at something. Then he leaned over and picked something out of the ashes. "Get a rake, Nick," he said to me. I went to the basement and brought a rake and my father raked very carefully in the ashes. He raked out stone axes and stone skinning knives and tools for making arrow-heads and pieces of pottery and many arrow-heads. They had all been blackened and chipped by the fire. My father raked them all out very carefully and spread them on the grass by the road. . . .
> "The best arrow-heads went all to pieces," he said.

Whether or not this episode reflects an actual event in Hemingway's childhood, he used it to epitomize his mother's proclivity for burning things and her long record of domination over her husband. For the smile on Nick's mother's face is the sign of her triumph, while the ruined weapons and tools and the blackened and broken arrowheads are the tokens—as are the popping bottles and burning snakes in the previous episode—of his father's humiliation. The possibility that the scene is a masked memory of a humiliation that the lieutenant himself had once suffered is explicitly ruled out by his presentation of the boy he used to be as uninvolved in the ugliness he has witnessed; in this memory, he says, "there were only two people, so he would pray for them both." Yet the tone of voice in which the lieutenant recounts the story is taut with emotion; conceivably, he has more of a personal stake in what he remembers than he is conscious of.

In one haunting piece of fiction after another, the early Hemingway probed at the quick of his deepest anxieties, at the same time that he did not directly acknowledge them. "Now I Lay Me" is not an exception to this rule. What counts supremely in the story is not the northern Italian frame that has made so many readers regard it as a tale of war, but the childhood memories within the frame. Which is why it is just right that Hemingway took the story's title from the familiar prayer with which he had attempted as a young child to set his mind at rest while kneeling before his iconlike mother.

Now I lay me down to sleep,
I pray the Lord my soul to keep.
If I should die before I wake,
I pray the Lord my soul to take.

CHAPTER THREE

A Land of Magic

AT THE END OF AUGUST 1909 Grace took Marcelline off to Nantucket for four weeks, leaving her dutiful husband to close up Windemere by himself and get Ernest, Ursula, and little Sunny ready for school. A year later, it was Ernest's turn to accompany his mother to the island. After a long train ride from Chicago to Woods Hole, Massachusetts, they boarded a boat that stopped briefly at Martha's Vineyard before taking them on to their destination. Grace had written ahead to a women's rights activist who ran a boarding-house on Pearl Street, so that they had a room waiting for them when they arrived. Ernest swam in the ocean every day, went fishing for mackerel, swordfish, and sea bass, and on Sunday mornings listened to his mother sing from the choir loft of a church on Centre Street. On their way back to Oak Park, Grace showed him Paul Revere's house, the Concord bridge, and other historic sights of the Boston area, despite the fact that he was already late for school.

With the encouragement of his sixth-grade teacher, he tried to recapture the excitement he had felt upon first seeing the ocean by writing a short story—based on his maternal grandmother's child-hood trip to Australia, but told from a boy's point of view—about a voyage around Cape Horn. The only mention of the boy's mother in the story was in the opening paragraph. He was born, the narrator says, in a little white house on Martha's Vineyard, and "my mother died when I was four years old." If that sentence represented the author's first attempt to punish his mother literarily, it would not be his last.

In any event, "My First Sea Vouge"—as the author misspelled the title—was a story with a rollicking tone and an oceanic perspective that revealed Ernest's growing interest in foreign travel. Except for the excursion to Nantucket, he made no extensive trips during his boyhood, but in his reading he ranged far and wide. A series of books called *Little Journeys* transported him in his imagination to France, Switzerland, Germany, Denmark, Belgium, and the Netherlands. *Robinson Crusoe,* which he received for Christmas one year, carried him even further away from home, as did the tales of Robert Louis Stevenson. He also acquired a strong sense of what China was like from listening to his father's younger brother, Dr. Willoughby Hemingway, who was a guest at Windemere along with his wife for most of the summer of 1911, following eight years of service as a medical missionary in Shansi province. Uncle Will had been in some frighteningly tight spots, had seen some beautiful country and met some remarkable people in the course of his travels, including the Dalai Lama, whom he had caught up with in Mongolia during one of the Lama's rare forays beyond the borders of forbidden Tibet. Ernest later remembered that his father had been terribly envious of Uncle Will and had spoken bravely of practicing medicine himself someday in Guam or Greenland perhaps, but that Grace, the "arbiter," had "dealt firmly with his wanderlust." Yet if Uncle Will's exotic stories served to make his brother Ed feel more trapped by life than ever, they reinforced young Ernest's resolve to see the world as soon as he could.

In the meantime, northern Michigan lay before him, a land of magic in its own right, in which even as an infant he had been allowed to look like a boy.

2

BEHIND the Hemingways' cottage was a sandy road that started at Henry Bacon's farm and led over hills and through dense woods to Petoskey, where veterans of the Civil War still staged their annual encampments. Berry bushes grew along either side of the road, and when the red raspberries and blackberries were ripe, they were picked by Indians, who packed them in tin buckets and covered them with basswood leaves to ward off the sun and brought them to Windemere to sell. The Indians lived in a camp in the woods, a miserable huddle of shacks, and were always on the lookout for ways to make a little money. You never heard them coming, Ernest remembered, but suddenly there they were, with their tin buckets loaded with fruit. Sometimes when he was lying in the hammock reading a book he could smell the Indians before he saw them.

The only financially successful red man he ever knew was a large fat fellow named Simon Green, who owned a big farm along Horton Creek, about four miles from the Hemingways' cottage. Ernest loved to talk to Simon as the two of them sat perspiring in the sun in front of Jim Dilworth's blacksmith shop in the little town of Horton Bay over on Lake Charlevoix, or as they walked together through the woods looking for game birds—for when Dr. Hemingway took Ernest hunting he sometimes invited Simon to join them. One morning, the trio came upon a covey of ruffed grouse—the first ones Ernest had ever seen—feeding alongside Jim Dilworth's grist mill. Ernest was so excited by the size of the birds and the whir of their wings that he missed both of the shots he had, but his father, shooting in rapid succession, killed five of them. Long after his father had committed suicide, Ernest would still remember fat Simon picking up the dead birds and laughing out loud in admiration of Dr. Hemingway's skill. "And when I look back at that shooting I am a great admirer of my father too," Hemingway wrote in *Esquire* in 1935. "He was a beautiful shot, one of the fastest I have ever seen; but he was too nervous to be a great money shot."

Another of Ernest's Indian acquaintances was a muscular and thoroughly disagreeable lout named Nick Boulton, a sawyer by trade, whom Dr. Hemingway sometimes hired to cut up the logs that drifted onto the Hemingways' beach from the big log booms that were forever being towed to a sawmill at the foot of Walloon Lake by a majestically slow-moving steamer called *Magic*. Most people believed that Boulton was a half-breed, although some of the farmers around the lake were certain he was a white man. Boulton lived in the Indian settlement in the woods and had had a son by one squaw and a daughter and a son by another. His daughter Prudy, who was three years younger than Ernest, occasionally did housework at Windemere. One summer during his middle teens, Ernest frequently went hunting for black squirrels with Prudy and her brother Billy. Prudy may have fallen into the habit of putting an exploring hand in Ernest's pocket while the three of them sat quietly in the middle of the woods listening for squirrels in the top branches, she may even have lain on her back on a bed of pine needles and allowed Ernest to climb on top of her while Billy watched. In his youth, Nick Adams declares in "Fathers and Sons," these things happened to him with an Indian girl named Trudy. Like many readers, Hemingway's widow has always regarded Nick's testimony as a reflection of real-life fact. Prudy Boulton was the first girl my husband ever "pleasured," Mary Hemingway asserts in her autobiography. (She also did not doubt him when he told her in a London restaurant in 1944 that her legs were just like Prudy's.) Other readers, though, are of the equally firm opinion that Hemingway's fictional account of his sexual initiation by Prudy is just that, a fiction, made up out of whole cloth, and that he and the Indian girl were just friends. The truth may lie somewhere in between. It would appear that, for a time at least, before Prudy started having more serious liaisons with older white boys and mature men like the fellow from Charlevoix with whom she would eventually make a death pact, Ernest thought of her as his girl and that their encounters in the woods were not entirely platonic.

The story of their breakup is told in "Ten Indians." A boy named Nick knows an Indian girl named Prudie Mitchell. Although she smells no less strongly than any other Indian, he is in love with her. Consequently, when his father informs him that he has seen her "threshing around" in the woods with another boy, he cannot keep from crying. Burying his face in the pillow on his bed that night, he tells himself that this is what it feels like to have a broken heart. During the night, he wakes up and listens to the wind in the hemlock trees outside the cottage and to the waves breaking on the shore. "In the morning," runs the final sentence, "there was a big wind blowing and the waves were running high up on the beach and he was awake for a long time before he remembered that his heart was broken."

Back in Oak Park, there were perhaps as many as half a dozen girls who were Ernest's pals. He did not have his first date, though, until he was 15½, when he escorted a freshman named Dorothy Davies to a basketball game. ("All his bachelor friends were nearly in a state of apoplexy over it," his mother remarked with amusement.) The following May, he invited Frances Coates for a couple of moonlight canoe rides on the Des Plaines River. But his mother saw to it that he took his sister to the Junior-Senior Prom on the nineteenth of that month. ("Ernest and Marcelline went together, altho Marcelline had other invitations," Grace noted with satisfaction.) To his friends, the adolescent Ernest liked to appear supremely self-assured. Yet the expression on his face was often tense and his sleep was often broken by nightmares (an especially bad one that had him yelling bloody murder occurred one night at Windemere after he and Marcelline and another boy and girl stayed up late reading aloud to one another from Bram Stoker's *Dracula*), and with the girls of Oak Park High he didn't compile much of a record in the role of a swain. Wherefore his woodland trysts with Prudy Boulton. Somehow he didn't feel threatened by her—possibly because she was of a lower class, possibly because she belonged to a conquered race.

3

AT Walloon Lake in 1900, the summer of Ernest's first birthday, he and Marcelline had played naked on the narrow beach in front of their parents' newly completed cottage. Dr. Hemingway's snapshots of them in the buff, duly pasted into scrapbooks by Grace, are charming. But while splashing his feet in the water and exploring the rowboat pulled up on the shore, it can be presumed that Ernest had ample opportunity to notice—if he had not done so already— that he and his sister were not built identically.

Did the infant boy take pride in the equipment that set him apart from Marcelline? Or did the sight of her smoothness make him think that she had suffered some sort of dreadful accident which might soon befall him as well? Or were pride and fear intermingled in his turbulent imagination? Familiar Freudian speculations these, which acquire extra force in this case because Ernest would soon become aware that he and Marcelline were being treated like twins of the same sex. And in years to come, the horrific image of phallic loss would be made light of by Hemingway in tall-tale jokes about such matters as the hazards of skiing in subzero temperatures, and dealt with seriously in two anguishing works of fiction, "God Rest You Merry, Gentlemen" and *The Sun Also Rises*.

His developing relationship with his older sister may have been a source of emotional turmoil in other ways, too. Marcelline was a much steadier walker than he was and could easily outwrestle him. Far more often than not in authentic boy-girl twinhoods, the girl is larger and stronger than her brother until puberty; in the spurious Marcelline-Ernest twinhood, Marcelline's genetic advantage was compounded by the fact that she was eighteen months older. It was Grace's belief that her "twins" were the same size, but the photos of them belie that idea. As late as their freshman year in high school, Ernest was a whole head shorter than Marcelline. In addition to towering over her brother, Marcelline for a while was a more advanced reader, and during the five-year period when she was a year ahead of him in school she always knew more about the subjects they were studying than he did. The Canadian writer Morley Callaghan, who met Hemingway in Toronto in 1923 and subsequently saw a lot of him in Paris, has observed, "Something within him drove him to want to be expert at every occupation he touched." The amazing quickness with which Hemingway could master information was part of his genius, of course, but the competitive urge that drove him to do so had surely been enhanced by his rivalry with the know-it-all, hypertalkative, ultrahandsome Marcelline, who often won exemptions from her parents' rules by threatening to kill herself or run away.

Beneath his early displays of affection for his older sister lay a lasting grudge which grew more virulent as Hemingway grew older. In 1944 in London, for example, he startled his future wife, Mary Welsh, whom he had only recently met, by launching into an attack on Marcelline. In contrast to his younger sister Ursula, who had "saved the family from mediocrity" and was "quick and bright as well as pretty and a very good artist in clay," Marcelline was full of "precious mannerisms." A few years later, over drinks with Mary at the luxurious Locanda Cipriani across the lagoon from Venice, he adversely compared Marcelline to all his other sisters. Sunny had been "a great baseball player." Carol was not only "the most beautiful," but "looked as a girl exactly as I looked as a boy." Ursula was "the nicest and best" of the lot. Marcelline, on the other hand, had been "a crowder." That was the heart of the matter. In a competition in which the odds had been stacked against him, Marcelline had often crowded him out.

Once Dr. Hemingway started teaching Marcelline and Ernest to swim, he ordered both children to put on bathing suits. Still, on certain evenings he allowed them to take a goodnight dip in the nude. This privilege was soon extended to Ursula and Sunny as well, and then to Carol. Even in his teens, Ernest and his sisters went swimming in the dark without suits. It made all of us feel, Marcelline said later, like members of a "Secret Society." But within that Secret Society there was an even more intimate cabal, as the literary transformation of the incident of the blue heron would later reveal.

The incident involving the heron occurred one day in the summer of 1915, around the time of Ernest's sixteenth birthday. The day began innocently enough with a decision by Ernest and Sunny to take a picnic lunch and go exploring in a wild area called Cracken, far down on the western side of the lake. They got the family motorboat started, hitched a rowboat on behind and set off. Soon after they reached the area and went ashore, Ernest flushed a beautiful blue heron out of the high reeds and promptly shot it, even though he was aware of the illegality of such an action. A heron would make a dandy addition, he said, to their father's collection of stuffed birds.

Rather than carry his trophy with him to their picnic spot, Ernest rowed back to the launch, wrapped the bird in an old newspaper and placed it under the seat. On their return a few hours later, they discovered that the heron was missing and that the son of a local game warden was waiting for them in a sailboat. Holding up the dead bird, the youth demanded to know whether Ernest had killed it. Ernest replied that he had received the bird from a man whose name he did not know. Although plainly dissatisfied with this answer, the youth asked no further questions and sailed away. As soon as he was gone, Ernest and Sunny hurried back to Windemere to tell their mother what had happened. Taking command of the situation with her customary authority, Grace told Sunny to stick close to the cottage, but advised Ernest to leave at once for Longfield Farm, the Hemingway-owned property across the lake on which Dr. Hemingway had established extensive orchards and a huge vegetable garden. If Ernest would spend some time working on the farm while he was keeping out of the sight of the law, his busy father down in Oak Park would doubtless be pleased.

The next morning, two strange men appeared at Windemere and began asking questions about Ernest without revealing why they were doing so. Nothing could better illustrate the forcefulness of Grace's personality than the description of her confrontation with these two men that she shortly sent off to her husband.

> I thought them burglars or fiends of some sort. They had such a beastly, insinuating, sneering way, and would not state their business. They fired question after question. . . . I said if you know so much about my business and that of my family, you don't need to give me any further impudence. This tackling a lone woman and her little children without giving your business or authority and asking impudent questions is not the way to behave yourselves, and just you remember it the next time.

As the two utterly intimidated men beat a hasty retreat, one of them called out, "Lady, I've learned a lesson." The only detail Grace neglected to pass on to Dr. Hemingway was that at some point she had ordered Sunny to bring her a shotgun.

Grace's next move was to send word to her son directing him to go into deeper hiding. After a fast walk over the ridge between Longfield Farm and Horton Bay, Ernest spent a few hours with the blacksmith, Jim Dilworth, and his jolly-faced wife, Liz, who ran a chicken-dinner place called Pinehurst Cottage overlooking Lake Charlevoix. Some of Liz's famous cooking was just what Ernest needed to prepare him for the second and longer stage of his flight, which finally brought him to his Uncle George's summer home near Ironton, Michigan. Except for a surreptitious trip back to Longfield Farm to pick some string beans and dig some potatoes as a present for his mother, Ernest stayed with Uncle George until the game wardens' tempers had cooled. At his father's suggestion, he then pleaded guilty before a judge in Boyne City and paid a fine of fifteen dollars.

In the wake of his mother's death some thirty-six years later, Hemingway turned back to the adventure of the blue heron and tried to write a novel about it. He kept fussing with the manuscript for the better part of ten years, but never came close to finishing it. Eleven years after his own death, most of the fragments (but not the one that asserts that Nick Adams got Prudy Boulton pregnant) were published as a lengthy short story called "The Last Good Country" in an edition of *The Nick Adams Stories.*

One of the many changes Hemingway made in recapitulating the adventure was in the role played by his mother. Nick Adams's mother doesn't defy the inquisitorial game wardens, she gives them lunch and supper, before retiring to her room with a headache. There is also no direct reference in the story to a blue heron. Nick's little sister says to him, "You killed what they took from your boat," but this vague allusion is never clarified. The game-law violation with which he is specifically charged is of a more serious nature: the killing of a twelve-pointed deer out of season. Another difference between fact and fiction is that instead of seeking refuge in his Uncle George's home, Nick flees into a virgin wilderness— "the last good country." Still another, and certainly the most remarkable, difference is that he does not flee alone. For Hemingway intended "The Last Good Country" to be his *Huckleberry Finn,* with Nick as the picaresque hero and Nick's little sister, Littless, as the hero's faithful sidekick.

Which of his real little sisters the author placed in his imaginary wilderness can be determined by a process of elimination. Inasmuch as his "littlest" sister, Carol, was only four years old in 1915, she is not a strong candidate. But Sunny at 10½ and Ursula at thirteen were both within hailing distance of Littless's "eleven or twelve." The fact that Sunny was with Ernest when he shot the heron and that she possessed tomboyish traits not unlike some of Littless's are further reasons for wondering if Hemingway had her in mind. Littless, however, has "dark brown eyes and dark brown hair," whereas little Sunny was a blue-eyed blonde. It is much more likely—indeed all but certain—that brown-eyed, brown-haired Ursula was the principal model for Littless. For "The Last Good Country" is a filial love story, and as Hemingway twice told Mary Welsh before he began to write it, Ursula had always been his favorite sister. (In another compliment that was probably intended for Ursula, he confessed through Nick Adams in "Fathers and Sons," "There was only one person in his family that he liked the smell of, one sister.") Although in later years Ursula lived in Honolulu, she and Ernest kept in touch with one another, and after his death she established the Ernest Hemingway Memorial Award for creative writing at the University of Hawaii. Yet this gesture could not dispel the long shadow cast by his suicide. When her doctors told her she had cancer, Ursula quickly made up her mind. In the fall of 1966, she too committed suicide, by swallowing a poisonous medicine.

People who kill themselves are apt to have had a history of anger toward loved ones. Both Nick and Littless are full of anger about their family. "[Littless] and Nick loved each other and they did not love the others. They always thought of everyone else in the family as the others." One of Littless's dreams is to set up a family of her own, with her brother as her husband. "I want to be your common-law wife," she says to Nick. "I've thought it out lots of times. I'll get cards printed Mrs. Nick Adams, Cross Village, Michigan—common-law wife." Nick amusedly replies that he doesn't think the scheme will work, but she refuses to be discouraged. "We'll have a couple of children while I'm a minor. Then you [will] have to marry me."

The further the fugitives retreat from civilization, the more incestuous they become. Thus, the kisses they exchange at the outset of the story are merely warm-ups for the moment when Littless sits on Nick's lap and he gets an erection. The aggressive Littless also leads her passive brother into a whole series of sexually suggestive conversations, about whores, menstrual periods, and above all, androgyny. Her interest in the latter topic reflects another of her personal dreams. In addition to dressing in overalls and a boy's shirt, Littless desperately wants to cut her hair short. "I always wanted to be a boy," she admits. (Hence the appropriateness of her desire to live with her brother in "Cross Village.") Two evenings later, she and Nick set up their lean-to on the edge of a swamp, deep inside the woods. After going off to catch some fish for their supper, Nick returns to find his sister lying on her side, reading. He asks what she has been doing.

> She turned and looked at him and smiled and shook her head.
> "I cut it off," she said.

"How?"

"With a scissors. How did you think?"

"How did you see to do it?"

"I just held it out and cut it. It's easy. Do I look like a boy?"

"Like a wild boy of Borneo."

"I couldn't cut it like a Sunday-school boy. Does it look too wild?"

"No."

"It's very exciting," she said. "Now I'm your sister but I'm a boy. . . ."

Hemingway's favorite sister had, in fact, once looked like a boy —but only at the age of three, when Grace outfitted Ursula in a campaign hat, a Rough Rider kerchief and fringed trousers. (The effect was so successful that Grace had started calling her Teddy.) Ursula's hair, however, was never cut so crudely that she looked like a wild boy of Borneo; Hemingway took that detail from a memorably painful moment in Marcelline's childhood. As to whether Ursula ever voiced the wish that she were a boy, there is no way of knowing. Nor is it known whether she and Ernest were sexually intimate in any way, even though Hemingway made a point of telling the critic Arthur Mizener in 1950 that after he came back from the war in 1919

> my [seventeen-year-old] sister Ura . . . always used to wait, sleeping, on the stairway of the third floor stair-case to my room. She wanted to wake when I came in because she had been told it was bad for a man to drink alone. She would drink something light with me until I went to sleep and then she would sleep with me so I would not be lonely in the night. We always slept with the light on except she would sometimes turn it off if she saw I was asleep and stay awake and turn it on if she saw I was wakeing [sic].

Thus it may very well be that Littless's androgynous and incestuous carryings-on in "The Last Good Country" had next to no real-life basis. Fantasies, however, can possess real-life significance. Ernest and Ursula not only were very close while they were growing up, but in Ernest's imagination, at least, their closeness would seem to have become incorporated into a larger drama of sexual confusion.

That drama had affected young Ernest's life for as long as he could remember. But in his boyhood years he made a major effort to conceal his continuing psychological involvement in it by showing the world how manly he was.

4

BECAUSE of all the time she spent in Hemingway's company after
he was hospitalized in 1918, Agnes von Kurowsky could not help
noticing how much the other men in the hospital—doctors and
patients alike—delighted in his company. "You know how he was,"
the erstwhile nurse remarked long afterwards, "men loved him." So
did most (although not all) of the boys at Oak Park High School
who knew him really well. There were some girls in the school who
knew him well and found him overbearing and stuck on himself,
but the boys tended to forgive his egotistical qualities on the grounds
that no one could talk more excitingly about baseball or boxing or
books, that no one had a better sense of humor or a keener wit and
that no one was more fun to be with on an overnight hike or a canoe
trip. Among the many signs of the esteem in which he was held was
his astonishing number of nicknames—Hem, Hemmie, Hemingstein, Nesto, Porthos, Butch, Eoinbones. Still another name that he
tried to hang on himself was "the Old Brute," but only Marcelline
was willing to adopt it. Of the names his schoolmates liked, his own
favorite was Hemingstein—sometimes abbreviated to Stein—for he
was enough of an anti-Semite to find Jewish names funny just because they were Jewish.

Several of the boys whom he was closest to were leaders in the
school, but after school they usually looked to Ernest. Whenever he
developed a new interest, most of his friends adopted it. Boxing was
a case in point. Ernest first saw a professional prizefight in Chicago
in 1916 and at once fell in love with the sport. Aided by an introduction from a friend of his father's, he gained access to a downtown
gym where boxers trained. A decade later he would boast that he
had learned to fight by sparring with such legendary figures as Sam
Langford, Jack Blackburn, Tommy Gibbons, and Harry Greb. But
in all probability he never even climbed into the ring with the little-
known club fighters who trained at the gym, let alone with any
luminaries. The sparring partners on whose hides he honed his skills
were his pals in Oak Park, most of whom knew considerably less
about the manly art of self-defense than he did.

Many of their bouts were staged in the Hemingway home.
Grace's music room was an ideal place to set up a ring, and spectators could watch from the balcony she had had installed to accommodate overflow audiences at her musicales. As long as the fighting
was not too bloody, Grace had no objections to pugilism, while
Ernest's sisters were delighted with it. "We girls watched from the

balcony," Marcelline recalled, "and teased the fighters by throwing paper wads and pillows down on top of them." Eventually, though, the fighting became quite violent, and Ernest and his friends were forced to move to Tom Cusack's house. The trouble was, Ernest not only wanted to win every match he fought, but to do so smashingly. The sweet smile on his face masked the savagery in his heart, and some of his opponents were rather thoroughly mauled, if not knocked out cold.

At the same time that he was indifferent to the bloody noses and puffy eyes of his friends, the sight of mere acquaintances in physical peril could cause him to spring to their rescue. In February 1917 three girls at Oak Park High accepted a dare from a friend to take a ride on the lunchroom dumbwaiter. The girls were "flying to destruction," the Oak Park newspaper, *Oak Leaves,* reported a few days later, "when Ernest Hemingway . . . saw and realized the danger. He grabbed the rope and was jerked off his feet and his bare hands engaged and blocked the pulley at the top." A minute or so later, four other boys came to his assistance and pulled the girls to safety.

In Michigan, his best friend was Bill Smith, who nicknamed him Wemedge. Bill had an older sister, Katy, whom Wemedge liked almost as much as he did Bill, and an older brother, Yeremya Kenley, understandably known as Y. K. Their mother had died in 1897, not long after Bill was born, and their father, a professor of mathematics at Tulane University, had been more interested in writing erudite jeremiads (yeremyads) criticizing Christianity for vulgarizing Hebraic thought, than in taking care of his offspring. Consequently, the job of raising them had been assumed by their socialite aunt, Mrs. Joseph William Charles, of St. Louis, Missouri, and Horton Bay. While the children saw very little of their father when they were growing up, he did succeed in conveying to all of them his love of literature. Bill was the only boy Ernest knew well who had read as much as he had, and he sought him out virtually every time he visited Horton Bay. Their days together often started with a few hours of wading in the chill waters of Horton Creek with fishing rods in their hands. (To keep warm, they went ashore from time to time for a slug of hard cider from a transparent jug of Hornsby's Best.) Once they had had their fill of fishing, they would go back to "Aunty Charles's" cottage and talk about their favorite British writers, some of whom Nick Adams and his friend Bill admiringly refer to in the wonderful story called "The Three-Day Blow." Hemingway's later feeling for understatement and his prejudice against talking about things too much owed a lot to his conversations with Bill

Smith about British phlegm. "We tended to buy the English gents' code of gallantry as revealed in fiction," Smith would recall in 1966. "The idea of being 'under wraps' was part of it. . . . I mean the kind of attitude Jake Barnes had about the newspaper business in *The Sun Also Rises*—one should never seem to be actually working or pressed —and yet the work must get done, etc., etc."

Of the modern British writers whom Bill and Ernest loved, Kipling was the one they made a cult of. "When I was your age," Hemingway recalled years later in a letter of advice to a young poet, "I guess I wrote like Kipling. I thought he was the best short story writer that ever lived and I still know that some of the short stories are the best. . . . Why don't you start again at the beginning and read . . . 'The End of the Passage,' 'The Strange Ride of Maraby [Morrowbie] Jukes,' 'The Mark of the Beast.' " The sense that Kipling communicated of possessing an insider's knowledge of things and his fascination with men of moral fortitude on the verge of collapse were qualities that would mark Hemingway's fiction as well.

Ernest also loved certain stories by other British writers that dealt with personal problems akin to his own. Of the various books that Nick Adams mentions in "The Three-Day Blow," none receives higher praise from him than Hugh Walpole's autobiographical novel, *Fortitude* (1913). "It's fine," says Nick. "That's a real book. That's where his old man is after him all the time." *Fortitude* is in fact an awkwardly told and overfurnished tale, but the hero's tortured life with his parents gave Ernest a lot to think about.

" 'Tisn't life that matters! 'Tis the courage you bring to it!" an old man in Treliss, Cornwall, tells twelve-year-old Peter Westcott at the outset of the story. The first test of the boy's courage occurs when his father commands him to strip naked and then savagely beats him with a cane for having stayed out late without permission. Although the pain is "intolerable," the boy proudly holds back his tears until after his father has left the room. A few days later, Mr. Westcott punishes Peter even more severely by sending him away to a miserably inadequate school—and after he is finally permitted to leave it, he is forced by his father to take a job in a solicitor's office in a town he does not care for. Only when it becomes apparent to Mr. Westcott that his chronically nervous wife is mortally ill does he summon Peter home.

On entering his mother's bedroom, Peter realizes that even though his father has hardly ever allowed him a moment's intimacy with her, he has always loved her dearly. As she gently strokes his hair, Peter confides to her that the dream of his life is to become a novelist. In reply, she tells him that she herself had once had artistic ambitions. Blessed with a lovely singing voice, she had actually given a few concerts before the collapse of her nerves compelled her to abandon the idea of a professional career. Under persistent questioning from Peter, she admits that her nervousness had been precipitated by her husband's unkindness to her in the early days of their marriage. "It gave him pleasure," she says, "to have something . . . that he could hurt." Deeply moved by this confession, Peter clasps his mother to his breast and kisses her passionately. Twice she asks him to kiss her again, and he smothers her mouth with his own. That evening, his father confronts Peter in the dining room and tells him he has done grave harm to his mother by his attentions. Rushing back to her room, Peter discovers that she is dying. "He . . . crossed to her, and she fell back, with a little sigh, dead."

In the last scene of the novel, Peter is several years older. He has endured a failed marriage and other disappointments, but his determination to achieve success as a writer is undiminished. A violent storm breaks out, and as the novel ends Peter prays to the rain and the wind, in words that ought to have reminded a young reader in the American Middle West of the motto of his boyhood: "Make of me a man—to be afraid of nothing."

As a child, Ernest had felt a kinship with his father that Peter Westcott had never enjoyed with his. On weekend hunting and fishing trips away from Oak Park, it had been a relief to them both to escape into a world of men without women. And because Dr. Hemingway had been far more interested in giving his boy a proper start in life, if he possibly could, than in maximizing his medical fees, he had made a point of being on hand in the early years at Windemere for the better part of every summer. At a time when Ernest had been confused and demoralized by his mother's changeable treatment of him, his father's steady support of his boyish interests had been vital. It is no wonder that he wanted to be a doctor when he grew up. Nor is it surprising that Dr. Hemingway's demonstrations of how to do things properly in the woods became a kind of religion for his son, or that for the rest of Ernest's life certain seasons of the year and certain outdoor settings would infallibly remind him of his father, as he would indicate in "Fathers and Sons."

His father came back to him in the fall of the year, or in the early spring when there had been jacksnipe on the prairie, or when he saw shocks of corn, or when he saw a lake . . . or when he saw, or heard, wild geese, or in a duck blind; remembering the time an eagle dropped through the whirling snow to strike a canvas-covered decoy, rising, his wings beating, the talons caught in the canvas. His father was with him, suddenly, in deserted orchards and in new-plowed fields, in thickets, on small hills, or when going through dead grass, whenever splitting wood or hauling water, by grist mills, cider mills and dams and always with open fires.

Young Ernest's view of his father gradually ceased to be worshipful, however. At first his adolescent rebellion against the hero of his childhood followed a normal developmental pattern for boys of his age. The estrangement between them was encouraged by Dr. Hemingway's decision in 1911, after Grace gave birth to baby Carol, that as the father of five children he could no longer afford to take long vacations at Windemere, thus reducing drastically the amount of time he and Ernest were able to spend in one another's company in the woods. Far more significant, though, was Ernest's growing realization of his father's degrading subservience to Grace, for it resulted in a loss of respect, which was then intensified by Dr. Hemingway's abject departure from home in 1912 to take a "rest cure" for his nerves. And working within Ernest's new attitude of condescension toward his father was a swelling anger about his disciplinarianism. Nick Adams's characterization of *Fortitude* as the book in which the boy's old man is "after him all the time" was no accident: there was no aspect of Peter Westcott's experience with which Ernest more fervently identified.

Unfortunately, the feelings that made for trouble between son and father were never resolved. To the contrary, Ernest's condescension and anger grew abnormally stronger with every passing year— which suggests that another sort of emotion was involved. From the toolshed behind Windemere, he could observe his father sweatily at work in his sunlit tomato patch. In the summer that Ernest turned eighteen—so he later confided to Bill Smith—he occasionally sat quietly in the doorway of the shed with a loaded shotgun beside him and, from time to time, would pick up the gun and carefully draw a bead on his father's head. Perhaps these mock assassinations arose out of a boy's desire to destroy the man he feared he himself would one day become.

To a casual observer, Ernest's adolescent relationship with Grace might have seemed delightfully warm, especially when they got to talking about music, for her interest in the subject had taken firm root in his own sensibility. On a more mundane level, baked goods were another bond between them. Although Grace generally tried to stay out of the kitchen, she did enjoy producing cakes and cookies

—much to the delight of the eternally hungry Ernest. Even after he went off to work in Kansas City, she continued to cater to his sweet tooth with packages sent special delivery.

A saccharine sweetness likewise characterized her manner of addressing him; indeed, as it became clear to her that he, not Marcelline, was her most gifted child, her gushing over him became so fulsome that it might have been an embarrassment, had he not learned to turn it aside with a bantering humor and Jewish nicknames. (Mother Hemingstein he called her, Mrs. Stein for short.) The light touch, in sum, became the socially acceptable means through which he was able to bring to the surface of their encounters his covert hatred and contempt for his mother. And when he reached his middle teens, these feelings were further darkened by an unconscious sense of betrayal. For in the summer of his fifteenth birthday he was given the astonishing news that his mother was once again pregnant. The baby arrived on April 1, 1915, and—April Fool!— turned out to be a boy. No sooner did his mother name him Leicester Clarence than Ernest started calling him Leicester De Pester, after a character in the comic strips. But the sobriquet was too cumbersome, as well as insufficiently expressive of how he felt about having a male sibling after so many years of being the only cock on the walk, so he reduced it to The Pest.

For her part, Grace never doubted that her handsome boy truly loved her. On February 15, 1916, she grouped together in one of her scrapbooks two recent photographs of him. One showed him looking glum with his mouth turned down; in the other, a shy smile wreathed his face. The first picture, Grace noted, is "the way he looks whenever his father speaks to him," and the second is "the way he looks whenever his mother speaks to him." Undoubtedly, she showed him the comment, but its coquettishness did not avail to halt his progressive withdrawal from her, a withdrawal that was particularly noticeable during the vacation months in Michigan. In the summers of 1915, 1916, and 1917 he slept most nights in a tent behind Windemere, or in another tent across the lake at Longfield Farm, or in a camp he established for himself at Murphy's Point, or in the homes of friends in Horton Bay. "Thinking of his mother's exuberant vitality, the rich curves of her every move, the warmth of her vital personality," Ernest's favorite teacher, Fannie Biggs, would reminiscently remark in 1952, "I wondered if Ern would find a wife with the lush motherhood he knew." This vibrant appreciation of another woman's ripeness may very well say less about Ernest than about Miss Biggs, for rumor had it that she was a lesbian. In assuming that he responded to his mother as she did, she did not reckon with the complexity of his feelings. While there is every reason to believe that he was entranced by the descriptions in *Fortitude* of the passionate embraces between Peter Westcott, the would-be novelist, and his mother, the onetime concert singer, within his own family he fled from the very possibility of restaging them.

With his departure for Kansas City in the fall of 1917, he placed a much greater distance between himself and Grace. She would send letters winging after him, however, one of which was highly critical of his conduct, and his instantaneous response to it would provide the first indication of his fate. Although he had reached the point of wanting to break completely free of her, he would not be able to bring it off, nor would he be able to do so in future years, not even after he had all but ceased to write to her. All his life, his mother would remain the dark queen of Hemingway's inner world.

CHAPTER FOUR

~~~~~~

The Championship Game

AMERICA'S DECLARATION OF WAR ON GERMANY in April 1917 moved Ernest to read the latest Hugh Walpole novel, *The Dark Forest,* for it was a war story grounded in firsthand experience. When England had gone to war in 1914, Walpole had attempted to join the British army; after being turned down because of poor eyesight, he had enlisted as a stretcher-bearer in Sanitar, the Russian Red Cross, and had reached East Galicia just in time to be caught up in the great retreat of the Russian Army that became the occasion for his novel.

The hero of *The Dark Forest* is a young Englishman, John Trenchard, who joins the Red Cross in Russia in spite of his having suffered since childhood from an inordinate fear of death. In the course of his rescue work, he falls in love with a nurse. Trenchard, however, is not at all forceful with women and ultimately loses his inamorata to an older, sexually experienced doctor. So great is Trenchard's distress about this that his errands of mercy into the forest of S———, wherein huge numbers of soldiers lie wounded or dead, gradually turn into a quest for oblivion. An Austrian bomb finally grants him his wish. The nurse he had loved is also killed by Austrian gunfire.

In the spring of 1917, Ernest was told in no uncertain terms by his father that he would have to postpone his wish to see action in the war. But if his father could arbitrarily decide that his son was too young to fight, he could not stop him from dreaming about Walpole's story of the Red Cross volunteer and the nurse. After reading a book, Jake Barnes says in *The Sun Also Rises,* it sometimes seemed as though the story "had really happened to me." The young Ernest Hemingway often felt that way, too. In the case of *The Dark Forest,* though, his imagination did its work somewhat differently. Consciously or not, he incorporated the story into his plans for the future, not his memories of the past.

2

THE question which was of more pressing concern to him during his final months in high school had to do with going to college. Marcelline had elected to enroll at Oberlin, and Dr. Hemingway definitely wanted Ernest to accompany her. Studying at Oberlin was a Hemingway tradition, which he felt his son should help to perpetuate. Ernest disagreed. He wanted to do something more exciting, like working on a newspaper. For he had had considerable success as a contributor to his high school literary magazine and as a reporter for the school paper and already knew that he wanted to be a writer. After much hesitation, Dr. Hemingway finally consented to write a letter to his brother Tyler, a prominent Kansas City lumberman, thanks to his marriage to an heiress, asking him if he would use his influence on Ernest's behalf at the Kansas City *Star*. Tyler's good friend, Henry J. Haskell, the chief editorial writer for the *Star,* liked what Tyler told him about his nephew in Oak Park. A cub reporter's position would be opening in the fall, Haskell told Tyler; all his nephew would have to do in order to be hired would be to show up at the proper time.

About his parting from his mother the following October, Ernest never said a word to anyone. But in *For Whom the Bell Tolls* he fictionally recreated in extremely condescending terms his final minutes at the train station with his father. Just before the conductor picked up the box that the novel's hero, Robert Jordan, would step up on to reach the steps of the day coach, "his father had kissed him good-by and said, 'May the Lord watch between me and thee while we are absent the one from the other.'" His father's mustache, Jordan remembers, had been moist and his eyes had been damp with emotion, and he himself had been very embarrassed and "felt suddenly so much older than his father and sorry for him that he could hardly bear it."

Uncle Tyler met his handsome and already physically imposing young nephew at Union Station in Kansas City and took him home to his Aunt Arabella. Although their three-story Victorian house on Warwick Boulevard had room to spare for several guests, Ernest felt constrained by their surveillance of his comings and goings. As soon as he decently could, he left them and moved in with a twenty-nine-year-old bachelor named Carl Edgar, whom he had come to know through Bill Smith's sister Katy at Horton Bay, for Odgar, as he was called, was hopelessly in love with Katy and hung around her every summer. Odgar was not only kind enough to share his apartment with Ernest for a couple of months, but on many a night stayed up to all hours listening to his youthful roommate's excited discourses on the romance of newspaper work. Ernest thought his host a splendid fellow and continued to see a lot of him even after moving to a dismal room of his own some distance away. Indeed, the easygoing Odgar was one of the three friends whom he would invite to join him on a final fishing trip to Michigan before going overseas.

At the Kansas City *Star,* Ernest's boss was the poker-faced assistant city editor, C. G. (Pete) Wellington. One hundred and ten rules for writing vigorous journalistic English had been worked out under the supervision of William Rockhill Nelson, the founder and first editor of the paper, and it was Pete Wellington's job to see that every reporter observed them. "Wellington was a stern disciplinarian, very just and very harsh," Hemingway told an interviewer in 1940, "and I can never say properly how grateful I am to have worked under him." Wellington had compelled him to write in short sentences, to stay away from slang phrases that had lost their freshness, and to cultivate a plainness of expression all but devoid of adjectives. "Those were the best rules I ever learned for the business of writing," Hemingway declared. "I've never forgotten them. No man with any talent, who feels and writes truly about the thing he is trying to say, can fail to write well if he abides by them." Maxwell Perkins, who would edit Hemingway's books at Scribners, was also of the opinion that his apprenticeship at the *Star* had taught him many valuable lessons about writing. It was in Kansas City, said Perkins, that Hemingway "began to learn."

Ernest's initial assignment was the Federal Building, which he found much too tame for his adventurous taste. In the succinct words of Frances Davis, a fellow reporter, "he wanted to ride ambulances," and after thirty days of boredom he finally cajoled Wellington into reassigning him to a beat that included the 15th Street police station, Union Station, and the city hospital, high atop a hill overlooking the train tracks. At the police station he covered reports of small crimes. At the railroad station he checked on the activities of various shady characters of his acquaintance and interviewed celebrities who were passing through. At the hospital he spoke to the

victims of accidents and crimes of violence. That the paper's strap-
ping recruit from Oak Park was "forever disappearing" into the
receiving ward of the hospital or into the back of an ambulance was
the visual impression of John Selby, an aspiring novelist who also
covered hospital stories for the *Star* in the early months of 1918.

Action was what Ernest craved, and action was what Kansas City
offered, in bloody abundance. "I never thought Chicago was a
tough place," he told a friend in 1953; Kansas City, on the other
hand, "was a little rough." The uninhibited violence of the jazz for
which Kansas City would become famous in the twenties, as
pounded out by Bennie Moten's band and Walter Page's Blue
Devils, had taken shape in a town where on one particularly notorious street the dives stretched for twenty-five blocks, three or four
doors apart. In places like The Bucket of Blood and The Yellow
Front, cutting scrapes occurred too frequently to warrant mention
and murder was the Saturday night special.

An aura of violence likewise hung over Lionel Calhoun Moise,
the *Star*'s most controversial reporter. Prodigally talented, Moise
admitted to having worked on nine newspapers across the country
and possibly had been fired from a couple of others because of his
penchant for brawling in barrooms, slugging cops, and throwing
typewriters out of office windows. From his vantage point on the
Star's sports desk, Russel Crouse, the future playwright, was interested to observe that Ernie Hemingway seemed to be modeling
himself on Moise. In Crouse's opinion, "Moise was the guy Ernie
eventually used as the basis for his 'character.' The two of them were
rough and tough but the only erudite rough and tough guys I ever
knew. They could clean out a bar and then quote Shakespeare to the
bartender." By his own admission, Ernest knew Moise "only
slightly," but he observed him from afar with such attentiveness
that some years later he wrote a sketch of him.

> Lionel Moise was a great rewrite man. He could carry four stories in
> his head and go to the telephone and take a fifth and then write all
> five at full speed to catch an edition. There would be something alive
> about each one. He was always the highest paid man on every paper
> he worked on. If any other man was getting more money he quit or
> had his pay raised. He never spoke to the other reporters unless he
> had been drinking. He was tall and thick and had long arms and big
> hands. He was the fastest man on a typewriter I ever knew. He drove
> a motor car and it was understood in the office that a woman had
> given it to him. One night she stabbed him in it out on the Lincoln
> Highway halfway to Jefferson City. He took the knife away from her
> and threw it out of the car.

In addition to being a superlative reporter, Moise could handle booze and he could handle women. Dr. Hemingway's son was impressed.

As for Ernest's own drinking, he was no longer content with the hard cider that he and Bill Smith had depended on. Wine, he decided, was a more worldly drink, and his favorite drinking companion was a worldly youth of twenty-two named Theodore Brumback who had joined the staff of the *Star* following three years at Cornell and four months of driving ambulances in France for the American Field Service. One Saturday night after they had finished work, Ernest insisted that Ted accompany him to his "lodgings," as he grandly called his little room. Although it was well past one in the morning by the time they arrived, Ernest produced a jug of "dago red" and a volume of Browning's poetry and proposed that they take turns reading aloud between sips. After about an hour, Ted fell asleep. A crick in his neck awoke him at four. Ernest, he discovered, was still as fresh as a daisy. "Sometimes I think that's the outstanding characteristic of genius—boundless energy," the hero-worshiping Brumback remarked in the thirties. "When the rest of us mortals have finished our work we're ready for play or bed. But your genius has only started."

Ernest also stopped going to church as soon as he moved out of Uncle Tyler's house. By January, his mother got wind of this and wrote him a letter in which she attempted to make him feel guilty by overstating the extent of his apostasy. In sorrowful tones she accused him of having ceased to be a Christian and of consorting with irreligious friends. On the same day that her accusations reached him he responded to them, in a letter that quickly moved from seemingly good-humored reassurances to lame excuses to unconcealed anger.

> Now dry those tears Mother. . . . Don't worry or cry or fret about my not being a good Christian. I am just as much as ever and pray every night and believe just as hard so cheer up! . . . The reason I don't go to church on Sunday is because always I have to work till 1 a.m. getting out the Sunday Star and every once in a while till 3 or 4 a.m. And I never open my eyes Sunday morning until 12:30 noon anyway. So you see it isn't because I don't want to. You know I don't rave about religion but am as sincere a Christian as I can be. . . . Now Mother I got awfully angry when I read what you wrote about Carl [Edgar] and Bill [Smith]. . . . Carl is a *Prince* and about the most sincere and real Christian I have ever known. . . . I have never asked Bill what church he goes to because that doesn't matter. We both believe in God and Jesus Christ and have hopes for a hereafter and

creeds don't matter. Please don't unjustly criticize my best friends
again.

There were any number of temptations for a young man in wartime Kansas City, prostitutes in particular. (According to local
wags, the thoroughfare for which the "Twelfth Street Rag" was
named deserved to be called Woodrow Wilson Avenue, since a piece
could be obtained there at any price.) Of the various indications that
whores were on Ernest's mind, the most direct was a feature article
he wrote for the *Star,* in which the lonely vigil of a streetwalker
standing in the falling snow outside the Fine Arts Institute is con-
trasted with the jolly time that some female students from the Institute are having at a dance inside the building with a group of soldiers
from Fort Leavenworth and Camp Funston. Ernest's inhibitions
were such that he probably only entertained fantasies about paying
a woman to have sex with him and didn't actually contract for
services. He may very well, however, have patronized one or more
of the city's striptease theaters, for in 1927 the manager of a burlesque show which had been booked into Kansas City would appear
in one of the sharply observed stories in *Men Without Women.*
For the first time in his eighteen years of life, Ernest was on his
own during his months in Missouri. Nevertheless, his mother's influence remained strong. If Grace did not call on her son in so many
words to keep his thoughts pure and his body unprofaned in this
time of trial, it was because she did not have to, for her lamentations
about his abandonment of Christianity sent him a message to that
effect in easily decipherable code. He got the moralizing message, all
right, and was upset by it, but his immediate reaction was mild
compared to the emotion he expressed fifteen years later. In the
gruesome story called "God Rest You Merry, Gentlemen," he
showed that after a decade and a half of brooding he now looked
back on his mother's veiled effort to ensure that he didn't have a sex
life in Kansas City as another attempt to unman him.
"God Rest You" takes place in the days before Kansas City's
protuberant hills were cut down; the setting is the city hospital; the
time is Christmas Day. Two ambulance surgeons, named Wilcox
and Fischer, are talking with Horace, the youthful narrator of the
story, who may or may not be a newspaperman and whose name
suggests what is on his mind, particularly if the second syllable is
dragged out (like this: whore-ass). According to the story that the
surgeons tell Horace, an excited, frightened boy of about sixteen had
come into the receiving room the afternoon before and told them

that he wanted to be castrated. Even though "I've prayed and done everything," the boy had said, an "awful lust" had taken control of his body. Fischer, a sardonically witty Jew with a history of lack of respect for Federal statutes (probably relating to abortion), had tried to persuade him that what was happening to his body was perfectly normal, but the boy refused to listen. "It is wrong," he had insisted. "It's a sin against purity. It's a sin against our Lord and Saviour." The boy had finally left the hospital, but at one o'clock on Christmas morning an ambulance had brought him back, "self-mutilated with a razor." Having known nothing about the physiology of desire, he has amputated his penis and may die from loss of blood. "On Christmas Day, too," Wilcox solemnly observes. Fischer at once objects that "the significance of the particular day is not important," but it is just another of his Jewish jokes, for only a few moments earlier he had reminded Wilcox with elaborate irony that the amputation has occurred on "the day, the very anniversary, of our Saviour's birth"—or rather, "*Your* Saviour."

While the moral spectacle of Kansas City in wartime did not cause the young Hemingway to lose all faith in the comfortable religion of his boyhood, it nevertheless opened his mind to a view of liberty as an unending ordeal and continuing agony very like that of a Puritan authority on the human condition. History, Jonathan Edwards had said two centuries before, displays a "prevailing, continual and generally effectual tendency . . . to the victory of evil appetites and lusts over men." Oak Park's liberal Protestantism contended to the contrary that history is a record of men's victory over themselves. Kansas City, however, did not support that view.

3

UPON arriving in Missouri, Ernest had initially thought that he would work on the *Star* for about seven months and then get in "one more good summer" in Michigan before enlisting in one of the military services. "I couldn't possibly stay out of [the war] any longer than that under any circumstances," he firmly informed his family on November 15. "It will be hard enough to stay out till then." In fact, he found it impossible. In his view, the "war to end all wars" was essentially like a championship football game in which America was the home team and the Germans and the Austrians were the visiting team. If he waited too long, he might miss it completely.

The only question that remained was what was the best way to take in the contest. In the course of the winter he led his family and friends to believe he had tried to enlist in the Army, but had been rejected because of poor vision in his left eye. To Marcelline he explained, "We all have that bad eye like Mother's but I'll make it to Europe some way, in spite of this optic," and he gave Ted Brumback the impression that the rejection "preyed upon his mind and made him morose at times." There is no record, though, of his having made a formal effort to sign up with the Army, while there is strong reason to believe that he would have been accepted if he had. The Army doctors in Kansas City put no roadblocks in the war path of Harry S. Truman, after all, despite the fact that without his glasses he was helpless. The likelihood, therefore, is that for all his patriotism the prospect of trench warfare put Ernest off. *The Dark Forest* had taught him that rescue work offered a splendid way to get close to the fighting without actually being a foot soldier, and this possibility was raised again by Brumback. The reason Ted had enlisted in the American Field Service rather than the Army was that he had lost an eye in an accident in college. Telling Ernest about his recent adventures in France had the effect of rekindling his own interest in driving ambulances at the same time that it brought Ernest's to a boil. Early in January, both boys volunteered for overseas duty with the American Red Cross (whose late founder, Clara Barton, was the sister of Oak Park's Dr. Barton). Four months later, they received notice that they would be assigned as second lieutenants in an ambulance unit in Italy if they could pass a physical exam at Red Cross headquarters in New York.

While Ernest had no difficulty with the exam, the Manhattan doctor who looked him over recommended that he start wearing glasses. That he paid no heed to this advice was not surprising, for this was how his mother had conditioned him to respond. Grace had been aware for years that Ernest and Marcelline both had eye problems, but because she herself disliked wearing glasses she discouraged her children from depending on them. When Marcelline complained one day that she couldn't see what was written on the blackboard at school, Grace told her to sit closer to the front of the room. In Ernest's case, uncorrected eyesight was one of the factors that made him accident-prone in later life. For even though he finally consented to be fitted for a pair of glasses when he was thirty-one, vanity would keep him from wearing them as consistently as he should have.

To the young volunteer's delight, the Red Cross issued him a regular U.S. Army officer's uniform with full insignia, leather aviation puttees, and officer's shoes, which Ernest promptly supplemented with a pair of cordovan leather boots that set him back thirty

dollars. Army privates and noncoms were required to salute "camouflaged 1st [*sic*] Lieuts" like himself, he told his family, and during
a walk up and down Broadway one evening, he wrote to a friend,
he counted 367 who actually did—or so he claimed. On May 17, he
was among the seventy-five thousand men and women who helped
launch a fund drive for the Red Cross by marching down Fifth
Avenue in a parade that was reviewed by President and Mrs. Wilson.
Because of his size and good looks, Ernest was chosen as the right
guide of the first platoon, which meant that when the command for
eyes right was given he had "a fine look at Woodrow."

Never before had he known such excitement. As the experiences
began to accumulate that would lead to his becoming one of the
most celebrated war writers of the twentieth century, his creative
imagination accelerated to the point where his communications with
his family and friends sometimes contained more fiction than fact.
Thus, his thoughts about the war in Europe made him think about
the war his two grandfathers had fought in, which in turn made him
think about a movie he had seen, D. W. Griffith's epic *The Birth of
a Nation* (1915), which in turn made him think of Mae Marsh, the
actress who had played the part in it of "the younger sister." The
result was a reiterated assertion that he was having a romance with
Miss Marsh, although in reality they had never met. "Miss Marsh
no kidding says she loves me," Ernest assured a newspaper buddy
back in Kansas City. "I suggested the little church around the corner
but she opined as how ye war widow appealed not to her. So I sank
the 150 plunks Pop gave me in a ring so I am engaged anyway."

While this yarn must have impressed the boys at the *Star*—if they
believed it, that is—it had a very different effect on his correspondents in Oak Park. On the morning that his letter arrived announcing his engagement, Grace was already in the midst of writing a
letter to him, in which she was doing her best to make him feel
uncomfortable about his failure to write home as often as she wanted
him to. "We are so eager to hear from you," she said. "Mrs. New-
burg gets a letter from her son every day, she is sorry for me and so
shares her news with me." At that point, the mail came.

When she picked up her pen and resumed writing, Grace's mood
was considerably grimmer. Combining mock self-abasement and
righteous wrath, she began by saying that she must have been a very
poor success as a mother, inasmuch as he had never admitted to
being serious about any girl and now he was speaking about an
engagement. He was only eighteen and had no income, she reminded him; if he persisted in this foolishness, he would be bound
to become a laughingstock. "Marriage," she sermonized,

is a beautiful and wonderful thing; but it is sacred in proportion to the prayerfulness with which it is entered into. You may come home disfigured and crippled; would this girl love you, then? A marriage ceremony should be followed by constant companionship, a little home nest, a bit of heaven roofed over and walled in. . . . Such marriage as you suggest would be unnatural and apt to bring great sorrow and misunderstanding. God help you, dear, I cannot.

Two days later, she tried a more seductive approach. It was "only yesterday," she emotionally reminded her son, that you were a "little yellow-headed laddie" who "used to hug me tight." Then she got down to business. "Don't forget, darling, that any girl who is worth while is worth waiting for and working for; and if she really loves you will be willing to wait till you are a man and able to take care of her. Oh, how I wish to help you at this time, but tho I cannot, God will, for He stands ready to guide your life ship." Forty-eight hours after this appeal, she again wrote to Ernest—but by this time she and Dr. Hemingway had received a telegram from New York saying CHEER UP AM NOT ENGAGED MARRIED OR DIVORCED THIS IS AUTHENTIC JUST JOKING. As a result, Grace was all smiles and eager to talk about other things. "My! but wouldn't the folks 'back home' like to have seen you leading the parade & saluting 'dear Woodrow.' We all swelled out at the very thought."

For all the floweriness of her language, Grace's arguments had been tellingly logical, and in less than a week she had forced Ernest to admit that his story wasn't true. But no one likes to be exposed as a liar, and her description of married life as "a bit of heaven roofed over and walled in" must have further enraged him by its almost comical hypocrisy. As for her shocking suggestion that he might come back from the war a cripple, it may have helped to provoke the tall tales he would soon be telling about the extent of his wounds.

4

THE French Line ship on which he crossed the U-boat–infested Atlantic was named, coincidentally enough, the *Chicago*. It was such a rotten old tub that when a storm came up she "pitched, rolled, stood on her ear and swung in wide lugubrious circles," Ernest reported to his family. Like most of the other passengers on board, he got sick to his stomach and felt miserable, but then the sun came out and he began to have a "grand time" with Ted Brumback, another ambulance driver named Howell Jenkins and a couple of Polish officers who were "dandy fellows." What he didn't tell his family was that there was a young French woman on board. Gaby had a raucous laugh, a bad odor of some sort, and blond hair that was always coming down, and she spent most of her time entertaining a succession of soldiers in a lifeboat. Although Ernest may not have joined the line, he at least remembered Gaby well enough to put her and the Polish officers into the first chapter of an abortive war novel called *Along With Youth* and starring Nick Adams.

Skirting south of the sea lanes in which the U-boats usually hunted, the *Chicago* finally reached Bordeaux, where Ted and Ernest had dinner in a cheap but good restaurant before boarding the night train for Paris. Shells from Big Bertha, a huge German siege gun, were falling indiscriminately on different parts of the city, someone at the train station told them the following morning. Ignoring Ted's idea that they hole up in a hotel, Ernest hailed one of the two-cylinder taxis that had helped to save Paris at the first battle of the Marne, threw his and Ted's luggage in the back, and told Ted to tell the driver to take them to "where those shells are falling." It appeared to Ted as though the driver was going to have a stroke, but when they offered him more money he became more cooperative. For the next hour or so they careened across the city in quest of the thrill of being under enemy fire. As they neared the Place de la Madeleine they at last heard a projectile rushing overhead. It made such a racket that Ted was afraid it was going to land in their taxi, but instead it hit La Madeleine, chipping off a foot of stone from the church's facade. Only then was Ernest willing to repair to the Hotel Florida on the Boulevard Malesherbes.

Along with more than a hundred other Red Cross volunteers, the two friends were soon on their way to Milan. There, too, they were reminded that a war was going on. On the morning of their arrival, a huge munitions factory outside the city was destroyed by an explosion, and Ernest and his comrades were ordered to help in the search for the dead. Years later, the author of *Death in the Afternoon* recalled that grisly day.

> Regarding the sex of the dead it is a fact that one becomes so accustomed to the sight of all the dead being men that the sight of a dead woman is quite shocking. I first saw the inversion of the usual sex of the dead after the explosion of a munition factory which had been situated in the countryside near Milan, Italy. . . . We were ordered to search the immediate vicinity and surrounding fields for bodies. We found and carried to an improvised mortuary a good number of these and, I must admit frankly, the shock it was to find that these dead were women rather than men. In those days women had not yet commenced to wear their hair cut short, as they did later for several years in Europe and America, and the most disturbing thing, perhaps

because it was the most unaccustomed, was the presence and, even
more disturbing, the occasional absence of this long hair. I remember
that after we had searched quite thoroughly for the complete dead we
collected fragments. Many of these were detached from a heavy,
barbed-wire fence which had surrounded the position of the factory
and from the still existent portions of which we picked many of these
detached bits. . . . The picking up of the fragments [was] an extraordinary business; it being amazing that the human body should be
blown into pieces which exploded along no anatomical lines, but
rather divided as capriciously as the fragmentation in the burst of a
high explosive shell.

He was shocked to come upon a sexual inversion; he was disturbed
by the sight of the dead women's long hair; he was even more
disturbed by the fact that some of them had short hair; he was
amazed by the number of different ways in which human bodies
could be maimed. Lombardy was a long way from home, but the
youth from Oak Park had brought with him a full set of old fixations
in which to pack new images.

On or about June 6, Ernest joined his ambulance unit—Section
Four, it was called—in the wool manufacturing town of Schio, sixteen miles northwest of Vicenza in the shadow of the limestone
peaks of the Dolomites. The unit was quartered in an old factory,
jokingly known as the Schio Country Club because of its stark
accommodations and pervasive smell of sheep. The wines, though,
were clear red, tannic and lovely, the game stews savory and the
servings of pasta large, and Ernest would have been content with his
lot if only he had been closer to the sound of battle.

His job was to drive a high-seated Fiat truck up into the mountains, take on a load of wounded soldiers and haul them down to a
distribution point, where they were given emergency treatment and
assigned to a hospital. Except for negotiating the hairpin turns on
Monte Pasubio, he found the work tedious. Literary legend has it
that one day he did have a lively encounter with a brilliant young
Harvard man named John Dos Passos, who had once driven ambulances for the socially prestigious Norton-Harjes unit in France and
was just now completing another tour of duty with an American
Red Cross unit stationed not too far from Section Four. Neither
young man caught the other's name, but after they became friends
in France in the twenties they discovered that they had both been in
the Dolomites at about the same time. Dos Passos then recalled that
he and another Harvard driver named Sydney Fairbanks had talked
with Hemingway for about two hours. Dos Passos's certainty about
this encouraged Hemingway to declare that he, too, remembered

their meeting. When Fairbanks was asked to confirm their recollections, he added a number of circumstantial details. Dos Passos and
Hemingway had instantly understood each other, he said; as for
Fairbanks's own reaction to Hemingway, he asserted that he had
found him opinionated but impressive. Remembrance, alas, is a
tricky business. Dos Passos's diaries and private papers reveal that
he was released from his unit and left for Rome on May 30, a full
week before Hemingway showed up in Schio.

Ernest was fed up, he told Ted Brumback after a week had gone
by. "There's nothing here but scenery and too damn much of that.
I'm going to get out of this ambulance section and see if I can't find
out where the war is." Almost at once his chance came. The chief of
Section Four asked for volunteers to man the chain of canteens the
Red Cross was setting up under the command of Captain James
Gamble in the Piave River Valley north of Venice. The canteens
would offer coffee, soup, candy and cigarettes to off-duty soldiers
and provide them with a place to write letters and listen to phono-
graph records. Until the canteens were operational, the *tenente* in
charge would be expected to bicycle up to the front twice a day and
pass out cigarettes and chocolates to the troops. Ernest immediately
volunteered, for he had heard that the fighting along the lower Piave
was the most intense since the Italian defeat at Caporetto the previous autumn.

By the fourth week in June, Lieutenant Hemingway was living by
himself in a small house in Fossalta di Piave, about a mile and a half
behind the lines. "Each aft and morning," he informed his high
school classmate Ruth Morrison in a somewhat lonely-sounding
letter, "I load up a haversack and take my tin lid and gas mask and
beat it up to the trenches. I sure have a good time but miss their [*sic*]
being no Americans. Gee I have near forgot the English language."
When his loneliness finally became more than he could bear, he took
a day off and cycled to a neighboring village where two other Red
Cross officers, Bill Horne and Warren Pease, were living on the
second floor of a silk factory housing thousands of silkworms.
Spending a night in that factory was an uncanny experience which
would later serve him well in "Now I Lay Me."

The Italian to whom he felt closest during the brief time he lived
in Fossalta was a young priest from Florence named Don Giuseppe
Bianchi. Most evenings Ernest ate dinner in the officers' mess of the
69th and 70th regiments of the Brigata Ancona, and it was there that
he encountered the priest. He "wore a uniform like the rest of us,"
Hemingway would say of Don Giuseppe's fictional counterpart in
A Farewell to Arms, "but with a cross in dark red velvet above the

left breast of his gray tunic." The priest was a great help to Ernest socially, speaking to him in pidgin English whenever he felt that the young American had lost the thread of what the other officers at the table were saying. In *A Farewell to Arms,* one of the Italian officers tells Lieutenant Frederic Henry, "Sometimes I think you and [the priest] are a little that way. . . . A little that way like the number of the first regiment of the Brigata Ancona." When Lieutenant Henry tells him to go to hell, the officer smilingly says that he was only teasing.

Much as he enjoyed the priest's company, Ernest did not appear in the mess hall on the night of July 8. Instead, he rode his bicycle far out along the west bank of the Piave to see what he could do for the morale of the men in a forward listening post. While he was passing out chocolates in a dugout, a trench mortar shell exploded a few feet away. Many years later he declared that the passage describing the wounding of Lieutenant Henry in *A Farewell to Arms* was an accurate account of what had happened to him. "I heard a cough, then came the chuh-chuh-chuh-chuh—then there was a flash, as when a blast-furnace door is swung open, and a roar that started white and went red and on and on in a rushing wind." Shell fragments tore into both of the American Tenente's legs, the novel says, knocking him off his feet and causing him to hit his head with stunning force against the side of the dugout. The soldier who was nearest to him was screaming in agony. The Tenente looked at him and saw that one of his legs was gone and that the other was held in place only by a few tendons and part of his trouser. He tried to come to the wounded Italian's aid, but found that he couldn't stand up. Pulling himself along the ground by his arms and elbows, he inched up to the soldier and unwound the puttee from his remaining leg to make tourniquets. By that time, though, the man was dead.

His legs felt warm and wet and his shoes were warm and wet inside. He reached for his knee but it seemed to be down on his shin. He asked God to get him out of there. A soldier took hold of him under the arms and another soldier lifted his legs. As the men were carrying him toward a dressing station, another shell landed nearby. Both soldiers fell to the ground to protect themselves, dropping their burden in so doing. With apologies, they picked the Tenente up again and resumed walking, only to drop him once more before reaching the station. A great many wounded soldiers lay on the ground, waiting for aid. A medical sergeant came out of the station and put bandages on his legs. The sergeant said that so much dirt had blown into his wounds that there had not been much hemorrhage. After a while, two stretcher-bearers and a tall Englishman came to fetch him inside. "I'd rather wait," he said. "There are much worse wounded than me." In spite of his protest, the Englishman ordered the stretcher-bearers to take him in. Attendants stripped off his trousers and the medical captain commenced dictating to the sergeant-adjutant while he worked. "Multiple superficial wounds on the left and right thigh and left and right knee and right foot. Profound wounds of right knee and foot. Lacerations of the scalp . . . with possible fracture of the skull." The captain removed as many of the *scaggia* from the Tenente's legs as he could under the circumstances, gave him an antitetanus shot and a snort of brandy and bandaged him up.

From the dressing station he was transported by ambulance to a field hospital. Here he remained, swathed in bandages, for several days before being sent on by train to a newly established American hospital in Milan for surgical removal of the remaining shell fragments.

5

FOUR documents lend credibility to Hemingway's assertion that he told the truth in *A Farewell to Arms* about the events of the night of July 8. First, there is the telegram that the Red Cross in Washington sent to his parents, informing them that their son had been hit by "a trench mortar bomb." Second, there is the cablegram that Ernest sent to them: WOUNDED IN LEG BY TRENCH MORTAR. WILL RECEIVE VALOR MEDAL. WILL WALK AGAIN IN TEN DAYS. Third, there is the reference to Hemingway in *Report of the Department of Military Affairs January to July, 1918,* a thirty-page pamphlet describing the work of the American Red Cross in Italy: "E. M. Hemingway was wounded by the explosion of a shell which landed about three feet from him, killing a soldier who stood between him and the point of explosion, and wounding others." Fourth, there is the citation appended to the Silver Medal of Military Valor which he received from the Italian government:

Ernest Miller Hemingway of Illinois Park (Chicago) Lieutenant of the American Red Cross.—Officer of the American Red Cross, responsible for carrying sundries (articles of comfort) to the Italian troops engaged in combat, gave proof of courage and self-sacrifice [*abnegazione*]. Gravely wounded by numerous pieces of shrapnel from an enemy shell, with an admirable spirit of brotherhood [*fratellanza*], before taking care of himself, he rendered generous assistance to the Italian soldiers more seriously wounded by the same explosion and did not allow himself to be carried elsewhere until after they had been evacuated.

In sum, Hemingway had been hit by shellfire, had responded courageously and had finally been borne to a dressing station.

Ambiguity about what had taken place dates from July 14, when Ted Brumback arrived in Milan. After spending the day visiting with Ernest, he wrote Dr. Hemingway a letter, setting forth everything he had learned. His first paragraph was compatible with the account that *A Farewell to Arms* would present.

> I have just come from seeing Ernest at the American Red Cross Hospital here. . . . Although some two hundred pieces of shell were lodged in him none of them are above the hip joint. Only a few of these pieces [were] large enough to cut deep; the most serious of these being two in the knee and two in the right foot. The doctor says there will be no trouble about these wounds healing and that Ernest will regain entire use of both legs.

"Now that I have told you about his condition," Brumback's next paragraph began, "I suppose you would like to know all the circumstances of the case." He then went on to tell how Ernest had been wounded and about the events that had happened next. In doing so, he had no reason to suspect that the heroic story he was relaying was not reliable.

> An enormous trench mortar bomb lit within a few feet of Ernest while he was giving out chocolate. The concussion of the explosion knocked him unconscious and buried him with earth. There was an Italian between Ernest and the shell. He was instantly killed while another, standing by a few feet away, had both his legs blown off. A third Italian was badly wounded and this one Ernest, after he had regained consciousness, picked up on his back and carried to the first aid dug-out. He says he does not remember how he got there nor that he had carried a man until the next day when an Italian officer told him all about it and said that it had been voted upon to give him a valor medal for the act.

In the rest of Brumback's letter there was nothing of comparable interest, except for one sentence near the close. "We have made a collection of shell fragments and bullets that were taken out of Ernie's leg which will be made up into rings." Neither the detailed description of Ernest's condition at the beginning of the letter nor the succeeding description of how he had been wounded had made reference to bullet wounds. What, then, did Brumback mean by saying that bullets had been taken from his leg? If Dr. Hemingway and Grace were confused by the wording of this sentence, they probably ascribed it to a carelessness of expression on Brumback's part, caused by fatigue at the end of a long day. It was their son, however, who was responsible for that mention of bullets, as he was for the assertion that after being wounded he had carried an Italian soldier on his back to a first-aid dugout. The astonishing details of this tale would only gradually emerge.

The telegram from Red Cross headquarters in Washington reached the Hemingways on July 15. A newspaper reporter who interviewed Grace later in the day found that in the absence of detailed information about what had happened to her son she mainly wanted to brag about his achievements as a newspaperman. After finishing high school, she proudly told the reporter, he "entered newspaper work, joining the editorial staff of the Kansas City *Star*. He made good with a vengeance there, and was considered a star of the staff, even if only a boy." A day or so afterwards, Ernest's cablegram arrived, with the news that he had been recommended for a medal. Grace waited until the twenty-first of the month—Ernest's nineteenth birthday—to respond to him. Nineteen years ago today, she began, "you were a mighty welcome laddie boy and it seems only yesterday that you were dependent upon me for everything." Having reminded him of his breast-feeding babyhood, she then saluted his manliness. "I know that you were rejoicing . . . to think that you were not found wanting when your supreme opportunity came; that you thought more of others than of yourself and so will be marked forever as a *brave* man." Not for the first time, she called Ernest's attention to the fact that he had been "named for great noble souls"—namely, her father and her uncle—which was her way of saying, of course, that he was a Hall, not a Hemingway. "It's great to be the mother of a hero," she glowed.

On that very same day her hospitalized son wrote his first letter home. "I'm the first American wounded in Italy," he announced, although as he well knew this wasn't so. Lieutenant Edward M. McKey, a fellow ambulance driver, had been killed by an Austrian shell in early June. A couple of shell fragments were still buried in his flesh, Ernest continued, and would have to be surgically removed, along with a machine-gun bullet from under his right kneecap and another bullet from his right foot. Otherwise, he was in fine shape. "All of the other bullets and pieces of shell have been removed," he said, and all 227 of his wounds—shades of 367 salutes on Broadway!—were healing nicely. Miraculously, none of the bullets he had been hit by had struck bone, not even the ones which were in his kneecap and foot. "There will be no permanent effects from any of the wounds," he emphasized, "as there are no bones shattered. Even in my knees." During the Civil War, a solitary minié ball had lodged in Ernest Hall's thigh. The bullet wounds sustained by his namesake were, or so he asserted, far more extensive, although their exact number had still not been specified.

It is difficult to imagine how he could have received such wounds. Inasmuch as the walls of the dugout he was in would have protected him from machine-gun fire altogether, a burst of bullets could have sprayed across his legs only after he had left it. But if he was borne to the dressing station by two soldiers, as the account in *A Farewell to Arms* suggests, would not a sequence of machine-gun fire have cut them down as well? Furthermore, how could the bullets he showed to Brumback have been recovered from *his* body? The machine guns of World War I fired pointed-nosed, low-velocity (2,500 feet per second), twisting bullets which did not lose their speed or tumble when they simply hit flesh. Consequently, they passed right through the body unless they struck bone—and in Hemingway's case they had not, as he himself had emphasized. As for the two bullets which he claimed would have to be surgically removed, given the boniness of the kneecap and the foot, what are the odds that bullets fired into them would *not* have caused fractures? Very long, indeed. Thus, even apart from the cablegram, the official Red Cross report, the medal citation, and *A Farewell to Arms,* Hemingway's talk of machine-gun wounds rings false. And so does the follow-up letter he sent to his family on August 18, in which he at last explained how he had sustained them.

In this letter, he did not speak of inching forward by his hands and elbows in an attempt to succor a soldier screaming in agony; he spoke rather of picking up a wounded Italian and carrying him an incredible 150 yards to the dugout of his company commander—in spite of being struck by machine-gun fire while doing so. "The machine gun bullet [sic] just felt like a sharp smack on my leg with an icy snow ball. However it spilled me. But I got up again and got my wounded into the dug out. I kind of collapsed at the dug out. The Italian I had with me bled all over my coat." The company commander was sure that this blood-drenched American was going to die. "You see they thought I was shot through the chest on account of my bloody coat." Thus did he confirm the story he had told to Ted Brumback.

With trench-mortar wounds in both legs and a badly lacerated head, could even the brawny and courageous Hemingway have

struggled to his feet, slung a grown man on his back and set off on
a walk half again as long as a football field? Could he have resumed
that burdensome walk after having his battered legs knocked out
from under him by machine-gun bullets? And what purpose did it
serve to hand over the wounded man to his company commander?
Would not Hemingway's Silver Medal citation have dwelt on this
remarkable—if futile—feat, instead of vaguely referring to generous
assistance offered to other victims before being carried from the
field? Indeed, would not the Italian government have been moved
to give him the more coveted Gold Medal? When it came to handing
out medals to their allies, after all, Italy's military commanders were
proverbially generous. While Italian soldiers had to do something
outstanding to qualify for the *medaglia d'argento,* Americans sometimes received it simply because they had been wounded. Lieutenant
McKey was an example. He was "killed by a shell while conferring
as to arrangements with two Italian officers"; yet even though he
had done nothing remotely heroic he was posthumously awarded
the Silver Medal.

A Farewell to Arms sheds further light on this point. Breezing into
Lieutenant Henry's room in the field hospital, Lieutenant Rinaldi
gives his American friend the good news. "They want to get you
the medaglia d'argento. . . . Did you do any heroic act?" When
Henry says he did not, Rinaldi presses him further. "Didn't you
carry anybody on your back? Gordini says you carried several people
on your back but the medical major at the first post declares it is
impossible. He had to sign the proposition for the citation." "I
didn't carry anyone. I couldn't move," Henry protests, but Rinaldi
brushes aside this honest statement as inconsequential. "Look how
you are wounded," he expostulates. "I think we can get you the
silver."

"In Another Country," one of Hemingway's own favorites
among his stories, is even more illuminating about the business of
medals. The young Italian officers whom the American narrator
meets in the physical-therapy room in the hospital in Milan are very
polite about his awards and ask him what he did to get them. "I
showed them the papers, which were written in very beautiful language and full of *fratellanza* and *abnegazione,* but which really said,
with the adjectives removed, that I had been given the medals because I was an American." The medals worn by the Italian officers
symbolized "very different things," the narrator realizes. "I had
been wounded, it was true; but we all knew that being wounded,
after all, was really an accident." His friends from the therapy room

"were like hunting-hawks; and I was not a hawk, although I might seem like a hawk to those who had never hunted."

Upon his return to Oak Park in early 1919, Hemingway would begin spreading stories around town that his parents must have known were deceptive. Nevertheless, their faith in the veracity of their limping son remained unshaken. To all appearances, the community as a whole was equally uninterested in challenging him. Thus, in the auditorium at Oak Park High School a week after he got back, he spoke in such circumstantial detail about the Italian shock troops called Arditi as to imply that after recovering from his wounds at Fossalta he had fought with them; yet even though everyone in the auditorium could see that he still could not walk comfortably without a cane, no pointed questions were put to him at the end of the talk. An interview he gave to the *Oak Parker* was no less expansive. He had been knocked down not once but twice by machine-gun fire, he told the hero-worshiping reporter who interviewed him, and had been hit thirty-two times all told by .45-caliber bullets. And when the ladies on the Memorial Committee of Oak Park and River Forest mailed him a questionnaire about his war service, he struck awe into them by replying that after a tour of duty with the American Volunteer Ambulance Service he had joined the 69th Infantry, Brigata Ancona as a first lieutenant and had fought in three major battles: along the lower Piave, on Monte Grappa and at Vittorio Veneto.

He continued to misrepresent his role in the war to friends in Chicago and Paris in the early twenties. But while lying about his experiences would seem to have become second nature to him, it also took an unforeseen toll, as he acknowledged in "Soldier's Home," written in 1924. A young man named Harold Krebs, a veteran of Belleau Wood, Soissons, St. Mihiel, and the Argonne, finds that the people in his home town have absorbed too many propaganda stories to be enthralled by unadorned truths. In order to be listened to, Krebs has to lie—but emotionally speaking he doesn't get away with it.

> A distaste for everything that had happened to him in the war set in because of the lies he had told. All of the times that had been able to make him feel cool and clear inside himself when he thought of them; the times so long back when he had done the one thing, the only thing for a man to do, easily and naturally, when he might have done something else, now lost their cool, valuable quality and then were lost themselves. . . . In this way he lost everything.

Perhaps in order to preserve the memory of those things that had made him feel justifiably proud of himself, Hemingway finally described what really occurred on the night he was wounded. He did so, however, in a work of fiction, *A Farewell to Arms,* which his readers would by and large refuse to accept as a summary of the whole story. Carlos Baker's standard biography speaks for myth-lovers everywhere as it moves from a description of how Hemingway "groped for [the wounded Italian's] neck and legs, heaved him up in a fireman's carry, and began to stagger back towards the command post" to an equally colorful evocation of the neatness of the scar on the future novelist's right instep, "where the copper-jacketed bullet had entered." The myth of what happened at Fossalta also survives in Jeffrey Meyers's *Hemingway* (1985), the most recent full-scale biography. Michael Reynolds, on the other hand, asserts in *The Young Hemingway* (1986) that the wounded lieutenant's August 18, 1918, letter to his family was "fiction," although Reynolds does not doubt that he had been hit by machine-gun fire.

The story of Hemingway's enlistment in the Italian army would likewise enjoy a remarkable longevity. Newspaper and magazine writers battened on it in the twenties and thirties; in the forties the critic Malcolm Cowley reaffirmed its authenticity by asserting in his introduction to the *Portable Hemingway* that after being patched up in the hospital in Milan the young hero "served for a time in the Italian shock troops, the Arditi." Philip Young and Robert Penn Warren subsequently repeated that statement in their own critical work on Hemingway, and in 1969 the biographical squib on the back of the Scribner Library reissue of *A Farewell to Arms* lent to it the imprimatur of the novelist's own publisher.

The critics would also fail to question Hemingway's account of how it was that he came to write a novel about a man who was not fully a man because he had been wounded in the crotch. In the course of his convalescence in Milan he had visited a genito-urinary ward in another hospital, the author of *The Sun Also Rises* would be wont to say. There he had talked to a number of soldiers who had suffered genital injuries, and as a result of wondering about their plight he had come to imagine Jake Barnes's. The only item of significance that was missing from this plausible-sounding story was a convincing explanation of why Hemingway had been so interested in the wounded in that particular ward.

6

MILAN'S Ospedale Croce Rossa Americana was located in a handsome stone mansion, with a gate and a courtyard, on the fashionable Via Manzoni, not far from La Scala and the Galleria. The patients were lodged on the top floor in lovely high-ceilinged rooms looking out on a balcony. Eighteen nurses were responsible for less than a third that number of patients, so that any new patient could expect a good deal of attention. The new patient who was wheeled in one sunny morning in July 1918 was a young man whose darkly handsome good looks were dramatically enhanced by the bandage around his head, even as his muscular upper body was set off by the bandages encasing his legs. Old and young, the nurses flocked around him.

With a nurse named Elsie Macdonald, a short, middle-aged woman with a burr in her speech that testified to her Scottish background, Hemingway quickly established a teasing relationship that facilitated his disobedience of hospital regulations. The patients were not permitted, for example, to keep wine or liquor in their rooms. Even though the boy from bone-dry Oak Park was not yet a regular drinker, he wanted to wet his whistle whenever he felt like it. On discovering that the wardrobe in his room contained some empty cognac bottles, the head of the nursing staff scolded him severely, but Nurse Macdonald made only a show of anger and looked the other way when he replenished his supply. She clucked around him constantly, *"like a good mother,"* as she later said in her emphatic way, going with him to another hospital to have x-rays taken before his surgery, and reminding him during his recuperation to protect his "poor lame foot" by wearing a slipper. In her view, Hemingway was "a broken doll who came all the way from the Piave to be *glued* together," and she did her best to make him as good as new.

Nurse Macdonald may have been like a mother to him—but she bore not the slightest resemblance to the real commodity. The same observation could not have been made of twenty-six-year-old Agnes von Kurowsky. At five feet eight inches tall, Agnes was the same height as Grace and her chestnut hair was almost exactly the same color. An important similarity also obtained in her personality—no shrinking violet was she. As a librarian in Washington, D.C., this self-dramatizing young woman had known and enjoyed the company of many men. Flirting with those she liked and refusing to be tied down by smitten suitors, she acquired a reputation for fickleness. After completing her medical training at Bellevue Hospital in New York, she had become engaged to a doctor, but once she reached Italy she no longer felt bound to him. Although Hemingway was certainly attracted to Agnes because of her beauty, their romance might never have developed had not her aggressiveness made it easy for him to know her.

For while he may have been bold when in the company of Prudy Boulton, he was still shy and uncertain about taking the lead with respectable young women. Furthermore, there was a passive streak in his restless nature, a streak that made him want to lie back and be ministered to. In the hospital, he of course had no choice but to be passive much of the time, especially after he was operated on and his right leg and foot were placed in a plaster cast. For weeks, their lovemaking routine was largely unvaried. As night fell, he would lie on his back in bed or recline in a chair on the balcony outside his room with his foot propped up on another chair. When he and Agnes embraced, the immobility of his leg presumably required that he stay beneath her. In years to come, there would be indications that he liked this posture—for reasons that would only gradually become clear.

In short order he told Agnes that he wanted to marry her. Yet if his nocturnal visitor was touched by his youthful ardor she was uneasy about the age difference between them and began calling attention to it by referring to him as Kid. He, however, positively reveled in the fact that she was seven and a half years his senior and promptly dubbed her Mrs. Kid. The nurse in Walpole's *The Dark Forest* may have thrown over the hero in favor of a doctor, but Hemingway was determined to reverse this denouement. When Agnes told him she had written to her fiancé and broken their engagement, Hemingway was exultantly sure he had won her. "I really honestly can't see what the devil she can see in the brutal Stein," he wrote to Bill Smith, "but by some very lucky astigmatism she loves me Bill." As soon as he got back to the States and got a job, he was going to send for Agnes. And when they walked down the aisle he wanted Bill to serve as best man.

Once he was able to get about on crutches, he and Agnes explored the shops in the Galleria together, took carriage rides out to San Siro to watch the horses run and drank white wine with peaches in it and held hands at Biffi's. By mid-September he was so certain of her love that he decided to go off on a holiday with a fellow ambulance driver, John W. Miller, Jr. The Gran Hotel Stresa on Lago Maggiore was their address for ten glorious days. When the sun was high in the sky Hemingway sat by the lake and read books, or had Miller take him rowing; in the evenings he gingerly played billiards with an incredibly old—a ninety-nine-year-old—Italian diplomat, Count Giuseppe Greppi. Not only was the Count an excellent player, but he treated his young American opponent to vintage champagne no matter who won, as well as to penetrating analyses of international affairs. In Hemingway's opinion, the Count was as wise as he was generous, and ten years later he portrayed him in those terms in *A Farewell to Arms*.

On returning to Milan, he was shaken to learn from Agnes that she was leaving almost immediately for Florence, in response to a call for more nurses from a hospital that was swamped with influenza victims. To keep himself occupied after she left, he went to visit a couple of his Red Cross friends in their new headquarters, sixteen miles east of Schio near the town of Bassano del Grappa. The very day of his arrival, October 24, the Italians kicked off the offensive that was destined to bring them a spectacular victory at Vittorio Veneto. Bassano, consequently, was teeming with soldiers, including several regiments of Arditi in their distinctive gray uniforms and black-tasseled caps. Out of Hemingway's week-long observation of these hardbitten, swaggering troops was born the fantasy that he had served with them; indeed, he fantasied that he had been wounded while doing so. But the only misfortune that actually befell him at Bassano was a case of jaundice that sent him back to Milan.

At the invitation of Red Cross Captain Jim Gamble, of the soap-rich Cincinnati Gambles, he also spent a week in Taormina, high above the sea in Sicily. Hemingway later swore to a British friend in Milan that he had never reached Taormina and in fact had seen nothing of any other part of Sicily, "except from a bedroom window," because his hostess in the very first hotel he had stopped at had hidden his clothes and kept him to herself for seven days. Although this story was completely made up, it may have been a screen for Hemingway's actual memory of his week in Taormina. For the suave, somewhat older Gamble was quite taken with his young friend. Not only did he foot his bills in Sicily, but offered to support him for an entire year so that the two of them could travel in Europe together. Although Hemingway was quite excited by the offer, Agnes wouldn't let him accept it. "My idea was to get him home to the United States," she later explained, "because he was very fascinating to older men. . . . I told him he'd never be anything but a bum if he sponged off someone else." After Hemingway returned to the States, he sent Gamble—whom he called Chief—an uncharacteristically gushy letter.

Gee you know I'd have written you before. In my day book for over
a month you could open it up and find "Write Jim Gamble," scrib-
bled. Every minute of every day I kick myself for not being at Taormina with you. It makes me so damned homesick for Italy and
whenever I think that I might be there and with you. Chief, honest I
can't write about it. When I think of old Taormina by moonlight and
you and me, a little illuminated some times, but always just pleasantly
so, strolling through that great old place and the moon path on the
sea and Aetna fuming away and the black shadows and the moonlight
cutting down the stairway back of the villa. Oh Jim it makes me so
damn sick to be there.

The British friend in Milan to whom he boasted about being held
sexual captive for a week was an Anglo-Irishman named Edward
Dorman-Smith, called Chink, whom he first met on the night of
Armistice Day at the Officers' Club. Only twenty-three years old,
this tall, spare man with blue eyes and a clipped red mustache held
the impressive rank of acting major in the Fifth Northumberland
Fusiliers, for he had been fighting more or less continuously since
1914, when the British army had gone into battle at Mons, Belgium,
in a vain effort to halt the surge of the German forces toward Paris.
Fearing that such a battle-toughened warrior would pay no attention
to him if he confessed to being nothing more than a Red Cross
officer, Hemingway told him, Dorman-Smith remembered, that he
"had been badly wounded leading Arditi storm troops on Monte
Grappa and was now in hospital in Milan, only recently able to get
about on crutches." Dorman-Smith might easily have exploded this
story by asking a few leading questions, but perhaps he recognized
that the youthful Hemingway was bidding for his friendship and
therefore refrained from pressing him.

Such forbearance would have been of a piece with Chink's under-
stated way of speaking, self-deprecating humor and casual air. It
took Hemingway more than one evening of drinks at the Cova and
dinner at Biffi's to persuade his new friend to tell him how he had
acquired the three wound stripes on his sleeve and the Military Cross
on his chest. To a nineteen-year-old Middle Western American boy
who had grown up on Kipling's stories of India, Dorman-Smith
seemed to incarnate all the virtues of the pukka sahib. In an age of
democracy, he stood for a nineteenth-century aristocratic ideal, as
did his bemonocled Prussian adversaries, whose legendarily fine
conduct under fire was also admired by Hemingway.

Distillations of two of Dorman-Smith's anecdotes about the war
would later appear in Hemingway's twenty-two-page mosaic of
modern violence, *in our time* (1924), and the book would be dedi-

cated, in part, to "edward dorman-smith, m. c., of his majesty's fifth fusiliers." It was Hemingway's view—as outlined in a letter to Ezra Pound on August 5, 1923—that in the beginning the war had been "clear and noble," and he attempted to convey this by recounting Dorman-Smith's early adventures in the latter's voice. "It was a frightfully hot day. We'd jammed an absolutely perfect barricade across the bridge. It was simply priceless. A big old wrought-iron grating from the front of a house. Too heavy to lift and you could shoot through it and they would have to climb over it. It was absolutely topping."

Later, in a hackwork introduction to *Men at War* (1942), an anthology of "the best war stories of all time," Hemingway would misremember the circumstances under which he first encountered Dorman-Smith. They had met, he said, while he was still in the hospital. He also said that "after being severely wounded a few weeks before my nineteenth birthday I had a bad time until I figured it out that nothing could happen to me that had not happened to all men before me," and that Dorman-Smith had written out for him some lines from Shakespeare, *Henry IV, Part Two*, that made him very happy: "*By my troth, I care not: a man can die but once; we owe God a death . . . and let it go which way it will, he that dies this year is quit for the next.*"

That he had been having "a bad time" was an admission he conspicuously did not make to any of the people to whom he wrote letters in the summer and fall of 1918. As far as his family, his Oak Park and Kansas City friends, and his fellow officers in Italy knew, his psychological health was remarkably sound, for he had not once mentioned to them any fear of death, or any difficulty in sleeping, or any other symptoms of what a later age would call combat fatigue, although in early August he did grumble a bit about being bedridden. An eagerness for experience and a patriotic pride at having contributed to the emerging Allied victory were the attitudes that came through to his correspondents; war, he made clear to them, was a terrific game, and he had been lucky enough to get into it. Another reason for his high spirits was left unstated. Passing out cigarettes and chocolates to soldiers could have been construed as woman's work—until a rain of mortar-shell fragments, boasts about bullet wounds and a story of the arduous rescue of a wounded Italian soldier made it seem like a man's. Compared to a warrior like Dorman-Smith, he had done almost nothing, but finally that didn't matter. What mattered was that his judgmental mother had called him a hero upon learning that he had been felled on a battlefield. As Ernest declared in a letter he mailed home from Milan on October 18, "It does give you an awfully satisfactory feeling to be wounded. It's getting beaten up in a good cause."

Indeed, he loved his wounds so much that he almost wished he had died of them—for his mother's sake and for his. "When a mother brings a son into the world," he expansively explained to her and the rest of the family, "she must know that some day the son will die, and the mother of a man that has died for his country should be the proudest woman in the world, and the happiest. And how much better to die in all the happy period of undisillusioned youth, to go out in a blaze of light, than to have your body worn out and old and illusions shattered."

PART TWO

1919–1923

CHAPTER FIVE

Rejection Slips

FROM GENOA IN EARLY JANUARY, Hemingway sailed for home on the S.S. *Giuseppe Verdi*. In the three months since Agnes had gone off to Florence, he realized while packing his trunk, he had had only three brief reunions with her. On the other hand, she had written to him regularly, and one of her letters had hinted that she might marry him in another year or so. As far as he was concerned, that tentative commitment had the force of a solemn pact.

Leaning heavily on a cane and dressed in a beautiful uniform and black cape custom-tailored by Spagnolini's, the most fashionable men's tailoring establishment in Milan, Hemingway looked like a man eminently worth talking to, in the estimation of a New York *Sun* reporter who met the landing of the *Giuseppe Verdi* in lower Manhattan ten days later. Indeed, of all the veterans interviewed either in Europe or America in the months right after the war, probably none was more romantic-looking or talked more rivetingly than Hemingway, not even the youthful commander of the Rainbow Division, General Douglas MacArthur, who likewise had a fondness for fancy uniforms and fanciful summaries of what had happened to him in the war. Having come under two mustard and tear-gas attacks which made him temporarily ill, MacArthur felt it appropriate in speaking to the press to make reference to "wounds."★

★ MacArthur's psychologically complex relationship with his soldier father and extraordinarily possessive mother also makes for an interesting comparison between him and Hemingway.

Hemingway gave the man from the *Sun* an earful. Yet in describing how he had been hit by machine-gun fire, he apparently spoke more modestly than he had to Ted Brumback or to his parents. For the story in the *Sun* said that after the shrapnel cut him down, two Italian stretcher-bearers

> started over the parapet with him, knowing that he needed swift attention. Austrian machine gunners spotted the party and before they could get over he and the stretcher-bearers went down under a storm of machine-gun bullets, one of which got Hemingway in the shoulder and another in the right leg. Two other stretcher-men took the tall American through the communication trenches to the rear, where he received first aid.

Still and all, the *Sun*'s man was bedazzled by Lieutenant Hemingway. His body, the reporter affirmed, bore more scars than that of "any other man, in or out of uniform, who defied the shrapnel of the Central Powers."

Only Dr. Hemingway and Marcelline were on hand to meet his train in Chicago, an arrangement that suggested the guiding hand of Grace. Ursula, to be sure, could not have been there because she was away at college, and his train arrived at an hour that was past the bedtime of seven-year-old Carol and four-year-old Leicester. There was no reason, though, for fourteen-year-old Sunny not to have joined the welcoming party—no reason besides Grace's wish to remind Ernest that he and Marcelline had a special kinship that set them apart from their siblings. During his absence from home, Ernest had seldom written to Marcelline, and Grace had been distressed about this.

Actually, her campaign to revive her son's sense of twinhood had been launched well before he arrived home. Three weeks after learning that he was due to have his knee and foot operated on, Grace had made a point of informing him that his older sister had been laid low by a badly swollen knee. "Marcelline feels very close to you, dear boy, while you are both lying in bed with 'legs.' " In the twelve months following his return to Oak Park, Grace made further attempts—all of which Ernest resented—to demonstrate to him how much he and Marcelline had in common. After he took a temporary job in Toronto in January 1920 she tried another tactic. She would rekindle his interest in his sister by making him jealous of her popularity. "I do not write to you about Marcelline's affairs because you do not care to hear, but she is a wonderful success socially," she informed him. When this tactic didn't work, either, she tried making him feel sorry for his sister. Thus, in the spring of 1921 she left word at his Chicago apartment that Marcelline had had to be operated on for appendicitis. The superficially friendly response to this news that he immediately sent off to his sister was in reality intended to cut her up further, for he snidely referred, not once but thirteen times in a letter not overly long, to her having been "under the knife."

Several months thereafter, as Ernest was preparing to marry Hadley Richardson, Grace again laid down the sympathy card. Marcelline is "played out," she dramatically announced to her son. "Nerves all gone to smash. Won't you write to her. . . . She keeps asking so longingly about your plans." This time, he didn't even bother to write something sardonic. For while Marcelline had such a crush on her brother that the news of his impending marriage was more than her nerves could bear, he had reached the point where he wanted to have nothing whatever to do with her if he could possibly help it. In a letter to Sunny at the age of fifty, he would declare that he had always thought of Marcelline "from when I first knew her, which goes back now half a hundred years . . . as a bitch complete with handles."

Profoundly hurt by Ernest's rejection of her, Marcelline would bide her time and take her revenge after he was dead. The one thing he had never wanted his public to know about him was the history of his peculiar childhood. Had it not been for Marcelline's *At the Hemingways* (1962), the most telling details of that story would never have been told.

2

IT was at an American military hospital near Padua that Hemingway had last seen Agnes. She had been transferred there following the completion of her work in Florence. Her letters to Oak Park came from yet another site, a hospital in Torre di Mosta that was jammed to the window ledges with wounded Italian officers. She was working hard and having a marvelous time, she reported, although she had been somewhat upset when one of the other nurses had accused her of playing up to the good-looking patients. "You know I don't do anything like that, don't you?" she asked. If her rhetorical question was designed to reassure Ernest, it did not succeed. The long letters he was writing to her every day suddenly became markedly longer. You mustn't write so much, she told him on March 1, 1919, in a letter that all but said that she had become involved with someone else. "I'm not [at] all the perfect being you think I am. But, as I am, I always was, only it's just beginning to creep out. I'm feeling very *cattiva* [naughty] tonight, so good-night, Kid, and don't do anything rash but have a good time. Afft., Aggie." Before the month was out, she confessed the truth. She had fallen in love with a titled Italian lieutenant, Duca Domenico Caracciolo. *The Dark Forest* had been prophetic, after all. Ernest had lost his nurse to a more experienced rival.

In her memoir of life in the Hemingway household, Marcelline would carefully refrain from saying how she herself had felt about the breakup of her brother's romance. She made clear, though, that she had paid close attention to Ernest's reaction. His disappointment was so intense, she said, that he actually ran a fever and had to go to bed. And for weeks thereafter, he was unable to think of anything else. Among the violent thoughts with which he consoled himself was the hope he expressed in a letter to Elsie Macdonald that when Agnes got back to New York she would trip and fall on the dock and knock out all of her front teeth. That his bitterness about her went on festering for years is evident in the tenth sketch in *in our time*. A nurse named Ag in a hospital in Milan sits on the narrator's bed and is cool to the touch in the hot night. After the Armistice, the two of them agree that he should go home and get a job so that they might be married, but once he is gone she allows an officer in the Arditi to make love to her. A few months after being told by Ag that "theirs had been only a boy and girl affair," the narrator contracts gonorrhea from a Loop department-store sales girl while fornicating in the back of a taxicab in Lincoln Park.

Ag was real, the sales girl was made up. "I set out to cauterize [Agnes's] memory and I burnt it out with a course of booze and other women," Ernest melodramatically informed his friend from Red Cross days, Howie Jenkins, but as usual he was overstating the case. When the weather got nice, he went canoeing with a pretty Oak Park girl named Kathryn Longwell; with a tough guy named Nicolas Nerone who had compiled a brilliant record in the war, he split an occasional flask of Chianti at the Café Venice in Chicago; and at a Michigan country club in early June he got drunk and passed out, after having consumed—by his count—"15 martinis, 3 champagne highballs and I don't know how much champagne."

On June 15 he received a letter from Agnes saying that her lover had thrown her over, but Ernest's wounded pride conquered any residual impulse he might have felt to take up with her again. "Poor damned kid," he wrote to Howie Jenkins, "I'm sorry as hell for her. But there's nothing I can do. I loved her once and then she gypped me. . . . She's all broke up and I wish there was something I could do for her tho. 'But that's all shut behind me—long ago and far

away and there ain't no buses running from the Bank to Manda-
lay.' " Not until he began to have trouble in his first marriage would
Agnes loom up in his imagination as the woman he had always
loved.

The main agent in his emotional recovery was not dissipation, but
work. Nearly every day that spring, he sat in his room and wrote
short stories, while puffing on the Russian cigarettes he had learned
to smoke overseas. The stories he liked best he typed up and sent off
to *Redbook* or the *Saturday Evening Post*. Without exception, they
followed popular-magazine formulas; without exception, they came
back to him with rejection slips. In a story he began the following
summer at Windemere, he revealed that he was making progress as
a writer, but that he still had a tremendous amount to learn. "The
Woppian Way" recounts the adventures of a ham-and-egg boxer by
the name of Neroni who fights under the monicker of Pickles
McCarty before joining the Arditi and learning to slaughter Austrians in hand-to-hand fighting in the mountains above Bassano. For
all its crudity, "The Woppian Way" was an ambitious story; as such,
it showed that its young author already believed that someday he
would own the war in Italy, in the way other writers had owned
other wars.

Grand dreams sustained him in bleak moments of disappointment. Those dreams, unfortunately, had no reality for his mother.
All she saw was a son who laughed at her recommendation that he
go to college, who showed no signs of wanting to get a job, and
who simply ignored her requests that he clean up his unspeakably
untidy room.

Besides being disappointed in Ernest, the forty-seven-year-old
Grace was having to cope with arthritis pain in her arms and shoulders—and in addition had probably entered menopause. By the
spring of 1919, her nerves were shot, as she made clear in a well-
nigh hysterical letter to her husband about her dread of Windemere.
"I had a nervous breakdown summer after summer when I was
forced to spend a summer there, shut in by the hills and lake, no
view, no where to go, acting the part of the family drudge, standing
at sink and cook stove until the agony in my spinal nerves forced me
to lie down and then turn up again and at it, day in and day out.
Too exhausted to swim or go anywhere when the opportunity afforded. These have been my summers for many years until the very
sight of Windemere brings tears to my eyes and a sob to my throat."

The occasion for this letter was her resentment of Dr. Hemingway's resistance to her plan for building a small cottage for herself
—Grace Cottage, she intended to call it—atop a hill on Longfield

Farm across the lake from Windemere. Yet even though he never did give his formal consent to the idea, she went ahead in the summer of 1919 and built the cottage anyway. "I love you all," she declaimed to her family in her most theatrical manner, "but I have to have a rest from you all now and then if I am to go on living."

The only person who seemed to understand Grace fully was one of her former voice pupils, a quiet, attractive young woman in her early twenties named Ruth Arnold. The daughter of a salesman in nearby River Forest, Illinois, Ruth had begun studying with Grace in 1907, when she was twelve. A year later, she moved into the Hemingways' Oak Park home as a part-time cook and mother's helper. It was a relief for the girl to get away from her dominating older sisters, her unsympathetic father, and her chronically ill mother. Besides, she worshiped Grace, whom she referred to as "Muv." "How I wish I cd [could] put my arms around you and kiss you," Ruth exclaimed to her in a typical letter. The adoring girl quickly picked up Grace's pet ways of talking about things, and she also loved playing with her "Muv's" lovely hair. "Wished you were here. I'd wash and curl your hair just beautifully," Ruth wrote to Grace and Marcelline in the summer of 1909, while mother and daughter were vacationing on Nantucket Island. "It is 9 p.m., Muv, and I must wash my hair and go to bed," she remarked to Grace in another revealing letter some years later, "I wish I could do yours and stroke your dear forehead as I enjoy doing each night that I could."

Early in the summer of 1919, Ruth accompanied Grace, Marcelline, Ernest, and the younger children to Windemere. After Grace Cottage was completed, Grace loved going over there with Ruth and just the two youngest children, Carol and Leicester, and staying for days on end. In the evenings, the two women made rag rugs together and talked and sang. Perhaps their relationship was sexually innocent; yet there was a "malicious story" in certain quarters-which would be renewed in the later years of Grace's widowhood, when she and Ruth lived together in River Forest—that they were lovers.

On August 2, 1919, Ruth left Windemere and returned to Oak Park, where the hard-working Dr. Hemingway was keeping house for himself. Within days, she discovered that she was persona non grata at 600 North Kenilworth Avenue, by order of a jealous husband who could contain himself no longer. When Grace heard from her spouse what he had done, she at once protested that "dear faithful Ruth, who has given me her youth and her loyal service for these many years, needs me . . . no one in the world can ever take my husband's place unless he abdicates it to play at petty jealousy with his wife's loyal girl friend who has an unhappy and unsympathetic home life." As for Ruth, she was both baffled and crushed by Dr. Hemingway's hostility. "It is hard enough to give up going to '600,' " she cried out in a letter to Grace, "but I could never give up *you,* or *your love*—you are such an ideal and always an inspiration to me."

Although Marcelline and Ernest were both witnesses of this drama, they took very different attitudes toward it. Whereas she pooh-poohed the idea that there was anything untoward going on, telling her mother that in her opinion her father was "insane on the subject," he believed that where there was smoke there was fire. This belief may have affected Ernest's innermost thoughts about his mother in a number of ways. Perhaps it merely confirmed an unconscious sense of her sexual complexity that he had had for a long time, dating back to the days when he had heard family stories about young Grace Hall, the bike-riding tomboy. Perhaps it seemed to him further proof that she was out to humiliate Dr. Hemingway in every way possible. Or perhaps it inspired a new awareness of her emotional vulnerability and therefore made him somewhat more sympathetic with her. But if so, it did nothing to decrease the escalating tension between mother and son.

Throughout the summer of 1919 that tension was terrific. From Grace's point of view, Ernest was never available to do any chores, even though the strength in his right leg had returned. When he wasn't writing stories that nobody would buy, or walking around lost in thought with a cigarette dangling from his mouth, he was off burning up back-country roads in Bill Smith's Buick, or watching the moon rise with a redheaded high school girl named Marjorie Bump who worked as a waitress in Liz Dilworth's dining room. Struggling—by her lights—to be fair, Grace observed to Marcelline that "Ernest is very like me. . . . When [he] gets through this period . . . of fighting himself and everybody else, and turns his energy toward something positive, he will be a fine man."

What was particularly maddening from Ernest's point of view was that his status hadn't changed after all. It was as if he had never ridden in the backs of ambulances on Saturday nights in Kansas City, or helped to remove the remains of dead women from a field in Lombardy, or felt the pain of shell fragments tearing into his flesh. On the night of his return to Oak Park, Grace had hailed him as a conquering hero—and the next day had resumed treating him as though he were still a boy. At times he couldn't stand the sight or the sound of her a moment longer. When that happened, he fled.

3

THE longest of the fishing trips he took in the summer of 1919 was into the woods in the upper peninsula of Michigan near the town of Seney, about fifteen miles south of Lake Superior. In seven days of casting in the Big Fox and Little Fox Rivers, Ernest and two friends, Al Walker and Jock Pentecost, caught about two hundred trout. One of the fish pulled in by Jock was fifteen and a half inches long, but it was Ernest who almost landed what would have been the prize catch. "I lost one on the Little Fox below an old dam," he wrote to Howie Jenkins, "that was the biggest trout I've ever seen. I was up in some old timbers and it was a case of horse out. I got about half of him out of wasser and my hook broke at the shank!" He did, however, gather in the materials for a notable piece of fiction.

In the fish story he had just finished writing, he told Gertrude Stein and Alice B. Toklas on August 15, 1924, he had been "trying to do the country like Cezanne and having a hell of a time and sometimes getting it a little bit. It is about 100 pages long and nothing happens and the country is swell. I made it all up, so I see it all and part of it comes out the way it ought to, it is swell about the fish, but isn't writing a hard job though?" His sense that the story was swell about the fish was not mistaken. ("He watched them holding themselves with their noses into the current, many trout in deep, fast moving water, slightly distorted as he watched far down through the glassy convex surface of the pool, its surface pushing and swelling smooth against the resistance of the log-driven piles of the bridge.") Nor was he speaking idly when he suggested that his recreations of landscape were like a series of pictures by Cézanne. ("Ahead of him, as far as he could see, was the pine plain. The burned country stopped off at the left with the range of hills. On ahead islands of dark pine trees rose out of the plain. Far off to the left was the line of the river.") In two respects, that is to say, his letter furnished the Misses Stein and Toklas with an accurate sense of what he had accomplished. But interestingly enough, he made no mention of the most difficult of all the objectives he had been seeking to attain in "Big Two-Hearted River": to endow a story in which "nothing happens" with an inner drama of terrific intensity.

As the solitary Nick Adams leaves the train station at Seney and walks across a "burned-over country" toward "the far blue hills that marked the Lake Superior height of land," he feels a wonderful sense of release. "He felt he had left everything behind, the need for thinking, the need to write, other needs. It was all back of him." Toward the end of the day, he pitches his tent and crawls inside, noting with pleasure how "homelike" the space seems. At last, he thinks, "he was settled. Nothing could touch him. It was a good place to camp. He was there, in the good place. He was in his home where he had made it."

From this point forward, the story abounds in details of how splendid the fishing is and of what a good time Nick is having. Nevertheless, dark thoughts of some sort are lurking on the margins of his consciousness. While he is finishing his supper the first night, he suddenly becomes aware that his mind is "starting to work," but because he is tired he is able to "choke it." The next day his happiness is again interrupted. An arduous battle with the biggest trout he has ever seen ends with the trout's escape, and as Nick is reeling in his line he feels "a little sick, as though it would be better to sit down." To avoid the possibility of a second defeat in one day, he thereupon modifies his plans. Instead of plunging into the armpit-deep water of a swamp overshadowed by big trees, where he might hook big trout in places impossible to land them, he decides to postpone the adventure. "There were plenty of days coming when he could fish the swamp," he says to himself, as the story ends.

What are the "other needs" Nick feels he has put behind him as he heads off toward the river? Why does he more than once refer to his tent as his home, and why does he feel so pleased to be in it? Why is it that failure to kill the big fish makes him feel sick? With the exception of "The Battler," "Big Two-Hearted River" raises more tantalizing questions than any other Hemingway story.

Plausible answers to these questions may be found by placing the story in its biographical context. Ernest spent the summer of 1919 thinking and writing. He also spent it in bitter contention with his mother. The following summer, the ill will between the two of them exploded into open warfare when she expelled him from Windemere within days of his twenty-first birthday and presented him as he was leaving with a letter that was indisputably the masterpiece of her epistolary career. Consequently, by the time he wrote the story about his fishing trip to Seney he was not only burdened by upsetting memories of the first summer after the war, but by even more upsetting memories of the second. Perhaps, then, the "other needs" Nick feels he has put behind him include a need to please his mother, while his talk of his tent as his home may represent a reaction to being thrown out of his parents' summer cottage. Perhaps, too, the burned-over country and the grasshoppers that have turned black from living in it constitute tacit reminders to him of his mother's penchant for burning things. And finally, the activity of his mind that keeps threatening to overwhelm his contentment could be rage.

The angler on the bank of the Big Two-Hearted River is clearly a man with a divided heart—but the precise nature of the division is never identified. "In the swamp the banks were bare, the big cedars came together overhead, the sun did not come through, except in patches; in the fast deep water, in the half light, the fishing would be tragic." The words apply well to the fisherman's efforts to shun the murky depths of his troubled inner life. First and last, Nick remains an enigma.

But to many readers in the twenties, Nick was not an enigma. For these people assumed that the key to Nick's secret was the fact that his creator was the archetypal representative of a war-scarred "lost generation." Ultimately, this assumption crept into formal assessments of the story. The experience that has given Nick "a touch of panic," Edmund Wilson announced in "Ernest Hemingway: Bourdon Gauge of Morale" (1939), is "the wholesale shattering of human beings in which he has taken part." Leading up to and away from this statement, "Bourdon Gauge" contains some wonderfully appreciative comments about the stifled pangs and undruggable disquiet that lurk beneath the most innocent surfaces in Hemingway's stories. In the case of "Big Two-Hearted River," however, Wilson felt a need to specify the malaise underlying it, and in doing so he could only think that it had to do with World War I. He cited no textual evidence in support of this diagnosis, for the simple reason that there was none. Not a single reference to war appears in the story, and it is highly doubtful, furthermore, judging by what can be observed of Nick's behavior, that panic is the feeling that he is fending off. Nor does battlefield trauma bear any discernible relation to those vague "other needs" that he feels he has put behind him, or to his strong expressions of contentment with his "homelike" tent.

Half a decade after "Bourdon Gauge," Wilson's interpretation was reinforced by Malcolm Cowley's introduction to the Viking *Portable Hemingway* (1944). To Hemingway, this essay could not have come as a surprise. For in *Exile's Return* (1934), Cowley had already proclaimed that the young American writers born in the years around 1900 were a lost generation, inasmuch as the war had shattered their relationship with the country of their boyhood and they had become attached to no other. That Hemingway felt precisely the way he himself did about the war was one of Cowley's cardinal beliefs, and he delighted in drawing other parallels between their lives. The equivalent for him of Hemingway's Michigan was Cambria County, Pennsylvania, on the western slope of the Alleghenies, where he had spent his boyhood summers fishing and shooting and walking in the woods, and his equivalent of Oak Park was a residential section of Pittsburgh, where his father practiced medicine, just like Dr. Hemingway. When America entered World War I, Cowley had wanted to join an ambulance corps in France, but because the demand for drivers had slackened by the time he got to Paris, he ended up driving a camion for the French military transport—which in his retrospective view was not all that different from driving a Red Cross truck in Italy. So closely did he identify himself with Hemingway that in his *Portable Hemingway* introduction he erroneously asserted that the novelist had been born in 1898, the year of his own birth. Hemingway's awareness of Cowley's habit of superimposing his own life on his was made explicit by him more than once. Thus, in a letter to Harvey Breit of the *New York Times* five years before his death, he sardonically observed that "Malcolm thot I was like him because my father was a Dr. and I went to Michigan when I was 2 weeks old where they had Hemlock trees." That Cowley would someday go on from the lost-generation argument of *Exile's Return* to a lost-generation interpretation of "Big Two-Hearted River" must have seemed to him like an inevitable development.

In the *Portable Hemingway* Cowley argued, not so much by direct statement as by artful implication, that Hemingway's fisherman, like Hemingway himself, was a war veteran who was trying to block out fear-ridden recollections of being wounded. Proof of Nick's state of mind was not to be found in the story, to be sure, but that didn't bother Cowley. Hemingway's stories "are most of them continued," he said, by which he meant that the emotions underlying "Big Two-Hearted River" could be understood in the light of the emotions expressed in "Now I Lay Me," written three years later. Since the hero of the latter story is an American lieutenant in wartime Italy who is afraid to close his eyes at night, "Now I Lay Me" has the effect, said Cowley, of giving readers "a somewhat different attitude toward the earlier story" and of drawing attention to something that "we probably missed at first reading; that there are shadows in the background and that part of the story takes place in an inner world."

In stressing an emotional consistency between "Big Two-Hearted River" and "Now I Lay Me," Cowley neglected to point out that the most emotional moment in the latter story is set in the hero's childhood and involves a confrontation between his parents. Nevertheless, Cowley's endorsement of the war-trauma argument soon became an inspiration to other critics, most notably to an impressionable young man named Philip Young, who "ported a *Portable Hemingway* halfway across Europe during World War II." In 1952, Young projected the admiration he felt for the Cowley introduction, amplified by his own reactions to war, into a book that proclaimed that the wound suffered by Hemingway in 1918 had so deeply affected him that he had spent his whole life as a writer composing variations on the story of the psychically crippled "sick man" in "Big Two-Hearted River." Ten years later, Mark Schorer spoke for what was now a critical cliché when he characterized Hemingway as the lifelong victim of the events that had befallen him at Fossalta di Piave. "Nothing more important than this wounding was ever to happen to him," Schorer sweepingly declared.

Thus, the war-wound interpretation of the story was established not by textual evidence, but by what the critics knew about the author's life—or rather, by what they thought they knew about his life. And after he was dead, they eagerly seized on his posthumously published comment in *A Moveable Feast* that "Big Two-Hearted River" was about "coming back from the war but there was no mention of the war in it" as clinching proof that they were right. They would have been better advised to wonder if a master manipulator was not making fools of them from beyond the grave, as he so often had in life.

For a quarter of a century after the story was published, Hemingway kept his own counsel about it. But in the aftermath of World War II he made a number of statements in which he related it to World War I. In all likelihood, though, these revelations reflected latter-day events. The late forties marked the beginning of the end for Hemingway. Fantasies of suicide thronged his mind, intermingled with fears of insanity, and his friend Buck Lanham saw him writing in the morning with a drink in his hand. For years, he had been given to saying that the first war had cost him a lot of sleep, but he had usually been careful to couple such confessions with manly assertions that he had finally put insomnia behind him and was once again in wonderful shape. The breathtaking tragedy that took form in the late forties exposed the hollowness of that boast. All too keenly aware of his problems and yet adamantly opposed to seeking professional help in understanding them, he more than ever felt the need of a heroic explanation for his life. In an effort to account for his imperiled sense of himself, as well as to preserve his macho reputation, he turned once more to Fossalta.

Thus, in a letter dated August 25, 1948, he informed Malcolm Cowley that he could now see that in the first war he had been hurt very badly in body, mind, and spirit and also morally, that "Big

Two-Hearted River" was about a man who was home from the war
and that he, the author, was still hurt in that story. The real truth
about himself, he assured Cowley, was that in the war "I was hurt
bad all the way through and I was really spooked at the end." And
in another letter a few years later to the *New York Times*'s Charles
Poore, he again characterized "Big Two-Hearted River" as "a story
about a boy who has come back from the war. The war is never
mentioned though as far as I can remember. This may be one of the
things that helps it." Private communications, however, were
merely warm-ups for the gloss he offered the public at large in *A
Moveable Feast*.

The book was written between 1957 and 1961, during which time
the author's long debate with himself about self-destruction was
moving inexorably toward violent resolution, despite his terrifying
belief that suicide was a cowardly, unmanly act. In the wake of his
death, his enemies in the critical world took the same line toward it,
as he had feared they would. To these commentators, his life had
ended with a whimper, not a bang. After 1930 he just didn't have it
any more, Dwight Macdonald fairly gloated in the pages of *Encounter* in January 1962, and by the summer of 1961—the critic savagely
continued—the position was outflanked, the lion couldn't be
stopped, the sword wouldn't go into the bull's neck, the great fish
was breaking the line, it was the fifteenth round and the champ
looked bad and the only way out was to destroy himself.

Even a Hemingway fan like Norman Mailer felt moved to confess
in a troubled essay in *Esquire* entitled "The Big Bite" that his suicide
had been "the most difficult death in America since [Franklin] Roosevelt's." What made it difficult for Mailer was that in taking his life
Hemingway had seemed to call into question all that he had represented. Consistently, he had presented himself as the champion of
whatever endeavor he had undertaken; consistently, he had proclaimed that the great thing was to last and get your work done.
How could such a life be reconciled with such a death?

Mailer's ultimate answer to this question was that "It is not likely
that Hemingway was a brave man who sought danger for the sake
of the sensations it provided him. What is more likely the truth of
his own odyssey is that he struggled with his cowardice and against
a secret lust to suicide all his life, that his inner landscape was a
nightmare, and he spent his nights wrestling with the gods. It may
even be that the final judgment on his work may come to the notion
that what he failed to do was tragic, but what he accomplished was
heroic, for it is possible that he carried a weight of anxiety with him
which would have suffocated any man smaller than himself."

As a hypothesis, Mailer's comment was marvelously suggestive and ought to have inspired searching examinations of the dynamics of Hemingway's early life. But it did not. Old habits of mind prevailed. Fossalta had been the break-point in a gallant hero's history. By seeming to imply in *A Moveable Feast* that "Big Two-Hearted River" was about a man who was doing his best to defend himself against memories of a dirty war, Hemingway himself helped to buttress that assumption.

4

ON his return to Windemere after fishing the Foxes, Ernest discovered that both his parents were in residence, but that Ruth Arnold was nowhere to be seen. In future years, Ruth would be able to visit Grace only in Dr. Hemingway's absence. It was one of the few enduring victories of his marriage.

When his parents closed up Windemere and returned to Oak Park, Ernest stayed on at the Dilworths' place until early October, writing stories in the morning and doing odd jobs for Liz in the afternoon as a way of earning his keep. He had always liked Liz. Her jolly face was a reflection of her warm and comforting personality, and her enthusiastic interest in going to concerts and lectures was charming. Now that he was getting along so badly with Grace, he more and more turned to Liz, as though he thought of her as the mother he would like to have had. He also was fond of her husband, Jim, the blacksmith. This short, dark, heavily mustached man was as easygoing as Dr. Hemingway was strict, especially about booze. For years, Jim had quietly supplied Ernest and Bill Smith with the hard cider they had drunk while fishing in Horton Creek.

Some of the same readers who discount the notion of Hemingway's sexual involvement with Prudy Boulton are equally certain— are dogmatically certain—that not until his stay with the Dilworths that fall did he lose his virginity. One cold night, the story goes, he escorted one of Liz's waitresses at Pinehurst Cottage—not Marjorie Bump, who had gone back to high school, but another young woman—out to the end of the Horton Bay dock and lay down with her on the splintery hemlock planking. Hemingway himself, however, in a short story based on the episode and bawdily entitled "Up in Michigan," has presented a different view. Although the waitress in the story is clearly inexperienced, her importunate partner appears to have had a fair amount of practice. It is altogether likely, of course, that the story departs from the truth. Nevertheless, it casts a shadow of doubt across the genteel assumption that until he was twenty Hemingway's body was the unprofaned temple his mother had always hoped it was.

"Up in Michigan" also raises the question of what had been going on in the author's mind in regard to the Dilworths. For the young man in the story is named Jim and the waitress he deflowers is named Liz. Jim, moreover, is "short and dark with big mustaches" and owns the Horton Bay blacksmith shop. And one of the things that Jim especially likes about Liz is that her face is "so jolly." Inasmuch as the story appeared in a little book called *Three Stories & Ten Poems* (1923) put out by an avant-garde press in Paris, the Dilworths remained blissfully unaware of "Up in Michigan," as did Hemingway's parents, but Marcelline read it, to her vast disgust. Even after her brother's death she was still indignant about its insult to the Dilworths. "The two main characters of the story, a man and a woman, had the same names as two of our family friends, a couple of whom we were particularly fond. The description of them in the tale, especially of the man, fitted our friends so accurately that as I read on . . . my stomach turned over."

The first version of "Up in Michigan" was written in Chicago in the late summer of 1921, just before Hemingway's marriage to Hadley Richardson on September 3; the second and final version was written in Paris five months later. By substituting two other recognizable individuals for himself and the waitress, Hemingway may have been trying to divert attention from the autobiographical nature of the story so that it would not make painful reading for his beloved, even though he would later compile a long record of ruthlessness about such matters. Yet assuming that sparing Hadley was indeed a consideration for him, why did he select Jim and Liz Dilworth, of all people, for his surrogates? Was he by any chance trying to rid himself, on the eve of taking a bride almost eight years his senior, of a sexual attraction to a much older woman?

Whatever the truth of this curious matter, "Up in Michigan" is a bracingly honest story, especially in its account of what happens after the seduction. Jim is so indifferent to the waitress, once he has had his way with her, that he falls asleep on top of her. Liz crawls out from under him, shakes him a few times and tearfully calls his name, but Jim merely rolls his head away and goes on sleeping. Finally, Liz takes off her coat and covers him with it, tucking in the edges neatly and carefully, as if she were his mother. "Then she walked across the dock and up the steep sandy road to go to bed. A cold mist was coming up through the woods from the bay." There is a "type" whose state of mind Hemingway understands very well, D. H. Lawrence once observed. "It is a state of *conscious* accepted indifference. . . . Nothing matters. Everything happens. One wants to keep oneself loose. Avoid one thing only: getting connected up." The observation is certainly applicable to the emotionally self-enclosed Jim in "Up in Michigan."

It is not applicable, however, to the story as a whole, for significantly, "Up in Michigan" is told from a female as well as male point of view. Moreover, the female viewpoint controls the narrative in the climactic final episode. From the moment that Jim and Liz lie down on the dock to the moment that Liz crawls out from under him and walks away, the reader feels what she feels.

> The boards were hard. Jim had her dress up and was trying to do something to her. She was frightened but she wanted it. She had to have it but it frightened her.
> "You mustn't do it, Jim. You mustn't."
> "I got to. I'm going to. You know we got to."
> "No, we haven't, Jim. We ain't got to. Oh, it isn't right. Oh, it's so big and it hurts so. You can't. Oh, Jim. Jim. Oh."
> The hemlock planks of the dock were hard and splintery and cold and Jim was heavy on her and he had hurt her. Liz pushed him, she was so uncomfortable and cramped. Jim was asleep.

The most familiar of all the charges that readers unsympathetic to Hemingway have leveled at him is that he has no perspective on the behavior of the men in his stories because he can't identify with the women. "Up in Michigan" reveals how impoverished an appreciation of his life and work lies behind that charge. On the planks of the Horton Bay dock a forcible seduction takes place that comes close to being an assault. In this situation, an author whose own sexual integrity had been tampered with was less strongly drawn to the brutally insistent aggressor than to his vulnerable prey. Abruptly relinquishing his off-and-on commitment to the point of view of the blacksmith, Hemingway kept strictly within the consciousness of the half-resistant, half-yielding, thoroughly frightened young woman lying on her back beneath him.

5

THERE was no use in his returning to Oak Park. He realized that even before he left the Dilworths'. After a couple of days of putting up with routines that made him feel like a prisoner, he told his parents that he wasn't getting any writing done and had to go back to Michigan. A week later, he reached Petoskey, where he rented a second-floor room in Mrs. Evva Potter's rooming house, unpacked his things, put on sweaters to ward off the chill and went to work. There was a diner on Main Street where he took most of his meals.

Sitting at his work table, he returned in imagination to Chicago. The vicious race riot that had broken out there the preceding summer held no literary interest for him, but the increasing power in the city of organized crime was a phenomenon he found fascinating. The buffoonish mayor, "Big Bill" Thompson, was reelected on November 4, so the lords of the underworld would continue to have a friend at City Hall. And the recent passage by Congress of the Volstead Act, which adopted a definition of intoxicating liquor that forbade all but the weakest beer, made it inevitable that bootlegging in Chicago and environs would develop into an enormously profitable business the instant that Prohibition went into effect in January 1920.

The Windy City's Italian gangs, restively united under the uncertain leadership of John (Machine-gun Johnny) Torrio, struck Hemingway as the American equivalent of the Arditi. While eating ravioli with Nick Nerone at the Venice Café on Wabash Avenue, he had seen so many hard-faced men come in for conferences and card playing in the closed-off back room that he had become a connoisseur of the type. The poet Wallace Stevens would say of Hemingway in 1941 that he, too, was a poet, "and I should say, offhand, the most significant of living poets, so far as the subject of EXTRAORDINARY ACTUALITY is concerned." Chicago gangsterdom was one of the extraordinary actualities he tried to capture for literature in Petoskey. In a story called "The Mercenaries," for instance, he spoke of "the Café Cambrinus on Wabash Avenue," where you couldn't get into the small smoke-filled room in the rear without the permission of the owner. Once you were in, "a sudden silence" would fall over the men already there, while their eyes looked you over "with that detached intensity that comes of a periodic contemplation of death." After a time, the talk would resume.

> But one time the door was pushed open, men looked up, glances of recognition shot across the room, a man half rose from one of the card tables, his hand behind him, two men ducked to the floor, there was a roar from the doorway, and what had had its genesis in the Malay Archipelago terminated in the back room of the Cambrinus.

In an effort to shore up his shaky rule, John Torrio in 1920 sent to New York for a helper. The helper was a plump young man whose fancy clothes always looked a little tight on him. By the mid-twenties, Al Capone had more power than any other mobster in the

Middle West. On an unseasonably cold day in the capital of Spain in 1926, Hemingway would decide to turn him into a work of art, and in the process of doing so he recalled the days toward the close of 1919 when he had written apprentice pieces like "The Mercenaries."

For although "The Killers" takes place on an autumn evening in a town called Summit outside of Chicago, Hemingway was actually thinking of Petoskey. In a second-story room in a rooming house, a big Swede named Ole Andreson, who "must have got mixed up in something in Chicago," lies on his rumpled bed, waiting for his gangland slayers to find him. At the diner not far away, young Nick Adams is talking to George, the counterman, when a stranger walks in. He is wearing a derby hat, a silk muffler and gloves and a black overcoat that is too tight for him. His name is Al, and he is looking for Ole Andreson. Alongside Al is another man, whom Al refers to as Max. "He was about the same size as Al. Their faces were different, but they were dressed like twins." "In their tight overcoats and derby hats they looked like a vaudeville team."

While Hemingway may have wanted to drop his twinhood experience down the memory hole of history, it had left an indelible imprint upon his mind, and in "The Killers" it served him well. For the free-floating hostility of the "twins" toward the world at large, as represented in the diner by Nick Adams, George the counterman and the Negro cook in the kitchen, and their prickly attitude toward one another as well are the frictional forces that generate the electricity for which the story is famous. Behind "The Killers" lay some obvious influences: Hemingway's firsthand acquaintance with petty criminals in Kansas City, his close observation of the men entering the back room in the Venice Café and the steady attention he paid in the twenties to journalistic accounts, in European as well as American newspapers, of the blood-drenched careers of Chicago hoodlums. But what is less obvious is that the story would not have taken the shape it did if the author had not once been a "twin" himself. Al's rebuke of Max, "You talk too much," could have been Ernest talking to Marcelline.

The perfection of "The Killers" took years of effort to attain. In the fall of 1919 in Petoskey, the best writing that Hemingway was capable of was a series of economically worded sketches of life in and around Horton Bay and Boyne City which he collectively entitled "Cross Roads." Among the people he portrayed were a lumberjack who once went six rounds with the celebrated boxer, Stanley Ketchel; an obnoxious braggart who is full of stories about the war, even though he reached France just in time for the Armistice; a beautiful girl named Pauline Snow who is seduced and abandoned and finally sent to correction school; and an Ojibway Indian named Billy Gilbert who has a daughter named Prudence. That Hemingway should have been thinking of his old girl, Prudence Boulton, was hardly surprising, for it was in the Petoskey *Evening News* that the report of her death had appeared. The story, to be sure, was now almost two years old, but the circumstances of her demise had been so sensational that she had become a subject of continuing gossip. In February 1918 the sixteen-year-old Prudy had been living with a white man named Richard Castle, from Charlevoix. She was pregnant, rumor had it, and Castle had been talking of marrying her, until the two of them decided upon a different course of action. Around seven o'clock one morning, they both swallowed strychnine.

Writing occupied Mrs. Potter's boarder from early in the morning until close to midday. After lunch, he worked for another couple of hours. When his brain finally began to fog over, he donned his sheepskin jacket and spent the rest of the afternoon shoveling gravel for the county in order to pay his rent or hanging around Petoskey High School waiting for Marjorie Bump to appear so that he could escort her home. On weekends, he took Marjorie to dances at the Elks Club. Another girl whom he enjoyed talking and dancing with was a lively fourteen-year-old named Grace Quinlan, whom he soon began to refer to as "Sister Luke," not only because he missed the companionship of his own younger sisters but because he didn't wish to call her Grace. He also had a couple of dates with Irene Goldstein, a good-looking Jewish girl who was just his age. His social life was hampered, though, by a shortage of funds. Unless something turned up, he would have no choice but to go back to Oak Park.

A talk he gave to the Ladies' Aid Society led to the lucky break he had been hoping for. The ladies wanted to hear some heart-stopping war stories, and he did not disappoint them. Afterwards, a distinguished-looking, white-haired woman came up to speak to him. She was in town visiting her mother, she explained, and her name was Harriet Gridley Connable. Her husband, Ralph, was the chairman of the Canadian division of the F. W. Woolworth chain. The Connables lived in Toronto, but would be going off to Palm Beach sometime in January with their twenty-six-year-old daughter Dorothy. Would Hemingway, she wanted to know, be willing to live in their house during their absence and look after Ralph, Jr.? Although the boy was in his late teens, he had been lame since birth and could not get out to plays, concerts, boxing matches, or hockey games unless someone went with him. Hemingway accepted her offer on the spot. As he wrote to Howie Jenkins on December 20, "this Toronto thing looks like the original Peruvian doughnuts."

Mainly because he wanted to see his sister Ursula, he went home at New Year's, but by the second week in January Mrs. Connable and Dorothy were showing him around the largest house he had ever been in. Not since the Gran Hotel Stresa had he seen such a billiard room; the music room, complete with pipe organ, was three times the size of his mother's; and the comfortable bedroom to which he was assigned had a table in it at which he could write. Outside, there was a tennis court that had been flooded for ice skating and a little cabin beside it where the skaters could get out of the wind and drink hot chocolate.

The job proved to be ridiculously easy. By and large, the "sitter" had his mornings to himself, and on those evenings when Ralph didn't want to go out he again was free to do what he wanted. Among the books he devoured while living under the Connables' roof were Joseph Conrad's *Victory* and Havelock Ellis's *Erotic Symbolism,* with its accounts of all the different positions that a man and a woman can assume in sexual intercourse and its detailed descriptions of various fetishisms, including some involving hair.

When the Connables returned to the city in February, he had a chance to talk at length with Mr. Connable and they hit it off very well. At the same time that Connable was a hard-driving, dynamic businessman, he was a practical joker. "His favorite escapade," it would be recalled years later by an obituary writer, "was to dress like a woman and walk into the men's locker room of the staid Lambton Golf Club. While men shouted and tried to hide behind doors, Connable would whisper, 'I'm looking for my gentleman friend.' " On learning that Hemingway had literary ambitions, the dime-store mogul took him downtown and introduced him to some of the executives at the Toronto *Star*. Gregory Clark, an ex-infantryman who was the features editor, was not initially impressed by this "large, rather heavy, loose-jointed youth, with a flushed face, dark loose hair and a big red mouth." He perspired freely, Clark further noted, could not pronounce the letter *l* properly and had a queer, explosive way of describing things. Even after he got to know and like Hemingway, Clark was of the opinion that "a more weird combination of quivering sensitiveness and preoccupation with violence never walked this earth." Hemingway's shyness, though, did not keep Clark and the other editors from proposing that he start contributing stories to the feature-laden Saturday edition called the *Star Weekly*. All told, the *Weekly* bought twenty-six pieces from him in 1920, on subjects ranging from how to rent an oil painting to the hazards of accepting free shaves at a local barbers' college.

6

ON March 18, Dr. Hemingway wrote to his son to bring him up to date on Grace's nerves. "Mother is a good deal better," he was happy to report, "and I hope this coming summer will bring things to a normal basis again." At Easter, Ernest tried to cheer her up by sending her a lily. Grace was thrilled by his thoughtfulness, to the point where she was finally able to say something nice about the newspaper stories he was writing. "I rejoice *so* in your professional success. It must be gratifying to have your ability recognized. Send me some clippings when you have time."

Yet no sooner were they reunited in May than they began to quarrel again. Instead of trying to land a job with a future, his mother noted with disgust, he was talking about shipping out to the Far East with Ted Brumback as a stoker on a steamship, Jack London style. When she remonstrated with him, he blew up. Dr. Hemingway would have liked his son to remain in Oak Park at least until the middle of June so that they could spend a couple of days together at the Republican National Convention in Chicago, but Ernest was too angry to stay and went storming off to Horton Bay. Full of trepidation about what the summer portended, his father wrote to him on June 4, urging him to develop more self-control.

> Do hope dear Ernest that you will think more of what others have done for you and try to be charitable and kind and gentle. Do not doubt that I am proud of your ability and independence, but try and soften your temper and never threaten your Father or Mother. We have both tried many trying years of your life to help you and I trust you will live to see the joy of a family of your own, with some of the cares and anxieties and responsibilities that go with the experience. I want you to represent all that is good and noble and brave and courteous in Manhood, and fear God and respect Woman.

The experience of being browbeaten all his married life did not mean, it was clear, that Dr. Hemingway would line up with Ernest in any showdown with Grace. No matter what, he would back his wife to the hilt.

Ernest's newly lacerated feelings about both his parents came out in his relations with friends in the form of a more than normally disagreeable competitiveness. A hike through the woods with Bill Smith was spoiled when Ernest accused Bill of trying to reach their

destination first. A talk with the Dilworths' son, Wesley, degenerated into a demonstration that only Ernest had the courage to walk
barefoot on broken glass. And in Petoskey one afternoon a couple
of sets of tennis with Irene Goldstein ended in such a display of bad
temper on his part that Irene was offended. Swallowing her feelings,
she invited him to stay for supper with her aunt and uncle, only to
have him embarrass them by bringing along a fish he had obviously
bought at a local market but which he told them he had caught
himself.

On the afternoon of his twenty-first birthday, he appeared at Windemere with Bill Smith and Ted Brumback, and Grace prepared
them a nice dinner. For the next few days, he hung around the
cottage, reading books, talking with Ursula and Sunny, flirting with
thirteen-year-old Jean Reynolds, a house guest at the nearby cottage
of the Loomis family, and making a show of his affection for Ruth
Arnold, who arrived on the twenty-fifth, Dr. Hemingway being in
Oak Park. Relations between Ernest and his mother had never been
worse. When he caught her leafing through a copy of *American*
magazine, he derided her for reading "moron literature" and inquired sarcastically if she subscribed to the *Atlantic Monthly* for pres-
tige reasons. If Grace did not answer him in kind, it was because she
was secretly engaged in drafting a letter to him that would take his
hide off.

The climax to their feud was not long in coming. Ursula and
Sunny were planning to stage a secret midnight supper on the
twenty-sixth, they confided to their brother, at Ryan's Point across
the lake. Jean Reynolds and Bob and Elizabeth Loomis were going
to sneak out and join them, and so was another girl who was visiting
the Loomises. If Ernest and Ted Brumback were to come along too,
the party would be even more fun.

The revelers ate, swam, sang songs, threw more chunks of wood
on their bonfire, and generally had a good time until three in the
morning; but as they were rowing home, they saw the light of a
lantern on the shore. Mrs. Loomis had missed her children. Frantic
with anger, she had gone to Windemere and awakened Grace, who
then discovered that there were empty beds in her cottage as well.
Mrs. Loomis and Grace both focused their outrage on the party's
two last-minute guests, Ernest and Ted. They were old enough to
have known better; they were guilty of corrupting the morals of
innocent young girls. Ernest's replies to these charges were apparently insolent. The next morning, Grace coldly informed him that
he and Ted would have to vacate the premises at once, whereupon,
as she later wrote to Dr. Hemingway, "Ernest called me every name

he could think of, and said everything vile about me; but I kept my tongue and did not get hysterical." Instead, she handed him the letter she had written to him. It was a rejection slip with a vengeance.

My Dear Son Ernest,

For three years, since you decided, at the age of eighteen years, that you did not need any further advice or guidance from your parents, I have tried to keep silence and let you work out your own salvation; by that I mean, your own philosophy of life—your code of ethics in dealing with men, women, and children. Now, at the age of twenty-one, and being, according to some of your best friends and well-wishers, so sadly in need of good guidance, I shall brave your anger, and speak this once more to you.

A mother's love seems to me like a bank. Each child that is born to her, enters the world with a large and prosperous bank account, seemingly inexhaustible. For the first five years he draws and draws—physical labor and pain—loss of sleep—watching and soothing, waiting upon, bathing, dressing, feeding, amusing. The Mother is practically a *body* slave to his every whim.

There are no deposits in the bank account during *all* the early years. "Cheery-o," thinks the mother, "some day he will be a comfort to me and return all I am doing for him," and she is content.

Then, for the next ten years, or so, up to adolescence, while the bank is heavily drawn upon, for love and sympathy, championship in time of trouble or injustice, nursing thru illnesses, teaching and guiding, developing the young body and mind and soul, at all and any expense to the often exhausted parents during this time—there are a few deposits of pennies, in the way of services willingly done, some thoughtfulness and "thank yous". . . .

Truly, the bank account is perilously low, for there is nothing coming in, no deposits, unless occasional spells of regret for past conduct make him come to her with an "I'm sorry and will truly try to do better."

But now, adolescence is past—full manhood is here. The bank is still paying out love, *sympathy* with wrongs, and enthusiasm for all ventures, courtesies and entertainment of friends who have nothing in common with Mother, who, unless they are very well bred, scarcely notice her existence.

The bank goes on handing out understanding and interest in budding love affairs, joy in plans of *every* sort. The account needs some deposits, by this time, some good sized ones in the way of gratitude and appreciation, interest in Mother's ideas and affairs. Little comforts provided for the home; a desire to favor any of Mother's peculiar prejudices, on no account to outrage her ideals. Flowers, fruits, candy, or something pretty to wear, brought home to Mother, with a kiss and a squeeze—The unfailing desire to make much of her feeble

efforts, to praise her cooking, back up her little schemes; a real interest
in hearing her sing, or play the piano, or tell the stories that she loves
to tell—A surreptitious paying of bills, just to get them off Mother's
mind; Thoughtful remembrances and celebration of her birthday and
Mother's day (the sweet letter accompanying the gift of flowers, she
treasures it most of all). These are merely a few of the deposits which
keep the account in good standing.

Many mothers I know are receiving these, and much more substantial gifts and returns from sons of less abilities than my son. Unless
you, my son, Ernest, come to yourself, cease your lazy loafing, and
pleasure seeking—borrowing with no thought of returning—stop
trying to graft a living off anybody and everybody—spending all
your earnings lavishly and wastefully on luxuries for yourself—stop
trading on your handsome face, to fool little gullible girls, and neglecting your duties to God and your Saviour Jesus Christ—unless,
in other words, you come into your manhood—there is nothing before you but bankruptcy: *You have over drawn.*

This world, which is your world, is crying out for men, real men,
with brawn and muscle, moral as well as physical—men whose
mothers can look up to them, instead of hanging their heads in shame
at having borne them. Purity of speech and life, have been taught you
from earliest childhood. You are born of a race of gentlemen—men
who would scorn to accept anything from anybody without rendering a just equivalent, men who were clean mouthed, chivalrous to all
women, grateful and generous. You were named for the two finest
and noblest gentlemen I have ever known. See to it that you do not
disgrace their memories.

Do not come back until your tongue has learned not to insult and
shame your mother.

When you have changed your ideas and aims in life, you will find
your mother waiting to welcome you, whether it be in this world or
the next—loving you and longing for your love.

The Lord watch between me and thee, while we are absent, one
from the other

Your still hoping and always praying mother

                                        Grace Hall Hemingway

When he finally was alone and had a chance to read the letter,
Ernest made no move to compose an answer—or if he did, he never
mailed it. But two weeks later he wrote to the other Grace in his
life, Grace Quinlan, his "Sister Luke." To this fourteen-year-old girl
he unburdened himself of the whole story of why he was no longer
living at home, topping it off with the most damaging explanation
of his mother's motives that his fertile mind could think of. "Mother
was glad of an excuse to oust me as she has more or less hated me
ever since I opposed her throwing two or three thousand seeds [dol-

lars] away to build a new cottage for herself when the jack should
have sent the kids to college." He also fired off a furious letter to his
father in Oak Park, who proceeded to anger him still further by
offering him no sympathy. "Ernest's last letter to me," Dr. Hemingway reported to Grace, "was written in anger and filled with
expressions that were untrue to a gentleman and a son who has had
everything done for him. . . . He must get busy and make his own
way, and suffering alone will be the means of softening his Iron
Heart of selfishness."

In early September, Grace sent her husband a copy she had made
of her letter to Ernest. Dr. Hemingway was full of admiration for
it. She had beautifully explained the "Mother's part of the game of
Family life," he told her, and he closed by calling on her to keep up
her courage. Yet if he fully supported his wife, he had no stomach
for further fighting. On September 18, Dr. Hemingway sent a letter
to his son in Boyne City, where Ernest was living in a down-at-the-
heels boardinghouse and earning enough money to keep alive by
doing odd jobs for people like Bill Smith's aunt, Mrs. Charles.

> I am wondering [Dr. Hemingway wrote] what are your plans for the
> Fall and Winter, inasmuch as the girls tell me you and Ted have given
> up the "Round the World" trip? . . . I have just written your dear
> Mother . . . that I would write to you to please go over to Grace
> Cottage and offer to help her to close up Windemere and Grace Cot-
> tage. Inasmuch as there were a few misunderstandings between you
> and your mother this summer I am sure if you make this effort you
> may right the matters and I will continue to pray that you will love
> one another as you should.

But Ernest preferred to repair relations with Grace by making her
feel sorry for him. During an afternoon of sailing on Lake Charlevoix with Katy Smith and Odgar (Carl Edgar), her perennial suitor,
he caught his navel on a boat cleat. Although an infection set in that
eventually forced him to see a doctor, the accident really wasn't
serious. In a letter to his mother, however, he explained that the
pain from the internal hemorrhages he had suffered would prevent
him from helping her to close down Windemere as his father had
suggested. The thought that her son had once again been wounded
was more than Grace could bear. On her return to Oak Park, she
dropped him a note. "I was sorry you failed to get over the day we
left. I had a nice lunch prepared for you. I hope your internal injury
is giving you no more trouble. I could not sleep the night after you
told me about it—(sympathetic nervous pain). So sorry you should
have to suffer so much torture. As always, Your loving Mother."

It was precisely the reaction he had hoped to evoke from her, and two months later, while she was spending Christmas in California with her brother Leicester, he cynically offered her a response to her reproofs that he was sure would mollify her. "Dearest Mother," he wrote to her from his apartment in Chicago, "Am being frightfully good in pursuit of your instructions. At least you told me to be good didn't you? Being so anyway."

The underlying mockery in these assurances was completely lost on Grace. Nor did she recognize the hostility to her that lay like a concealed knife inside his season's greetings. ("Well, Merry Christmas to you old dear—won't wish you Happy New Year because New Year is just one lurch nearer the grave and nothing to be happy over.") On the contrary, her view of her son in the final days of 1920 was that he had finally come to his senses. He had landed a well-paying job with a magazine. He had met a young woman named Hadley Richardson who sounded very nice. And he was once again writing loving letters to his mother.

7

"BY 1920," according to historian William E. Leuchtenburg,

> the nerves of the country had been rubbed raw by bitterness over the war, the debate on the League [of Nations], the Red Scare, and the postwar inflation. In a word, the nation had had enough of [Woodrow] Wilsonism. . . . Wilson had become, in [the newspaperman] Mark Sullivan's words, "the symbol of the exaltation that had turned sour, personification of the rapture that had now become gall, sacrificial whipping boy for the present bitterness."

But not every American was interested in politics. On the evidence of the letters he wrote in the aftermath of his return to the United States, the young Hemingway was indifferent to the debate on the League, the Red Scare and the inflation in prices; and while the paralyzed man in the White House may have become America's favorite whipping boy, Hemingway had nothing to say about Wilson one way or another. As for bitterness about the war, he would very shortly give way to it, but not even the rudiments of such a feeling can be found either in the press interviews he granted in 1919 or in the speeches he gave that year, while in the correspondence he conducted with former Red Cross officers rapturous nostalgia was the prevailing sentiment. He could hardly wait to get together with his pals again so that they could talk about the great adventures they had had. A letter to Grace Quinlan, written from Oak Park on New

Year's Day, 1920, catches the excitement he felt at the prospect of a reunion. "There's going to be an ARDITI dinner of 15 of the old gang from all over the country at the North Side Saturday night. Jenks [Howie Jenkins] had arranged it and he was going to WIRE me today to come down, called up to see when I'd be there. It'll be quelque occassion [sic] . . . 15 of the old gang!"

The first public event to engender a "postwar disillusionment" in his soul was the baseball scandal. On September 28, 1920, while he was still living in exile from his family in Boyne City, he learned that eight players on the Chicago White Sox had been indicted on charges of having thrown the 1919 World Series to the Cincinnati Reds in exchange for $100,000 from a syndicate headed by the New York gambler Arnold Rothstein. Some of the team's finest players were involved—Shoeless Joe Jackson, Happy Felsch, Eddie Cicotte.

Ring Lardner was so nauseated by the perfidy of the "Black Sox" that he ceased writing baseball fiction until 1925, the year in which his friend Scott Fitzgerald introduced readers of *The Great Gatsby* to a Jewish gambler named Meyer Wolfsheim, who reputedly had "fixed the World Series back in 1919." Although Fitzgerald was not a particularly ardent baseball fan, he had spent a lot of time listening to Lardner's mordant monologues; perhaps it was in the wake of one of them that he decided to include a fictionalized Rothstein in his symbology of American corruption. In contrast to Fitzgerald, Hemingway had been a close student of baseball all his life. Besides memorizing the sports pages every day, he had spent many an afternoon watching either the Cubs or the White Sox play. So angered was he by the revelation of the conspiracy that when Grace Quinlan's brother Deggie told him two days after the announcement of the indictment that he didn't see why anyone would want to blame the players for trying to earn a little extra money, Hemingway was barely able to restrain "a great and overpowering desire to spank him." In his fiction, his response to the scandal was equally unforgiving.

References in "The Three-Day Blow" to certain actual events serve to place the time of the story in the period prior to America's involvement in the war. But in the course of their drunken conversation, Nick Adams and his friend Bill give voice to the disillusionment with baseball that swept over Hemingway in 1920.

> "What'll we drink to?" Nick asked, holding up the glass.
> "Let's drink to fishing," Bill said.
> "All right," Nick said. "Gentlemen, I give you fishing."
> "All fishing," Bill said. "Everywhere."

"Fishing," Nick said. "That's what we drink to."

"It's better than baseball," Bill said.

"There isn't any comparison," said Nick. "How did we ever get talking about baseball?"

"It was a mistake," Bill said. "Baseball is a game for louts."

Nick's thirst for whiskey has also developed at an earlier point in his life than it had in his creator's. In an astonishingly short space of time, Nick and Bill both put away "glasses" of Irish, plus "awfully big" shots of Scotch, whereas Hemingway did not have his first taste of either Irish or Scotch until he joined the Officers' Club in Milan, and did not develop a dependency on drink until the stressful period following his big blow-up with his mother. Psychiatrist Ronald R. Fieve has conjectured in an interesting book on mood swings that "Hemingway's heavy drinking . . . might be considered his own form of self-treatment." Indeed it was. As he once confessed to Archibald MacLeish, "Trouble was all my life when things were really bad I could always take a drink and right away they were much better."

Fishing the Black River with Jock Pentecost, Ted Brumback and Howie Jenkins was another way in which he endeavored to cheer himself up in the late summer of 1920, and when the dejected Odgar returned to Kansas City in September, having failed once again to win the hand of Katy Smith, Hemingway found further solace in dating her himself. Butstein, as he suggestively called her, was twenty-nine to his twenty-one, but as it had with Agnes, the age discrepancy appealed to him.

One night, the two of them tested the alcoholic waters at a Boyne City joint called Martin's. While they were riding around Petoskey the next day in her brother Bill's Buick, Hemingway impulsively stopped at a Catholic church. By the flickering light of the votive candles they lit, he "prayed for all the things I want and won't ever get and we came out in a fine mood," he later reported to his teen-aged confidante, Grace Quinlan. Yet no sooner did they get back on the road than his prayers were answered, his letter to "Sister Luke" continued, for "the Lord sent me Adventure with a touch of Romance." (What he meant by that interesting remark, he didn't say.) Then a storm broke, and in the course of their drive home through the rain Katy fell asleep on the seat beside him.*

* It was under similar circumstances that she would die. Near dusk on September 12, 1947, as John Dos Passos was driving west on the Cape Cod Highway with his wife, Katy Smith Dos Passos, asleep against his shoulder, the blinding glare of the setting sun prevented the novelist from seeing a truck partially pulled off the road. Katy went through the windshield and died

That talking with the sympathetic Katy had something to do with Hemingway's surprising decision to stop at the Catholic church is certainly possible, for as the daughter of an authority on comparative religions Katy had thought a fair amount about the problem of faith. But at the heart of his decision there surely lay his feelings of anger and depression about his parents and his seething resentment of the religious morality by which they had recently judged him. To Sylvia Beach and other friends in Paris in the twenties, he would insist that his connection with Catholicism had begun on the night he was wounded, when his friend Don Giuseppe Bianchi, the Florentine priest, had come through the dressing station and—amazingly enough—had murmured some words over him from the baptismal ceremony. Such unlikely stories, though, are the stuff of which myths of war trauma are made. There is no persuasive evidence that he ever knelt in prayer in a church that was not Protestant until the day he and Katy lit the candles in Petoskey.

---

instantaneously as the top of her head was sliced off. Dos Passos lost his right eye but survived. Katy had lived on the lower Cape a long time, and in Provincetown, Wellfleet and Truro there were many people who loved her. In a letter to the still hospitalized Dos Passos, Edmund Wilson declared that he had never seen the local residents so stunned by anything as Katy's death. At the funeral, Wilson said, "Everybody seemed much older, both from strain and losing Katy, who had always remained so young. . . . [She] must have been a wonderful companion—I had the impression that you were never bored with her, and that—rather shy with most other people—she must have been inexhaustibly entertaining with you and inexhaustible in her gift of investing life with something that the statistics don't add up to but that is one of the only reasons why one would like to see life continue on this planet."

~~~~~~

CHAPTER SIX

"The World's a Jail and We're Going to Break It Together"

THE IDEA OF TAKING OFF FOR THE ORIENT had been abandoned because Ted Brumback lost interest in going and Hemingway had no wish to make the trip by himself. With the Far East no longer a live option, he linked up with Katy Smith in a more modest adventure. They would go to Chicago together and look for work. While she was looking, Katy planned to live at the Arts Club, but Hemingway could stay with Y. K. and Doodles for at least a few weeks. Her brother and sister-in-law were very generous about sharing their living quarters, Katy assured him. They already had given temporary shelter to three young men in their East Chicago Avenue apartment and wouldn't mind sheltering a fourth.

Shortly before she and Ernest hitched a ride to the city with her brother Bill, Katy wrote a letter to a young woman back home in St. Louis whom she had known since their days at Mary Institute, a private girls' school established by T. S. Eliot's grandfather. Hadley Richardson had recently lost her mother and needed to be distracted, Katy decided. Come up to Chicago for a few weeks, she urged her. Brother Y. K. would be delighted to put her up.

2

SOME of Hemingway's male friends could never understand what attracted him to Hadley. Shining red hair, a lively intelligence and musically talented, to be sure—but about to turn twenty-nine and no great beauty! Her appraisers overlooked the psychological factors. To begin with, Hemingway had arrived in Chicago hard on the heels of discovering in Boyne City that facing life alone was rough. Furthermore, there were similarities in his and Hadley's backgrounds, especially in the character of their parents, that instantly created something very like a brother-and-sister bond between them—at the same time that her age made her seem like a mother.

James and Florence Richardson had six children, of whom Hadley, born in 1891, was the youngest. Mrs. Richardson has been described by Hadley's biographer, Alice Hunt Sokoloff, as "a woman of strong personality and convictions" who was the "dominant influence in the Richardson family." Winning political rights for women was one of her major interests, and expressing herself through music was another. In the Richardsons' comfortable home in St. Louis's West End, where the oak trees soared like cathedrals into the sky, two Steinway grand pianos adorned the yellow music room. With groups of friends, Mrs. Richardson played symphonies and concertos there; on evenings when only the family was present, she provided a piano accompaniment to the songs her husband liked to sing in his richly colored baritone. Higher than politics and music, though, in her firmament of interests was her love of the mysteries of psychic phenomena. Theosophy, mental science, ouija boards, automatic writing, and communications with the dead consumed vast amounts of her imaginative energy.

Hadley's father was a charmingly humorous, financially incompetent, desolately unhappy, thoroughly daunted man who took no satisfaction in running the pharmaceutical business he had inherited from his hard-driving, socially prominent father and who found marriage to the self-absorbed Florence more trying than he dared to say. In the middle nineties, he started drinking heavily, in spite of the manifest disgust of his teetotaling wife, and in 1903, when Hadley was twelve, he put a revolver to his head and killed himself.

Tragedy stalked the Richardson household in other ways. Two children died in infancy, and one day little Hadley fell out of a window in the second-floor nursery, injuring her back so severely that she was confined to a wheelchair for almost a year. A decade and a half later, Hadley's pregnant sister, Dorothea, was badly burned in a fire and died a few days later, after giving birth to a stillborn child.

As a little girl, Hadley's impulsively affectionate manner won her many friends, but between the ages of twelve and fourteen her gregariousness gradually evaporated. The death of her father, to whom she had been very close, had a great deal to do with this, but so did her mother's intense preoccupation with restoring the fortunes of her late husband's business, her consequent lack of concern with the questions of growing up that Hadley wanted to ask her, her clear preference for the company of her next-to-youngest child, on whom Mrs. Richardson had bestowed her own Christian name, and her insistence that Hadley had never been the same since her childhood accident. Although the adolescent Hadley withdrew more and more from social challenges, she continued to do well in her studies at Mary Institute and ultimately graduated with honors (but was too unsure of herself to accept the assurance of her teachers that she had literary gifts). On a calamitous postgraduation tour of Europe with her mother and sister Florence, she suffered a nervous breakdown— fainting fits and persistent headaches were its leading signs—in a city that was also named Florence. Upon entering Bryn Mawr College, she performed poorly in her courses and was often ill, and at the end of her freshman year her mother withdrew her. She simply didn't have the strength to be a college student, Mrs. Richardson demoralizingly informed her.

Fulfillment for this troubled girl came only through music. By the time she was in her middle teens her accomplishments as a pianist were not far from professional caliber, and after dropping out of Bryn Mawr she returned to her piano with more dedication than ever. Old friends from Mary Institute dropped by to tell her of their plans for marriage, but Hadley had learned from her parents' incompatibility that "marriage was a trap"; a concert career was the goal she dreamed of, and she was prepared to "throw over everything for it—people, parties, beaux," although for a time she wistfully hoped that her piano teacher, a young aesthete named Harrison Williams who had studied in Italy, would take a personal interest in her.

Yet even her marvelous skills as a musician did not prompt her mother to become less pessimistic about her. Mrs. Richardson worried aloud that Hadley was pushing herself too hard, and in time Hadley had to admit that she deteriorated physically beyond a certain amount of work. For a while she tried resting fifteen minutes for every half hour she practiced, but the scheme didn't work and she gave it up—along with all thoughts of becoming a concert performer.

Not until 1919, the year in which she turned twenty-eight, did she at last emerge from the shadows. She started seeing school friends again and at one of their parties met Leo Loeb, a forty-eight-year-old physician, who persuaded her to go out with him. In another bold step, she took up tennis—and made spectacular progress.

Unfortunately, her delight in these developments was distinctly not shared by her mother. Now that her daughter Florence was married and had children of her own, Mrs. Richardson more than ever wanted Hadley at her beck and call. The strain that developed between mother and daughter was suddenly broken in the summer of 1920 when Bright's disease claimed Mrs. Richardson. The compassionate Hadley did all she could to assist her mother through her final days.

At the funeral service in October, she felt emotionally drained, physically exhausted. As to what she was going to do next, she hadn't the slightest idea. A few days later, a letter arrived from Katy Smith, inviting her to come to Chicago.

3

AT the party in the Smiths' apartment on the night of Hadley's arrival, she met a number of interesting men, Don Wright, Bobby Rouse, Bill Horne and a "hulky, bulky" fellow named Wemedge— or was it Hemingstein?—who had also just arrived. He had a habit of standing on the balls of his feet and weaving his head back and forth like a boxer. When he laughed, his mouth stretched from ear to ear. As he talked to you, his eyes focused directly on yours. His enthusiasm about reading, fishing, hunting, going back to Italy, or whatever else bubbled up from his mind, was amazing. He was intensely alive, this man. It was no wonder that everyone in the room, male and female alike, seemed eager to get his attention.

To Hadley's surprise, Hemingway kept coming back to her side throughout the evening. The moment he saw her, he later told his brother Leicester, "an intense feeling came over me. I knew she was the girl I was going to marry." During the three weeks of her visit, they were together every day. By the time he put her on the train for St. Louis, they realized how much they had in common, how many ideas they shared, how many tastes.

That Hadley had a fondness for hard liquor was a discovery that particularly pleased him. As it did for many Americans in the twenties, drinking possessed a special excitement for Hadley because society had attempted to prohibit it. But in her case there was an additional reason for excitement: every time she took a drink she certified herself as her father's daughter, not her mother's. At a time when drinking had only recently become a daily habit of Hemingway's, the inexperienced but compliant Hadley became his companion in alcoholic exploration. One of the first letters she wrote to him after she went back to St. Louis revealed the importance of this link between them. "I still cherish, you know, the remark you made that you almost worshipped me as a drinker, tho (Falstaff old bean) I wouldn't repeat it to just everybody. *You* know?"

To have been told that she was loved by the handsomest, most charming man she had ever met had also been intoxicating. But what took the edge off her exhilaration on her return to St. Louis was the fear that some other woman might snare him. Dorothy Connable, of the Toronto Connables, seemed especially threatening. She had showed up in Chicago during Hadley's visit and it hadn't taken Hadley long to figure out why. In a letter to Hemingway on November 11, she voiced her misgivings about this good-looking Wellesley graduate. "Connable is a strangerish creature, what? Nice and nervously shy and yet Don [Wright] says fastish and avid for pleasure. Do let me know, man, when the going [i.e., the getting rid of her] is good. Will that cut out the Toronto writing?" One night at a party, Hemingway made advances, not to the avid Dorothy, but to two other young women. Full of remorse on the morning after, he told Hadley at least a part of the story of what had happened and tacitly begged for forgiveness. "I understand," she sympathetically replied, "how many different grains of personality must go to make up the experience of an intelligent and normally curious man and perhaps you really *are* young, Ernest. . . . Can't imagine, personally, shining up to a man who didn't attract me other ways than physically. . . . So glad you did tell me—anything goes, doesn't it, between honest men?"

Among her other rivals was Katy Smith, who once confided to Edmund Wilson's daughter Rosalind that she and Hemingway had been romantically involved for a time. Just how physical their involvement was, she did not say, but in any case it probably began in the summer of 1920, when Odgar was still courting her, if the repulsive and possibly wish-fulfilling Nick Adams story, "Summer People" (1926), was in any way based on fact.

Again Hemingway used real names. With every passing summer, Nick remarks, the desire of "poor old Odgar" to win Kate's hand has grown more "pitiful." Besides being over thirty, he has been "twice operated on for varicocele" and gets a "fried-fish" look in his eyes whenever he looks at his beloved. While Kate can't bear to have Odgar touch her, she is very attracted to Nick, and the final third of the story is taken up with an account of their lovemaking. Kate is profoundly aroused by the controlled power of Nick's performance as he takes her from behind, but is somewhat unsure about her own performance. When she asks, "Was I bad, Wemedge?" he assures her she was good. At the same time, it is clear that at least some of

Nick's satisfaction has come not from Kate's body, but from the knowledge that Odgar would "kill himself" if he were to learn of their liaison.★

It is also possible that Hemingway and Katy continued to be more than just friends all through the fall of 1920 and into the early months of 1921, by which time he was living in rather splendid digs that seemed made for dalliances. For Y. K.'s advertising business had been so profitable in 1920 that toward the end of the year he decided to lease a seven-room apartment in a monument to conspicuous waste called the Belleville, and when his wife went off to New York to study music he invited several friends to move in with him, rent-free. Among those who took him up on his invitation were Bobby Rouse, Don Wright, and Hemingway—who for the two months previous had been living as Bill Horne's guest in a flat not much bigger than a postage stamp on North State Street. In his letters to Hadley, Hemingway spoke of his new life with an elusive openness that made it impossible for her to pursue him with questions, even when he told her that he and Katy Smith had gone out dancing. For all his guile, however, he was full of guilt, with the result that his letters soon began to be marked by ambivalent comments about the durability of his commitment to her, which gave her a chance to ask him a frank question or two. When he told her, for instance, that he expected to go on loving her for "a little while at least," she immediately sought clarification of this tepid confession. "Do you mean at all that you don't feel the capacity to stand the long strain of things and circumstances on our companionship?" If that was the case, she said, now was the time for him to speak up.

But since he didn't speak up, she gladly put aside her suspicions. As she repeatedly admitted, she was madly in love with him, and besides which she was as eager as he was to find a mate. Having lived so reclusively for so many years, she longed to see the world, but just as Hemingway did, she wanted to have a partner along for the ride. "Together" was such a magic word for her that she felt sorry for other young women who were never able to find a kindred spirit. In a comparison of herself to Carol Kennicott, the heroine of Sinclair Lewis's recently published *Main Street,* Hadley observed to Hemingway that what Carol had "needed *so much* in the lonely town was someone *to tell what she tho't* to. Whoops—I shudsay!"

In March he went down to St. Louis to see her, wearing a new Brooks Brothers suit and his Italian cape. Two weeks later, she came

★ Although "Summer People" was of publishable quality, it never saw the light of day in the author's lifetime. Thus, Odgar and Katy were spared the sort of humiliation that Hemingway visited upon so many other people in his fiction and nonfiction alike.

up to Chicago, carrying a suitcase containing her own latest purchase, a satin dress with Bulgarian embroidery. Feelings of fright overtook her for some reason as she walked into Y. K.'s apartment, but her sweetheart's exuberance carried her past it, and on a visit to Oak Park a few days later she got along swimmingly with Dr. Hemingway and passed muster with Grace as well. On the last night of her stay she told Ernest that she had a trust fund that paid her three thousand dollars a year. Supplemented by the money he could earn as a foreign correspondent for the Toronto *Star,* her income put living in Italy well within their grasp. Suddenly, it was all decided. They would get married in Horton Bay at the end of the summer and leave for Europe sometime in the fall. "The world's a jail," Hadley exclaimed, "and we're going to break it together."

4

DURING his first months in Chicago, Hemingway couldn't find a suitable job. Not until December of 1920 was he finally hired as a writer and editor by a monthly magazine called *The Cooperative Commonwealth,* whose sole reason for being was to stimulate investor interest in the corporation which owned the magazine, the Cooperative Society of America. The head of the parent organization was a smooth-talking swindler named Harrison Parker, who would eventually be taken to court by his irate stockholders for having driven the corporation into bankruptcy with an incredible fifteen million dollars in acquired liabilities. Hemingway was able to tell right away that there was something fraudulent about the Society, but since its journalistic offshoot was paying him forty dollars a week, he decided not to "play the role of the rats deserting the stinking ship," as he wrote to his vacationing mother in California. Another compensation was that there were some interesting people who worked for the magazine, one of whom was a young man with the odd name of Krebs Friend. Krebs had fought in France and was planning to go back there to live.

In his spare time, Hemingway plucked out of the shadows of his psyche a curious, untitled tale about a British soldier named Orpen.*

---

* The British painter, Sir William Newenham Montague Orpen, was appointed an official artist by the British government during World War I. His paintings included portraits of Woodrow Wilson, Marshal Foch, and other wartime leaders. But the work of Orpen's with which Chicagoans were familiar was a painting from 1908 that the Art Institute acquired not long before Hemingway's arrival in the city in 1920. Entitled "Woman in Grey," it depicts the artist's wife in a full-length dress. Despite the changes in women's fashions after the war, Grace Hemingway had continued to wear such dresses and in fact would go on doing so for the rest of her life. Perhaps this was the reason why the painting reminded Hemingway of the woman he wanted to write about in the story of the soldier he named Orpen.

As the story opens, the exhausted Orpen is lying on a foggy hillside defending a bridge against German attack. A gray-coated enemy rides onto the bridge on a bicycle and Orpen raises his rifle and fires. The stricken man falls from his bike and flops about grotesquely like a spider with a leg torn off. Before the front wheel of his bike stops turning, the man is dead.

Sinking into a reverie made possible by a lull in the attack, Orpen compares a machine gunner's dependence on manual dexterity to a pianist's. The comparison comes easily to him because he has always wished to be a concert pianist and play at Albert Hall. Suddenly, he recalls the music room at home in which he used to play Chopin for his mother. "That's so sweet my dear," he remembers her saying to him. "Will you play some more. I just don't see any sense to Schönberg, my dear. Should I?"

The fighting resumes. Orpen is wounded by a shell burst and becomes delirious. In his feverishness, he dreams that he has died a hero's death and has entered Valhalla, the Hall of Heroes, high above heaven itself. He recognizes Lord Nelson, Sir Francis Drake, General Grant, General Custer, General Sherman, Eric the Red, and Tamerlane, among others. A ridiculous quarrel breaks out among these famous figures and they begin to fight. The fighting is enjoyable to them, though, for in Valhalla "there is the fun of killing, but none of the drawbacks of dying." Thus when Orpen runs his bayonet into the groin of George Washington, the father of his country simply laughs and says, "Oh, good thrust. . . . I forgot you were British." Being stabbed in the chest by Washington is not Orpen's idea of fun, however, and he wishes he could leave Valhalla and its "hateful game." A staircase leading downward to heaven is his avenue of escape. Upon descending it, he finds himself in a country lane. "It looked much like the lane at home to Orpen with great elms meeting overhead." Walking along "without hesitation," he comes to a door, turns the handle and enters. A smiling woman is waiting within. "Mother," he cries. "I've been a long way." "I knew you'd get here, son," she says.

Across the room he recognizes his old concert grand piano. His mother says that all of his compositional materials are still intact. "I've kept them . . . waiting. There is pen and ink." Orpen is overcome with joy. "Now I can really go on with the symphony tomorrow." Alas, no sooner does he say this than he recalls with a start that he is supposed to fight the next day in Valhalla. ". . . to cut to slice is the greatest joy of man," he says defiantly. His mother smiles, looking "like the mother of all wisdom." He resumes talking about the delights of warfare. "Today we slashed and slashed. I ran

George Washington through as I battled down the road to you . . . [and] the joy of battle was in my heart." Again his mother smiles. Angrily, he insists that she must believe what he is saying. It is clear, though, that she doesn't, and "somehow before he knew it he was on his knees before her and she was holding his head." At her touch, Orpen's bravado collapses. "It wasn't wonderful mother," he confesses. "It was terrible. I wanted to stay and do my music mother. I don't want to be in Valhalla!" "I know son," his mother says, stroking his head. Her touch and her words make Orpen feel like a boy again.

There is no reason for him to be anxious about shirking his manly duty, his mother reveals. Not only he but all the inhabitants of Valhalla are now living in peace right there in her home as household gods. Fighting bores them so much that they return to Valhalla only in order to greet new members, of whom there have recently been an unusual number because of the world war. After proudly showing Orpen the medals that were awarded to him when he died, she assures him that he was a hero for having defended the bridge and that now he can stay at home and work on his music. Orpen breaks out into a dance, "a curious dance—great high leaps in grace note form with quaver duration." Unfortunately, the violent exercise causes a pain in the section of his chest where George Washington had stabbed him. A second surge of pain convulses him, and he awakes from his delirium. A small piece of shrapnel is removed from his chest. "Tell them I don't want to go back to Valhalla," he mumbles. "No, you won't have to," a woman's voice answers.

A dead cyclist and a still-turning bicycle wheel; a bayonet thrust at the groin of a father figure; a young man's discovery of a heavenly vision of his boyhood home and his further discovery of his mother in the music room; the false front the young man puts up about his love of fighting; his mother's disbelief in what he is saying; the pride she nevertheless takes in the way he had conducted himself at the bridge; her revelation that he no longer has to prove that he is a man; the permission she grants him to devote himself full-time to his art: in these and other ways the story of Orpen is such an unmediated mixture of raw hopes and fears that the author must have made next to no effort to control his dreaming imagination.

Hemingway the Chicagoan also began and abandoned work on a novel, collaborated with his high school chum Morris Musselman on a worthless theatrical farce appropriately called *Hokum,* tried his hand at writing poetry, turned out several more stories that the slick magazines didn't want, and immersed himself in Havelock Ellis's *The Psychology of Sex,* Sinclair Lewis's *Main Street* and every history he could lay his hands on about the war he had just served in, including ancillary studies like Isaac Don Levine's *The Russian Revolution*. ("He sat there on the porch reading a book on the war," Hemingway would say of Harold Krebs in "Soldier's Home." "It was a history and he was reading about all the engagements he had been in. It was the most interesting reading he had ever done. . . . Now he was really learning about the war.") *

On forays away from home base, he absorbed such varied sights and sounds as the schmaltzy music of the German band that played at a North Avenue beer hall called Wurz 'n' Zepp's, the size of the morbid crowd outside the County Jail a few hours before the hanging of two gangland figures named Cardinella and Cosmano and of "some other Wop killer" whose name escaped him, and the wailing of dark-skinned jazz babies in black-and-tan nightclubs. "Aggravatin' papa, don't you try to two-time me. . . . Aggravatin' papa, treat me kind or let me be. . . . Stop messin' round, sweet jelly roll." (In time, a snatch of that beat would be heard in *The Sun Also Rises*.) And on nights when he was feeling flush, he sampled the city's first-run theatrical fare, from Ethel Barrymore in Zoë Akins's *Déclassée* to Belle Bennett in *Happy Go Lucky* to Ann Pennington in *George White's Scandals of 1920*. His appetite for new experiences was immense.

At the same time, he continued to be vulnerable to bouts of depression. So far as he could tell, what was plaguing him was the fear that marriage might prove to be a form of death. In late March, Howie Jenkins made matters worse by taking him aside and warning him not to get hitched if he knew what was good for him, and by the end of April he had "damn near [gone] cuckoo," as he confessed to Bill Smith, from thinking about all the bachelor fishing trips to the north country that he would never take again.

> Guy loves a couple or three streams all his life and loves 'em better than anything in the world—falls in love with a girl and the goddam streams can dry up for all he cares. Only the hell of it is that all that country has as bad a hold on me as ever—there's as much of a pull this spring as there ever was—and you know how it's always been—just don't think about it at all day times, but at night it comes and ruins me—and I can't go.

In the poems he wrote in this period, he sometimes was able to slough off at least some of his black feelings by making savage

---

* Among the books Hemingway may have read in this period were C. F. Horne and W. F. Austin's five-volume anthology, *The Great Events of the War* (1920), and Thomas N. Page's *Italy and the World War* (1920), both of which contained details that would prove valuable to him in writing *A Farewell to Arms*.

comments about the war. His own brief tour of duty had given him "an awfully satisfactory feeling," of course. On the other hand, most of the books on the conflict that were coming out presented it as a colossally mismanaged butchery—and this was the view of the latter years of it that he, too, now adopted, for reasons that surely had to do with a larger pessimism about human life.

Somewhat surprisingly, the target he took dead aim at in the first of his antiwar poems was Gabriele D'Annunzio. For as a novelist, D'Annunzio was one of Hemingway's principal postwar enthusiasms, mainly because of his superbly romantic account in *The Flame* (1900) of a young poet's erotic involvement with an older actress. The story was based on D'Annunzio's famous affair with Eleonora Duse, and the young novel-reader who had once boasted to his family and friends of being engaged to the actress Mae Marsh found it easy to project himself into the role of the hero. But in addition to being a writer, D'Annunzio was a fanatical nationalist and war lover. Overjoyed by the Italian government's belated decision to enter the war against the Central Powers, the novelist had fought for his country with both the army and the navy, had lost an eye in a military plane crash and had made countless fervent speeches to men under arms. In *Across the River and Into the Trees* (1950), Hemingway would have the aging Colonel Cantwell remember the time when, as a young lieutenant in the Veneto in 1918, he had stood in the pouring rain with his platoon of assault troops listening to D'Annunzio address a huge assemblage of Italian soldiers. With his dead eye covered by a patch and his face "as white as the belly of a sole, new turned over in the market, the brown side not showing, and looking thirty hours dead," he was revoltingly ugly, and in Lieutenant Cantwell's opinion his speech had been even more revolting. "Morire non è basta," D'Annunzio had shouted at the rain-soaked throng, and the young Cantwell had thought, "What the muck more do they want of us?" Which is precisely how, in the early months of 1921, the young Hemingway felt, even though he himself had never heard the orator perform.

> D'ANNUNZIO
> *Half a million dead wops*
> *And he got a kick out of it*
> *The son of a bitch.*

That a fear of marriage as an equivalent of death was also at work in his war poems became obvious in only one of them. Unable to get to sleep, a young woman lies torturing herself with recollections of sexual intercourse with her soldier lover. Suddenly he reappears and embraces her once more—to the extent, that is, that a dead man can.

> *KILLED PIAVE—JUNE 15—1918*
> *Desire and*
> *All the sweet pulsing aches*
> *And gentle hurtings*
> *That were you,*
> *Are gone into the sullen dark.*
> *Now in the night you come unsmiling*
> *To lie with me*
> *A dull, cold, rigid bayonet*
> *On my hot-swollen, throbbing soul.*

Hemingway would often remark in later years that war was one of the great subjects for a writer; and for a writer as secretive as he was one of the greatest things about it was that the maimings it caused could serve as metaphors for less tangible forms of disablement. Thus, his inability to match Hadley's ardent love for him did not have to be directly acknowledged so long as it could be expressed through a poem about a sexually aroused young woman who can no longer be satisfied by her lover because he was killed on the Piave during the same summer that Lieutenant Hemingway was struck down. The symbolic reformulation of the author's underlying emotion was certainly odd, but perhaps no odder than the reformulation he would come up with four years later in *The Sun Also Rises.**

At times, his mood swung so fast from low to high and back down again that one could almost say that he was simultaneously exhilarated and depressed. Shortly before his twenty-second birthday, for instance, the after-taste of a just-concluded visit by Hadley moved him to write a bitterly discouraged poem called "Flat Roofs."

> *It is cool at night on the roofs of the city*
> *The city sweats*
> *Dripping and stark.*
> *Maggots of life*
> *Crawl in the hot loneliness of the city.*
> *Love curdles in the city*

* In order to bring "Killed Piave" even more directly in line with his own experience, Hemingway later changed the date in the title to July 8, 1918.

Love sours in the hot whispering from the pavements.
Love grows old
Old with the oldness of sidewalks.
It is cool at night on the roofs of the city.

Yet on the day of his birthday, July 21, he fairly overflowed with enthusiasm in a letter to "Sister Luke."

> Suppose you want to hear all about Hadley. . . . She's a wonderful tennis player, best pianist I ever heard and a sort of terribly fine article. Spite of the [enclosed] clipping prophecying [*sic*] a big wedding in the fall in St. Louis, we're going to fool them and be married at the Bay in that small, trick church there. Then going to kinda bum around for about three weeks and then go back to Chicago . . . stay there through November I guess and then allez to Italy for a year or maybe two years. . . . We're going to Naples and stay there till it gets warm in the spring. Living at Capri I guess, and then go up into Abruzzi. Capracotta probably—there's a fine trout stream there—the Sangro River—and tennis courts and it's 1200 meters above sea level—most wonderful place you ever heard of.

Not long thereafter, he again felt awful, as another poem bore witness.

BIRD OF NIGHT
Cover my eyes with your pinions
Dark bird of night
Spread your black wings like a turkey strutting
Drag your strong wings like a cock grouse drumming
Scratch the smooth flesh of my belly
With scaly claws
Dip with your beak to my lips
But cover my eyes with your pinions.

As in "Killed Piave," the speaker is a woman in the love-grip of death.

5

A middle-aged writer whose fiction had earned him more esteem than cash was still working, in the winter of 1921, for a Chicago advertising firm and still hobnobbing with other ad men in the city, of whom Y. K. Smith was one. It was at a typically big party in Y. K.'s spacious sublet that the writer was approached by a broad-shouldered young man with admiration shining in his eyes. Of all his literary mentors, none would have a greater influence on Hemingway than Sherwood Anderson.

The writer's wiglike clump of unruly black hair, blazing dark eyes, full-throated laugh and bright-colored shirts were the outward signs of what seemed to be an incorrigibly youthful spirit; at forty-four, Anderson still became as wide-eyed as a boy whenever he talked about boxing, baseball, or horse racing, and he had a wonderfully romantic history that he would recount to new friends at the drop of a hat. In the fall of 1912, he had been the president of a prosperous paint factory in Elyria, Ohio. Unhappily married, repelled by business, and bored by Elyria, he walked out of the office one day—and kept on walking. Thenceforward, he vowed, his only master would be literature.

Anderson's boyish openness, however, was not to be trusted. A need to escape had been a recurrent phenomenon in his emotional life from an early age; in Elyria, the need had climaxed in a mental breakdown. That he told conflicting stories about his departure from the town, occasionally acknowledging that he had been teetering on the brink of insanity at the time but for the most part making himself out to have been heroically rebellious, was typical of a man for whom there was no distinct borderline between reality and make-believe.

Anderson's secretary at the paint factory remembered that on Thursday morning, November 28, 1912, he came into the office and "acted queerly." After opening his mail, he approached her and said with a laugh, "I feel as though my feet were wet, and they keep getting wetter." With this oblique indication that he was drowning in obligation, he then left the office, saying he was going for a walk. Three days later, he was discovered in a Cleveland drugstore, haggard, unshaven, and suffering from amnesia. At Huron Road Hospital, his identity was learned from papers found in his clothes.

For at least two years before his breakdown, Anderson had been working dangerously hard. At the end of a day's stint at the office, he was wont to lock himself in an upper room of his house and write, often all night. Cornelia, his loving, anxious wife, thought he was slightly crazy. To relieve the pressure he could feel building inside him, he took long walks alone in the woods. He also started drinking heavily and "did a lot of woman chasing." Although he would later say that his mind was a blank for the entire period of his disappearance from Elyria, the fact is that he wrote and mailed a seven-page letter to his wife during the course of his wanderings. Ostensibly a set of notes on the events of the trip, the letter ran heavily to images of filth, aggression, and escape that seemed to

reflect a terror of grown-ups and an identification with the feelings
of crying children. The jottings on pages one and two leave little
doubt of how close to insanity he had come:

> Why do the children cry. They are everywhere underfoot. Among
> them ran yellow dogs with brown dirt stuck on their backs. The dogs
> howl and the children cry. At night the dogs howl and the children
> cry and your head hurts. There are so many children and so many
> dogs and so many long streets filled with dirty houses.
>
> If one does ask he could find Cornelia but if you ask the people
> they will hit you. Mrs. Leonard had a book in her hand and tried to
> hit me with it. There is a place near Bedford. A child that cried looked
> at a man with a pipe in his mouth who growled like a yellow dog. I
> tried to drink some beer but it was bitter and the room was full of
> men who would have hit me but I ran.

Under Cornelia's care, he returned to Elyria in late December.
After disposing of his paint business, he left for Chicago—where he
had worked in his late teens as a common laborer in a warehouse—
and took a job in advertising. While he pointedly did not take his
wife and children with him, divorce proceedings were not initiated
until 1916, when he finally decided to legalize his relationship with a
music and dance teacher named Tennessee Mitchell. (Like Hemingway, he would marry four times in all.) His first novel, *Windy
McPherson's Son,* appeared that same year, quickly followed by
Marching Men (1917), *Mid-American Chants* (1918), *Winesburg, Ohio*
(1919) and *Poor White* (1920).

A troubled psychological history, a passion for sports and a rebellious spirit were by no means the only similarities between Anderson
and Hemingway. Anderson's wish to make literature reveal once
again "the terrible importance of the flesh in human relations" was
certainly shared by Hemingway, and Anderson treated the subject
of androgyny, which would also figure in Hemingway's work, in a
story titled "The Man Who Became a Woman," later collected in
Horses and Men (1923).

In his youth, the narrator of the story remembers, he had worked
as a swipe for the owner of a race horse named Pick-it-boy, which
he loved with a strange passion. Often the horse would put its nose
against his face, and sometimes this experience would make him
wish that Pick-it-boy was a girl, or that he himself was a girl and
the horse was a man. One cold rainy night, the narrator further
remembers, he wandered away from the fair grounds where the
horse was stabled and walked into a saloon in a nearby mining town.

After ordering a drink at the bar, he glanced at the cracked looking-glass behind it and caught sight of his reflection, except that it "wasn't my own face at all but the face of a woman. It was a girl's face, that's what I mean . . . and a lonesome and scared girl too." Three whiskeys later, the shaken youth returned to the stable, stripped off his soaking wet clothes and tucked himself naked into a pile of horse blankets above Pick-it-boy's stall. During the night, two liquored-up Negro bucks discovered him there and yanked off his blankets. In the light of their smoky, dirty lantern, his pretty, white and slender body looked like a young girl's. Figuring that he couldn't be a very respectable female to be in such a place, the Negroes decided to take advantage of the situation. "Jes' you lie still honey. We ain't gwine hurt you none," one of them said with a chuckle. When the boy squirmed, both of the black men jumped at him, but he got away from their grasp and fled into the black night and the rain, running like a crazy man. In a slaughterhouse field filled with bones, he stumbled and fell into the skeleton of a horse. His hands, clutching upwards, "got hold of the cheeks of that dead horse and the bones of his cheeks were cold as ice with the rain washing over them." Terror washed over the youth like a big wave. Yet the terror also felt like a burning, and it finally "burned all that silly nonsense about being a girl right out of me." Not even the strangest of Hemingway's cross-sexual scenarios would exceed the strangeness of "The Man Who Became a Woman."

The concept of adolescence constituted another link between the two writers. In Anderson's opinion, he himself was an eternal adolescent. "When in speaking of *Winesburg* you used the word 'adolescence,' " he wrote the literary critic Van Wyck Brooks in December 1919, "you struck more nearly than you know on the whole note of me. I am immature, will live and die immature. A quite terrible confession that would be if I did not represent so much." That he, too, was fated to live and die immature was not an admission that Hemingway was willing to make, of course, for it ran directly counter to his wish to believe that he was already a man. As a means of encouraging his new friends in Chicago to share that belief, he exaggerated how old he was by two or three years, if not more; even Hadley did not learn he was only twenty-one until she had known him for more than six months—and by the time of their divorce in 1927 he would be known as Papa. Yet at the same time that he wanted to be thought of as a man of transcendent maturity, he was drawn as if by a magnet to the stories of adolescence that had made Anderson famous. In the early stages of Anderson's career, Hemingway observed in 1929 to Owen Wister, he "wrote some stories that I thought were lovely—all the time he was working as an advertising writer but he wrote simply and to me, anyway, very beautifully—about people and the country and, it's true, best of all about adolescence." So taken was he by Anderson's portrait of an adolescent in "I Want to Know Why" that in an early story of his own he imitated it. To the considerable embarrassment of some of his friends, he would always deny that "My Old Man" was derivative, but it clearly is in every important respect, from its focus on a young boy's initiation into the disillusioning world of adulthood to its racetrack settings and artfully naive vernacular voice.

In less obvious ways Hemingway also built upon the example of *Winesburg,* absorbing and transmuting its sensitive registrations of young George Willard's feelings into his own accounts, in such stories as "The End of Something" and "The Three-Day Blow," of young Nick Adams's state of mind. Readying himself for the emotionally arduous task of writing about his parents' marriage, he carefully studied how Anderson had dealt with the unhappy relationship of George Willard's mother and father. Anderson's sympathetic treatment of the indomitable Mrs. Willard did not correspond, to be sure, to the kind of portrait of a mother that Hemingway had in mind, nor was he tempted to emulate Anderson's recapitulation of Mrs. Willard's history of sexual confusion. Even so, there was at least one reference to her girlhood that may have sounded a note that he found familiar: "Once she startled the town by putting on men's clothes and riding a bicycle down Main Street."

A heightening of his consciousness about *Huckleberry Finn* was almost surely another result of his friendship with Anderson. Although the book had been valued by Hemingway in his boyhood, it wasn't his favorite. To Anderson, on the other hand, Mark Twain's masterpiece was in a class by itself. Its name seemed to be always on his lips, and never more so than in the winter he met Hemingway, for Van Wyck Brooks had recently published a study of Mark Twain that had created a sensation. Anderson admired *The Ordeal of Mark Twain* (1920) as an emblematic analysis of the difficulties besetting all writers in America, but felt that it hadn't sufficiently praised *Huckleberry Finn.* Well before *The Ordeal* was put to paper, he had repeatedly urged Brooks to grant that at least once in his life Mark Twain had heard the whispering of the gods. "I believe he wrote that book in a little hut on a hill on his farm," he reminded Brooks in an eloquent letter.

It poured out of him. I fancy that at night he came down from his hill stepping like a king, a splendid playboy playing with rivers and men,

riding on the Mississippi, on the broad river that is the great artery
flowing out of the heart of the land.

To Brooks, to Paul Rosenfeld, to Waldo Frank, to all of his literary
friends, Anderson proclaimed that *Huckleberry Finn* had in effect
been responsible for his career. It had inspired the vision of American loneliness that informed everything he had written; it had shaped
his responses to the "lovely stillness" of the Mississippi River in the
opening section of *Poor White;* it was the source of the rhythm and
swing of the poems in *Mid-American Chants* and of the groping,
stumbling, yearning style of the *Winesburg* stories. Is it any wonder
that half a decade after meeting such an enthusiast Hemingway
would reread *Huckleberry Finn* and judge it anew for himself?

In all likelihood, he also heard the older writer speak in praise of
Gertrude Stein. In the beginning, Anderson had scorned her work,
some said, but if so, he had quickly changed his mind. Her drastically simple syntax and diction demonstrated that the demolition of
traditional literary language could be carried even further than Mark
Twain had dreamed, while her trick of repeating certain key words
opened up a new means of communicating emotion. As Anderson
often emphasized—possibly in his conversations with Hemingway
as well—Miss Stein was a wholesome cook, working in a "kitchen
of words."

Private tutor to a young man who had spurned the idea of going
to college: this was the role that the author of *Winesburg* played in
Hemingway's life in Chicago. Indeed, there was a father-and-son
quality in their relationship. For although Hemingway had been
relieved to be freed of his father's guidance, he still felt the need of
an older man to tell him what was right, and Anderson had a great
gift for saying just the right thing to people who needed help. In the
words of the newspaper critic, Burton Rascoe, who knew him well,
"People hurt by life, women entangled with psychic conflicts,
bruised, saddened and disillusioned spirits find in him a consoler."
Anderson for his part considered Hemingway "a young fellow of
extraordinary talent" who was "instinctively in touch with everything worth-while going on." He liked to be in the young man's
company as much as the young man liked to be in his, and he easily
fell into the habit of inviting him out to his little house in suburban
Palos Park.

In the spring of 1921, however, their meetings temporarily came
to a halt, when Anderson and his wife went off to Europe as the
guests of his literary admirer Paul Rosenfeld. During his absence
from Chicago, he was not a good correspondent, so it was not until

he returned that Hemingway learned of his fortunate encounter with an American woman named Sylvia Beach, the owner of a Paris bookshop called Shakespeare and Company, who had kindly introduced him to a number of writers, including Gertrude Stein and James Joyce. Paris, Anderson told him, was where the future of literature was being forged, and where Hemingway ought to be.

6

WHILE Anderson and his wife were enjoying themselves abroad, Hemingway had hung on at *The Cooperative Commonwealth,* methodically extruding feature stories from his typewriter, painfully extracting paychecks from an organization whose financial sponsor was clearly on the verge of collapse, and in his spare hours giving himself up to the joys of reading modern fiction, including Floyd Dell's *Moon-Calf* and *The Briary-Bush,* Somerset Maugham's *The Moon and Sixpence* and *Mrs. Craddock,* Knut Hamsun's *Hunger,* Rose Macaulay's *Potterism* and Boni and Liveright's reissue of Conrad's *The Nigger of the "Narcissus"* with its famous Preface in which Conrad had written that the task of the writer was "to make you hear, to make you feel . . . to make you see. That—and no more, and it is everything."

Hadley came up from St. Louis for a weekend in July and made arrangements to have a new Corona typewriter delivered to him on his birthday. At the end of the month she came up again and stayed a whole week. Every day they had lunch together and afterwards went for a walk, her hand on his arm, "wonderful times of . . . breathing together, stepping together," she later recalled. In the evenings they sought to be alone, but unfortunately the arrangements in Y. K.'s apartment made that all but impossible. For Y. K. had by this time left the commodious Belleville and gone back to his old quarters at 100 East Chicago Avenue, taking Hemingway and Bill Horne along with him as freeloaders and welcoming as well his errant wife, Doodles, whom Hemingway suspected of being sexually unfaithful and whom he cordially disliked in any case. In order to be by themselves, Hemingway and Hadley took to going up to the roof, where they couldn't be seen from neighboring buildings as long as they huddled beneath the parapet. "I wish I could have you now to pet," Hadley wrote to him in early August from the fishing camp where she spent the final weeks before their marriage. "Remember how we both tried to be the little, small, petted one the last night on the roof?" They were already taking turns being the passive lover.

Hemingway also enjoyed talking about sex and called on Hadley to describe to him every romantic adventure in which she had ever been involved, as well as all of her current fantasies. Her experience as a lover was so limited that the only interesting anecdote she could come up with had to do with the discovery that the mother of her Bryn Mawr roommate, Edna Rapallo, was a lesbian. She managed to show me, Hadley related, how much pleasanter life was for women who loved women, and "being very suggestible I began to imagine I had all this low sex feelin' and she for me." In retrospect, Hadley was sure that the attraction hadn't amounted to much; if only her life with her mother hadn't been so unsatisfactory, she said, she probably wouldn't have been attracted to Mrs. Rapallo in the slightest. As for her current fantasies, they were varied, albeit entirely focused on the man she was going to marry. In a burst of passion on August 21, she confessed that "I need you in *every* part of my life. I wanta be kissed. I wanta pull your head down on my heart and hold it very close and cradle you there for hours, you blessed thing—love you, love you—your ownest in the world."

Their wedding, everyone agreed, was beautiful. The third of September was a brilliantly clear day in northern Michigan, and the little church at Horton Bay had been handsomely decorated with swamp lilies, balsam boughs, and goldenrod. With almost a hundred people from St. Louis supplementing all the friends of the Hemingway family, there were no empty pews. Bill Smith was best man and his sister Katy one of the bridesmaids.

Hemingway got dressed for the ceremony at Pinehurst Cottage, while a couple of his friends from Petoskey, Dutch Pailthorp and Luman Ramsdell, looked on and made comments. In a Nick Adams sketch called "Wedding Day," Hemingway subsequently insisted that Dutch and Luman had been nervous, whereas Nick had not been, but it was Grace's opinion that her son had been exceedingly apprehensive all day, while seven-year-old Leicester claimed that his brother's legs were clearly shaking as he came down the aisle. The stress of the occasion was further increased by a fifteen-minute delay in Hadley's arrival at the church. She had gone for a swim that afternoon and had underestimated the time it would take to dry her hair. Because her hair was fairly long and quite thick, it was still damp when she finally appeared, but the wreath around her head, the soft veil cascading down her back and her ivory lace dress and bouquet of baby's breath were enough of a distraction so that no one noticed, she was sure. After the ceremony, the wedding party gathered outside Pinehurst Cottage for pictures, most of which proved to be reasonably flattering to the bride, at the same time that they revealed how much less good-looking she was than the bride-groom's sister, Ursula. (The wonderfully handsome Marcelline, be it said, was not on hand for the ceremony. Upset by her brother's lack of attention to her, she had contrived to be unavoidably detained in New England.)

Toward the end of the chicken dinner that Liz Dilworth laid on, the newlyweds piled into a Ford belonging to a local character named John Kotesky and roared away in the twilight. For five dollars, Kotesky had agreed to drive them over the hill road to Walloon Lake where, after considerable difficulty, they located the oars of Dr. Hemingway's rowboat and rowed across to Windemere. Grace had not only offered the cottage for their honeymoon, but in a further gesture of conciliation toward her son had had a new roof put on the porch and had the floors freshly varnished. "It was a long row across the lake in the dark," the author of "Wedding Day" would write, in a description that foreshadowed the account of the escape of the lovers across Lago Maggiore in *A Farewell to Arms*. As soon as Nick had helped his bride from the boat, he kissed her, the author continued. "She kissed him back hard the way he had taught her with her mouth a little open so their tongues could play with each other." Then they walked up to the cottage and Nick unlocked the door and lit the lamps and they looked through the cottage together.

Grace's bed was the principal scene of their lovemaking, and if *Islands in the Stream* can be biographically relied upon, the posture they assumed may sometimes have resembled Lieutenant Hemingway's acceptance of Nurse Kurowsky's embraces. The hero of the novel, the painter Thomas Hudson, asleep on his boat off Cuba, dreams that his first wife is sleeping with him, sleeping on top of him, that is,

> as she liked to do sometimes. He felt all of this and the tangibility of her legs against his legs and her body against his and her breasts against his chest and her mouth was playing against his mouth. Her hair hung down and lay heavy and silky on his eyes and on his cheeks and he turned his lips away from her searching ones and took the hair in his mouth and held it. . . . Then he lay under her weight with her silken hair over his face like a curtain and moved slowly and rhythmically.

Because Windemere had almost no insulation, it was difficult to heat, so that when the weather turned chilly for a couple of days both the honeymooners came down with bad colds. Hemingway's throat was so sore that he didn't even feel like taking walks, but one day he did make the effort to take Hadley to Petoskey, where he proceeded to nettle her by introducing her to Marjorie Bump, as well as to a couple of other girls whom he tactlessly identified as additional losers in the competition for his hand. Except perhaps for the sex, the honeymoon was not a great success, in short, and at the end of two weeks they were only too happy to return to Chicago.

Originally, their plan had been to live at Y. K.'s, for he had generously told them that one of the bedrooms in his apartment was theirs for the asking. But Hemingway had had a quarrel with Y. K. a few weeks before the wedding, as a result of his having talked rather too freely about the free-swinging morality of Y. K.'s wife.* When Y. K. angrily told him that he and Hadley would have to look elsewhere for a place to live, Hemingway rented a fifth-floor walkup in a rundown building on North Dearborn Street. With its leaky pipes and swaybacked bed, the apartment was even more disagreeable than he had assumed it would be, and from the day that he and Hadley moved in he spent as little time there as possible. Taking long walks across the city by himself was much more to his taste than assisting his wife in making their quarters more livable. For company during the day, the lonely Hadley had to depend on conversations with the corner grocery man.

One day while she was alone, Grace arrived, apparently for the purpose of discussing the satisfactions of marital love. By way of illustrating her theme, she told her daughter-in-law that she and Dr. Hemingway were going to hold a reception on the first of October to celebrate their twenty-fifth wedding anniversary and that they wanted Hadley and Ernest to be the guests of honor. They also had invited a number of Ernest's friends, out of a wish to make the party even more enjoyable for him. On learning that the friends on his mother's list included Y. K. and Doodles Smith, Hemingway at once sent Y. K. a letter in which he brutally rescinded Grace's invitation, made mocking reference to Doodles's opinion of Y. K.'s manliness and warned that he would shortly be coming by to "collect the residue of my clothes and my probably well-thumbed correspondence." In reply, Y. K. coldly informed him that he had placed Hemingway's clothes in a storeroom and that he could get the key from the janitor. "You can readily understand," he finished by saying, "that your having written me as you have makes your

---

* What Hemingway in his residual innocence did not understand about the Smiths was that they both had a bohemian attitude toward marriage. If Doodles felt that she could play around, so did Y. K. Three years later, however, their open marriage would collapse in scandal when Y. K.'s mistress attempted to kill Doodles and then took her own life.

presence in my house quite impossible, at any time, under any circumstances."

It was Y. K.'s generosity that had enabled Hemingway to bank the money he would otherwise have had to spend on rent, which is to say that Y. K. had enabled him to pay for his upcoming passage to Europe. Moreover, it was at Y. K.'s parties that he had met Sherwood Anderson—and Hadley. Yet none of this counted for Hemingway, once his anger was aroused. At that point, all he could think of was how to hurt his benefactor, and he did so by aiming at his groin, as he so often would in future quarrels with other men. His implicit reminder to Y. K. of the infidelity of his wife was a prophecy of the sort of humiliating attack he would make on Harold Loeb, Chard Powers Smith, and F. Scott Fitzgerald, among others.

Having decided that it was financially useless to prolong his association any further with *The Cooperative Commonwealth,* Hemingway began his married life by living almost exclusively on the income from Hadley's trust fund. The situation was strikingly reminiscent of the first year of his parents' marriage, when his father's meager fees had merely supplemented Grace's earnings. Although he occasionally turned out an article for the Toronto *Star Weekly,* these sporadic efforts were mainly for the purpose of reminding the managing editor of the paper, John Bone, that he would make a good foreign correspondent. But before negotiating the specifics of a regular arrangement with Bone, he and Hadley had to decide where in Europe they were going to live.

At a dinner at the Andersons' one evening, the older writer reiterated his recommendation that the Hemingways settle in Paris. The strength of the dollar against the French franc made living there wonderfully cheap, and until they found a flat of their own they could stay at the same Left Bank hotel where the Andersons had stayed, the Jacob et d'Angleterre in the rue Jacob, just off the Place St-Germain-des-Prés. Not only was the Jacob full of interesting Americans but it was an easy walk from there to the hearth and home of literary Americans in Paris, Sylvia Beach's bookshop in the rue de l'Odéon. If Hemingway wanted him to, Anderson would be glad to write letters of introduction for him to Miss Beach, Gertrude Stein, and James Joyce, as well as to Ezra Pound, whom Anderson had also met during his visit to Europe, and to Lewis Galantière, a former Chicago newspaperman who was now the Paris secretary of the International Chamber of Commerce. Galantière had acted as the Andersons' guide around Paris and would doubtless be willing to share his knowledge of the city with the Hemingways as well. By the time Anderson finished this little speech, his listeners were convinced that Paris was the place for them.

Thereafter, everything fell into place very quickly. John Bone formally hired Hemingway as the *Star*'s first European correspondent. Whenever he was on assignment, he would be paid seventy-five dollars a week, plus expenses, and for every unassigned piece that the paper accepted he would be paid at the rate of a penny a word. The editor of the *Star Weekly* also asked him to keep sending in stuff. As for the five letters of introduction that Anderson had offered to write, he came through with all of them, which the Hemingways could drop into Paris mailboxes at their convenience.

The ship they decided on was a French Line relic called the *Leopoldina,* leaving New York the second week in December and landing at Le Havre four days before Christmas. On the eve of their departure from Chicago, Hemingway gathered up all the canned goods in their apartment and took them out to the Andersons. Long after his novel *Dark Laughter* had been cruelly satirized by his erstwhile pupil, Anderson would still cherish the memory of his earlier thoughtfulness.

CHAPTER SEVEN

Americans in Paris

HEMINGWAY'S FIRST LETTERS FROM PARIS were full of enthusiasm about the low cost of living. To the Andersons he reported on December 23 that "the Restaurant of the Pre aux Clercs at the corner of the Rue Bonaparte and the Rue Jacob is our regular eating place. Two can get a high grade dinner there, with wine, a la carte for 12 francs. We . . . usually average about 2.50 F. for breakfast. Think things are even cheaper than when you all were here." Three days later, he wrote Howie Jenkins that a two-room suite at the Jacob came to 12 francs a day, "and there are 12.61 to the paper one." A bottle of rum could be had for 14 francs and a bottle of "good Pinard" for 60 centimes. In a second letter to Jenkins on January 8, he announced that just after Christmas he had paid a visit to the Paris branch of a men's clothing store called Cook and Company, "a famous London house," and for the equivalent of fifty dollars had had a suit made to measure of the finest Irish tweed in the place. Behind the good fortune of the Hemingways, and of other Americans in Paris, lay some grim historical facts.

Nearly a million and a half French soldiers lost their lives in battle between 1914 and 1918, an awesome 10.5 per cent of France's economically productive male population, and another 1.1 million soldiers were permanently disabled. In the areas of France overrun by the Germans, more than a million people were forced to flee from their homes, thousands of buildings were partially or totally de-

stroyed, livestock herds were all but wiped out, and factory machinery was systematically disassembled and shipped to Germany.

A policy of compensating citizens who had suffered war damage
was pursued by every postwar prime minister, but the methods used
to finance this policy helped to set off and to perpetuate a pernicious
inflation. In 1920, it took twelve francs to purchase a dollar; in 1925,
it took twice that number. Widespread anger about the inflation
made it politically impossible to lift the rent controls which had been
imposed as a war measure in 1914, with the result that landlords
refused to install electricity, modern toilets, and other conveniences
that many of their buildings lacked, while economically nervous
investors became particularly loath to put their money into the construction of new dwellings. On the eve of World War I, France had
9.5 million housing units; on the eve of World War II, 9.75 million,
of which almost a third had been officially declared unfit for human
habitation. Uncertainty about the nation's economy also discouraged farmers from buying motorized equipment and caused automobile manufacturers to shy away from the challenge of producing
a cheap car for the masses. As late as the midthirties, there were as
many horses on French farms as in 1850 and as many horse-drawn
carriages on the streets of French cities and towns as in 1891.

These conditions signified that France was in deep trouble, but in
the twenties they helped to make living there extraordinarily attractive to Americans. From 1920 onward, the transatlantic migration
steadily grew from a trickle to a flood, so that by 1927 there were
fifteen thousand American residents in Paris alone, in the judgment
of the American Chamber of Commerce, thirty-five thousand by
the reckoning of the Paris police. From the expatriate perspective,
horse-drawn carriages were not frustrating reminders of France's
technological lag, but evocative examples of Old World charm;
while sitting on the terrace of the Café Napolitain, sipping an aperitif
and savoring the evening air, Jake Barnes in *The Sun Also Rises* is
appreciatively conscious of "the horse-cabs clippety-clopping
along" and finally climbs into one, along with the *poule* he has selected to have dinner with him. Rent-controlled housing constituted
another reason for the expatriates' choice of France, and if having to
contend with outdated facilities was apt to be bothersome, the problem could usually be alleviated by hiring a maid. For the ever more
favorable rate of exchange put servants, as well as many other amen-
ities of life, within the financial grasp of even marginally well-off
American residents.

2

ONE of the first members of the American colony whom the Hemingways met was Lewis Galantière, who came round to the Jacob immediately upon receiving the letter of introduction that Hemingway had mailed to him and invited them to have dinner with him at the Restaurant Michaud. The food at Michaud's was very good, but the Hemingways were a little nervous about its prices, so they were relieved when their new acquaintance told them that he intended to foot the bill. In addition to being generous, the twenty-six-year-old Galantière was a man of exquisite taste and mimetic wit who spoke perfect French and knew Paris intimately. At the outset of the meal Hemingway found him delightful, but as it became clear that Hadley felt the same way Hemingway's competitive ire was aroused. Wherefore he brought up the subject of boxing. When Galantière admitted to a slight acquaintance with the sport, Hemingway invited him back to the Jacob for a few rounds of postprandial sparring. He had two pairs of regulation boxing gloves in his trunk, so there would be no problem about proper equipment. On the way across the Atlantic, he further informed Galantière, he had fought a three-round exhibition match in the dining salon of their steamship with an Italo-American fighter from Salt Lake City and had beaten him badly. Galantière's reluctance to accept Hemingway's invitation became pronounced at this point. He didn't really like to hit other people, he explained, any more than he liked being hit himself. But Hemingway refused to take no for an answer.

In the living room of the Hemingways' suite, the two men touched gloves and commenced to circle one another, while Hadley acted as timekeeper. After a minute or two, during which time neither man threw a single punch, Galantière straightened up and laughingly said that he had had enough. After removing one glove, he put on his glasses and began to unlace the other glove. In the meantime, Hemingway had been shadow boxing, throwing lefts and rights and dancing about. Suddenly, he lunged at Galantière and hit him in the face, breaking his glasses. Luckily, no fragments flew into the victim's eyes or cut his face. Hemingway was obviously relieved about this, but he felt no contrition, in Hadley's opinion. He had effectively demonstrated his masculine superiority.

Somehow, Galantière's wish to be friends survived the incident and a few days later he met with the Hemingways again in order to help them in their search for an apartment. A good many Americans had chosen to live right there amongst the plain eighteenth-century facades and antique stores of the rue Jacob, but Hemingway wanted a flat that was much, much cheaper than anything they could possibly have found nearby. After several hours of looking in other parts of the sixth arrondissement, Galantière finally led them to a poor working-class neighborhood on the Montagne Ste-Geneviève in the fifth arrondissement. A two-room apartment, someone told them, was available on the fourth floor of an old building at 74 rue du Cardinal Lemoine. On every landing on the dingy spiral staircase was a squat toilet with two cleated cement elevations, one on each side of the hole. The apartment itself seemed to be all angles and corners and was difficult to move around in. A massive fake-mahogany bed dominated one room and an ugly oak dining table and two chairs the other. The bathroom was a closet, containing a pitcher, a bowl, and a slop jar. No more than one person at a time could squeeze into the kitchen and the ancient stove had only two burners. The slop jar had to be emptied on the landing and the garbage toted down to the street. Egg-shaped lumps of coal dust called *boulets,* which could be burned in the fireplace in the bedroom, were the only source of heat. Not until after the Hemingways moved in—which they did on January 9—did they become aware of two other disadvantages. Music from the *bal musette* next door could be heard far into the night in their bedroom, and the Place Contrescarpe just down the street was the site of a human cesspool called the Café des Amateurs, which they couldn't bear to use as a neighborhood bar because of "the smell of dirty bodies and the sour smell of drunkenness."

In *A Moveable Feast* Hemingway would summon up remembrances of "how Paris was in the early days when we were very poor and very happy." Happy, he and Hadley surely were. Poor, they were not. Their actual financial situation was accurately revealed in the description of Robert Cohn's in *The Sun Also Rises*. Although Cohn is a descendant of one of the richest Jewish families in New York, he himself is not rich. Ever since squandering the bulk of the inheritance that had come to him from his father, he has been living on an allowance settled on him by his mother of three hundred dollars a month. The allowance is modest by the standards to which he had been accustomed, but in France his money goes a long way. Between them, the Hemingways in 1922 had an even higher income. Hadley's trust fund gave them three thousand dollars a year, while Hemingway earned at least fifteen hundred more as a journalist. And just as Cohn still had a little money left from his father's bequest, so Hadley had come to Europe with a windfall of eight thousand dollars that she had inherited a month after her marriage from the estate of an uncle. Thus she and Hemingway could easily have afforded to live in more agreeable surroundings, and in fact she would have been relieved if they had. His travel plans, though, were far more ambitious than she had realized, and he was determined in addition to eat and drink well and to follow, either as spectator or participant, at least half a dozen sports. To achieve these goals would require all the cash they could muster, aside from the sum they had determined to save. Hence his ruthless insistence on living in a slum, in spite of Hadley's uneasiness about the roughness of the men and women she saw in the streets and her discouragement at not understanding their argot. The one concession he was willing to make to her—and he made it quite readily—was to hire a *femme de ménage*. The woman they settled on was a hefty, sweet-tempered Breton peasant who asked them to call her Marie Cocotte and who managed to produce wonderful meals from menus they themselves made up of "all the things we've ever heard of or eaten," as Hemingway happily described them.

In the mornings, he had breakfast with Hadley in preoccupied silence and then went off to write in the sixth-floor room he had rented in a scruffy hotel in the rue Mouffetard, where Verlaine had not died, despite Hemingway's assertion in *A Moveable Feast*. Not surprisingly, the hotel had no central heating, so that after climbing six flights of stairs Hemingway had to build a fire in his room— thanks to his father, he was good at building fires—out of the bundles of twigs and kindling wood and the small hardwood logs he bought from a merchant on the corner. On days when he was sure that his chimney wouldn't draw, he didn't bother to go up to the room. Instead, he kept on walking, by a route he would always remember, past the Lycée Henri Quatre and the ancient church of St-Étienne-du-Mont and the Panthéon to the Boulevard St-Michel, and then down past the Cluny Museum and the Boulevard St-Germain to a café he liked on the Place St-Michel. But whether he settled down to work in his solitary aerie or in the café with a cup of coffee or a rum St. James in front of him—"genuwind 7 year old rum as smooth as a kitten's chin," he assured Howie Jenkins—the words in his blue notebooks piled up steadily during those cold and rainy weeks in January. In *A Moveable Feast* he would remember that one of his accomplishments was a short story about Michigan, and since he wrote it on "a wild, cold, blowing day" he made it "that sort of a day in the story." His memory, however, had played him false, for he was alluding to "The Three-Day Blow," which he would not write for another two years. The story he actually composed—or revised, to be more precise—did not have to do with two boys getting drunk on a blowy afternoon, but with a man and woman having sex on the Horton Bay dock as a cold mist comes up from the water.

3

INSTEAD of mailing Sylvia Beach the letter of introduction from Anderson, Hemingway simply brought it with him on the day he first entered her shop. A bookstore and rental library combined, Shakespeare and Company was a cheerful, homey place, with a big stove glowing with heat and antique chairs and tables scattered about. On the floor were white woolen rugs that Sylvia had bought in Serbia during her work there for the Red Cross in 1919. New books filled the window and covered some of the tables, and hundreds of other volumes were crammed into shelves as high as the ceiling and stretching into the back room. Along one wall were racks of literary periodicals, mainly English and American, and another was hung with pictures of Walt Whitman, Edgar Allan Poe, Oscar Wilde, Sherwood Anderson, and other writers.

The owner of Shakespeare and Company proved to be a petite, energetic woman of thirty-four with a lively, sculptured face, brown eyes as sparkling as a girl's, and pretty legs, Hemingway approvingly noted, as he told her his name. Yet if her feminine charms did not escape his glance, he was also keenly conscious of her mannish velvet jacket and boyishly bobbed hair, which she wore "brushed back from her fine forehead and cut thick below the ears." These details of her appearance were the expression of a sexual preference, it turned out. The love of Sylvia's life was a matronly-looking French woman four years her junior named Adrienne Monnier, whose own rue de l'Odéon bookstore and rental library had been the model for Shakespeare and Company.

Another woman who had realized (during a disastrous marriage) that she had no sexual interest in men, but who could be, Hemingway discovered, as steadfast a friend as a man could want, was an aspiring novelist who arrived in Paris in the fall of 1922. As her prominent nose, strong mouth, and springing chestnut mane suggested she might, Janet Flanner had exceptional strength of character and independence of mind. Rising above the failure of her early writing, she would go on to a notable career as *The New Yorker*'s "Genêt." No other intimate of Hemingway's, male or female, understood his fascination with bullfighting better than Janet, or derived greater satisfaction from matching wits with him. She also took pleasure in mothering her handsome friend from Illinois, where she herself had been a student at the University of Chicago. In her apartment in the Hôtel Napoléon Bonaparte, there was a chair covered in a print of galleons and tall sailboats that she called "Ernest's chair," and whenever he came to call she always sat him down in it, as if he were a boy who had come home again.

Sylvia Beach mothered him too. During their long chat on the day they met, she drew him out on his life experiences, and Hemingway responded with a series of poignant stories that elicited clucks of sympathy from her. "I . . . learned that he had spent two years in a military hospital, getting back the use of his leg," she recalled at the age of seventy-one. "In the hospital they had thought he was done for; there was even some question of administering the last sacraments. But this was changed, with his feeble consent, to baptism—'just in case they were right.' " Her new friend then turned, she further remembered, to the subject of his boyhood, confiding to her that "before he was out of high school, when he was still 'a boy in short pants,' his father had died suddenly and in tragic circumstances, leaving him a gun as a sole legacy. He found himself the head of a family, his mother and brothers and sister dependent on him. He had to leave school and begin making a living. He earned his first money in a boxing match, but, from what I gathered, didn't linger in this career." At some point in this touching recital, Sylvia said, he pulled up his pants leg and took off his shoe so that she could examine his scars.

Although he didn't have enough money with him to join the rental library, she told him that he could pay the deposit any time and invited him to take as many books as he wished. Turgenev's *A Sportsman's Sketches,* which he would borrow time and again, D. H. Lawrence's *Sons and Lovers* and Dostoevski's *The Gambler and Other Stories* were the choices he walked out with. That afternoon, he came back with Hadley and paid the deposit. Sylvia found "Feather Cat" —as he currently was calling his wife—an "attractive boyish-looking girl" and a "delightfully jolly person." Hadley asked her if she had any books by Henry James, which she did, and Hemingway wanted to know when James Joyce was apt to stop by. "If he comes in, it's usually very late in the afternoon," he was told. In the course of the coming months, Hemingway would not only meet Joyce at Shakespeare and Company, but numerous French and American writers as well, including Ezra Pound.

"No one that I ever knew was nicer to me," Hemingway said of Sylvia in *A Moveable Feast,* and over the years he was consistently nice to her in return. His first act of kindness had to do with Joyce's *Ulysses,* in whose forthcoming publication she had a sizable financial stake. In February 1921 the avant-garde editors of *The Little Review,* Margaret Anderson and Jane Heap, had been found guilty of obscenity by a three-judge panel in New York City for publishing the Nausicaa portion of the novel, and the book publisher Ben W. Huebsch had thereupon announced that he was no longer interested in taking the risk of sponsoring the publication of the full text. A month later, Joyce related these catastrophic developments to Sylvia. In a tone of complete discouragement, he finished his tale of woe by expressing the fear that *Ulysses* would never be published. When Sylvia suggested that he permit Shakespeare and Company to bring out the book and sell it by subscription, Joyce accepted the idea with alacrity. By the following January, publication was imminent, and the bill from the printer was clearly going to be far larger than Sylvia had anticipated. Consequently, she was grateful to Hemingway for volunteering to help collect subscriptions. Furthermore, he came up with a plan for smuggling copies of the book into the United States. A newspaperman named Barney Braverman whom he had known in Chicago had recently taken a job with an advertising agency in Windsor, Ontario, and was commuting to it by ferry from his new apartment in Detroit. As a close student of the methods used by Chicago bootleggers to supply their customers with Canadian whiskey, Hemingway felt that Braverman was in a splendid position to aid the cause of modern literature. Once the plan was in place, Braverman rented a room in Windsor, to which Sylvia then mailed a large carton containing forty copies of *Ulysses.* Canadian customs law imposed a duty on foreign books of 25 percent of the selling price. This meant that Braverman ought to have been charged $300, but because he was able to convince the customs inspector that the books in the carton were cheap novels worth no more than fifty cents apiece, he got away with a payment of $6.50. A few nights later, he took a wrapped copy of *Ulysses* home with him to Detroit. The ten-minute ferry ride seemed endless. As he passed through U.S. customs, an officer instructed him to unwrap the package. The novel that would have set off alarm bells in the New York customs shed aroused no sign of recognition in Detroit. In Braverman's triumphant words, he had put one over on the Republic and its Methodist smut-hounds. All forty copies of the book were subsequently mailed from within the United States to such subscribers as the Washington Square Book Shop in New York City, the publisher Alfred A. Knopf, and Sherwood Anderson.

4

TWO advance copies of *Ulysses,* with its Greek-blue cover and white lettering, reached Paris from the printer in Dijon on February 2, in time for Joyce's fortieth birthday. Sylvia presented one copy to the author and "unfurled" the other, as an English friend put it, "like the flag of freedom on the Left Bank," in the window of Shakespeare and Company.

The Hemingways, however, were not on hand to witness this historic event. At the end of January they had decided—Ernest had decided—that it was time for them to go to Switzerland and learn to ski. After outfitting themselves with skis and boots and sweaters and caps, they left by train for Chamby in the mountains above Montreux, where they rented a room with a big double bed in a chalet that he had heard about. Every morning while they still were luxuriously dozing, Madame Gangwisch, the wife of the owner, came in with an armload of wood for their tall porcelain stove. After closing the windows and getting a roaring fire going, she brought them breakfast in bed. There was plenty of snow at Chamby and they both found skiing as exciting a sport as they had ever tried, although after a few hours on the slopes Hemingway tended to be bothered by stiffness in his battered right knee. Sliding down icy mountain roads on a luge provided further exhilaration. A luge, Hemingway was pleased to explain to the readers of the Toronto *Star Weekly,* is "a stout sled of hickory built on the pattern of little girls' sleds in Canada." From the top of the four-thousand-foot Col du Sonloup, he went on, a lugeur can

> go down a long steep stretch of road flanked by a six hundred foot drop-off on the left and bordered by a line of trees on the right. The sled goes fast from the start and soon it is rushing faster than anything you have ever felt. You are sitting absolutely unsupported, only ten inches above the ice, and the road is feeding past you like a movie film.

But it was in the letter he wrote from Chamby to Katy Smith, urging her to come on over, that his enthusiasm for living abroad really soared. "Suisse is a wonderful country," he exclaimed.

> We live at a chalet run by an english speaking Swiss named Gangwisch and have breakfast in bed and two enormous meals besides. Mrs is a high grade cook and we rate meals like roast beef, creamed cauliflower, fried potatoes, soup before and blueberries after with

whipped cream for two seeds a day. . . . What's the use of trying to live in such a goddam place as America when there is Paris and Switzerland and Italy. My gawd the fun a man has. When people lie to you and say America is as beautiful, or as much fun to live in, give them the razz.

While his dismissal of America was sophomoric, his excitement about Europe was undeniably infectious and prophesied one of the cultural functions that his fiction would perform. Beginning in the midtwenties, Hemingway's stories of Americans in Europe would serve as guidebooks for generations of tourists—as Henry James's stories had for earlier generations—informing them about where to go and how to have a good time. And as his letter to Katy Smith suggested he would be, he was especially adept at conveying the pleasures of the table. The *omelette aux tomates* and bottle of straw-colored Chablis that are set before Strether and Madame de Vionnet in James's *The Ambassadors* are a feast for the eyes but not for the palate; Hemingway, on the other hand, actually makes you hungry and thirsty for the fare he describes. "The beer was very cold and wonderful to drink. The *pommes à l'huile* were firm and marinated and the olive oil was delicious. I ground black pepper over the potatoes and moistened the bread in the olive oil. After the first heavy draft of beer I drank and ate very slowly. When the *pommes à l'huile* were gone I ordered another serving and a *cervelas*. This was a sausage like a heavy, wide frankfurter split in two and covered with a special mustard sauce."

That description also testifies to the heartiness of Hemingway's appetite, which he combined with a capacity for alcohol that not even his punishingly hard-drinking editor, Maxwell Perkins, would be able to match, although some of the characters in his fiction were certainly in his class. (In the final chapter of *The Sun Also Rises,* Jake Barnes and Brett Ashley sit on high stools at the bar of the Palace Hotel in Madrid and drink three "coldly beaded" Martinis apiece, before going on to Botín's—"one of the best restaurants in the world," Hemingway the travel writer asserts—where they order a lunch of roast suckling pig and a bottle of *rioja alta*. Brett doesn't eat very much, but Jake consumes "a very big meal" and downs the better part of five bottles of the *rioja*—or is it six?) Yet a further advantage he had as a writer about food and drink was that he was eternally curious—the trait was another legacy from his father—about the taste of things he had never eaten before and about the best ways of preparing them. In a letter he wrote to Dr. Hemingway in the spring of 1922, he vividly described a forty-mile hike that he and Hadley had recently taken through a chain of forests north of Paris. His itemization of the animals they had seen—"deer and wild boar and foxes and rabbits"—predictably led him to add that "I've eaten wild boar twice and it is very good. They cook it up into a pasty with carrots and onions and mushrooms and a fine brown crust." Although Hemingway, unlike his father, was not a reliably good cook, he was almost always able to provide succulent meals to his readers.

5

A BOTTLE of kirsch was one of the mementoes he brought back with him from Switzerland, and after a long morning of work in his little room in the rue Mouffetard he would take a swig from it. Sometimes when he was starting a new story and couldn't get it going, he would sit in front of the fire and eat clementines and squeeze their peel into the edge of the flame and watch the sputter of blue they made, or stand at the window and look out over the roofs of Paris. Besides writing stories about Michigan, he wanted to record his impressions of the French capital. But in order to let these realities shine through, he first had to teach himself to avoid using words that did not correspond to things.

In his pursuit of a purer prose style he was driven by a wish, it has been said many times, to dissociate himself from a wartime rhetoric of glory and honor. But while an acquired distaste for the oratory of demagogues like Gabriele D'Annunzio ("Morire non è basta") undoubtedly contributed to his hostility to bombast, so did memories of his mother's operatic language. "Marriage is . . . sacred in proportion to the prayerfulness with which it is entered into." "A Mother's love seems to me like a bank." "You were named for the two finest and noblest gentlemen I have ever known." Hemingway's epochal determination to forge a new style originated, like his myth, in a drama of family life. All he had to do, he told himself, as he stared into the flames in his little fireplace, was to "write one true sentence and then go on from there." But the tightness and transparency he sought were not easily come by. The sentences in his blue notebooks were a palimpsest of erasures, deletions, and insertions.

After he had closed his notebooks for the day, he often strolled through the Jardin du Luxembourg to the picture galleries in the Musée du Luxembourg, where he reveled in the Monets and Manets but spent most of his time in front of the Cézannes. On other afternoons he walked down to the Seine and along the quais, looking for new English and American books that were sometimes on sale in the bookstalls for bargain prices. In the small park at the head of the Ile de la Cité he liked to watch the fishermen with their long cane poles trying to catch a dace-like fish called *goujon.* "Plump and sweet-fleshed with a finer flavor than fresh sardines even," *goujons* made a delicious *friture,* and in little restaurants on the Ile St-Louis the hungry author ordered them by the plateful, when he did not go home for lunch with Hadley, which usually included three courses and several glasses of the Beaune that they bought by the gallon at a wine cooperative.

In the evenings he was ready more often than not to go out on the town. With Hadley almost always on his arm, he traveled near and far, from the bal musette beside their front entrance, which was crowded six nights a week with working people from the quarter, to the Stade Anastasie, where the boxers served as waiters at the tables set out under the trees and the ring was in the garden. Yet for all his kinetic energy, he also stayed at home a fair amount, for he always had a pile of books on hand that he wanted to read, as well as an ever-growing correspondence to keep up. Furthermore, he enjoyed just sitting and listening to Hadley play Ravel, Brahms, or Scriabin on the small upright piano she had rented. The sound of music had filled the house he had grown up in and he craved it still.

At prizefights, Janet Flanner has testified, Hemingway exhorted and derided the combatants in the argot of the fight fans around him. In her words, he was "a natural quick linguist who learned a language first through his ears because of his constant necessity for understanding people and for communicating." Another way he picked up colloquial French was by perusing sports journals, for in order to master the ins and outs of any sport he felt that he had to study the opinions of the critics. Of the various sports journals that he regularly read in the spring of 1922, the ones to which he paid the most careful attention were devoted to horse racing. Arising at dawn, he would sit by an open window in the dining room and write something while Hadley still slept. After a while, if he knew that the horses were running that day at Enghien or Auteuil, he would go down and buy a racing paper. Then around noon he and Hadley would set out for the track, carrying their lunch, a bottle of wine, and a form chart. They called what they were doing going racing, although it really wasn't, as Hemingway painfully acknowledged in *A Moveable Feast.* "It was gambling on horses. But we called it racing." He kept a sum of money apart from all their other money, so that they would always be able to bet, and when they won he spent a quarter of their earnings on himself, gave a quarter to Hadley to spend and put the rest back into their racing capital.

Gradually, these activities ceased to be merely an amusement for him and became what he termed his "avocation." At times he went off to the track by himself, where he invested long hours in talking to jockeys, trainers, and owners in an attempt to improve his handicapping. Apart from the money they earned him, such tactics could be justified, he told himself, on the grounds that they enabled him to write several short stories about horse racing; yet even these accomplishments could not wipe out his intermittent sense of unease. The dilettantish Americans who spent their days and nights crowded around café tables in Montparnasse, talking about what they were going to do but never doing it, were contemptible, in Hemingway's estimation. "The scum of Greenwich Village, New York," he wrote in a strong piece for the *Star Weekly,* "has been skimmed off and deposited in large ladlesful on that section of Paris adjacent to the Café Rotonde." The ex-Greenwich Villager whom he considered the scummiest piece of scum was Harold Stearns, the editor of a widely talked-about symposium on *Civilization in the United States: An Inquiry by Thirty Americans* (1922). The implicit message in Stearns's introduction to the volume was that his native land was much too stuffy for a lively fellow like him, and in the summer of 1921 he had left New York for Paris, with the announced intention of writing books of bold consequence in more congenial surroundings. Instead, he quickly degenerated into a drunk and a deadbeat, whose only claim to fame was the racing column he produced under the name of Peter Pickem for the Paris edition of the Chicago *Tribune.* By becoming more involved in horse racing than he had ever imagined he would, was Hemingway running the risk of becoming another Stearns? As he himself phrased it many years later, he was betting on horses rather than on his work and his life with Hadley. Just how he managed to stop gambling he never satisfactorily explained, but it took him three or four years to put the addiction behind him. And while he felt glad at having finally done so, his achievement "left an emptiness," which was his way of saying that he sank into a depression—as he always did, he added, whenever he lost anything, whether good or bad.

6

SHORTLY after he and Hadley got back from Chamby, Sylvia Beach gave him a copy of *Ulysses,* in gratitude for his help in finding subscribers for it. He couldn't wait to start reading the book, or to pass on his opinion of it to Sherwood Anderson. "Joyce has a most god-damn wonderful book," he wrote to Anderson on March 9. "It'll probably reach you in time," he added consolingly. In his eagerness to speak familiarly about the novel Hemingway was not alone. As Joyce's biographer, Richard Ellmann, has remarked, to have read *Ulysses* was considered the mark of the sophisticated expatriate. Particularly among the literati on Paris's Left Bank, admirers of the novel thought of themselves as a happy few, despite the fact that it was steadily acquiring an audience on both sides of the Atlantic. The young Hemingway, for instance, would inform the young Morley Callaghan on arriving in Toronto in the fall of 1923 that Joyce was "the greatest writer in the world," and he spoke in a tone of voice, said Callaghan, which suggested that he was "letting [me] in on something."

Unquestionably, Hemingway was staggered by the multilayered richness of Joyce's book; nevertheless, his interest in the story gave out well before he finished it. In the copy that Sylvia Beach presented to him, which now rests with his papers in the John F. Kennedy Library in Boston, only the pages of the first half and of Molly Bloom's concluding soliloquy are cut. More than anything else, it was the characterization of Stephen Dedalus that put him off. "The weakness of Joyce," in his opinion, was his failure to understand that "the only writing that was any good was what you made up, what you imagined. . . . Daedalus [*sic*] in *Ulysses* was Joyce himself, so he was terrible. Joyce was so damn romantic and intellectual about him. He'd made Bloom up, Bloom was wonderful. He'd made Mrs. Bloom up. She was the greatest in the world."

For his part, the author of *Ulysses* had considerable admiration for Hemingway. Neither as a man nor as an artist was he as simple as he seemed, Joyce realized. Which was not to say, of course, that sheer physical strength was not one of the keys to understanding him. As Joyce remarked to a Danish interviewer in the thirties, Hemingway was "a big powerful peasant, as strong as a buffalo. A sportsman. And ready to live the life he writes about. He would never have written it if his body had not allowed him to live it." Hemingway's body further enabled him to guarantee the Irishman's safety whenever the two writers went café-crawling together. "We would go out to drink," Hemingway told a reporter for *Time* magazine in the midfifties, "and Joyce would fall into a fight. He couldn't even see the man so he'd say: 'Deal with him, Hemingway! Deal with him!' " Nevertheless, Joyce insisted, Hemingway was no mere roughneck. "Giants of his sort are truly modest," he emphasized to the Danish interviewer. "There is much more behind Hemingway's form than people know." One day at Shakespeare and Company Joyce offered Sylvia Beach an instructive analysis of the equally misleading images that Hemingway and the American novelist Robert McAlmon cultivated about themselves. Hemingway liked to be thought of as "such a tough fellow," while McAlmon tried to pass himself off as "the sensitive type." The truth, however, was the other way around. To which Sylvia added, as she finished recording these remarks, "So Joyce found you out, Hemingway!"

Unlike so many of Hemingway's literary friendships, his association with Joyce was never marred by a quarrel. Behind the Irishman's back, it is true, he did not hesitate to make fun of his foibles, such as his willingness to allow his patroness, Harriet Weaver, to subsidize his taste for eating in expensive restaurants. The report on Joyce, Hemingway told Sherwood Anderson, is that "he and all his family are starving but you can find the whole celtic crew of them every night at Michaud's. . . . Gertrude Stein says Joyce reminds her of an old woman out in San Francisco. The woman's son struck it rich as hell in the Klondyke [sic] and the old woman went around wringing her hands and saying, 'Oh my poor Joey! My poor Joey! He's got so much money!' The damned Irish, they have to moan about something or other, but you never heard of an Irishman starving." When Hemingway was in Joyce's company, however, he treated the prince of avant-garde Paris with a respect that amounted to "worship," as Janet Flanner's lover, Solita Solano, observed.

Ezra Pound was another writer with whom Hemingway never had a falling out, although at the outset of their relationship they came within an ace of becoming enemies when Hemingway misjudged the poet on the basis of his operatic appearance. The showy blue-glass buttons on Pound's jacket, his open-throated shirt, his unclipped goatee—his apparent imitation, in short, of Rodolfo in Puccini's La Bohème—served to convince Hemingway that he was a colossal fake. In Pound's studio in the rue Notre-Dame-des-Champs, to which he and his handsome wife Dorothy invited the Hemingways for tea in the late winter of 1922, there were a number of paintings by Japanese artists, but Hemingway decided that the manifest pride Pound took in them was just another sign of his vaingloriousness. A day or so later, a bitingly satirical characterization of the poet's artsy way of life emerged from Hemingway's typewriter. It was his intention to submit the piece to Margaret Anderson and Jane Heap at The Little Review—until Lewis Galantière explained to him that both women felt deeply indebted to Pound for his years of service without pay as a talent scout for their magazine. At which point Hemingway began to realize that Pound was a more complicated piece of machinery than he had assumed.

The report of the four psychiatrists who examined the poet at St. Elizabeths Hospital in Washington, D.C., at the end of World War II advised against his being compelled to stand trial for treason, on the grounds that the pro-Fascist broadcasts he had made over Rome radio during the war were the work of a man who somewhere along the line had gone insane. Having no clinical knowledge of his earlier history, the psychiatrists did not venture to say exactly when he had lost his sanity, but his old friend Hemingway chose to believe that his madness dated from the early thirties. "When I last saw him in 1933 at Joyce's," Hemingway told Allen Tate in 1943, after perusing the transcripts of the poet's "loony" radio broadcasts, "Joyce was convinced that he was crazy then and asked me to come around when Pound was present because he was afraid he might do something mad. He certainly made no sense then and talked as utter rot, nonsense and balls as he had made good sense in 1923." Therefore, instead of being hanged "he ought to go to the loony bin, which he rates and you can pick out the parts in his cantos at which he starts to rate it." With our knowledge of "how he went nuts," Hemingway reaffirmed to Tate with a rising note of passion in his voice, "how gradually and steadily he became irresponsible and idiotic, and what a great, sound and fine poet he was, and what a generous and really noble person he was in aiding all those he believed in back in the old days, such as Elliot [sic], Joyce, many many others including the worthless [Ralph Cheever] Dunning, I think we have an absolute and complete obligation to oppose any hanging, even though we all should have to get up on the scaffold with the rope on our own necks."

The one question about Pound that Hemingway would always dodge was whether he had not been mentally unbalanced throughout the entire period of their acquaintance. According to the description of him by the St. Elizabeths examiners, Pound was eccentric, querulous, egocentric, grandiose, expansive, and exuberant. All of those adjectives apply to the man Hemingway met in 1922. Moreover, the broadcaster who warned the people of Britain and the United States that Jewish propagandists had deceived them into entering the war against Mussolini and Hitler and that "Mr. Squirmy and Mr. Slime are still feeding it to you right over the BBC radio and every one of the Jew radios of Schenectady, New York and Boston" had talked precisely that way in an essay of 1921 called "Kongo Roux," the thesis of which was that a conspiracy by Jews —"totem de tribu SHEENY, Yid, taboo"—had hatched World War I.

The Pound of the Depression era who talked obsessively about "usura" in the Cantos in which Hemingway said he detected signs of madness had also given evidence much, much earlier of being out of control on the subject of money-lending. In an essay he gave to *The Little Review* in 1920, for instance, Pound hailed *Economic Democracy*, by the anti-Semitic economist, Major C. H. Douglas, as a program for saving modern civilization from the abomination of usury, and his uncritical devotion to Douglas's primitive ideas (as John Maynard Keynes would observe in his *General Theory*, among economists Douglas deserved the rank of a "private, perhaps, but not a major") was further revealed in a series of Cantos he had completed before Hemingway knew him.

The relationship between sexuality and art was another subject on which Pound had long cherished strange opinions. Thus, in the summer of 1922 he published a translation of Rémy de Gourmont's *Physique d'amour; essai sur l'instinct sexuel* under the title *The Natural Philosophy of Love*. In a translator's postscript Pound not only endorsed Gourmont's dubious belief that there was a connection between "la copulation complète et profonde et le développement cérébral," but proclaimed that the brain itself in all likelihood was "a sort of great clot of genital fluid held in suspense or reserve." Creative thought, Pound averred, was a masculine power, and he likened it to a "phallus or spermatozoide," whose natural target was the "female chaos" of life. "Even oneself has felt it," he added, in obvious reference to his embattled years in England, "driving any new idea into the great passive vulva of London, a sensation analogous to the male feeling in copulation."

"Utter rot, nonsense and balls," in short, were already staples of Pound's thinking in the early twenties. Yet in reminding Allen Tate of what the poet had been like in those days, Hemingway kept silent about the fatuousness—or the craziness—of his nonliterary beliefs and stressed instead how much Pound had cared about his fellow writers and how much he had done for them. This emphasis on the positive was not surprising. For in "Homage to Ezra," published in the expatriate magazine *This Quarter* in May 1925, Hemingway had long since made clear his gratitude to Pound for his many favors to him.

So far, we have Pound the major poet devoting, say, one fifth of his time to poetry. With the rest of his time he tries to advance the fortunes, both material and artistic, of his friends. He defends them when they are attacked, he gets them into magazines and out of jail. He loans them money. He sells their pictures. He arranges concerts for them. He writes articles about them. He introduces them to wealthy women. He gets publishers to take their books. He sits up all night with them when they claim to be dying and he witnesses and dissuades them from suicide. And in the end a few of them refrain from knifing him at the first opportunity.

Pound's first effort to help Hemingway began with a request to see some of his poems and stories. "Swell" was his verdict on the poems, and with the author's permission he immediately sent off six of them to *The Dial* in New York, with a covering letter to the coeditor, Scofield Thayer, stating his opinion of them. He also took it upon himself to accept one of the stories for *The Little Review*. Unfortunately, Margaret Anderson countermanded the acceptance and Thayer turned down every one of the poems, but Hemingway was at least able to take comfort from the fact that a major American poet was sympathetic to his work.

The poet's "fine bitter tongue" and impressive command of juicy gossip about writers on both sides of the Atlantic also helped to convince Hemingway that he and Pound were kindred spirits. But of all the ways in which Pound reached out to this young man who had initially distrusted him, none was more effective than his surprising announcement that he wanted to learn to box. "I've been teaching Pound to box wit little success," Hemingway shortly informed Sherwood Anderson. "He habitually leads wit his chin and has the general grace of the crayfish. . . . Going over there this afternoon for another session but there aint much job in it as I have to shadow box between rounds to get up a sweat. Pound sweats well, though, I'll say that for him. Besides, it's pretty sporting of him to risk his dignity and his critical reputation for something that he don't know nothing about." In ensuing days, however, Pound caught him off guard with a couple of solid punches, and Hemingway's respect for him increased in direct ratio to their effectiveness. "I'm boxing regular with Ezra Pound," he wrote Howie Jenkins, "and he has developed a terrific wallop. I can usually cross myself though before he lands them and when he gets too tough I dump him on the floor. He is a good game guy and has come along to beat hell wit the gloves—and some day I will get careless and he will knock me for a row of latrines. He weighs about 180."

When Hemingway asked his new friend to take a look at the writing in his notebooks, Pound offered him quite specific advice— the most practical he ever received, the recipient would later say. Pound had performed a similar favor some months earlier for T. S. Eliot, when Eliot had given him the manuscript of "a sprawling chaotic poem called 'The Waste Land.' " With the singularly touchy Hemingway, Pound was careful to preface his criticisms with flattery, or, if a letter written some years later can be taken as characteristic, in man-to-man language from the world of sports that somehow took the sting from his words. ("I think you are more intelligent than this mss.," he brusquely told Hemingway on January 25, 1927. But then he added, "HELL, I want stuufffff that'll END discussion. I want to say: me frien Hem, kin knock yew over the ropes; and then I want to see the punch delivered. I dont want gentle embraces in the middle of the ring.") It also helped that these very different writers shared the desire to seize passing moments for their own sake. While walking out of a train in the Place de la Concorde station of the Paris Métro a decade earlier, Pound had suddenly seen a beautiful face, and then another and another, and out of this experience had come, after eighteen months of trying, a two-line poem:

> The apparition of these faces in the crowd;
> Petals on a wet, black bough.

After half a year in Europe, Hemingway succeeded in distilling some of his own adventures in Paris into six long sentences. All six were marked by a visual intensity that the author of "In a Station of the Metro" surely must have admired, especially these three:

> I have stood on the crowded back platform of a seven o'clock Batignolles bus as it lurched along the wet lamp lit street while men who were going home to supper never looked up from their newspapers as we passed Notre Dame grey and dripping in the rain. . . . I have seen the one legged street walker who works the Boulevard Madelaine between the Rue Cambon and Bernheim Jeune's limping along the pavement through the crowd on a rainy night with a beefy red-faced Episcopal clergyman holding an umbrella over her. . . . I have watched two Senegalese soldiers in the dim light of the snake house of the Jardin des Plantes teasing the King Cobra who swayed and tightened in tense erect rage as one of the little brown men crouched and feinted at him with his red fez.

Speed was another of Pound's aesthetic principles, and he occasionally was able to show Hemingway how he could tell his stories faster and better—for example, "An Alpine Idyll," which Hemingway mailed to him from Paris after Pound had gone off to live in Italy and was about to start a magazine called *The Exile*. Speaking in the accent of an American hick, as was his wont, Pound told him in effect that he wouldn't publish the piece unless Hemingway were willing to cut the beginning.

> This is a good story (Idyl) but a leetle litterary and Tennysonian. I wish you wd. keep your eye on the objek MORE, and be less licherary. Do you onnerstand what I mean about bein licherary. Bein licherary mean that the reader (even the interested and in my case abnormally HOPING reader) has to work to keep his eye on the page during the introductory pages. . . . ANYTHING put on top of the subject is BAD. Licherchure is mostly blanketing up a subject. Too much MAKINGS. The subject is always interesting enough without the blankets.

In this particular case, Hemingway refused to heed the poet's advice and published "An Alpine Idyll" just as it stood in an anthology edited by Van Wyck Brooks. Yet even before the anthology appeared Hemingway admitted to Pound in a letter that the story really wasn't satisfactory, for precisely the reason he had singled out. Hemingway's other mentor in Paris, Gertrude Stein, rarely if ever made criticisms that specific.

7

IT was in 1907 that Alice B. Toklas first called on Miss Stein in the two-story apartment at 27 rue de Fleurus where she lived with her brother Leo. The whitewashed walls of the adjacent studio room were lined with paintings right up to the ceiling, Renoirs, Gauguins, Manguins, two rows of Matisses, enormous Picassos of the Harlequin period, a big portrait of a woman by Cézanne, some little Cézannes, many Cézanne water colors, a big nude by Vallotton, a portrait of Gertrude by Vallotton, a Toulouse-Lautrec, a Maurice Denis, a Bonnard, a little Daumier, a little Delacroix, a moderate-sized El Greco, and many more. When Hemingway and Hadley were ushered into the studio some fifteen years later, they felt as if they were in "one of the best rooms in the finest museum." The collection that all but overwhelmed them, however, was not as ample as it had been before the war, for after an unamicable parting with Gertrude in 1913 Leo had sent word from Florence, where he had gone to live, that half of the Cézannes and all of the Renoirs were to be sent to him.

If he had chosen to do so, Leo could have asked for many more paintings, inasmuch as Gertrude had displayed virtually no independent judgment in the visual arts in the glory years of their collecting. In the informed opinion of the American painter Maurice Sterne, her artistic sensibility had merely been a "reflection" of her brother's. The observant newspaper reporter Agnes Ernst, who would later marry the financier Eugene Meyer, had been even less impressed with Gertrude. "When I first knew her in 1909," she recalled long afterwards, she had considered Gertrude "a humbug" who "lived on what she could assimilate from Leo."

A humbug she may have been as a connoisseur of art, but as an analyst of the psychology of artists she was extremely shrewd, not only because she had observed a great many of them but because she had "plenty of brains," as Bernard Berenson's wife, Mary, noted in her diary in 1903, following Gertrude's initial visit to the Berensons' Villa I Tatti outside Florence. Besides brains, she possessed a piercing wit, a gift for coining phrases, and a flair for self-advertising that her brother's overbearing personality could not obscure forever. Over a period of several years she gradually stopped listening to Leo's monologues at their parties and began thinking about speaking out herself. When she finally did begin, there was no stopping her.

On the Hemingways' first afternoon at the rue de Fleurus, it was made clear to him that he was to sit beside Gertrude in front of the fireplace at one end of the studio while Hadley was to talk to Alice Toklas at the other end. By the time the visit was over, something else was coming into focus as well. In Oak Park, "Mrs. Stein" had been one of Ernest's nicknames for his mother; in Paris, Miss Stein would become Grace's most encompassing replacement. Although the two women could not have been more different in some respects, the several similarities between them were significant.

To begin with, they were only twenty months apart in age. Both liked to dominate conversations, and Gertrude spoke, as Grace did, in a contralto voice that commanded attention by its velvety loveliness as well as by its tone of assurance. As for Gertrude's attachment to Alice Toklas, Hemingway may have thought of it as a bolder, Parisian variation on his mother's relationship with Ruth Arnold. Finally, there was the impact created by physical presence. Gertrude's body seemed even fuller than Grace's, even though Grace had ballooned to 180 pounds by the time Ernest was four years old. Mary Berenson, who had a weight problem herself, simply could not get over Gertrude's avoirdupois. In 1903 she described her as a "fat unwieldy person, the colour of mahogany, but with a grand monumental head." Three years later, as Mary and her cousin Emily Dawson were driving back to the Villa I Tatti on a splendid Tuscan afternoon, "we saw on the hill a most fearful apparition—a round waddling mass, and a tall blaze of bright brown beside it. These queer things turned out to be Gertrude Stein and her brother, she fatter than ever (but fairly clean). . . . They simply hurt one's eyes, and Emily and I drove on, after shaking hands with them, in pained amazement." To her parents, Mary confided on the first day of summer 1908 that "[today] we had a glorious swim of 'ladies only,' Miss Stein going in clad in nothing but her Fat. I really didn't know such enormities existed." As for Hemingway's impression of Gertrude's amplitude, his first thought was that she "was very big but not tall and was heavily built like a peasant woman." The size of her breasts especially interested him, and he wondered how much each one weighed. "I think about ten pounds, don't you, Hadley?" he asked his wife after they left.

Her hair was of equal interest. Gertrude had not yet settled on the Julius Caesar haircut by which most of the world now remembers her, but wore her hair "put up in the same way she had probably worn it in college," according to the author of *A Moveable Feast.* It was "lovely, thick, alive immigrant hair," and it went well, Hemingway implied, with her "beautiful eyes" and "strong German-Jewish face." The sort of sexual undercurrent that may have figured in his relationship with Liz Dilworth was explicitly singled out by him as an element in his relationship to Gertrude. Shortly after reading W. G. Rogers's *When This You See, Remember Me: Gertrude Stein in Person* (1948), he told Rogers that "I liked her better before she cut her hair and that was sort of a turning point in all sorts of things. She used to talk to me about homosexuality and how it was fine in and for women and no good in men and I used to listen and learn and I always wanted to fuck her and she knew it and it was a good healthy feeling and made more sense than some of the talk."

At the same time that he was vividly aware of her female fleshiness, he was also capable of talking about her as though she were a man. "Gertrude Stein and me are just like brothers," he exclaimed in a letter to Sherwood Anderson. His perception of her as double sexed was underscored by Gertrude's sense of herself. She subscribed to the notions put forth in a book called *Sex and Character* (1906), by the Viennese psychologist Otto Weininger, who maintained that completely female women were devoid of imagination and that the only ones who possessed it were those who were part male. To an expert, he declared, "all women who are truly famous and are of conspicuous mental ability reveal some of the anatomical characters of the male, some bodily resemblance to a man." He further argued that "the woman who attracts and is attracted by other women is herself half male." Lesbianism, in other words, was sometimes the mark of mental power. No wonder that Gertrude liked to talk to Hemingway about sexual inversion.

Yet it seems that she had another motive for doing so. Initiating such discussions gave her a chance to size up Hemingway's responses. Normally careful to the point of calculation in what he said to new friends, he apparently failed to realize that at 27 rue de Fleurus psychological intuitiveness was the *spécialité de la maison*. When Gertrude savaged him eleven years later in *The Autobiography of Alice B. Toklas,* she showed how well she had figured him out, even though she knew none of the bizarre details of his background. "What a book," she venomously remarked, "would be the real story of Hemingway, not those he writes but the confessions of the real Ernest Hemingway. It would be for another audience than the audience Hemingway now has but it would be very wonderful."

Did she sense on the day she met him that this muscular young man was hiding something? If so, she kept her thoughts shielded from him. Gertrude and her companion both "seemed to like us," Hemingway recalled, and when the two ladies climbed four flights of stairs a few days later to pay a visit to the Hemingways' apartment, "they seemed to like us even more." Gertrude sat on the bed and courteously asked if she could see some of Ernest's work. While everyone else talked, she went through his poems, a fragment of a novel and several stories. The poems, she evasively declared, were "direct, Kiplingesque." The novel she didn't care for because the descriptions weren't concentrated enough. The stories, though, she liked very much, except for "Up in Michigan." It was *inaccrochable,* that is to say unhangable, she explained, like a picture that a painter paints and can't exhibit because of its moral offensiveness. No American publisher would accept the story, she warned, just as no American publisher had been willing to take a chance on Joyce's *Ulysses.* Turning to the subject of pictures, she told Hemingway and Hadley how to buy them. "You can either buy clothes or buy pictures," she advised them. "It's that simple. No one who is not very rich can do both." As she and Alice bade the young couple goodbye, she invited them to come to call again at the rue de Fleurus.

Possibly it was on the occasion of the Hemingways' second visit that Gertrude got out a pair of scissors and showed Ernest how to trim his wife's hair. Since arriving in Paris Hadley had been wearing her hair in a bob, and because her husband wanted it to be even shorter, she too wanted it that way. Probably no other piece of advice that Hemingway received from Gertrude in the early months of their acquaintance served more effectively than this haircutting demonstration to make him think of her as "family."

Before the year was out the rapport between them had developed to the point where, upon running into him one day in the Jardin du Luxembourg, she issued him a blanket invitation to come by the studio any afternoon after five. Dropping in to see her unannounced was awfully pleasant, he discovered. There were always delicious little cakes to eat and a choice of fragrant, colorless alcohols to drink that had been distilled from purple plums, yellow plums, or wild raspberries and were served from cut-glass carafes in small glasses. As he sipped his liqueur and she replenished his glass, the two of them talked about the pictures on the walls, although Gertrude had more interesting things to say about the painters who had painted the pictures than about the pictures themselves. She also talked about her work and showed Hemingway thousands of pages of it, all of which had been neatly typed by the faithful Alice. Gertrude wrote every day, disliked revising, and paid no attention to the criticism that her writing was often unintelligible, with the result that she still hadn't achieved the recognition she felt her genius deserved. Jealous of the success of D. H. Lawrence and James Joyce, she disparaged their books and made nasty cracks about the fiction of many other contemporary writers as well, the conspicuous exceptions being those, like Sherwood Anderson, who had nice things to say about her books. Yet in spite of her competitiveness, Hemingway found it a great help to talk to her about his own writing. Unlike Ezra Pound, she did not deal in details, for she was no editor—as her unwillingness to revise her own manuscripts indicated. In her criticism she stuck strictly to what she called "general principles," but she talked brilliantly well about them, sitting the while in her special chair with her elbows resting on her knees like a washerwoman, while Hemingway hung on her every word.

Under his rapt and increasingly frequent attention, Gertrude became even more expansive than usual; as she acidly confessed years later, she had a "weakness" for this young man. Her interest in him was not lost on Alice Toklas. Gertrude's companion lived for Gertrude. She cooked for her, typed for her, and talked to the unscintillating wives of the scintillating painters and writers who clustered around Gertrude in front of the fireplace. Selflessness, however, was a source of power. "Care for me," Gertrude had implored, on the afternoon in Fiesole when she had asked Alice to become her wife. "A wife hangs on her husband that is what Shakespeare says a loving wife hangs on her husband that is what she does," and Alice had cried, "I am your bride," or so Gertrude remembered the event at any rate. Always, though, there was the frightening possibility that Alice would find another lover and withdraw. As Alice's biographer, Linda Simon, has observed, "Gertrude's fear of Alice's infidelity was hidden in her writings," a fear that caused her to become abjectly submissive whenever Alice demonstrated displeasure.

Over the years, Alice had allowed Gertrude to enjoy intimate friendships with such handsome men as Sherwood Anderson and Pablo Picasso, for she didn't feel threatened by them. Hemingway, however, with his "dark luminous eyes," "flashing smile," and overlong hair that "made him look like an Italian" was different from other men. From the very first, apparently, she viewed him with suspicion, although she was perfectly cordial to him for Gertrude's sake and continued to be. Thus, it was she who probably picked out the casaba melon that Gertrude sent the Hemingways from the south of France in the fall of 1922, and it was she who recommended that the young couple visit Pamplona in the summer of 1923. But because Hemingway immortalized the town in *The Sun Also Rises,* it was spoiled forever for Alice; even after his death she said that "on account of Hemingway" she had no wish to go back there.

Gertrude was aware, said Hemingway, that he wanted to fuck her. But if Gertrude knew this, then Alice knew it too, for she was a student of Gertrude's mind. Nevertheless, she bided her time. Not until Hemingway had begun to take Gertrude's friendship for granted would she finally lay down the law about this bold fellow. "You know, I made Gertrude get rid of him," she told a friend later.

Dragons' Teeth

By attending the weekly meetings of the Anglo-American Press Club over on the Right Bank, Hemingway came to know a number of other foreign correspondents, of whom the most congenial as far as he was concerned was Guy Hickok of the Brooklyn *Daily Eagle*. An avid sports fan and redoubtable bon vivant, Hickok was impressively well informed about race horses, boxers, and French wines. Hickok's neat black mustache was impressive too, and during a visit to Germany in the summer of 1922 Hemingway more than matched it with a dark brown brush of his own.

He also let the hair on his head grow over the tops of his ears and thicken up in back, as Alice Toklas disapprovingly noted. According to an unpublished passage that he probably wrote with the idea of including it in *A Moveable Feast,* some of his Press Club acquaintances were quite put off by his bohemian appearance. Occasionally one of them would take him aside and speak to him about it. "You mustn't let yourself go, Hem. It's none of my business of course. But you can't go native this way. For God's sake straighten out and get a proper haircut at least." While the story may be too good to be true, it does illustrate the storyteller's continuing consciousness of the question of hair length—as well as his vivid sense of being a maverick in the journalistic herd. He didn't really want to be a newspaperman any more, and he was appalled at how much of his time it took up. "This goddam newspaper stuff is gradually ruining me," he complained to Sherwood Anderson only three months after leaving Chicago.

What prompted this outburst was an instruction from the *Star* to show up in Genoa on April 9 for the opening of the much-heralded International Economic Conference. Cursing but complying, he got himself a haircut, put on his Irish tweed suit and the good pair of English shoes he had bought and headed for Italy. He may not have felt like a diplomatic reporter, but at least he looked the part.

The Genoa Conference of 1922 was the most picturesque gathering of its kind that the world had witnessed since the Congress of Vienna more than a century earlier. Above the narrow, stone-paved streets of the old city, flags hung from every gable, as if a festival were in progress. Every morning, secretaries, financial experts, hundreds of newspapermen and delegates from more than forty nations, including defeated Germany and revolutionary Russia, poured into the great hall of the palace of the Genoa bankers' guild, the Palazzo San Giorgio, where the plenary sessions of the conference were being held. The delegates had come to discuss the reconstruction of Europe. Of the many high-powered statesmen on hand, the star of stars was the British Prime Minister, David Lloyd George. He had taken the lead in convening the conference, and when the white-haired Welshman first appeared on the speaker's platform he brought the entire hall to its feet in a spontaneous outburst of appreciation. But the delegates who cheered Lloyd George in unison could get together on little else. Once it was clear that the conference was hopelessly deadlocked, the Germans and Russians began to talk in secret sixteen miles away at Rapallo. To the amazement of the Genoa conferees, they quickly concluded a treaty of friendship. Both powers canceled all prewar debts as well as all war claims. A trade agreement was also signed, and in exchange for Germany's willingness to become the first country to accord diplomatic recognition to the Soviet regime, the Russians secretly agreed to permit the joint manufacture of arms inside Russia and the training of German soldiers there, in direct violation of the Versailles peace treaty.

Hemingway's reporting from Genoa was inadequate. Unversed in economics to begin with, he made next to no effort to understand the significance of the proceedings, contenting himself instead with dashing off dramatic accounts of rhetorical clashes between rival delegations and vivid descriptions of various people who caught his eye, from Dr. Wirth, the German chancellor, "who looks like a tuba player in a German band," to two young Russian secretaries, whose "fresh faces, hair bobbed in the fashion started by Irene Castle, and modish tailored suits" made them "the best-looking girls in the conference hall." As for the developments in Rapallo, he was much more interested in talking about the glass of marsala he drank with Max Beerbohm at the humorist's villa there than in reporting even the announced details of the shocking Russo-German rapprochement.

He also spent a lot of time drinking and eating at a trattoria with Lincoln Steffens, Max Eastman, George Seldes, and Sam Spewack, who were supposed to be covering the conference too, and occasionally the five of them were joined by the sculptor Jo Davidson, who had come over from New York to make portrait heads of some of the political dignitaries. "I have been over into the future, and it works," Steffens had been famous for saying ever since his visit to Red Russia in 1919, and Messrs. Eastman, Seldes, Spewack, and Davidson also regarded the Russian revolution as the red dawn of freedom and social justice throughout the world. The talk of such well-informed and self-assured companions was heady stuff for Hemingway, and while he did not believe everything they had to say, he did not question their utterly benign view of the Communist movement in northern Italy.

"The North Italian Red," he soon was telling the readers of the *Star,* is the "father of a family and a good workman six days out of seven [and] on the seventh he talks politics. His leaders have formally rejected Russian communism and he is Red as some Canadians are Liberal. He does not fight for it, or convert the world to it, he merely wants to talk about it." If the North Italian Red sometimes committed acts of violence, it was only because he had been provoked by his enemies, Hemingway implied.

Yet if he waxed sentimental about Italian Communists, the *Star*'s reporter had no illusions about Benito Mussolini and company. The Fascists are "a brood of dragons' teeth," he said, which had cropped up after the war when it had looked as though Italy might go Bolshevik at any moment. Ever since then, these bullyboys had been taking to the streets, tricked out in their black-tasseled caps, armed with knives, bombs and ammunition, and singing the Fascist hymn, "Giovinezza" (which Hemingway would always spell "Giovanezza"). Whenever they came upon a political meeting that didn't please them, be it Communist, Socialist, or Republican, they stabbed and killed if their fists weren't sufficient to break it up. "The fascisti," Hemingway said, "are young, tough, ardent, intensely patriotic, generally good looking with the youthful beauty of the southern races and firmly convinced that they are in the right."

"Give peace in our time, O Lord." Hemingway had learned those words as a very little boy from listening to his Episcopalian grandfather read aloud from the Book of Common Prayer. But in postwar Italy there was no peace. From 1919 onward, hundreds of fatal clashes between the Fascists and the Reds had taken place up and down the peninsula, Hemingway reported. In Tuscany and the north, bloody fighting, murders, reprisals, and pitched battles had occurred in just the past few months. The government had brought fifteen hundred picked military policemen into Genoa to crush any Red or anti-Red demonstration that might be triggered by the arrival at the conference of the Soviet delegation, but this was merely a stopgap measure. Once the troops were removed, the violence would resume, Hemingway was convinced, as were his trattoria pals.

The left-wing journalists he consorted with at the Genoa Conference further influenced his views by their characterization of the reforms of the Progressive era in the United States as patch jobs on a socioeconomic system that wasn't worth saving. "We Americans made a great mistake having that brief period of muckraking," Lincoln Steffens was wont to argue in the twenties, even though he himself was the author of a muckraking masterpiece, *The Shame of the Cities* (1904). "It set back our death more years than we devoted to it," his enthrallment with the Soviet experiment would lead him to say. "It protracted the age of folly, did harm, and no good." Shortly after his first exposure to such cynicism, the credulous Hemingway got off a few cynical remarks of his own about the life and times of his boyhood hero, Theodore Roosevelt.

> *Workingmen believed*
> *He busted trusts,*
> *And put his picture in their windows.*
> *"What he'd have done in France!"*
> *They said.*
> *Perhaps he would—. . . .*
> *Perhaps,*
> *Though generals rarely die except in bed,*
> *As he did finally.*
> *And all the legends that he started in his life*
> *Live on and prosper*
> *Unhampered now by his existence.*

The poem was a tissue of ironies, but its greatest irony was lost on the author. In the last three lines, Hemingway inadvertently composed a prophetic description of the power that his own legends would acquire.

2

ON RETURNING to Paris, he came down with one of the worst of the many severe sore throats he had endured since childhood. The weakness was traceable, he was certain, to an accident that had befallen him as a boy when a stick had pierced the back of his throat. Too ill to concentrate on any new work, he mailed off six poems to Harriet Monroe at *Poetry* magazine—one of them was entitled "Roosevelt"—and daydreamed about the trip to Soviet Russia that he expected to take very soon at his newspaper's expense. But when the assignment failed to materialize, he decided to take some more time off and go fishing and mountain climbing with Hadley and his old pal from Milan, Chink Dorman-Smith, who agreed to meet the Hemingways in the middle of May at the *pension* in Chamby where they had stayed before.

The three of them began their vacation by climbing the Cap au Moine, a steep and dangerous ascent of seven thousand feet. From a point about a mile high, they had a marvelous time coasting down the snowfields simply by sitting down and letting go. The next big challenge they took on didn't work out so well. At Chink's urging, they set off on a walk across the St. Bernard Pass into Italy, not realizing that the pass wasn't open yet and that no one had walked up it that year from the Swiss side. At times, they waded in snow up to their knees. The situation was toughest of all on Hadley. "Vanity and ignorance," she ruefully recalled, "induced me to wear a light pair of American Oxfords, suitable for neither terrain nor weather. I believe I wanted Chink to admire my trim legs." As they struggled on, she was freezing cold and possibly somewhat frightened, but at last they came upon the Hospice of St. Bernard, where they were given refuge for the night. The next morning, Hadley discovered that her feet had swollen and her shoes had shrunk. Nevertheless, the two men were in favor of pushing on. All the way to Aosta, they walked for twenty minutes and rested for ten. Even so, Hadley's ability to ignore the pain of her tight shoes finally gave out a few miles short of the town and she had to be more or less carried the remaining distance. "I was a human blister," she remembered. "I did not leave my bed for two days."

As she always would, she had done her gallant best to keep up with her husband. Yet in writing to Gertrude Stein and Alice Toklas about the walk, Hemingway told the story from a somewhat different angle. Except for a passing reference to "Mrs. Hemingway's feet swelling on her at Aosta," he made no mention of her ordeal, at the same time that he let the ladies know how difficult the ascent to the hospice had been for him. "It took the combined efforts of the Captain and Mrs. H. and a shot of cognac every two hundred yards to get me up the last couple of kilometers of snow."

Chink parted company with them a few days later and returned to his military post in the Rhineland. Hemingway then conducted Hadley on a fascinating tour of all the places in Milan that had meant something to him in 1918. Their strolls would later become the model for the twenty-third chapter of *A Farewell to Arms,* wherein Lieutenant Henry and Catherine Barkley pause in front of the Duomo, "white and wet in the mist," walk on to do some window-shopping in the Galleria and end up in a hotel, on the night before he has to return to the front.

Fascination of another sort attached to the interview Hemingway had in Milan with the renegade Socialist, Benito Mussolini. He found the Fascist leader seated at a desk in the office of his newspaper, *Il Popolo d'Italia,* fondling the ears of a wolfhound pup. Mussolini talked like an intellectual, yet he commanded an organization of half a million men that was at once a political party and a military force. The question of what he would attempt to do with his power was left open by Hemingway in his accounts of their meeting, but he strongly implied that the answer would be bitter.

Pursuing remembrances of things past still further, the travelers took a bus from Milan to Schio and went on from there by train and hired car to Fossalta. Unfortunately, neither town was recognizable to him, Schio because it was a much meaner place than the erstwhile lieutenant remembered and Fossalta because its devastated center had been rebuilt in offensively bad modern taste. The final blow to nostalgia came when their driver drove them out along the Piave and Hemingway couldn't find a single trench or dugout anywhere near the spot where he had been wounded.

3

IT TOOK only two months back in Paris for him to become restless again. A hiking and fishing trip through the Black Forest, he proposed to Hadley, would be an ideal way to beat the August heat. As usual, she was game. He then cajoled Lewis Galantière and his fiancée, Dorothy Butler, into coming along, and the newspaperman Bill Bird and his wife Sally as well. The hikers would all meet in Strasbourg, it was agreed, because the Hemingways intended to fly there instead of taking the train with the rest of the party.

The silver-painted biplane rose in the air, Hemingway related to his readers in Toronto, as though the pilot and his two passengers were being lifted slowly by some giant. "The ground began to flatten out beneath us. It looked cut into brown squares, yellow squares, green squares, and big flat blotches of green where there was a forest. I began to understand cubist painting." It was a sight he may have described to Gertrude Stein as well, for when she took her first flight during a visit to the United States twelve years later her reaction was very similar. "It was then in a kind of way that I really began to know what the ground looked like. Quarter sections make a picture and going over America . . . made any one know why the post-cubist painting was what it was."

While the flight to Strasbourg was a thrill for Hemingway, the rest of the trip drove him crazy. The Black Forest was too tidily maintained to suit a man who was used to the wilds of Michigan; fat German tourists with loutish manners threw their weight around everywhere; and bureaucratic red tape made obtaining group fishing licenses frustratingly difficult. To top everything off, Hemingway conceived a violent dislike for Dorothy Butler. Two years later, he would tell her what he thought of her, in the sort of killer letter he loved to send. "Even though I kissed you Dorothy, even while I kissed you, I never liked you, but I was willing to make the effort to like you for the sake of seeing Lewis occasionally. I made this effort successfully numberless times. Finally it could no longer be made."

Hadley didn't enjoy the Black Forest any more than her husband did, and within days of their return to Paris their frayed nerves led them into their first major quarrel since their honeymoon. What precipitated the dispute was a cable from John Bone in Toronto, ordering Hemingway to Constantinople to cover the bitter consequences of the war between Greece and Turkey. Hadley was vehemently opposed to his going. She disliked staying in their apartment alone, and anyway the trip might endanger his life, for even if the fighting had ended epidemics were rumored to be raging. He said she was out of her mind. Hadley reiterated her position. Suddenly, they both were furious. "It was just awful," she said in retrospect. For three solid days before he left, she wouldn't speak to him. After he was gone, her loneliness was made more acute by the realization that she had placed her own preferences above his career. There was no one to whom she felt she could unburden herself, least of all to her mother-in-law. In writing to Grace she spoke cheerfully of "practising [the piano] 3 hours a day and gadding about with all the gay people here." She missed Ernest, she admitted, but "everyone assures me that he is safe as anything down there and will probably

be home soon." Unfortunately, she added, his trip had got off to a
bad start, as he had "sprained his ankle on the way to the train and
the taxi driver broke his typewriter."

Constantinople would be mentioned by Hemingway a decade
later in the puzzling first sentence of "God Rest You Merry, Gentlemen." "In those days the distances were all very different, the dirt
blew off the hills that now have been cut down, and Kansas City
was very like Constantinople." The reference to the trimming off of
Kansas City's hills correlates with the ghastly surgery that the sexually disturbed boy in the story performs on himself. But what
purpose did it serve to say that Kansas City was "very like" Constantinople? After that first sentence, the city on the Bosporus is
never mentioned again. Why bother, then, to introduce the comparison? There was, perhaps, an association between Hemingway's
state of mind in Kansas City in the fall of 1917 and his state of mind
in Constantinople five years later. Kansas City had been a town full
of sinful temptations, and he had felt their tug, despite his mother's
encoded admonitions that had so angered him. In the autumn of
1922, Constantinople was likewise renowned for its wickedness,
despite the victorious Mustafa Kemal's announced intention of
cleaning it up. As Hemingway toured the nightclubs and dancehalls
of the sleazy Galata district that he would evoke so memorably in
"The Snows of Kilimanjaro," was he tempted to be unfaithful to the
wife with whom he had just quarreled? If so, as locales where he had
been torn apart by conflicting feelings of anger, lust, and guilt, Kansas City and Constantinople were indeed "very like." And "Kilimanjaro" is very like "God Rest You" in that it, too, was written
out of a despairing sense of the tragedy of sex. In the midst of the
heaped-up wreckage of his marriage to Pauline Pfeiffer, the author
of "Kilimanjaro" conjured up the first bad moment in his marriage
to Hadley—and his earlier loss as well of Agnes von Kurowsky.

After the dressing has been changed on his gangrenous right leg
and Helen, his present wife, has gone in to bathe, a dying writer
named Harry lies on his cot in the hot African darkness, watching
the shadow of the firelight jumping on the tents and thinking about
the time he had been "alone in Constantinople," after having quarreled in Paris with his first wife. "He had whored the whole time
and then, when that was over, and he had failed to kill his loneliness
but only made it worse," he had written a letter to the very first
woman he had loved, "the one who left him," telling her how he
had never been able to kill his love for her. He wrote the letter, cold
sober, at the Press Club high above the Bosporus, asking her to
answer him at the office in Paris. Whatever the biographical truth

about all that whoring, the part about writing a letter to an earlier
love was taken straight from life, albeit Hemingway's letter to
Agnes was written upon his return to Paris, rather than in Constantinople, and its tone was friendly, not ardent.

4

THE hero of "Kilimanjaro" also remembers crossing Anatolia on a
train, riding all day through fields of poppies that were raised for
opium, until finally he got to the place where armed Turks were
coming steadily and lumpily forward, the skirted Greek soldiers
were running and their officers were shooting into them and then
running themselves. "That was the day he'd first seen dead men
wearing white ballet skirts and upturned shoes with pompons on
them." Hemingway himself never saw such a sight. The Turks had
driven the Greeks out of Anatolia in August, while he was still on
vacation in Germany, and the Greek infantrymen whom he followed
across Thrace in mid-October were dressed in surplus U.S. Army
uniforms. The dead soldiers in skirts had been described to him in
Constantinople by a British captain in the Indian cavalry who
worked as a liaison officer at the Press Club. Perhaps it was the
conjunction of death and crossed sex that made the description as
vivid to Hemingway as his firsthand memory of the dead women
with short hair in the field outside of Milan.

The Hôtel de Londres, where he stayed during his first days in
Constantinople, was filled with what Baedeker guidebooks of the
period still referred to as "enemies of repose." Malaria struck the
badly bitten correspondent a day or so after he had moved to a
cleaner place. Although doses of quinine made him feel somewhat
better, he was too feverish to attend press briefings for about a week.
His inability to do his job properly aggravated another problem he
was having with his managing editor. Before leaving Paris, Hemingway had duplicitously agreed to send dispatches from Turkey
and Greece to Hearst's International News Service, even though his
agreement with Bone gave the *Star* exclusive rights to his work.
Back in Toronto, Bone noticed that the stories coming over the INS
wire were virtually identical to those he was receiving from the
Star's own correspondent. He cabled his suspicions to Constantinople. Hemingway ultimately managed to squirm out of trouble, but
his relations with the *Star* were never quite the same again. Certain
powerful men in the organization flatly disapproved of him, although Bone remained in his corner.

By terms of the agreement signed at the hastily assembled Mu-

dania Conference, eastern Thrace was handed over to Mustafa
Kemal and the Greek army was given seventy-two hours to get out.
In the wake of the retreating Greek forces, a quarter of a million
Thracian Christian refugees poured onto the stony road leading into
western Thrace and Macedonia. The afternoon of October 17 found
Hemingway on a train to Adrianople to observe the evacuation. At
eleven o'clock that night, he alighted in a muddy chaos of soldiers,
bundles, babies, bed-springs, bedding, sewing machines, and broken carts, all exposed to the endless rain. Faced with the choice of
sleeping in the mud or in a hotel room seething with lice, he chose
the hotel room.

The next morning he went out to inspect the "silent, ghastly
procession" of humanity streaming across the Maritza valley in the
direction of Karagatch. For some miles he walked along with the
refugees, dodging camels that swayed and grunted and flat-wheeled
ox carts piled high with bedding, mirrors, furniture, pigs tied flat,
and mothers huddled under blankets with their babies. Occasionally
a line of ammunition mules came along loaded with stacks of rifles
tied together like wheat sheaves, or a battered Ford car sped by
carrying Greek staff officers, their red eyes grubby with lack of
sleep. But in between these interruptions there was nothing to be
seen except "the slow, rain soaked, shambling, trudging Thracian
peasantry, plodding along in the rain."

Hemingway's reporting from Adrianople was superb. As a writer
of fiction the Thracian evacuation also represented an important
moment for him. For in time it would become one of the principal
sources for his account in *A Farewell to Arms* of the Italian army's
retreat from Caporetto.

Of all the events he witnessed on the Karagatch road, the sight
that he lingered longest over in his dispatches was of a man holding
up a blanket to keep the driving rain off a woman in labor in one of
the ox carts. She was the only person in the entire procession who
was making a sound, Hemingway reported, until her little daughter
began to cry. The vignette about the evacuation that he would include a year and a half later in *in our time* would tell the story slightly
differently. "There was a woman having a kid with a young girl
holding a blanket over her and crying." In a subsequent rumination
on the art of writing, he would come up with a second variant,
saying this time that he himself had tried to help the woman. Somehow, he couldn't stop thinking about the incident, and his inability
to do so deeply affected his creative imagination. A woman in
agony, someone trying to help and a third person transfixed by
helpless horror: this scene, with variations, would surge up in his

work again and again, for reasons that had their roots in his early life.

Childbirth had figured prominently in Hemingway's upbringing, first of all because he was the son of an obstetrician and a mother who had four more children after his own birth, the last when he was fifteen. Grace, moreover, often told the tale of the pain and danger that had attended his sister Marcelline's delivery. Pregnant with her first child, she had consulted an older Oak Park physician of some prominence. On January 15, 1898, she entered into labor, attended by this physician and a nurse, in a second-floor bedroom of her father's house. Despite the fact that it was snowing, Dr. Hemingway was out making house calls in his horse and buggy. In the middle of the delivery, Grace's doctor suffered a heart attack and passed out. Summoned by telephone either by his father-in-law or the nurse, Dr. Hemingway made his way home through the snowstorm, administered first aid to the unconscious physician, gave his wife a second anesthetic and performed a high-forceps delivery. Dr. Hemingway attended other harrowing births over the years in Oak Park and environs, and in 1908 he spent four months in New York taking a postgraduate course in obstetrics at New York Lying-In Hospital. Thus, childbirth as both familiar and frightening was etched in Hemingway's recollections of growing up, and the mental picture of the woman in the ox cart in the pouring rain on the Karagatch road would have an important future in his life, as it had had an important past.

5

THE *Star*'s correspondent returned to Paris in style, aboard the Orient Express. Having parted from his wife in anger, he brought her peacemaking gifts, necklaces of amber and ivory and a bottle of attar of roses. Although touched by these gestures, Hadley was shocked by Hemingway's filthy clothes, bug-bitten face and shaven head— for he had been forced to get rid of his hair to get rid of his lice. As for his reaction to Hadley's appearance, he thought she was "more beautiful than ever and we loved each other very much and went everywhere together, the races at Auteuil with everybody crowded around the big charcoal brazier and a November bright blue sky and the turf hard and the fields good and we watching each race from the top of the stands." Yet his mood that something had been lost prevailed and he sent off a letter to Agnes von Kurowsky, catching her up on the news of his marriage and telling her how she could get in touch with him at the office.

Four weeks after his reunion with Hadley, he left for Lausanne. The *Star* had asked him to cover the Peace Conference that was scheduled to open there on November 21 for the purpose of drafting a settlement of the territorial questions engendered by the Greco-Turkish War. Soviet Russia, Great Britain, and Italy were among the other powers that would be sending delegations. Hadley planned to join Hemingway a few days after the opening of the conference, but she caught such a bad cold that she didn't feel up to it. He then caught a cold himself, which only made him miss her all the more. "I've been crazy for you to come and would love so still," he told her, and he urged her to believe that "I want you and wasn't trying to stall."

Yet if he was intent on convincing Hadley that he was an honorable husband, his journalistic ethics were even shabbier in Lausanne than they had been in the Levant. Not only did he continue to send reports to INS—being careful this time to avoid duplications of phrasing, so that Toronto wouldn't know what he was doing—but he entered into a clandestine arrangement with Universal News Service as well. As he himself admitted a decade later, he was "running a twenty-four hour wire service for an afternoon and morning news service under two different names." How much Universal News paid him is unclear, but Frank Mason of the INS office in Paris was sending him $90 a week, in addition to compensation for his expenses. However, when Hemingway asked INS in mid-December for 800 Swiss francs to reimburse him for the telegraph tolls he asserted he had paid, Mason objected. According to his books, INS could not possibly owe him more than 500 francs, so Hemingway would have to back up his claim to the extra amount with a set of receipts. The claimant's inability to produce them was promptly made clear in furious cablese: INTER NEWS PARIS SUGGEST YOU UPSTICK BOOKS ASSWARDS HEMINGWAY.

While journalistic triple-dipping kept him on the run, he still found time to relax with friends, one of whom was Lincoln Steffens. Impressed by Hemingway's dispatches from Adrianople, Steffens asked if he had any of his fiction on hand. Hemingway dug the manuscript of "My Old Man" out of his suitcase. Steffens was so taken with the story—despite its echoes of Sherwood Anderson—that on his own initiative he mailed it to Ray Long, the cruelly brilliant editor of *Cosmopolitan,* whose blazing career would eventually be snuffed out in the company of his secretary-mistress in a double suicide. A new friend whom Hemingway took up with in Lausanne was William Bolitho Ryall, the European correspondent for the Manchester *Guardian,* who later worked for the New York

World as William Bolitho, the same name under which he wrote a best-selling book of biographical portraits called *Twelve Against the Gods*. In his long fur-collared coat, Ryall rather looked like a ham Shakespearean actor, but in fact he was an ex-soldier from South Africa who had been badly blown up in the war while commanding infantry. Afterwards he had joined the British intelligence service, which assigned him the job of influencing public opinion. In Lausanne he was still bribing Continental journalists into giving their stories a pro-British slant. Ryall's view of politicians was no less cynical than his opinion of newsmen. Power was a malady, he said. It bred suspiciousness, touchiness, and finally a conviction of personal indispensability in the breast of everyone who possessed it. Hemingway ate dinner practically every night with Ryall, roaring with laughter at his jaundiced comments about the statesmen at the conference. Almost surely it was Ryall who disabused Hemingway of his previously high opinion of the quality of Mussolini's intellect and who filled his willing ear with gossip about the inverted sex lives of the Turkish puritan, Mustafa Kemal, the Soviet Commissar for Foreign Affairs, Grigori Chicherin, and the British Foreign Secretary, Lord Curzon, whose appetite for little boys was legendary. A young Foreign Office employee, so the latest Curzon story ran, put through a call to the Beau Rivage Hotel in the hope of speaking to his chief. He asked the flunky who answered the phone in Curzon's suite, "I say, is the Imperial Buggah in?" Somehow, the young man survived the clear, cool-toned reply. "*This* is the Imperial Buggah speaking."

In a piece for the *Star* that showed the influence on him of Ryall's down-putting wit, Hemingway described the press conference that Mussolini staged. The Fascists' "march on Rome" three weeks before had enabled Mussolini to take over the government, and at the Lausanne Conference he was very full of himself, strutting about and striking attitudes that befitted a Duce. When it was announced that he would hold a press conference in the reception room of his suite, reporters crowded into the room, Hemingway related. "Mussolini sat at his desk reading a book. His face was contorted into the famous frown. He was registering Dictator." For some time he held that pose, as if oblivious of the presence of the reporters. Finally, Hemingway tiptoed over behind him to see what the book was. "It was a French-English dictionary—held upside down." Later the same day, Hemingway continued, a group of Italian women living in Lausanne came to the dictator's suite to present him with a bouquet of roses. "Mussolini came out of the door in his frock coat, his gray trousers and his white spats. One of the women stepped forward and commenced her speech. Mussolini scowled at her, sneered, let his big-whited African eyes roll over the other five women and went back into the room." Apparently no member of the delegation had been sufficiently attractive to suit his lubricious interests. A little later, he opened the door and admitted a pretty young reporter named Claire Sheridan, who did not reemerge for half an hour.

No country was ever riper for Communist revolution than Italy after the war, so Hemingway had thought when he left the country at the beginning of 1919. By the time of the Genoa Conference in early 1922 he no longer believed this, but a number of leftist diehards still did. Yet the revolution had not only not come off, but the Fascists had jailed or killed its leaders or driven them into exile. Seven months after satirizing the chesty Duce at Lausanne, Hemingway recalled the mistaken optimism of some of his Genoa friends in a biting little story about a starry-eyed radical.

The year is 1919, in the months following the crushing of Bela Kun's Hungarian Reds by Admiral Horthy's Whites. A young Hungarian Communist is traveling on the railroads of Italy, carrying a square of oil cloth from "the headquarters of the party in Budapest," saying that he has "suffered very much under the Whites" and requesting comrades along the way to help him out. Since he has no money, the Italian train men pass him from one crew to another and feed him in railway eating houses.

The young man loves Italy. Its people are beautiful, and so are the paintings of Giotto, Masaccio and Piero della Francesca. He buys reproductions of their work and wraps them in a copy of the Socialist newspaper, *Avanti*. The paintings of Mantegna, on the other hand, are not to his taste.

In spite of all he has endured at the hands of Horthy's men, the young man believes "altogether" in the inevitability of Communist world revolution. Thus, when he inquires of the narrator of the story how the revolutionary movement is going in Italy and is informed that it is going very badly, he is not at all discouraged. "But it will go better," he avows. "You have everything here. It is the one country that every one is sure of. It will be the starting point of everything."

After a walking trip with the revolutionist up into the Romagna, the narrator bids him goodbye in Bologna. The young man intends to take a train to Milan and then go on to Aosta. From there he will walk over the St. Bernard Pass into Switzerland—the reverse of the walk that the Hemingways had taken with Chink Dorman-Smith. Before the young man's train leaves Bologna, the narrator tells him where to eat in Milan, gives him the addresses of several comrades who might help him while he is in the city and speaks about the Mantegnas there. The young man indicates that he does not like Mantegna. It is the second time in a story of approximately four hundred words that this aversion is stated. He sets out on his journey and the last the narrator hears of the revolutionist is that the Swiss have put him in jail.

Several names in the story have stories behind them. *Avanti* had been edited by Il Duce in his Socialist days; in order to emphasize his repudiation of this association, a flying squad of Fascists invaded the paper's offices on April 15, 1919, destroying its subscriber lists and ruining its linotype machinery. The Romagna was the birthplace of Mussolini. Bologna, a historic center of Communist strength, was seized and terrorized by fifteen thousand Fascist Arditi in the spring of 1922, as Hemingway reported in a story for the *Star*. As for Mantegna, his paintings were revered by Hemingway, above all, the uncompromisingly grim *Dead Christ* in Milan. "Very bitter" is the way Lieutenant Henry describes the painting in the thirty-seventh chapter of *A Farewell to Arms*. "Lots of nail holes," he explanatorily adds. Perhaps it is for that reason that the young Hungarian revolutionist so dislikes Mantegna's work. An idealist adrift in a dream world, he cannot stomach the painter's portrayals of Christ's suffering any more than he can face up to the accumulating portents of Communist defeat.

First published as one of the eighteen brief, untitled chapters in *in our time* (1924), the story of the revolutionist said farewell to easy talk of red dawns. It did not, however, say farewell to the proposition that the Communist movement was the enemy of tyranny and the people's champion. A dozen years later, Hemingway's renewed susceptibility to Red propaganda would lead him into dreadful errors of judgment about the Spanish Civil War.

6

HAVING recovered from her cold, Hadley started packing for her trip to Switzerland. As soon as he was finished at Lausanne, Hemingway had told her, he wanted to go back to Chamby for a long holiday, so she made room in her bags for their ski clothes. And in a separate valise, she carefully placed the original manuscripts, the typescripts, and the carbons of all the literary work her husband had done in Europe, on the assumption that he would want to revise some of it on days when the ski slopes didn't beckon. On her arrival at the Gare de Lyon, she asked a porter to carry her luggage on board the train. By the time she entered the compartment, the valise had been stolen. A frantic search of other compartments proved fruitless.

Hemingway was waiting to meet her at the station in Lausanne. She cried and cried and couldn't tell him what had happened. He told her that no matter what the dreadful thing was that had happened nothing could be that bad, and whatever it was she shouldn't cry any more. At last she gasped out the story. He was sure she could not have packed the carbons as well. After arranging for someone to cover for him at the conference, he took the train for Paris alone. All that he found were the manuscript of "Up in Michigan," hidden away in a drawer because Gertrude Stein hadn't liked it, and three pencil drafts of "a bum poem." Because "My Old Man" was under consideration at *Cosmopolitan* and *Poetry* had accepted six of his poems, these pieces survived as well. Otherwise the slate was wiped clean. As he sardonically remarked in a letter to Ezra Pound in Rapallo, "Hadley had made the job complete."★

All his life he would remember "what I did in the night" after he let himself into the apartment and confirmed that his wife's tale of disaster was true. Perhaps he got drunk and sought out a whore, or thought about killing himself. These are only guesses, however, for he never revealed the details of the rituals he went through. The next morning he made a beeline for 27 rue de Fleurus, even as he had hurried back to his mother at Windemere after he knew he was in trouble about the dead blue heron. Miss Stein and Miss Toklas, as he still called them, were very sympathetic and gave him a fine lunch. For the rest of the afternoon he sat in the studio with Gertrude, talking his head off and reading some of her recent work. On the way back to Lausanne that night, he drank a big bottle of Beaune in the dining car and wrote a nasty poem about various luminaries at the conference, from Lord Curzon, the lover of little boys, to Mussolini with his "nigger eyes" to the flat-chested wife of the American ambassador.

Another product of this period of extreme emotional turbulence was a piece he wrote for the *Star* about the Russian diplomat, Chicherin. The scion of a noble family, Chicherin had a wispy red beard and mustache, big eyes and a high forehead, and walked with a slouch "like an old clothes man." Although in his manner he appeared to be "a man without a weakness," this was a false impres-

---

★ The six sentences of "Paris 1922" were later discovered in a forgotten notebook, at which point he copied them over on telegraph forms picked up in Lausanne.

sion. For while Chicherin loved wearing military uniforms, he actually was "timid, personally" and had never been a soldier. Indeed, "until he was twelve years his mother [had] kept him in dresses." Hemingway seemed to take a particular pleasure in purveying this last bit of information and in the closing paragraph he repeated it. "The boy who was kept in dresses until he was twelve years old always wanted to be a soldier."

7

AN organizer as always, Hemingway lured a succession of friends and acquaintances into joining him and Hadley at Chamby, including an Oak Park chum of his named Isabel Simmons and a St. Louis family, Dave and Barbara O'Neil and their seventeen-year-old son, George, whom Hadley had known for years. Hemingway and young George teamed up on a two-man bobsled in the Canton de Vaud races down the Col de Sonloup *piste*. Most days, though, the organizer led parties of skiers up to the Dent de Jaman or the Dent du Lys, where the slopes were long, the snow crisp and there weren't a lot of other people around. After drinks in the evening in front of the fire, Hemingway would retire to bed to read "the Roosians and Joe Conrad . . . because they're so long," as he explained to Isabel Simmons.

But beneath the daily excitement of life at Chamby there was renewed alienation. In early January, Hadley obliquely referred to it in a letter to Grace that was ostensibly written in reply to the news Grace had given them about Marcelline's recent marriage to Sterling Sanford of Detroit. Hadley was very interested to think of Marcelline, she told her mother-in-law, embarking on a life that was "far from her family and old companions and spent entirely for a new person that can't quite absorb you all at first." Within the quietness of that remark lay a wistful acknowledgment that her own husband was not fully absorbed in her.

In "The Snows of Kilimanjaro" the dying writer remembers that after returning to Paris from the Greco-Turkish War the office sent his mail up to the apartment. On top of the batch was a reply to the letter he had written from the Press Club in Constantinople to the woman whom he had never been able to forget. "So then the letter in answer to the one he'd written came in on a platter one morning and when he saw the handwriting he went cold all over and tried to slip the letter underneath another. But his wife said, 'Who is that letter from, dear?' and that was the end of the beginning of that." A similar incident occurred at Chamby. The office in Paris forwarded Hemingway's mail to him, and in the batch was a lengthy letter from Agnes von Kurowsky.

"After I recovered from the surprise," the letter began, "I was never more pleased over anything in my life. You know there has always been a little bitterness over the way our comradeship ended, especially since I got back and Mac [Elsie Macdonald] read me the very biting letter you wrote about me. . . . Anyhow I always knew that it would turn out right in the end and that you would realize it was the best way, as I'm positive you must believe, now that you have Hadley. Think of what an antique I am at the present writing." (Apparently, Hemingway had not told her that Hadley was her age.) After being jilted by her Italian lieutenant, Agnes had returned to New York, "a sadder but wiser girl—feeling that I'd like to break something and preferably somebody, and life really wasn't worth living." After six months at Bellevue, her old hospital, she had signed up to work for the Red Cross in Rumania and had stayed there until the fall of 1920. Since then, she had visited some of the cities that he knew something about, including Constantinople and Paris. There was no place like Paris. "I'm homesick for the smell of chestnuts on a grey, damp Fall day—for Pruniers . . . and my pet little restaurant behind the Madeleine—Bernard's where I ate creme chocolat every night." Now she was back in the States again. "It is so nice," she said in conclusion, "to feel I have an old friend back because we were good friends once, weren't we?" She was proud to know that he was a writer, and she hoped they could correspond occasionally. It had been "priceless" to have had the chance to talk with him this way. "With best wishes to you and Hadley. . . . And a strong grasp of the hand, as they say in Rumania. Your old buddy. Von (Oh, excuse me, It's Ag.)"

Judging by Hadley's jealous reaction to Marjorie Bump and the other old girlfriends of Ernest's whom she had been forced to meet on her honeymoon, she may not have been at all pleased to learn that he was once again in touch with Agnes. But if she made her feelings known, as her fictional counterpart does in "The Snows of Kilimanjaro," her doing so could only have made him more impatient with her than ever. For it was thanks to Hadley's busybodiness that he had had to start all over again as a writer, as he would broodingly remind himself for the rest of his life. In a letter written from Chamby on January 29, he informed Ezra Pound that "this high altitude has made me practically sexless. I don't mean that it has removed the sexual superiority of the male but that it has checked the activity of the glands." It was his attitude, however, not the altitude, that had reduced his sex life with Hadley.

Reduced it, but not eliminated it. Despite the precautions she said she always took, Hadley discovered in February that she was pregnant. For a woman of her age it was high time, she felt, but Hemingway did not share her joy. This was a further instance of her bungling. It was also, perhaps, another symptom of a growing concern about the state of her marriage. Just as her loss of his manuscripts may have represented a subconscious attempt on her part to deprive her husband of the literary livelihood that would enable him to break free from dependence on her trust fund, so her pregnancy might not have been as accidental as she made it out to be—for if she bore Ernest's child, would that not bind him to her?

But to her dismay, Hemingway continued to be angry, and the next time he was in Paris he went round to the rue de Fleurus to unburden himself to Gertrude Stein, whom he was sure would be sympathetic. Perhaps she was—but that was not how she would write about it. "[Hemingway] and his wife went away on a trip and shortly after Hemingway turned up alone," Gertrude would relate in her most malicious manner in *The Autobiography of Alice B. Toklas*. "He came to the house about ten o'clock in the morning and he stayed, he stayed until about ten o'clock at night and then all of a sudden he announced that his wife was enceinte and then with great bitterness, and I, I am too young to be a father. We consoled him as best we could and sent him on his way."

Slightly over a year later, by which time he was acquainted all too well with the obligations created by parenthood, Hemingway would recall in the story called "Cross-Country Snow" how depressed he had felt upon learning Hadley's news. Nick Adams is having a fine time skiing in the mountains above Montreux with a younger friend whose name is George. What they would like to do, they agree, is to bum together and run the slopes indefinitely, beginning where they are and continuing right across the Oberland, up the Valais, all through the Engadine and into the Schwarzwald, where Nick had done some fishing the previous summer. The trouble is, George has to go back to school and Nick's wife, Helen, is going to have a baby. "Will you go back to the States?" George asks. "I guess so," says Nick. "Do you want to?" George asks. "No," says Nick. Too young to be a father! That cri de coeur rings out with anguished clarity in "Cross-Country Snow."

Sports

IN THINKING ABOUT the unpleasant fishing trip to the Black Forest that had been the prelude to his and Hadley's big fight in Paris, Hemingway decided that the moments he had enjoyed the most had been his conversations with Bill Bird. A tall, angular man with a professorial demeanor, Bird was fun to be with because he was full of ideas. He and another enterprising young newspaperman, the soon-to-be-famous David Lawrence, had founded the Consolidated Press Association on a shoestring, and since 1920 Bird had been working out of Paris as the Association's European manager. Somehow, he had also found the time to turn his long-standing interest in hand printing into a promising adventure in publishing.

While walking the narrow streets of the Ile St-Louis, he had noticed a small printery that set books by hand on an ancient press. As a means of sharpening his typesetting and printing skills, Bird apprenticed himself to the owner. After several months of training, he rented the empty shop next door, purchased a wonderful old Mathieu press, and went into business on his own. The Three Mountains Press was the name he chose, in honor of the three mountains of Paris, Ste-Geneviève, Montparnasse, and Montmartre, but he would always print the name entirely in lower case, as he would the titles of the books he printed.

At first, Bird contented himself with republishing classic works of literature, until Ezra Pound, whom he met through Hemingway, urged him to do a series of "strictly modern" books. Bird said he would, if Pound would hunt up the authors. After agreeing to do so, Pound proposed that the series be thought of as an "inquest" into "the present state of English prose." He himself offered to contribute an autobiographical fragment called *Indiscretions,* covering his life up to his sixteenth year, and he asked for additional contributions from seven other writers, T. S. Eliot, Wyndham Lewis, William Carlos Williams, Ford Madox Ford, Ernest Hemingway, and two thoroughly obscure Britishers whom he knew, a sometime wood merchant, B. Cyril Windeler, and an upper-class lady who wrote under the name B. M. G. Adams. Eliot and Lewis excused themselves, but all the others accepted, although Hemingway wasn't sure what his book would be about, and his unsureness increased after his manuscripts were stolen. Consequently, in the first announcement of the series that Bird cranked out, the titles of the books as well as the authors' names were listed in every instance except one. Opposite Hemingway's name in the brochure the word *blank* appeared.

The solution to the problem of filling in *blank* was provided by Bird. During the Hemingways' long sojourn at Chamby and their ensuing visit to Rapallo, Hemingway produced six prose sketches of various kinds of physical violence, and Margaret Anderson and Jane Heap promptly printed them all in the Spring 1923 "Exiles" issue of *The Little Review,* under the heading provided by the author, "In Our Time." On reading these sketches, Bird proposed that Hemingway revise them and write perhaps a dozen more. Eighteen sketches would make a manuscript of book length, and *in our time,* with its ironic echo of the Book of Common Prayer, would make a wonderful title. If Bird had the manuscript in hand by the end of the summer of 1923, he could promise publication in early 1924.

Bird also intended to ask Hemingway to let him publish "Up in Michigan" and "My Old Man," but by the time he got around to popping the question both stories had been preempted by another publisher, Robert McAlmon, who never hesitated to muscle in on the easygoing Bird, even though the two men were friends.

McAlmon habitually betrayed his friends, out of a sense of having been betrayed himself. The last of ten children born to a Presbyterian minister and his wife in the dusty town of Clifton, Kansas, he had grown up with the feeling of being unwanted. "Even as a little boy," one of his sisters would remark, he "had believed everyone was out 'to get him.' " He had feared betrayal, she said, long before "he had been so bitterly betrayed." Eventually his very appearance was affected by his paranoid fantasies. Acquaintances could tell just by looking at Bob McAlmon how full of suspicion and hatred he was.

William Carlos Williams, for example, who met McAlmon in New York in 1920, was amazed by the hardness of the expression in his eyes, as well as by the coldness of his manner.

Determined to achieve the notice that he felt had never been given to him at home, McAlmon used his blistering wit, his talent for telling untrue but believable stories about people, and above all his sharp good looks as attention-getting devices. At the time that William Carlos Williams first knew him, he was earning his living by posing in the nude for mixed classes at Cooper Union. "He had an ideal youth's figure," Williams recalled, "such a build as might have served for the original of Donatello's youthful Medici in armor in the niche of the Palazzo Vecchio." The painter Marsden Hartley was one of the many men who were physically attracted to him, as were numerous women, and McAlmon obliged both sexes. In Paris, he spent his nights drifting from fashionable Left Bank bars in which he could count on meeting well-heeled expatriate Americans to dance halls where French workingmen danced with drag queens. Yet no matter what sort of crowd he was with, he was never lost in it. As Sylvia Beach succinctly put it, "he attracted people" and "dominated whatever group he was in."

McAlmon had reached Paris by marrying Bryher, the English poet and novelist, whose real name was Annie Winifred Ellerman. Winifred's father was the shipping magnate, Sir John Ellerman, easily one of the richest men in England. As a child, Winifred had not been allowed to have friends or even pets, for Sir John himself had no need for any sort of close companionship and saw no reason why his daughter should be indulged. Once she came of age, her "one overmastering passion was to be free," as she would confess in her memoir, *The Heart to Artemis*. She wanted to travel to all the places she had read about, preferably in the company of women on whom she could lavish her pentup love.

Sir John disapproved of his daughter's peripatetic behavior. Flitting about the world without male protection was dangerous for a woman, especially if her father was rich. Faced with the implicit threat of losing Sir John's financial support, Bryher felt like killing herself. In New York, luckily enough, she happened to meet "a young American writer, Robert McAlmon, who was full of enthusiasm for modern writing. He wanted to go to Paris to meet Joyce but lacked the passage money. I put the problem before him and suggested that if we married my family would leave me alone. I would give him part of my allowance, he would join me for occasional visits to my parents, otherwise we would lead strictly separate lives." And so they were married, on St. Valentine's Day, 1921.

Following a "honeymoon" voyage across the Atlantic, McAlmon settled in Paris and Bryher went on to Switzerland.

As Bryher saw it, their marriage was a business deal, as coldly calculated as any of her father's. As for McAlmon, it would appear that he had been equally calculating. Yet there is also reason to believe that he developed a genuine attraction to his wife, both intellectually and physically, and that her spurning of him was the experience that intensified as nothing else in his later life ever would his childhood conviction that the world was against him. In any event, he quickly became notorious in Paris for heavy drinking, a propensity for fistfights and prodigal generosity with his wife's money.

Some expatriates were of the opinion that McAlmon was a better writer than Hemingway, to whom he was often compared. Ernest Walsh, for instance, the tubercular coeditor of *This Quarter,* called McAlmon "the most honest and authentically American of our writers, and the only man writing who can seriously compete with Joseph Conrad and James Joyce." But McAlmon's early promise as a writer was destined never to be fulfilled. The most significant mark he left on the literary history of his time was as an editor and publisher. In New York, he launched a poetry magazine called *Contact,* which he used to promote the reputations of William Carlos Williams and other undervalued poets. In Paris, he wangled a gift of fourteen thousand pounds sterling out of his father-in-law and founded the Contact Publishing Company. Dedicated to bringing out the work of writers "whom America . . . finds it hard to tolerate," as the critic Edwin Muir observed in a congratulatory letter to McAlmon, the firm got off to a memorable start, publishing William Carlos Williams's *Spring and All;* a collection of Mina Loy's poems called *Lunar Baedecker* (the misspelling of Baedeker was McAlmon's fault); Marsden Hartley's *Twenty-Five Poems;* two collections of sexually disquieting short stories by McAlmon himself; a thinly disguised autobiographical novel by Bryher, in which she gave voice to her sense of herself in adolescence as an obedient girl on the one hand and as an adventurous boy on the other; and a slender volume of stories and poems by Ernest Hemingway.

2

HEMINGWAY met McAlmon for the first time in February 1923 at the Hotel Splendide in Rapallo. At the invitation of Ezra and Dorothy Pound, who were spending the winter there, Hemingway and Hadley had come down from Chamby to play tennis with Ezra and

a painter whom they had become friends with in Paris, Henry Strater by name, nicknamed Mike. Strater had painted a brooding portrait of Hemingway after his return from the Greco-Turkish War
and in Rapallo he would paint another, as well as a portrait of Hadley. A pacifist and political radical in his collegiate days at Princeton
—his friends would later recognize him as Burne Holiday in Scott
Fitzgerald's *This Side of Paradise*—Strater in the spring of 1917 had
been one of the ringleaders of the brave but futile boycott of the
university's undergraduate eating clubs. This six-foot, two-
hundred-pounder had also done some boxing at Princeton—a detail
that Hemingway would appropriate for his characterization of the
Princetonian Robert Cohn in *The Sun Also Rises*. Having gone a few
rounds with him in Paris, Hemingway challenged him again as soon
as he got to Rapallo, but Strater promptly sprained his ankle and
couldn't box or play tennis either.

On the night Hemingway ran into McAlmon, he had the hob-
bling painter in tow. McAlmon warmed to Strater immediately, as
most men did—and women as well. (Henry the Satyr was another
of his nicknames.) With Hemingway, though, McAlmon came to
feel uneasy, because of what he regarded as his two-facedness. At
times, Hemingway was "deliberately hard-boiled, case-hardened,
and old." At other times, he was "the hurt, sensitive boy, deliberately young and naive, wanting to be brave, and somehow on the
defensive, suspicions lurking in his peering, analytic glances at the
person with whom he was talking. He approached a café with a
small-boy, tough-guy swagger, and before strangers of whom he
was uncertain a potential snarl of scorn played on his large-lipped
rather loose mouth." A devastating assessment certainly—but it was
not formulated at Rapallo. By the time McAlmon wrote those
words he had been verbally roughed up so often by Hemingway—
and on one occasion socked in the jaw as well—that all he was
interested in was getting even. In Rapallo, however, the bisexual
editor was quite taken with Hemingway's swagger, and three
months later the two men would travel through Spain together at
McAlmon's expense. Furthermore, in the course of their trip
McAlmon would ask Hemingway to become one of *Contact*'s authors.

After Pound left town to do some research for his Malatesta Cantos, Hadley whiled away her days talking about pregnancy with
Strater's wife, who had recently had a baby, and Hemingway took
the occasion to finish writing the half-dozen miniature studies of
violence that he planned to send to *The Little Review*. Of the six,
only one was based on firsthand experience, the account of the

woman having a baby in the rain on the Karagatch road. Two others were fashioned out of Chink Dorman-Smith anecdotes about the fighting around Mons, Belgium, in August 1914. The sketch of a battery of drunken American troops riding along a road in the dark somewhere behind the lines in France derived from a source that has never been satisfactorily identified. The physical exhaustion of a very young matador who has to kill five bulls in a row after the two other matadors of the afternoon are badly gored was imagined by Hemingway following several conversations about bullfighting with Mike Strater, for he himself had yet to witness a *corrida*. The final sketch, about the execution of six cabinet ministers, was inspired by a story he had read in the London *Daily Express* during his stay in Chamby.

The liberties he took with the story in the *Express* demonstrated how conscious he had become of the limitations of journalism as a means of getting at the meaning of events. Journalists focused on facts; writers created visions. Gertrude Stein had already warned him about the difference. "If you keep on doing newspaper work," she had said, "you will never see things, you will only see words." In a letter to her from Rapallo, he told her that he had thought a lot about what she had said and was "working hard about creating and keep my mind going about it all the time."

The story in the *Express* had caught Hemingway's attention because it dealt with the recent execution in Athens of the cabinet ministers considered responsible for Greece's disastrous defeat in the war with Turkey. On the morning of the execution, the newspaper's correspondent related, one of the men, ex-Premier Gounaris, was in a hospital in extremely critical condition. Nevertheless, at eleven o'clock he was

> taken out on a stretcher, placed in a motor van and driven to a place about one and a half miles outside of the city. He was left lying on his stretcher in a dying condition while the car went back to fetch five others from the prison where they had all been confined in a single room.
>
> To begin the horrors of that morning, it was discovered by the guards that one of the five had died in the van on the way out from heart failure.
>
> On the arrival of the van Gounaris was lifted out of [the] stretcher to stand up and face a firing party. It was then found that this wretched man, who, after all, had been a figure in the recent history of Europe, was unable to stand at all. He was thereupon given sufficient injections of strychnine to strengthen the action of his heart to enable him to stand up in front of the firing party. The man who had

died on the way out was propped up beside him—a ghastly line of four live men, one half alive and one dead man. . . .

The order to fire was given. The moment the prisoners fell the firing party rushed forward and emptied their revolvers into the corpses, including that of the man who died on the way from the prison. The bodies were then thrown into a lorry and taken to a public cemetery just outside of the city and were thrown out casually in a heap in the mud which covered the ground.

Hemingway kept re-working these facts until finally he transformed them:

They shot the six cabinet ministers at half-past six in the morning against the wall of a hospital. There were pools of water in the courtyard. There were wet dead leaves on the paving of the courtyard. It rained hard. All the shutters of the hospital were nailed shut. One of the ministers was sick with typhoid. Two soldiers carried him downstairs and out into the rain. They tried to hold him up against the wall but he sat down in a puddle of water. The other five stood very quietly against the wall. Finally the officer told the soldiers it was no good trying to make him stand up. When they fired the first volley he was sitting down in the water with his head on his knees.

The short and simple sentences are like a series of hammerblows. All the words in the *Express*'s account that betray emotion—"horrors," "ghastly," "wretched"—have been stripped away. The drama has been heightened by shifting the execution to an earlier hour of the day and by moving it from an indefinite location outside the city to the courtyard of a hospital. The focus on the minister who is deathly ill is unrelieved by any mention of a minister who is already dead. Pools of water, dead leaves and hard rain create a fearsome atmosphere. That supposedly merciful doctors and nurses have turned a blind eye to what is being done to one of their patients is symbolized by the hospital's nailed-shut windows. Try as he might, the sick minister is unable to face the firing squad standing up. With every shred of his human dignity gone, he is shot while sitting in a puddle with his head on his knees. "Give peace in our time, O Lord." Into a paragraph as pointed as an epigram, Hemingway packed everything he had learned since his return to Europe about the pitiless, endless violence of twentieth-century history.

3

THE pieces for *The Little Review* were completed in good time. Thereafter, Hemingway was literarily impotent at Rapallo. With his and Hadley's very differing views about parenthood much on his mind, he jotted down some notes for a story to be called "Cat in the Rain," about an unhappy American woman and her husband who are staying in a resort hotel room that faces the sea on one side and the public garden on the other, as the choicest rooms did in the Hotel Splendide, but he simply couldn't get beyond the notes. It was a very depressing time, he said later, "and I did not think I could write any more."

A boost to his morale was unexpectedly provided by a shy gentleman with pale blue eyes and straight lanky hair who was living as a boarder in a monastery in the hills above the town. He was Edward J. O'Brien, the editor of annual volumes of the best short stories of the year. Hemingway told him about the theft of the valise containing his work and then mournfully showed him the dogeared manuscript of "My Old Man," his sole surviving racetrack story, which had recently been turned down by *Cosmopolitan*—showed it to him, Hemingway would remember in *A Moveable Feast,* "as a curiosity, as you might show, stupidly, the binnacle of a ship you had lost in some incredible way, or as you might pick up your booted foot and make some joke about it if it had been amputated after a crash." To his surprise, O'Brien loved the story. Even though it was the editor's custom to include only previously published works in his anthologies, he forthwith accepted "My Old Man" for publication in *The Best Short Stories of 1923.* Indeed, O'Brien ultimately decided to dedicate the volume to Hemingway.

Upon Pound's return from his research trip, the poet and his wife and the Hemingways set off on a walking tour. Despite leisurely picnic lunches every day, they reached Pisa quite quickly and Siena in even better time. The always competitive Hemingway had probably set the pace, but in any event he found it punishing. After depositing the Pounds aboard a train for Rapallo, he was forced to spend a few days in bed. "Angina," he jokingly informed Ezra in a letter. Actually, the trouble was in his scarred right knee. After unusually strenuous exertion, it still could cause him acute discomfort.

Even so, he craved more exercise. At Cortina d'Ampezzo, spectacularly situated in a high-sided bowl in the ruggedly beautiful eastern Dolomites, the spring skiing was very good, he had been told. On their arrival there, he and Hadley took a room in the Hotel Bellevue on the crowded Corso Italia, a few blocks north of the bustling piazza with its charming baroque church and 250-foot campanile. But Cortina was not a large town and it did not take them too many minutes of walking to get out into gorgeously empty country.

Although Hadley tried hard to have a good time, the effort failed miserably. Besides being resentful of her husband's attitude toward parenthood, she was in the first trimester of her pregnancy and feeling increasingly rotten. Then, to her consternation, Hemingway received a message from John Bone, asking for a series of firsthand reports on the current unrest in the Ruhr. French troops had occupied the valley in January, in retaliation for Germany's failure to send sufficient quantities of coal to France to meet the inexorable schedule of its reparations payments. Hemingway cabled Bone that he was on his way. Hadley agreed to stay on in Cortina, rather than returning to Paris.

It was not only the French who were the targets of German anger in the spring of 1923, Hemingway discovered. When German Communists and German Nationalists confront one another, he advised the *Star*'s readers, "they look each other in the face or look at each other's clothes with a hatred as cold and final as the towering slag heaps back of Frau Bertha Krupp's factories." The Ruhr was a boiling caldron of hatred, and in two weeks of hard-driving work Hemingway did a good job of reporting that fact. In addition, he made a serious effort to deal with economic questions, as he had never done before. Bone was delighted with his performance.

En route to the Ruhr, he had paused in Paris long enough to complain bitterly to Gertrude Stein about the fact of Hadley's pregnancy. On the way back, he again stopped in the city, this time to pick up some fishing tackle. The higher slopes at Cortina would still have good snow on them, but there were also some lovely trout streams in the area. Hadley would enjoy fishing them too, for under his tutelage she had become as adept with a rod as he was.

The trip back to Italy took the better part of two days and he arrived feeling awfully tired. In a little over a year he had logged nearly ten thousand miles on trains. Six times he had gone back and forth from Switzerland to Paris and he had crossed into Italy on four separate occasions. For the moment at least, he had a belly full of traveling. And Hadley had a belly full of being left behind. During her husband's absence, she had succeeded in making friends with an Italian concert pianist, Renata Borgatti, the sometime lover of the wealthy and talented painter Romaine Brooks, but by and large she had felt terribly isolated. The natives spoke both Italian and German in dialects she could barely understand. She was also disturbed by the fact that there was no doctor in the village whom she trusted enough to consult. At the Hotel Bellevue, then, the weary Hemingway embraced a wife who was none too happy with him.

What made matters even worse, as Hemingway in years to come

would encourage Scott Fitzgerald and other friends to believe, was his and Hadley's frustrating discovery that the fishing season at Cortina had not yet officially begun. A gardener at the hotel whose breath betrayed his fondness for wine was nevertheless prepared, he said, to guide them to a spot on the Bigontina River where the trout were biting. But the brown and muddy river proved to be unfishable, and the spot of which the gardener had boasted had a refuse dump beside it.

On reentering the Bellevue, a thoroughly angry fisherman reported the gardener to the owner, who forthwith fired the man—so Hemingway assured Fitzgerald in a letter written in Schruns, Austria, on Christmas Eve, 1925—"and as that was the last job he had in town and he was quite drunk and very desperate [he] hanged himself in the stable." No sooner did he hear the news of the gardener's death than Hemingway sat down and wrote, "right off on the typewriter without punctuation," a short story, "Out of Season," that was "an almost literal transcription of what [had] happened." The only difference of any importance between fact and fiction was that he left out the gardener's suicide. At the time, he explained to Fitzgerald, he had been engaged in writing his sketches of violence for *The Little Review,* "and I wanted to write a tragic story *without* violence. So I didn't put in the hanging. Maybe that sounds silly. I didn't think the story needed it." Three decades later, in *A Moveable Feast,* he restated his reason for leaving out the suicide. "This was omitted on my new theory that you could omit anything if you knew that you omitted and the omitted part would strengthen the story and make people feel something more than they understood."

Like Hemingway's letters from the hospital in Milan about what happened to him at Fossalta, the anecdote about the gardener is fascinating, but doesn't hold up under scrutiny. As a sportsman, Hemingway had been schooled by an excellent teacher. In fishing and hunting there were proper ways to do things, his father had repeatedly told him, there were rules by which one must abide. While Hemingway as a boy had illegally killed a blue heron, Hemingway the man rigorously adhered to his father's philosophy. He was disgusted by fishermen who used types of lines and hooks that didn't give the fish a fighting chance, by hunters who shot from cars, by bullfighters who shaved the horns of their bulls. The idea that he would have been interested in fishing out of season at Cortina is therefore not plausible. Nor is it plausible that a gardener would promptly hang himself upon being told by a hotel manager that he was fired, or that Hemingway, having heard the news, would at once sit down at his typewriter and pound out a tragedy without violence, according to a new theory of omission he had just evolved. And the final implausibility is the idea that the omitted hanging strengthens the story, for there is nothing, absolutely nothing, about the conduct of the bold, devilish fishing guide in "Out of Season" that could lead the reader to suspect him of having suicidal tendencies.

The overwhelming likelihood is that the story was wholly invented by Hemingway, that the marital dispute it depicts took place mainly in his mind and that the dispute arose out of his conflicted feelings about Hadley's pregnancy. Upon being informed of her condition, he had been furious. Thereafter, he didn't warn her to slow down and take care of herself; rather, he put her through the paces of a strikingly energetic exercise program—tennis at Rapallo, a rapid walking trip to Pisa and Siena, skiing in the Dolomites. Whether consciously or subconsciously, had he been trying to terminate her pregnancy by natural means? Having failed in this attempt, did the thought of surgical abortion then cross his mind? "Out of Season" subtly indicates that it did and that he hated himself for it.

On a windy spring day in Cortina with "the sun coming out from behind clouds and then going under in sprinkles of rain," a young American couple is walking through the town with a gardener named Peduzzi. (Hemingway took the name from one of the Italian soldier-servants who had waited on the American ambulance drivers in Section Four at Schio.) The wife is carrying several fishing rods, unjointed, and "rather sullenly" lags behind her companions. Her name is Tiny—one of Hemingway's several nicknames for Hadley. The husband's name is never given. Instead, he is referred to throughout as "the young gentleman," a distancing device that is one of many indications in the story that the wife's alienation from her husband is shared by the author. The young gentleman does not appear to be altogether happy with himself, either. Like the rain clouds that keep obscuring the sun, a guilt-stricken tenseness shadows his self-possession, most noticeably so during his exchanges with his wife.

> "I'm sorry you feel so rotten, Tiny," he said. "I'm sorry I talked the way I did at lunch. We were both getting at the same thing from different angles."
>
> "It doesn't make any difference," she said. "None of it makes any difference."

"Are you cold?" he asked. "I wish you'd worn another sweater."
"I've got on three sweaters."

Ostensibly, the disagreement between Tiny and her husband relates to his stubborn refusal to abandon the idea of doing some
fishing out of season, in spite of her opposition. "Of course you
haven't got the guts to just go back," she tauntingly says to him as
they walk along. Go back by yourself, he urges her, and when he
says it a second time, she does. "You're cold in this wind anyway,"
he calls to her.

A mere difference of opinion about unlicensed fishing, however,
cannot be the reason for his uneasy apology to her for having "talked
the way I did at lunch," or for her singularly cold response to him.
Nor can it account for the sense that something morally unclean is
at issue in the story, a sense that is communicated through the dirti-
ness of the imagery—manure, mud, and the like—as well as by the
gardener's sly winks at the young gentleman and the impertinent
familiarity with which he calls him "caro." Clearly, something of
considerable importance has been submerged in the story.

Although at the beginning Tiny sullenly lags behind the two men
and there is not much conversation, after she is persuaded to walk
abreast of them Peduzzi begins to talk to her very rapidly. "Part of
the time he talked in d'Ampezzo dialect and sometimes in Tyroler
German dialect. He could not make out which the young gentleman
and his wife understood the best so he was being bilingual." Pointing to a girl standing in the doorway of a house, the voluble gardener
says, "My daughter." "His doctor," Tiny says with some annoyance, "has he got to show us his doctor?" Apparently, she has taken
the German word for daughter (tochter) to be the Italian word for
doctor (dottore). The substitution is no accidental slip: it reveals
what is on her mind, and why she is so angry. The young gentleman
belatedly responds to her outrage by reassuring her that they both
have the same objective in mind, which presumably is to be happy
in their marriage ("We were both getting at the same thing from
different angles"). Tiny, however, coldly rejects his blandishments
("It doesn't make any difference"), even though he makes a show of
being concerned about her condition ("Are you too cold?").

Among the unfortunate consequences of Hadley's pregnancy,
from Hemingway's point of view, was that at some point she
wanted them to return to the United States or to Canada, on the
grounds, as she put it, that the "doctors, nurses, hospitals, would be
better there than in Paris." Because of his own anxieties about the

birth process, Hemingway was impressed by this argument. On the other hand, he was exceedingly loath to leave the new life he had made for himself. The idea that Hadley should cross the Atlantic by herself may also have been among the thoughts that entered his mind. For when the wife in "Out of Season" tauntingly remarks, "Of course you haven't got the guts to just go back," the young gentleman parryingly replies, "Why don't you go back?"

Yet "Out of Season" was clearly not the work of a man who wished to perpetuate marital differences. To the contrary, the story reads as though it was inspired by Hemingway's sudden surrender of all his oppositional ideas and by an attendant feeling of being washed morally clean. The textual evidence that supports this supposition is that upon reaching the river the young gentleman changes his mind about fishing out of season. To begin with, he suddenly feels "uncomfortable and afraid that any minute a gamekeeper or a posse of citizens would come over the bank from the town." And when he finds that he won't be able to fish after all because he has forgotten the lead sinkers for his line, he is "relieved. He was no longer breaking the law." Peduzzi tries to persuade him to go fishing with him the next morning, but as the story concludes it is clear that he doesn't intend to. "I may not be going," he tells Peduzzi, "very probably not. I will leave word with the padrone at the hotel office."

Just why his arrival at the river produces such a radical change in the young gentleman is a question that Hemingway leaves unanswered. The spring of the year is the spawning season for trout; fishing is barred by law in the hatching grounds so as to protect the egg-bearing females. The law is thoroughly understandable, yet not until he actually sits down on the river bank and joints up and threads his rod does the young gentleman's intention to flout it at last dissolve. In front of him is the river, swollen and discolored by melting snow, a tacit reminder of the miracle of renewal. Behind him, he can see something else that conceivably could have checked his disregard of the sacredness of life: the campanile of Cortina's church looming over the edge of a hill.

4

THE metaphorical congruence between the revealed and hidden halves of the young couple's quarrel was an unmistakable sign that Hemingway was gaining the artistic control of an important writer. Nevertheless, he did not even try to get the story published in an American magazine, because he had been so discouraged by his inability to place "My Old Man." After Ray Long informed him that

Cosmopolitan would not be publishing his racetrack story, he sent it, at Edward J. O'Brien's suggestion, to Arthur T. Vance, the editor of *Pictorial Review,* only to receive another rejection letter. From Paris, Hemingway wrote O'Brien on May 21 to let him know the verdict and to confess that Vance's comments had "made me feel pretty low. Got drunk on the strength of it and feel lower still now. [Vance] so obviously was hanging on to it all ready to buy if someone would tell him it was good. Guess it's a hopeless game to buck. . . . It is ridiculous, of course, but it frightens me so when the storys [*sic*] come back when there are letters like that. Throws me all off and makes it almost impossible to write. Seems to destroy any reason for publishing." In a poignant one-sentence paragraph he added, "And yet I want, like hell, to get published."

Even the beauties of Paris in the spring failed to lift him out of his depression. Indeed, he felt mocked by them. Everything looked just a little too beautiful. Not until he was about to set off for Spain with Bob McAlmon was he able to start smiling again. Mike Strater predicted he would love bullfighting, as did Gertrude Stein and Alice Toklas. Strater also drew him a fine map of Spain on the back of a restaurant menu and gave him the names of various places he himself cherished, including a little restaurant in Madrid where the specialty was suckling pig, roasted on an oak plank and served with a mushroom tortilla and *vino rioja,* and a *pensión* in the Calle San Jerónimo where bullfighters lived. Just before leaving Paris, Hemingway urged Bill Bird to come along, and the future publisher of *in our time* agreed to meet him and McAlmon a little later in Madrid.

The travelers' first night on the train was well lubricated with alcohol. The next day, McAlmon felt decidedly queasy, and his nausea increased when the train stopped alongside a flatcar, upon which lay the maggot-eaten corpse of a dog. Fearing that he might be sick at his stomach, McAlmon looked away, much to his companion's disgust. During the war, said Hemingway, he had seen maggot-eaten corpses of men stacked up like cordwood; such sights were awful, he admitted, but members of their generation simply had to inure themselves to awfulness. As he raved on, McAlmon recalled a remark that Ezra Pound had made to him about "Hemingway's self-hardening process."

Yet while Hemingway wanted to show McAlmon that he himself was much the tougher man, he did not fail to join the publisher for a few fortifying drinks at a big café near the Puerta del Sol before they went off to their first bullfight. They agreed, McAlmon remembered, that they might be bothered by what would probably happen to the horses, for in those days horses entered the ring un-

protected by any sort of padding. The two men also took the pre-
caution of carrying a bottle of whiskey with them to the arena, just
in case they were shocked and felt the need of a few calming swallows.

"My reactions to the bullfight were not at all what I had anticipated," McAlmon recorded in his autobiography a decade later. "At
first it seemed totally unreal, like something happening on the
screen. The first bull charged into the ring with tremendous violence. When the horses were brought in, it charged head on and
lifted the first horse over its head. But the horns did not penetrate.
Instead of a shock of disgust, I rose in my seat and let out a yell.
Things were happening too quickly for my mind to consider the
horse's suffering. Later, however, when one of the horses was galloping around the ring, treading on its own entrails, I decidedly
didn't like it." By the end of the afternoon, McAlmon's mood had
changed to resentment. "I resented the crowd's brutality and the
way people threw mats and articles of clothing into the ring at
moments in which the matadors were in danger. The crowd itself
was taking no chances. . . . The matadors did their dance well,
moved beautifully, and played seriously with death. The role of the
horses I decided to overlook as confirmation of Spanish brutality,
which was probably no worse than many French and Anglo-Saxon
cruelties."

Hemingway, meanwhile, was going wild with excitement. The
first bull, he stated in a feature article for the *Star Weekly,* was

> absolutely unbelievable. He seemed like some great prehistoric ani-
> mal, absolutely deadly and absolutely vicious. And he was silent. He
> charged silently and with a soft galloping rush. When he turned he
> turned on his four feet like a cat. When he charged the first thing that
> caught his eye was a picador on one of the wretched horses. The
> picador dug his spurs into the horse and they galloped away. The bull
> came in on his rush, refused to be shaken off, and in full gallop crashed
> into the animal from the side, ignored the horse, drove one of his
> horns high into the thigh of the picador, and tore him, saddle and all,
> off the horse's back.

Hemingway's contempt for McAlmon's negative reactions was
enormous—and enduring. Nine years afterwards he published a savagely condescending description of him in *Death in the Afternoon.*

> X.Y., 27 years old; American; male, college education; ridden horses
> on farm as boy. Took flask of brandy to his first bull fight—took
> several drinks at ring—when bull charged picador and hit horse,

X. Y. gave sudden screeching intake of breath—took drink of brandy
—repeated this on each encounter between bull and horse. Seemed to
be in search of strong sensations. Doubted genuineness of my enthusiasm for bullfights. Declared it was a pose. He felt no enthusiasm
and declared no one else could. . . . Does not care for sport of any
sort. Does not care for games of chance. Amusements and occupation
drinking, night life and gossip. Writes. Travels about.

The possibility cannot be ruled out that McAlmon further incurred
Hemingway's disgust on this trip by picking up young men. Then
too, there was the fact that McAlmon was paying all the bills, and
as Hemingway had already demonstrated in his dealings with Y. K.
Smith, he had a penchant for repaying generosity with viciousness,
possibly as a means of freeing himself of all sense of obligation.
Unlike Y. K., however, McAlmon did not get angry enough to
shut off his largesse. Instead, he kept on doling out money and
absorbing the recipient's insults.

Relations between them improved somewhat after Bird arrived,
and Hemingway's interest in insulting McAlmon was further diverted by the matadors whom they met at the *pensión* in the Calle
San Jerónimo and whom they accompanied to Seville for the feast
of Corpus Christi bullfights. From listening to these men Hemingway not only picked up an impressive amount of colloquial Spanish,
but a host of fine points about the art of bullfighting, including a fair
amount of its technical terminology. As always, he wanted to be an
expert.

Even though the fiesta in Seville was wonderfully colorful, the
three Americans left early in order to take in a few fights in the
ancient bullring in Ronda, a breathtaking mountain town which
Hemingway would always love. While walking away from the Plaza
de Toros one afternoon toward the edge of a precipitous cliff overlooking El Tajo gorge, they came upon a statue of an eighteenth-
century bullfighter, Pedro Romero, whose name Hemingway filed
away in his memory for future reference. Granada, their next stop,
was a letdown after Ronda. The bullring was beautiful, to be sure,
but the scheduled *novillada* (young bulls and not-yet-accredited matadors) was rained out, and the gypsy caves were a bore as far as
Hemingway was concerned. Projecting his annoyance with Granada
upon McAlmon, he now seized every opportunity to taunt him.
Although McAlmon's hard face took on a look of loathing, he kept
his usually ready fists in his pockets and curbed his rough tongue as
well. On finding that he couldn't provoke him, Hemingway re-
doubled his insults, at which point Bird told him to lay off. But all

the peacemaker received for his pains was an assurance that Hemingway wasn't angry at him. "You know," he told Bird, "I'll take
anything from *you*." Yet he knew in his heart how badly he was
behaving, and in a gesture of reconciliation that foreshadowed similar gestures toward other men whom he would offend in the future
he treated McAlmon with marked courtesy upon their return to
Paris.

If McAlmon had physically challenged Hemingway, he would
have been severely beaten. His awareness of this doubtless helped
him to control himself. So did his desire to sign up Hemingway for
his newly founded publishing house. Bird was going to publish *in
our time,* as soon as Hemingway got around to writing another dozen
sketches. But because the printing at the Three Mountains Press was
done by hand, it would take Bird five months to bring out the book
after receiving the completed manuscript. McAlmon, on the other
hand, intended to avail himself of the much faster printing facilities
of Maurice Darantière in Dijon, the printer whom Sylvia Beach had
hired to produce *Ulysses.* Because Hemingway was eager to have a
book to his credit right away if not sooner, he was excited by
McAlmon's guarantee that he could have "Up in Michigan," "My
Old Man," and "Out of Season" between hard covers by the end of
the summer. The deal was sealed with a handshake. To fatten up the
book a bit, it was further agreed that McAlmon would include a
selection of Hemingway's poems. McAlmon's private view was that
the poems were unimportant, and he didn't care for "My Old Man,"
either. What disturbed him about it was the falsely naive attitude of
the adolescent narrator. As in Sherwood Anderson's "I Want to
Know Why," "My Old Man" sentimentalized the facts of childish
life, in McAlmon's view. "Children of my experience," he once
said, were "much colder and more ruthless in their observations than
the child characters . . . in this type of writing." There was a de-
plorable trend in American writing, he felt, toward celebrating "the
fake child-mentality . . . as the true American." "Up in Michigan"
and "Out of Season," by contrast, were fine pieces of work. It was
for the sake of these two stories alone that McAlmon published
Three Stories & Ten Poems.

5

BACK in Paris, Hemingway addressed himself to the task of producing the rest of the sketches that Bill Bird wanted, but quickly realized
that in order to do justice to his thoughts and feelings about bullfighting he had to know more about the subject. Alice Toklas passed

on the information to him that some of the very best bullfighting in Spain took place in July at the festival of San Fermín in Pamplona, a white-walled, sun-baked town high up in the hills of Navarre. Pamplona is the World Series of bullfighting, he duly reported to Hadley, who was delighted to be invited to go with him. It was now the fifth month of her pregnancy, and they agreed that the experience wouldn't hurt her. Bullfighting might even have a "stalwart" prenatal influence upon the child that both parents were sure was going to be a boy.

They entered Pamplona by bus at night. Every seat was taken in every café under the wide arcades around the Plaza de la Constitución. The streets were jammed with jostling bands of blue-shirted peasants whirling and lifting and swinging in the traditional Basque riau-riau dances. Fife and reed instruments were wailing and big drums were throbbing. Fireworks were being set off every minute or so. A rocket exploded overhead and came swirling and whishing down. Dancers bumped into them as the Hemingways struggled to get their bags down from the top of the bus. Finally, they made their way to the hotel where Hemingway had reserved a double room two weeks in advance.

Nothing had been saved for them. In a mixture of French and Basque-accented Spanish the broad-hipped landlady informed them that they could have a small room with a single bed opening on to the kitchen ventilator shaft for seven dollars a day apiece, or a better room for ten dollars apiece. Hemingway said it would be preferable to sleep in the streets with the pigs. The landlady said that could be arranged. Hemingway said he would prefer it to such an inhospitable hotel. Hadley sat down on their rucksacks and prepared for a long siege. At last, the landlady said that she could get them a room in a house in the town and that they could eat in her place, for five dollars apiece everything included.

The boy from the hotel who carried their rucksacks led them to an old house with walls as thick as a fortress. The room was lovely and cool, with a red tile floor and two comfortable beds set in an alcove. A window opened on to an iron-grilled porch over the street. The sound of music filled the air.

Perhaps they were happier that week in Pamplona than at any time since their first month in Paris and first visit to Chamby. They went everywhere together and saw wonderful things—men and boys running as hard as they could through the cobblestoned streets at dawn, as the bulls that were going to be killed that day came galloping toward the pens in the Plaza de Toros; gorgeous dark-eyed girls with beautiful shawls over their shoulders and black-lace mantillas over their hair walking with their escorts through the evening crowds; tall pilgrim-father sombreros from Andalusia perched over the same café tables with straw hats from Madrid and flat blue caps of the Basque country.

"By God they have bullfights in that town," Hemingway exclaimed in an exultant letter to his old roommate in Chicago, Bill Horne. Eight of the best matadors in Spain fought in the Pamplona fiesta that year, and five of them were gored before the week was out. Of the famous ones, only Nicanor Villalta, who walked with the suppleness of a young wolf yet stood as straight as a lance, managed to escape injury. Hemingway had seen Villalta fight in Seville, but it was not until Pamplona that he became such an ardent fan of his that he thought of naming his unborn son Nicanor. "Nick" also struck him as a good name for a fictional hero.

On the most remarkable of the afternoons that he and Hadley spent watching the fights, three splendid matadors were on the card: a long-legged fellow named Olmos who reminded Hemingway of Tris Speaker, the center fielder for the Cleveland Indians; Algabeno, a slim young Andalusian whose high cheekbones resembled a real Indian's; and the incomparable Manuel García, called Maera, a dark, spare, and deadly-looking man already suffering from the tuberculosis that would finally kill him.

Hemingway never forgot that the second bull of the afternoon belonged to Maera. The matador began by snarling at the beast, and as the bull charged him he leaned back against the fence and the searching horns struck on either side of his body. When Maera at last decided it was time to kill the bull, he made "absolutely unbelievable passes" with the muleta, then drew up his sword and thrust it, as the bull charged and caught him on its horns. Maera was thrown up into the air and came down hard on his right wrist. The wrist was sprained so badly that every time he raised it to sight for a thrust the effort brought out beads of sweat on his face. Again and again he tried to make the death thrust, only to lose his sword on every attempt. The bull nearly hooked him about twenty times, but finally he was able to put it away. When the victorious matador came to the side of the barrera below the Hemingways' seats, Hemingway saw that his wrist was swollen to twice the normal size. "I thought of prize fighters I had seen quit," Hemingway said later, "because they had hurt their hands." Maera was one tough man. "Era muy hombre," as he would phrase it still later in *Death in the Afternoon*.

6

HEMINGWAY had acquiesced to Hadley's wish not to have her baby
in Europe, and during the month that remained to them before their
departure in mid-August for the home base of the paper he worked
for, he finished the batch of sketches for Bill Bird.★ Four of them he
set in Italy. In the first, a wounded soldier named Nick is sitting
against the wall of a church, looking "straight ahead brilliantly."
Turning his head carefully, he peers at the wounded soldier named
Rinaldi who is lying face down beside him. "You and me we've
made a separate peace," Nick says. In the second, a soldier lying flat
under night bombardment at Fossalta di Piave prays in terror to
Jesus to get him out of there—and the next night in Mestre goes
upstairs with a whore. In the third, a wounded soldier goes home to
Chicago following a hospital romance in Milan and contracts a case
of gonorrhea. In the fourth, a young Hungarian Communist is certain that a red dawn is breaking in Italy. Two other sketches were
products of the author's fascination with crime in America. The first
deals with two crooks in Kansas City who are gunned down by a
policeman after breaking into a cigar store. The second portrays the
hanging in the county jail in Chicago of a well-known mobster, Sam
Cardinella. (It was an execution that Hemingway could have personally witnessed if he had wanted to, for he had passed by the jail only
a few hours before. Having not seen it, he felt free to imagine that
the mobster lost control of his sphincter muscle as the two guards
came toward him with a cap to put over his head.) Still another
sketch was based on a story that an American filmmaker named
Shorty Wornall had recently told Hemingway about an encounter
he had had with the king of Greece in the garden of the royal palace
in Athens. The king had been confined to the palace grounds by a
revolutionary committee headed by a strong man named Plastiras.
At the end of their talk, said Wornall, the disconsolate king had said
that he wanted to go to America. Hemingway appropriated the
anecdote lock, stock and barrel, but recounted it in a voice that was
more British than American.

The five remaining sketches all came out of his recent experiences
in Spain. "They whack-whacked the white horse on the legs" focused on the poor animal whose impalement Hemingway and
McAlmon had witnessed at the amphitheater in Madrid. (Hemingway hadn't averted his eyes from the agonizing sight and didn't want

★ Hoping for magazine publication as well, he mailed several of the sketches to the *Dial,* but
the editors rejected them, as they earlier had rejected his poems.

his readers to do so, either. The horse's entrails, he wrote, hung down in a blue bunch and swung backward and forward as he ran; blood pumped regularly from between his front legs.) "The crowd shouted all the time and threw pieces of bread down into the ring" was again a memory of that first afternoon with McAlmon in Madrid. "If it happened right down close in front of you" paid tribute to Nicanor Villalta's marvelously accomplished cape and sword work. "I heard the drums coming down the street" depicted Maera's disgust with an ignorant Mexican matador who becomes inebriated on a day he is supposed to perform. "Maera lay still, his head on his arms, his face in the sand" envisioned the great matador's death in the ring from repeated gorings.

Not since Goya's *Tauromaquia* etchings had bullfighting been as intensely conveyed as in these five sketches—and a little over a year later the level of intensity would be raised still higher in "The Undefeated." By the late twenties, Hemingway's name had become virtually synonymous with the sport. When people thought about bullfighting, Hemingway came to mind; and when they thought about Hemingway, bullfighting was one of the first things they associated with him. He was an enthusiast about many sports, of course, but there was something about bullfighting that made it special to him. At his very first corrida he displayed a wild enthusiasm and he remained an ardent fan for the rest of his life.

To the question of why his consciousness was so conspicuously heightened by the sport, the young correspondent for the Toronto *Star* had a resounding answer ready to hand. The significance of bullfighting, he announced in a piece which appeared in the paper on October 20, 1923, is that it is "not a sport. It is a tragedy, and it symbolizes the struggle between man and the beasts." Those sentiments would eventually be echoed and amplified in the solemn references to ritual and tragedy in *Death in the Afternoon* that Max Eastman, in a corrosive review, would deride as sentimental poppycock. In the style he forged in his first years in Paris, Hemingway worked enormously hard to purge it of words that had a big sound but were spiritually empty—the sort of words, that is, that his mother loved. Nevertheless, in the public comments he made in his character as Ernest Hemingway about what the corrida meant to him, he resorted to rhetoric. The exigencies of self-concealment simply did not permit him to speak as plainly as he might have.

The bulls selected for combat in the arena may weigh half a ton or more. Heavily muscled, amazingly fast on their feet and armed with dagger-sharp horns that they can wield with terrifying dexterity, they are truly awesome concentrations of male power. For a lone man to take on one of these creatures requires *cojones,* and the Spanish use the word advisedly, for the genitalia are placed at risk in the contest, along with the abdomen, the buttocks, the intestines, the thighs, and life itself. To conquer a bull, a matador must therefore first conquer a host of fears, including the fear of sexual violation and the loss of his manhood. To paraphrase Gertrude Stein's famous taunt, what a disquisition about bullfighting the real Ernest Hemingway could have written!

Only in his fiction did he achieve philosophical significance as well as dramatic excitement in writing about the sport, and that happened only once, in "The Undefeated." His fiction is also the only place in which one can gain a sense of how caught up he was in the sexual imagery of bullfighting. And the only revealing example of this among the five vignettes he wrote about Spain after his and Hadley's return from Pamplona is "Maera lay still, his head on his arms, his face in the sand."

> He felt warm and sticky from the bleeding. Each time he felt the horn coming. Sometimes the bull only bumped him with his head. Once the horn went all the way through him and he felt it go into the sand. . . . Maera felt everything getting larger and larger and then smaller and smaller. Then it got larger and larger and larger and then smaller and smaller. Then everything commenced to run faster and faster as when they speed up a cinematograph film. Then he was dead.

From his seat in the Pamplona amphitheater, Hemingway had admired Maera's toughness in refusing to quit fighting after spraining his wrist. But admiration passed over into empathy, the spectator became the matador, only in a totally imagined scene in which mortal wounds had finally robbed the man in the arena of all of his manly resistance. In "Up in Michigan" Hemingway had projected himself into the consciousness of a woman who was being sexually penetrated by a blacksmith who wouldn't take no for an answer. While "Maera lay still" was a very different story, it, too, involved the sensation of lying helpless beneath an unstoppable male assault.

7

AT the end of long days of work on the *in our time* sketches, Hemingway usually relaxed by playing tennis with Ezra Pound. Afterwards the two friends would repair to the poet's studio to talk about the problem of how to order the sketches so that they would "all hook up." The arrangement that the author finally settled on was as carefully thought out as the order of the sections in Pound's "Hugh

Selwyn Mauberley." "The bulls start, then reappear and then finish," Hemingway explained in a summarizing note to Pound on August 5. "The war starts clear and noble just like it did, Mons etc., gets close and blurred and finished with the feller who goes home [to Chicago] and gets clap. The refugees leave Thrace, due to the Greek ministers who are shot. The whole thing closes with the [Shorty Wornall] talk with the King of Greece. . . . The radicals start noble in the young Magyar story and get bitched. America appears in the cops shooting the guys who robbed the cigar store. It has form all right. The king closes it in swell shape. Oh that king."

One day, his brainstorming with Pound was interrupted when a young American poet named Malcolm Cowley was ushered into the studio. Pound introduced him to Hemingway and Cowley at once said he had heard about him. By way of reply, Cowley remembered years later, "Hemingway gave a slow Midwestern grin." The grin may have been prompted by Hemingway's recollection of why he knew Cowley's name. Only a couple of weeks earlier, on Bastille Day to be precise, the young poet had been arrested and jailed and threatened with a jail sentence of several months for punching the proprietor of the Café Rotonde. As a radical, Cowley valued the Rotonde. It had "long been patronized by revolutionists of every nation." The proprietor, however, was notorious for treating young American women as if they were prostitutes. After an evening of sipping drinks with the Dadaist Tristan Tzara at the Dôme, Cowley decided to call the ill-mannered Frenchman to account by making a Dadaist "significant gesture of violence." Following his arrest by the police, several of the Left Bank's most belligerent expatriates, including Robert McAlmon and the current husband of superrich Peggy Guggenheim, the wildly erratic Laurence Vail, sprang to their countryman's defense. McAlmon's testimony that the proprietor had an evil disposition was instrumental in securing Cowley's release. His willingness to help the poet did not mean, however, that McAlmon either admired or liked him. On the contrary, he regarded Cowley as a "duly ponderous" fellow, "fairly slow on the uptake." It was only because he was an American that McAlmon had testified in his behalf.

A passage in the first version of "The Snows of Kilimanjaro" makes clear that Hemingway soon came to share McAlmon's low opinion of Cowley. As the gangrene-ridden hero is thinking about his early days in Paris, he recalls a walk through Montparnasse: "And there in the café as he passed was Malcolm Cowley with a pile of saucers in front of him and a stupid look on his potato face talking about the Dada movement with a Roumanian who said his name was Tristan Tzara. . . ." But shortly before Hemingway published "Kilimanjaro"—in the August 1936 issue of *Esquire*—he had second thoughts about that bit of frankness. By the middle thirties, Cowley had attained through his literary editorship of the *New Republic* a considerable influence in the world of books. Consequently, he was in a position to retaliate against writers who insulted him. In private correspondence with friends like John Dos Passos, who also had contempt for Cowley, Hemingway would never make any bones about how he felt about him. A "twirp" he called him on one occasion; on another, a "fool." In public, however, he decided to be more circumspect. As a result, Cowley's name was dropped from the final draft of "Kilimanjaro" and an innocuous reference to "that American poet" was substituted.

The question of how they felt about Cowley may have occasionally arisen during Hemingway's fence-mending conversations with McAlmon in the second half of the summer of 1923. Mainly, though, the two men talked about the imminent appearance of *Three Stories & Ten Poems*. When the proofs arrived in early August, Hemingway wrote McAlmon how impressed he was by them, how "very good and clean" they looked. Concerned that the volume was still going to be "too goddam thin," he asked his publisher if it would be possible to thicken it with lots of blank pages. "I've been checking up the blank page stuff on books here in the house," he said. "Find in Three Soldiers, Daws Passos, 8 blank pages without a goddam thing on them immediately after cover. Find in Seven Men, Max Beerbohm, four blank pages but evidence of two having been torn out by owner for can paper. Find in cheap edition of Madam [*sic*] Bovary by Gus Flaubert four blank pages." McAlmon obliged him with eight blank pages in front of the text and five behind. He also acceded to Hemingway's request that the full table of contents be printed in bold black type on the front cover of the grayish-blue jacket. And he made sure that Hemingway had bound copies of the book in hand before his and Hadley's departure for Toronto on August 17.

8

ABOUT a month before they sailed, Hemingway revealed that reservations about becoming a father were once again on his mind. On a visit to Guy Hickok's Brooklyn *Eagle* office, he got involved in a discussion of birth control, and in a startlingly vehement voice he burst out with the warning that there was no sure preventative. For the most part, though, he was loud in his expressions of delight

about the prospect of being joined by a "young feller." In a letter to
Bill Horne that reflected his upbeat mood more than it did the facts,
he declared that "Hadley hasn't been sick a minute or even nauseated
all the time. She never felt better and looks wonderfully, Bill."
Being in love, he added, was "the only thing worth a damn to be.
No matter how being in love comes out it's sure worth it all while
it's going on."

A last-minute sobering note was sounded by Ezra Pound. Taking
Hadley aside for a moment when she and Hemingway came to the
studio to say goodbye, he advised her that she mustn't try to change
the man she had married. "Most wives try to change their husbands.
With him it would be a terrible mistake. When you come back from
Canada with a baby, you won't be the same. Women's minds
undergo a softening process when they become mothers." Hadley
resented this advice, even as she privately resented the man who had
voiced it. She knew he was an adulterer and looked down on women
as inferior creatures. Right from the beginning, she decided, she had
never really liked Pound. Nevertheless, she couldn't help worrying
about what he had said.

PART THREE

1923–1926

CHAPTER TEN

"Nick in the Stories Was Never Himself"

THE BAGGAGE HEMINGWAY CARRIED aboard ship in Cherbourg was inordinately heavy because of all the copies of *Ulysses* that Sylvia Beach had given him. On reaching Toronto, he successfully arranged to have all of them smuggled into the United States. Aside from this coup and the "corking" apartment he and Hadley found for themselves on the edge of a ravine across from the Connables' estate, nothing pleased him. Canada was "the fistulated asshole of the father of seven among Nations," and Toronto was just a larger version of the dull Ohio town from which Sherwood Anderson had fled. "If anybody pulls any more of that stuff about America, Tom Mix, Home and Adventure in search of beauty," he wrote to Pound, "refer them to me."

At the *Star,* he expected to be assigned strictly to local stories, so that he would be able to take Hadley to the hospital when she went into labor. Unfortunately, the sadistic city editor, Harry Hindmarsh, under whom he now was working, felt that Hemingway was a cocky, duplicitous young man who needed a few lessons in humility. No sooner did he show up at the office than Hindmarsh ordered him to cover a story in Kingston, Ontario—and saw to it that the long article that Hemingway submitted was run without a byline. A week or so later, Hindmarsh sent him up to the Sudbury Basin in the back of the beyond north of Georgian Bay, and in early October assigned him to report on the arrival in New York City of Britain's ex-Prime Minister, David Lloyd George.

During the four days he was in New York, Hemingway tried without any luck to get in touch by telephone with Sherwood Anderson, but even if he had managed to do so he couldn't have spent any time with him because of the number of stories he was required to file. The people he observed in the streets seemed to be just as harried as he was. "All the time I was there I never saw anybody even grin," he observed to Gertrude Stein and Alice Toklas. New York in the autumn was beautiful, he conceded, but even so he didn't care for the city. As for Lloyd George, he found him "cantankerous, mean, temperamental and vicious," although the Welshman never manifested these characteristics in public. The symbol of Lloyd George's hypocrisy, Hemingway suggested, was "all that long hair" on his head.

On October 9, the *Star*'s reporter left New York on the special train that the New York Central had made available to the ex-Prime Minister to convey him and his entourage to Toronto. On the morning of the tenth, ten miles short of the city, the trainmaster handed Hemingway a message from the Connables, saying that Hadley had been taken to Wellesley Hospital the previous night. When he finally reached her side, he looked quite broken-down from "fatigue and strain," Hadley later noted in a letter to Isabel Simmons. The final minutes of his trip had clearly been a nightmare for him. Hadley, however, had had a very easy delivery, and to her anxiety-ridden husband she looked amazingly relaxed and fresh. As both he and Hadley had predicted, the baby was a boy, whom they promptly named John Hadley Nicanor Hemingway. His hair was like his father's and so was his nose, although Hemingway claimed to detect in his face a "remarkable resemblance" to the king of Spain.

At the office later that day, he replied to Hindmarsh's criticism of him for not coming directly to work by spelling out his "utter contempt and hatred for him and all his bunch of masturbating mouthed associates." He also offered to knock the editor down if he opened his trap again. Instead of firing him, Hindmarsh merely upped his work load unmercifully. "Shot from nervous fatigue," Hemingway found it impossible to sleep at night or keep food on his stomach. And his anger at Hindmarsh was so intense that he feared for the quality of any serious writing he might attempt, even though he kept telling himself that the "diseased oyster shits the finest pearl." In a letter to his friends in the rue de Fleurus, he confessed that he now "understood for the first time how men can commit suicide simply because of too many things in business piling up ahead of them that they can't get through." Yet the depression into which he had fallen probably had less to do with his work days at the *Star,* exhausting though they were, than with the appalling disruption of his domestic tranquillity by John Hadley Nicanor. "The Baby has taken to squawling and is a fine nuisance," he remarked with rueful humor in a letter to his father. "I suppose he will yell his head off for the next two or three years. It seems his only form of entertainment. No one gets as much pleasure out of it as he does."

2

THE lack of reviews of *Three Stories & Ten Poems* was another source of frustration for him. Combing through the newspaper exchanges at the *Star,* he came upon a paragraph in Burton Rascoe's weekly column of social and literary notes in the Sunday New York *Tribune* which stated that Edmund Wilson had recently shown Rascoe six sketches in *The Little Review* by a writer named Hemingway. They were "amusing stuff," Rascoe declared. The same writer, he went on to say, was also the author of a book of stories and poems. Rascoe's friend Lewis Galantière had sent him a copy from Paris, but he hadn't yet got around to reading it. Given his extraordinarily strong sense of entitlement, it is not surprising that Hemingway was irate. Rascoe had had the book for more than two months, but still hadn't read it, still hadn't reviewed it! The columnist couldn't do that to him, any more than the landlady in Pamplona could get away with saying that she had no room reserved in his name.

Despite his anger, he kept control of himself. Instead of telling Rascoe what he thought of him, he wrote a winning note to Edmund Wilson.

November 11, 1923

Dear Mr. Wilson:

In Burton Rascoe's Social and Literary Notes I saw you had drawn his attention to some writing of mine in the *Little Review*.

I am sending you *Three Stories and Ten Poems*. As far as I know it has not yet been reviewed in the States. Gertrude Stein writes me she has done a review but I don't know whether she has gotten it published yet.★

You don't know anything in Canada.

I would like to send out some for review but do not know whether

---

★ Gertrude's review appeared on November 27 in the Paris edition of the Chicago *Tribune:* "Three stories and ten poems is very pleasantly said. So far so good, further than that, and as far as that, I may say of Ernest Hemingway that as he sticks to poetry and intelligence it is both poetry and intelligent. . . . I should say that Hemingway should stick to poetry and intelligence and eschew the hotter emotions and the more turgid vision. Intelligence and a great deal of it is a good thing to use when you have it, it's all for the best."

to put a dedication, as compulsory in France, or what. Being an unknown name and the books unimposing they would probably be received as by Mr. Rascoe who has not yet had time, after three months, to read the copy Galantière sent him. . . .

I hope you like the book. If you are interested could you send me the names of four or five people to send it to to get it reviewed? It would be terribly good of you. This address will be good until January when we go back to Paris.

Thanking you very much whether you have the time to do it or not.

Yours sincerely,
Ernest Hemingway

Wilson admired the book and told Hemingway he was willing to write a note about it in the "Briefer Mentions" section of *The Dial*. At the same time, he indicated disappointment in the close resemblance of "My Old Man" to Anderson's "I Want to Know Why." Hemingway was quick to reply to him. "I am very glad you liked some of [the book]," he wrote. "As far as I can think at the minute yours is the only critical opinion in the States I have any respect for." He begged to differ with Wilson, though, about "My Old Man." The story was about a boy and his father and race horses, and while it was true that Anderson had also written about boys and horses Hemingway was sure that his story wasn't derivative. "I know I wasn't inspired by him," he insisted. Having denied an indisputable indebtedness, he then proceeded to disparage Anderson's current work. "[It] seems to have gone to hell," he said, "perhaps from people in New York telling him too much how good he was."

Moving on to other recent developments in American literature, he informed Wilson that of all the books published in 1922 he liked E. E. Cummings's *The Enormous Room* the most. On the other hand, Willa Cather's Pulitzer Prize–winning *One of Ours* was not to be taken seriously, certainly not as a portrayal of World War I. "You were in the war weren't you?" he asked. "Wasn't . . . [Cather's] last scene in the lines wonderful? Do you know where it came from? The battle scene in *Birth of a Nation*. I identified episode after episode. Catherized. Poor woman she had to get her war experience somewhere."

At the heart of this second letter lay a proposal. Suppressing his fervent wish to be reviewed at once, Hemingway urged Wilson not to publish a brief notice of *Three Stories*. Within a month, he pointed out, copies of *in our time* would be available, and as soon as they were he would send one to Wilson. "You can get from it what I am trying to get at and the two . . . [books] together could make one review." They could and they did. Eleven months later, in the October 1924 issue of *The Dial,* Wilson signaled to the world of letters the arrival of a genius by hailing the author of *in our time* and *Three Stories* as a writer of prose of "the first distinction." The pride Wilson took in having discovered Hemingway is clear from the long account of the event in his literary chronicle of the twenties and thirties, *The Shores of Light.* Yet Wilson's own evidence demonstrates that his discovery was masterminded by Hemingway himself. Ever since coming upon the racks of periodicals in Sylvia Beach's shop, Hemingway had been reading literary criticism with a great deal of care and rising impatience. In electing to initiate a correspondence with a twenty-eight-year-old Princeton graduate whose work had appeared in *The New Republic, Vanity Fair* and *The Dial,* he singled out the only critic who in his opinion possessed the wide curiosity, the seriousness of purpose, the capacity to formulate his thoughts with precision and the forcefulness of style that really influential reviewing required. Two years after his innocent-sounding initial letter to Wilson, a reviewer for *The New Yorker* would note that Hemingway "has only to publish to be read by a certain circle of the intelligentsia, and not even to publish to be discussed." A key element in this public-relations triumph was the review that he manipulatively proposed that Wilson write.

3

AFTER giving Sylvia Beach the joyous news about the baby's arrival, Hadley admitted to her that coming to Canada was "the first big mistake" that she and Ernest had made. "Our hearts are heavy, heavy," she told another correspondent, "just when we ought to be so happy." Besides his wife, Hemingway enjoyed the company of the Connable family, a few of the older men at the *Star* and a college student named Morley Callaghan who worked part-time at the paper, but otherwise he was bored out of his mind by the people he encountered. "He seemed to feel smothered," Callaghan remembered, and his judgments of many of his fellow reporters were scathing. This one had "no shame." That one had a "homosexual style." On one occasion Callaghan, too, felt the whip of his scorn. Hemingway asked him if he wrote fiction. The youngster said that he did, and promised to bring some of his work to the office and show it to him. The following week, Hemingway rather snappishly reminded him of his promise. Callaghan explained that he had been so busy it had slipped his mind. To his amazement, Hemingway took his forgetfulness as a personal insult. The only reason he had wanted to see Callaghan's stories, he sneered in reply, was that "I just wanted to see if you were another god-damned phoney."

To keep from going crazy, Hemingway tried to keep his mind on Spain. Much as he missed Paris, it was his Spanish memories that soothed his soul and renewed his faith in the worthwhileness of life. Spain was "the best country in Europe" in his opinion, "unspoiled and unbelievably tough and wonderful." Galicia, various friends had told him, had the best trout fishing on the Continent, and he intended to sample its rivers himself in the summer of 1924. Another trip to the Iberian peninsula would take money, of course, and in the coming year his financial situation was going to be unprecedentedly tight. For he had finally become so fed up with newspaper work that he had resigned from the Star, effective January 1, thereby cutting off a significant part of his and Hadley's income. Bad investments, furthermore, by Hadley's broker in St. Louis had diminished the value of her securities. Nevertheless, he was determined to get back to Spain, no matter what.

Just before Christmas, he made a quick trip to Oak Park. Everyone in his family was disappointed at not seeing Hadley and the baby, but she had been afraid that the fatigue and nervous strain generated by such a visit would cause her milk to dry up. Grace's gifts for her grandson were consequently handed to her son, rather than to her daughter-in-law. In the largest of the packages there were a pair of silk stockings, a pair of pink shoes and an exquisite dress— not unlike the one he himself had worn in infancy, as Grace did not fail to remind him.

To add to the difficulty of the occasion, Marcelline was also on hand, for she had come down to Oak Park for Christmas from her suburban home in Michigan, along with her husband, Sterling Sanford, an engineer with Detroit Edison. Despite his aversion to his sister, Hemingway was elaborately polite to both the Sanfords upon his arrival, and that night after Dr. Hemingway and Grace had gone upstairs to bed he sat talking with them in front of the fire in the living room. As if eager to prove to his sister that he really was a writer, he suddenly left the room for a moment and came back with a copy of Three Stories & Ten Poems. Dropping the book in her lap, he told her she could have it if she wished, but that she should wait to read it until she got home. He didn't want the old folks to know of the existence of the book because it included a story called "Up in Michigan" that he knew they would find offensive. In the seclusion of a Pullman berth several nights later, Marcelline pulled out

the book and immediately turned to "Up in Michigan." She was
filled with revulsion—which was possibly the reaction her brother
had been counting on.

Inasmuch as his stay in Oak Park was extremely brief, there was
no time for a quarrel to develop between him and his mother. Besides, she was impressed by his mustache, his mature appearance (he
could have passed for thirty-five) and his knowledge of French.
After he left, she wrote him what was intended to be a highly complimentary letter. "I cannot tell you how much it meant to me to
have you come here this time, and find you so mature in judgment,
and so like my father, for whom you were named. As you sat and
talked, Sunday night, you expressed the very same views of life
which he held—a big world vision that cannot place any arbitrary
boundary lines to the mercy and justice of God."

Back in Toronto, he found a package waiting for him containing
several copies of *in our time,* the harbingers of a limited—and today
very valuable—edition of 170 copies. The book had an arresting
cover designed from scrambled newspaper clippings and the text
was handsomely printed on deckle-edged paper. Because he was
anxious to place copies in the hands of Edmund Wilson and other
people who could aid his career, he did not even consider sending
one to his parents. He did instruct Bill Bird, though, to mail them
an order form. On receiving it, Dr. Hemingway contracted to buy
half a dozen copies. When they finally reached Oak Park, he and
Grace each sat down with one and started to read. Their mutual
horror attained its apogee in the final sentences of chapter ten, which
informed them that the war veteran who had been thrown over by
a nurse named Ag had contracted gonorrhea from a salesgirl while
riding in a taxicab through a Chicago park. Grace wept and Dr.
Hemingway raged. He would not tolerate such "filth" in his house,
he sputtered. As he was wrapping up the books preparatory to shipping them back to Paris, Grace pleaded with him to retain one copy,
for as far as they both knew this was their son's very first book.
Surprisingly enough, Dr. Hemingway's will prevailed. The Three
Mountains Press got all six of them back. Marcelline, who happened
to be in Oak Park at the time, warned her parents that Ernest would
be sure to hear of their action and would resent it terribly.

4

FOLLOWING a rough mid-January crossing on the Cunard Line's
Antonia—whose name he Catherized into *My Antonia*—Hemingway
and Hadley and the baby camped out for a couple of weeks in the

Pounds' damp and unheated studio, the Pounds themselves having gone off once again to Rapallo for the winter. A diligent search for a place of their own ultimately led the Hemingways to a flat that was quite close by, at 113 rue Notre-Dame-des-Champs. Well-kept trees and a clean, well-lighted café made the neighborhood far more attractive than their old one, but the flat itself had no electricity and only slightly less primitive plumbing than the staircase facilities they had formerly put up with. Moreover, there was a noisy sawmill adjacent to the building. While music from a bal musette would no longer trouble the Hemingways' sleep, the whine of a circular saw and the put-put of a donkey engine were bound to annoy them from seven in the morning until five in the afternoon.

On February 10, in the midst of packing up to move, Hemingway took time out to write Pound a gossipy letter that reflected the fact that he had a lousy cold and was feeling especially mean and combative. Laying about him like Douglas Fairbanks in one of his swashbuckling movies, he cut down literary figures left and right. On the basis of a brief stopover in New York before they sailed, he asserted that there was now a "tremendous reaction" in America against Sherwood Anderson and the "Broom boys," by whom he meant Harold Loeb, Matthew Josephson, and the other editors of the little magazine whose title had promised a clean sweep. The two-thousand-dollar prize given annually by *The Dial,* he continued, had just been awarded to the author of *The Ordeal of Mark Twain,* whom he scoffingly identified as "Wickham Brooks or Van Wyck Steed or somebody." Further news about *The Dial* was that Gilbert Seldes had quit the staff, "his sphincter muscle no doubt having lost its attractive tautness," and his place had been taken by "an aged virgin," to wit, Marianne Moore. As for the literary scene at the moment in Paris, "the town seems, when you can distinguish faces through the rain and snow, to be full of an enormous number of shits." If Pound's faithful correspondent was nevertheless a happy man, it was thanks to the oysters he had been eating and the wine of the country he had been imbibing—and to the exciting knowledge that he had "about 7 stories to write."

A portion of his writing got done on the dining-room table in their new apartment. But when the baby started to cry or he could no longer stand the incessant racket of the sawmill, he gathered up his writing materials and walked to the Closerie des Lilas. People from fashionable cafés like the Dôme and the Rotonde never came to the Lilas. Most of its clients were elderly bearded Frenchmen and their wives or mistresses. "They were all interested in each other and in their drinks or coffees, or infusions, and in the papers and periodicals which were fastened to rods, and no one was on exhibition," Hemingway would recall in *A Moveable Feast*. Somewhat younger men who lived in the quarter were also habitués of the Lilas. Some of them wore the Croix de Guerre and others wore in addition the Médaille Militaire, "and I watched how well they were overcoming the handicap of the loss of limbs, and saw the quality of their artificial eyes and the degree of skill with which their faces had been reconstructed. There was always an almost iridescent shiny cast about the considerably reconstructed face, rather like that of a well packed ski run." Thus, it was in front of an unwitting audience of *mutilés de guerre* that Hemingway sat writing sentences about a mutilation that Nick Adams witnesses as a boy in an Indian encampment in the woods of Michigan. By the end of February he had finished the story.

Originally, "Indian Camp" contained some flashback material about young Nick going to church back home and singing a hymn about the breaking of the silver cord and then staying up all night reading *Robinson Crusoe*. But on reconsideration Hemingway cut this material, because he wanted his narrative to consist of nothing but a series of moment-to-moment events in a continuously unfolding present. And within each moment he adhered to a behavioristic mechanism of stimulus and response.*

In the middle of the night, Dr. Adams, his son Nick and his brother George enter a shanty where an Indian woman is screaming in pain. For two days she has been trying to have her baby. In the bunk above her, her silent husband lies smoking his pipe. The extent of Dr. Adams's concern that Nick not become frightened is made evident by the careful way in which he explains to him what is going on. "Oh, Daddy," says Nick, "can't you give her something to make her stop screaming?" "I haven't any anaesthetic," Dr. Adams replies. "But her screams are not important. I don't hear them because they are not important." When the doctor starts to operate, it takes his brother George and three Indian men to hold the laboring woman down. Her husband, still in his bunk, rolls over against the

---

* Whether Hemingway had read any of the books or articles by the founder of behavioristic psychology, John B. Watson, is uncertain, but he need not have done so in order to have been familiar with his ideas, for Watsonianism was very much "in the air" in the twenties. Watson's notion that fits of depression could be overcome if the sufferer picked his environment with care not only interested Hemingway personally, but as a writer as well, as "Big Two-Hearted River" shows. For the fisherman's decision to stay out of the swamp where the fishing might be "tragic" is a perfect illustration of Watsonian self-management. As for Watson's view of Hemingway, he was an admirer, even though Hemingway in his work was not a strict behaviorist for long. A ruggedly handsome man, much given to colorful cursing and the pursuit of women, Watson was thought of as "Hemingwayesque." The sole encounter between the two men occurred in 1929 in Paris.

wall and covers his head with a blanket. A Caesarean section is performed with a jack-knife. It takes a long time. The baby turns out to be a boy and screams lustily. Dr. Adams sews up the incision he has made, using nine-foot, tapered gut leaders as sutures. On completing his work, he feels as "exalted and talkative as football players are in the dressing room after a game." George, however, does his sarcastic best to deflate his brother's exhilaration. "Oh, you're a great man, all right." Dr. Adams peers into the upper bunk and pulls the blanket off the Indian husband's head, remarking as he does so that fathers are "usually the worst sufferers in these little affairs." The Indian has cut his throat from ear to ear and a razor lies, edge up, in the blankets. Dr. Adams is upset that Nick has seen the mutilation. "Why did he kill himself, Daddy?" Nick asks as they walk back to their boat on the shore of the lake they had crossed to reach the Indian camp. "I don't know, Nick," says Dr. Adams. "He couldn't stand things, I guess." Nick's next question is, "Do many men kill themselves, Daddy?" "Not very many, Nick," his father says. In the boat, Nick sits in the stern and his father rows. The sun is coming up over the hills. A bass jumps, making a circle in the water. Nick trails his hand over the side of the boat and notices that the water is warm. "In the early morning on the lake sitting in the stern of the boat with his father rowing, he felt quite sure that he would never die."

"Indian Camp" first appeared in print in the April 1924 issue of Ford Madox Ford's new magazine, the *transatlantic review*. By the time the ensuing summer was half over, so many readers had asked Hemingway whether the story was based on personal experience that he felt moved to declare in a digression on the art of writing in the midst of "Big Two-Hearted River"—a digression he finally decided to eliminate from the story—that "Nick in the stories was never himself. He made him up. Of course he'd never seen an Indian woman having a baby. That was what made it good. Nobody knew that. He'd seen a woman having a baby on the road to Karagatch and tried to help her. That was the way it was."

In fact, Nick in "Indian Camp" *was* Hemingway, although not in the way that literal-minded readers assumed when they asked him about the laboring Indian woman he had seen in the woods in his childhood. A miracle of verbal compression, "Indian Camp" filters a remarkable amount of autobiographical emotion through its fictive events, from the closeness that the author had once felt to his father to his longtime dislike of his Uncle George to the fact that from a very young age he had always found something frightening in the trauma of childbirth. But a major portion of the inspiration for

"Indian Camp" came from a less obvious cluster of emotions, all of which had been generated by the circumstances surrounding the birth of John Hadley Nicanor. The Indian husband in the upper bunk was Hemingway's symbolic equivalent of himself being handed a telegram on the train to Toronto. With his extraordinary capacity to visualize, he had apparently been able to imagine his wife in Wellesley Hospital almost as clearly as if he had been right there in the operating room; at the same time, he was beside himself with fear (unwarranted fear, as it turned out) about the extent of her suffering and swamped by a sense of helplessness at the realization that he would probably arrive too late to be of assistance to her. (No wonder that he looked utterly exhausted when he finally reached her side!) The Indian husband, correspondingly and conversely, is so demoralized by his wife's agony that he cannot bring himself to help her in any way, or even to watch the birth of his son; it is as if he were not really there, even though, terribly, he is. There is yet another parallelism between the Indian husband and the author. When the Indian slits his throat, he acts out the thoughts of suicide to which Hemingway had made reference in his letter to Gertrude Stein and Alice Toklas after Hadley and the baby came home from the hospital. The probability that in describing the awful fate of the Indian Hemingway achieved catharsis is evident in the story's final moments of peace. For modern readers, however, the ending of "Indian Camp" cannot help but be shadowed by the awareness that the real-life counterparts of both the occupants of that boat on the lake would one day do away with themselves.

5

IF Ford Madox Ford at fifty looked like Lord Plushbottom in the comic strip *Moon Mullins,* as Robert McAlmon wisecracked, he was a woefully untidy version thereof. Tall, fat, and pink-faced, Ford sported a mustache that was habitually stained, wore suits that were seldom sent to the cleaners and spoke in a low, explosive mumble that even fellow Englishmen had difficulty with. A carelessness about all these matters was matched by what H. G. Wells called "a copious carelessness of reminiscence" about the famous men of letters he had known. Yet as a novelist Ford was a meticulous craftsman, and he had a well-earned reputation for making accurate judgments about the work of other writers. During his prewar editorship of the *English Review* he not only had cajoled "The Jolly Corner" out of Henry James and *Tono-Bungay* out of H. G. Wells, but had published the submissions of such unheralded talents as

D. H. Lawrence, Norman Douglas, H. M. Tomlinson and Wynd-ham Lewis.

Fed up with the dampness of the English climate and the isolation of his home in the Sussex countryside, Ford shifted his base to France in the fall of 1922. A little over a year later he launched the *transatlantic review,* with the promise that he would make it an outlet for younger writers. In Hemingway's case, this promise was kept, for Ford "did not read more than six words of his before I decided to publish everything that he sent me." During the *review*'s brief lifespan—only a year separated its demise from its birth—Ford printed three of his stories. At Ezra Pound's recommendation, he also hired Hemingway as one of his subeditors. "He's an experi-enced journalist," Pound told Ford, as they sat watching him pranc-ing about on his toes and throwing punches at imaginary targets in the dim reaches of Pound's studio one day. "He writes very good verse and he's the finest prose stylist in the world."

The offices of the *review* were located in the loft above Bill Bird's Three Mountains Press on the Ile St-Louis. Owing to Ford's admin-istrative inefficiency and the editorial inexperience of all the subedi-tors, the task of putting out the magazine was accomplished in conditions of the utmost confusion. Everything that could possibly go wrong with regard to printing, paper, packing, forwarding, and distribution infallibly did go wrong, issue after issue. The turmoil in the building was further increased by the tea parties that Ford held there every Thursday. "You should have seen those Thursday tea-parties!" the erstwhile editor exclaimed eight years later in the intro-duction he contributed to the Modern Library edition of *A Farewell to Arms.*

> The French speak of "la semaine à deux jeudis" . . . the week with two Thursdays in it. Mine seemed to contain sixty, judging from the noise, lung-power, crashing in, and denunciation. [Guests] sat on forms—school benches—cramped round Bird's great hand press. They all shouted at me: I did not know how to write, or knew too much to be able to write, or did not know how to edit, or keep accounts, or sing "Franky and Johnny" or order a dinner. The ceiling was vaulted, the plane-leaves drifted down on the quays outside, the grey Seine flowed softly.

When the size of the teas got completely out of hand, Ford shut them down and started giving weekly dances instead, at the bal musette in the rue du Cardinal Lemoine beneath the Hemingways' old apartment. And when the number of crashers made the dances unmanageable as well, Ford canceled that arrangement and enlarged the number of candlelit soirees he had been holding in the barnlike apartment on the Boulevard Arago that he shared with his mistress, the young Australian painter Stella Bowen. As a result of all this entertaining by Ford, Hemingway's acquaintanceship expanded exponentially. Harold Loeb, Nancy Cunard, Josephine Herbst, John Herrmann, Djuna Barnes, Samuel Putnam, Nathan Asch, Glenway Wescott, Scofield Thayer, E. E. Cummings and Chard Powers Smith were among the scores of people whom he either met for the first time or came to know better at his boss's parties. Yet no matter how many guests he assembled, Ford generally managed to be the star of the shows he staged. "The Leviathan of the Quartier Montparnasse," Herbert Gorman dubbed him, and Samuel Putnam recalled in his autobiography that the most marvelous aspect of the gatherings in the Boulevard Arago was the chance it gave to young Americans like himself to "listen to the onetime collaborator of Conrad and discoverer of D. H. Lawrence as he reminisced of his yesterdays."

Hemingway, too, was fascinated by what Ford had to say about Conrad. But Ford's memories of Henry James may have meant even more to him, because of his rapidly growing interest in American literature in general and James in particular. Thus, his somewhat inaccurate account in *The Torrents of Spring* (1926) of the aged James's instruction to his nurse, on the day that Britain's Order of Merit was brought to his bedside, to "turn off the light so as to spare my blushes," was based—the author made clear a few pages later— on an anecdote of Mr. Ford Madox Ford's. Another James story that he probably heard from Ford concerned the black and yellow bruises the Master sustained while learning to ride a bicycle in the Devonshire resort town of Torquay in 1895. Ford himself may have picked up this story secondhand, but it is also possible that James had personally told him about his biking misadventures when he gave the youthful Ford lunch at his house in Rye in the late summer of 1896. In any event, the idea of James suffering injuries as a result of riding a bicycle acquired a complicated significance for Hemingway, and he would make reference to it in an important passage in *The Sun Also Rises*.

6

THE savagely hostile feelings that soon overwhelmed and obliterated Hemingway's initial fondness for Ford were formed out of a number of elements. Like Henry James before him, Hemingway found many

of Ford's mannerisms quite tiresome, especially his pretense that he
was one of the last of the Old Tory squires. "He is so goddam
involved in being the dregs of an English country gentleman that
you get no good out of him," Hemingway complained to Pound
only two months after going to work for the *review*. He also was
put off by Ford's frequent references to his having volunteered for
active duty in World War I, even though he was then in his forties,
and to the gas attack he had gone through that had altered the quality
of his voice. "De Maupassant, Balzac, the Chartreuse de Parme guy,
they all made the war, or didn't they," Hemingway exasperatedly
asked Pound. "In any event they just learned from it. They didn't
always go on under the social spell of it. I'm going to start denying
I was in the war for fear I will get like Ford to myself about it."
What really outraged Hemingway, though, was not Ford's personal
style but his editorial stance.

In the very first issue of the *review,* Ford ran a long letter of
lukewarm encouragement from his friend T. S. Eliot, in which Eliot
took exception to Ford's statement that he wanted the *review* to be a
vehicle for young writers. "I object that this is an unnecessary dis-
crimination in favor of youth," said Eliot. A review is not measured
by the number of scoops that it gets, he insisted. "Good literature is
produced by a few queer people in odd corners; the use of a review
is not to force talent, but to create a favorable atmosphere. And you
will serve this purpose if you publish . . . writers of whatever age
who are too good and too independent to have found other publishers." Eliot also took this occasion to argue that there was no such
thing as an American literature, as distinct from English literature,
and that claims to the contrary were merely manifestations of the
"mistaken nationalism" of the "singularly stupid" present age.
Hemingway knew from a piece Ford had published the preceding
autumn in Eliot's review, *The Criterion,* that he was capable of making what Hemingway regarded as even more obnoxious cultural
judgments. "What stands out in our world of Thought and Art,"
Ford had written, is that "it is only England and France that matter. . . . *Let* us, for heaven's sake, be insular and—as long as we
include France—bold, bad, remorselessly exclusive."

Almost immediately after expressing those sentiments, though,
Ford had regretted them. Not only did he entitle his projected magazine the *transatlantic review,* but in one of the early issues he announced that the United States appeared to be coming of age,
literarily speaking, whereas England was "bled too white—and of
our best blood." Nevertheless, he continued to publish far too many
English and French writers for Hemingway's taste. Moreover,

Hemingway was convinced that Ford had cravenly abandoned the idea of favoring young writers. The result was that he was accepting stories by recognized writers that were not much different in spirit from the fiction one could find in mainstream magazines in America. "Ford's running [the] whole damn thing as a compromise," Hemingway raged in a letter to Pound in May. "In other words anything Ford will take and publish can be took and published in Century, Harpers, etc, except [Tristan] Tzara and such shit in French. That's the hell of it. Goddam it he hasn't any advertisers to offend or any subscribers to discontinue so why not shoot the moon?" In September he exclaimed to Gertrude Stein and Alice Toklas that he was "sick of Ford and his megalomaniac blundering" that had "spoiled the chance he had with the review," and a month later he favored these ladies with his definitive judgment of the man. "[He] is an absolute liar and crook and always motivated by the finest synthetic English gentility."

Ford had launched the *review* with the expectation of maintaining an approximately even balance between British, French and American contributions. But thanks to Hemingway's machinations inside the office and Pound's harassments from outside, the *review* actually ran a total of sixty British pieces, forty French and ninety American, the latter by such writers as William Carlos Williams, Lincoln Steffens, H. D., Natalie Barney, John Dos Passos, Nathan Asch, Djuna Barnes, and Gertrude Stein. In retrospect, Ford took pride in having published all these Americans, but without Hemingway's and Pound's energetic interventions in behalf of some of them it is unlikely that the magazine would have accumulated such an impressive roster of contributors.

In the case of Gertrude Stein, for instance, Ford let it be known that he would be pleased to publish something of hers someday. Hemingway seized on this vague remark as a cue for action. Gertrude wasn't a young writer, but her work was underrecognized; hence the *review* ought to support her. "Hemingway came in then very excited," according to *The Autobiography of Alice B. Toklas,* and said that

> Ford wanted something of Gertrude Stein's for the next number and he, Hemingway, wanted The Making of Americans to be run in it as a serial and he had to have the first fifty pages at once. Gertrude Stein was of course quite overcome with her excitement at the idea, but there was no copy of the manuscript except the one that we had had bound. That makes no difference, said Hemingway, I will copy it. And he and I between us did copy it and it was printed in the next

number of the *transatlantic*. So for the first time a piece of monumental work which was the beginning, really the beginning of modern writing, was printed, and we were very happy.

Well before the first installment of Gertrude's manuscript appeared in the April issue, Hemingway assured her that Ford had agreed to publish the whole thing, even though the editor had been informed that the manuscript was unusually long. It is all but certain, however, that this statement of Hemingway's was a barefaced lie, and that the truth of the matter lay in Ford's complaint that his subeditor had not only concealed from him that *The Making of Americans* was six volumes long but had described it to him as an extended short story—for no editor who had not taken leave of his senses would have embarked upon the complete serialization of a work of such length. By deceiving Ford, Hemingway forced him into the embarrassing position of having to explain to Gertrude that he couldn't possibly publish her manuscript in its entirety. Suspicious as always of Hemingway, Alice Toklas wondered whether "some other story" lay beneath the surface of this contretemps, and she was almost surely right. Hemingway in his anger at Ford was out to make trouble between him and other writers any way he could.

Another American writer whose work Hemingway shepherded into print was Nathan Asch, the son of the Yiddish novelist and playwright, Sholem Asch. A native of Poland, the young Asch had grown up in Switzerland, Germany, and France, but with the outbreak of the war in 1914 he and his parents had fled to America. College work at Syracuse and Columbia was followed by employment as a stockbroker in New York City, but after two years on Wall Street Asch decided that he wanted to devote his life to literature. Shortly after arriving in Paris in 1924, he mailed one of his stories to the *transatlantic review*. Hemingway found the unopened manuscript on Ford's desk one morning as he was headed for the toilet and took it along with him. Asch's recollection of Hemingway's recollection of what happened next was that "he got so excited about my story, he forgot to button up his pants." And Harold Loeb would remember a friend of his telling him that Hemingway had gone over Asch's work "paragraph by paragraph," much to the young author's benefit. What surprised Loeb about this anecdote was not that Hemingway's comments had been helpful, but that he had been "so eager to help" another writer.

The task of subverting the editor's authority over the magazine was made easier for his discontented subeditor when Ford left Paris in late May for a six-week visit to the United States. During his absence, Hemingway altered the basic character of both the July and August issues. In the July issue, he ran three pieces that Ford would never have sanctioned: a satirical story about college fraternity life and football fever by the humorist Donald Ogden Stewart, who had recently become Hemingway's bosom buddy; a nonsensical skit by Ring Lardner that made fun of Dadaism, a movement that Ford took with the utmost seriousness; and an unsigned editorial by himself in which he ridiculed three writers whom Ford thought well of, Jean Cocteau, Tristan Tzara and Gilbert Seldes, whose spirited new book on *The Seven Lively Arts* Hemingway might have approved of, too, had he not suspected that Seldes in his capacity as an editor of *The Dial* had been responsible for turning down the chapters from *in our time* he had submitted to the magazine the year before. In the August issue, Hemingway's biggest affronts to Ford consisted of his exclusion of an installment of Ford's novel *Some Do Not,* which the magazine had been serializing for some months, and his inclusion of a nosegay of pidgin-English poems by Elsa von Freytag von Loringhoven. Rumored to be the widow of a German nobleman, the eccentric Elsa had gained notoriety in Greenwich Village almost a decade earlier by wearing an inverted coal scuttle for a hat, a vegetable grater as a brooch, long ice-cream spoons for earrings, and metal teaballs attached to her pendulous breasts. Hemingway thought her poetry was as absurd as she was, but in an effort to annoy Ford he had been trying for months to sneak some of it into the magazine, only to have Ford discover it at the last moment and take it out. The August issue also featured, thanks to Hemingway, a story by Donald Ogden Stewart, another by Nathan Asch, an article by Guy Hickok, and a complimentary assessment of the fiction of Robert McAlmon by William Carlos Williams that Ford had previously refused to publish because he didn't like McAlmon's work.

By the time the wandering editor returned to the office on July 4, the July issue had long since come out and the August issue was at the printer and beyond recall. Ford did manage to squeeze in an editorial comment, however, on his subordinate's subversive performance. "During our absence," he said, "this Review has been ably edited by Mr. Ernest Hemingway, the admirable young American prose writer." With only two exceptions, the editor was at pains to point out, "the present number is entirely of Mr. Hemingway's getting together. It must prove an agreeable change for the Reader and it provides him with an unusually large sample of the work of that Young America whose claims we have so insistently—but not with such efficiency—forced upon our readers."

Although Ford at once attempted to reemphasize the English and French character of the *review,* he no longer had as much power as before. For the famous New York lawyer, John Quinn, the magazine's principal backer and a thoroughgoing admirer of Ford's policies, had suddenly died in July. For weeks, the *review*'s financial situation seemed hopeless—until Hemingway came up with another angel. Krebs Friend had been an associate of his on the *Cooperative Commonwealth* in Chicago. Marriage to a fantastically rich woman forty years his senior had subsequently enabled Friend to return to the French capital—which he had first come to know as a soldier convalescing from a severe case of shellshock—and to rent an apartment in the same exquisitely located building that housed the Tour d'Argent restaurant. (Instead of doing any cooking themselves, the Friends simply had the restaurant send in their meals.) When Friend agreed to keep the *review* afloat for another five months, he automatically became president of the Transatlantic Review Company— and Hemingway automatically acquired more editorial clout. By the end of the year, Ford's control of the magazine had so diminished that American contributors simply overran the final issue. Short stories by Hemingway, Don Stewart, Nathan Asch, Bob McAlmon and several less talented writers—including Elizabeth Friend, the sexagenarian wife of Krebs—were flanked by the latest installment of *The Making of Americans* and a sampling of the poetry of Evan Biddle Shipman, the raunchily dressed twenty-year-old scion of a wealthy family from Plainfield, New Hampshire, whose excuse for hanging around Paris was that a magazine called *The American Horse Breeder* had asked him to serve as its European correspondent.

7

ASCH and Shipman have had a fight, Hemingway reported to McAlmon during his final days at the *review,* "and after ½ hour of slugging no one had a mark. Neither packs much of a punch I guess. Shipman's girl has left him and he has gone back to Belgium after her. She left him because he loaned Asch money to get new teeth. Asch hit him out of kike gratitude. Ca va." In the same era in which Anthony Patch, the hero of Scott Fitzgerald's *The Beautiful and Damned,* detected something sinister in the faces of Semitic New Yorkers and T. S. Eliot defined the universalist Jew in terms of "A saggy bending of the knees/And elbows, with the palms turned out,/Chicago Semite Viennese," Hemingway found it easy to revile Jewish acquaintances with anti-Semitic epithets, especially those he hated, like Lincoln Steffens's new wife, Ella Winter. "You heard of course of Steffens marriage to a 19 year old Bloomsbury kike intellectual," he wrote to Pound from Burguete, Spain, on July 19, 1924, having forgotten that two and a half months earlier he had written him from Paris to say that "Abe Linc Steffens [has] gone off to Italy with objectionable 22 year old Jewine who treats him like Gaugin [*sic*] treated Van Gogh."

Of homosexuals he was even more intolerant. Take, for instance, his reactions to the author of a 1924 novel called *The Apple of the Eye*. As a boy in Kewaskum, Wisconsin, Glenway Wescott had wept over the novels of Henry James and acquired speech mannerisms that were more girlish than his sisters'. By the time he reached Paris he had picked up in addition an English accent. Ford liked both the man and his work, but Hemingway couldn't stand either. Wescott's prose style was a "fake," his stories were "fundamentally unsound" and his affected way of speaking was utterly nauseating—as he would attempt to show in a thumbnail sketch of a fruity young man in the bal musette scene in *The Sun Also Rises*. Roger Prescott is the young man's name—or was, until Maxwell Perkins at Scribner's objected to the obviousness of Wescott equals Prescott and made Hemingway change it to Robert Prentiss. "He was from New York by way of Chicago," Jake Barnes explains, "and was a rising new novelist. He had some sort of an English accent. I asked him to have a drink."

> "Thanks so much," he said, "I've just had one."
> "Have another."
> "Thanks, I will then."
> We got the daughter of the house over and each had a *fine à l'eau*.
> "You're from Kansas City, they tell me," he said.
> "Yes."
> "Do you find Paris amusing?"
> "Yes."
> "Really?"
> I was a little drunk. Not drunk in any positive sense but just enough to be careless.
> "For God's sake," I said, "yes. Don't you?"
> "Oh, how charmingly you get angry," he said. "I wish I had that faculty."
> I got up and walked over toward the dancing-floor.
> Mrs. Braddocks [Ford Madox Ford's mistress] followed me. "Don't be cross with Robert," she said. "He's still only a child, you know."
> "I wasn't cross," I said. "I just thought perhaps I was going to throw up."

Sometimes Hemingway verbally abused people for no apparent reason at all, and every now and then he gave way to even darker feelings and abused them physically. One of his victims became known to him through Harold Loeb. On the red clay tennis courts on the Boulevard Arago, near the prison where the guillotine was kept, Loeb and Hemingway fell into the habit of playing tennis together. "Ernest's game was not too good," according to Loeb, because of his bad eye and trick knee, "but he tried so hard and got such pleasure out of a successful shot that it was good fun notwithstanding." It was even more fun when they were joined for sets of doubles by two of Loeb's friends, Paul Fisher and Bill Bullitt. Fisher was a socially prominent American architect whose athletic good looks put Loeb in mind of an Arrow-collar ad. Bullitt was a diplomat from Philadelphia who had married John Reed's widow, Louise Bryant, and was reputedly working on a novel of manners about the Main Line. Boxing with Hemingway was another pastime that Loeb enjoyed, and so did Paul Fisher—for a while, that is. For on a hot September afternoon, Hemingway suddenly and without warning stepped up the force of his blows and began to beat Fisher unmercifully. Afterwards, Hemingway explained to Loeb that he had just felt "like blasting hell out of him."

Perhaps he blasted hell out of the architect because Fisher came from a well-to-do family. At a time when he and Hadley were strapped for money, Hemingway was extremely envious of people who had never had that problem—and all around him in the expatriate community he saw such people. Even though Loeb had run through most of his initial inheritance, it still galled Hemingway to remember that this Princeton Jew was the grandnephew of one of the founders of Kuhn, Loeb and Company and that his mother was the second daughter of Meyer Guggenheim, the legendary copper king. Bill Bullitt, of the Philadelphia Bullitts, had been reared in Rittenhouse Square and continued to live opulently wherever he went, from Paris to the Riviera to the Bosporus. Evan Shipman in his dirty white shirt and wrinkled gray suit may have looked like a bum, but he had attended Groton and his mother was a Biddle. Scofield Thayer was another fellow who had been born with a silver spoon in his mouth. Slim, bisexual Nancy Cunard, whose Ile St-Louis apartment made a convenient stopping-place for Hemingway on his way home from the *transatlantic review,* was the daughter of Sir Bache Cunard, a grandson of the founder of the shipping line. Natalie Barney's exquisite house in the rue Jacob reflected the fact that she was rich twice over, through her paternal grandfather, a manufacturer of railroad cars in Dayton, Ohio, and her maternal grandfather, the most successful businessman in Cincinnati. Krebs Friend and Robert McAlmon were both married to money, and a nice guy named Barklie Henry had recently fallen into the lap of luxury by becoming the husband of a Whitney heiress, as Hemingway informed Gertrude Stein and Alice Toklas in the same month in which he beat Paul Fisher.

The financial shape that Hemingway the writer was in during 1924 was summarized by him in a letter to Edward J. O'Brien in May. "I'm about broke," he said, "as I've never yet gotten any money except 150 francs from Ford's Transatlantic for anything I've written." All the copies of *in our time* had been sold, but the profits had been preempted by Bill Bird to offset the losses on other books he had published. *Three Stories & Ten Poems* had likewise earned him nothing. Recompense for his editorial labors on the *review* consisted of invitations to Ford's parties, period.

To economize, he stopped buying clothes for himself; when the elbows of his jackets wore thin, he patched them. Hadley also made do with the clothes she had on hand, and they both skimped on lunch and allowed other people to pay for the piles of saucers they accumulated in cafés. (According to the composer Virgil Thomson, Hemingway never bought anybody a drink until "he paid them off in *The Sun Also Rises*. . . . He bought all his friends drinks in that book.") Because all of these economies were conspicuous, they created an impression in the minds of sympathetic souls like Sylvia Beach that the Hemingways were eking out a hand-to-mouth existence. Yet in most respects they continued to live in their customary manner, by the anxiety-building device of dipping into principal. They rehired Marie Cocotte as their maid as a matter of course, and washed down the meals she prepared for them with the same good grade of wine as before. Their frequent attendance at prizefights at the Cirque de Paris did not cost them anything because Guy Hickok kept them supplied with press tickets, but in order to nourish his brand-new interest in six-day bicycle racing, Hemingway had to pay his and Hadley's way into the Vélodrome d'Hiver. Night after night, they could be found eating a picnic supper in their seats at the Vel d'Hiv, usually in the midst of a group of friends, for in John Dos Passos's words, "Hem . . . had an evangelistic streak that made him work to convert his friends to whatever mania he was encouraging at the time." Another sign of Hemingway's obsession with bike racing, according to Dos Passos, was that he "used to get himself up in a striped jumper like a contestant in the Tour de France and ride around the exterior boulevards with his knees up to his ears and his chin between the handlebars"—all of which suggests that in order to act out his fantasy Hemingway had not hesitated to buy himself an expensive bicycle. Nor did he hesitate to indulge his devotion to Spain and to bullfighting with another trip to Pamplona in the summer of 1924, during which he and Hadley discovered that the fiesta-inflated rates for food and lodging had been jacked up considerably higher than the year before.

In an effort to reduce the discrepancy between income and outgo, Hemingway hired himself out as a sparring partner for professional fighters who worked out in a gymnasium in the rue Pontoise. He also invested a number of evenings in playing poker for money with a group of men that included Harold Loeb, and he stepped up his bets at the horse tracks as well. Although he assured Dos Passos that he was winning "great sums" at Auteuil and Longchamps, it was the sort of claim one would expect him to have made. As for his luck at poker, Loeb's recollections imply that it was mixed, while the boxers he sparred with paid him a mere ten francs a round.

As he raided his and Hadley's savings account, Hemingway probably kept telling himself that he would cease to do this as soon as well-paying magazines like the *Saturday Evening Post* started accepting his stories. During 1924 he turned out ten pieces of work of which he was extremely proud. None, however, was taken by a national magazine in America. Three little magazines whose editors were known to Hemingway, the *transatlantic review*, *The Little Review* and Ernest Walsh's and Ethel Moorhead's *This Quarter,* would collectively take six, for which they would pay him the grand total of sixty dollars, and he earned some inflated marks for one of them when it was published in German in an avant-garde magazine in Berlin called *Der Querschnitt* (i.e., The Cross-Section). Not even in the world of the little magazines, however, was he able to count on unanimous support of his work. Thus, the New York-based *Dial,* which unlike most of its highbrow counterparts had the financial resources to pay its contributors something more than a pittance, repeatedly spurned his stories, as it had his poetry and *in our time* sketches.

Frustrating though it was to find that the *Saturday Evening Post* still wasn't interested in his work, it was the rejection by *The Dial* that drove him wild. In his anger, he tried to dismiss the magazine as the plaything of aesthetically precious Harvard snobs—Scofield Thayer, James Sibley Watson, Jr., and Gilbert Seldes—who made adoring references to Proust in practically every issue and gave their annual prize to fellow Harvardians like T. S. Eliot and Van Wyck Brooks. Another Harvardian, John Dos Passos, said of Hemingway in this period that he felt "sorry for himself," and that "one of the things he'd get sorriest for himself about was not having been to college." Without a certain refinement that statement is unfair. It was only in the presence of graduates of Harvard, Yale, and Princeton that Hemingway was sometimes overcome with self-pity. They all seemed to know one another, these Ivy Leaguers, and they thought nothing of excluding him, not only from the magazines they controlled but from the parties they gave, such as the great bash on a barge restaurant in the Seine that a wealthy dandy named Gerald Murphy and his wife Sara held on June 17, 1923, in connection with the premiere of the Ballet Russe's presentation of Stravinsky's *Les Noces*. Don Stewart had been invited, because both he and Murphy had been Skull and Bones at Yale, and so had Dos Passos, Scofield Thayer, and other Harvardians. But not Hemingway.

His self-pity, however, did not mean that he was about to let a snob like Thayer ignore him and his work with impunity. Two widely spaced literary events involving two famous writers supplied him with the grist he needed to grind out a revenge on *The Dial*. The first event had to do with the death in 1922 of the author of *A la recherche du temps perdu*. Much to Hemingway's disgust, the event had occasioned yet another adulatory essay in Thayer's precious magazine. The essay—called "A Monument to Proust"—appeared in the March 1923 issue and was the work, predictably enough, of another Harvardian, in this case Malcolm Cowley. The second event involved an insult to Ezra Pound. For several years, Pound had acted as *The Dial*'s Paris correspondent and literary agent, but Thayer had never been entirely happy about the arrangement. His dissatisfaction increased after he and his fellow editors began serializing Pound's translation of some writings of Rémy de Gourmont's, which Pound called *Dust for Sparrows*. Impatient with the seemingly endless length of the work, Thayer started referring to it as *Shit for Sparrows*. The jibe got back to Pound—as Thayer seems to have hoped it would— and at his leisure the editor then added injury to insult by terminating Pound's role as the magazine's agent. In a poem which appeared in *Der Querschnitt* in the fall of 1924, Hemingway struck back at this high-handed, to him typically Harvardian, treatment of his friend and ally with an extended series of excremental allusions built around an echo of the title of Cowley's essay of the year before on Proust.

> *They say Ezra is the shit.*
> *But Ezra is nice.*
> *Come let us build a monument to Ezra.*
> *Good a very nice monument.*

You did that nicely.
Can you do another?
Let me try and do one.
Let us all try and do one.
Let the little girl over there in the corner try and do one.
Come on little girl.
Do one for Ezra.
Good.
You have all been successful children.
Now let us clean the mess up.
The Dial does a monument to Proust.
We have done a monument to Ezra.
A monument is a monument.
After all it is the spirit of the thing that counts.

8

EXCREMENT, however, was not his favorite smear. Accusations of
sterility, impotence, and homosexuality were the weapons the embattled Hemingway most frequently resorted to in his public and
private wars on literary figures whom he felt were a threat to him in
some way. "E. E. Cummings married to Scofield Buggaring Thayer's first wife," he announced in telegraphic style to Pound on May
2, 1924. "That may explain award of Dial prize to Van Wyck
Brooks," he added, thereby implying that upon being abandoned
by his wife, Thayer had turned for sexual solace to the critic to
whom he had later given two thousand dollars in prize money. In
the next paragraph, Hemingway informed Pound that Gilbert
Seldes's brother George—also a graduate of Harvard, also a writer
—had found a woman to marry him. "Let us hope the marriage will
be consummated," the letter writer commented. These social notes
were followed a few weeks later by the appearance of a travel letter
by Hemingway in the *transatlantic review,* wherein he again found a
way to suggest that Van Wyck Brooks wasn't really a man. "For
every writer produced in America, there are produced eleven critics.
Now that the Dial prize has gone to a critic, the ratio may be expected to increase to 1/55 or over," said Hemingway. "As I have
always regarded critics as the eunuchs of literature. . . . But there is
no use finishing that sentence. If this letter is accepted that means
one hundred and fifty francs which relieves one of that responsibility
to follow through which is imposed on golf and creative writing."

Brooks was either a homosexual or a eunuch. Hemingway
spewed out innuendoes to this effect because, in his paranoiac alertness to any sort of challenge to himself, he believed that Brooks had

cast doubt on his manhood as well as on his future as a writer through a series of essays in *The Dial* that were chapters from a work-in-progress on Henry James. While the essays praised the author who, in his American phase, had produced such books as *Washington Square* and *The Bostonians,* they clearly implied—and literary gossip confirmed—that this praise was but preparation for a scathing analysis to come of what happened to the author's talent when he ultimately sought a field for his art in English society.

The chapters that appeared in *The Dial*—and the book called *The Pilgrimage of Henry James* (1925) into which they would be integrated —were Brooks's way of warning gifted American writers in the twenties who had elected to live abroad of the dangers inherent in their choice. His argument about James, in other words, was designed to be taken personally by younger expatriate writers, and that is precisely how Hemingway took it. Enraged by the sexually charged implication—as he construed it, at any rate—that the artist who cut his American roots ran the risk of emasculating his art, he struck back at Brooks with sexual insults. If his remarks were unconscionable, they were also diabolically clever, in the sense that he rightly suspected simply from reading and hearing about Brooks that something was amiss with him. Hemingway, a man of many secrets, believed that other men had them, and he delved for them with the same assiduity with which he guarded his own.

The Pilgrimage of Henry James was "the book of a sick man," Brooks's biographer, James Hoopes, has written. Already breaking down under the strain of the manic-depressive illness that would lead him from making threats of suicide to actual attempts at self-destruction and prolonged incarceration in mental hospitals, Brooks in the early twenties had hopelessly confused the anxieties in his life with James's. (And in his room in a mental hospital, Brooks's confusion would some day cause him to be terrorized by hallucinatory visions of James standing at the end of his bed and turning "great luminous menacing eyes" upon him.) The critic who attacked James for losing contact with reality was worried that his own mental grasp of the world around him was giving way. Furthermore, Brooks was obsessed by fears of sexual inadequacy. "When Eleanor [Brooks's first wife] returned with her mother and children in April," biographer Hoopes relates, "she found Van Wyck more depressed than ever before and unlike himself in a 'cold, terrible way.' She could not reach him emotionally or physically. He said he was impotent and he probably was, impotence being a symptom of manic-depressive illness." Mr. Hoopes locates this encounter in the spring of 1926, but it is eminently possible that episodes of impotence had been bedeviling Brooks from the very outset of his emotional illness. In any event, Hemingway caught a whiff of sexual anxiety in Brooks's essays on James, and his retaliation against him was guided by that.

9

GOLDEN young men from Harvard, Yale, and Princeton could also offend Hemingway by being nice to him. Such was the fate of the poet Chard Powers Smith.

Smith had been Archibald MacLeish's contemporary at both Yale College and Harvard Law School before becoming a member of the MacDowell Colony in Peterborough, New Hampshire, where Edwin Arlington Robinson adopted him as a pupil. In the early twenties, Smith and his wife, Olive, an Alabamian in her middle thirties who was in the early stages of a difficult pregnancy, rented a splendid château in the south of France. On trips to Paris they spent much of their time going to literary parties. More than once in early 1924 they invited their new friends, the Hemingways, to visit them. It was while he was a guest under their roof that Hemingway became aware of a tension in the Smiths' relationship that also involved a woman friend of theirs who was clearly in love with Smith. Nevertheless, Hemingway was contemptuously sure that there was a lot less to this cultivated young man's manliness than met the eye, and out of this conviction there came a story entitled "Mr. and Mrs. Smith."

A twenty-five-year-old Harvard man of independent means is married to a sickly Southern woman of forty. Following their wedding in Boston, they "tried very hard to have a baby." They tried on the boat coming over to Europe. They tried in Paris. And they tried again after renting a château in Touraine. A woman friend who is living with them is very fond of the wife. By the end of the story, the two women have begun sleeping together in a "big medieval bed." The husband has taken to drinking white wine and lives apart in a room of his own. In the evenings they all sit at dinner together in the garden under a plane tree and the hot evening wind blows and the husband drinks wine and the wife and the woman friend make conversation and they are "all quite happy."

In order to intensify the Smiths' discomfiture, as well as to secure his own vision of unhappiness, Hemingway heightened their marital troubles by turning Olive and the other woman into lovers, by widening the age gap between husband and wife and by insinuating that Smith was either sterile or impotent. Completed in the spring

of 1924, the story was first published in *The Little Review* the following October—the very month in which Olive Smith died while
giving birth to twins—and republished a year later in *In Our Time*.
Still another year passed before Chard Smith was moved to write a
letter of protest to the author. But the letter simply inspired Hemingway to humiliate him anew.

> Gstaad, Switzerland
>
> My dear Smith:
>
> I received your letter several weeks ago but did not wish to answer
> it hastily. It is very interesting to find you identifying yourself with
> characters in [my book of stories] and I hope it may induce you to
> purchase several copies of the book which, on my next visit to Paris,
> I will be very glad to inscribe for you or for any of your friends.
>
> Your letter too, in spite of certain defects in construction, seemed a
> very interesting example of a letter written to some one you were
> sure was out of town. I noted too, how, unable to rely absolutely on
> this premise (my absence) you brought in a hope-for-better things
> note at the end; very nicely designed to remove the danger from the
> first part. May I congratulate you on the improvement of your prose
> style?
>
> Your application of the term "contemptible worm" to myself was
> very flattering. I feel you must be an authority on anything contempt-
> ible and will not attempt to dispute your classification. I remember
> the feeling of contempt I had for you on meeting you and regretted it
> intensely as a very cheap emotion and one very bad for literary pro-
> duction. I feel we are in accord on this. However, this feeling, con-
> tempt, has persisted, greatly to my regret, and has, in fact, increased
> the more I have heard of you and your adventures in America. I am
> sure I am a contemptible worm to you, because you have told me,
> and I feel very humble beside you; because to me, my dear Smith,
> you are a very contemptible mountain.
>
> It will be a great pleasure to see you again in Paris and somewhat
> of a pleasure to knock you down a few times, or perhaps once, de-
> pending on your talent for getting up; although I am sure I should
> feel very sorry afterwards. . . .
>
> You must believe, my dear Smith, that this letter does not end on
> anything but a note of sincere and hearty contempt for you, your
> past, your present and your future—and—lest you should have been
> deceived in an earlier paragraph—for the prose style of your letters.
>
> Your admiring friend,
> Ernest Hemingway

Had he chosen to say something comforting, he might have
pointed out to Smith that before publishing the story he had offered

him and his wife at least a slight degree of protection by changing the title and the names of the characters. Yet it was not out of any wish to be merciful that he had made those changes. They were prompted instead by the realization that he could injure two poets with a single stone. Accordingly, he had changed the title from "Mr. and Mrs. Smith" to "Mr. and Mrs. Elliot." That he chose not to call it "Mr. and Mrs. Eliot" did not, once again, have anything to do with mercy, but stemmed rather from his habitual uncertainty about how to spell T. S. Eliot's name. In his correspondence, he occasionally got the spelling right, but generally he referred to him as "Elliot" or "Elliott."

Were it not for his obvious resentment of him, one could argue that Hemingway adored Eliot, for he read and reread his poetry and paid close attention to discussions in literary journals of its intellectual origins. Explanations of how Eliot had taken the scheme for "The Waste Land" from Jessie L. Weston's book on the Grail legend, *From Ritual to Romance* (1920), in which Miss Weston had demonstrated that behind the legend lay ancient fertility myths personified in the figure of a sexually maimed Fisher King who is magically restored, may have been of more than passing interest to Hemingway, while the writer who placed the fisherman of "Big Two-Hearted River" in a "burned-over land" had surely paid attention to the description in "The Waste Land" of a fisherman sitting on the edge of an "arid plain." Hemingway was also moved to read Andrew Marvell's "To His Coy Mistress" because he had been told that Eliot admired the poem, and he appropriated the Marlovian title of his story "In Another Country" from the epigraph to Eliot's "Portrait of a Lady," rather than from the passage in Marlowe's *Jew of Malta* in which Eliot found those words.

He resented Eliot because the poet had used his authority to influence the policies of the *transatlantic review* in ways that Hemingway did not approve of, and he punished him for this in every way he could think of. In Pound's presence, he always referred to Eliot as Major Eliot, "pretending to confuse him with Major Douglas an economist about whose ideas Ezra was very enthusiastic," the point of the joke being that Eliot was just as much of a crackpot in his way as Douglas was in his. In the "Conrad Supplement" to the September issue of the *transatlantic review* Hemingway gratuitously remarked in the course of his tribute to the late novelist that if he knew that "by grinding Mr. Eliot into a fine dry powder and sprinkling that powder over Mr. Conrad's grave in Canterbury Mr. Conrad would shortly appear," he would "leave for London early tomorrow morning with a sausage-grinder." (Death and renewal, with a vengeance.) In the pages of *Der Querschnitt* two months later he parodied Eliot's attachment of footnotes to "The Waste Land" in a foul piece of work called "The Lady Poets With Foot Notes," the other nasty aspects of which included the assertion that Edna St. Vincent Millay was a "college nymphomaniac," that Sara Teasdale "couldn't have a baby" and that Zoë Akins was the mistress of William Marion Reedy, the publisher of the St. Louis *Mirror*. "Mr. and Mrs. Elliot," though, was the cruelest blow that he aimed at Eliot.

In the twenties, most admirers of the achievement of Eliot the poet responded to his work along lines laid down by Eliot the critic, and Eliot the critic had proclaimed in the most notable of his early essays, "Tradition and the Individual Talent," that "the progress of an artist is a continual self-sacrifice, a continual extinction of personality." Thus, "The Waste Land's" condemnation of the modern age as emotionally sick unto death, and the images of sterility and impotence, the scenes of meaningless fornication and vulgar talk of abortion in which that condemnation was clothed, were not usually viewed as oblique expressions of the personal problems of the poet and his wife, even though Eliot's friends were aware that the English woman he had married, Vivien Haigh-Wood, was "an invalid, always cracking up, & needing doctors," as Ezra Pound summarized her condition, and that Tom had written the bulk of "The Waste Land" while undergoing treatment in Lausanne for troubles he himself described to Richard Aldington as "an aboulie and emotional derangement which has been a lifelong affliction."

That the author's personality had not been fully eliminated from "The Waste Land," that the poem projected a private agony upon a portrait of civilization, were realizations that a great many readers did not squarely confront until the 1980s, when the Eliots' private lives were portrayed on stage and discussed at length in a biography of the poet. Hemingway, in all probability, would not have been surprised by these latter-day developments. Between 1922 and 1924, he undoubtedly heard stories about the Eliots from Pound. But more important than the gossip he absorbed was the fact that he read "Mr. Apollinax," "Rhapsody on a Windy Night," "The Love Song of J. Alfred Prufrock" and "The Waste Land" with the same scornful, searching eye for authorial vulnerability that he was training on the essays of Van Wyck Brooks. His conclusion was that Eliot, like Chard Powers Smith, was absolutely panicked by the challenge of adult sexuality. Once this resemblance occurred to him, he moved to exploit it. "Mr. and Mrs. Smith" accordingly became the mocking story of Hubert and Cornelia Elliot.*

If his manifestations of contempt for Eliot said something about the poet, they also contributed to a portrait of Hemingway at this moment in his life. Collectively, the assaults he mounted on men of Harvard in the middle twenties revealed him to be an envious, ferociously egocentric, and hugely ambitious writer with the bravado of a competitive athlete. Even if it took locker-room rhetoric and threats of physical violence, he would allow no one to stand in his way. In taking particular aim at sexual vulnerabilities he appeared to be proclaiming his own invulnerability. Yet that very choice of target sprang from similar concerns about himself. If Hemingway often seemed gratuitously mean and vicious, it was because he was a very tormented young man.

---

* Sexual derision would also figure in Hemingway's attack on the Humanists—one of whom, Irving Babbitt, had been Eliot's teacher at Harvard—in *Death in the Afternoon*. "In my musings as a naturalist it has occurred to me that while decorum is an excellent thing some must be indecorous if the race is to be carried on since the position prescribed for procreation is indecorous, highly indecorous, and it occurred to me that perhaps that is what these people [the Humanists] are, or were; the children of decorous cohabitation. But regardless of how they started I hope to see the finish of a few, and speculate how worms will try that long preserved sterility; with their quaint pamphlets gone to bust and into foot-notes all their lust.

   Old lady: That's a very nice line about lust.

   Author: I know it. It came from Andrew Marvell. I learned how to do that by reading T. S. Eliot.

   Old lady: The Eliots were all old friends of our family. I believe they were in the lumber business.

   Author: My uncle married a girl whose father was in the lumber business."

CHAPTER ELEVEN

"We Have More Fun Together All the Time"

ALL THEIR MARRIED LIFE, Hadley would recall in her seventies, she only twice saw Hemingway on his knees in a house of worship. The two occasions were her wedding day and the afternoon of March 10, 1924, when they had John Hadley Nicanor christened in St. Luke's Episcopal Chapel in the rue de la Grande Chaumière. Bumby, as he now was known to his parents, wore the lace-trimmed dress and booties that Grace had bought for him, and Gertrude Stein and Chink Dorman-Smith were on hand to assure the minister that as the child's godparents they would oversee his religious upbringing—even though one of them was a Jew and the other a Catholic, as Hemingway observed with a big grin. After the ceremony, Hadley served sugared almonds and the proud father broke out bottles of champagne at a small party in their apartment.

Hadley continued to nurse her infant son until the end of May, when William Carlos Williams, a physician as well as a poet, advised her during a social call that her milk supply must have dwindled because Bumby was underweight. (Dr. Williams also retracted the baby's foreskin to see if it was too tight, at which point Bumby "naturally cried," Williams noted, "much to his parents' chagrin.") Thereafter, the preparation of formula, the boiling of rubber nipples, and the filling of bottles became a way of life at 113 rue Notre-Dame-des-Champs. When the spirit moved him, Hemingway performed these duties himself, and it was not unheard of for him to change the baby's diaper or give him his bath. Sylvia Beach, who dropped by one morning, expressed amazement at his deft handling of his son. "Hemingway *père* was justly proud, and asked me if I didn't think he had a future as a nursemaid." He also brought Bumby with him on occasion to Shakespeare and Company. "Holding his son carefully, though sometimes upside down," Sylvia remembered, Hemingway would stand in the middle of the shop reading the latest periodicals.

The task of caring for Bumby, however, mainly fell to his mother. So that his boisterous cries for attention wouldn't disrupt his father's concentration on his writing, Hadley took him out in his carriage in nice weather for hours at a stretch, and it was usually she who fed him, changed him, put him down for his nap. Going to bed early was an idea that powerfully appealed to her on days when Bumby had been especially demanding, but she resolutely ignored her fatigue so as to provide Hemingway with the companionship he absolutely had to have, no matter whether he intended to stay at home and read a book or go out to a party or take in the bike races at the Vélodrome d'Hiver. "We have more fun together all the time," Hemingway made a point of writing to Howie Jenkins, the friend who had warned him against getting hitched to Hadley. "She is keeping her piano up and runs the house and the baby damned smooth and is always ready to go out and eat oysters at the café and drink a bottle of Pouilly before supper. We have good whiskey in the home and a swell lot of books, open fire places and it's comfortable, and a guy can read or lie around and go out when he feels like it." That she could do much more than she imagined she could was Hemingway's constant message of encouragement to Hadley, as it would be to all his wives. "Hem was hard on his women," Dos Passos would ruminatively observe in his autobiography. "Yet I'm convinced that he was more of a builderupper than a breakerdowner. He left them more able to cope with life than he found them." But messages of encouragement were of little avail in the upper stands of the Vel d'Hiv at three o'clock in the morning. Dos Passos was able to "sneak out and make for my lodgings," when he had had his fill of the racing, but "Hem used to make poor Hadley sit there all night." When she got to the point where she couldn't keep her eyes open a minute longer, she would curl up on a bench and go to sleep, while her indefatigable husband went on cheering his favorite riders with undiminished enthusiasm. Despite her all-out efforts to be a constantly available playmate as well as the efficient manager of a household and a loving mother, Hadley simply could not maintain the pace of the considerably younger man she had married.

Harold Loeb's companion, Kitty Cannell, an erstwhile ballerina with golden hair and outspoken opinions, was outraged by Hemingway's apparent belief that he had the right to shape his wife's whole existence to his. At the Nègre de Toulouse restaurant in the Boulevard Raspail where Harold and Kitty sometimes had dinner with the Hemingways, Kitty couldn't help noticing that Hadley never looked as attractive as she might have. In an effort to persuade her to take better care of herself, Kitty took her out shopping and later made her a present of some of her jewelry. When Hemingway saw the jewelry he recognized its tacit rebuke of his lack of concern for Hadley's womanly tastes and was filled with resentment, which in turn filled Kitty with satisfaction for having set "a bad example to a submissive wife." How to make Kitty rue her minor success in sowing marital discord in his house was a question that Hemingway at once began to ask himself.

The answer came in a caricature of her as Frances Clyne, the very tall girl in *The Sun Also Rises* who speaks "in a sort of imitation joyful manner" but is frantically unhappy because her lover is leaving her. In addition to that cruelty, Kitty later told an interviewer, Hemingway had explicitly assured her while writing the novel that although the book would tear that "bastard" Loeb apart, he had left her out of it altogether. "To see whether I was buying [this assurance]," she said, "he looked at me with what I called his 'shining morning face'—rosy cheeks with white teeth and the sudden marvelous smile of a good little eight year old boy. It made you feel like giving him an apple—or maybe your heart."

2

WHAT Kitty actually gave him was a kitten. The presentation occurred shortly after her troublemaking gift of jewelry to Hadley and was partially intended as a peace offering. The principal motive for her generosity, however, was that the kitten was rapidly destroying the array of Sèvres jars on the mantelpiece in her living room by nosing them over the edge. In offering such a "wonderfully bad" creature to a man who had already been offended by her, Kitty did not neglect to warn him about its destructive propensities. But because Hemingway and Hadley were both very fond of cats (and owned nothing breakable of any value), he accepted Kitty's gift without a moment's hesitation.

After a few weeks of observing Mr. Feather Puss—as he named the kitten—happily playing in their apartment with Feather Cat—as he still called Hadley from time to time—Hemingway wrote a story about a woman who feels a kinship with a cat. First conceived in

Rapallo over a year earlier, when the disagreement between him and Hadley about her pregnancy had been uppermost in his mind, "Cat in the Rain" as finally written concentrated on the more recent disharmonies in the Hemingway household stirred up by Kitty Cannell, and it did so from a point of view that might be considered astounding, were it not for "Up in Michigan" and "Out of Season." The author of those stories had already manifested an ability to look critically at the insensitive ways in which men handled women, and in "Cat in the Rain" he manifested it again. Fictionally he was able to acknowledge, as he could not in reality, that in expecting Hadley to live her life as though she were merely a duplicate of himself he was doing violence to her nature, even as his mother had interfered with his.

A young American woman is standing, as the story begins, at the front window of her bedroom in an Italian seaside resort hotel, gazing out at the steadily falling rain. Underneath a dripping green table she sees a cat trying to keep from getting wet. Impulsively announcing to her husband, George, who is lying on their bed reading, that "I'm going down and get that kitty," she leaves the room. Yet even with the help of a maid she cannot find the cat, and her failure to do so serves to darken her already discouraged mood. The woman is unhappy because nothing in her life is sufficiently feminine to suit her, as she makes explicit when she picks up a mirror from her dressing table and studies her profile and the back of her head and neck. The unhappiness she expresses about her hair is particularly striking.

> "Don't you think it would be a good idea if I let my hair grow out?" she asked, looking at her profile again.
> George looked up and saw the back of her neck, clipped close like a boy's.
> "I like it the way it is."
> "I get so tired of it," she said. "I get so tired of looking like a boy."
> George shifted his position in the bed. He hadn't looked away from her since she started to speak.
> "You look pretty darn nice," he said.
> She laid the mirror down on the dresser and went over to the window and looked out. It was dark.
> "I want to pull my hair back tight and smooth and make a big knot at the back that I can feel," she said. "I want to have a kitty to sit on my lap and purr when I stroke her."
> "Yeah?" George said from the bed.
> "And I want to eat at a table with my own silver and I want candles.

And I want it to be spring and I want to brush my hair out in front
of a mirror and I want a kitty and I want some new clothes."

"Oh, shut up and get something to read," George said. He was
reading again.

His wife was looking out of the window. It was quite dark now
and still raining in the palm trees.

"Anyway, I want a cat," she said. "I want a cat. I want a cat now.
If I can't have long hair or any fun, I can have a cat."

A moment later, there is a knock at the door. The maid is standing
in the hallway, holding a big tortoiseshell cat. The hotelkeeper has
told her to bring it to the American signora.

It is obvious whom the wife is speaking for when she talks of
being tired of looking like a boy. But the tone of bitter despair in
which she reveals that she thinks of a cat as a consolation prize for
the total lack of fun in her life is not at all Hadleyesque. At that
point, the wife is expressing the depressed feelings of the author of
the story—as Kitty Cannell unwittingly discovered a few days after
she gave the kitten to Hemingway. She ran into him in a café, she
later told an interviewer, sitting by himself and feeling, in his words,
"terribly low." "I have just one consolation in my life," he glumly
told her. Since Kitty expected him to make mention either of his
wife or his infant son, she was startled to hear him say, "My kitty."
At the close of the tale, Hemingway went beyond sympathy with a
restless wife and voiced his own unhappiness through a female
mask.

3

NEAR the end of 1924, much to his surprise, he received a letter from
Bill Smith. For years, Bill had been full of anger at him for insulting
his brother Y. K. But it had finally subsided and now he was ready
to resume his friendship with Hemingway. In his generously long
reply, Hemingway began with an apology for making "an offensive
bludy ass of myself with Y. K." Since he and Bill had last been in
touch, he went on to say, he had been doing a lot of writing, and of
all the work he had thus far produced "almost everything worth a
damn" had been about Michigan. The country that he and Bill had
known in their boyhoods was on his mind all the time, he averred,
"the swell times we used to have with Auntie [Mrs. Charles] at the
farm, the first swell trips out to the Black and the Sturgeon and the
wonderful times we had with the men and the storms in the fall and
potato digging and the whole damn thing." As if anxious not to

give Bill the idea that fond recollections of the past were an indication of present misery, he then launched into a glowing account of his marriage. He and Hadley "have had and have a damn good time," he emphasized. "We pastime the fights and the concerts, bull fights and the finnies. She fishes not with the usual feminine simulation of interest but like one of the men, she's as intelligent about fights as she is about music, she drinks with a male without remorse, and turned out Bumby the boy spring off who is built like [Luis] Firpo, sleeps all night and is cheerful as a pup. . . . Hash [Hadley] hasn't lost any looks and gets better all the time. She runs the house like a Rolls Royce."

In short, the endless honeymoon he and Hadley had enjoyed during their first two years in Europe had resumed without a hitch. But the truth of the matter was very different. The baby's presence had profoundly altered their lives, as he had feared it would. "It is just about morning," Hemingway grumpily informed Robert McAlmon in a letter written in the predawn darkness on November 15. "Bumby had a night when he didn't sleep and Hadley and I've been up with him alternately and together. . . . Bumby is getting some new molars through I think." Another annoyance was that whenever Hemingway felt like going out for the evening he and Hadley first of all had to arrange with Madame Chautard, the wife of their landlord, the sawmill proprietor, to look in on Bumby every hour or so. And because Hemingway adamantly refused to take an infant along with them on trips, he and Hadley had to shell out extra money to Marie-Cocotte to take care of their son in their absence.

Such interferences with his freedom certainly contributed to the melancholia that Kitty Cannell glimpsed in the café that day. A more basic problem was depressing his spirits, however. For reasons he would never fathom, he was falling out of love. Hadley hadn't lost any looks, he insisted; indeed, she was getting better all the time, he claimed. But in two stories about Michigan, both written well before his glowing letter to Bill Smith, he confessed, through Nick Adams, that actually he was looking for a way out of their relationship.

Although Nick Adams's girlfriend in "The End of Something" is named Marjorie, this is no warrant for the widespread assumption that she was modeled on the author's redheaded flame from Petoskey, Marjorie Bump. That Marjorie loves to fish, that she and Nick have been good buddies as well as sweethearts, and that she is desperately in love with him, are characteristics which identify her as a younger incarnation of Hadley. As the author of the story imagined Nick and Marjorie building a fire on a sandy point and watching it get dark, he was rehearsing a scene that he would eventually stage in his own life. "There's going to be a moon tonight," Nick says. "I know it," Marjorie replies. Without warning, Nick turns on her. "You know everything," he says. "I've taught you everything," he goes on, "and now it isn't fun any more." Marjorie asks, "Isn't love any fun?" "No," says Nick, his head in his hands. The laconic answer suggests how utterly empty he feels. And without further protest, Marjorie rows away into the night. The story ends with the sudden appearance of Nick's friend Bill, who asks him, "Did she go all right?" making it clear that the breakup has been coldbloodedly planned. Thus "The End of Something" was a veiled expression of Hemingway's feelings about his marriage—with a dash of wish fulfillment thrown in. For in real life the rejected woman would not depart without setting a difficult condition.

That Hemingway's feelings about Hadley and their life together were ambiguous is strongly conveyed in the followup story, "The Three-Day Blow." "You were very wise, Wemedge," Bill says to Nick, after the two friends have been guzzling whiskey for a while and the first storm of the autumn continues to rage around the cottage in which they have taken refuge. "What do you mean?" asks Nick. "To bust off that Marge business," Bill explains. "If you hadn't by now you'd be back home working trying to get enough money to get married." Nick says nothing, so Bill resumes his drunken attempt to comfort him. "Once a man's married he's absolutely bitched. . . . He hasn't got anything more. Nothing. Not a damn thing. He's done for." Once again, Nick says nothing. His feelings of emptiness have reduced him from laconicisms to silence. Only in his thoughts can he acknowledge the cost of what he has done.

> The big thing was that Marjorie was gone and that probably he would never see her again. He had talked to her about how they would go to Italy together and the fun they would have. Places they would be together. It was all gone now.

4

WHEN Bill Bird informed him that six copies of *in our time* had been returned to the Three Mountains Press by his parents, Hemingway retaliated by not sending them a copy of the issue of the *transatlantic review* in which "Indian Camp" appeared. He was too eager, though, to make them aware of his work not to send them a copy of the issue containing "The Doctor and the Doctor's Wife." That the story would win their praise was his sincerest hope. Yet he also wanted to wound them with it, for he was still smarting from their rejection of his earlier work.

Dr. Hemingway, it turned out, simply thought of "The Doctor and the Doctor's Wife" as a fanciful story decked out with recognizable details. "I have read your article on 'The Doctor and the Doctor's Wife' in the Dec. no. of Transatlantic Review," he wrote his son. "I know your memory is *very* good for details and I surely saw that old log on the beach as I read your article—I got out the Old Bear Lake [Walloon Lake] book and showed Carol & Leicester the photos of Nic [Nick] Boulton and Billy Tabeshaw on the beach sawing the big old *beech* log. That was when you were 12 yrs old. . . . Wish, dear boy, you would send me some of your work often." Ernest promptly replied. "Thanks for your fine letter," he began. "I'm so glad you liked the Doctor story. . . . I've written a number of stories about the Michigan country—the country is always true—what happens in the stories is fiction." But while the events in the story were made up they nevertheless placed an all too recognizable couple in a terribly unflattering light, especially the doctor's wife.

Dick Boulton—as Hemingway calls Nick Boulton in the story—is an oafish half-breed who lives in the Indian camp in the woods. At Dr. Adams's request, Dick and two helpers have come to the beach below the Adamses' cottage to cut up some logs which have drifted ashore after becoming separated from one of the big log booms that the steamer *Magic* had been towing down the lake to a sawmill. Unlike the actual Boulton, his fictional counterpart does not carry out his assignment. Instead, he insults his employer, accusing him of having stolen the logs and impudently referring to him as "Doc." The infuriated Dr. Adams tells the half-breed that "If you call me Doc once again, I'll knock your eye teeth down your throat," but Boulton coolly replies, "Oh, no, you won't, Doc." At which point Dr. Adams stalks away toward the cottage and the Indians depart.

Later, Mrs. Adams calls to her husband and asks if anything is the matter. She is lying down in her bedroom with the blinds drawn. On the table beside her bed are "her Bible, her copy of *Science and Health* and her *Quarterly*." (Just as Hadley's mother had been a devotee of various mental faiths, so Mrs. Adams is apparently a Christian Scientist.) While he is explaining to his wife that Dick Boulton had picked a quarrel with him, probably because "Dick owes me a lot of money for pulling his squaw through pneumonia," Dr.

Adams tries to get a grip on himself by cleaning a shotgun. After ejecting the magazine full of heavy yellow shells onto the bed in his bedroom, he wipes the gun with a rag and pushes the shells back in again. His task completed, he sits silently with the gun on his knees, for "he was very fond of it." Defending Boulton, Mrs. Adams says, "Dear, I don't think, I really don't think that any one would really do a thing like that." When she repeats this piety, Dr. Adams abruptly stands up, puts the shotgun in the corner behind his dresser and announces that he is going for a walk. Mrs. Adams asks him to tell young Nick that his mother wants to see him. As the doctor leaves the house, he allows the screen door to slam. All of his impotent rage is summed up in that gesture; nevertheless, he apologizes for it. "Sorry," he says outside his wife's window with the blinds drawn. "It's all right, dear," she says. Dr. Adams finds Nick sitting in the woods with his back against a tree, reading. He tells his son that his mother wants him. "I want to go with you," Nick says. "All right. Come on then," his father says. "I know where there's black squirrels, Daddy," Nick says. "All right," says his father. "Let's go there."

Huck Finn sliding into the river instead of returning to Miss Watson's reproofs; Rip Van Winkle taking off into the woods to escape his termagant wife: the fantasy of fleeing from female authority is a familiar one in American literature. "The Doctor and the Doctor's Wife," however, has a special quality, as Scott Fitzgerald would point out in an admiring review of Hemingway's work in the May 1926 issue of *Bookman*. Fitzgerald had himself grown up in the shadow of a father who was haunted by a sense of personal inadequacy, so he was speaking from the heart when he said that "the quality of humiliation in the story is so intense that it immediately calls up every such incident in the reader's past. Without the aid of a comment or a pointing finger one knows exactly the sharp emotions of young Nick who watches the scene." Less than three years after the appearance of Fitzgerald's review, Dr. Hemingway would take himself beyond the reach of his wife's voice forever by putting a bullet in his brain in his bedroom back in Oak Park. That is how Hemingway, at any rate, would come to view the meaning of the choice his father made. Dr. and Mrs. Adams are Dr. and Mrs. Hemingway, and the depiction of Dr. Adams sitting silently in his bedroom in Michigan with a shotgun on his knee while his wife unsparingly rebukes him for his lack of Christian charity chillingly foretells the tragedy that would soon overtake the house of Hemingway.

5

THE devastating sketch of the doctor's wife was not the only example of how thoughts of Grace affected Hemingway's work during
1924. Although in "Big Two-Hearted River" he made no specific
mention of the fisherman's mother, the story nevertheless took off
from recollections of the summer of 1919 when he had fled from
Windemere to the banks of the Big Fox and the Little Fox. And in
"Soldier's Home" he dreamed up a face-to-face conflict between
mother and son, on a battlefield that was normally off limits to his
fictive imagination. In the story, Oak Park is called a "home town
in Oklahoma."

The emotional complexity of "Soldier's Home" begins with the
hero's name, Harold Krebs, for Hemingway borrowed the unusual
second half of it from his friend Krebs Friend, who had married a
woman fully old enough to be his mother. Home from the war,
young Krebs sleeps late in the morning, walks down to the library
to get a book, practices his clarinet and watches the girls go by. Yet
Krebs doesn't feel the need of a girl. Getting to know one isn't worth
the trouble, he tells himself. He would rather read a history of the
war, or talk to "his best sister," Helen, who has a crush on him.

> "We're playing indoor over at the school this afternoon," [Helen]
> said. "I'm going to pitch."
> "Good," said Krebs. "How's the old wing?"
> "I can pitch better than lots of the boys. I tell them all you taught
> me. The other girls aren't much good."
> "Yeah?" said Krebs.
> "I tell them all you're my beau. Aren't you my beau, Hare?"
> "You bet."
> "Couldn't your brother really be your beau just because he's your
> brother?"
> "I don't know."
> "Sure you know. Couldn't you be my beau, Hare, if I was old
> enough and if you wanted to?"
> "Sure. You're my girl now."

A significant weakness in the story is that its most memorable
character, Mrs. Krebs, is not linked in any way to this quasi-
incestuous byplay going on in her household between two of her
children. The intense if not unnatural fondness for one another of
Ernest and Ursula Hemingway had not developed in a vacuum; yet
for all of the determination to achieve self-understanding that Hem-

ingway seems to have brought to the composition of "Soldier's Home," he was only able to dramatize the intimacy between Krebs and his kid sister, not account for it.

Where the story triumphs is in its portrayal of Mrs. Krebs's tyranny. From the doorway of the kitchen she keeps an eye on her son while he eats a bowl of cereal, and when he folds open the morning paper—it is the Kansas City *Star*—and props it against the water pitcher, she admonishes him for mussing it up. He then addresses himself to two fried eggs with bacon and a stack of buckwheat cakes, but she spoils his enjoyment by asking whether he doesn't think it is time he decided what he is going to do for a living.

> "I hadn't thought about it," Krebs said.
> "God has some work for every one to do," his mother said. "There can be no idle hands in His Kingdom."
> "I'm not in His Kingdom," Krebs said.
> "We are all of us in His Kingdom."

The excruciatingly painful finale of this scene commences with a question by Mrs. Krebs. "Don't you love your mother, dear boy?" Krebs's blunt answer is, "No," and as his mother starts to cry he blurts out a more sweeping confession. "I don't love anybody." In that terrible admission, Hemingway for the first time showed a glimmering of understanding that his eternally tense involvement with Grace was somehow disabling his entire emotional life. Yet while Krebs knows how much is at stake for him in his being able to break free of his mother, he still feels the orbital pull of her personality. "I didn't mean it," he hastens to tell her as he sees her tears. "I didn't mean I didn't love you," he adds, and in a gesture that for Hemingway was full of reverberations, he kisses her hair. "I'm your mother," she says. "I held you next to my heart when you were a tiny baby." Her words cause Krebs to feel "sick and vaguely nauseated." They both kneel down beside the dining-room table—but when she asks him to pray, he says he can't. Would he like her to pray for him, she asks, and he says yes. With the conclusion of her prayer, he kisses her again.

On leaving the house a few moments later, he tells himself that what happened in the dining room hasn't really touched him, that he had simply felt sorry for his mother. After enduring maybe one more scene with her, he thinks, he will get a job in Kansas City and then his mother will "feel all right about it." Buoyed up by the prospect of independence, Krebs is full of hopeful thoughts as the story ends. "He wanted his life to go smoothly. It had just gotten

going that way. . . . He would go over to the schoolyard and watch
Helen play indoor baseball.''

"Soldier's Home" is the story of a young man's struggle to separate from home, and Hemingway packed it with a lifetime of revulsion and outrage. Nevertheless, the utterly unrelenting, utterly
unqualified characterization of Mrs. Krebs as a monster revealed that
the author was in fact still in thrall to her flesh-and-blood counterpart. Only a man who was truly free could have seen that she had
done her best to be a good mother, that she had not meant to harm
her son and that she, too, had been tossed about by psychological
impulses she did not understand.

6

"I'VE never seen a man," Archibald MacLeish would say of the
Hemingway he knew in the midtwenties, "go through the floor of
despair as he did." Yet when he wasn't in despair, the poet remarked
on another occasion, no one had a keener sense of life's brimming
possibilities.

Hemingway's happiest time in 1924 came just after he had finished
a big stint of work for the *transatlantic review* and he and Hadley took
off for Spain. In Madrid, their first stop, they rented a room in the
boardinghouse frequented by bullfighters where he and McAlmon
had stayed. At Aranjuez, twenty miles south of the capital, they
witnessed a spectacular corrida in which the supple Nicanor Villalta
dispatched a total of six bulls in brilliant fashion. From there they
journeyed north to Pamplona for the fiesta of San Fermín, and this
time they had no trouble about their hotel reservations.

"The godamdest wild time and fun you ever saw," Hemingway
wrote Howie Jenkins. "Everybody in the town lit for a week, bulls
racing loose through the streets every morning, dancing and fire
works all night and . . . us guys practically the guests of the city."
The friends he had assembled around him to heighten his fun included Chink Dorman-Smith, Bob McAlmon, Don Stewart, John
Dos Passos, Bill and Sally Bird, and young George O'Neil. On her
first visit to the arena, Sally Bird was horrified by the suffering of
the bulls and the horses and never went back. Hadley, the eternal
good sport, was not only on hand every afternoon but got up in the
morning after very little sleep to watch her husband in action in the
free-for-alls, in which amateurs were permitted to act out moments
of truth with three or four small bulls whose horns were padded so
as to prevent serious injury. On entering the ring—as he did every
morning for five straight days—Hemingway would entice a bull to

charge by waving a red cape and shouting "*Huh, toro, toro!*" As the animal was about to slam into him, Hemingway would grab his horns, twist his neck and wrestle him to the ground.

Although he kept challenging Don Stewart to join the fray, Yale's gift to American humor did not feel that the bulls were particularly small. Every morning, therefore, he wandered miserably around the edge of the arena, hoping that Hemingway would become so caught up in his own exhibitions of courage that he would forget about his indecisive friend. Unfortunately for Stewart, events ultimately made his decision for him. A bull lowered his head and charged a young Pamplonian who was taunting him. At the last moment, the youth leaped over the barrier at the foot of the stands to what he thought was safety, only to have the bull come leaping after him. The youth and various spectators, including Dos Passos, hastily vacated the premises by scrambling upwards over several rows of seats, but Stewart for some reason jumped down into the arena. Two youths who seemed anxious to show him that they bore no ill will toward America for winning the Spanish-American War thrust a cape into his hand, led him across the sand and introduced him to another bull. As hundreds of spectators gave him their full attention, Stewart tried to fool the charging animal with a graceful swirl of his cape. Alas, "the bull did not swerve as I had expected," Stewart would recall in his autobiography, *By a Stroke of Luck!* "I was hit full force," he regretted to say.

> My glasses flew in one direction, the cape in another, and I was tossed in the air amid a great gleeful shout from the spectators. When I hit the ground, however, an amazing thing happened. I lost my fear completely. And not only that—I got mad. I grabbed the cape and started to chase my enemy. When I got to him I held the cape once more in front of me, yelling "Come on, you stupid son of a bitch!" The bull . . . again tossed me triumphantly in the air and galloped away. . . . Ernest clapped me on the back and I felt as though I had scored a winning touchdown. After we left the arena I discovered that a couple of my ribs had been fractured, but that couldn't spoil the last frenzied night of drinking and dancing. It had been a memorable week, a male festival, a glorified college reunion.

Other accounts of Stewart's brief career as a bullfighter substantially confirm his own. With one exception. On July 29, the Chicago *Tribune* ran as a front-page headline BULL GORES 2 YANKS ACTING AS TOREADORS. Ernest Hemingway, the accompanying story breathlessly related, had recently had a brush with death in Pamplona,

Spain. A bull had gored him as he was rescuing his friend Donald
Ogden Stewart from a mauling on the floor of the arena. The reporter who filed this story made it sound as if he had actually witnessed Hemingway's heroism, but chances are he was in another
country at the time. For the dateline on the story suggests that upon
his return from Spain Hemingway had told the story to someone he
knew in the Paris office of the *Tribune*. In any event, the story
marked the take-off point of the general public's awareness of Hemingway the man. Five years earlier, of course, the New York *Sun*
had proclaimed that Lieutenant Hemingway had taken more punishment than any other man who had fought the Central Powers, a
judgment that the Chicago *American* had echoed by saying that Lieutenant Hemingway was "the worst shot-up man in the U. S."
Thereafter as a reporter Hemingway had included many an adver-
tisement for himself in his stories for the Toronto *Star Weekly*. But
it was not until the appearance of the *Tribune* piece that the press
began to puff him up with any degree of regularity.

The mileage he got out of the Pamplona story alone was quite
impressive. In 1926, a literary columnist in the New York *Herald
Tribune* took Don Stewart's glorious injuries away from him and
gave them to Hemingway by asserting that the latter had once suffered three broken ribs from "an annoyed toro." In 1927, Burton
Rascoe passed along to the readers of the magazine *Arts and Decoration* an anecdote that he had heard from Ford Madox Ford about
Hemingway's dramatic rescue of John Dos Passos from a goring in
Pamplona. Just as the bull that had tossed him was about to impale
the prostrate Dos Passos with its spearlike horns—Ford had apparently failed to mention to Rascoe that in free-for-alls the horns were
padded—Hemingway had grabbed the animal by the neck and
dragged him away. Also in 1927, *Time* magazine's review of *Men
Without Women* stated that "Author Hemingway was a football star
and boxer at school. In the War he was severely wounded serving
with the Italian Arditi, of whom he was almost the youngest member. Since the Armistice he has lived . . . in Paris. Every spring he
goes down to Pamplona to watch the bullfights; on an occasion
when he entered the arena himself, several of his ribs got broken by
a bull." In 1928 a writer in *Bookman* declared that Hemingway was
not only "a semiprofessional prizefighter" and "an expert at skiing,"
but "an amateur toreador."

As a result of such reports Hemingway came to be regarded by
the public as a sports hero as well as a war hero, a perception that
enormously enhanced his glamour, for in the emerging mass culture
of the twenties superlatively talented athletes loomed very large,

especially in the United States. Babe Ruth, Red Grange, Bobby Jones, Bill Tilden, Jack Dempsey—to tens of millions of Americans these were household names. Blessed, in Archibald MacLeish's words, with a "tremendous physical presence," Hemingway certainly looked as though he, too, was a star athlete, and his circumstantial accounts of his prowess reinforced that impression. He had mixed it up in the boxing ring with the likes of Sam Langford and Harry Greb; he had been the mainstay of the line on a redoubtable varsity football team at Oak Park High; as a skier he was virtually a professional; and in the arena at Pamplona he had had the courage and strength to grapple with a dangerous bull that was about to gore Don Stewart, or was it John Dos Passos. All of these balloons were filled with hot air, yet no one bothered to prick any of them. In the sports-crazy twenties, Hemingway found that he could count on the press to repeat and indeed to enlarge upon his every claim to athletic fame.

His confidence that he could manipulate the engines of mass publicity without any cost to himself in any way was sublime. This confidence, alas, was hubris. His work would soon become subject to interpretations that he didn't care for. In his daily life he would feel impelled to live up to his public image in order to sustain its credibility. And from the early thirties onward the pitiless glare of the spotlight and the endless clamor of the crowd would interfere with the free working of his creative imagination.

CHAPTER TWELVE

Harold and Horace, Scott and Zelda

AT THE CLOSE OF THE FIESTA IN PAMPLONA, the Hemingways took a bus filled with Basque peasants to Burguete, high in the Pyrenees near the ancient monastery of Roncevalles. From there they hiked through virgin forests of enormous beeches to the ice-cold headwaters of the Irati River. It was "the wildest damn country" Hemingway had ever seen. "Even the mules pass out on the trail," he later told Howie Jenkins. Robert McAlmon and the Birds trudged along with them, and a day or so after making camp they were joined by Dos Passos, Chink Dorman-Smith, and George O'Neil. During their first go at fishing, Hadley outdid all the men by catching six trout in less than half an hour out of a pool beneath a waterfall. (In *The Sun Also Rises,* her achievement would be given to Jake Barnes.)

Dos Passos, McAlmon, Dorman-Smith, and George O'Neil had planned in addition a two-week walking trip to Andorra. When they at last set out, Hemingway surprised everyone including Hadley by accompanying them. At nightfall, however, he reappeared in camp, much to Hadley's relief. It was his duty, he explained, to stick by his wife. He may have been sincere in what he said, although Dos Passos's biographer, Virginia Spencer Carr, implies that he may have been motivated by more selfish considerations. "He was never the hiker Dos Passos was." For Dos Passos's father, John R. Dos Passos, Sr., a dynamic, hugely successful, highly sexed corporation lawyer, had kept his bantam-rooster body in trim by taking long walks at a punishingly fast pace. As a boy, his son had been an unathletic string bean, but a bastard's dream of legitimating himself in the eyes of his father had inspired him to emulate the senior Dos Passos's feats as a walker. If Hemingway had accompanied Dos Passos into the higher reaches of the Pyrenees, he might have been forced to call it quits before the hike was over—as McAlmon was compelled to do after six blistering days. Returning to Hadley ruled out the danger of being humiliated by a literary rival.

2

THUS far, there was very little published proof that he really was a writer. On the other hand, he had worked extremely hard in 1924 and had built up a backlog by September of nine new stories: "Indian Camp," "Big Two-Hearted River," "The Doctor and the Doctor's Wife," "The End of Something," "The Three-Day Blow," "Soldier's Home," "Mr. and Mrs. Elliot," "Cat in the Rain," and "Cross-Country Snow." By combining them with the three stories the Contact Press had published, "Up in Michigan," "Out of Season," and "My Old Man," and then weaving through this assemblage the sketches from Bill Bird's edition of *in our time,* he at last had a manuscript in hand that was strong enough, he believed, to capture the interest of a publisher in the United States.

The stories were intensely personal and imbued with emotional violence; the sketches focused on incidents, culled from two continents, of physical violence; taken together, they constituted an existential reflection on modern life. As Hemingway explained to Edmund Wilson in October, he wanted "to give the picture of the whole between examining it in detail. Like looking with your eyes at something, say a passing coast line, and then looking at it with 15X binoculars. Or rather, maybe, looking at it and then going in and living in it—and then coming out and looking at it again." To make the alternation work out exactly, he treated the sketch about the wounded American in northern Italy who falls in love with a fickle nurse and the sketch about the Hungarian revolutionist as though they were stories.

The collection was superb, its arrangement artful. Nevertheless, Hemingway encountered almost as much difficulty in persuading an American publisher to accept *In Our Time*—as he had decided to call his book—as he had in interesting American magazines in its component parts. Toward the end of September, he sent a copy to Don Stewart at the Yale Club in New York, because Stewart had said he wanted to help him. The humorist's first thought was to give the manuscript to his own publisher, George Doran. After holding on to it for three months, Doran turned it down, however, with mumbo-jumbo regrets. As the frustrated Hemingway remarked to Harold Loeb in a profane and slightly incoherent letter on January 5, 1925,

> Mr. Doran felt they couldn't go all the way with me on the matter of sex in a book of Short Stories as Mr. Doran didn't like to "center the shocks in a series of shocks" or some such shit altho he would go all the way with me in a novel and should they write to me suggesting this and then maybe leave the publishing of the short stories as a 2nd volume in abeyance or something like that but that they were all agreed on the power of my stuff and what a great book it was only they didn't want to publish it. Don said it was all horse cock except they didn't want to lead off with a book of short stories no matter whether good or not. So he has given the book to Menken [H. L. Mencken]—that shit—to recommend to [Alfred] Knopf.

Mencken had doughtily defended the sexual frankness of Theodore Dreiser's fiction, Stewart reasoned, and therefore ought to be sympathetic with Hemingway's. Although he fervently hoped that Stewart was right about this, Hemingway was all but convinced from the beginning that he wasn't. Mencken had never had anything but jeering comments to make about American expatriates in Paris, and anyway the Baltimorean was no longer interested in literature. *The American Mercury,* which he and George Jean Nathan had started in 1924 with the backing of Alfred Knopf, was primarily intended to further Mencken's career as a social critic. When Mencken eventually bore out Hemingway's pessimism by not even troubling to tell Knopf about *In Our Time,* the angered author made a mental note of it. And he made a second mental note about Mencken when he subsequently came across his brief review of *in our time:* "The sort of brave, bold stuff that all atheistic young newspaper reporters write. Jesus Christ in lower case. A hanging, a carnal love, and two disembowelings. Here it is set forth solemnly on Rives handmade paper, in an edition limited to 170 copies, and with the imprimatur of Ezra Pound." Somehow, Hemingway vowed, he would make Mencken regret his indifference to him.

In the meantime, Harold Loeb was trying as hard as Don Stewart to be of assistance to Hemingway. Upon being told in the early fall of 1924 that his tennis pal had a manuscript he wanted to market, Loeb thought it would be wonderful if the Boni and Liveright firm, which had recently agreed to publish his first novel, *Doodab,* were to bring out *In Our Time* as well. At a meeting with Leon Fleischman, the firm's European agent, who had just returned to Paris with a contract for Loeb to sign, Loeb asked if he could bring Hemingway along with him some evening to Fleischman's luxurious flat off the Champs-Elysées. Perhaps it was the costliness of Fleischman's velvet smoking jacket or his air of self-satisfaction that set him off, but in any case Hemingway's mood darkened as soon as the agent greeted them. While Loeb valiantly tried to keep a conversation going, Hemingway sat brooding over a Scotch and soda. Fleischman finally turned to him and said that he had heard good things about his stories and would like to read them; if his reaction was favorable, he would send the manuscript to Horace Liveright in New York. Hemingway detected patronization in these remarks. As he and Loeb walked down the stairs into the street a short while later, he could contain himself no longer. Fleischman was a low-down kike, he burst out, ignoring the fact—or was he, on the contrary, remembering it?—that Loeb was Jewish, too.

As soon as he calmed down, his ambition reasserted itself and he duly sent the agent a copy of his manuscript—only to discover that Fleischman was in no more of a hurry than George Doran to make up his mind. As a result, a second wave of anger surged through him, weighted down by depression, and these feelings were further deepened by what he regarded as the stupidity of the reviews that his first two books were receiving. In a bitter moment in Toronto, he had brought up the subject of suicide in a letter to Gertrude Stein and Alice Toklas. Now he brought it up again in a letter to Ezra Pound via an allusion to the recent tragic death of U.S. Senator Frank Brandegee of Connecticut—but he buried his implicit cry for help beneath a boast that his own view of life was getting brighter. "Did you see that when Sen. Brandegee committed suicide he was found with the gas tube *In His Mouth?* I still claim that anybody that wants to can do it. Things are looking better and I look forward to not giving a demonstration of my theory for some time."

As a means of managing his tensions, he plunged into writing a story which symbolically dealt with their causes, as he understood them. Toward the end of November, after weeks of work, he finally finished "The Undefeated." Besides taking aim at critics like Burton Rascoe, who had condescendingly announced that *Three Stories & Ten Poems* was full of echoes of Ring Lardner and Sherwood Anderson, Hemingway may also have been trying to work off a residue of irritation with Edmund Wilson.

In some respects, Wilson's review of his first two books in *The Dial* had been as complimentary as any author could have wished.

About *in our time* Wilson had said, "I am inclined to think that [this] little book has more artistic dignity than anything else about the period of the war that has as yet been written by an American." He had also called Hemingway's talent "strikingly original" and had said of his prose that it was of "the first distinction." For these judgments Hemingway was grateful. In the letter he wrote to Wilson in October, he told him that he thought his review was "cool and clear minded and decent and impersonal and sympathetic. . . . You are the only man writing criticism who or whom I can read when the book being criticized is one I've read or know something about." On the other hand, Wilson had said of "Up in Michigan" that it had failed when it ought to have been a masterpiece, because it had the "curious defect of dealing with rude and primitive people yet leaving them rather shadowy." It would have been out of character for the thin-skinned Hemingway not to have taken umbrage at this comment, and he must also have bridled at Wilson's insistence that he and Sherwood Anderson had both been taught by Gertrude Stein. Mr. Hemingway, Wilson asserted,

> must be counted as the only American writer but one—Mr. Sherwood Anderson—who has felt the genius of Gertrude Stein's *Three Lives* and has evidently been influenced by it. Indeed, Miss Stein, Mr. Anderson and Mr. Hemingway may now be said to form a school by themselves. The characteristic of this school is a naiveté of language, often passing into the colloquialism of the character dealt with, which serves actually to convey profound emotions and complex states of mind. It is a distinctively American development in prose—as opposed to more or less successful American achievements in the traditional style of English prose—which has artistically justified itself at its best as a limpid shaft into deep waters.

The praise was glowing, but it had not been lavished upon Hemingway exclusively.

Underlying "The Undefeated" was Hemingway's belief that bullfighters were like writers, in the sense first of all that their artistry, too, was at the mercy of know-it-all reviewers. Interpolated into the story of the aging Manuel "Manolo" Garcia's heroic attempt to pull off a comeback in the arena are a series of quotations from the notes being taken at ringside by the second-string bullfight critic of *El Heraldo*. "The veteran Manolo designed a series of acceptable veronicas, ending in a very Belmontistic recorte," the critic notes, even as influence-mongering journalists had talked of Hemingway's work in terms of his predecessors'.

Long before the evening is over, the critic departs, so that he misses the matador's finest moments of capework, his awful luck in hitting bone with his sword while attempting to finish off the bull, his humiliation at the hands of the spectators who throw cushions and empty bottles down upon him, and his refusal to be treated for the painful wounds he receives until after he has completed his performance. All the anger and frustration and feelings of defeat that gnawed at Hemingway in the autumn months of 1924—as well as his gritty determination to succeed as a writer no matter what critics or publishers said of his work—went into the making of "The Undefeated." In his opinion, it was the best piece of fiction he had written to date—and the day would come when existentialist philosophers would agree with him. Bullfighters were not only like writers, but Manolo was an exemplar of Man, that peculiar creature in the world of being who can achieve "authenticity" only by confronting the burden of his freedom to make choices and by embracing the awareness, without allowing it to demoralize him, that someday he will die.

In rapid-fire succession, *The Dial* and the *Saturday Evening Post* both rejected the story. Once again, Hemingway was forced to turn for literary recognition to little magazines in Europe. "The Undefeated" first appeared in a German translation in *Der Querschnitt,* and in the late fall of 1925 Ethel Moorhead and Ernest Walsh finally published it in English in *This Quarter.*

3

AT the urging of Bertram Hartman, an American painter who had become a friend of theirs, the Hemingways spent most of the winter with him at the Hotel Taube in Schruns, Austria. Because of the runaway Austrian inflation, full *pension* came to a mere dollar and a quarter a day per person, and a lovely young woman who lived across the street from the hotel was eager to look after Bumby for far less money than baby care cost in Paris. The only thing wrong with life in Schruns was that the snow came late that year, but Hemingway bowled with Hartman every day in the Taube's bowling alley and took interesting walks in the mountains with Hadley. Wherever they went, he reported to Harold Loeb four days after Christmas, they encountered "good crucifixes with Herr Gott in the act of [taking?] any amount of punishment and fine little pubs full of chamois hunters."

Hemingway also posted letters and cards from Schruns to Sylvia Beach, Gertrude Stein and Alice Toklas, Howie Jenkins, and other friends, but it was Loeb that he wrote to most often and seemed to miss the most. Addressing him in the sort of mock-insulting way that usually bespeaks affection, he warned that "if you don't come [visit us] you are not only a low son of a bitch but also ignorant. It is a pipe to get here as all the customs etc, are made on the train and you only have to get off at Buchs, walk across the tracks, change a little money and buy a ticket to Bludenz." When Loeb wrote back and said that he was sailing for New York in order to talk to his editor at Boni and Liveright about his novel, Hemingway was distressed. "What a lousy business," he replied. "We're all sad as hell this morning that you're not coming. We'd have had such a hell of a good time." In retrospect, though, he admitted that it was lucky for him that Loeb had not come to Schruns. For by returning to New York Loeb was able to join forces with other friends of the author in a concerted—and ultimately successful—effort to find a publisher for *In Our Time*.

As soon as the attempt to reach Knopf through Mencken had clearly failed, Don Stewart had taken his copy of the manuscript to Horace Liveright, who turned out to know nothing about it, thanks to the dilatoriness of Leon Fleischman. When Loeb arrived in New York, he, too, spoke to Liveright about *In Our Time,* and so did Dos Passos and Sherwood Anderson. Collectively, these endorsements packed a considerable wallop, which caused their recipient to sit up and take notice.

A born gambler who had quit a flourishing Wall Street brokerage business to enter publishing with the Greenwich Village radical, Albert Boni, Liveright had been astonishing the book trade for years by his willingness to take chances, of which the chanciest had been his scornful refusal to be intimidated by John S. Sumner, Anthony Comstock's equally blue-nosed successor as the head of the quasi-official New York Society for the Suppression of Vice. In 1915, Sumner and his minions had gone through Dreiser's The *"Genius"* "with the terrible industry of a Sunday-school boy dredging up pearls of smut from the Old Testament," as Mencken had described their activities, and after adjudging the novel immoral had succeeded in coercing the John Lane firm into withdrawing it from sale in the United States. The ban lasted into the early twenties, when an unexpurgated edition of the book was brought out by Liveright. This brash publisher's next act of defiance took him to the state house in Albany, where he lobbied against a Sumner-backed proposal called the Clean Books Bill. The bill had already passed the state assembly and seemed certain to pass the senate, but with the help of an immortal quip from the flamboyant Senator James J. Walker, "I do not know of any young woman who has been ruined by a book," it was narrowly defeated.

Having overcome Comstockery, the victorious Liveright was not disposed to find too much that was objectionable in Hemingway's manuscript. A passage in "Mr. and Mrs. Elliot" struck him as obscene, and "Up in Michigan" was ruled out by him altogether because of its explicitness about the pains of sexual intercourse. Otherwise, he loved the book and was prepared to publish it, he informed Stewart and Loeb. Both writers immediately flashed the good news to Austria.

On the evening that their cables reached the Hotel Taube, Hemingway was engrossed in playing poker at the Madlenerhaus, an alpine hut built into the flank of a nearby mountain at an altitude of two thousand meters. By the time the cables were delivered to the hut the next morning, Hemingway had left for the day in the company of Walther Lent, the head of the local ski school, to try a five-mile run down the icy face of the Vermuntgletscher. A blizzard made the 1,200-meter climb to the top of the glacier unusually difficult. ("Jesus it was cold," Hemingway fancifully recalled in a letter to Loeb a few weeks later. "My genital organ to wit penis, pecker, cock or tool froze or damn near froze and had to be rubbed with snow.") Not until dusk did the two skiers reappear at the Madlenerhaus. Hemingway's first reaction to the cables was that Stewart and Loeb must be kidding, but after deciding that their messages were on the up and up he got very excited and couldn't get to sleep that night in spite of his weariness.

The next day at the Taube, a confirming cable from Liveright arrived, followed shortly thereafter by a letter. Without delay, the revved-up author set to work on a story about a prizefighter that could serve to fill the hole created by the banning of "Up in Michigan." On February 13, after having worked through the night on revising it, he had a typescript of "The Battler" ready for transmission to New York. And in a somewhat later letter to Liveright he told him what he thought of it. "The new story makes the book a good deal better. It's about the best I've ever written and gives additional unity to the book as a whole." He might have added that the story had the quality of a recurrent dream.

As the teenaged Nick Adams struggles to his feet alongside a railroad track somewhere near Mancelona, Michigan, he gingerly puts his fingers on the swelling bump over his eye. The bump is the handiwork of "that lousy crut of a brakeman" on the freight train just disappearing from sight around a curve up ahead. Instead of riding the rails to Mancelona, Nick will have to walk. A camp fire on the edge of the woods catches the boy's attention and he decides to investigate it. Seated in front of the fire with his head in his hands is a punchdrunk, self-admittedly crazy, ex-champion boxer by the name of Ad Francis. Nick can see from the fighter's putty-colored and misshapen face that he has taken a lot of punishment around his head. "His nose was sunken, his eyes were slits, he had queer-shaped lips." Even more revoltingly, he has only one ear. "It was thickened and tight against the side of his head. Where the other ear should have been there was a stump."

Out of the darkness appears a gentle-voiced, crazy black man named Bugs. Bugs and Ad had first met when they were both serving prison sentences. Since their release, the two men have been traveling around the country together. In the manner of Nigger Jim with Huck Finn, Bugs mothers Ad, cooking him delicious fried ham and egg sandwiches and referring to him with unfailing politeness as Mister Francis. But the solicitous Negro is also a sadist, as the worn black leather on the blackjack he carries silently testifies. Master as well as slave, destroyer as well as caretaker, this black man is another of Hemingway's dark mother figures. Thus, when Ad becomes violently angry at Nick for no good cause, Bugs does not attempt to reason with his paranoid companion, but simply saps him across the base of the skull with his blackjack.

While the unconscious battler lies breathing deeply beside the fire, Bugs addresses himself to Nick's bluntly phrased question, "What made him crazy?" "He took too many beatings, for one thing," the Negro replies, and then drastically qualifies this answer by adding, "But that just made him sort of simple." His more considered opinion is that Ad was driven crazy by events in his personal life. "His sister was his manager," the black man explains, "and they was always being written up in the papers all about brothers and sisters and how she loved her brother and how he loved his sister, and then they got married in New York and that made a lot of unpleasantness. . . . Of course they wasn't brother and sister no more than a rabbit, but there was a lot of people didn't like it either way and they commenced to have disagreements, and one day she just went off and never come back." The Negro swallows some hot coffee, wipes his lips and somberly says, "He just went crazy."

If Ad's face were not all busted, Bugs continues after a moment, he would not be a bad-looking man. As for his wife, "she was an awful good-looking woman. Looked enough like him to be twins." For some reason, Bugs elects to repeat this interesting fact. "She looks enough like him to be his own twin." Abruptly, Bugs asks Nick to leave; apparently, there is nothing further about the fighter that he wishes to tell him. As Nick walks away from the fire, he becomes aware that Bugs has succeeded in awakening the "little man" he serves (and whose mutilated face had "looked childish" in repose) and that Ad is babyishly whining about a headache. "You'll feel better, Mister Francis," Nick hears the fighter's motherly attendant tell him. "Just you drink a cup of this hot coffee."

Of all the stories in *In Our Time,* the dreamlike "Battler" is the most problematic, biographically speaking. Hemingway wrote it against the backdrop of the news that Liveright was going to publish his manuscript. At last, he had reason to hope that he was on his way to the literary championship of the world. But was his excitement unalloyed, or was it edged with a gathering dread? The question arises because of the story's prophetic dimension. Nick Adams has a black eye and a bump on his forehead, and the first syllable of his last name is "Ad." The youth's future, it would appear, hovers before him in the fearful sight of a punchy ex-prizefighter with a hideously battered head. "He says he's never been crazy," Ad remarks about Nick. "He's got a lot coming to him," the Negro replies. In the late 1950s, Hemingway would reveal to his friend, A. E. Hotchner, an astonishing touchiness about those ominous words, as though he considered them to be a prophecy fulfilled.

The marital break-up of Ad and his ambiguously twinlike wife and manager is also a cause for wonder about the relationship of art to life. For their fatal disagreements, Bugs's yarn about the couple makes clear, grew out of the unpleasantness created by people who did not like it whether they were actually brother and sister or just rumored to be. In relating this strange tale of how a marriage failed, Hemingway may have been voicing his own dissatisfaction with Hadley and her ambiguous sister-wife-mother-manager role in their relationship. Or could it be that, in conjuring up Ad's marriage to "an awful good-looking woman" who looked enough like him to be his own twin, Hemingway was toying with a long-suppressed fantasy about himself and Marcelline, the handsome "twin" sister whom he professed to despise?

4

DELIGHTED ACCEPT, Hemingway cabled Liveright from Schruns, only to discover upon his return to Paris that if he had held off committing himself just a little while longer he probably could have signed on with the far more prestigious firm of Charles Scribner's Sons, whose publishing achievements included not only the monumental New York Edition of Henry James's novels and tales, Galsworthy's *Forsyte Saga,* and the work of Edith Wharton, but several books by the golden boy of the early twenties, F. Scott Fitzgerald. For in a stack of mail that Sylvia Beach had been holding for him was a letter from Fitzgerald's editor at Scribners, Max Perkins, saying he had heard from Fitzgerald's friend from Princeton days. John Peale Bishop, who had made Hemingway's acquaintance in Paris, that Hemingway had completed a new book. "I hope this is so and that we may see it," Perkins's letter continued. "We would certainly read it with promptness and sympathetic interest if you gave us the opportunity."

Perkins had received an earlier tip about "a young man named Ernest Hemmingway [*sic*]" in a hurriedly scrawled note that Fitzgerald had sent to him the previous October from the villa in the south of France where he was engaged in completing *The Great Gatsby.* Fitzgerald had described Hemingway as an American expatriate who wrote for the *transatlantic review* and was destined to have a brilliant career. "Ezra Pound published a collection of his short pieces in Paris, at some place like the Egotist [*sic*] Press. I haven't it here now but it's remarkable and I'd look him up right away." In a Jamesian phrase, Fitzgerald had added, "He's the real thing." After determining that the collection of short pieces was actually a publication of the Three Mountains Press, Perkins ordered a copy from Paris. The package cleared customs in December, but he was too busy to inspect its contents until February, at which point he reported his reaction to Fitzgerald. "[The book] accumulates a fearful effect through a series of brief episodes, presented with economy, strength and vitality. A remarkable, tight, complete expression of the *scene,* in our time, as it looks to Hemingway." Perkins then repeated the substance of this judgment in a letter to the author himself, although he felt constrained to voice the doubt that "we could have seen a way to the publication of this book . . . on account of material considerations: it is so small that it would give the booksellers no opportunity for substantial profit if issued at a price which custom would dictate. This is a pity, because your method is obviously one which enables you to express what you have to say in a very small compass." In closing, Perkins emphasized that if Hemingway happened to be writing something that would not raise practical objections to trade publication, Scribners would like to consider it.

Somehow, this letter went astray in the mails, so that Hemingway would have remained oblivious for quite some time of Perkins's interest in his work if the editor had not written him again a few days later, upon receiving word from John Peale Bishop that the author of *in our time* had indeed been doing some writing that might interest Scribners.

"I cannot tell you how pleased I was by your letter," Hemingway replied to Perkins on April 15, and he feelingly added that "you must know how gladly I would have sent Charles Scribner's Sons the manuscript." According to the contract he had agreed to sign with Boni and Liveright, he explained, "they are to have an option on my next three books, they agreeing that unless they exercise this option to publish the second book within 60 days of the receipt of the manuscript their option shall lapse, and if they do not publish the second book they relinquish their option on the third book." Thus, at the very moment of becoming a Boni and Liveright author, Hemingway let Perkins know that he could easily sever his connection with the firm by writing a book that Liveright would be compelled to turn down. "If I am ever in a position to send you anything to consider I shall certainly do so," he told Perkins. He didn't care, though, about writing a novel, he warned the editor, for it seemed to him "an awfully artificial and worked out form." (Which was his way of saying, perhaps, that he was intimidated by the greater length and freedom of the novel.) On the other hand, he pointed out, a few of his short stories were now stretching out to 8,000 to 12,000 words, so someday he might write a novel after all. (By which he meant that he was on the brink of deciding to do so, despite the hazards.)

"What rotten luck—for me I mean," Perkins wrote back, but if he was genuinely discouraged he need not have been. Less than ten months later, Hemingway would sign a contract in Perkins's office in New York, having found a way to force Liveright into releasing him.

5

EVER since reading Edmund Wilson's copy of *in our time* in the late winter or early spring of 1924, Fitzgerald had had it in mind to arrange a meeting with Hemingway in May, when he and his wife Zelda planned to be in Paris for a week and a half. The idea didn't pan out, however, because most of the Fitzgeralds' time in the French capital was unexpectedly taken up by their excited pursuit of two other expatriates, the painter Gerald Murphy and his wife Sara, whom they had looked up at the behest of their Long Island neighbor, Gerald's sister Esther.

The Murphys were ensconced that spring in a house in St-Cloud which had formerly belonged to the composer Gounod, but like the Fitzgeralds they were going to the Riviera for the summer, in the Murphys' case to the Hôtel du Cap on the Cap d'Antibes, so that Gerald—who had thought at one time of becoming a landscape architect—could personally oversee the renovation of the villa they had recently purchased. The assertive, handsome Gerald and the calmly beautiful Sara appeared to be leading lives of perfect self-realization, and the imperfectly self-realized Fitzgeralds at once fell worshipfully in love with them. Even after many hours in the Murphys' company, they could hardly bear to tear themselves away, and on one occasion they reappeared beneath the darkened windows of the St-Cloud house in the dead of night, in the hope that their plaintive calls of greeting would gain them admission. More flattered than annoyed by such naked adoration, the Murphys assured their new friends that they hoped to see a lot of them during the summer. Scott, to be sure, had a novel to write, but that didn't mean that he and Zelda couldn't come to Sara's parties, or take the sun with them at midday.

The summer led to stresses and strains that neither couple had bargained for. As Fitzgerald would recall in the thirties, he had to drag *The Great Gatsby* "out of the pit of my stomach in a time of misery." But at the end of October the novel was finally put in the mail to Max Perkins and a month later the Fitzgeralds left the Riviera for what would prove to be a bad winter for both of them in Rome and Capri. With the return of spring *Gatsby* would be coming out, and the thought of that event filled Fitzgerald with gloomy forebodings that grew worse with each passing week. Supposing, he wrote to Perkins from Capri on the day of publication, April 10, 1925, that "women didn't like the book because it has no important women in it, and critics didn't like it because it dealt with the rich and contained no peasants borrowed out of *Tess* in it and set to work in Idaho? Suppose it didn't even wipe out my debt to you—why, it will have to sell 20,000 copies even to do that! In fact, all my confidence is gone—I wouldn't tell you this except for the fact that by the [time] this reaches you the worst will be known."

Too nervous about the fate of his book to stay where he was and try to relax, he persuaded Zelda that they should sail from Naples to Marseilles on the next available ship. Perkins's cable about the book's initial reception reached him at sea. SALES SITUATION DOUBTFUL EXCELLENT REVIEWS. From Marseilles, he cabled Perkins that he was "depressed" by the news and then agitatedly set off with Zelda for Paris in the Renault that they had had shipped with them. But the Fitzgeralds had been abusing the car—they always abused their cars—ever since they had bought it, and upon arriving in Lyon they were forced to garage it for extensive repairs and continue on by train. At Zelda's insistence, the mechanic agreed that in addition to getting the Renault to run properly again he would saw off its roof. The lady preferred, it seemed, to travel in open cars.

Impulsively deciding that it would be a good idea to remain in Paris until his next novel was finished, Fitzgerald signed an eight-month lease on a pretentiously furnished apartment in the rue de Tilsitt. (*Tender is the Night* would take eight years, not eight months, to complete.) Shortly before he and Zelda moved in, he wandered away from their hotel without her one evening to have a couple of drinks. In a Montparnasse watering-hole called Le Dingo (The Crazy), he caught sight at the bar of a handsome fellow whose face was still tan from skiing. With him were an English woman in her early thirties and a young Scotsman. Their sexually ambiguous first names were Duff and Pat and they had an interesting relationship. But it was their handsome companion whom Fitzgerald really wanted to talk to.

6

FITZGERALD was three years older than Hemingway and far, far better known. Nevertheless, Hemingway lorded it over him right from the start, both as a man and a writer. A letter he wrote to his new friend from Burguete, Spain, two months after their encounter at the Dingo drew the sort of personal contrast between them that would forever be a feature of his attitude toward Fitzgerald.

> I wonder what your idea of heaven would be—A beautiful vacuum filled with wealthy monogamists, all powerful and members of the best families all drinking themselves to death. . . . To me heaven would be a big bull ring with me holding two barrera seats and a trout stream outside that no one else was allowed to fish in and two lovely houses in the town; one where I would have my wife and children and be monogamous and love them truly and well and the other where I would have my nine beautiful mistresses on 9 different floors.

Fitzgerald, in brief, enjoyed getting drunk, whereas Hemingway enjoyed getting laid.

Instead of insulting him back or telling him to shut up, Fitzgerald treated Hemingway's sexually aggressive putdowns as statements of symbolic truth. For Hemingway in Fitzgerald's conjuration was endowed—as he believed Gerald Murphy and the ten-goal polo player,

Tommy Hitchcock, also were—with a splendidly masculine animus
which he himself could only vampirishly dream of draining them
of. "When I like men I want to be like them," he confided to his
Notebooks. "I want to lose the outer qualities that give me my
individuality and be like them. I don't want the man, I want to
absorb into myself all the qualities that make him attractive and leave
him out."

Hemingway the writer was worshiped no less abjectly by Fitzgerald than Hemingway the man. In Fitzgerald's self-denigrating opinion, Hemingway was the "one true genius" of their literary
generation, and he could not imagine how any fair-minded and
informed person could disagree. Drawing Glenway Wescott aside
on a Riviera beach in the summer of 1926, Fitzgerald asked him
whether he didn't think that *The Great Gatsby* and Wescott's own
novel, *The Apple of the Eye,* had been inflated in value by the critics,
in contradistinction to the literary achievements of Hemingway,
which had been neglected, misunderstood, and insufficiently remu-
nerated. What could Wescott do to help Hemingway, Fitzgerald
wanted to know, impatiently grasping and shaking his fellow novelist's elbow. Perhaps, Fitzgerald ventured, Wescott would be willing to write a laudatory essay about him. "It simply had not
occurred to him," Wescott wrote in the *New Republic* in February
1941, two months after Fitzgerald's death, that

> unfriendliness or pettiness on my part might inhibit my enthusiasm
> about the art of a new colleague or rival. . . . [Fitzgerald] not only
> said but, I believe, honestly felt that Hemingway was inimitably,
> essentially superior. From the moment Hemingway began to appear
> in print, perhaps it did not matter what he himself produced or failed
> to produce. He felt free to write for profit, and to live for fun, if
> possible. Hemingway could be entrusted with the graver responsibil-
> ities and higher rewards such as glory, immortality.

A remarkable upward revision in the estimates of Fitzgerald's
achievement brought him posthumous glory in abundance, however, and in the last dozen years of his life an astounded Hemingway
responded to this threat to his accustomed primacy by trying to cut
his rival back to size. His first notable effort along these lines occurred on April 22, 1950, in a letter to Arthur Mizener, who had
initiated a correspondence with Hemingway at his villa in Cuba in
connection with the biography of Fitzgerald he was working on.
Although the master of the Finca Vigía was just about to begin
correcting the galley proofs of *Across the River and Into the Trees,* he

took time with his letter to Mizener. Behind its composition lay not only jealousy of Fitzgerald's belated good fortune, but nervousness about the quality of *Across the River*. The result was that black toads leapt out of all ten paragraphs, of which the last is a fair sample:

> He was romantic, ambitious, and Christ, Jesus, God knows how talented. He was also generous without being kind. He was uneducated and refused to educate himself in any way. He would make great studies about foot-ball say and war but it was all bull-shit. He was a charming cheerful companion when he was sober although a little embarrassing from his tendency always to hero-worship. . . . Above all he was completely undisciplined and he would quit at the drop of a hat and borrow some-ones hat to drop. He was fragile Irish instead of tough Irish. I wish he were here and I could give him this letter to read so he would not ever think I would say things behind his back.

Although Hemingway was obviously hoping to influence Mizener's judgment of Fitzgerald, he didn't allow him to quote from this letter because he had earmarked its most arresting materials for use by himself in *A Moveable Feast*. Public disclosure of what he knew —or said he knew—about a writer whose literary reputation was fast overtaking his own was a task that was too important to Hemingway to entrust to someone else.

His first impression of Fitzgerald that night in the Dingo, according to *A Moveable Feast,* was that in appearance he was both boyish and girlish.

> Scott was a man then who looked like a boy with a face between handsome and pretty. He had very fair wavy hair, a high forehead, excited and friendly eyes and a delicate long-lipped Irish mouth that, on a girl, would have been the mouth of a beauty. His chin was well built and he had good ears and a handsome, almost beautiful, unmarked nose. This should not have added up to a pretty face, but that came from the coloring, the very fair hair and the mouth. The mouth worried you until you knew him and then it worried you more.

The memoirist further emphasized Fitzgerald's femininity by contrasting his nervous volubility with the easygoing manner of the manly fellow who was with him. For Fitzgerald had not entered the Dingo alone, by Hemingway's account, but was in the company of an erstwhile Princeton varsity baseball player named Duncan Chaplin, who was "extraordinarily nice, unworried, relaxed and friendly and I much preferred him to Scott." Alas for damaging contrasts,

Duncan Chaplin later told one of Fitzgerald's biographers that he had not been in Europe at all in 1925.

Having polished off his rival's face, the memoirist moved on to his legs. As Fitzgerald plunked himself down on a bar stool, Hemingway could not help noticing that "he had very short legs. With normal legs he would have been perhaps two inches taller." As for the clothes he was wearing, his Brooks Brothers suit "fitted him well," but unfortunately he had chosen a Guard's tie to go with his white button-down shirt. "I thought I ought to tell him about the tie, maybe, because they did have British in Paris and one might come into the Dingo—there were two there at the time—but then I thought the hell with it. . . . It turned out later he had bought the tie in Rome."

After champagne was ordered and poured, Fitzgerald's face again caught Hemingway's attention. "As he sat there at the bar holding the glass of champagne the skin seemed to tighten over his face . . . and then it drew tighter until the face was like a death's head." How many glasses of wine it took to produce this startling metamorphosis is unclear, but the implication is that the number was small. The evening ended, the memoir relates, with Duncan Chaplin helping Hemingway to pour poor Scott into a taxi and send him home.

A few days later, the two writers met again at the Closerie des Lilas, where Fitzgerald, says Hemingway, drank two whiskey and sodas without visible effect and was "cynical and funny and very jolly and charming" as he talked about "writers and publishers and agents and critics and [the *Saturday Evening Post's*] George Horace Lorimer, and the gossip and economics of being a successful writer." Did they eventually get around to talking about more personal matters? All that *A Moveable Feast* says is that they sat on the terrace of the Lilas for quite a long time, watching it get dusk and the people passing on the sidewalk and the gray light of the evening changing, and that before they parted Fitzgerald asked Hemingway if he would like to go down to Lyon with him on the train and pick up his repaired Renault and drive back to Paris. He accepted the invitation, the memoirist explains, because "it was late spring now and I thought the country would be at its best and . . . I would have the company of an older and successful writer." That Hemingway viewed the trip as a means of cementing a friendship which, in the space of less than a week, had acquired as much importance for him as it had for Fitzgerald is nowhere acknowledged in the memoir.

A Moveable Feast presents the Lyon expedition as a comedy of Fitzgeraldian ineptitude and self-pity that an exasperated but forbearing Hemingway endured without uttering a single harsh word, because "you could not be angry with Scott any more than you could be angry with someone who was crazy." On the morning of their departure they were to meet at the train station and Fitzgerald was to bring the tickets. When it got close to the time for the train to leave and Fitzgerald had still not appeared, Hemingway bought an entry ticket to the track and walked the length of the train looking for him. It was a long train and Fitzgerald was not on board. Even though he and Hadley were on a tight budget, Hemingway felt he had no choice but to shell out more money for a train ticket and proceed to Lyon by himself.

As he was shaving the next morning in the first-class hotel in Lyon where he had spent the night, Fitzgerald rang him up from the lobby. Hemingway suggested that they have a quick breakfast in a café, but Fitzgerald preferred a more expensive meal right there in the hotel. Fitzgerald also insisted that the hotel make them a picnic lunch for the road, even though Hemingway pointed out that they could buy a bottle of Mâcon in Mâcon and the makings of sandwiches in a *charcuterie*. At the garage, Hemingway was surprised to find that the Renault no longer had a roof. The mechanic pleaded with him to persuade Fitzgerald to have new piston rings installed once they got to Paris. "Try and make Monsieur be serious," the mechanic begged. "At least about the vehicle," he entreated. "Ah," said Hemingway.

About an hour north of Lyon the travelers were halted by rain. Further downpours halted them possibly ten times more. Still and all they had a marvelous lunch from the hotel in Lyon, truffled roast chicken, delicious bread, and white Mâcon wine. On reaching Mâcon, Hemingway bought a few more bottles and uncorked them as the need arose. "I am not sure," the memoirist remarks, that Fitzgerald had ever drunk wine from a bottle before, and "it was exciting to him . . . as a girl might be excited by going swimming for the first time without a bathing suit."

By early afternoon, unfortunately, the cold and rainsoaked Fitzgerald began to worry about his health. Two people in Italy, he gloomily announced, had recently died of congestion of the lungs, a statistic which appeared to impress him deeply. Despite Hemingway's attempt to cheer him up by informing him that congestion was just an old-fashioned term for pneumonia, Fitzgerald was inconsolable. As the intensifying rain pelted down upon them, Fitzgerald asked Hemingway if he was afraid to die and Hemingway replied, more at some times than at others. On reaching Chalon-sur-Saône, Fitzgerald abruptly stopped the car, booked a room in a hotel, and went to bed. He did not mind dying of congestion of the lungs, he said. Hemingway told him that his pulse was normal and that he hadn't any fever to the touch. Fitzgerald asked Hemingway in the name of friendship to send for a thermometer. Hemingway rang for room service. Fitzgerald closed his eyes. With his waxy color and his perfect features, he looked like a little dead crusader. At this point, the memoirist confesses, "I was getting tired of the literary life." No deadpan comment in the collected works of Mark Twain was ever delivered better.

The thermometer, when it came, turned out to be meant for the bath, but Hemingway concealed this fact, placed the business end of the instrument under Fitzgerald's arm for four minutes and assured him that the reading was normal. The next day the sun came out, and while they were bowling along through the vineyards of the Côte-d'Or Fitzgerald brought up the subject of Michael Arlen. In current literature he was the man to watch, in Fitzgerald's opinion, from which Hemingway dissented by saying that he himself couldn't read Michael Arlen's books. You don't have to, Fitzgerald exclaimed, as he launched into a recapitulation of the plots of each and every one of them. On reaching Paris, Hemingway got out of the Renault at Fitzgerald's apartment building and taxied home, and "it was wonderful to see my wife and we went up to the Closerie des Lilas to have a drink."

What portion of this wonderfully funny, savagely destructive story is believable? That Fitzgerald had in truth become thoroughly chilled while driving in the rain can be ascertained from a letter Hemingway wrote him the following December. "Know you will be glad to read in N. Y. Herald that 2 men died of cold in Chalons Sur Saone where you nearly did same." On the other hand, Hemingway gave Max Perkins a strikingly different impression of the trip than he would the readers of A Moveable Feast. "We had a great trip together driving [Scott's] car up from Lyon through the Cote d'Or," he informed the editor a few weeks after their return to Paris, and with equal enthusiasm he added, "I've read his Great Gatsby and think it is an absolutely first rate book. I hope it is going well." Fitzgerald, too, spoke glowingly of the trip. Within days of his companion's letter to Perkins, he told Gertrude Stein that "Hemingway and I went to Lyons . . . to get my car and had a slick drive through Burgundy. He's a peach of a fellow and absolutely first-rate."

7

THREE chapters in *A Moveable Feast* are devoted to making Fitzgerald look bad, of which the most frequently talked about is the last. For in "A Matter of Measurements" Hemingway elaborated upon the nastiest of the tales that he had told Arthur Mizener.

Four years after the two writers' first meeting, the story begins, in the time after Zelda had suffered "what was then called her first nervous breakdown," Fitzgerald and Hemingway both happened to be back in Paris, and at Fitzgerald's urging they had lunch at the Restaurant Michaud. Fitzgerald wanted to ask Hemingway about something important. Yet it was not until they were eating their dessert—it was cherry tart, Hemingway remembered—that he finally got up the courage to reveal what was bothering him. He had "never slept with anyone except Zelda," he began, and as a result there was no woman to whom he could turn for relief from the terrible doubts his wife had aroused in him about the adequacy of his lovemaking equipment. Therefore, he was turning to Hemingway. Zelda had told him he was built in such a way that he could never make any woman happy. It was a matter of measurements, she had said. Hemingway promptly escorted his agonized friend to the men's room, and after inspecting him carefully pronounced him "perfectly fine." Fitzgerald's anxiety was not assuaged, however, so they repaired to one of the statuary rooms in the Louvre, where Hemingway gave an impromptu lecture on the phenomenon of phallic expansion. "It is not basically a question of the size in repose," he pointed out. "It is the size that it becomes. It is also a question of angle." He explained in addition the uses of a pillow and concluded with the warning that "Zelda just wants to destroy you." Despite the lecture, Fitzgerald was obviously still upset, so Hemingway proposed that they go look at some paintings. Fitzgerald, however, said he wasn't in the mood and besides which he had promised to meet some people at the Ritz bar.

That this "astonishing incident took place" is accepted without question by a number of authorities on Fitzgerald and Hemingway. Judging by the way they talk about it, these critics find the incident credible because it fits the long-term pattern of self-doubt in Fitzgerald's behavior as well as his hero-worship of Hemingway, and because Hemingway's recollection of what happened is filled with accurate-sounding quotes and belief-compelling circumstantial details, like that cherry tart for dessert. But in putting cherry tart on the table at the very moment when Fitzgerald begins to disclose his woeful innocence about the facts of life the author of *A Moveable Feast* was indulging in the sort of double-entendre joke he always delighted in, and which could have been a signal that other elements in his story were no less fanciful.

How likely is it, for instance, that Fitzgerald would have told Hemingway that he had never slept with any woman besides Zelda? In one of his remembrances of undergraduate days at Princeton, Fitzgerald states that on the night after being informed of his suspension from college for scholastic deficiencies and of his consequent ineligibility for the Triangle Club presidency, he had sought consolation in hunting down a prostitute. A much more telling rebuttal of the notion that Fitzgerald's sexual experience was as limited as Hemingway said he said it was has been provided by the English actress Rosalinde Fuller, who talks at length in her unpublished autobiography about her romantic fling with Fitzgerald in and around New York City during the autumn preceding his marriage to Zelda. There was "no end to our delight and discovery of one another," Miss Fuller remembers. "We made love everywhere, in theatre boxes, country fields, under the sun, moon and stars," and one night in Fitzgerald's hotel room they both took Spanish fly in an effort to heighten their ardor. Zelda, moreover, was certain that in the first summer of their marriage Fitzgerald made love to another Alabama girl, Tallulah Bankhead's older sister Eugenia, and she was also concerned about Scott's attentions to yet another Southern belle who was cutting a wide swath in New York in the early twenties, the beautiful and talented actress Miriam Hopkins.

Even if Fitzgerald had slept with no other woman than his wife, that experience alone ought to have made him quite conversant with all the copulatory lore about pillows and such which Hemingway claimed he didn't possess. To be sure, the idea that Zelda might have complained to her husband about not being sexually satisfied by him is not hard to believe. Nor is it hard to believe that Fitzgerald might have mentioned her complaint to Hemingway toward the end of a wine-blown lunch. But the scene in the men's room and subsequent lecture at the Louvre bear the hallmarks of fantasy. Two things and two things only can be said with certainty in regard to the notorious "matter of measurements." The first is that Hemingway, ever competitive, ever preoccupied with his own literary reputation, set out in *A Moveable Feast* to remind the world of Fitzgerald's inferiority. And the second is that Hemingway was himself obsessed with masculinity and its outward manifestations. Commenting on the androgyny of Fitzgerald's appearance was a familiar tactic. Describing a man with his pants open, pathetically waiting for an experienced friend to render a verdict about his manhood, was, in Hemingway's view, the final humiliation.

8

A Moveable Feast asserts that Fitzgerald told Hemingway the story of his courtship of Zelda on their way back from Lyon. He talked about how he had met her during the war and then lost her and won her back. He talked, too, about "something tragic" that had taken place on the Riviera in the summer of 1924. Zelda and a French naval aviator, Edouard Jozan, had fallen in love, and Fitzgerald wanted Hemingway "to know and understand and appreciate what it was that had happened." He made it so clear, Hemingway remembered, "that I could see the single seater seaplane buzzing the diving raft and the color of the sea and the shape of the pontoons and the shadow that they cast and Zelda's tan and Scott's tan and the dark blonde and the light blond of their hair and the darkly tanned face of the boy that was in love with Zelda."

While Fitzgerald's romantic description of his twenty-four-year-old wife may have caused Hemingway to assume that she must be a beauty, his first impression of her looks was unfavorable, or so he later claimed. In *A Moveable Feast* he recalled that on the late spring afternoon when he and Hadley were introduced to Zelda at a lunch in the Fitzgeralds' apartment her face had been "taut and drawn," her eyes had been "tired" and her hair "had been ruined temporarily by a bad permanent she had gotten." Not until the second to last paragraph of the chapter he devoted to her did the memoirist finally say something seemingly ungrudging about her appearance. At a party on the Riviera in the summer of 1926, she had been "very beautiful and was tanned a lovely gold color and her hair was a beautiful dark gold." There was malice at work, however, even in this tribute, for he quickly undercut it with a concluding anecdote about her emerging madness. That night on the Riviera, "her hawk's eyes were clear and calm. I knew everything was all right and was going to turn out well in the end when she leaned forward and said to me, telling me her great secret, 'Ernest, don't you think Al Jolson is greater than Jesus?'"

The author of *A Moveable Feast* also insisted that during the spring in which he met Zelda "she was making [her husband] jealous with other women." That charge, like his attack on Scott's masculinity, was in all likelihood a fabrication and a further attempt to degrade the Fitzgeralds. It also smacks of revenge, for Zelda had surely aroused his ire by impugning his masculinity.

If she made sexual overtures to anyone that spring, Zelda's long
flirtatious history indicates that she made them to a man—conceivably to Hemingway himself. And if she tried and failed to work her
charms on him—for she was the kind of insistently feminine woman
he was ordinarily not attracted to—the rebuff could have supplied
her with her first reason for suggesting that he was homosexual. A
second might have been to sow suspicion and dissension between
her husband and his new friend. A third to heap another emotional
burden on the already overladen Scott.

Not long after meeting Hemingway, she surprised and annoyed
Fitzgerald by calling his new friend "bogus," and she subsequently
derided his muscular exhibitionism as "phony as a rubber check."
While he came across as all male, no man could be "as male as all
that," in her acidulous opinion, and the more she thought about it
the more she became convinced that there was something ambiguous about the relationship between Hemingway and her husband.
Thus, during their overlapping sojourns in Paris in 1929, the Fitzgeralds and Hemingway and his second wife, Pauline Pfeiffer, had
dinner together one night in the Hemingways' apartment. Several
bibulous hours later, the Fitzgeralds returned home, and as Scott
was getting into bed he drunkenly murmured, "No more, baby."
Zelda took his words to mean that he was having a conversation in
his mind with Hemingway (which may have been true), and from
this conclusion she leapt to the conviction that the two men were
lovers. In 1930, she would list this event as one of the precipitating
causes of her mental breakdown. "We came back to the Rue Palatine," she reminded Fitzgerald, "and you in a drunken stupor told
me a lot of things that I only half-understood; but I understood the
dinner we had at Ernest's." Beside himself with rage, Fitzgerald
cried out, "The nearest I ever came to leaving you was when you
told me you thot I was a fairy in the Rue Palatine."

The only compliment Zelda ever paid to Hemingway was that he
had nice manners, by which she meant that he paid attention to her.
What she didn't realize was that his attentiveness was literarily motivated. For he was studying her for the sake of the novel he had
decided to write. Her nonchalant charm and ready retorts, her zest
for parties that went on all night, her appetite for male admiration,
her compulsive fondness for taking baths, as though she were trying
to wash away a sense of moral uncleanliness, would all contribute to
the characterization of Brett Ashley in *The Sun Also Rises*.

There was yet another aspect of Zelda, and her relationship to
Scott, that would figure in Hemingway's later work. Zelda, on the
basis of the theosophical doctrines imparted to her by her mother,

Minnie Machen Sayre—a frustrated operatic contralto and actress—
had arrived at a belief in spiritual twinhood. Thus, in the summer of
1919 this belief enabled her to escape the feelings of "vague despondency" she had been having about her engagement to the unwealthy
and unsung Princetonian whom she had met during the war. She
had been to see a spiritualist in Montgomery, she elatedly reported
to Scott, in a letter that reached him at the address on the upper West
Side of New York where he was living in a dreary one-room apartment. The message she herself had received from the spiritualist's
Ouija board had spoken only of death, but the message the spiritualist obtained "told us to be married—that we were soul mates."
To anyone who knew how to interpret it, the message was profoundly important, because theosophy, Zelda explained, taught that
"two souls are incarnated together—not necessarily at the same time
but are mated—since the time when people were bi-sexual, so you
see 'soul mate' isn't exactly snappy storyish, after all."

Fitzgerald was utterly beguiled by this letter. Scott was Zelda and
Zelda was Scott: the more he thought about this idea, the more
meanings he discovered in it, as did Zelda. They both were conscious of being slender and handsome and golden, of having shrewd
opinions and amazing perceptions and of speaking in marvelously
original ways, of worshiping success and fame and of wanting to be
the toast of the town—and of being so much in love with death that
they were forever egging one another on to ever more dangerous
feats of high-diving and reckless driving. On occasion, their sense
of identicalness even led them to dress alike. Three months after
they were married in New York they set off by car for the south,
wearing matching white knickers and preppy jackets. In *The Beautiful and Damned* (1922), Fitzgerald dramatized the vision they shared.
Gloria Gilbert assures Anthony Patch that "We're twins," by way
of summing up the belief she has absorbed from her mother that
"two souls are sometimes created together . . . and in love before
they're born," and Anthony is "ecstatic" at the idea.

The Fitzgeralds' relationship would prove to be mutually destructive. Yet the author of *A Moveable Feast,* overwhelmingly, laid the
blame on Zelda's doorstep. Not only was she an everlasting cock-
teaser, but she used the temptations of strong drink to erode Fitzgerald's ability to write, of which she was exceedingly jealous. Hemingway first became aware of her alcoholic wiles, he claimed, on the
very day he met her. She had a bad hangover and kept treating
Fitzgerald "as though he were a kill-joy or a spoilsport." Apparently
she had flung those words at him the night before, at a party in
Montmartre where they had quarreled because of his unwillingness

to join her in getting drunk. After a disastrously alcoholic winter in Rome and Capri, Fitzgerald had resolved upon his arrival in Paris to forgo all-night drinking sessions, get some exercise each day and work regularly, Hemingway further recalled. But as soon as he was working well, "Zelda would begin complaining how bored she was and get him off on another drunken party. They would quarrel and then make up and he would sweat out the alcohol on long walks with me, and make up his mind that this time he would really work, and would start off well. Then it would start all over again." As Hemingway watched Zelda watching her husband drink more than was good for him, he soon came to appreciate that the thin-lipped smile on her hawklike face "meant she knew Scott would not be able to write."

Zelda, in sum, was precisely the kind of manipulative, man-destroying, work-destroying female that Hemingway most feared. Even though he wrote about her in his late middle age, at a time when he himself was tormented by alcoholism and fears of insanity, he was unable to enlarge her into a figure of tragedy and portrayed her instead as an object for contempt. Only in the Zelda-like crazy wife in *The Garden of Eden* would he be able to see himself in such a woman.

Grace Hemingway wrote "summer girl" in her scrapbook alongside this photograph of her son Ernest, taken a month before his second birthday. (Oak Park, Illinois, June 1901)

Raising them as twins, Grace imposed both boyish and girlish costumes and hairstyles on Ernest (in his mother's lap) and his older sister, Marcelline (in her father's). At the family cottage on Walloon Lake, Michigan, in the summer of 1901, they were dressed as "lads" or "chaps," as she called them.

3

Out for a stroll with their baby sister, Ursula, the "twins," Ernest (left) and Marcelline (right), were dressed as girls. (Oak Park, October 1902)

4

With the birth of Madelaine ("Sunny"), the Hemingways numbered six: (left to right)
Marcelline, Sunny, Dr. Hemingway, Grace, Ursula and Ernest. (Oak Park, 1906)

The spacious house in Oak Park that Grace designed for her growing family (shown here in 1906, the year of its completion) included offices for Dr. Hemingway and a music conservatory for herself. During his teens, Ernest staged boxing matches in the conservatory.

Seventeen and a graduating senior at Oak Park High School in 1917, Ernest was both an athlete and a clever writer. Refusing to go to college, he got a job through family connections as a reporter for the Kansas City Star.

Eager to go to war, Hemingway volunteered for the American Red Cross and was struck by mortar fire while passing out chocolates to Italian soldiers on the front lines. He cheerfully recovered from his wounds in the American Red Cross Hospital in Milan in July 1918.

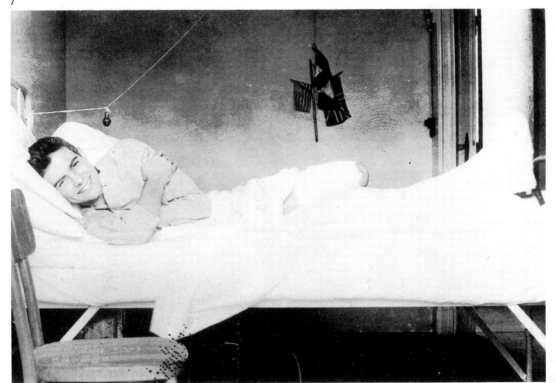

Hemingway fell in love with and planned to marry *Agnes von Kurowsky*, his American Red Cross nurse. Although she jilted him for an Italian officer, their romance inspired the love story of Frederic Henry and Catherine Barkley in A Farewell to Arms *(1929)*.

Back home in Oak Park in the winter of 1919, Hemingway told tales of his experiences under fire that were as melodramatic as his custom-tailored Italian cape.

His ambition to become a writer dominated Hemingway's thoughts during the summer of 1919 at the family cottage on Walloon Lake. A fishing trip he took that summer became the basis for his hauntingly enigmatic story "Big Two-Hearted River" (1924).

11

*Hemingway married Hadley Richardson in Horton Bay, Michigan, on September 3, 1921.
To their right: his sisters Ursula and Carol; to their left: his mother, his brother Leicester and
his father. Hadley's small trust fund would enable the newlyweds to live in Paris.*

By the time of his return to Oak Park at Christmas, 1923, Hemingway (posing here with his brother, Leicester) had become a published author. But when his parents received copies of his collection of sketches entitled in our time, *Dr. Hemingway returned them to the publisher, refusing to have such "filth" in the house.*

Hemingway's sojourn in Pamplona, Spain, during the fiesta of San Fermín in July of 1925 with (to his left) Duff Twysden and Hadley, among others, led very quickly to The Sun Also Rises *(1926). The stylish, sexually tortured heroine, Brett Ashley, was partly based on Duff.*

14

Scott and Zelda Fitzgerald met Hemingway in Paris in 1925. Scott's admiration for Hemingway both as a writer and a man bordered on idolatry. In Zelda's opinion, her husband's friend was "bogus" and as "phony as a rubber check."

Hemingway with the two women in his life at Schruns, Austria, on or near New Year's Day, 1926: (left) Hadley, his wife and the mother of his son; and (right) the well-to-do Pauline Pfeiffer, already campaigning to become his second wife.

15

16

Hemingway and his friends Gerald Murphy (left) and John Dos Passos (right) at Schruns, Austria, March 1926. Murphy invited Hemingway to occupy his Paris studio after he separated from Hadley. Almost always jealous of fellow writers, Hemingway later vilified Dos Passos as Richard Gordon in To Have and Have Not *(1937).*

Pauline and Hemingway on the beach at San Sebastián, Spain, in July 1927, two months after their wedding.

A favorite among the expatriate literary ladies of Paris, including for a time Gertrude Stein, Hemingway posed with Sylvia Beach (on his right) and two of her friends in front of Beach's Left Bank bookshop, Shakespeare and Company, in March 1928. He had pulled a skylight down on his head, one of several head injuries he would sustain in the next three decades.

Dr. Hemingway visited his now famous son in Key West, Florida, in April 1928, eight months before he committed suicide, an act that would torment Hemingway for the rest of his life.

Chap!

In the late summer of that year
we lived in a house in a village that

In the August we heard the troops
looked across the river and the plain to the
mountains. The water in the river clear
boulders are the river ran was clear
the water was clear and swiftly moving and dry white
bed of white pebbles and white boulders and
troops went by the house
and down the road road and the dust
they raised powdered the leaves of the trees,
the trunks of the trees too were dusty and the
leaves fell early that year and we saw
the troops marching along the road and
the dust rising and leaves stirred by the breeze
the soldiers marching and afterwards the
road bare and white except for the leaves.

A draft of the opening sentences of A Farewell to Arms *(1929), whose publication solidified Hemingway's reputation as one of the foremost novelists of his generation.*

CHAPTER THIRTEEN

Betrayals

THE COUPLE WITH WHOM HEMINGWAY had been drinking at the Dingo on the spring night in 1925 when Fitzgerald came up and introduced himself were Duff Twysden and her young cousin, Pat Guthrie. Besides being blood relatives, Duff and Pat were lovers; indeed, they had been living together for some time, in accommodations that ranged from the Ritz Hotel to fifth-arrondissement flea-bags, depending on the flow of remittances from home. That Duff had a live-in bed partner did not prevent her, however, from becoming involved with other men, and Hemingway quickly became a member of her inner circle. A barman in Montparnasse who poured a lot of drinks for Hemingway in the twenties could never understand what he saw in Lady Twysden. She was just one of those horsey English girls, in his sturdy opinion. That Hemingway thought she had class was the only explanation of her appeal he could think of. They used to go dancing over on the Right Bank, the barman remembered.

As far as it went, his explanation made sense. Having been exposed as a boy to the Anglophilia of the Hemingway family in particular and of Oak Park in general—the Oxford Room and all that—Hemingway tended to be automatically impressed by titled English women. In casting about for a suitable last name for the titled heroine of *The Sun Also Rises,* he would finally decide to borrow Edwina Ashley's. For in 1922 this elegant, vital, hectically pleasure-seeking, enormously rich young woman had married

Queen Victoria's great-grandson, Louis Mountbatten, in the most important society wedding in Britain since the war. If it amused Hemingway to name his heroine after "Dickie" Mountbatten's bride, he also derived a snobbish pleasure from doing so, just as he did from taking Lady Twysden dancing.

Duff Twysden had actually started out in life as plain Dorothy Smurthwaite. But while her father was an unassuming if well-off Yorkshire shopkeeper, her mother came from a socially pretentious Scottish family named Stirling that kept horses and claimed aristocratic ties. After her parents were divorced, Duff took her mother's maiden name, and it was as Dorothy Stirling that she was presented at court.

Her first marriage, to an older man named Luttrell Byrom, was a product of World War I and a fairly prompt victim of it, as Duff found herself unwilling to fend off the flattering attentions of the young officers she met in connection with her courier work for the British Secret Service. Toward the end of 1916, Byrom divorced her on the grounds of adultery. A few weeks later, she married Roger Twysden, a Royal Naval Commander and a baronet, in the teeth of the fierce opposition of Twysden's mother. Even after Duff gave birth to a son, her mother-in-law continued to despise her as an unprincipled social climber and an alcoholic besides who was leading her innocent son into debauchery. Duff, for her part, recalled her second marriage rather differently. Her husband was a drunk, she said succinctly, who got ugly when he was in his cups. Hemingway also remembered her telling him that Sir Roger had insisted on sleeping with a drawn sword between them, but the all but certain truth of the matter is that Hemingway took this detail from a book he had read. For as the conversation between Nick Adams and Bill in "The Three-Day Blow" reveals, one of the novels that Hemingway was fond of in his youth was Maurice Hewlett's *The Forest Lovers* (1898), in which—to quote Nick— the lovers "go to bed every night with the naked sword between them."

In any event, relations between Duff and Roger were never smooth. Their frequent separations, during which Duff was apt to flee to her grandmother's stone mansion in Scotland, ultimately led her into the arms of her cousin, Pat Guthrie. Guthrie's drinking problems, which occasionally required him to "dry out" in a hospital, his history of bisexualism, his habit of leaving large unpaid bills behind him and his vicious temper were the signs of a possibly unbalanced, certainly ruthless personality. His ruthlessness, though, struck an answering chord in Duff. When she finally ran off to Paris with him, leaving her little boy in the care of his two grandmothers, her husband filed suit for divorce.

On May 22, 1925, Duff turned thirty-three, which is to say that she was only slightly younger than Hadley Hemingway and Agnes von Kurowsky. Like her tweed skirts, her face was "well-tailored," as someone remarked, while her eyes were expressive and her complexion fresh, even though she was a drinker. But the aspects of Duff's appearance that caught Hemingway's eye were undoubtedly the ones he would emphasize in his description of Brett Ashley in *The Sun Also Rises*. Lady Ashley, says the appreciative Jake Barnes, has curves "like the hull of a racing yacht," yet her cropped hair is "brushed back like a boy's." Furthermore, she affects a man's felt hat, just as Duff did, and can hold her liquor with an equivalent gallantry. Hemingway's lady friend, in short, would make the journey from life to art virtually intact.

2

TO add to her many other attractions, Duff Twysden had wit and a hearty sense of humor. "When she laughed," Hadley recalled a quarter of a century later, "the whole of her went into that laughter. Lots of broad language, certainly, but it went over with all kinds of people." Someone who found her laugh particularly entrancing was Harold Loeb. It had, he said, the "liquid quality of the lilt of a mocking bird singing to the moon." If those words reflected Loeb's lifelong admiration for the prose of W. H. Hudson, they also were a measure of the romantic passion that had once consumed him.

Having wearied of the long-legged charms of Kitty Cannell, Loeb approached Duff one afternoon at the Café Select and asked her to have a drink with him the next day in an out-of-the-way bar where neither of them was known. It was a rendezvous that began with an aperitif and ended in bed. The experience was sufficiently satisfactory to Duff that she was persuaded to go off to northern Spain with Loeb for a week. To her, their holiday was a glorious little dream; to him, it was the beginning of their life together. On realizing that her companion took their affair much more seriously than she did, she tried to warn him against her fickleness. "I think . . . that you see me as someone that I'm not," she told him. "I could disappoint you horribly." At the end of the week Duff took a train back to Paris. But Loeb chose to stay on for a while at St-Jean-de-Luz, savoring what he was certain was his romantic conquest and wondering how Hemingway and Pat Guthrie would take the news that he had supplanted them in Duff's affections.

Hemingway, meanwhile, had been engaged in completing the details of another visit to Spain. This time he wanted to begin with a week of trout fishing at Burguete and then go on to the fiesta in Pamplona. Bill Smith, who had recently arrived in Paris, jumped at the chance to join him and Hadley for the fishing as well as the bullfighting. Don Stewart told Hemingway to count him in as well. And so did Loeb. After learning of Loeb's dalliances with Duff, Hemingway might have responded by telling him to get lost, but by not doing so he meant to convince his friend that he bore him no animosity. Loeb, after all, had worked hard to get him into Boni and Liveright.

Hemingway, however, did not like feeling indebted to anyone, and particularly to Loeb. Furthermore, he was secretly furious that a Jew had muscled his way into Duff's Gentile affections. Wherefore, he invited Duff and Pat to join the fun. "Pamplona's going to be damned good," he deceitfully assured Loeb in a letter he mailed to St-Jean on June 21. "Pat and Duff are coming too," he added with elaborate casualness. "Pat has sent off to Scotland for rods and Duff to England for funds." Thus, having been shown by his mother that the best way to punish someone was to humiliate him, he set up a confrontation that would cause Loeb excruciating pain— and which when recreated in *The Sun Also Rises* would haunt him for the rest of his life.

Although Loeb was relieved by the friendly tone of this letter if not by its surprising news, two worried-sounding messages that he received from Duff were somewhat troubling to him, despite their tender protestations of how much she missed him. "I'm miserable without you," she said in the first of them. "Now for a doubtful glad tidings. I am coming on the Pamplona trip with Hem and your lot. Can you bear it? With Pat of course. If this appears impossible for you, let me know and I'll try to get out of it. But I'm dying to come and feel that even seeing you and being able to talk to you will be better than nothing." Three days later, she again voiced her uneasiness. "It will be a great joy to see you again," she began, "though I expect I shall have a bit of a time managing the situation. Hem has promised to be good and we ought to have really a mar-velous time."

Suddenly convinced that it would behoove him to cut back a bit on the amount of time he had been planning to spend in Heming-way's company, Loeb wired him that he had changed his mind about coming to Burguete for the full week. Instead, he would wait at St-Jean for Duff and Pat to arrive and come on with them. That way, he would be able to deal with his rivals one at a time. For they both would surely be trying hard to hold on to Duff, even though they both would surely fail.

3

THE trip to Burguete was a huge disappointment to all concerned, especially to the man who had planned it. In the first place, Duff and her two companions never did show up, having decided for some reason to tarry at St-Jean until the festivities at Pamplona were about to begin. Second, the wonderful stream he remembered from the year before had been ruined by logging and was full of trash. The fish had been killed, the pools destroyed and the dams broken down. "Made me feel sick," Hemingway told his father.

Pamplona had likewise been profaned. "The Garden of Eden wasn't the same," Don Stewart lamented. The sort of crowd that a later age would refer to as the Beautiful People had discovered the fiesta of San Fermín. Big cars from Biarritz were parked in the streets and uniformed chauffeurs idled beside them. One could hear English being spoken in the cafés; it was more difficult to get good tickets to the bullfights; and the prices of hotel rooms were noticeably higher than in 1924. Stewart also felt personally let down. For with the intrusion of that "devil, sex" the atmosphere of "male revel" had disappeared from the gatherings of the Hemingway circle. Loeb was in an unshakably sullen mood and no wonder; at St-Jean, Duff had disappointed him terribly, just as she had predicted she might. Over a drink in the hotel bar one night, while Pat was out of the room, she had bluntly told him she no longer desired him. "Pat broke the spell," she said. "He worked hard at it." Nevertheless, Loeb had accompanied them to Pamplona, hoping against hope that he could win her back, only to find that in addition to sharing a bedroom with Pat she blatantly went after Hemingway. She was "wild about Ernest," in Bill Smith's opinion, and Hemingway was so tactless about returning her signals of interest that Hadley in her distress took to excusing herself and retiring early, pleading that she was awfully tired or had a headache.

Hemingway and Duff sometimes appeared for drinks wearing matching berets and held whispered conversations that tended to exclude everyone else. Their affectionate behavior did not seem to anger Pat, however; instead, he reserved all his venom for the hang-dog Loeb. Perhaps because she felt sorry for him, perhaps for other reasons, Duff went off alone with Loeb on Friday night for an hour or so. The next day at lunch her cameo face was marred by a black eye and an ugly contusion on her forehead. Astonished and deeply upset, Loeb started to ask her what had happened, but Hemingway interrupted, Loeb recalled in his autobiography, "saying she had fallen against the railing. I boiled, but could think of no retort. Pat was sour, ugly. Hadley had lost her smile. Don tried a quip that went lame. Bill looked grim." Clearly, Pat had punished Duff with his fists for offering encouragement to a Jew. Just as clearly, Hemingway intended to defend Pat against any criticism coming from Loeb.

That night, Hemingway's vengeful plan reached its climax. Loeb expressed his disgust with Pat, so the account in Loeb's autobiography began. "You lay off Pat," Hemingway interjected. "You've done enough to spoil this party." Pat interpreted this remark as the cue for a showdown. "Why don't you get out?" he shouted at Loeb. "I don't want you here. Hem doesn't want you here. Nobody wants you." Loeb looked straight at Duff. "I will," he said, "the instant Duff wants it." Duff shook her head with seductive slowness. "You know . . . that I do *not* want you to go." Loeb's appeal to Duff to protect him from expulsion filled Hemingway with contempt. "You lousy bastard," he sneered. "Running to a woman."

All his life Loeb would remember that he then rose to his feet and asked Hemingway to step outside. Hemingway obliged him. In a dark street a short distance away, they stopped. If Loeb felt a twinge of fear—Hemingway outweighed him, after all, by forty pounds— he was also saddened. This man had been his friend; now he had become his "bitter lashing enemy." Loeb stripped off his jacket, carefully removed his horn-rimmed glasses, put them in one of the pockets and looked around for a safe place to lay the jacket down. He didn't want his glasses to get broken, he muttered, since he might not be able to get them properly repaired in a town like Pamplona. Suddenly, he became aware that Hemingway was smiling at him, with that mischievously boyish smile "that made it so hard not to like him." Loeb said, "I don't want to hit you." "Me either," said Hemingway. Together they walked back to the café.

The next morning the concierge in Loeb's hotel handed him a note from Hemingway. "I was terribly tight and nasty to you last night and I don't want you to go away with that nasty insulting lousiness as the last thing of the fiestas [*sic*]. I wish I could wipe out all the mean-ness and I suppose I can't but this is to let you know that I'm thoroly ashamed of the way I acted and the stinking, unjust uncalled for things I said."

Hemingway had belatedly expressed deep regret to Bill Smith for his intolerably offensive remarks about Bill's older brother, Y. K. He had tacitly apologized to McAlmon for his beastliness to him in

Granada by being nice as pie upon their return to Paris. A third episode in which a remorseful Hemingway tried to make amends for untoward behavior had occurred in the fall of 1924. He and the unmuscular Nathan Asch had a fistfight, and Asch was knocked unconscious. In Asch's own words, "He knocked me cold on the Boulevard Montparnasse, after telling me there wasn't anything I had [as a writer] that was original except maybe a little freshness. That night as I slept in my room on the Rue Campagne Premiere he broke into my room drunk and in tears and told me he could never forgive himself and that I had more [talent] than anybody."

A rearranged version of this episode resurfaced a year later in Hemingway's account in *The Sun Also Rises* of his contretemps with Loeb. At the height of their quarrel in the Café Suizo in Pamplona, Robert Cohn (Loeb) knocks out Jake Barnes (Hemingway). Jake enters Cohn's room later that night and finds him lying face down on his bed in the dark, overcome with contrition and crying silently.

> "I'm sorry, Jake. Please forgive me."
> "Forgive you, hell."
> "Please forgive me, Jake."

A complicated man, Ernest Hemingway. Enraged by Loeb's sexual success with Duff, he set up a social situation that exposed his rival to Pat Guthrie's savage abuse. Then he himself spoke so outrageously to Loeb that the man had no choice but to challenge him to a fight—a fight that Loeb would have lost very badly. Yet at the moment of truth Hemingway's mood abruptly shifted; instead of smacking Loeb he smiled at him, and sealed his peacemaking the following morning with a written apology. *The Sun Also Rises,* however, registered a shift back in the direction of his original mood. For the novel is unsparing in its account of Robert Cohn's swellheadedness about women, his caddish treatment of his faithful mistress, Frances Clyne, his sophomoric acceptance of W. H. Hudson's *The Purple Land* as a guidebook to what life holds, his "hard, Jewish, stubborn streak" and his abysmal lack of personal dignity in following Brett (Duff) around Pamplona "like a bloody steer," as the Pat Guthrie character, Mike Campbell, sneeringly puts it. To make Cohn—that is, Loeb—look even worse, Hemingway then topped off all of these recognizable aspects of Loeb's life with an incident drawn from his own in which he had looked bad from beginning to end—from the knockout punch he had thrown at the physically outclassed Asch to the unmanly tears that wouldn't stop coming when he broke into his victim's room and apologized.

Yet the incorporation of his beating of Asch into the portrait of Cohn can be viewed another way, as a testimony not to Hemingway's insensate desire to "get" Harold Loeb, as he assured Kitty Cannell he was going to, but to the degree of his identification with the character he created in Loeb's image. Left Bank readers in 1926 gleefully assumed that *The Sun Also Rises* was a straightforward roman à clef. Jake Barnes was Hemingway, Brett Ashley was Duff Twysden, Robert Cohn was Harold Loeb, Bill Gorton was Don Stewart, Mike Campbell was Pat Guthrie, and so on. But this assumption overlooked—among other things—Hemingway's imaginative involvement with Cohn. The author of *The Sun Also Rises* took sadistic delight in degrading the fictional stand-in for Harold Loeb, only to become ashamed of himself in the process and ambivalently sympathetic with Cohn as a result. Through Jake Barnes, Hemingway gave voice to his on-again, off-again feelings. "I liked to see [Mike Campbell] hurt Cohn," the sleepless Jake tells himself in bed one night. But in his next breath he admits that "I wished he would not do it, though, because afterward it made me disgusted with myself." At another point Jake says of Cohn, "He can be damn nice." At yet another point he says, "I hate him, myself." And at still another he says, speaking directly to the reader, "Somehow I feel I have not shown Robert Cohn clearly." Perhaps it was Ernest Hemingway that he was unable to show clearly.

4

AT the bullfights in Madrid, which the Hemingways headed for by themselves as soon as the Pamplona fiesta ended, the matador Juan Belmonte dedicated one of his bulls to them and Hadley was presented with an ear, which she wrapped in a handkerchief and stuck away in a bureau drawer, just as Brett Ashley would do with the ear given to her. But despite Belmonte's great reputation, the matador who most impressed the Hemingways was a young man they had first seen in Pamplona, Niño de la Palma. "He did everything Belmonte did and did it better," Hemingway told Gertrude Stein and Alice Toklas on July 15, "all the adornos and desplantes and all. Then he stepped out all by himself without any tricks—suave, templando with the cape smooth and slow—splendid banderillos and started with 5 Naturales with the muleta—beautiful complete faena all linked up and then killed perfectly." A native of Ronda, Niño had every aficionado in Spain talking about him. One afternoon he asked Hadley to hold his cape, and her thrilled acceptance of it seems to have given Hemingway an idea. He could channel the action of the novel he had just started to write toward a climactic love affair between the thirtyish heroine and a boyish bullfighter whom he would call Pedro Romero.

Trial drafts of the first section of the book—which at first he called *Fiesta*—were produced in Madrid, Valencia, and San Sebastián in late July and early August, and many of the pages were of shockingly low quality. In some there were characters completely unleavened by literary imagination named Hem, Hadley, Duff, and Dos Passos; in others the narrator talked about the heroine in a tone of voice that made him sound like a teenager. "She had been turning all this sex appeal on me all the time we were talking." That Hemingway had had a preliminary conversation with a knowledgeable friend in Paris about the risks of writing a novel about a man who has lost his penis was made clear by the sentence which read, "Scott Fitzgerald told me once it couldn't be treated except as a humorous subject." Not until the Hemingways left San Sebastián, where they greatly enjoyed the swimming and there were wonderful trees along the promenade above the beach, and moved into the Grand Hotel at Hendaye across the border in France did the struggling author finally hit his stride, albeit his story still began quite confusingly *in medias res,* rather than chronologically in Paris as the published version would.

Despite long stints of writing in Hendaye that filled up notebook after notebook, he still found the time and energy to start reading *War and Peace*. The choice of Tolstoy's novel was not without significance. Back in Paris in June he had started writing a novel that he tentatively thought of calling *Along with Youth*. The hero, Nick Adams, is introduced on the manuscript's first page. He is aboard the troopship *Chicago* as it nears the French coast. A couple of Polish officers, a sexually complaisant French girl and a likable youth nicknamed—like Howie Jenkins—"The Carper" are also on board. Apparently, the author expected to follow Nick to Italy, where the focus would alternate between scenes of war in the mountains and valleys of the Veneto and scenes of romance in Milan with a nurse named Agnes. The story died on page twenty-seven. But Hemingway was not disheartened. Someday he would write another novel about the war in Italy, and in Hendaye it appears to have struck him that the story might include an episode involving childbirth—told from the expectant father's point of view. For although he didn't record this idea as a literary note, he talked about it in a general way in a letter to Barklie Henry, from whom he would eventually take the names of both the hero and the heroine in *A Farewell to Arms*. Barklie's wife had recently had a rough time giving birth to their first child. She now felt fully recovered from her ordeal, but Hemingway wanted the Henrys to know that he was thinking of them. On August 12, accordingly, while feeling somewhat lonely because Hadley had left that very morning for Paris—she had been away from Bumby for much too long, she said—he sat down and wrote to Barklie. "I'm terribly glad Barbara is fit again," he began. "That was rotten she was so ill. God how you must have worried. Somehow I don't think many people realize what kind of things young fathers go through. When you really love someone it can certainly give you hell. Motherhood is so darn spectacular that fatherhood's never gotten much publicity!"

Some nights he worked on his fiesta novel until his head felt like a frozen cabbage, but always he got up early the next morning and plunged onwards. By August 19, when he boarded the train for Paris, he figured that another month of work at the same pace would bring him to the end of the story.

"Toward the last it was like a fever," he told his pen friend Bernard Berenson twenty-seven years later. "Toward the last I was sprinting, like in a bicycle race, and I did not want to lose my speed making love or anything else and so had my wife go on a trip with two friends of hers down to the Loire." And when he finally crossed the finish line, he sank into a depression. "I . . . was hollow and lonely and needed a girl very badly," he confessed to Berenson.

> So I was in bed with a no good girl when my wife came home and had to get the girl out onto the roof of the saw mill . . . and change the sheets and come down to open the door of the court. Everybody happy at the surprise return except the girl on the roof of the sawmill. . . . But I had written too fast and the excitement was all in me and almost nothing in the book. So I fornicate into that terrible, dreadful state of absolute clear-headed-ness that is non-believer's limbo and then we go down to Schruns in the Vorarlberg and have a wonderful, healthy, happy life and I re-write. Then you re-write again. Then you have a book. With all sorts of various dreadful things happening all the time.

It was a good story, but somehow Hemingway had forgotten that Hadley's trip to the Loire did not take place until the spring of 1926. Still, he was right in remembering that the preceding September he had been sexually involved with another woman, for his impulse to kick over the traces of marital fidelity had been overmastering him more and more, in spite of guilt feelings that would soon have him talking of suicide.

As to who his regular sex partner actually was that fall, it was not Duff Twysden. After his return from Pamplona he made no effort to see her, and the letter she sent to him around the first of October indicates unmistakably that their relationship had lost its magic for both of them. The letter was written on the stationery of a studio-apartment hotel in the rue Delambre, but actually Duff was living outside the city in order to economize, which she desperately needed to do. Don Stewart at her urging had paid her hotel bill in Pamplona, and now she was looking to other friends to help her out with other bills.

> Ernest my dear, forgive me for this effort but can you possibly lend me some money? I am in a stinking fix but for once only temporary and can pay you back for *sure*. I want 3000 francs—but for Gods sake lend me as much as you can. . . . If you can—and will be an angel will you leave an answer here with Fred—at the bar as soon as you get this? I'm in such a stew so hope you'll really forgive this. . . . Best luck. As ever, Duff Twysden.

The message was strictly business. Duff wanted her former drinking and traveling companion's money, nothing else. The romantic gaze of Lady Twysden had shifted to new horizons. Then too, she may have heard someone in the Dingo say that Hemingway had lately been seen fairly often with two well-to-do young women from the United States, Pauline and Jinny Pfeiffer.

5

PAULINE and Jinny's father—like Hadley's father, coincidentally—was a St. Louisan who as a young man had gone to work for a drug business owned by his family. Hadley's father, however, was a most reluctant businessman, whereas Paul Pfeiffer burned to get rich. After building a chain of successful smalltown drugstores, he branched out into agriculture. Near the town of Piggott, Arkansas, an imperium of 60,000 acres was methodically assembled by him for the shrewd price of a dollar an acre. Tenant farmers were recruited from as far away as Iowa and Illinois to produce crops of cotton, corn, wheat, and soybeans. In short order, Pfeiffer owned Piggott's bank and Piggott's cotton gin, as well as the largest house in town, which he filled with massive, German-style furniture that reminded him of the fatherland of his ancestors. At his further instruction, one of the rooms in the house was converted into a chapel, for although Pfeiffer himself had no interest in religion his wife was an ardent Catholic who wanted their four children to be raised in her faith.

Pauline, an intelligent and serious-minded girl who loved to read and had a flair for writing, did her high-school work at the Visitation Convent in St. Louis, majored in journalism at the University of Missouri and in 1918 took a job on the Cleveland *Star*. Her next move was to the New York *Daily Telegraph,* where after a time her writing caught the eye of Frank Crowninshield, the editor of *Vanity Fair,* who was looking for a fashion reporter and publicist. Although her tenure at *Vanity Fair* overlapped with Edmund Wilson's, no mention of her appears in his journals of the period. It was not that she wasn't bookish or had no interest in the intrigues of the in-house literati, but rather that her social orbit never intersected with Wilson's. After business hours Pauline was apt to relax in the sumptuous Manhattan pied-à-terre of her favorite relatives, Uncle Gus Pfeiffer and his wife, Louise. Gus and yet another of the talented Pfeiffer brothers owned Richard Hudnut Perfumes, Sloan's Liniment and William Warner Pharmaceuticals. Through Uncle Gus, Pauline was introduced to and then impulsively agreed to marry a Hudnut official named Matthew Herold. On reflection, she was not entirely certain that she loved him. So when Mainbocher, the editor of the Paris *Vogue,* offered her a position as his assistant, she jumped at it. At a distance of three thousand miles, her feelings about her fiancé would surely come into sharper focus.

She was accompanied across the Atlantic by her younger sister Jinny, who always had free time on her hands because, unlike Pauline, she saw no earthly reason why young women of means should work for a living. In the early months of 1925 in Paris, the sisters enjoyed hobnobbing with fellow Americans from financially substantial families—Gerald and Sara Murphy, for instance, and Archibald MacLeish, and Harold Loeb. On a raw March afternoon in Loeb's apartment, their host and his girl friend, Kitty Cannell, brought them together with the Hemingways, who were just back from Austria. Loeb wanted to toast his fellow writer's new contract with Boni and Liveright.

Hemingway could not doubt that Pauline and Jinny were sisters. Both had bobbed their dark-brown hair to a "Dutch-girl" length and combed it forward in bangs. Both were small in stature, delicately boned, younger looking than their age and, unlike Hadley, who had not shed any of the weight she had gained in her pregnancy, pencil-thin. Another plus for Pauline in Hemingway's eyes was that she was dressed with the chic that one would expect from Mainbocher's assistant—her coat in particular on that cold afternoon in Loeb's apartment was really smashing—while Jinny's attractiveness was enhanced by her sardonic wit and the proud,

commanding way in which she held her head. Like Pauline, Jinny
was a woman who knew what she wanted—and high on her list
was the loving companionship of other women. Although she was
willing to go out with men, her sexual perferences were plainly
lesbian and would remain so. About Pauline's preferences there are
questions. In the forties, Hemingway would tell the chauffeur and
handyman, Toby Bruce, who had worked for him and Pauline in
Key West, that Jinny was trying to persuade her sister to switch
over to her side of the sex business. Even though this statement
probably represented conjecture, Pauline did have love affaires
with several women following her divorce from Hemingway. That
she had had similar affairs before she met him is also possible.
Indeed, it may have been Hadley—once the object of the affections
of her college roommate's mother—who was the first member of
the Hemingway family on whom Pauline trained her sights. For
when she and Jinny stopped by the Hemingway's apartment a few
days after their meeting at Loeb's, it was Hadley whom they came
to see. Moreover, Pauline's sensibilities were affronted by the brief
glimpse she had of the unshaven master of the house stretched out
reading on a rumpled bed; as she later told Kitty Cannell, she did
not see how Hadley could stand to live in such mean suroundings,
or in the company of such a lout. Nevertheless, Hadley was deeply
in love. Upon realizing this, did Pauline then decide to go after her
husband?

In any case, she soon went through a sea change in her attitude
toward Hemingway. He was as brilliant as he was handsome, as
humorous as he was courageous; Matthew Herold, her fiancé,
wasn't in the same league with this man. In an effort to catch his
attention, she resorted to schoolgirlish stratagems. "I was talking to
someone about you just the other day," she would say, and Hemingway would reply, "Oh? And what did he say?" For although he
had initially been more attracted to Jinny ("I'd like to take her out in
her sister's coat," he confided to Kitty Cannell), Pauline's efforts to
charm him easily won him over.

Throughout the remainder of the spring and into the early summer of 1925, she continued to massage him with flattery whenever
they met. By means of voluble opinions about novels old and new
and of somewhat long-winded anecdotes about office life at *Vanity
Fair,* she sought to demonstrate that she was more literary than his
current wife. With displays of vim and vigor, she also reminded him
of how much trimmer she was than Hadley, and how much
younger, although she was four years older than Hemingway. On
his return to Paris in August, she resumed her campaign. If Hadley
gave any sign of awareness that she now was engaged in a fight for

her husband, it was through the number of new pieces she mastered
to play for him on the piano. As the autumn leaves flamed up and
fell, Hemingway found himself trapped between conflicting alle-
giances. "I said perfectly calmly and not bluffingly," he would later
remind Pauline, "that if this wasn't cleared up by christmas I would
kill myself—because that would mean it wasn't going to clear up."

Unlucky in love, lucky at dice. That connoisseur of horseflesh and
sometime poet, Evan Shipman, had been promised by the Paris art
dealer who handled the work of Joan Miró that for five thousand
francs he could have a coveted canvas of the Spaniard's called *The
Farm*. But the guilt-riddled Hemingway wanted to present *The Farm*
to Hadley in honor of her thirty-fourth birthday on November 9.
On learning of his friend's interest in the painting, Shipman sport-
ingly offered to shoot dice with him for the right to buy it. Hemingway won, and with a little help from Dos Passos and other well-
heeled friends he raised the five thousand francs. Whereupon he
carried the painting home in triumph in a taxi and hung it above his
and Hadley's bed. Looking at *The Farm* together for the first time
proved to be a poignant moment for them both, for it brought back
memories of Spain, where they had once been happy.

6

ANOTHER landmark occasion that fall generated new tensions between them which Pauline did her best to take advantage of. On
October 5, Boni and Liveright published *In Our Time,* in an edition
of 1,335 copies that only Hemingway was sure would sell out right
away. The dedication page read "To Hadley Richardson Hemingway." On the back of the light-gray dust jacket were appreciations
of the author's talent by an array of recognized writers and critics,
including Edward J. O'Brien, Sherwood Anderson, John Dos Passos and Ford Madox Ford. Hemingway immediately regretted the
use of the Anderson blurb because it simply encouraged readers to
keep on comparing their work. He was sick and tired of hearing that
he was a disciple of Anderson's and that his debt to Gertrude Stein
was equally obvious. Somehow, he had to get both these monkeys
off his back. He could do so, he realized in a flash of illumination,
by writing a pocket-sized parody of Anderson's latest novel, *Dark
Laughter,* which he considered atrociously bad, and by salting and
peppering at least a couple of its pages with a little ridicule of his
redoubtable friend in the rue de Fleurus, who had lately been giving
him a hard time anyway, thanks no doubt to the machinations of

Miss Toklas. ("Ah," the parodist would exclaim, apropos of the achievement of Miss Stein, "there was a woman! Where were her experiments in words leading? What was at the bottom of it?") Such a book would also enable him to break his contract with Boni and Liveright, for, as Anderson's publisher and personal friend, Horace Liveright would have to reject it, and Hemingway would then be free to sign with Scribners or Harcourt, Brace, or some other house of greater distinction.

The idea was flawless—as long as he didn't allow himself to remember how very kind Anderson had been to him over the years. Hadley, though, was not about to allow him to forget it. She thought his idea "detestable" and told him so, which he didn't appreciate any more than he had his mother's moral advice in years past, and which didn't deter him.

Borrowing his title, *The Torrents of Spring,* from Turgenev, he started writing the little book in mid-November and finished by Thanksgiving. After she read it, Hadley felt even sorrier for Anderson than before and expressed the hope that Hemingway wouldn't publish it. Dos Passos likewise recommended that he keep the manuscript to himself. There were some laughs in it here and there, he conceded, but on the whole he felt it wasn't "quite good enough to stand on its own feet as a parody," and besides which, why would Hemingway wish to chop up an aging author who at one time had written some remarkable stories? Scott Fitzgerald, on the other hand, told Hemingway what he wanted to hear. As did Pauline. "About the best comic book ever written by an American," said Fitzgerald. It's great, agreed Pauline; by all means, she urged, send it to Liveright.

The disagreement between Hadley and Pauline about *The Torrents* was at once literary and moral. It was also a function of their overarching struggle for possession of the man they both loved. The stakes in this struggle meant so much to them that not even the frank-speaking Hadley, let alone the politic Pauline, dared to talk with Hemingway about the book's black-humored account of their triangular troubles. For beneath its surrealistic send-ups of *Dark Laughter* in which, to paraphrase a few of Peter Quennell's admiring comments in the *New Statesman and Nation,* the wild, distant war whoops of mysterious Indians take the place of the dusky laughter of Negro maid servants, and the alcoholic Scripps O'Neil struggles like Anderson's Sponge Martin with his formless, but portentous, thoughts, dragging them across the page like flies newly escaped from a bath of molasses—beneath its crazily random references to Huysmans, Wordsworth, Calvin Coolidge, Steve Brodie, Coxey's army, Scott Fitzgerald, John Dos Passos, Frank Crowninshield's *Vanity Fair,* Mencken's *American Mercury* and Scofield Thayer's *Dial* —beneath the deftly tempered ribaldry and marvelously well sustained irony that would inspire Allen Tate to hail it in the pages of the *Nation* as "a small masterpiece of American fiction"— *The Torrents of Spring* was about Hemingway and his women, told in Anderson's clodhopper style.

Scripps O'Neil, a tall, lean man with a tall, lean face, pushes his way into a popular beanery in Petoskey, Michigan. "The Best by Test," the beanery's motto flatulently promises. Inside is an elderly waitress with a curious story to tell, a story which symbolically makes Hadley Richardson out to have been Grace Hemingway's daughter. The elderly waitress, whose name is Diana, was born and brought up in England, she says, in the Lake Country to be precise. ("A field of golden daffodils," Scripps thinks to himself. "The wind blowing at Windermere.") As a jeune fille, the waitress continues in her inimitable way, she had been taken to Paris by her mummy. It was about the time of the Paris Exposition of 1900. (The year in which Hadley turned eight.) They stopped at a coiffeur's shop to purchase some smelling salts and then took adjoining rooms in a hotel. When Diana awoke the next morning, she found that the person lying in her mummy's bed was an elderly French general. (Mother into military man: an interesting metamorphosis.) Where is my mummy, the little girl asked, but the general said he didn't know what she was talking about. It was he and Diana who had taken the suite in the hotel, he assured her, and when the little girl ran downstairs and looked at the hotel register, she discovered that it told the same story. Later on in the coiffeur's shop, she again was informed that the day before she had come in with an elderly French general. Never again did the jeune fille see her mummy. On bidding goodbye to her, the French general gave her a hundred francs. With this gift, she had been able to go to America and thus to meet, many, many years later, the tall and lean Scripps O'Neil.

Scripps likes being with the elderly waitress. He likes listening to her "picturesque" speech and thinking about her "strange background." Scripps marries the elderly waitress. Not long afterwards, though, a "relief waitress" appears in the beanery, "a buxom, jolly-looking girl." The new waitress's name is Mandy. Mandy's vigor and health appeal to Scripps. He also is excited by her story of the aged Henry James's instruction to his nurse to turn off the light so as to spare his blushes when Britain's Order of Merit was presented to him, and by the other literary anecdotes she has on the tip of her tongue. Scripps likes Mandy, he decides.

In the opinion of Scripps's spouse, Mandy is "no better than a slut." Trembling with indignation and a sense of threat, she asks herself, "Was that the way to do? Was that the thing to do? Go after another woman's man? Come between man and wife? Break up a home? And all with these interminable literary reminiscences. These endless anecdotes." Trying desperately to compete intellectually with Mandy, the elderly waitress buys a subscription to *Harper's* magazine. She is not sure, though, that it will do the trick. Can she hold him? Can she hold him? she nervously wonders.

Finally, only three people are left in the beanery, Scripps, his aging wife, and the robust Mandy. Scripps has eyes only for Mandy. His wife feels that the time has come to walk away from her marriage. "She knew it was over." In a last-ditch effort to recapture Scripps's attention, she mentions a new article in the *American Mercury*—on chiropractors, by Mencken. It is no use. Scripps's wife leaves the beanery. "You are my woman now," Scripps tells Mandy. Yet by the end of the evening Scripps is no longer sure about his feelings, and the little drama closes on a note of uncertainty.

> It grows late in the beanery. Mandy talks on. She is his woman now. He is her man. But is he her man? . . . Mandy talking on. Telling literary reminiscences. Authentic incidents. . . . But were they enough? Scripps wondered. She was his woman. But for how long?

The Torrents of Spring is a funny story, at times a very funny story. It deserved the encomia of Peter Quennell and Allen Tate. But when the parody is set in the context of Hemingway's marital crisis, when it is remembered that Hadley and Pauline were both hovering over him as he wrote it and read the manuscript the instant it was available to them, its detestability cannot be blinked. The author, to be sure, was contending at the time with onslaughts of depression; black humor served as a substitute for pistol and ball. Then, too, his narcissism may have made him oblivious, as it so often did, to the feelings of others. Or he may have recognized that his broodings were all but undisguised and he didn't care. He and Hadley would not separate for many months, and his union with Pauline would last for years. Nevertheless, the marital doom of both women is written on the wall for all to see in *The Torrents*, along with some insulting reasons why they would be cast off. The parodist portrayed Hadley and Pauline as abjectly anxious to please—as waitresses in the most degrading sense of the term—but then indicated that sooner or later they would have to go, Hadley because she was too old, Pauline because she was too talkative. Given the hopes that both women cherished in their hearts in the fall of 1925, denial must have ruled their minds. *The Torrents* referred to characters in *Dark Laughter,* not to them. But did either of them fully believe this? It is hard to imagine that they escaped the shadow of doubt so easily.

7

PAUL Rosenfeld's review of *In Our Time* in the November 25 *New Republic* confirmed Hemingway in his belief that it was absolutely essential to his chances for fame that he distance himself from Sherwood Anderson. For while Rosenfeld praised Hemingway's prose for its "lyricism, aliveness and energy tremendously held in check" and likened his rhythms to "the trip-hammer thud" of Stravinsky's *Le Sacre du Printemps,* he also pointed out that the diction in *In Our Time* was akin to Anderson's vernacular usages and that its "steady reiterations" of certain words derived from a practice of Gertrude Stein's. In the only negative review the book received, from Herschel Brickell in the New York *Evening Post,* Anderson's name again came up. Hemingway's stories were hardly stories in the accepted sense, Brickell declared, except "My Old Man," which not even the author of "I Want to Know Why" could have improved upon.

To convince himself that his double cross of Horace Liveright would be justified, Hemingway took another tack. Instead of pointing to book reviews, he held up sales figures. In the two months since its publication, the small first edition of *In Our Time* hadn't come close to selling out. Did the fault lie with the reading public, which historically wasn't much interested in buying collections of short stories? No, it lay with Liveright, the disgruntled author decided. Because the publisher had not believed in the book's salability, he hadn't pushed it, hadn't advertised it. In a letter to Liveright on December 7, Hemingway let him know that under separate cover he was sending him the manuscript of *The Torrents of Spring,* that he wanted a decision on it by cable "at once," and that he hadn't been happy with the way *In Our Time* had been handled. The massing of "all those blurbs on the cover, each one of which would have made, used singly, a valuable piece of publicity," had been a bad idea, he told him, because it had "simply put the reader on the defensive."

Ever since quitting the *Star,* Hemingway reminded himself, he had had virtually no income. He had had to pay for his and Hadley's trips by depleting their savings and he had had to borrow money to buy Miró's *The Farm.* He was fed up with living like that. As he warmed to the task of covering up his consciousness of what a dirty trick he was playing on Liveright, it further occurred to him that he was a family man, whose wife and child had basic needs that royalties from *In Our Time* ought to have enabled him to supply. The more he thought about Liveright, the angrier he became. If marital relations in the rue Notre-Dame-des-Champs were rocky, it was partly because of his and Hadley's financial worries, which that Jew publisher in New York had done nothing to alleviate. ("To hear him talk," Fitzgerald reported to Max Perkins, "you'd think Liveright had broken up his home and robbed him of millions.") As a responsible husband and father, Hemingway concluded, he had been compelled to write *The Torrents of Spring*. Offering Liveright a manuscript which he knew in advance would be turned down was the only way to get out of his Semitic clutches and move on to a more honorable publisher. It wasn't he, in short, who had double-crossed Liveright; it was Liveright who had double-crossed him.

A self-induced anger, a self-pitying sense of victimization and a convenient anti-Semitism did more than put the torch to Hemingway's piled-up guilt. They also lit the flame that led to "Fifty Grand." He started writing the story in early December and finished it within a week. It was "easy for me to write," he told Fitzgerald.

In a typically Hemingwayan leap, the author's mind moved from the world of literature to the world of sports, translating nasty thoughts about Horace Liveright into nasty thoughts about the renowned Jewish boxer whose ring name was Benny Leonard. At the New York Hippodrome on June 26, 1922, in the thirteenth round of a fifteen-round fight, Leonard, the world lightweight champion, hit Jack Britton, the welterweight king, a low blow, and Britton was declared the winner on a foul. Again and again, Hemingway mulled over the events of that fight, rearranging and expanding them until they could carry everything he wanted to get out of his system about Liveright—and about a couple of other Jews, while he was at it.

Welterweight Jack Brennan is a devoted family man. At Hogan's health farm over in Jersey, where he is training for a defense of his title, he keeps telling his trainer, Jerry Doyle, the narrator of "Fifty Grand," how much he misses his wife, and Jerry notices on his own that Jack writes his wife a letter every day. Jack is also having trouble sleeping at night, for reasons that further reveal how seriously he takes his family responsibilities. "What do you think about, Jack, when you can't sleep?" Jerry asks. "Oh, I worry," Jack says. "I worry about property I got up in the Bronx, I worry about property I got in Florida. I worry about the kids. I worry about the wife. . . . I got some stocks and I worry about them. What the hell don't I think about?"

Over lunch at Hanley's tavern, Jack reveals to Jerry that he is doubtful about his chances against his upcoming opponent. "I'm going to need a lot of luck with that boy," he says. "Handle him like you handled Kid Lewis," Jerry tells him. All at once, the narrative erupts with references to kikes. "Kid Lewis," Jack snorts. "That kike!" A couple of women who have been drinking for some time at a nearby table overhear this remark and one of them objects to it. "What do you mean, kike?" she says. "What do you mean, kike, you big Irish bum?" "Sure," Jack says. "That's it." The woman goes on. "Kikes," she says. "They're always talking about kikes, these big Irishmen. What do you mean, kikes?" Jack suggests to Jerry that they leave. "Kikes," the woman says again. "Whoever saw you buy a drink? Your wife sews your pockets up every morning. These Irishmen and their kikes!" Jack has the final word. "Sure," he says. "And you give away a lot of things free too, don't you?"

It is mainly by inversion that these stinging exchanges measure the intensity of the author's anti-Semitic rage. For all but one of the exclamatory references to kikes come out of the mouth of a person who is seemingly protesting against such references. Jack Brennan, whom Hemingway sides with from beginning to end in "Fifty Grand," is protected against forfeiture of the reader's sympathy—which would have happened if he had fulminated excessively about Jews—by his creator's cunning introduction of a drunken "broad" who echoes Jack's epithet seven times in less than half a page.

A much more self-controlled bigot than his friend Ezra Pound (and a good thing, too: Hemingway did, after all, want to sell "Fifty Grand" to a mainstream American magazine like *Collier's* or the *Saturday Evening Post*), he further muted the signs of his prejudice by being somewhat vague about the ethnic identity of the fighter who finally squares off against Jack in Madison Square Garden. Hemingway certainly thought of him as Jewish, not only because he had written "Fifty Grand" with the Jack Britton-Benny Leonard fight in mind, but because he identified his hero's opponent with Horace Liveright. Solly Freedman, the challenger's manager, is clearly Jewish, but Solly says his fighter is "some sort of a Dane," possibly because he is blond. The boy who brings the gloves to ringside firmly asserts to the contrary that the challenger is a Bohemian. To add further confusion, and the opportunity for another slur, Jimmy Walcott is the challenger's ring name but not his real name. ("What do you call yourself 'Walcott' for?" Jack tauntingly asks his opponent as the two men come to the center of the ring to touch gloves. "Didn't you know he was a nigger?")

Two other characters in the story are Jews—at least in Hemingway's mind. At the training camp one afternoon, a couple of pool-
room operators show up in the company of John Collins, Jack's
manager. Morgan and Steinfelt are their names and gambling on the
outcome of sports events could be called their game, except that—
in Jack's words—"they don't take any chances, those two." Jack is
not likely to beat Walcott anyway, but to make sure that he doesn't
these two sharply dressed strangers talk him into betting fifty thousand dollars of his own money on his favored opponent. "I'll get
twenty-five thousand bucks [profit]," Jack later tells Jerry. Presumably, Morgan and Steinfelt will also be betting heavily on Walcott.
But, in fact, in an elaborate double cross, they have bribed Walcott
to throw the fight by fouling Jack. Their money is on Jack. Despite
his unawareness that he is being set up, Jack sarcastically says of
these sharks, they are a "fine bunch," and through their slimy presence Hemingway covertly degraded two Jews whom he had gone
after before. In Steinfelt, he struck at Gertrude Stein for the second
time in less than a month. In Morgan—a name that was even more
legendary on Wall Street than Kuhn, Loeb—he made a contemptuous addition to the assault on Harold Loeb that he was in the
process of mounting in *The Sun Also Rises.*

The account of Jack Brennan's last fight is the high point of "Fifty
Grand." It was an achievement for which Hemingway could be said
to have been preparing himself for a decade. To begin with, the
knowledge he could call on about boxing was impressive. Not only
had he himself been boxing since high school, but by hanging
around gyms where professionals trained he had picked up vast
quantities of anecdotal lore. He had seen scores of fights in arenas on
both sides of the Atlantic and had read follow-up accounts of countless others in the newspapers. Finally, there were Ring Lardner's
short stories and columns about boxing, which he had studied with
loving care. (It was sadly indicative of Hemingway's tendency to be
ungrateful to mentors that he went out of his way in "Fifty Grand"
to take a potshot at Lardner, simply because he was annoyed with
reviewers who had referred to the two of them as being somewhat
similar writers. "This Lardner," says Jerry Doyle, recalling the sun-
baked afternoon when Jack Dempsey had taken the heavyweight
crown from the giant Jess Willard, "this Lardner, he's so wise now,
ask him about when he picked Willard at Toledo.") Yet if Hemingway conceivably could have written an encyclopedic history of boxing, he did not forget as a writer of fiction that less is more. His
sense of selection is "unerring," Dorothy Parker would say of him
in her *New Yorker* review of *Men Without Women* (1927), the book of

stories in which "Fifty Grand" first appeared in hard covers. "He discards details with a magnificent lavishness; he keeps his words to their short path."

After a grueling battle through the early rounds, Jack is knocked down for an eight-count. When he gets up again, Walcott starts toward him. His purpose in doing so, however, is to lose the fight, and he does his best to do so by socking his right into Jack's body just as hard as he can and just as low as he can—an appalling five inches, in fact, below the belt. Jack's eyes are bulging out of his head with the pain. He walks as though all his insides are falling out. But if he goes down, there goes his fifty grand. "Come on and fight," he croaks to Walcott. Jack swings wildly at Walcott's head and the challenger covers up.

> Then he swung the left and it hit Walcott in the groin and the right hit Walcott right bang where he'd hit Jack. Way low below the belt. Walcott went down and grabbed himself there and rolled and twisted around.

The fight is over, Walcott has won on a foul, the double cross hasn't worked. The sums that Morgan and Steinfelt had secretly bet on Jack have been lost and the large bribe that they must have dangled before Walcott will not be paid.

Dorothy Parker would speak in her *Men Without Women* review of the "dangerous influence" Hemingway had come to exert on other writers by 1927. "The simple thing he does looks so easy to do," she would observe. "But look at the boys who try to do it." "Fifty Grand," however, was not a simple thing. Behind the facade of a cynical and brutal boxing story lay Hemingway's ugly wish to believe that a Jewish publisher had hit him in the groin, so to speak, and that therefore it was all right for him to reply in kind. Two wrongs, in this case, made a right. By that deft inversion of morality, Jack Brennan became a hero—and Hemingway's own greed was justified.

8

SCHRUNS was the place to read, Hemingway remarked to Archibald MacLeish, and during the winter of 1925–1926 he managed to do a fair amount of it there. The first book he read was Turgenev's *Fathers and Sons,* followed by Thomas Mann's *Buddenbrooks,* half of which he thought was "pretty good," but not as enjoyable as the next book he turned to, Wilkie Collins's *The Moonstone.* Thereafter he was engaged by Captain Marryat's *Peter Simple,* which he hadn't read since boyhood but found he still loved, Somerset Maugham's *Of Human Bondage,* Conrad's *Within the Tides* and two illustrated German war books, the first a description of the mountain fighting on the Italian front which would someday aid him in envisioning certain events in *A Farewell to Arms,* the second a history of the Württemberg Artillery. Understandably, he also devoured the Autumn-Winter issue of *This Quarter,* for among other items of interest it contained "The Undefeated," as well as the editor Ernest Walsh's review of *In Our Time.* ("The first impression one gets on reading a story by Hemingway," Walsh observed, "is that this writer has been getting ready inside himself and outside himself for a long time before he began to write.") Hemingway thought the review was "swell," but rereading "The Undefeated" proved to be disillusioning. The story wasn't as good as he had been convinced it was when he wrote it. "Oh Christ," he exclaimed to Walsh, "I want to write so well and it makes me sore to think that at one time I thought I *was* writing so well and was evidently in a slump."

Also distressing to him was Walsh's extremely laudatory judgment of a new collection of Robert McAlmon's stories. Hemingway had long had a low opinion of McAlmon as a writer, and this opinion had been reinforced in the fall of 1925 by a resurgence of his low opinion of him as a man. In his viciously gossipy way, McAlmon had taken to spreading the story that Scott Fitzgerald was a homosexual. Hemingway rebuked the rumormonger to his face when he heard of this. For a couple of nights thereafter, so a couple of Hemingway's friends reported to him, McAlmon had gone about declaring that the author of *In Our Time* was an ungrateful swine who had forgotten he owed his start as a writer to Contact Press. At which point Hemingway decided that McAlmon was "a son of a bitch with a mind like an ingrowing toe nail." Yet he surely would have objected to Walsh's praise of McAlmon's book even if his personal relations with the author had still been cordial. For McAlmon's talent, in Walsh's rash judgment, was superior to Mark Twain's. You are right, Hemingway replied, but only in the sense that "Mark Twain wrote great, vast quantities of Hog Wash."

> He also wrote one, and one only very wonderful thing—Huck Finn.
> And if you will, now, read Huckleberry Finn, honest to God read it
> as I re-read it only about three months ago, not anything else by Mark
> Twain, but Huckleberry Finn, and the last few Chapters of it were
> tacked on to finish it off by Howells or somebody. The story stops
> when Jim, the nigger, is captured and Huck finds himself alone and

his nigger gone. That's the end. Well you read Huckleberry Finn and
if you really, honest to ourselves believe McAlmon has ever written
anything or everything together that deserves to be mentioned in the
same room, house, city, continent or magazine with Huckleberry
Finn, I will stop writing because there will be no damn use to write if
such a state of things can be.

Most of the books he read at Schruns would have engrossed him
at any time. But he turned to them with a special eagerness that
winter in order to escape from thinking about his personal life. He
had told Pauline that if by Christmas the split in his affections was
not resolved he would kill himself. Christmas Day, 1925, found him
playing in the snow with Hadley and two-year-old Bumby—and
awaiting the arrival that afternoon of Pauline. She would be staying
right there with them in the Hotel Taube. For the man in the triangle, the situation was flattering—and nightmarishly awful. In a letter
to Fitzgerald, he spoke of all the "sons of bitching things I've done"
that loomed up in his mind when he couldn't get to sleep at night.
In his anguish, he also invoked the name of Christ a number of
times: "Christ nose," "for Christ sake," and "seem to be in a mood
of Christ like bitterness this A.M." At Schruns, he confessed months
later to the same correspondent, he had descended into hell, "with
plenty of insomnia to light the way around so I could study the
terrain." Only one means of deliverance occurred to him. With the
example of Pauline's devout Catholicism before him in the Christmas season in Catholic Austria, he asked for God's help.

Unlike the religion preached by Dr. Barton in Oak Park, Pauline's
faith had not forgotten the Cross, and this fact constituted one of its
chief appeals to Hemingway; as his fascination with Mantegna's
Dead Christ had long since indicated, he was deeply in love with the
image of Jesus Christ crucified. Yet at the same time that Catholicism envisaged a community of suffering, it offered forgiveness for
one's sins here and now, and this fact, too, was critically important
to a man who was being driven crazy by guilt. Ever since the early
summer, Pauline had almost certainly been leading him into
churches and then talking to him afterwards about the habit of
prayer, she stressing its rewards, he doubting its efficacy, for just
such differences in attitude toward prayer crop up in the conversations between Jake Barnes and Brett Ashley in *The Sun Also Rises*.

> "I've never gotten anything I prayed for. Have you?"
> "Oh, yes."

"Oh rot," said Brett. "Maybe it works for some people, though. You don't look very religious, Jake."

"I'm pretty religious."

"Oh, rot," said Brett. "Don't start proselyting to-day."

Hemingway's friends in Paris had for years been familiar with his claim that a priest had murmured some baptismal words over him on the night he was wounded. He did not flatly describe himself as a Catholic, however, until January 2, 1926, in a letter written from Schruns to Ernest Walsh, who was a Catholic himself. Thus, it was the spiritual torment created by his affair with the very woman who had been telling him she knew how he could get relief from torment that spurred his acceptance of her faith. And the further irony is that Pauline's proselytizing success promptly gave her another advantage in her deadly, undeclared war with Hadley. Catholicism was a bond between *her* and Ernest, and Hadley was left out in the cold.

The Sun Also Rises would soon make clear, however, that prayer worked only intermittently well for Jake Barnes, despite his description of himself as "pretty religious." On the afternoon, for instance, of his arrival in Pamplona he goes into the cathedral and kneels with his head on the wood in front of him and prays for himself. Nothing happens. Finally he admits, "I was a little ashamed, and regretted that I was such a rotten Catholic, but realized that there was nothing I could do about it, at least for a while, and maybe never, but that anyway it was a grand religion, and I only wished I felt religious and maybe I would the next time; and then I was out in the hot sun on the steps of the cathedral, the forefingers and the thumb of my right hand were still damp, and I felt them dry in the sun." The honesty of the scene is admirable, the physical details are graphic, but no reason has been offered for the failure of Jake's prayers. To understand that requires an appreciation of the author's situation. While Hemingway had violently rejected the Protestantism of his childhood, its moral critiques were not so easily put behind him. Long ago, Dr. Hemingway had spoken of his son's iron heart of selfishness; long ago, his mother had accused him of trying to graft a living off other people. Those appraisals were still valid, and Hemingway's tortured awareness that they were was by no means always assuaged by Catholic methods—as he understood them—of off-loading mental burdens. "Listen, Jake," Bill Gorton confidentially says to him, "are you really a Catholic?" "Technically," Jake laconically replies. "What does that mean?" Bill asks. "I don't know," is the painfully brief and bewildered answer he receives, and underneath it can be felt the religious disappointment that Hemingway first endured in Catholic churches in Paris before he began to write *The Sun Also Rises* and that he again endured in Austria during the months in which he rewrote the novel.

Strongly attracted to Catholicism but deeply discouraged by its failure to help him consistently, he concomitantly adopted a privately formed and far more pessimistic religious vision which stressed that human life was hopeless, that God was indifferent, and that the cosmos was a vast machine meaninglessly rolling on into eternity.

9

LIVERIGHT's cable reached the Hotel Taube on December 30: REJECTING TORRENTS OF SPRING PATIENTLY AWAITING MANUSCRIPT SUN ALSO RISES WRITING FULLY. "So," said Hemingway, "I'm loose." Hadley could not find it in her heart to encourage her husband to seek another publisher for the parody, but Pauline, with her terrier-like feistiness, clenched her fists and said he must do so at once.

Three options lay before him. Louis Bromfield, the Ohio-born novelist whose bestseller, *The Green Bay Tree* (1924), had permitted him to take up the life of a country squire in a showplace outside of Paris, had written to Schruns a week or so earlier to say that he had mentioned Hemingway's possible availability to his own publisher, Alfred Harcourt. Bromfield was pleased to report the publisher's reaction. Harcourt was an admirer of *In Our Time* and would love to see the book about Sherwood Anderson. It "might rock the country," Bromfield quoted him as saying. In addition, Hemingway had received a letter from William Aspenwall Bradley at Knopf, expressing keen interest in signing him up. Finally, there was Max Perkins, to whose inquiry the preceding spring Hemingway had replied by promising that if he were ever free to do so he would send him a manuscript. In a sentence that would have given a moment of ironic amusement to Horace Liveright if he had known of it, Hemingway announced to Fitzgerald which option he had chosen. "I am not going to Double Cross you and Max Perkins to whom I have given a promise."

The best way to dicker was the next question he faced. At first, he thought of wiring Don Stewart at the Yale Club in New York to pick up the manuscript from Liveright and deliver it to Scribners, after which he himself would take over and negotiate with Perkins by letter. But after a night of worry he decided to deal with Perkins in person. That way, he explained to Fitzgerald, he could settle everything without a "six week lapse between every proposition." Hadley and Bumby could stay in Schruns while he was away and he would return to them as soon as possible. His departure for New York would have to be delayed for a couple of weeks, however, because his old passport had expired and he hadn't as yet received a replacement.

By the time it came through, Pauline had long since gone back to Paris in order to cover the new designer shows for *Vogue*. Nevertheless, she found the time to post a letter to Schruns nearly every day, sometimes writing to Ernest and sometimes to Hadley. For Hadley's benefit she maintained the pretense that her relationship with them both was strictly a matter of palship—of all-male palship, one might say, if one were to take seriously the curious letter in which she exclaimed, "Oh, my soul, I wish I woz in Schruns. I miss you two men. How I miss you two men!" Only in one letter did she speak her mind with a clarity that must have made Hadley wince. Why don't I tag along with Ernest to New York, she asked. Failing that, she continued, she would certainly welcome his arrival in Paris and cling to him like a millstone, old moss, or winter ivy.

Which she did, being a woman of her word. As she delighted in recounting to Hadley, she and Ernest spent a lovely afternoon together looking at pictures in a museum. But about the evening she had nothing to say. Officially, Hemingway was staying at the Hôtel Venézia in Montparnasse; Pauline's lovely apartment was in the rue Picot. Presumably, they slept together at her place.

In New York he registered at the Brevoort and met "hells own amount of people," most of whom loomed up before him out of a fog of bootleg Scotch and endless martinis. With Liveright he had a couple of drinks in a speakeasy, where he told the publisher how sorry he was about the way things had turned out. Well before they parted, they were on a first-name basis. No hard feelings, Horace; no hard feelings, Ernest. In a more sober interval, the visiting author had a long and gratifying talk with Max Perkins in the editor's uncarpeted office in the Scribner Building. Perkins was forty-one years old, spoke in a rasping but well-bred Yankee voice, wore his fedora the way Walt Whitman did, indoors and out, and had pale blue eyes that—as Thomas Wolfe would eloquently observe—were "full of a strange misty light, a kind of far weather of the sea in them, eyes of a New England sailor long months outbound for China on a clipper ship, with something drowned, sea-sunken in them." Perkins pronounced Hemingway's parody "grand" and offered him an advance of fifteen hundred dollars for both *The Torrents* and *The Sun Also Rises,* against a flat royalty of 15 percent. In Hemingway's judgment, Perkins was "very damned nice" and his contract offer "awfully swell." As soon as the document was typed he signed it, after which, by his own admission, he was "cockeyed" on booze most of the time, with further stimulation being provided by encounters with Marc Connelly, Ernest Boyd, Dawn Powell, Robert Benchley, Dorothy Parker, Elinor Wylie, and John Herrmann and Josephine Herbst, who were married now, after having been lovers in Paris.

Benchley and Dorothy Parker also accompanied him back to Europe, aboard a ship whose staterooms had been oversold. As a result, Benchley had to sleep in a maid's room. The fourth day out, the humorist said it was funny but he felt just like the time he had crabs, and the sixth day out he *had* crabs. For Hemingway, though, the trip was a triumphal progress—or so he made it seem. He had hitched up with one of New York's most prestigious editors and boozed it up with the local literati. The only trouble was, his personal and emotional life was a shambles.

CHAPTER FOURTEEN

Double Meanings

TOWARD THE END OF THE VOYAGE, Hemingway borrowed a copy of Anita Loos's *Gentlemen Prefer Blondes* from one of the other passengers, most of whom seemed to possess two or three copies. Apparently, the book was sweeping America like the flu of 1918, but Hemingway thought it second-rate Lardner. On reaching Schruns once again, he read nothing to speak of for more than a month, for he was too busy revising *The Sun Also Rises*. Moreover, some new guests shortly appeared at the Hotel Taube who expected him to spend time with them.

Originally, Gerald and Sara Murphy had invited the Hemingways, whom they really didn't know very well, to join them in March at their Villa America on the Cap d'Antibes and go sailing with them on the Mediterranean. But Hemingway missed several weeks of skiing by going to New York, so upon his return he persuaded the Murphys and John Dos Passos, who was staying with the Murphys at the time, to come to Austria, even though Sara Murphy had never been on skis before and Dos Passos's last time had been fifteen years earlier. Possibly afflicted by a fear of heights, Sara never graduated from the "bunny" slopes, but her husband and Dos Passos were even willing to essay a few of the challenging descents on which Hemingway doted. While Gerald acquitted himself with his usual grace, Dos Passos was self-admittedly "too damn clumsy." When he felt he was about to lose control, he simply sat down on his skis and turned them into a toboggan. "Was I razzed," he good-humoredly recalled, "when it was discovered . . . that I'd worn a hole in the seat of my pants."

At the dinner table, though, Dos Passos recovered his honor, for he was a notable trencherman. Their appetites satisfied, the party would then reassemble in front of the fire and talk, although sometimes Hemingway read from his manuscript, which he expected to finish reworking in just a few weeks. Finally, everybody would get sleepy and go upstairs, where they all, in Dos Passos's words, "slept like dormice under the great featherbeds."

For the rest of his life, Dos Passos would look back on Schruns as the place where he had had his "last unalloyed good time" with Hemingway and Hadley as a team. They had seemed to him to be wonderfully happy, and he had loved being with them, this restless, lonely bachelor who scuttled about the world like a cockroach running away from a light. When he heard that Hemingway had walked out on Hadley, he was shocked, and when he learned he was planning to marry Pauline Pfeiffer, he wrote a letter to him saying that he would like to knock his and Hadley's heads together and that Hemingway should consider becoming a Mormon.

2

TO be a boy but to be treated like a girl. To feel impelled to prove your masculinity through flat denials of your anxieties (*Fraid a nothing* had been your motto as a child) and bold lies about your exploits. To be forced to practice the most severe economy in your attempts to "render" your life artistically, because your capital of self-understanding was too small to permit you to be expansive and your fear of self-exposure too powerful. To make a virtue of necessity by packing troubled feelings below the surface of your stories like dynamite beneath a bridge. To be tempted by your enormous ambition into writing a novel, despite the risks inherent in amplitude. To ascribe your protagonist's disablement to a flying accident in wartime Italy (an echo of the way in which D'Annunzio lost an eye), rather than to a subtler malaise. To turn the Great War, in fine, into a Great Explanation and proceed from there.

But *The Sun Also Rises* was not merely a portrait of the artist. A social as well as a personal essay, the novel also arose out of the sexual turmoil of the twenties, as viewed from Paris.

In 1922, the year in which Hemingway took in the spectacle of postwar life in the City of Light with the special alertness of the newly arrived resident, Coco Chanel was wowing visitors to her fashion house in the rue Cambon by using flat-busted, boyishly hipped models with helmetlike coiffures to show off her linear dresses and suits that didn't cover the knees and her cloche hats that fit the head like a second helmet. In 1922, the best-selling novel in France was Victor Margueritte's *La Garçonne*—*The Tomboy*—whose nineteen-year-old heroine decides to have a baby and raise it by herself, without any advice or support from the contemptible species known as men. (While President Poincaré did not suppress this scandalous book, as he was repeatedly urged to do by indignant editorialists, Margueritte did endure the disgrace of expulsion from the Légion d'Honneur.) In 1922, Genica Athanasiou played the leading role in Jean Cocteau's production of *Antigone* with her head shaved androgynously bald and her eyebrows plucked bare. And in 1922, Ezra Pound escorted Hemingway to the *salon* conducted on Friday afternoons by the forty-nine-year-old "Popess of Lesbos," Natalie Barney, at her house in the rue Jacob.

Before the war, Miss Barney had ridden horseback every day in the Bois de Boulogne dressed in a mannish outfit topped off with a black bow tie and a bowler. Defiantly lesbian and rampantly lustful, she had been the lover—by her own account in her *Souvenirs Indiscrets*—of upwards of forty women. Belly dancers performed before all-female audiences in her high-walled garden, at the bottom of which was a replica of a Greek temple called the Temple à l'Amitié, wherein homage was ritualistically offered to Sappho. Plays in which Natalie might appear as a shepherd or a sailor and masquerade balls that gave her a chance to wear a cape, a cocked hat, and polished black boots further helped to keep life interesting at 20 rue Jacob, as did the hostess's increasingly famous "Fridays," at which one might encounter André Gide, Jean Cocteau, Raymond Radiguet, Robert de Montesquieu, Djuna Barnes, Renata Borgatti, Romaine Brooks, and Edna St. Vincent Millay. Romaine Brooks disliked large gatherings, but came to the "Fridays" as a favor to Natalie, with whom she had had a love affair that had lasted, off and on, for years. Like Natalie's mother, Alice Pike Barney, of Sheridan Circle, Washington, D.C., Romaine was a portrait painter—who concentrated her artistic attention exclusively, however, upon such inverts as Jean Cocteau, Robert de Montesquieu, Una Troubridge and Radclyffe Hall, whose novel, *The Well of Loneliness,* featuring a transparently disguised Natalie Barney as the heroine, would be the Anglo-American succès de scandale of 1928.

In the America of Hemingway's early experience—Oak Park, northern Michigan, Kansas City, New York, Chicago—homosexuals, male and female together, kept a low profile. "Queer," to use the language of the day, was after all a scornful term overlaid with moral opprobrium, and very few deviates from the norm were daring enough to come out of the closet. Paris in the twenties was explosively different.

Sexual inversion was everywhere, it seemed—in the haut monde that Hemingway knew about only at thirdhand from talking to friends who had pored over Proust's revelations in the two volumes of *Sodome et Gomorrhe* (1921–1922), in the French literary world with which he became somewhat familiar through his friendship with Sylvia Beach and his acquaintance with Natalie Barney, and in the world of the English-speaking expatriates within which he lived.

His contempt for the male homosexuals of the Quarter was so overwhelming that he got to know comparatively few of them well. Like the white-faced, wavy-haired "crowd of young men, some in jerseys, and some in their shirt sleeves," whom Jake Barnes observes coming into the bal musette with Brett Ashley, the men-loving men of the young Hemingway's acquaintance have largely remained anonymous, the three most notable exceptions being Bob McAlmon, Pat Guthrie, and Glenway Wescott.

The women who loved women, by contrast, he looked at not as a crowd but as individuals, and he formed judgments of them which ran the gamut from affectionate to ambivalent to hostile. From his very first days in Paris, he began encountering their kind with such frequency that it was as though he had a tropism for them. First of all, there were Sylvia Beach and Adrienne Monnier, and next there were Gertrude Stein and Alice Toklas. One glance at Jane Heap's severely masculine haircut was sufficient to alert him to her sexual persuasion, and then from Lewis Galantière he learned that Jane's coeditor at *The Little Review,* the arrestingly beautiful Margaret Anderson, was hopelessly involved with the eccentric actress and singer Georgette Leblanc. (Hemingway's dislike of Georgette, in contradistinction to his warm feelings about Margaret, whom he enjoyed taking to prizefights, was privately communicated to Pound in a letter which referred to her in devouring terms as "Georgette Mangeuse le Blanc" and subsequently made publicly clear in the bal musette scene in *The Sun Also Rises.* Jake and the French whore with bad teeth whom he has picked up in order to have company for the evening approach a table occupied by people he knows. "I wish to present my fiancée, Mademoiselle Georgette Leblanc," he announces.)

Wherever Hemingway turned, there were new women-loving women to observe and talk to, from Bryher to Jinny Pfeiffer. Several of them had subscription cards at Shakespeare and Company, and their presence was even more noticeable in the neighborhood of St-

Germain-des-Prés. At the Café de Flore, Janet Flanner, Nancy Cunard, and the short-story writer Solita Solano made a striking threesome as they sat in a row like the Fates, each wearing a black tailored
suit, a white satin scarf and a pair of white gloves and each sipping a
martini. In time, Solano and Flanner would also make a striking
twosome when Djuna Barnes presented them as the sisters Nip and
Tuck in her sexually satirical *Ladies Almanack* (1928). The sapphic
Miss Barnes was a sight all by herself. Tall, ramrod-straight, and
handsome, she ranged the Latin Quarter in a black cape that set off
her fair complexion and fine head of glossy auburn hair. On first
coming to Paris she had put up at the Hôtel Jacob, where the Hemingways perched upon their arrival in the city. After a sojourn in
Berlin—the homosexual capital of postwar Europe—she again
dropped anchor in Paris. Hemingway spoke well of some of her
writing, admired her good looks and in all likelihood was delighted
to hear of the trap she set for Harold Loeb. Prior to his romance
with Kitty Cannell, Loeb had sexually exploited a secretary who
worked for him at *Broom*. Eventually he brought her to Paris and set
her up in a room at the Jacob. (The secretary's last name has never
been satisfactorily established, but her first name was Frances, and
in *The Sun Also Rises* Hemingway would give his readers two of
Loeb's mistresses for the price of one by dubbing the Kitty Cannell
character Frances Clyne.) Once Loeb took up with Kitty, he cut the
secretary off cold turkey. It was Djuna Barnes's thought that Loeb
should be entrapped into giving the girl some money. The secretary
should plead with him to come to see her at the hotel one last time.
As soon as he entered the room, Djuna would swoop in from the
hall and say that his presence proved his involvement with the young
woman and that he was financially obligated to her because she was
pregnant. Whether the plan paid off is unclear, but for Hemingway
at least that detail can't have mattered much. For him, the thought
of Loeb's discomfiture at the sudden appearance of black-caped
Djuna must have been satisfaction enough.

How numerous were the lesbians of Hemingway's acquaintance!
How numerous, how intelligent, how high-spirited! Yet with his
abiding interest in human vulnerability, Hemingway would not
have been Hemingway if his imagination had not been engaged by
the dark side of lesbian life, by Djuna Barnes's drunkenness and
nervous collapses, by the pathological infidelity of Natalie Barney,
and by the humiliating drama that sometimes broke out behind the
scenes at 27 rue de Fleurus and that would one day serve as the
subject for the chapter called "A Strange Enough Ending" in *A
Moveable Feast*.

The spring weather was lovely that day, the memoirist remembered, as he walked across the Luxembourg Garden to pay a call on Miss Stein. The great chestnut trees had blossomed, children were playing in the graveled walks, and wood pigeons were cooing. The maidservant opened the door before he could ring the bell and told him to come in and wait. Miss Stein would be down in a moment. The maidservant gave him a glass of eau-de-vie. As he was savoring it, he "heard someone speaking to Miss Stein as I had never heard one person speak to another; never, anywhere, ever." Then Miss Stein's voice could be heard, pleading and begging. "Don't, pussy. Don't. Don't, please don't. I'll do anything, pussy, but please don't do it. Please don't. Please don't, pussy."

By the time he set down those words, Hemingway had come to hate Gertrude with all his heart for the terrible, manhood-insulting things she had said about him in *The Autobiography of Alice B. Toklas*. Thus, "A Strange Enough Ending" was an act of revenge, and every sentence in it may have been made up. Nevertheless, the chapter sets forth a symbolic truth about the power relationship that obtained between Gertrude and Alice.

Fancifulness, then, is not the most serious flaw in "A Strange Enough Ending." Omission is. As in his portrayal of Fitzgerald's helpless inability to resist Zelda's attempts to destroy him, the memoirist did not acknowledge the dimension of symbolic self-involvement in the love affair he was describing. Hemingway was not only acquainted with a remarkable number of lesbians, but, far more remarkably, was able in his imagination to identify himself with them. It was no accident that from "Soldier's Home" to "The Last Good Country" he would write about tomboyish girls, or that he was sexually attracted to Jinny Pfeiffer and Gertrude Stein, or that he valued Hadley—as he would his other wives—as a good buddy who could drink with him and share his sporting enthusiasms. His mother's longtime relationship with Ruth Arnold had, of course, brought the drama of single-sex intimacy right into the Hemingway household. Yet it surely was his firsthand experience of knowing how it felt to look like a girl but feel like a boy that was the fountainhead of his fascination with the ambiguities of feminine identity. Ironically enough, Hemingway was psychologically readied for his role as an observer of postwar Paris by an Oak Park upbringing.

Herbert Gorman and other early reviewers of *The Sun Also Rises* who were familiar with life on the Left Bank would be beguiled in the fall of 1926 by the number of actual men and women whom they could identify in its pages, from Ford Madox Ford and Stella Bowen to the drunken racetrack columnist, Harold Stearns, to the homosexual novelist, Glenway Wescott. There was, however, an empty space in the author's lineup of fictionalized portraits. Not one of his characters was a lesbian. After a couple of "Fridays" *chez* Natalie Barney in 1927, Scott Fitzgerald turned out a twenty-page jeu d'esprit on Parisian lesbianism in which Miss Barney figured as Miss Retchmore, and reverberations from this unpublished effort would eventually be recorded in *Tender Is the Night*. Yet the author of *The Sun Also Rises* had avoided the subject of women-loving women altogether, despite his awareness of how important it was in the Left Bank life he was writing about. Or so it might seem.

In fact, he had not avoided the subject at all. In fact, he had imported it, albeit obliquely, into the very center of his novel by encapsulating it within the story of its two principals. The only clear reference to the book's duality that the caution or perhaps the subconscious of the author allowed him, however, was in the name he bestowed on his hero. "Barnes!" Braddocks calls out to Jake in the bal musette. "I say, Barnes! Jacob Barnes!" A few pages later, Jake's proper name is dramatically reemphasized when Robert Cohn asks Brett to dance and is refused. "I've promised to dance this with Jacob," she explains. "You've a hell of a biblical name, Jake," she laughingly adds. Natalie Barney, 20 rue Jacob; Djuna Barnes, Hôtel Jacob. From these two associations Hemingway derived the name of a man who is passionately in love with a sexually aggressive woman with an androgynous first name and a mannish haircut, a man whose dilemma is that, like a lesbian, he cannot penetrate his loved one's body with his own.

Having set up a lesbian parallelism, Hemingway did not thereupon abandon it; the name Jacob Barnes was not simply an inside joke inserted for the delectation of Left Bank readers. In a novel in which double meanings abound, the story of Jake and Brett seems in two or three places like two stories, most strikingly so in chapter seven. Tired and headachy at the end of a long day, Jake returns to his flat and takes a shower. He is rubbing himself with a towel when he hears the door-bell pull. Putting on a bathrobe and slippers, he opens the door. Brett and Count Mippipopolous, the champagne-loving Count Mippipopolous, have brought him a huge bunch of roses. After letting them in, Jake excuses himself and goes to his bedroom. Sitting on the bed, he slowly gets dressed. He is feeling pretty rotten. Brett enters the bedroom and sits down beside him.

> "What's the matter, darling? Do you feel rocky?"
> She kissed me coolly on the forehead.
> "Darling," she said. Then: "Do you want me to send him away?"

"No. He's nice."

"I'll send him away."

"No, don't."

"Yes, I'll send him away."

"You can't just like that."

"Can't I, though? You stay here. He's mad about me, I tell you."

She was gone out of the room. I lay face down on the bed. I was having a bad time. I heard them talking but I did not listen. Brett came in and sat on the bed.

"Poor old darling." She stroked my head.

"What did you say to him?" I was lying with my face away from her. I did not want to see her.

"Sent him for champagne. He loves to go for champagne."

Then later: "Do you feel better, darling? Is the head any better?"

"It's better."

"Then," followed by a colon. "Then later," followed by a colon. Both usages indicate a passage of time and an omitted action. The first usage introduces a question from Brett that is clearly prompted by a sexual idea of some sort. The second results in the revelation that a tension has been released in Jake; his head feels better now. There is no way to be utterly positive, of course, about Hemingway's meaning, for in order to keep Max Perkins's blue pencil still, an artful vagueness was essential. Nevertheless, the implication is fairly clear that, while the full extent of his injury is unspecified, Jake remains capable of achieving a degree of satisfaction through oral sex, and that Brett has been a most willing mangeuse. Jake and Brett have apparently made love in a fashion often associated with lesbian as well as heterosexual intercourse.

Thoughts of such creatures as Djuna Barnes aside, Hemingway's portrait of Jake is a portrait of himself. The portrait of the thirty-four-year-old heroine, by contrast, is a complicated composite, involving close approximations first of all of Duff Twysden's mannish appearance and brittle way of talking and Zelda Fitzgerald's madcap charm and habitual bathing. Three other real-life women also figured in the conception of Brett. The woman whom Jake loves but cannot find sexual contentment with is the counterpart of Hadley, and the woman who met Jake in a hospital during the war represents a memory of Agnes von Kurowsky. As for the woman who humiliates the men in her life, either Duff or Zelda could easily have sat for the portrait—as a substitute, that is, for Grace Hall Hemingway. A literary model was also helpful to Brett's creator, although he made a point of denying it. In *A Moveable Feast* he would emphasize that he had never been able to read a book by Michael Arlen, but this was a sign that he actually had, and that Edwin Muir and other reviewers of *The Sun Also Rises* had not been altogether wrong in referring to Brett as an imitation of the devil-may-care heroine of Arlen's *The Green Hat* (1924).

Yet if women real and imaginary can be discerned in Brett, Hemingway himself implied that she had been modeled on a man. Each of his books, he told Archibald MacLeish in 1943, was grounded in a new truth he had learned. "Promiscuity no solution" was the bitter wisdom that had given rise, he said, to *The Sun Also Rises.* In her inability to accept Jake as he is and live with him simply because she loves him, in her raging need to fornicate at no matter what cost to the feelings of others, and in her unquenchable unhappiness, Brett was Hemingway.

3

THE novelist had reread *Huckleberry Finn* and it showed, in *The Sun Also Rises,* in some of the most moving writing about landscape in American literature. Toward the end of a particularly splendid passage, Jake Barnes even mimicked Huck's phrasings.

> After a while we came out of the mountains, and there were trees along both sides of the road, and a stream and ripe fields of grain, and the road went on, very white and straight ahead, and then lifted to a little rise, and off on the left was a hill with an old castle, with buildings close around it and a field of grain going right up to the walls and shifting in the wind. . . . Then we crossed a wide plain, and there was a big river off on the right shining in the sun from between the line of trees, and away off you could see the plateau of Pamplona rising out of the plain.

In the scenes in the Irati River country, where Jake and the Don Stewart character, Bill Gorton, go fishing before the fiesta begins, the precedent of *Huckleberry Finn* again comes to mind, for just as the beauty and humor of Huck's narrative are crossed with sadness and horror, so the physical appetite for life and free-wheeling wit that Jake and Bill display *con brio* are intermingled with a sense of irreparable discord, a consciousness of "the falsity or tragedy of a moral situation," as Edmund Wilson would remark in the *New Republic* in December 1927. This consciousness, Wilson would discerningly go on to say, "does not arouse Hemingway to passionate violence; but it poisons him and makes him sick, and thus invests with a singular sinister quality—a quality perhaps new in fiction—

the sunlight and the green summer landscapes of *The Sun Also Rises*."

Jake and Bill's repartee is full of literary and political digs, risqué remarks and blasphemies, all delivered at the bing-bang pace that the wisecracking twenties loved. Max Perkins, it may be assumed, did not catch the off-color jokes that he let pass, for he was opposed to them on principle. As he wrote to Hemingway in justification of his prudential blue pencilings, if "a lot of cheap, prurient, moronic yappers" began raising a cry about indecency in *The Sun Also Rises*, the significance of the novel would be overwhelmed.

The first of Bill and Jake's comic routines slyly pokes fun at *The Great Gatsby* by picking up on the words "irony and pity" and riding them hard. "Irony and pity" were Anatole France's touchstones for good writing, and the French-literature-loving Gilbert Seldes had invoked them in his *Dial* review of *Gatsby*. Fitzgerald, Seldes proclaimed, now surpassed all the writers of his generation; although he had taken only a tiny section of American life for his province, he had reported on it "with irony and pity and a consuming passion." Fitzgerald proudly showed these comments to Hemingway, who didn't like Seldes in any case because of what he regarded as his Harvard-bred intellectual snobbery and who probably didn't feel too good in addition about the lavishness of Seldes's praise of a rival. In *A Moveable Feast* he would dismiss the review with the sour remark that it "could not have been better. It could only have been better if Gilbert Seldes had been better." But in *The Sun Also Rises* he made it the occasion for a vaudeville turn, sung to the tune of "The Bells Are Ringing for Me and My Gal."

Go out and dig some more worms, slugabed Bill says to Jake in their bedroom in the inn at Burguete, as he finally throws off the covers and starts to dress. "Work for the good of all," Bill tells him, stepping into his underwear. "Show irony and pity."

> I started out of the room with the tackle-bag, the nets, and the rod-case.
> "Hey! Come back!"
> I put my head in the door.
> "Aren't you going to show a little irony and pity?"
> I thumbed my nose.
> "That's not irony."
> As I went down-stairs I heard Bill singing, "Irony and Pity. When you're feeling . . . ["shitty" was the rhyme, but Hemingway didn't even try to get it past Perkins]. Oh, Give them Irony and Give them Pity. Oh, give them Irony. When they're feeling . . . Just a little

irony. Just a little pity . . .'' He kept on singing until he came downstairs.

Over coffee and toast, Bill kicks off their second routine. "You
know what's the trouble with you?" he says to Jake, and then answers the question himself.

> "You're an expatriate. You've lost touch with the soil. You get
> precious. Fake European standards have ruined you. You drink your-
> self to death. You become obsessed by sex. You spend all your time
> talking, not working. You are an expatriate, see? You hang around
> cafés."
> "It sounds like a swell life," I said. "When do I work?"
> "You don't work. One group claims women support you. Another
> group claims you're impotent."
> "No," I said. "I just had an accident."
> "Never mention that," Bill said. "That's the sort of thing that can't
> be spoken of. That's what you ought to work up into a mystery. Like
> Henry's bicycle."
> He had been going splendidly, but he stopped. I was afraid he
> thought he had hurt me with that crack about being impotent. I
> wanted to start him again.
> "It wasn't a bicycle," I said. "He was riding horseback."

Hemingway's typescript had read, "Like Henry James's bicycle."
Perkins, though, found this flip reference to James distasteful, and
he called on Hemingway to cool off this "hot spot," which Hemingway then did in the galley proofs, thus leaving future readers to
wonder about what person Bill Gorton had in mind. There was
something else besides the excision of an identifying last name, however, that made "Like Henry's bicycle" a curious reference.

In his autobiographical *Notes of a Son and Brother* (1914), James had
circumlocutorily related the story of a physical mishap that had overtaken him "at the same dark hour" as the Civil War. Fort Sumter
was fired upon, Mr. Lincoln called for volunteers, and James eventually answered the call—to help put out a "shabby conflagration,"
that is, as a volunteer fireman in Newport, Rhode Island. Jammed
into an "acute angle between two high fences," as he and his fellow
volunteers struggled to induce "a rusty, a quasi-extemporised old
engine" to work and "a saving stream to flow," he had suffered a
"horrid, even if an obscure hurt." One had the sense, James said
looking back, of having "kept company" with the country at large.
"One had the sense, I mean to say, of a huge comprehensive ache,

and there were hours at which one could scarce have told whether it came most from one's own poor organism, still so young and so meant for better things, but which had suffered particular wrong, or from the enclosing social body, a body rent with a thousand wounds that thus treated one to the honour of a sort of tragic fellowship.''

Bill Gorton was right: James had suffered an accident, but hadn't spoken of it. Instead, he had worked it up into a mystery, via elaborate euphemisms centering on words like "horrid" and "odious" and an extended comparison of his hurt to the social body of Civil War America "rent with a thousand wounds." The young Glenway Wescott, among others, was nevertheless sure that he understood *Notes of a Son and Brother* perfectly well, and eventually he would spell out his views in the fabled Henry James number of the magazine *Hound & Horn* (April–June 1934). "Henry James; expatriation and castration. . . . Henry James, it is rumored, could not have had a child.''

Bill Gorton clearly has this interpretation in mind (did Hemingway pick it up in conversation with Wescott?), for his remarks about James take off from the unfortunate joke he has made about impotency. What is not clear, though, is why Bill alludes to "Henry's bicycle." The allusion was simply a "non-sequitor [*sic*]," Hemingway explained to Perkins, "and had nothing to do with James." Except that it did. For in Hemingway's mind James's wartime injury had become conflated with the black and yellow bruises James had sustained in England three decades later while learning to ride a bicycle. And it was no accident that this conflation had occurred. On the night of July 8, 1918, an American Red Cross lieutenant attached to the Italian army had ridden a bicycle out along the Piave River, en route to a rendezvous with injury whose exact nature he, too, would obscure.

Years after his divorce from Hadley, Hemingway musingly remarked to her that he thought it possible that he would "turn out to be the Henry James of the People or the comic strips." One of the technical lessons he learned from the Master had to do with the uses of dialogue; there were times, indeed, when he carried his Jamesian facility for talk too far and allowed his characters to indulge in more of it than was wise—which is why Pound's letter of criticism about the "blanketing up" of the beginning of "An Alpine Idyll" specifically accused him of following too closely "in the wake of H. J." The substance of a famous speech in James's *The Ambassadors* likewise left a deep impression on Hemingway, as one of the key speeches in *The Sun Also Rises* reveals. "Listen, Jake," Robert Cohn says in the second chapter. "Don't you ever get the feeling that all your life is going by and you're not taking advantage of it? Do you realize you've lived nearly half the time you have to live already?" In more casual parlance, Cohn is echoing the words of James's Lambert Strether, as he unburdens himself to Little Bilham in Gloriani's beautiful Paris garden. "Live all you can; it's a mistake not to. It doesn't so much matter what you do in particular, so long as you have your life. If you haven't had that, what *have* you had?"

Yet if Hemingway cherished James as his great predecessor, he also displayed great contempt for him, especially when confronted with what he regarded as unmanly behavior on the part of James's men. "Pauline has been fine and has read Henry James (The Awkward Age) out loud," he reported in 1927 to Waldo Peirce, the bearded and bawdy-minded painter from Bangor, Maine, who had recently become one of his closest friends. The novel is "shit," Hemingway succinctly continued. "The men all without any exception talk and think like fairies except a couple of caricatures of brutal 'outsiders.' " In a later letter to another close friend, Hemingway spoke even more contemptuously of James's lack of understanding of masculinity. "For your information," he told Charles Scribner in 1949, "I started out trying to beat dead writers that I knew how good they were. (Excuse vernacular) I tried for Mr. Turgenieff and it wasn't too hard. Tried for Mr. Maupassant (won't concede the de) and it took four of the best stories to beat him. . . . Mr. Henry James I would just thumb him once the first time he grabbed and then hit him once where he had no balls and ask the referee to stop it." James may have made sexual renunciation look splendid in *The Ambassadors,* but Hemingway wanted his own readers to know that having to live without Brett Ashley was sheer torture for Jake Barnes. While cracking wise with Jake at breakfast, Bill Gorton makes a slip and mentions impotency; beneath the even tone of Jake's patient reply, "I just had an accident," one can feel how he really feels.

Following a splendid morning of fishing, the two friends knock off for lunch and another comic routine, this one lubricated by two bottles of wine that have meanwhile been chilling in a nearby spring. Their patter ranges far and wide across the contemporary American scene, from Calvin Coolidge, John D. Rockefeller, Henry Ford, and Bishop Manning to Jo Davidson, Frankie Frisch, and Wayne B. Wheeler of the Anti-Saloon League. Two of the leading exemplars of the nation's division of opinion about Darwinian evolution, William Jennings Bryan and H. L. Mencken, are also featured in a mock communion service. Hemingway had already ridiculed Mencken as an intellectual has-been in the Paris section of the novel, but he wanted to embarrass the sage of Baltimore one more time.

After "utilizing" a little of the wine, Jake and Bill open the parcels of hard-boiled eggs and cold chicken that will be their meal. "First the egg," says Bill. "Then the chicken. Even Bryan could see that." Bryan is dead, Jake says, having seen the story in a newspaper the day before. "Gentlemen," says Bill, unwrapping a drumstick, "I reverse the order. For Bryan's sake. As a tribute to the Great Commoner. First the chicken; then the egg." With the drumstick serving in lieu of the communion wafer, Bill calls on Jake to "accept on faith" what is before him and join him in saying—

> "What shall we say, brother?" He pointed the drumstick at me and went on. "Let me tell you. We will say and I for one am proud to say —and I want you to say with me, on your knees, brother. Let no man be ashamed to kneel here in the great out-of-doors. Remember the woods were God's first temples. Let us kneel and say: 'Don't eat that, Lady—that's Mencken.' "

In brandishing the drumstick about, Bill has noticed its configuration. It is not of the body of the Lamb that the chicken leg reminds him, but of Mencken's member. A couple of fast exchanges later, Jake demonstrates that he has had no difficulty in following his friend's thinking. "You're cock-eyed," he tells Bill.

Once again, their ribaldry has veered perilously close to the topic of Jake's disability. In seeking to ignore his situation, the two men continually reveal their oppression by it.

4

HEMINGWAY'S art, Edmund Wilson would go on to say in his 1927 *New Republic* piece, is "a clairvoyant's crystal" in which we may find "an image of the common oppression." In the long run, though, the clairvoyant was unable to maintain a steadiness of vision in *The Sun Also Rises*. A master miniaturist, a poet essentially, Hemingway was not accustomed to the amplitude of the novel form and he partially lost control of his materials. The diametrically opposed assessments of the novel by its two ablest reviewers in 1926 pointed up its contradictions.

The Sun Also Rises achieves "a quite extraordinary effect of honesty and reality," Conrad Aiken wrote in the New York *Herald Tribune* on October 31.

The half dozen characters, all of whom belong to the curious and sad little world of disillusioned and aimless expatriates who make what home they can in the cafés of Paris, are seen perfectly and unsentimentally by Mr. Hemingway and are put before us with a maximum of economy. In the case of the hero, through whose mind we meet the event, and again in the cases of Brett, the heroine, and Robert Cohn, the sub-hero, Mr. Hemingway accomplishes more than this— he achieves an understanding and revelation of character which approaches the profound. When one reflects on the unattractiveness, not to say the sordidness, of the scene, and the (on the whole) gracelessness of the people, one is all the more astonished at the fact that Mr. Hemingway should have made them so moving. These folk exist, that is all; and if their story is sordid, it is also, by virtue of the author's dignity and detachment in the telling, intensely tragic.

Allen Tate, writing in *The Nation* six weeks later, took a very different view.

Mr. Hemingway has produced a successful novel, but not without returning some violence upon the integrity achieved in his first book. He decided for reasons of his own to write a popular novel, or he wrote the only novel which he could write.

To choose the latter conjecture is to clear his intentions, obviously at the cost of impugning his art. One infers moreover that although sentimentality appears explicitly for the first time in his prose, it must have always been there. Its history can be constructed. The method used in *In Our Time* was *pointilliste,* and the sentimentality was submerged. With great skill he reversed the usual and most general formula of prose fiction: instead of selecting the details of physical background and of human behavior for the intensification of a dramatic situation, he employed the minimum of drama for the greatest possible intensification of the observed object. . . .

In *The Sun Also Rises,* a full-length novel, Mr. Hemingway could not escape such leading situations, and he had besides to approach them with a kind of seriousness. He fails. It is not that Mr. Hemingway is, in the term which he uses in fine contempt for the big word, hard-boiled; it is that he is not hard-boiled enough, in the artistic sense. . . . And he actually betrays the interior machinery of his hard-boiled attitude: "It is awfully easy to be hard-boiled about everything in the daytime, but at night it is another thing," says Jake, the sexually impotent, musing on the futile accessibility of Brett. The history of his sentimentality is thus complete.

Was Jake unsentimentally observed, had the author told his story with dignity and detachment, as Aiken believed, or did the novel expose Hemingway as insufficiently hard-boiled, as an incorrigible sentimentalist in fact, as Tate contended? The answer is that both reviewers were right. *The Sun Also Rises* is informed by an impartial and intensely tragic vision of human life—that is forever dissolving into self-exculpatory self-pity. The spiritual difference between the two quotations that Hemingway placed in front of the novel symbolizes the inconsistency of attitude in the story. One of the quotations (which he slightly reduced in the third and all subsequent editions of the novel) was from *Ecclesiastes:*

> Vanity of vanities, saith the Preacher, vanity of vanities; all is vanity. . . . One generation passeth away, and another generation cometh; but the earth abideth forever. . . . The sun also ariseth, and the sun goeth down, and hasteth to the place where he arose. . . . The wind goeth toward the south, and turneth about unto the north; it whirleth about continually, and the wind returneth again according to his circuits. . . . All the rivers run into the sea; yet the sea is not full; unto the place from whence the rivers come, thither they return again.

A conversation with Gertrude Stein was the source of the other: "You are all a lost generation." Once the novel was published and he saw to his dismay how much attention the latter quote was getting, Hemingway hastened to assure various correspondents that he regarded Gertrude's remark as laughable. How refreshing it is, he wrote Max Perkins in November, "to see someone [i.e., the reviewer for the Boston *Evening Transcript*] have some doubts that I took the Gertrude Stein thing very seriously—I meant to play off against that splendid bombast (Gertrude's assumption of prophetic roles). Nobody knows about the generation that follows them and certainly has no right to judge." As late as 1932, he was still protesting—in a letter to a scholarly gentleman named Paul Romaine—that his purpose in quoting from a modern as well as an ancient authority had merely been "to show the superiority of the earlier Hebrew writers over the later."

These protestations are belied, however, by the blue notebook he took with him on a short trip to Chartres following the completion of the first draft of the novel. For the notebook shows that he seriously considered calling his novel *The Lost Generation* and that he even went to the trouble of roughing out a foreword explaining how the phrase had originated. In the summer of 1925, he wrote, Gertrude Stein and Alice Toklas stopped in a village in the Jura Mountains to have the malfunctioning engine of their Ford repaired. A strikingly youthful garage mechanic told them that one of the valves was stuck, and he fixed it right away. Gertrude was curious to know where the owner of the garage had found such efficient workers. He had trained them himself, said the owner. His very youngest recruits had learned very fast, but the same could not be said of those between the ages of twenty-two and thirty, all of whom had ultimately proved to be unteachable. "C'est une génération perdue," the owner declared.

In reworking the Frenchman's opinion into a comment of her own, Gertrude may very well have been making her first face-to-face attack on Hemingway, the jealous Alice having at long last laid down the law about getting rid of him. Hemingway would assert in *A Moveable Feast* that Gertrude not only told him that "all of you young people who served in the war . . . are a lost generation," but went on to say, "You have no respect for anything. You drink yourselves to death." He had immediately objected to these remarks, the memoirist further claimed, and on his way home had become very angry. "The hell with her lost-generation talk and all the dirty, easy labels," he said to himself.

Is it likely that a writer who felt this way would thereupon have been tempted to call the novel he was working on *The Lost Generation?* Gertrude may indeed have intended to be insulting to Hemingway, but at the time, it would appear, her words had excited him, and it is easy to understand why: they contained a phrase that was truly catchy. In 1920, a young American writer had become famous overnight as the spokesman of a generation "grown up to find," as he had written in *This Side of Paradise,* "all Gods dead, all wars fought, all faith in man shaken." Conceivably, the author of a novel called *The Lost Generation* might have been able to take that self-dramatizing role away from Scott Fitzgerald.

Yet in making his final selection of a title Hemingway chose against the theme of generational disillusionment in favor of a broader view of human existence. As he later told Max Perkins, he hadn't set out to write "a hollow or bitter satire." To the contrary, it had been his intention to write a "damn tragedy"—a tragedy whose melancholy outlook on life was very like that of the sage in *Ecclesiastes.*

An observer of society, standing aloof from its passions and ambitions and interested primarily in pointing out their emptiness, the sage had maintained a predominant attitude of calm hopelessness, tinged on occasion by disgust or contempt and an unspeakable weariness. His deliberate conclusion was that life had nothing of permanent value to offer. An inscrutable God was the absolute determiner of man's fate; wherefore it was impossible to add to the content of the world or take from it, impossible to change the nature of things or to effect any radical betterment in relations. No goal or purpose was discoverable in the earth's eternal round; if the sun rose and journeyed across the sky, it was merely to come back to the place whence it rose, while rivers flowed forever into the sea without filling it. To what purpose, then, was the world created? It was impossible to say. Nevertheless, the sage affirmed that life with its limitations was worth living. Man ought to face the facts and accept the given as unchangeable, but he also ought to enjoy whatever good things God permitted—until death brought oblivion, just as it did to beasts.

In detailing the atrocious behavior of his characters at the orgiastic fiesta in Pamplona, Hemingway was uncompromising. That latter-day Circe, Brett Ashley, not only can't take her eyes off the eviscerated horses in the arena—"Brett's not a sadist," her drunken lover, Mike Campbell, declares, "she's just a lovely, healthy wench"—but is indifferent to the sufferings of the men in her life; thus, it is not of Jake's feelings but of her own that she is thinking when she enlists his aid in setting up her first assignation with the handsome matador who is fifteen years her junior.

The only moral relief from the accumulating squalor is provided by the performances of Romero in the arena. Bullfighters were like writers: Hemingway had already established that identification in his account of the battered and aging Manolo in "The Undefeated," but now he symbolically did so again, in a phrase that would become famous. At nineteen, Romero reminded Hemingway of himself at that age—deeply in love with an older woman and dreaming of the career that lay before him; and by saying of Romero's work as a matador that he "had the old thing, the holding of his purity of line through the maximum of exposure," he was tacitly enunciating a literary ideal.

In keeping, though, with the pessimism of his Biblical vision, Hemingway did not exempt even bullfighting from his demonstration of the emptiness of society's passions. One of the men racing ahead of the bulls through the streets of the town early one morning is overtaken and gored in the small of the back. A few hours later, Jake describes the incident to a waiter in a café. The man had been "badly cogido," Jake says. "Badly cogido," the waiter says, nodding his head. "All for sport. All for pleasure." He goes away and comes back with coffee and milk. "Badly cogido through the back," he says. "A big horn wound. All for fun. Just for fun." Two grave-looking men pass by on the street. "Muerto!" one of them calls out to the waiter. Walking back to Jake's table, the waiter says, "You hear? Muerto. Dead. He's dead. With a horn through him. All for morning fun. Es muy flamenco." The bull who killed the man, it develops, was killed in the arena by Romero. By popular acclamation, the animal's ear was cut off and handed to the young matador, who in turn gave it to Brett. After wrapping it in a handkerchief belonging to Jake, she "left both ear and handkerchief, along with a number of Muratti cigarette-stubs, shoved far back in the drawer of the bed-table that stood beside her bed in the Hotel Montoya, in Pamplona." Vanity of vanities; all is vanity!

"It is awfully easy to be hard-boiled about everything in the daytime, but at night it is another thing." The sentence that Allen Tate singled out for scorn is by no means the only instance in the book of the defeat of Hemingway's tragic intention by his inability to stifle his sentimentality. For a man who is supposedly stoic, Jake certainly does not restrain himself from telling us how low he feels and how drunk he gets, and even more blatant appeals for our sympathy are contained in his seemingly offhand revelations of how generous he is with his money and how selfless it is of him to interrupt the San Sebastián holiday he is enjoying near the end of the story in order to take care of Brett in Madrid. Furthermore, the double-entendre references to his disability gradually lose their dramatic effectiveness as a result of being resorted to too often, until finally they become embarrassing. Tell Romero, the drunken Mike says mockingly, that "Brett wants to see him put on those green pants." "Pipe down," says Jake, setting up the joke. "Tell him Brett is dying to know how he can get into those pants," says Mike. "Pipe down," says Jake. The Hotel Montana in Madrid, says Jake, by way of introducing an even more lamentable witticism, is a second-floor establishment. But "I could not make the elevator work," he explains, "so I walked up." And at the desk he encounters a landlady who tells him that the patrons of the hotel have been "rigidly selectioned."

Yet if the author's emotional discipline broke down badly in his handling of Jake, it held up beautifully in regard to Brett—although Hemingway himself would not have agreed with this judgment. In Pamplona, Brett doesn't care about her moral reputation; in Madrid, she does, but her efforts to make herself look good merely augment her degradation. "I'd have lived with [Romero]," she bursts out, upon admitting Jake to her hotel room, "if I hadn't seen it was bad for him." In other words, she would have Jake believe that it is not temporarily sated nymphomania that has caused her to give up Romero, but a concern for his career as a bullfighter. "He wanted to marry me, finally" is another of her renunciatory announcements that can't bear scrutiny. (Brett Ashley as a Spanish *señora?* The idea that she could be content in such a role is preposterous. Why, then, should she expect Jake to admire her rejection of it?) On the verge of tears she theatrically proclaims, "I'm thirty-four, you know. I'm not going to be one of these bitches that ruins children." It is this speech that becomes the basis for the self-congratulation she voices in between sips of a martini in the Palace bar. "You know it makes one feel rather good deciding not to be a bitch. . . . It's sort of what we have instead of God." "Some people have God," Jake informs her. "Quite a lot."

And so off to lunch at Botín's they go, and in the taxicab afterwards there is only time for one last phallic symbol, sandwiched in between a final bid for Jake's pity on her part and a final bid for the reader's on his.

> "Oh, Jake," Brett said, "we could have had such a damned good time together."
> Ahead was a mounted policeman in khaki directing traffic. He raised his baton. The car slowed suddenly pressing Brett against me.
> "Yes," I said. "Isn't it pretty to think so?" *

5

"BABES in the Bois," by a journalist named Richmond Barrett, described for the readers of *Harper's* in the spring of 1928 the effect that *The Sun Also Rises* had been having on young people in the year and a half since its publication. They have taken it as their Bible, Barrett began. They have "learned it by heart and deserting their families and running away from college . . . [have taken] ship to Paris to be the disciples of the new faith under the awnings of the Dôme and the Rotonde and the other sidewalk cafés." Beneath the journalistic hyperbole there was a residue of interesting fact. *The Sun Also Rises* had become a cult book in the colleges. "So many young men get their likes and dislikes from Mencken," Jake Barnes sarcastically observes. But beginning in 1926 they got them as well from *The Sun Also Rises*. From New Haven, Connecticut, Thornton Wilder reported that the Yale undergraduates were very much taken with the novel, while in New York, according to Malcolm Cowley, girls down from Smith "were modelling themselves on Lady Brett."

---

* It was an ending which illustrated a theory of fiction that Hemingway would successfully urge Fitzgerald to adopt. As the author of *Tender Is the Night* would explain in April 1934, in a letter to John Peale Bishop, "I believe it was Ernest Hemingway who developed to me, in conversation, that the dying fall was preferable to the dramatic ending under certain conditions. . . ."

In the twenties, the disequilibrium of life gave rise to a romantic sensibility, especially among pacesetting young people. It was their sense of themselves as historical victims that led them to interpret *The Sun Also Rises* in the light of its modern epigraph and to identify with Jake and Brett as fellow lost souls. "The point of the book to me," Hemingway protested to Max Perkins four weeks after it was published, "was that the earth abideth forever," but that was not how it was destined to be read. Broadening out the definition of young people to include not only the college students of the middle twenties but a somewhat older crowd, Edmund Wilson said of the author of *The Sun Also Rises* that he "expressed the romantic disillusion and set the favorite pose for the period. It was the moment of gallantry in heartbreak, grim and nonchalant banter, and heroic dissipation. The great watchword was 'Have a drink'; and in the bars of New York and Paris the young people were getting to talk like Hemingway."

In terms of augmenting and solidifying his fame, it was Hemingway's great good luck to speak for a special moment in history. Nevertheless, he continued to resist the "lost generation" label that had been pinned on his book, mainly by continuing to make cracks about Gertrude Stein. At one point, though, he abruptly dropped his dismayed defense of his tragic aspirations and announced that the book was a failure and that the fault was his. In the emotionally tumultuous aftermath of his father's suicide, he began corresponding with the sixty-nine-year-old author of *The Virginian,* Owen Wister, out of his need to have father-figures to talk to. One of his most painfully honest communications with the older novelist dealt with his early years as a writer in Paris. He confessed:

> My life was more or less shot out from under me and I was drinking much too much entirely through my own fault. I was writing better and getting so I could link up sentences occasionally instead of having them all go put put put. Then wrote the Sun also in 6 weeks. . . . I tried to give the destruction of character in the woman Brett—that was the main story and I failed to do it. . . . I thought the Pamplona part was all right and the rest interesting enough to carry it even though to me it was a failure and I wouldn't have published it except that that was the only way I could get it behind me. If I'd destroyed it I might have thought it was better than it was.

PART FOUR

1926–1936

CHAPTER FIFTEEN

"I Loved Her Fine"

HE CARRIED THE COMPLETED MANUSCRIPT of *The Sun Also Rises* back from Schruns to Paris in a suitcase. It came to "330 typewritten pages in my typing which is without margin," he reported to Max Perkins on April 1, 1926. To Scott Fitzgerald a few weeks later, he said that he was thinking of dedicating *The Sun* to his son.

His inclination not to include Hadley in the dedication was apparently reinforced by the quarrel they had after her return from an unhappy trip to the Loire Valley that spring with the Pfeiffer sisters. The first days of the trip had been delightful, but then Pauline had become curiously moody, snapping at Hadley when she tried to make conversation and withdrawing into herself. Although Jinny lamely explained that her sister had been that way all her life, Hadley felt that the time had finally come to put aside polite evasions. "Is Ernest any way involved?" she asked Jinny. "Has Pauline fallen in love with him?" Jinny reluctantly said that she knew they were very good friends. On reaching Paris, Hadley could hardly keep from crying as she blurted out to her husband that she suspected him of being in love with Pauline. Flushing bright red, Hemingway angrily rebuked her for bringing the "thing" out into the open. "What he seemed to be saying to me," Hadley recalled, "was that it was my fault for forcing the issue. Now that I had broken the spell our love was no longer safe."

Out of this troubling confrontation Hemingway produced, around the first of May, a particularly brutal and guilt-drenched story called "An Alpine Idyll," in which he symbolically dramatized both his callous treatment of Hadley as nothing more than a convenience to him during their months together in wintry Schruns and the effective burial of their marriage in springtime France. For years, so the story reveals, a bestial Austrian peasant by the oafish name of Olz had lived with his wife in an isolated house high up in the Silvretta Valley above the village of Galtur. A chronic sufferer from heart trouble, Frau Olz had finally died, but it was the middle of December and Olz had been unable to transport her corpse down into the village until the snow was gone. On the spring day that he arrived with his burden, the priest who was to bury the dead woman had uncovered her face and was horrified by its disfigurement. Under pressure, the peasant confessed to the priest why her features were damaged. After her death he had laid out her body in the woodshed, and after it was stiff he had stood her against the wall. Her mouth was open and whenever he had come into the shed at night to cut some wood he had hung his lantern from it. What he had done was very wrong, the priest tells him, and he asks the peasant if he had loved his wife. "Ja, I loved her," Olz answers. "I loved her fine."

Even the lighthearted passages in Hemingway's letters to Fitzgerald that spring were built around brutal images. Sometime this coming summer, he informed his friend, he would like to show him a carbon copy of *The Sun Also Rises,* and if the novelist would be so good as to read it he would welcome his advice. In the meantime, Fitzgerald might be interested in a résumé of the plot.

> I have tried to follow the outline and spirit of the Great Gatsby but feel I have failed somewhat because of never having been on Long Island. The action all takes place in Newport, R.I. and the heroine is a girl named Sophie Irene Loeb who kills her mother. The scene in which Sophie gives birth to twins in the death house at Sing Sing where she is waiting to be electrocuted for the murder of the father and sister of her, as then, unborn children I got from Dreiser but practically everything else in the book is either my own or yours. I know you'll be glad to see it. The Sun Also Rises comes from Sophie's statement as she is strapped into the chair as the current mounts.

The emotional stress that elicited this fantasy from him also led him to coin a phrase in the self-same letter about the measure of a matador's bravery in the face of death. Something else was required, he told Fitzgerald, besides sheer guts: "Grace under pressure." Guts, he added, "never made money for anybody except violin manufacturers."

2

THEY had talked, he and Hadley, of going back to Spain together in the middle of May, but now they used the bad cough that had been plaguing Bumby as an excuse for altering their plans. Hadley would stay with the child and Hemingway would go to Madrid by himself. There were novilladas that he was eager to see, and he had a couple of stories to write. Being alone wouldn't be pleasant, but he couldn't invite Pauline to accompany him because she was off on an Italian holiday with her Uncle Gus and his wife.

Madrid was fine and cold and dry, he found, so cold in fact that on Saturday, May 15, it snowed, thereby forcing the cancellation the next day of the festival of San Isidro bullfights. To keep warm in his heatless room, he stayed in bed that Sunday and wrote, not only all day but far into the night, since he knew he couldn't sleep in any event.

The Sun Also Rises, he had spoofingly assured Fitzgerald, dealt with an execution. This was actually true of the two stories he turned out in Madrid. Ole Andreson, an ex-heavyweight-boxer whose body is too long for the roominghouse bed he is lying on, waits inertly for the twinlike hit men from Chicago, Max and Al, to carry out their assassination assignment. "The Killers" was classic Hemingway. "Today is Friday," on the other hand, a playlet involving three Roman soldiers and a Hebrew wineseller who are discussing the Crucifixion in tough-guy lingo ("I tell you, he was pretty good in there today"), was shoddy goods. Biographically, though, the playlet's emphasis on how it "must get to you pretty bad" when they pound in the nails, and how far worse it must be when they lift you up and your "weight starts to pull on 'em," is not without interest, for it suggests how much Hemingway craved the experience of pain as a penitence, if only because Dr. Hemingway had always required him to ask the Lord for forgiveness after beating him. I went to Mass this morning, he wrote to his father one week after composing "Today is Friday."

Most of the guilt that gave him trouble in Madrid had to do with Hadley, but every now and again he remembered someone else whom he had betrayed. Wherefore he wrote a letter—a quite incoherent letter—to Sherwood Anderson about *The Torrents of Spring,* which was due to be published on May 28. "You see I feel that if among ourselves we [writers] have to pull our punches," he explained to his old mentor,

> if when a man like yourself who can write very great things writes something that seems to me, (who have never written anything great but am anyway a fellow craftsman) rotten, I ought to tell you so. . . . It looks, of course, as though I were lining up on the side of the smart jews like Ben Hecht and those other morning glories and that because you had always been swell to me and helped like the devil on the In our time I felt an irresistable [*sic*] need to push you in the face with true writer's gratitude. But what I would like you to know, and of course that sounds like bragging, is—oh hell I can't say that either.

Trying once more to justify the unjustifiable, he told Anderson that "outside of personal feelings nothing that's any good can be hurt by satire." Quite possibly, this utterly grotesque argument was the work of a man who was drunk.

3

THINKING that the Riviera sunshine would be good for Bumby's alarmingly persistent cough, Hadley accepted the Murphys' invitation to bring him south. The guest house on the grounds of their Villa America estate proved to be enchanting, and Bumby picked up a fine sunburn playing on the beach with the Murphys' children. The health-conscious Sara, however, didn't like the sound of his hacking, and a British doctor whom she summoned diagnosed whooping cough and said that the child would have to be quarantined. The Fitzgeralds, providentially, were just about to vacate the Villa Paquita in Juan-les-Pins, even though their lease had not yet expired, in favor of a larger and more comfortable place, the Villa St. Louis, that had a private beach and was nearer to the casino. Hadley and Bumby forthwith moved in, along with Hadley's ever-faithful Breton servant, Marie Cocotte, and after his three-week visit to Spain Hemingway also joined them there.

Daily letters from Ernest reached Pauline in Paris, who said she felt like an exile. Supposing, she said, with her usual boldness, she were to come to Juan-les-Pins and share the Hemingways' quarantine; having had whooping cough as a child, she wasn't afraid of contracting it again. Hemingway enthusiastically agreed to her proposal. Thus, Hadley soon found herself living once again, as she had at the Hotel Taube, in a ménage à trois, and when the Fitzgeralds' lease on the villa finally ran out, the ménage simply moved to the nearby Hôtel de la Pinède. "Here it was," Hadley remembered, "that the three breakfast trays, three wet bathing suits on the line, three bicycles were to be found. Pauline tried to teach me to dive, but I was not a success. Ernest wanted us to play bridge but I found it hard to concentrate. We spent all morning on the beach sunning or swimming, lunched in our little garden. After siesta time there were long bicycle rides along the Golfe de Juan." ★

That the Murphys were visibly awed by Hemingway's literary achievements and commanding personality, and increasingly irritated by Fitzgerald's antic behavior, created another sort of triangular tension that summer. At a party at the casino that the Murphys threw in Hemingway's honor, champagne and caviar were served, which Fitzgerald in his jealousy derided as pretentious fare. Ostentatiously turning his chair away from the table, he stared with such rude persistence at the attractive young woman who was being entertained at the next table by a considerably older man that the couple complained to the headwaiter. Throwing ashtrays on the floor was Fitzgerald's next attention-seeking stunt. Gerald Murphy became so annoyed by this "sophomoric and—well, trashy" conduct that he got up and left the party, even though he was its host.

Besides finding his childishness tiresome, the Murphys were put off by Fitzgerald's constant third-degreeing of them about their feelings, as if he would never be able to publish another novel until he knew absolutely everything about them. "You can't expect anyone to like or stand a *Continual* feeling of analysis & sub-analysis & criticism—on the whole unfriendly—Such as we have felt for quite awhile," Sara told him in a reproving note. "*You ought to know at your age,*" she emphatically added, "that you *Can't have Theories about friends.*"

Fitzgerald's anguished realization that there had been a shift in the Murphys' loyalty from him to Hemingway did not prevent him, however, from reading the carbon typescript of *The Sun Also Rises* with the utmost care, or from giving Hemingway the benefit of his superbly intelligent criticism. High on the list of his recommendations was that the background material on Jake, Brett, and Mike Campbell be cut back or eliminated—and Hemingway responded to this piece of advice by ruthlessly lopping off the novel's first fifteen pages. Fitzgerald also observed that Jake's narrative contained too many "sneers, superiorities and nose-thumbings-at-nothing," that he was given on occasion to clichés ("Quarter being a state of mind,

---

★ On automobile rides with the Murphys, they got as far as La Napoule, where much of *The Garden of Eden* takes place.

etc. This is in all guide books.") and that there was a tone at the beginning of "elephantine facetiousness" that he hoped Hemingway would fix in the proofs. Yet if Fitzgerald knew how to criticize, he also knew how to praise, how to comfort and how to encourage. "God! the bottom of p. 77 *jusque* the top of p. 78 are wonderful," he exclaimed, and he called on Hemingway to remember that writing a novel was "a new departure for you, and I think your stuff is great. You were the first American I wanted to meet in Europe—and the last."

All in all, the critique was splendid. There was one observation, though, that stood apart from the others. He was convinced that there was a cover-up in the novel, although he didn't use that word, having to do with Jake's emasculating injury and his inability to follow through on Brett's bid to be seduced by him. "The heart of my criticism," he told Hemingway, "beats somewhere upon p. 87. I think you can't change it though. I felt the lack of some crazy, torturing tentativeness or insecurity—horror, all at once—that she'd feel—and he'd feel—maybe I'm crazy. He isn't *like an impotent man. He's like a man in a sort of moral chastity belt.*" That Jake cannot make love to the woman he loves is the consequence not of a war wound, Fitzgerald all but said, but of something more deeply rooted in his psychological history.

4

BY late June, the Fitzgeralds were back in Paris, where Zelda underwent what was officially billed as an appendectomy in the American Hospital in Neuilly, although there is reason to believe that the operation she actually had was an abortion.

As for Hemingway, he was still fixated on the Pamplona fiesta, despite the fiasco of the year before. This time he took Pauline and the Murphys with him, in addition to Hadley. Expensive barrera seats, paid for by Gerald, were occupied by their party every afternoon. At one of the morning free-for-alls, Hemingway challenged Gerald to join him in the arena. Waving his raincoat around like a cape, Gerald gave a reasonably good imitation of a matador, although being a perfectionist about everything he was unhappy with his performance. "Next year," he promised, "I'll do well, Papa," using the nickname that Hemingway—just turning twenty-seven—was now actively engaged in hanging on himself.

At the conclusion of the fiesta, the Murphys went back to the Riviera, Pauline returned to Paris and the Hemingways went on to Madrid, Valencia, and San Sebastián, "all the time bitterly unhappy," said Hadley. The letters that reached them from her rival made her feel even worse. "I'm going to get a bicycle and ride in the bois," Pauline wrote. "I am going to get a saddle, too. I am going to get everything I want." There was the sound of rich-girl certainty in her voice.

Early in August, the Hemingways reappeared at the Villa America, all their pretenses to being happily married utterly gone. The Murphys were amazed to learn that they were splitting up, while Don Stewart, who was honeymooning at the time on the Cap d'Antibes, had even greater difficulty in accepting the news. To him, Hemingway and Hadley had seemed a perfect match. Gerald said that in Paris he kept a studio in the rue Froidevaux and that Hemingway should feel free to live there as long as he wanted. His offer was immediately accepted.

The train that bore the Hemingways north on the last of their many trips together gave them a glimpse of the sea for a while before moving inland through flat fields of grapes with gray-stone hills behind them, so Hemingway would remember in the short story called "A Canary for One," into which he would also weave accusatory thoughts about his mother. As it is getting dark, the story relates, the train passes a burning farmhouse. Motor-cars have stopped along the road and things from inside the farmhouse are spread out around it. The station platform at Avignon is crowded with Negro soldiers, commanded by a short, white sergeant. In the morning near Paris, as the train passes through carefully tended forests and towns with tram-cars and big advertisements for Dubonnet, Pernod, and the Belle Jardinière, a young American couple in the *lit salon* compartment is informed by an older American woman, who is traveling with a canary in a cage, that she had once been forced to break up her daughter's passionate romance with a European student because she didn't approve of her marrying a foreigner. The caged canary is the symbol of the woman's control of her daughter. In the shadowy cavern of the Gare de Lyon, the young couple follows a porter who is in charge of their bags down the platform. At the end of the platform is a gate and a man who takes their tickets. "We were returning to Paris," the story ends, "to set up separate residences."

5

UNABLE to face living in their apartment with all its reminders of Ernest, Hadley rented a room for herself and Bumby in the Hôtel Beauvoir across from the Closerie des Lilas. She was completely

shattered by what had happened and kept breaking into tears at odd
moments. Don Stewart, who walked her back to the hotel one night
after a party, remembered that she wept all the way. As a youngster,
she had been traumatized by the suicide of her father and the insistence of her mother that the back injury she had suffered in childhood had permanently affected her ability to lead a normal life. After
dropping out of college, she had lived in the shadows for years. At
the end of her twenties, miraculously, she had met and married an
exuberant man who had showed her the world, and after their son
was born she had driven herself to the edge of exhaustion in an effort
to go on being his ever-ready companion. That she did not lose the
weight she had gained during pregnancy was a sign, however, of
her mounting sense of defeat. Excessive eating and drinking served
as compensations for the obvious leeching away of her husband's
fidelity. But to face the future without this difficult but unforgettable
man, to watch their son growing up—as she herself had—in a fatherless household, were prospects for which she could foresee no
compensation.

Even though the battle for Ernest had ended, she made one last
try to win it. Because she knew that he hated to live alone, she wrote
out a formal proposal, affixing her signature to it and personally
delivering it, in which she swore that if he and Pauline would remain
apart for a hundred days and were still in love at the end of that
time, she would grant him a divorce. What she secretly hoped
against hope would happen was that in the course of this period he
would find out how much he missed his wife and son and come
back to them.

Hemingway's first reaction was that he and Pauline should simply
ignore this little piece of paper and start living together at once. In
time, he was sure, Hadley would give in and agree to a divorce.
Pauline was more tough-minded. All that they had to do in order to
get what they wanted was to practice self-discipline for three
months. Wherefore she took a leave of absence from *Vogue* and
booked passage on the Red Star liner *Pennland,* leaving Boulogne for
New York on September 24.

The night before the *Pennland* sailed, the lovers dined together on
sole and partridge and decided on a set of code words for use in their
transatlantic cables. "Pilar," they agreed, would be their name for
Pauline. No sooner had the ship cleared the port the next morning
than "Pilar" dispatched her first cable, and followed it with another
when the ship put in at Southampton. In her first letter at sea, she
told Hemingway she was passing the time by studying French and
conversing with other passengers on subjects ranging from the effec-

tiveness of Mussolini's dictatorship to the state of the harbors in Brazil. On reaching New York, she bought some lovely white shirts for her future husband, ran into Robert Benchley on the street, who wanted to hear all about Ernest, and stopped in at Scribners, where she was informed that publication of *The Sun Also Rises* had been set for late October. Her sympathetic Uncle Gus was predictably very supportive of what she was engaged in doing, but when she got to her parents' place in Arkansas and told her mother she was going to marry a man who was still married to another woman, she was distressed to find herself the object of opprobrium. The devoutly Catholic Mrs. Pfeiffer's first question to her daughter was "And how does she [Hadley] feel?" At the end of their talk, Mrs. Pfeiffer said that perhaps the best thing for the two of them was not to discuss the matter again, and she instructed Pauline not to mention it at all to her father.

For solace, Pauline turned to the woods and fields of her father's vast acreage. Early October in Piggott, she wrote to her beloved, was "very much on the bright side with a swell kick in the air," and the overgrown and untended countryside was far more to her liking than "smug New England." Yet if nature buoyed her up, it finally let her down. On a dark Monday morning following a weekend of rain that left the autumn leaves on the ground dark brown and soggy, "a madhouse depression" descended upon her. Borrowing a neighbor boy's bike, she cycled down a muddy road, trying to recover her morale. Back at the house, though, she began weeping bitterly and continued to do so, off and on, for hours. In the letter she wrote to Hemingway that afternoon, she confessed that "You got your terrible hell being day after day with Hadley and I think I'm getting mine with Mother. . . . in addition to feeling that her daughter has broken up a home and feeling so terrible about Hadley, she worries about me. . . . if there is anything Hadley wants you to do for her or Bumby, ever, no matter what, you gotta do it don't you. And any amount of money settlement." Financial generosity would always seem to the second Mrs. Hemingway to be the best way to deal with vexing problems in human relations.

6

FROM the moment that he parted from Hadley outside the Gare de Lyon, Hemingway had tried to hold on to himself through hard work. The first thing he did was to correct and revise the proofs of his novel that Scribners had sent him. On August 26, having finished this task, he returned the proofs to "Mr. Perkins," as he still called

his editor, aboard the *Mauretania*. In the same packet he enclosed a
copy of "The Killers," which had been "typed up by the well
known, admired author on a six year old Corona," and which he
hoped that Perkins would be able to sell to *Scribner's Magazine*. (The
editor of *Scribner's,* Robert Bridges, accepted the story at once and
ran it in the March 1927 issue.) The third and last of his enclosures
in the packet was the dedication page for *The Sun Also Rises:* THIS
BOOK IS FOR HADLEY AND FOR JOHN HADLEY NICANOR. His inclination
to exclude Hadley from the dedication had been no match, finally,
for the mounting surge of his guilt feelings about her.

During the first week in September, he began and finished "A
Canary for One" and started another story of far greater importance.
Gerald Murphy's thirty-foot-high studio in the rue Froidevaux opposite the Cimetière du Montparnasse was the scene of his labors,
and an interesting scene it was. The walls were hung with the over-
sized canvases on which Murphy had attempted to assimilate and
transform the principles of Synthetic Cubism and other movements
in modern art into a vision of his own. It was Murphy's passion to
present the reality of everyday objects—a razor, a watch, a cigar box
—on a giant scale and with the utmost precision. In order to do so
he first spent months reducing these objects to purely abstract forms,
until at last he felt ready to *"re-*present them," as he punningly
described his method. In the admiring words of his fellow Yale man,
Archibald MacLeish, Murphy's aesthetic aim was to make visible
" 'the thing itself"—the 'thing' so like 'itself' that it would *become* its
implications." Gerald "painted an Edwardian cigar box," MacLeish
further explained, that was "so totally representative of itself that it
became its world. He painted a wasp so like a wasp that no one
looking at it could take a wasp for granted ever again." The huge
examples of his art adorning his studio provided a stunning backdrop for Hemingway's own pursuit of reality. Murphy had really
been a prince to let him have the place. Unfortunately, his sense of
indebtedness to the painter was one of the chief reasons why their
friendship would eventually wither and die.

When Hemingway's bank statement from the Paris branch of the
Guaranty Trust came in at the end of September, he discovered that
Murphy had quietly assisted him in another way by depositing four
hundred dollars in his account. This gift, too, would irritate the
recipient.

The second of the two stories he wrote in the studio was less than
three thousand words long but required much effort to complete. In
between sessions of work on it he wrote frantic letters to Pauline in
Piggott which vividly illustrated what an emotionally dependent

person he was. Hadley knew her husband well: living alone was all but intolerable for him. In a tone of voice that approached hysteria he cried out to Pauline that "All I can think is that you . . . are all I have and that I love more than all," that "All day long I think of things to say to you and things to tell you," that "all I want is you Pfife and oh dear god I want you so," that "[missing you] doesn't take any particular form outside of the horrors at night and a black depression" and that "when two people love each other terribly much and need each other in every way and then go away from each other it works almost as bad as an abortion."

He also spent a good deal of time with Archie and Ada MacLeish during these nightmarishly lonesome months, biking with Archie to Chartres and other points around Paris and dragging him off to Zaragoza for the October bullfights there. With Ada he went to prizefights, at which she was embarrassed by her escort's truculent responses to anyone in the crowd who jostled her; more than once, she remembered, he threatened to slug the unwitting offender. One night at the MacLeishes', he vomited forth a few more of the scorpions that were crawling around on the rocks inside him by hauling out a poem he had just written about Dorothy Parker and insisting on reading it aloud. Don Stewart, who was there that night, was so sickened by it that his affection for Hemingway was permanently compromised.

The story behind the poem had begun the previous April, when *The New Yorker*'s witty Miss Parker had visited Spain with Gilbert Seldes and his wife and a historical writer of uncertain health named Seward Collins. On her return to Paris, she had let Hemingway know, much to his annoyance, that she hated the damn country. Subsequently, she had annoyed him further by borrowing his typewriter and failing to return it promptly, possibly because she was so thrilled at being able to compose on it. For Hemingway was one of her idols. She had come to France in order to visit him, even as she would follow him to Sun Valley and to Spain during the Civil War and would entertain for him when he came to Hollywood. Virtually every word of the journalistic pieces that she would publish about his life and work would be adulatory, and she constantly measured her own work habits against his legendary dedication. Her last recorded words, to her friend Beatrice Ames, would poignantly reveal her utter adoration of him—as well as her insecurity about how he felt about her. "I want you to tell me the truth," she urged. "Did Ernest really like me?" Yet if Hemingway was flattered to have such a worshipful fan, he also was disgusted by her. She could never stop talking about being half Jewish, or about her attempted suicides, or

about the grisly details of her abortion, or about her sexual infidelities. In the midst of his raging discontent with everything in the
autumn of 1926, it seemed to him that she amply deserved "To a
Tragic Poetess." The first twenty-nine lines of the poem are representative of the vileness of the whole:

> *O thou who with a safety razor blade*
> *a new one to avoid infection*
> *Slit both thy wrists*
> *the scars defy detection*
> *Who over-veronaled to try and peek*
> *into the shade*
> *Of that undistant country from whose bourne*
> *no traveller returns who hasn't been there.*
> *But always vomited in time*
> *and bound your wrists up*
> *To tell how you could see his little hands*
> *already formed*
> *You'd waited months too long*
> *that was the trouble.*
> *But you loved dogs and other people's children*
> *and hated Spain where they are cruel to donkeys.*
> *Hoping the bulls would kill the matadors.*
> *The national tune of Spain was Tea for Two*
> *you said and don't let anyone say Spain to you—*
> *You'd seen it with the Seldes*
> *One Jew, his wife and a consumptive*
> *you sneered your way around*
> *through Aragon, Castille and Andalucia.*
> *Spaniards pinched*
> *the Jewish cheeks of your plump ass*
> *in holy week in Seville*
> *forgetful of our Lord and of His passion.*
> *Returned, your ass intact, to Paris*
> *To write more poems for the New Yorker.*

But as a new piece of fiction demonstrated, his most deeply felt
anger that fall was directed at the idea of marriage. If only he hadn't
got married, he wouldn't be in this horrible fix. Feelings of self-pity
compounded his anger, and so, apparently, did sporadic wishes that
Hadley were dead, a panicky sense that he would be lost without
her and a lacerating guilt. So terribly wrought up was he that when
he delivered a load of furniture in a handbarrow to her new apartment at 35 rue de Fleurus, he broke down in tears at the sight of her.
A few years before in Toronto, he had feared that a consuming anger

might interfere with his ability to write; this fear came back to him
now, in the terrible image of a deformed right hand. Somehow he
had to regain control of himself, which meant getting rid of his
feelings by writing about them. But in order to establish artistic
control, he found it necessary to place a certain distance between
himself and his emotions by projecting them upon some other character than an alter-ego narrator. The difficulty of this task was considerable. In the end, it took him two months to write the story
whose title he lifted from the quotation from Marlowe's *The Jew of
Malta* with which T. S. Eliot had prefaced his "Portrait of a Lady":

> *Thou hast committed—*
> *Fornication: but that was in another country*
> *And besides, the wench is dead.*

Among Hemingway's short works of fiction, the opening paragraph of "In Another Country" is matchless. The rising and falling
cadences, the visual and tactile values, the strung-up dead animals
and birds that serve as objective correlatives to the story's disabled
men strapped into therapy machines, are the creations of a poet
working at the pinnacle of his power. The descriptive exactitude of
the writing also had behind it the meticulous paintings of Gerald
Murphy in the presence of which the paragraph was composed.

> In the fall the war was always there, but we did not go to it any more.
> It was cold in the fall in Milan and the dark came very early. Then
> the electric lights came on, and it was pleasant along the streets look-
> ing in the windows. There was much game hanging outside the
> shops, and the snow powdered in the fur of the foxes and the wind
> blew their tails. The deer hung stiff and heavy and empty, and small
> birds blew in the wind and the wind turned their feathers. It was a
> cold fall and the wind came down from the mountains.

The young American narrator of the story is receiving physical
therapy on an outpatient basis for the wounds he has sustained in his
knee and leg. Every afternoon he walks to the hospital with three
Italian officers who have also been wounded. While none of them
has suffered, so far as the reader is aware, the sort of damage that
disabled Jake Barnes, a fourth Italian officer who occasionally joins
them wears a black handkerchief across his face because he has lost
his nose.

Still another Italian officer, a major with a withered right hand,
works in the machine next to the tricycle-like apparatus in which the

American usually sits. The doctor who supervises their therapy is optimistic about their chances for recovery, but the major is profoundly skeptical. He winks sardonically at the American when the doctor examines his hand, which is being held between two leather straps that bounce up and down and flap the stiff fingers. To inspire him, the doctor brings out a photograph of a hand that had been almost as small as the major's but that after a course of machine work was a little larger. "Very interesting," says the major. "You have confidence?" says the doctor. "No," says the major.

Even though the major had been the greatest fencer in Italy before the war, the anger that is in him seems out of proportion to the injury that has ended his career. Not only does he become quite vituperative about the machines—they are "idiotic," he says—but he loses his temper at the young American for speaking Italian without troubling to learn the grammar. "He said I was a stupid impossible disgrace," the narrator relates, "and he was a fool to have bothered with me." And when he starts to quiz the American about his personal life, the major flies off the handle completely.

> "What will you do when the war is over if it is over?" he asked me. "Speak grammatically!"
> "I will go to the States."
> "Are you married?"
> "No, but I hope to be."
> "The more of a fool you are," he said. He seemed very angry. "A man must not marry."
> "Why, Signor Maggiore?"
> "Don't call me 'Signor Maggiore.'"
> "Why must not a man marry?"
> "He cannot marry. He cannot marry," he said angrily. "If he is to lose everything, he should not place himself in a position to lose that. He should not place himself in a position to lose. He should find things he cannot lose."
> He spoke very angrily and bitterly, and looked straight ahead while he talked.
> "But why should he necessarily lose it?"
> "He'll lose it," the major said. He was looking at the wall. Then he looked down at the machine and jerked his little hand out from between the straps and slapped it hard against his thigh. "He'll lose it," he almost shouted. "Don't argue with me!" Then he called to the attendant who ran the machines. "Come and turn this damned thing off."

What ails the major is the knowledge that his young wife is dying of pneumonia. It is the prospective loss of her that has made him so angry, that has prompted him to warn the American that he must not marry.

Yet after he has been out of the room for a while, the major comes back in a somewhat different mood. He apologizes to the American for having been rude to him and pats him on the shoulder with his good hand. Suddenly, the reader glimpses the grief beneath his anger, the awful fear of loneliness that lies behind his bitter assertion that men should find things they cannot lose. On the telephone just now, he has learned that his wife is dead. "It is very difficult," he says, biting his lower lip. "I cannot resign myself." With tears on his cheeks and biting his lips, he walks past the machines and out the door.

7

THE psychological conditions under which "In Another Country" was composed were dramatically eased on November 17, even as Hemingway was preparing to mail the story to the States for consideration by *Scribner's Magazine*. For on that day he received a letter from Hadley saying that even though he and Pauline had lived apart for less than two-thirds of the time she had stipulated, she no longer wished to stand in the way of the divorce that he so obviously desired. "I took you originally for better, for worse (and meant it!)," she told him, "but in the case of your marrying some one else, I can stand by my vow only as an outside friend."

Hemingway's reply, dated November 18, said in effect that he had never loved her more than in this moment in which she was giving him up forever. Here was the permissive mother he had always dreamed of, the mother who would not hold him morally accountable for obligations he wanted to shirk, the mother who would let him do exactly what he wanted. "My dearest Hadley," he began, and he went on from that term of endearment to tell her that her letter, "like everything that you have ever done," was "very brave and altogether unselfish and generous." He would shortly be instructing Scribners, he said, that "all royalties from The Sun Also Rises should be paid to you," and that she could also count on all the royalties from Jonathan Cape, the novel's British publisher, "which are very generous," he informed her, "on a book that might have a great sale in England." These arrangements were only fair, he continued, for "I would never have written . . . In Our Time, Torrents or The Sun if I had not married you and had your loyal and self-sacrificing and always stimulating and loving—and actual cash support backing." In addition, he was making a will and writing to his agents and publishers to tell them that in the case of his death the money from all his books, "past and future," was to go to Bumby, in a trust that Hadley could hold for him. In conclusion, he wanted to say to her that "perhaps the luckiest thing Bumby will ever have is to have you for a mother. And I won't tell you how I admire your straight thinking, your head, your heart and your very lovely hands and I pray God always that he will make up to you the very great hurt that I have done to you—who are the best and truest and loveliest person I have ever known."

Thus was Hadley transformed into a fantasy figure, in which Hemingway at once began to invest an enormous amount of imaginative capital. Pauline may have taken Hadley's husband away from her in real life, but real life was not the only realm in which he lived.

8

WITH his actual mother he had had very few direct dealings since she had deeply disappointed him by not commenting on "The Doctor and the Doctor's Wife" in the December 1924 issue of the *transatlantic review*. When *In Our Time* was published on October 5, 1925, he heard by the grapevine that his father had bought a copy, but two months later he still hadn't received a word from either of his parents about it. "Think the family are praying over what they should say to me about this last book," he exasperatedly remarked two months later to his high school friend, Isabel Simmons, who was married now to the classics professor Francis R. B. Godolphin.

Shortly before Christmas of that year, he finally received a letter from his father, saying that he had heard "many compliments" around town about *In Our Time* and intimating that he was proud of his son. At the same time, Dr. Hemingway remained the moralist who had returned the six copies of *in our time* to the Three Mountains Press. "Trust you will see and describe more of humanity of a different character in future," he emphasized. "Volumes of the brutal you have surely shown the world. Look for the joyous uplifting and optimistic and spiritual in character. . . . Remember God holds us each responsible to do our best." As for his mother, she had nothing at all to say about a book that contained "Soldier's Home" as well as "The Doctor and the Doctor's Wife." Thus while she clipped out Paul Rosenfeld's *New Republic* review of *In Our Time* and enclosed it in a Christmas letter to Paris, along with Archibald MacLeish's *Atlantic Monthly* review of Sherwood Anderson's *Dark Laughter,* she pointedly spent the bulk of the letter talking about her own burgeoning career as a landscape painter.

In Hemingway's reply to her from Schruns, pseudo-heartiness reigned. "Congratulations on your success with your paintings! Thank you for the New Republic review. Also the review of Anderson's Book for the Atlantic Monthly. Archie MacLeish is very intelligent. He voiced my own opinion of Dark Laughter." Turning from literary to personal matters, he ended the letter by casually remarking that a woman named Pauline Pfeiffer would be coming to Schruns to spend Christmas with him and Hadley. A week later, he revealed at least some of his annoyance with his mother in a note to MacLeish. "My mother sent me your review of Dark Laughter from the Atlantic Monthly," he wrote. "It is a damned good review. My mother always sends me everything that shows up Sherwood or when he gets a divorce or anything because she has read that I am much the same thing only not so good and she naturally wants me to know how the Master is getting along."

Hemingway heard from both his parents twelve months later, and about the same two things: The Sun Also Rises and his marital troubles. "You surely are now famous as a writer and I shall trust your future books will have a different sort of subject matter," his father tactfully told him. "You have such a wonderful ability and we want to be able to read and ask others to enjoy your works." In a paragraph that was even more painful for him to write, Dr. Hemingway then added that "the gossip is about a serious domestic trouble, please write to me the truth, so I can deny the awfull [sic] rumors that you and Hadley have had a break."

His mother's response to the rumors about the "cooling off of affection between you and Hadley" was quite gently phrased. "Trust they are not true," she said, "but you have not mentioned her in any recent letters and I can't help but worry a little concerning your happiness." On the subject of The Sun Also Rises, however, she fired off a devastating barrage of moral judgments. The novel was selling, she was glad to hear, even though it seemed to her "a doubtful honor" to have produced "one of the filthiest books of the year." Surely Ernest must know other words besides damn and bitch. It was a pity that she had had to miss the last meeting of her Current Books Study Group, but she simply "could not face being present" during the discussion of The Sun Also Rises. "What is the matter?" she asked her son. "Have you ceased to be interested in loyalty, nobility, honor and fineness of life—Why life is more wonderful and beautiful to me every day of my life—I have found my heaven here—in the opportunity to create beauty and exalt the nobility of life." If Ernest was having romantic troubles or if drink had "got" him, then he must break those bonds and rise up and be the man and the writer that God had intended him to be. Even before his conception his parents had dedicated him to God in the hope that he might make the world a better place. "I love you dear," she closed by saying, "and still believe you will do something worthwhile to live after you."

Within days of the appearance of Allen Tate's adverse appraisal of *The Sun Also Rises,* Hemingway banged out a caustic complaint to the poet about it. But his mother's criticisms pierced him more deeply than any professional reviewer's could. So hurt and angered was he by her words that he couldn't respond, even as he had been unable to speak to her "bank account" blast six and a half years earlier. When she didn't hear from him, Grace wrote again, on January 31, 1927. It was a cheerful note, all about herself. "Did the family tell you that I was getting big fees for my pictures, 250.00 per," she wanted to know, and she enclosed a catalogue of the recent Marshall Field exhibit of her work that contained a reproduction of the painting she called *The Blacksmith Shop.* By this maneuver, she virtually compelled him to reply, and he obliged her on February 5.

Following a couple of sentences of perfunctory thanks for sending him the Marshall Field catalogue, he explained to her that he hadn't answered her comments about *The Sun Also Rises* "as I could not help being angry and it is very foolish to write angry letters; and more than foolish to do so to one's mother. It is quite natural for you not to like the book and I regret your reading any book that causes you pain or disgust." End of paragraph. But not end of subject. Not only did he go on to say that he himself was in no way ashamed of the book, but he tried to hurt her by making sarcastic reference to the long history of her bad relations with his father. My book, he declared, is no more unpleasant than "the real inner lives of some of our best Oak Park families." The only difference, he said in effect, was that she was a hypocrite about human life and he was not. "You must remember that in such a book all the worst of the people's lives is displayed while at home there is a very lovely side for the public and the sort of thing of which I have had some experience in observing behind closed doors."

Nor did he stop there, for now that the dam of his silence had been breached he simply could not restrain himself from sneering at her friends as well. If "the good ladies of the book study club under the guidance of Miss [Fanny] Butcher [of the Chicago *Tribune*] who is *not* an intelligent reviewer—I would have felt very silly had she praised my book—agree unanimously that I am prostituting a great talent etc. for the lowest ends—why the good ladies are talking about something of which they know nothing and saying very foolish things."

In regard to Hadley and himself, he wished his mother to know that "we are the very best of friends" and that she and Bumby "are both well, healthy and happy and all the profits and royalties of The Sun Also Rises, by my order, are being paid directly to [her], both from England and America." As for Grace's speculation that he had become an alcoholic, he lyingly assured her that he had "been drinking nothing but my usual wine or beer with meals," that in fact he had been leading "a very monastic life" and that "I have never been a drunk nor even a steady drinker (You will hear legends that I am —they are tacked on everyone that ever wrote about people who drink) and that all I want is tranquillity and a chance to write."

Finally, he picked up on her question of whether he had ceased to be interested in loyalty by accusing her of disloyalty to him, whereas "Dad has been very loyal." In the course of my life, he ended by saying, "you will find much cause to feel that I have disgraced you if you believe everything you hear. On the other hand with a little shot of loyalty as anaesthetic you may be able to get through all my obvious disreputability and find, in the end, that I have not disgraced you at all."

"Your statement that I have not been loyal to you would make me *very unhappy* were it the truth," his mother shot back on February 20. "Our Heavenly Father hates the sin and loves the sinner. In my feeble way I am still taking a Mother's privilege and prerogative of urging you to cut loose from the coarse and low things and aim higher. . . . As long as I live I shall believe in you, believe in the ultimate triumph of your better self over degrading influences and low appeals. God will bring this to pass, just as soon as you give him the controlling hand, in your life."

They had traded their best shots, but Grace, seemingly, had had the last word. Two months later, though, he struck back at her in a different way by writing "Now I Lay Me," wherein a triumphantly smiling woman stands on the porch and watches her husband rake chipped and blackened arrowheads, stone axes and stone skinning knives out of the ashes of the fire that has been burning in the roadway in front of their home.

9

The Sun Also Rises appeared in the bookstores on October 22, 1926, in a dust jacket that was printed in gold, black, and tan, with a gold apple on either side of the title and beneath it the figure of a drowsing woman clothed in the style of Greek antiquity. A Pan's pipe lay near her sandaled foot and another gold apple rested in the palm of her left hand. At the bottom, Hemingway was identified as the author of *In Our Times* [sic] and *The Torrents of Spring*. The first edition consisted of 5,090 copies. By mid-December, it had sold out completely, as had a second printing of 2,000 copies. In the course of the next month, 3,000 more copies were sold, with no signs of a letup in the public's interest. "The Sun has risen . . . and is rising steadily," Max Perkins remarked.

At the same time, Hemingway was no longer simply collecting rejection slips from popular American magazines. Besides "The Killers," *Scribner's Magazine* took "A Canary for One" and "In Another Country," and the *Atlantic Monthly,* amazingly enough, accepted "Fifty Grand." While the author of these stories could not yet command the sort of fees that his friend Fitzgerald had been accustomed to for years, he was clearly headed in that direction.

But the marked shift in his style of life that occurred in the winter of 1927 was primarily underwritten by Mr. and Mrs. Paul Pfeiffer —Mrs. Pfeiffer having become reconciled to the idea of having Hemingway as a son-in-law—and even more so by Pauline's Uncle Gus. Thus, after meeting Pauline's ship in Cherbourg, Hemingway took off with her and Jinny and the MacLeishes for an extended skiing vacation. The Hotel Taube in Schruns, however, was no longer good enough for him; now he preferred the grander *luxe* of the Hotel Rossli in Gstaad. It was there that he learned that Hadley had been granted a divorce in Paris on January 27.

On their return to the French capital in March, Pauline was shocked to discover that although their marriage was set for early May, Hemingway had no intention of helping her to find an apartment for them. Instead, he set off with his pal Guy Hickok on an "Italian tour for the promotion of masculine society," as Pauline acidly described it. After she had hunted for days without any luck, a tip from Ada MacLeish finally brought the bride-to-be to an apartment in the rue Férou, a picturesquely narrow street behind the Church of St-Sulpice. The place had been freshly painted and included a large bedroom, a formal living room, a dining room, a spacious kitchen, two bathrooms, a study, and a maid's room. It was just what she wanted, Pauline enthusiastically wrote to her Uncle Gus, who at once let her know that he was coming to Paris soon and that if he liked the place he would pay the rent.

With Hickok at the wheel of his battered Ford coupe and Hemingway reading the road maps, the tour for the promotion of masculine society was meanwhile proceeding very nicely. Entering Italy through Ventimiglia, the two friends headed first for Rapallo, where Hemingway spent an evening reminiscing with Don Giuseppe Bianchi, who was still a simple priest, about old times in the officers' mess in Fossalta.

The next afternoon the travelers stopped for lunch in Spezia. Stenciled eye-bugging portraits of Il Duce with handpainted "vivas" in black beneath them were everywhere. Because it was Sunday, crowds of men and women dressed in their fanciest attire were strolling up and down the streets that led to the harbor. In the restaurant in which Hemingway and Hickok elected to eat, their order was taken by a girl who put her arm around Hickok's neck while they were looking at the menu. Another girl stood in the doorway, and the funny thing was that she wasn't wearing anything under her house dress. A third girl also stood in the doorway from time to time. All three of them seemed to be under the control of an old woman who sat at a table in the back. The first girl brought out the spaghetti and red wine that the diners had ordered and sat down with them. Leaning forward against the table and putting her hands on her breasts, she asked Hickok if he liked her. "He adores you," said Hemingway, considerately answering for his friend. "But he doesn't speak Italian." Hickok asked Hemingway if it was necessary for him to let the girl put her arm around his neck again. "Certainly," Hemingway replied. "Mussolini has abolished the brothels. This is a restaurant."

For dessert, they were offered bananas. "Bananas are all right," said Hickok. "They've got the skins on." The girl embraced Hickok. Hemingway explained that the girl was pleased about his taking the bananas. "Tell her I don't take bananas," said Hickok. Hemingway communicated this information and then asked for the bill. After paying it, he and Hickok walked out and got in the car. The girl who had waited on them came out and stood in the door. Hemingway waved to her, but she didn't wave back.

During the next ten days, the two men paid their passing respects to Pisa and Florence, drove across the Apennines to Rimini and circled back via Bologna, Parma, Piacenza, and Genoa. "Italy, 1927," the semifactual, semifictional account of the trip that Hemingway quickly wrote and sent to Edmund Wilson at the *New Republic,* contained a number of impressions of life under Fascism that were worth thinking about, but the best part of the report was the wonderfully heightened description of that Sunday lunch in Spezia, although Guy Hickok may be pardoned for not agreeing. So many of his friends sent him clippings from the *New Republic* with red underscorings or comments appended that he at last understood, he wrote Hemingway with rueful amusement, "why everybody you use in your stuff goes and gets a gun." Come in and see me this week, he urged. "I keep my gun here in the desk."

Inasmuch as Hemingway wanted a Catholic wedding as much as Pauline did, he willingly accepted the Church's interpretation of his Protestant marriage to Hadley as a nonevent. That Hadley had never been his wife, that his son Bumby was a bastard, were religious rigmaroles that utterly disgusted Ada MacLeish, although she breathed not a word of her feelings to Hemingway and indeed staged a lunch for him and Pauline following the ceremony. As for Hadley, she mildly observed that the conclusions of the Church struck her as strange, but said no more than this out of consideration for her ex-husband, with whom she had been getting along so well since her decision to divorce him. His attentions to Bumby during the ten days that the boy spent with his father in Gstaad had especially pleased her, and when she and Bumby left Paris in mid-April for a trip to the United States, she was touched by Hemingway's courteousness in escorting them to the boat train and seeing them off.

Pauline and Hemingway were married on May 10 in the fashionable church of St-Honoré-d'Eylau in the Place Victor-Hugo. The groom wore a three-piece tweed suit, the bride a stylish silk dress straight out of the pages of *Vogue*—from whose employ she had now resigned—and a single strand of pearls. Her dark hair had been bobbed above the ears and she looked like a boy. Jinny Pfeiffer, who had become such a favorite of Hemingway's that he was thinking of dedicating his next collection of short stories to her, was Pauline's only attendant. Other members of the Pfeiffer clan nevertheless made their presence felt through the thousand-dollar checks they sent.

For their honeymoon, Hemingway chose the unspoiled fishing village of Le Grau-du-Roi in the marshy flats below Aigues-Mortes at the foot of the Rhône estuary. Under commission from Philippe le Hardi, Simone Bocanegra had built magnificent ramparts at Aigues-Mortes in the late thirteenth century, and as a student of warfare Hemingway enjoyed clambering about them. While walking naked on deserted stretches of beach, the newlyweds also developed deep tans, which they further augmented one day by staining their faces with berry juice, for they had decided to bicycle to a local festival disguised as gypsies. In their costumes they looked surprisingly like blood relatives, and two decades later the lingering memory of that family resemblance would inspire Hemingway to set the opening episodes of his strange novel of sexual transference, *The Garden of Eden,* in Le Grau-du-Roi.

The wasted and whitened landscape, the absence of shade and the baking heat of the Rhône delta had a more immediate effect on his imagination. They served to remind him of the conditions he had described in a short story he had started writing earlier and then put aside. "The hills across the valley of the Ebro," his manuscript had begun,

> were long and white. On this side there was no shade and no trees and the station was between two lines of rails in the sun. Close against the side of the station there was the warm shadow of the building and a curtain, made of strings of bamboo beads, hung across the open door into the bar, to keep out flies. The American and the girl with him sat at a table in the shade, outside the building. It was very hot and the express from Barcelona would come in forty minutes. It stopped at this junction for two minutes and went on to Madrid.

During his three weeks in Le Grau-du-Roi, Hemingway spent several days completing "Hills Like White Elephants." It seemed a curious choice of subject matter for a honeymooner to make, for the idea for the story had arisen out of a what-might-have-been fantasy about his first wife, centering on a replay of the tension he had expressed in "Out of Season." Once again, the author wanted sympathy to be with the woman, who is resisting the idea of an abortion. Nevertheless, there can be no question that the brutal persistence with which the man in the story makes a case in favor of it was an expression of Hemingway's latest theory about the failure of his marriage to Hadley: if only the two of them had not allowed a child to enter their lives they would never have parted.

That some such idea was festering within him in the fall of 1926 is revealed in his curious use of the word abortion in one of the letters he had written to Pauline in Piggott: "You see Pfife I think that when two people love each other terribly much and need each other in every way and then go away from each other it works almost as bad as an abortion." But it was not until some months after he had mythologized Hadley into the best and truest and loveliest person he had ever known that the atrocious notion of retroactively thwarting the birth of Bumby became so real to him that he had to write a story about it. "Out of Season: Part Two," he might have called it.

"I know you wouldn't mind it, Jig. It's not really anything. It's just to let the air in," the man says to his female companion as they sit drinking beer in the patch of shadow beside the station across the valley from the hills that look to her like white elephants. "We can have everything," he tells her. "We can have the whole world." But "I don't want anybody but you," he emphasizes. "I don't want any one else." To this nameless man—nameless like the young gentleman in "Out of Season"—a child would truly be a white elephant. The woman named Jig resists him, though, by giving in to his demands on terms he can't accept. "Then I'll do it," she says. "Because I don't care about me." Yet when he says in reply that "I don't want you to do it if you feel that way," he is not conceding defeat, but merely regrouping for another attempt to wear her down, an attempt that goes on and on until finally she says, "Would you please please please please please please please stop talking?"

In his frustration, the man walks into the bar by himself and orders an Anis. Nothing has been resolved. Unlike the young gentleman in "Out of Season," he hasn't changed his mind, and yet he hasn't won, either. "Do you feel better?" he asks Jig, on returning to their table. "I feel fine," she says. "There's nothing wrong with me. I feel fine." The bright falsity of these closing sentences offers a final measure of the dreadful ugliness of their dispute. From bitter beginning to bitter end, the story reflects the terrific conflict inside Hemingway's mind between an obsessive dream of killing his son in utero and the realization that such a dream was monstrous.

In a penciled note at the end of the manuscript, the honeymooning author wrote, "Mss for Pauline—well, well, well." His choice of words implied both surprise and wonder. It may also have been intended to convey a warning.

A Hollow Man

LIKE SO MANY OF HEMINGWAY'S EXPEDITIONS in years to come, the trip to the Rhône delta was marred by an accident. While swimming one day, he cut his foot on a rock; an anthrax infection set in, his temperature soared, his foot swelled up and on his return to Paris he was forced to spend ten days in bed.

After he was up and about again, he gratified a long-deferred wish to dress like a fashion plate by ordering a hand-tailored suit from a shop in the rue St-Honoré, and a splendid fedora and overcoat as well. The prices he was charged seemed to be almost a matter of indifference to him. Not only was the dollar still exceptionally strong against the franc, but Pauline's Uncle Gus was paying the rent on their apartment, sales of *The Sun Also Rises* had reached the twenty thousand mark and in the fall Scribners would be publishing a new collection of his stories.

Men Without Women was the excellent title he chose for the collection, although its subtlety would be lost on devotees of the Hemingway myth. The title certainly implied that he had written about the self-sufficiently masculine worlds of crime, boxing and bullfighting —which is the interpretation that the mythophiles would put upon it. But he also meant to suggest that the alienation of women from men (as well as vice versa) was one of his themes, and he was conscious, too, that in one of the stories he was proudest of he had depicted the inconsolable sorrow of a man who has lost his wife. Four of the stories that he felt would have the biggest impact upon

readers he placed at the beginning of the volume, "The Undefeated," "In Another Country," "Hills Like White Elephants," and
"The Killers." Two other strong stories, "Fifty Grand" and "An
Alpine Idyll," he wanted in the sixth and tenth positions respec-
tively. And just as he had ended *In Our Time* with the memory-
haunted "Big Two-Hearted River," so he decided to end *Men
Without Women* with the memory-haunted "Now I Lay Me." "Che
Ti Dice La Patria" (which was "Italy, 1927" under a title that derived
from a D'Annunzio slogan), "Ten Indians" (the tale of how Prudie
Mitchell broke young Nick Adams's heart), "A Pursuit Race" (a
sketch about an advance man for a burlesque show), "A Simple
Enquiry" (an account of a homosexual Italian officer's interest in his
young orderly), "Banal Story" (a salute to the dead matador,
Maera), "A Canary for One," and the mediocre "Today is Friday"
rounded out the volume. If *Men Without Women* was not destined to
become the most widely influential book of short stories ever published by a twentieth-century American author, that was only because it followed *In Our Time*.

With the scheme for his new book complete, he began thinking
about where he and Pauline should spend the summer, for his wish
was her command, just as it had been Hadley's. Despite a gracious
letter from Sara Murphy on June 17, inviting them to the Villa
America, he decided that he would rather go back to Spain, and they
did. While their return to the Pamplona festival must have evoked
unfortunate memories, they apparently did not speak of them, and
afterwards they chose, like Jake Barnes, to swim and rest at San
Sebastián. From there they went on to Valencia and Madrid, both
of which were hellishly hot, but northwestern Spain, which they
reached at the end of the first week in August, was cool and rainy
and delightful. La Coruña was "a grand town as far out in the old
Atlantic as Europe can get," Hemingway reported to Barklie Henry
in a glowing letter, with "fine wide streets with no sidewalks or
gutters and the first good food I've had all summer." Santiago de la
Compostela appealed to him even more—"the loveliest town in
Spain" he pronounced it—and he and Pauline happily remained
there for almost two weeks, reading proof of *Men Without Women*
and wandering the aisles of the great cathedral.

2

IN the mail waiting for them at Hendaye Plage, where they spent
the last two weeks of their trip, was a letter from Dr. Hemingway that had been forwarded from Paris. Although he and Grace

had continued to write him, Ernest had not communicated with either of them, not even about his marriage to Pauline, since the bitter exchange with his mother the previous winter, and Dr. Hemingway was upset about this. "Had you answered any of my letters since last December and given me your confidence," he wrote, "I would have been oh so happy and had less sleepless nights & fewer explanations, which I have been unable to make. . . . God bless you dear boy, but remember—'What do it profit a man, if he gain the whole world & lose his Soul?' Let us hear from you often—please!"

Hemingway's response to these reproofs was six pages long, largely untruthful and in a couple of places quite moving. The first subject he addressed himself to was his separation from Hadley. They had simply "split up," he assured his father, and if anything the decision was more hers than his. "I did not desert her nor was I committing adultery with anyone. I was living in the apartment with Bumby—looking after him while Hadley was away on a trip and it was when she came back from this trip that she decided she wanted the definite divorce." For over a year, he continued, "I had been in love with two people and had been absolutely faithful to Hadley. . . . After we were divorced if Hadley would have wanted me I would have gone back to her. She said that things were better as they were and that we were both better off. I will never stop loving Hadley nor Bumby nor will I cease to look after them. I will never stop loving Pauline Pfeiffer to whom I am married." He knew that he was "a rotten correspondent," and he was very sorry about that, but "the only way I could keep my private life to myself was to keep it to myself—and I did owe you and Mother a statement on it. But I can't write about it all the time."

Turning to the question of his writing, he revealed how raw the wounds still were that had been caused by his mother's condemnation of *The Sun Also Rises*.

> I know you don't like the sort of thing I write, but that is the difference in our taste and all the critics are not Fanny Butcher. I *know* that I am not disgracing you in my writing but rather doing something that some day you will be proud of. . . . You could if you wanted be proud of me sometimes—not for what I do for I have not had much success in doing good—but for my work. My work is much more important to me than anything in the world except the happiness of three people and you cannot know how it makes me feel for Mother to be ashamed of what I know as sure as you know that there is a God in heaven is *not to be ashamed of.*

At the end, he tried to speak of love, but couldn't keep from dissolving into self-pity and getting angry again before he was through.

> I love you very much and love Mother too and I'm sorry this is such a long letter—it probably doesn't explain anything but you're the only person I've written six pages to since I learned to use a pen and ink. I remember Mother saying once that she would rather see me in my grave than something—I forget what—smoking cigarettes perhaps. If it's of any interest I don't smoke. Haven't for almost 3 years altho you will probably hear stories that I smoke like a furnace. . . . I wish you'd let Mother read this letter. She wrote me a fine letter last Spring and I'm afraid I never answered it. The reason I haven't made either of you a confidant was because I was so upset about Mother accusing me of pandering to the lowest tastes etc in my writing that I shut up like a hermit crab. . . . But anyway I hope you have the dope you both want in this letter—and I'll write often if we can lay off of literary criticism and personalities.

The letter was dated September 14. In exactly one month's time, as Hemingway well knew, Scribners was going to issue *Men Without Women*. The final story in that book, his parents and Grace's book club were going to discover, was full of recognizable details. Lying on the floor of a silk factory in Italy, the hero remembers his grandfather's house, where he and his family had lived when he had been a very little boy, and the "new house designed and built by my mother" to which the family had later moved. "You cannot know how it makes me feel," Hemingway had cried out in the most poignant sentence in his letter, "for Mother to be ashamed of what I know as sure as you know that there is a God in heaven is *not to be ashamed of.*" "Now I Lay Me," however, with its devastating portrait of Grace, was bound to bring shame to her.

3

BACK in Paris, Pauline informed him she was pregnant. Whatever the twinges of panic he may have felt, he made no protest, lest it disrupt the domestic tranquillity he craved at the moment. For at Hendaye Plage he had begun work on a new novel, entitled *Jimmy Breen*, that was giving him difficulties. A kind of modern *Tom Jones*, as he called it, the novel was slated to follow the picaresque hero and his revolutionist father from Oak Park to Chicago, thence to New York, and ultimately to Paris, the home of Jimmy's mother. By mid-October, the furiously industrious author had thirty thousand words in hand, and by the following March when he finally gave up on the book his manuscript was half again as large.

Men Without Women appeared in the midst of these frustrating labors. Its end papers were yellow with three deeper yellow bands centered on the silhouette of a charging bull in a yellow circle. Although the amount of attention the book received from reviewers was gratifyingly large—a fact which helped to account for its sale of fifteen thousand copies in three months, an amazing figure for a collection of short stories—the reviewers' opinions were deeply divided. In a front-page assessment in the Sunday book section of the New York *Herald Tribune* on October 9, 1927, Virginia Woolf showed her capacity for malice by fastening upon a publisher's blurb for which Hemingway had not been responsible. "The softening feminine influence is absent—either through training, discipline, death, or situation," the blurb writer had proclaimed. Mrs. Woolf remarked,

> Whether we are to understand by this that women are incapable of training, discipline, death, or situation, we do not know. But it is undoubtedly true, if we are going to persevere in our attempt to reveal the processes of the critic's mind, that any emphasis laid upon sex is dangerous. Tell a man that this is a woman's book, or a woman that this is a man's, and you have brought into play sympathies and antipathies which have nothing to do with art. The greatest writers lay no stress upon sex one way or the other. The critic is not reminded as he reads them that he belongs to the masculine or the feminine gender. But in our time, thanks to our sexual perturbations, sex consciousness is strong, and shows itself in literature by an exaggeration, a protest of sexual characteristics which in either case is disagreeable.

And her final judgment of Hemingway was that while he was modern in manner he was not so in vision, that his talent had lately contracted rather than expanded and that compared with his novel his stories were "a little dry and sterile."

Cyril Connolly, writing in the *New Statesman,* felt that the stories were "a blend of Gertrude Stein's manner, Celtic childishness, and the slice of life . . . redeemed by humour, power over dialogue, and an obvious knowledge of the people [described]" and that in spite of America's judgment of their author as a second Joyce he was "more of a dark horse than a white hope." H. L. Mencken, in the *American Mercury,* observed that Hemingway and Thornton Wilder "have made huge successes of late, and received a great deal of critical homage," but that it was merely "technical virtuosity" that had won them attention, while Percy Hutchison, in *The New York Times Book Review,* was of the opinion that Hemingway's art was merely "the art of the reporter, carried to the highest degree."

William Curtis, on the other hand, told the readers of *Town & Country* that *Men Without Women* was "probably the best volume of short stories published since the days of the younger Kipling." Dorothy Parker, having heard about but risen above Hemingway's scathing poem about her, hailed the book in *The New Yorker* as "a truly magnificent work. . . . I do not know where a greater collection of stories can be found." Edmund Wilson's encomium to Hemingway in the *New Republic* began with the trenchant assertion that his reputation "has, in a very short time, reached such proportions that it has already become fashionable to disparage him." And the reviewer for the *Dial,* N. L. Rothman, described Hemingway as "our outstanding realist" and ventured to predict that someday he "could write a great tragedy."

4

SHORTLY after Christmas 1927, the four-year-old Bumby ruined a visit to Switzerland with Hemingway and Pauline by sticking a finger in his father's right eye and severely scratching the pupil with his nail. For a week, Hemingway was in considerable pain and could barely see, as both of his eyes kept watering. Three months later, he sustained a more serious injury. At two in the morning he entered the bathroom of his and Pauline's apartment, after having dined with Archibald and Ada MacLeish. Perhaps because he was sleepy, more likely because he was drunk, he did not pull the chain of the flushbox above the toilet, but instead yanked the cord of the skylight, bringing down the whole frame with its thick glass panes upon his head. The resulting moonshaped gash just below his hair part required nine stitches to close and left a scar that he carried for the rest of his life.

The accident was duly described in various wire-service accounts, for by 1928 almost anything that happened to him was regarded by the press as newsworthy. Ezra Pound caught up with the story in Rapallo and at once dispatched a facetious message to his wounded friend. "Haow the hellsufferin tomcats," he wrote on March 11, "did you git drunk enough to fall upwards thru the blithering skylight!!!!!!" On the same day, Hadley also sent him a letter of sympathy that surely must have reminded Hemingway of the loveliness of her spirit. "You poor dear old thing! What rotten, rotten luck to have such a thing happen to a truly beautiful mitten like you! I expect you [and Pauline] are both a bit discouraged about how life *is* one damn thing after another."

Hadley and Bumby had returned to Paris the previous October, and on seeing her again Hemingway had been instantly struck by the thought that she not only was beautiful but happy. The reason for her happiness, it turned out, was that during her stay in the United States she had had an important talk with Paul Mowrer, the Paris correspondent for the Chicago *Daily News*. Her acquaintance with Mowrer had begun in Paris a year earlier, just after her separation from Hemingway. They had played tennis together a few times and had cooled off afterwards over a beer at the Café de l'Observatoire. Mowrer liked "the clean way she hit the ball" and her "barbless wit and generous good humor." No romance had developed, however, for the forty-year-old Mowrer was married and the father of two teenage sons. But at their meeting in the States, he told Hadley his situation had changed. His wife had decided to move in with a woman friend of hers who owned a studio in Paris. Mowrer himself intended to buy a country property near Crécy-en-Brie and commute to his Paris office. If Hadley was willing, said Mowrer, he would like to start taking her out. Hadley indicated that that would please her very much.

Perhaps it was the realization that his ex-wife not only intended to go on living in Paris but had taken up with another man that started Hemingway thinking about leaving the city. Seeing her with Mowrer would be an uncomfortable reminder of the happiness they themselves had once shared. A more certain reason why he found the idea of pulling up stakes appealing was that a lot of Left Bankers were gunning for him. Although Ford Madox Ford would eventually forgive him, Stella Bowen, Harold Loeb, and Kitty Cannell had been permanently offended by his portraits of them in *The Sun Also Rises,* while Duff Twysden, on reconsideration, was miffed as well. Gertrude Stein also had it in for him, and her sharp wit made her a formidable enemy. His Parisian nest had not been completely befouled, to be sure. Sylvia Beach and Janet Flanner were still as fond of him as ever, and he remained close to Fitzgerald and Dos Passos. But at the end of 1926 Fitzgerald and Zelda had abruptly returned to the United States; following an interlude in Hollywood, they leased a Greek Revival mansion called Ellerslie, on the Delaware River, not far from Wilmington. As for the peripatetic Dos Passos, he hardly considered the French capital his home; indeed, he, too, was currently in the United States, working with an experimental theater group in Manhattan called the New Playwrights. The size of the American expatriate population in Paris was still growing, but a countercurrent was now running westward.

The appeal of the States may have been further enhanced for Hemingway by the realization of how little he knew about his native land. While he had been to New York a number of times, he really couldn't claim a familiarity with the city. Nor had he ever fished in Florida, or hunted in the Rocky Mountain West. During his years in Europe, his interest in sports had hardly been neglected, of course. Just recently, he had spent six weeks at Gstaad for the second year in a row, and before that had made a quick trip to the Sportspalast in Berlin to take in the six-day bike races. But now it was obvious that between Pauline's financial resources and his own rising income he could afford to lead the life of a sportsman on a much grander scale. America as well as Europe could become his playground— and possibly Africa as well. Thus, while he wasn't quite prepared to give up on Paris, he nevertheless conceived of his and Pauline's upcoming holiday in the States as a hunt for a new base of operations.

5

THEIR departure date was governed by Pauline's desire not to have her baby in Europe. For in spite of her insistence that she had as much energy as a pack of fleas, she had been having an uncomfortable pregnancy and was worried in addition about the quality of European medical care. While the baby was not due until the end of June, her physician in Paris advised her to cross the ocean no later than the end of the seventh month and preferably earlier. Late in March, therefore, she and Hemingway left for Havana in an English ship called the *Orita* and from there took a boat to Key West, ninety miles away. The dilapidated village on the southernmost island in the insular chain stretching south of mainland Florida had been selected by him on the recommendation of Dos Passos as the place to start renewing his acquaintance with American life. In one of the many suitcases they arrived with were two works in progress, a novel and a short story. The novel was *Jimmy Breen,* and although he had written forty thousand words he wasn't sure he knew enough to finish it. The short story, on the other hand, was coming along much better than he had expected.

A sassy yellow Ford, a gift from Pauline's everloving Uncle Gus, was delivered to them on the Key West dock. In it they reconnoitered the village. Blacks, Cubans, and white American "conchs,"

whose ancestors mainly came from New England and the Middle
States, not from the South, made up the bulk of the declining population, which in 1928 numbered only ten thousand. Most of the
houses were venerable, unpainted wooden structures that nevertheless possessed a seedy charm. A naval station and a military reservation occupied a good deal of the waterfront. Purple and dark red
bougainvilleas, pink and red hibiscuses and oleanders, and mango,
guava, lime, and coconut trees flourished in the tropical air. Although Key West had once boasted a prosperous cigar industry,
most of its workers in the late twenties were connected with the sea
one way or another, if not as fishermen then as ships' carpenters or
as civilian employes of the naval station. All businesses shut down
in the middle of the day. There were no streetcars or buses. Coffee
shops along Duval Street sold strong Cuban coffee, sweetened with
condensed milk, and tasty little cakes called *bollos*. In bars like
Sloppy Joe's, the well-to-do owners of cabin cruisers who had put
into port for the night drank their bootleg rum and Coca-Colas
cheek by jowl with merchant sailors on leave.

The man who taught Hemingway how to fish for tarpon and red
snapper was a husky fellow of about his age named Charles Thompson, whose family owned a variety of island businesses, including a
fish-house, a cigarbox factory, a hardware store, and a fishing tackle
shop. With his usual competitive zeal, Thompson's pupil informed
Max Perkins on April 21 that he had caught "the biggest tarpon
they've had down here so far this season. Sixty-three pounds." At
the same time, he assured his watchful editor, he was not neglecting
his work. Although he had been forced to shelve *Jimmy Breen,* the
short-story manuscript was now more than ten thousand words
long and "going very well." Over the next four months, it would
grow into the first draft of *A Farewell to Arms.*

The visitors' first visitors during their five weeks in Key West
turned out to be Dr. Hemingway and Grace. They were vacationing
in St. Petersburg, as it happened; on discovering this, Ernest invited
them by telegram to come on down. While the apartment that he
and Pauline had rented was too small to accommodate overnight
guests, the nearby Overseas Hotel wasn't filled and his parents could
stay there at not too great an expense. While his epistolary relations
with his mother had not been good, to say the least, he wanted her
to meet—and approve of—Pauline.

In a story about her blossoming career as a painter, Grace had
recently been described by a newspaper reporter as "radiant with
enthusiasm. . . . She looks as much the prima donna as Schumann-
Heink. . . ." Two months shy of her fifty-sixth birthday at the mo-

ment when her son leaned forward to give her a kiss of welcome, she did indeed put one in mind of the prima donna she might have been. Her great bulk was sheathed in an ankle-length dress, her immaculately groomed hair was attractively set off by a white felt hat, her ruddy cheeks testified to undiminished vigor and her twinkling eyes to joie de vivre. The contrast between her appearance and her fifty-six-year-old husband's was dramatic. For Dr. Hemingway had developed diabetes, and this condition in combination with several angina attacks had aged him shockingly. Worry about his financial condition had also taken its toll. Like many Americans in the feverishly speculative twenties, Dr. Hemingway had been drawn into the booming market in Florida real estate, and the subsequent collapse in land values had cost him dearly, in spirit even more than in net worth. His hair and beard had gone gray and straggly, the wing collar he still wore no longer fit his neck and from time to time his eyes filmed over with tears. Even though Pauline got along well with both his parents and they with her, Hemingway expressed no satisfaction about their visit. *The Sun Also Rises* had been written out of a pessimism about the unimprovability of human relationships; seeing his parents again could only have made him surer than ever about this dark conclusion.

Dos Passos was the next visitor to sign in at the Overseas Hotel. Although he didn't much care for ocean fishing, he went out with Hemingway in Charles Thompson's boat for friendship's sake—and found that he loved the look of the islands from the sea and the blaze at the horizon line of the tropical sunsets. In the few remaining cigar factories on Key West, he also enjoyed chatting with the workers in Spanish and was impressed to learn that out of their own pockets they paid readers to recite Spanish translations of Tolstoy to them as they stood at their work tables.

Just as Dos Passos was on the verge of leaving Key West for an extended tour of the Soviet Union, the Hemingways' next visitor arrived. It was Katy Smith, whom Hemingway hadn't seen since the day he married Hadley. In recent years, he knew, she had been living with her brother Bill and two other women in a cooperative establishment called Smooley Hall in Provincetown, Massachusetts. One of her housemates was Edith Foley, a friend from Chicago days, whom Hemingway had also known in that period. Edie, like Katy, wrote trashy magazine stories for a living, partook liberally of "The Boy" and "The Fruit of the Worm," as the alcoholic Bill called the home brews he produced, and was the subject—in conjunction with Katy—of sexual gossip. Some people on the lower Cape were convinced that the two women were lovers. According to Mary

McCarthy, Edmund Wilson regarded Katy's whole circle of female intimates as a "lesbian enclave," and in his journals of the thirties Wilson would describe how attached to Katy his wife, Margaret Canby, was, even after Katy married Dos Passos. "Glimpse of her," Wilson noted, "chasing Katy Dos Passos . . . in the front room of Susan Glaspell's house in Provincetown—somehow, this glimpse made me feel badly [sic]: masculine impulses helplessly, awkwardly, ludicrously in little feminine body—impulse automatic, she didn't know what she was doing or why." In Key West in 1928, Dos Passos, too, was attracted to Katy, with her yellow-green cat's eyes and her shy but ready wit, although his active pursuit of her would not begin for another year, when they both returned to Key West to be with the Hemingways.*

6

HAVING sent Pauline on ahead by train, Hemingway drove the yellow Ford to Arkansas in the midst of a brutal heat wave. Aside from the droll stories told by Pauline's mother about the scandalous doings of local white folks, there was nothing in Piggott that pleased him. Quail hunting was out of season, the heat wave was relentless and he found no graceful way of withdrawing from family get-togethers so that he could get on with his novel.

His mood improved somewhat once he and Pauline moved on to Kansas City. For she had elected to have her baby in the city's well-appointed Research Hospital, and two wealthy friends of hers, Ruth and Malcolm Lowry, had opened their spacious suburban home to them. After a morning of work that often began at dawn, Hemingway unwound by attending polo matches in the afternoon, and one day out of passing curiosity he dropped by the convention hall where the Republican party was in the process of choosing Herbert Hoover as its Presidential candidate, but came away disgusted by the hypocrisy of politics. Before supper he usually cooled off with a dip in the Lowrys' pool and afterwards went to bed with Zane Grey's latest treatise on fishing or some similar entertainment.

On June 17, he reached the end of Book Two of his novel. The

---

* In inviting them at the same time, was it Hemingway's intention to play matchmaker? Not at all. In 1929, he brought Dos Passos to Key West in order to introduce him to his sister Sunny. "When he invited Dos Passos down," Sunny would recall, "he built him up to me at every opportunity. I began to look forward to Dos's arrival and had a fine mental picture of him. But when he arrived, I was shocked to see a bald man with nervous, jumpy movements. Ernie had neglected to give me a physical picture of his friend, who was nine years older than I. Of course, I didn't play up to Dos, and Ernie was put out by my lack of interest and apparent rudeness."

hero, Frederic Henry, having recovered from his wounds and having said goodbye to the pregnant Catherine Barkley, leaves Milan aboard the crowded train that will bear him back to the front and, ultimately, the Caporetto disaster. In a letter which the author wrote that June morning to the painter Waldo Peirce, he triumphantly announced that he now knew how the story was going to come out. Presumably, this meant that he knew that Catherine Barkley was going to die in a hospital in Switzerland following a long and difficult labor climaxing in a Caesarean operation. It was a foreknowledge that came uncannily close to being an accurate forecast of Pauline's experience in the delivery room at Research Hospital. Her labor pains began on June 27. Eighteen hours later, the sleepless father was informed that a 9½-pound baby boy had finally been delivered by Caesarean section. The Hemingway equation of childbirth and death had been avoided, but only after considerable danger and pain.

"[My wife] had a very bad time," he tersely wrote Max Perkins a few weeks later, "and a rocky time afterwards." As for the boy, who had been named Patrick, he was "very big dark and strong seeming." After signing the letter, Hemingway apparently remembered that Perkins, who would have given the world for a son, had sired five daughters. From one disappointed father to another, he added in a postscript, "I wish the boy had been one of your girls." Perpetuation of himself in female form was a delight that he would never know, however, and in future years he would have to content himself with referring to virtually every woman he liked as "Daughter."

Incipient hostility to his newborn son became livid fact during an appallingly humid, twenty-one-hour train ride from Kansas City to Piggott, following Pauline's release from the hospital. Patrick was built like a bull and had bellowed like one practically the whole way, Hemingway disgustedly reported to Waldo Peirce. Being a father was enough to drive a man "bughouse," especially when the man in question was writing a novel. *A Farewell to Arms* was a story of escape, and in order to finish it, the author seemingly believed, he himself would have to run away—at least for a while. Accordingly, on the night of July 25 he returned alone to Kansas City, picked up the yellow Ford, joined forces as per arrangement with his old friend Bill Horne and took off for Wyoming. His "monumental opus," he informed Guy Hickok in a hasty note, had now reached page 482. In other words, he had now locked up the magnificent account of the retreat from Caporetto and of Frederic's desertion.

For three blissfully cool, family-free weeks, Hemingway wrote in the morning, fished for trout in the afternoon and tried not to drink too much bootleg whiskey at night. Only thirty pages or so of the manuscript remained to be written when his wife appeared, looking ready to resume her primary role. Being a good mother was a Hadleyesque idea that had little appeal to the second Mrs. Hemingway. "With you away," she had written her husband on July 31, "it seems as tho I was just a mother, which is certainly not very gripping." When her sister Jinny said that she would be willing to take care of Patrick, Pauline blessed her for the offer and accepted it. "Hurry up and send for your wife," she pleaded with Hemingway on August 4. "I'll even pay my own passage." At times, her letters almost made it appear that Patrick was Jinny's child. "Jinny was cutting out the two o'clock feeding because the doctor said he gained too fast and he has started on orange juice. I think we may like him very much."

At the dude ranch in Sheridan, Wyoming, where she joined her husband, she did everything possible to make him think of her as the perfect playmate. If he preferred to hunt for sharp-tailed grouse rather than write, she picked up a gun and went with him, and while she would never match Hadley's skill with rod and reel, it wasn't for lack of trying. After Hemingway informed Perkins on August 22 that the novel was finished, he proposed to Pauline that they might enjoy exploring the Snake River Valley and the Bighorn Mountains, and off they duly went. "This is a cockeyed wonderful country, looks like Spain," he reported to Waldo Peirce a couple of weeks later. A particularly "sweet old guy [who] writes damned well too," his note to Peirce continued, was Owen Wister. Almost as long as Hemingway could remember, he had admired *The Virginian,* but another reason for looking him up at his place in Shell, Wyoming, was Hemingway's awareness, through Barklie Henry, that the old novelist had been very impressed by *The Sun Also Rises* and "Fifty Grand." "Were I thirty," Wister had written to Henry, "that's the way I would wish to write."

When Hemingway swung the yellow Ford into Pauline's parents' driveway in late September, he was still riding the wave of a manic high. "I've . . . never felt better or stronger or healthier in the head or body—nor had better confidence or morale—haven't been sick since I've been in America—knocking on wood—nor had an accident—more knocking," he boasted to Perkins. All sorts of pleasant schemes were simmering in his brain. Although he was eager to start revising his manuscript, he decided to let it cool until his return to Key West, where he and Pauline would spend the winter in the nice house that Charles Thompson's wife, Lorine, would surely be able to find for them. But before heading for Florida, they once again dumped Patrick into Jinny's lap and set off for Chicago and

points east, including Conway, Massachusetts (for a long weekend
with the MacLeishes at their country place), New York City (to talk
with Perkins about publication schedules and to take in a couple of
prizefights with Mike Strater and Waldo Peirce) and the mansion
called Ellerslie on the Delaware River (where Fitzgerald was so upset
by the news that Hemingway had finished a draft of his novel that
he swore he was working eight hours a day on his own).

7

THE white frame house that Lorine Thompson had picked out for
the Hemingways contained half a dozen bedrooms. Thus, without
jeopardizing the possibility of entertaining a stream of house guests,
they were able to provide baby Patrick with a room of his own and
another room for Hemingway's sister Sunny, who arrived just after
Thanksgiving for an extended visit. To pay her way, so to speak,
Sunny had offered to help take care of Patrick and of five-year-old
Bumby, who would shortly be arriving in the United States to visit
his father, and to type at least a portion of the final draft of her
brother's manuscript. But before Hemingway could settle down to
the task of producing that draft, he had to meet Bumby's ship at a
Manhattan dock.

On the afternoon of December 6, father and son left Penn Station
in New York for the return run to Florida. At Trenton, Hemingway
was handed a telegram. His father had died that morning, it said. At
Philadelphia, he left the train, having consigned Bumby to the care
of a responsible-looking porter, and caught a night express to Chicago. From his sister Carol, now a high school student, rather than
from his mother, who was under heavy sedation, he learned what
had happened. Dr. Hemingway had awakened the previous morning with a pain in his foot. His demoralized mind had started racing.
The pain probably represented an arterial obstruction, which could
lead to gangrene, which could lead to amputation. Over breakfast,
he told Grace he was frightened. She urged him to consult another
doctor. Although he promised he would, he did not. Around noon
he returned home and went to the basement, where he burned some
personal papers. He was very tired, he told his wife, and was going
up to his room and rest until lunchtime. The only other people in
the quiet house besides himself and Grace were thirteen-year-old
Leicester, who was in bed with a cold, and the cook in the kitchen.
A few minutes after closing his bedroom door, he shot himself in
the right temple with a Civil War "Long John" revolver he had
inherited from his father at the latter's death two years before.

Although Hemingway was able to take command of the funeral arrangements, his mind was numbed and his remarks inconsistent. Following the services at the First Congregational Church, he infuriated Marcelline by saying that Catholicism had taught him that suicide was a mortal sin and that consequently their father would languish in hell forever. On the other hand, he comfortingly assured young Leicester and Carol that there was nothing to be ashamed of in their father's death. Because of all his ailments, the old boy had been temporarily knocked in the head and wasn't responsible for what he had done.

Leicester, however, would never get over the sound of the gunshot that he had heard so distinctly down the hall. In his autobiographical novel, *The Sound of the Trumpet* (1953), he would recall that when he heard the shot he had got out of bed and tried the door of his father's room. "It opened, and in the darkened room, all shades drawn except one, there on the bed lay his father, making hoarse breathing noises. His eyes were closed, and in that first instant as he saw him there in the half-dark, nothing looked wrong. He put his hand under his father's head. His hand slipped under easily and when he brought it out again, it was wet-warm with blood." But writing about his father's death only heightened Leicester's memory of the event, and after the thunderclap of his brother's suicide he was a haunted man. Upon being informed by his doctor in 1982 that as a result of his diabetes he would have to have his legs amputated, Leicester killed himself with a single shot to the head.

Once Dr. Hemingway was in his grave, Leicester asked his mother to give him the "Long John" as a keepsake. But so did Ernest, and upon his return to Key West she sent it to him—although she wanted it back, she said. "I will take care of it for you," she promised. In a characteristic effort to speak cheerfully, she urged her older son in a Christmas letter not to "worry a moment about us. All is going well. Leicester . . . [is] being such a comfort to me —My! but he loves you. . . . So much to be thankful for. God bless you, *each* and *every one,* and give you much joy. Your own loving Mother." She was masking, though, a growing anxiety about her finances, and by the beginning of February she had to admit that she had taken on three pupils in painting and two in voice and was hoping to rent out rooms. In his response to this letter, Hemingway told her he had decided that for the rest of her life he would send her a monthly check of one hundred dollars.

If the terrible accusation that she was a husband killer had already formed in his mind, he was not yet ready to broadcast it. To Max Perkins he quietly said on December 16 that "What makes me feel the worst is my father is the one I cared about," while in a letter to Guy Hickok he wisecracked that he might be willing to give his relatives money if they agreed not to write to him. These remarks, however, were mildness itself in comparison to those to come. Of much greater interest in his correspondence in this period than any of his comments about his mother were, first, the admission that the revisions he was making in the manuscript of *A Farewell to Arms* were taxing him to the utmost ("I've had hell's own time writing and worse rewriting it," he confessed to Owen Wister), and, second, the striking upsurge in his use of violence-haunted language. In telling Wister, for example, what his life had been like at the time he wrote *The Sun Also Rises,* he said that it had been "more or less shot out from under me," and in a note to Dos Passos informing him of his father's suicide he added, "I have my bloody book all gone over in pencil and another third typed." But his most telling self-revelations were contained in the changes he made in the final draft.

8

MAJOR deletions were indicated on the pages he began to feed to his two typists, Pauline and Sunny, in mid-December, and the most important of them had to do with the elimination of Frederic Henry's feelings, such as they were. For example, the description at the beginning of chapter seventeen of how Henry feels after he awakens from the operation on his legs originally began as follows:

> My legs hurt so that I tried to get back into the choaked [*sic*] place I had come from but I could not get back in there but threw up again and again and nothing came. They gave me water to rinse out my mouth and then I lay still and waited for the pain to reach the top and go down but there was no limit to the pain and it had long passed the point where pain had always stopped. I thought how our Lord would never send us more [than] we could bear and I had always believed that meant me, became unconscious when it became too bad, hence the success of martyrs, but now it was not so but the pain went way beyond what I could bear in the bone and everywhere there was and then inside my chest it started to jerk and jerk and then I cried and cried without any noise only the diaphragm jerking and jerking and then it was better and I knew I could bear it but gave no credit to our Lord. . . .

In the revised version, the entire passage was reduced to four sentences: "When I was awake after the operation I had not been away. You do not go away. They only choke you. It is not like dying it is just a chemical choking so you do not feel, and afterward you might as well have been drunk except that when you throw up nothing comes but bile and you do not feel better afterward." Frederic Henry had been a remarkably unresponsive man in the first draft of the novel; he became even less responsive as a result of the deletions in the final draft.

The lengthiness of Hemingway's debate with himself about the fate of Catherine Barkley's baby likewise reveals something about the disorienting effect upon him of his father's suicide. In the summer of 1928 in Wyoming, he had written a scene in which the nurse tells Henry that his infant son has been choked to death by his umbilical cord. On the very same day, though, he discarded this scene and substituted a more hopeful one, in which the nurse tells Henry:

> "The baby is alive you know."
> "What do you mean?"
> "It's alive that's all."
> "You want to be more careful what you tell people."

A month after Hemingway buried his father, he cut these lines and changed Henry's last-minute plea to God from "Take the baby but don't let her die" to "You took the baby but don't let her die." This reversion to his original plan did not represent, however, a final decision. Even after he and his family returned to Paris in April 1929, he continued to brood about the fate of the baby. During May, he wrote a new ending that restored the baby to life, only to follow it with a number of others that did not. Not until June 24, a mere three months before the book's publication, did he irrevocably decide not to mitigate death's triumph in *A Farewell to Arms*.*

An effect of a different sort that resulted from Dr. Hemingway's death was a deepening of the editorial relationship between Hemingway and Max Perkins into a more personal pact, even though Perkins was just in the process of becoming similarly involved with another writer. On January 2, 1929, the editor had looked up from his desk at Scribners to discover a six-foot-six-inch giant named Thomas Wolfe filling the doorframe. The author of a sprawling manuscript called *O Lost,* much of which was spread out on Perkins's desk at that very moment, Wolfe rather desperately needed a

---

* The author found his title in the *Oxford Book of English Verse*. George Peele's poem, "A Farewell to Arms," published in 1590 and dedicated to Queen Elizabeth, salutes a knight named Henry Lee who has grown too old to serve any longer as the Queen's champion in tournaments.

father, and he found him in Perkins, who had always wanted a son. Twenty-nine days after that legendary encounter, Perkins arrived— at Hemingway's urgent invitation—in Key West. From that point onward, Perkins assumed a fatherly role in his life as well, albeit on more moderate terms than Wolfe required.

On each of the eight days that Perkins remained in Florida, his host had him out fishing at six in the morning and did not bring him back until late afternoon. In the evenings, Perkins addressed himself to the typescript of *A Farewell to Arms,* which he kept declaring was magnificent. Shortly after his return to New York, he ebulliently wired Hemingway that Robert Bridges, the editor of *Scribner's Magazine,* had agreed to serialize the novel prior to book publication and was proposing to pay him sixteen thousand dollars. But in a follow-up letter on February 13, Perkins spoke more austerely of "certain words" in the text which "must be concealed by a white space" and of "several passages" which "we will have to raise the question of omitting, chiefly because they contain certain words which could not be deleted without spoiling the sense of the passages." While Perkins was not as straitlaced as his Vermont Yankee forebears, he still had only a limited sympathy with Hemingway's compulsion to put foul language into print—and the same was true of Robert Bridges.

In addition to eliminating *shit, fuck, son of a bitch, whore, whorehound, balls, cocksucker,* and *Jesus Christ,* Bridges cut out the bulk of a discussion between Rinaldi and Lieutenant Henry about the pain that sexual intercourse causes any girl "who has always been good" and reduced a fornication scene between Catherine and Henry to an exchange of remarks about their beating hearts. While these bowdlerizations infuriated Hemingway, they did not suffice to prevent Michael H. Crowley, the intensely Irish superintendent of police in Boston (who depended for advice on these matters on the Beacon Hill Yankees in the Watch and Ward Society) from banning the June issue of *Scribner's* from newsstand sale in the city.

When Hemingway received the galleys of the novel that Perkins proposed to print in book form, he was pleased to note that his editor had reinstated *Jesus Christ, son of a bitch, whore,* and *whorehound.* Although Hemingway tried hard to save *balls* as well, Perkins would only let him have *scrotum.* In regard to the author's proposal that they compromise on *cocksucker* by printing *c—s—r,* Perkins yielded not an inch in his insistence on a blank space, but he did withdraw his hyperprudish suggestion that *bedpan* be excised as well.

Without asking Hemingway's permission beforehand, Perkins sent a set of galleys in early April to Owen Wister, possibly because he was hoping for a blurb, but possibly, too, because he had some troubling questions about the book which he hoped that the older novelist might raise on his own volition. In the first of two replies to Perkins, Wister told him that although he was still reading the book he was already prepared to "frame my enthusiasm into something you can use to help [Hemingway] and his book and his publisher."

After finishing the story, Wister again wrote Perkins. He was still enthusiastic about it, he said, but was somewhat disappointed that love and war, its two main themes, had not been brought together at the end, although he granted that love was by all odds the main theme. In his answer to Wister, Perkins indicated that in more drastic form he shared his disappointment.

Wister thereupon passed on his critique to Hemingway, and on May 24 Perkins finally divulged to the author his own negative thoughts.

> [My] first point relates to the combination of the two elements of the book—Love and War. They combine, to my mind, perfectly up to the point where Catherine and Lieutenant Henry get to Switzerland; thereafter, the war is almost forgotten by them and by the reader, though not quite. And psychologically it should be all but forgotten; it would be by people so profoundly in love, and so I do not think what I at first thought, that you might bring more news of it or remembrances of it into this part. Still, I can't shake off the feeling that War, which has deeply conditioned this love story—and does so still passively—should still do so actively and decisively. It would if Catherine's death might probably not have occurred except for it, and I should think it likely that the life she had led as a nurse, and all the exposure, etc. might have been largely responsible. If it were, and if the doctor said so during that awful night, in just a casual sentence, the whole story would turn back upon the War in the realization of Henry and the reader.
>
> I say this with the realization that a man in this work may make a principle into an obsession, as professors do. Unity? Nothing is so detestable as the *neat* ending. . . . I know, by the way, that Wister wrote you about these two elements of War and Love, and that he saw the question differently, as if the story was really only of Love with War as the impressive and conditioning background, or almost only that. But I could not quite see it that way.

Although Perkins was an admirably conscientious editor, he did not understand *A Farewell to Arms*, let alone its tortured author. At the time that Hemingway received Perkins's letter, he was feverishly

reworking the final paragraphs of his manuscript because he couldn't
get them to sound right, try as he might. Caught up in an agony
that led him to produce thirty-two variant endings, he had no interest in complicating matters further by factoring in a subject that had
not conditioned the story of Henry and Catherine in anything like
the degree that Perkins believed.

9

IN the five paragraphs that make up the novel's first chapter, the
word "and" is employed again and again, "in conscious imitation,"
Hemingway would boozily claim in the course of a visit to New
York City more than twenty years later, "of the way Mr. Johann
Sebastian Bach used a note in music when he was emitting counter-
point." Whether or not the work of Bach actually figured as a model
in his composing, the repetitions of "and" indubitably contribute to
the flow of a beautiful music of seasonal change. "In the late summer
of that year," so the first paragraph begins, and down through the
end of the second the imagery holds us within that time frame even
as it prepares the reader to be carried beyond it. The bed of the river
is filled with pebbles and boulders, dry and white in the sun, the
water is clear and swiftly moving and blue in the channels, the
trunks of the trees are dusty "and the leaves fell early that year. . . ."
The constrictions of autumn are defined in the third paragraph by
the rain-blackened trunks of the chestnut trees, the thin and bare-
branched vineyards, "and all the country wet and brown and
dead. . . ." In the final paragraph, "permanent rain" announces the
start of the winter.

   To paraphrase a famous tribute to the novel by Ford Madox Ford,
the words of the first chapter are like a tessellation of pebbles fetched
fresh from the riverbed that it describes—and are as impressive as
the riverbed's boulders, owing to the symbolic freight they carry.
The fallen leaves of late summer augur the doom of the troops
whose marching feet briefly stir them up, while the wet and muddy
troops of autumn, with their bulging capes that make them look "as
though they were six months gone with child," compose a forecast
of Catherine Barkley's fatal pregnancy. But the somber narrative
voice of Frederic Henry does not merely bespeak an afterknowledge
of terrible events. It also defines the speaker's frame of mind in the
very moment in the late summer of 1915 in which the story begins.

   Before the war, Henry had been living in Rome—"a filthy place,"
in his opinion—because he wanted to be an architect. But after
Italy's entrance into the conflict he had enlisted in the ambulance

corps of the Italian army, for reasons he won't discuss and possibly doesn't understand. "There isn't always an explanation for everything," he tells Catherine Barkley. So profound is his emotional uninvolvement in the struggle that he can't even believe in its capacity to harm him. "[The war] did not have anything to do with me," he says. "It seemed no more dangerous to me myself than war in the movies."

Just before he hears that the Germans and Austrians have broken through in the north at Caporetto, Henry confesses—in what would quickly become the most celebrated passage in all of Hemingway's work—his utter repugnance for high-flown rhetoric. His confession is not, however, an expression of battlefield-induced disillusionment, as so many readers in 1929 and afterwards would suppose, for he makes clear that he has "always" felt this way. The war has simply intensified a nausea of indeterminate origin, until "finally" his faith in language has been reduced to a reliance on certain numbers, certain dates, and the names of places. Contrary to popular impression, the narrator of *A Farewell to Arms* does not suggest that stirring words had had anything to do with inspiring his enlistment in the army:

> I was always embarrassed by the words sacred, glorious, and sacrifice and the expression in vain. We had heard them, sometimes standing in the rain almost out of earshot, so that only the shouted words came through, and had read them, on proclamations that were slapped up by billposters over other proclamations, now for a long time, and I had seen nothing sacred, and the things that were glorious had no glory and the sacrifices were like the stockyards at Chicago if nothing was done with the meat except to bury it. There were many words that you could not stand to hear and finally only the names of places had dignity. Certain numbers were the same way and certain dates and these with the names of places were all you could say and have them mean anything.

Nineteen twenty-nine represented, in the United States at least, the high-water mark of postwar revulsion. The horrendously isolationist Hawley-Smoot tariff bill (1930) was working its way through the Congress at the time, and it was the big year as well for antiwar books. For reviewers and readers alike, the most important of these books—apart from Hemingway's—was the English translation of Erich Maria Remarque's *Im Westen nichts Neues* (*All Quiet on the Western Front*). The intention of Remarque's novel, as he himself explained, was to present "the fate of a generation of young men who, at the critical age when they were just beginning to feel the pulse of life, were set face to face with death." Hemingway's intention was very different. As Owen Wister came close to realizing, the story Hemingway told in *A Farewell to Arms* was not really a war story. While Lieutenant Henry's account of his retreat after Caporetto and of the "separate peace" he finally makes is deservedly famous, in the last analysis it serves the novel as a metaphor. For the portrait of Frederic Henry is a study in affective disorder, and retreat and desertion are functions of a larger disengagement from life.

An emotional reticence amounting to apathy governs a wide range of his reactions, as he reveals in the early chapters of the novel. He is content, for one thing, to send postcards that say nothing to the members of his family back in the States, for although he used to care for them, as he says later, "we quarrelled so much it wore itself out." He also keeps a certain distance between himself and his army friends. When, for instance, he returns from leave and Rinaldi puts his arm around his neck and kisses him, Henry's one-word reaction is "Oughf." While Rinaldi is too outgoing to be put off by such aloofness, the uniformed priest from Abruzzi who had wanted Henry to visit his family there and who "had written to his father that I was coming and they had made preparations" is quite hurt when he doesn't go. Just why he decides not to is as much of a mystery to Henry, apparently, as it is to the priest, for "it was what I had wanted to do," he says, and "I . . . could not understand why I had not gone." As for the whores in whose beds he ends up on drunken nights, he cares and he doesn't care, and in the morning there is "sometimes a dispute about the cost." A deleted reference in the manuscript of the novel reveals that T. S. Eliot's "The Hollow Men" (1925) was very much on Hemingway's mind in the late twenties, and the hollowness of Henry's responses to the world makes clear why. "Between the idea/And the reality," Eliot had written, "Between the motion/and the act/Falls the Shadow."

Even when Henry meets Catherine Barkley, a beautiful young English woman whose jittery, neurotic manner calls Brett Ashley to mind, his pursuit of her is nothing more than a "chess game," in which he pretends to be in love with her, although what he is really thinking is that she is a little crazy. "I did not care what I was getting into," he says. "This was better than going every evening to the house for officers where the girls climbed all over you and put your cap on backward as a sign of affection between their trips upstairs with brother officers." Although Catherine finally lets him know that she knows that he is playing a "rotten game," he merely responds with a new outburst of cynicism. "But I do love you," he protests.

The morning after the wounded lieutenant is carried into the American hospital in Milan, Catherine looks in on him, for she has just been assigned to work there. "Hello, darling," she says eagerly. "Hello," Henry replies, with what seems for a second like his usual reticence. But then he adds, "When I saw her I was in love with her. Everything turned over inside me." And the novel turns over as well, shedding consistency of character right and left as it flees toward dream. Not only does a hollow man discover passion, but his Brett Ashleyesque lady suddenly becomes a mother figure whose character is a mix of Agnes von Kurowsky's and Hadley's.

Fitzgerald, who read the novel before it was published and offered the author some comments about it, thought that Catherine seemed markedly older than Henry, even though she was not supposed to be. His theory about this, Fitzgerald explained, was that "You're seeing him [Frederic] in a sophisticated way as now you see yourself then—but you're still seeing her as you did in 1917 [sic] thru nineteen yr.-old eyes. In consequence unless you make her a bit fatuous occasionally the contrast jars—either the writer is a simple fellow or she's Elenora [sic] Duse disguised as a Red Cross nurse." As usual, the perceptive Fitzgerald was on to something, although he would have got further if he had been able to figure out the author's reason for having Rinaldi repeatedly refer to Henry as "baby." For Henry falls in love with Catherine while lying helplessly in a hospital bed like a baby in a bassinet, as the critic Millicent Bell would astutely observe in 1984 in a pathbreaking reconsideration of the novel. As Nurse Gage washes his body with a cloth and soap and warm water and Catherine takes his "lovely temperature," or watches him sleeping like "a little boy," he appears wonderfully content in his dependency upon them. When Catherine returns to him in the night, he seems like a small child whose mother has allowed him erotic privileges.

The miraculously transformed woman whom Henry loves owes her pinned-up coiffure (although not her blondness) to the nurse Hemingway fell in love with in 1918, to the wife he took in 1921 and to the mother of his childhood. Dipping down to kiss Henry from time to time, Catherine sits patiently on the edge of his bed and lets him take her hair down, which he loves to do, he makes clear. "I would take out the pins," he says,

> and lay them on the sheet and it would be loose and I would watch her while she kept very still and then take out the last two pins and it

would all come down and she would drop her head and we would
both be inside of it, and it was the feeling of inside a tent or behind a
falls.

Her "wonderfully beautiful hair" is clearly an indispensable part of
his sexual pleasure, and Catherine understands this very well.
"Would you like me to take my hair down?" she asks at one point.
"Do you want to play?" The questions are meant to arouse him, and
they do not fail to do so.

Transsexual fantasies are also built into their bedtime games, although it takes time for this to become evident. At first, Catherine
speaks so urgently of her wish to be swallowed up in her lover's
identity that she creates a misleading impression of what she and
Henry are up to. "I'm you," she says to him. "Don't make up a
separate me." All she wants is "what you want. There isn't any me
any more. Just what you want." Such statements would someday
give rise to the opinion—as advanced by feminist critics, the vehement opinion—that the author of *A Farewell to Arms* was dramatiz-
ing a rude vision of male domination over a degradingly submissive
female. Yet even in the early stages of their liaison Henry says things
that have a qualifying effect upon Catherine's comments. Merging,
he implies, is a two-way street. "Besides all the big times we had
many small ways of making love and we tried putting thoughts in
the other one's head while we were in different rooms. It seemed to
work sometimes but that was probably because we were thinking
the same thing anyway." Each of them apparently wants to enter
into the other, and mentally at least this appears to be possible. After
they have been living for some time in a Swiss *pension*—it is the
same *pension* where Hemingway and Hadley had felt so cozy in bed
in the winter of 1922—Catherine finally brings up the question of
their becoming interchangeable in appearance as well as thought.
That she shows more eagerness than he is a sign not of submissive-
ness on her part, but rather of Henry's passivity:★

> "Darling, why don't you let your hair grow?"
> "How grow?"
> "Just grow a little longer."
> "It's long enough now."
> "No, let it grow a little longer and I could cut mine and we'd be
> just alike only one of us blonde and one of us dark."
> "I wouldn't let you cut yours."

★ The same observation applies to Littless and Nick in "The Last Good Country" and to
David and Catherine in *The Garden of Eden*.

"It would be fun. I'm tired of it. It's an awful nuisance in the bed at night."

"I like it."

"Wouldn't you like it short?"

"I might. I like it the way it is."

"It might be nice short. Then we'd both be alike. Oh darling, I want you so much I want to be you too."

"You are. We're the same one."

"I know it. At night we are."

"The nights are grand."

In the night, Catherine says, "I want us to be all mixed up." The statement reinforces the reason why Hemingway took the last name of both his principals from Barklie Henry: he thought of them as the two halves of an androgynous whole.

Enveloped in a snowbound world, the lovers have "a fine life," Henry declares in the first sentence of chapter forty. Nevertheless, the narrative is filled with a sense of dread. On learning months before that Catherine was pregnant, Henry had despairingly spoken of being biologically trapped, and in chapter forty—the next to last in the book—the theme of entrapment is reintroduced in an existential meditation in which one can more clearly hear the voice of the author than at any other point in the book.

The meditation immediately follows the opening statement, "We had a fine life." Before turning the lens of his attention upon himself, Henry briefly considers the case of the good priest from Abruzzi, "who has always loved God and so is happy and I am sure that nothing will ever take God away from him. But how much is wisdom and how much is luck to be born that way? And what if you are not built that way?" A more personal restatement of these desolate questions then makes plain his conviction that his own luck in life has been extremely bad.

> But what if you were born loving nothing and the warm milk of your mother's breast was never heaven and the first thing you loved was the side of a hill and the last thing was a woman and they took her away and you did not want another but only to have her; and she was gone, then you are not so well placed and it would have been better to have loved God from the start. But you did not love God and it doesn't do any good to talk about it either, nor to think about it.

How many times in his boyhood had Hemingway pored over the passage in Grace's scrapbook record of his early life in which she had talked about his having slept in her bed for half a year and lunched all night at her breast? That an echo of that passage should have turned up in a meditation written in the summer following his encounter with his mother in all her buxom majesty in Key West was a testimony to the power of his attachment to her. At the same time, his hatred of Grace—his wild certainty that she wanted him to taste her all his life and that her milk was poison—impelled him to deny that he had ever felt close to her. Nevertheless, he ultimately decided to cut the entire meditation from the final draft of the novel. There was poignancy in this act. Every word of the passage implied a terrible longing on his part to start talking—at long last!—about the remote origins of his emotional problems. But as a disquisition on how and why he couldn't love, it represented only the barest beginning of a confession, and he just couldn't make it longer and clearer, he just couldn't.

Not even *The Sun Also Rises,* not even *The Torrents of Spring,* has a more crippled ending, emotionally speaking, than *A Farewell to Arms.* For in the wake of having willed Catherine's death, Hemingway was all but incapable of expressing a grief about it. After Henry shoos the nurses out of the room and he is at last alone with Catherine's body, he shuts the door and turns off the light. "But . . . it wasn't any good. It was like saying good-by to a statue. After a while I went out and left the hospital and walked back to the hotel in the rain." His reaction, in sum, is virtually a nonreaction, and he does not, furthermore, appear to be in shock.

Among the variant endings over which the author agonized in the spring of 1929 were two of considerable length that read as if he were trying to discover feeling by continuing to write. But finally he seems to have realized that he was merely filibustering and that, faute de mieux, it was better to be brief. As Henry walks back to the hotel in the rain, he is once again the hollow man he had been at the beginning of the story. Only a regressive relationship with a mother figure who also wanted to become "all mixed up" with him had been unable to lift him out of his death-in-life, so that with her passing he, too, is finished. The baby he has sired can thus be said to symbolize the babyish Henry himself, for it has choked to death on its umbilical cord. "I wished the hell I'd been choked like that," Henry says, and in effect he has been.

10

THE white dust jacket was garishly printed in blue and orange and the front flap carried a synopsis in which Catherine Barkley's name was spelled "Katharine Barclay." But the packaging did not seem to matter. By October 22, four weeks after publication, sales of the novel reached 33,000; a month later, they topped 50,000, despite the cataclysmic collapse of the stock market; and on January 8, 1930, Hemingway was informed that more than 20,000 additional copies had been sold.

Superlatively favorable reviews in American journals by Malcolm Cowley, Clifton Fadiman, Henry Seidel Canby, and T. S. Matthews, among many others, plus equally enthusiastic comments in England by Arnold Bennett, J. B. Priestley, and the anonymous reviewer for the *Times Literary Supplement,* helped to create the demand for the book and to spread the author's fame more widely than ever. Indeed, a *New Yorker* "Profile" by Dorothy Parker on November 30, 1929, may be said to have marked the point at which Hemingway passed beyond mere fame into living legend.

Her awe of Hemingway, Miss Parker confessed, was akin to the reverence that a tourist might feel at the majestic sight of a Grand Canyon sunset. Yet for all of his eminence he was greatly misunderstood, she continued. Supposedly, he was a barely literate ruffian who had once been a hobo, a safecracker, and a stockyard worker and who was now an habitué of the Café Select, an absinthe drinker, a womanizer, and an America hater. Fortunately, Miss Parker was in a position to set the record straight. He had left home at an early age, she averred, with the intention of becoming a prizefighter, but had landed a job as a foreign correspondent instead. With the outbreak of the war he had joined the Italian army and had suffered seven major wounds. An aluminum kneecap was only one of his mementoes of the battlefield. As a fiction writer, his willingness to work "like hell and through it" was exemplified by the fact that he had rewritten the ending of *A Farewell to Arms* seventy times. For his professional and personal conduct were a seamless whole:

> He has the most profound bravery that it has ever been my privilege to see. . . . He has had pain, ill-health, and the kind of poverty that you don't believe—the kind of which actual hunger is the attendant; he has had about eight times the normal allotment of responsibilities. And he has never compromised. He has never turned off on an easier path than the one he staked himself. It takes courage.

According to Hemingway, Miss Parker added, courage was "grace under pressure." His life has met that definition, she admiringly concluded.

One of the sources of error in this spectacular mishmash was a false assumption about the relationship between Frederic Henry's war career and his creator's. The guileful realism of Hemingway's method of describing the Caporetto retreat—his trick, for instance, of throwing in slightly irrelevant details now and then so as to give the impression that his narrator is yielding to spur-of-the-moment flashes of memory—seduced his profilist into believing that the novelist had had the same experience as his narrator, even though at the time of the novel's beginning Hemingway had never been further east than Nantucket Island and was just about to begin his junior year in high school.

Miss Parker was not alone in her confusion. So many other readers were similarly fooled that Hemingway felt constrained to add a disclaimer to the second edition of the novel saying that "None of the characters in this book is a living person, nor are the units or military organizations mentioned actual units or organizations." He also instructed Perkins to issue a similar statement to the press. Three years later, while the film version of *A Farewell to Arms* was playing in American movie houses, Hemingway again protested against "the romantic and false military and personal career" which had been attached to his name. These efforts were of no help, though, to those who did not wish to be helped. As late as 1949, a writer for *Coronet* magazine would characterize Hemingway's description of Caporetto as "a vivid fragment of memory." Five years later, an Italian critic, Giacomo Antonini, writing in *La Fiera Letteraria,* would speak of the novelist's decision to "enlist and leave for the front during his stay in Italy" and then praise him for evoking "the climate of the first two years of [Italy's participation in] the war until the disaster of Caporetto with extraordinary vivacity."

But if Frederic Henry influenced the world's impression of Hemingway, the reverse was equally true and then some. For the author bulked even larger than his book in the public mind, with the result that readers automatically imposed his image upon his protagonist. Inasmuch as it was common knowledge that Hemingway had become disillusioned after being wounded, the weary tone of voice that informs *A Farewell to Arms* was duly interpreted as emanating from battlefield memories. And because most of the world also believed that Hemingway was blunt-minded and two-fisted (the principal dissenters from this view at this point were cynics like Zelda Fitzgerald and Robert McAlmon), J. B. Priestley was speaking for many more readers than himself when he characterized the novel as "a brutally masculine performance" that somehow achieved "a beautiful tenderness and pathos in [its] love story." As for the wounded Lieutenant Henry's manifest contentment with being taken care of, it was diagnosed as an expression of macho dominance if it was diagnosed at all. "He, the male, is served and adored and complacently spreads his peacock tail before her who serves and adores," Lewis Galantière asserted in *Hound & Horn*. Galantière could appreciate male passivity when he encountered it in Proust, but not in Hemingway, who had once knocked his glasses off, after all.

At the same time that Hemingway was disgusted by the inaccurate responses to his book, he also sought to nullify any publicity that threatened to blemish his tough-guy reputation. Thus when the book section of the Sunday New York *Herald Tribune* printed a story on November 24, 1929, asserting that the author of *A Farewell to Arms* had been carrying on in a bullying way at the Dôme one night about Morley Callaghan's ignorance of prizefighting, and that the young Canadian, after challenging him, had proceeded to knock the bully out, Hemingway was enraged, not amused. Since Fitzgerald had served—ineptly served—as the timekeeper in a friendly match that Callaghan and Hemingway had fought the previous summer, Hemingway coerced him into sending a collect cable to Callaghan demanding a public retraction. But because Callaghan had instantly realized that the *Tribune* story might destroy "a legend very important to Hemingway," he had already sent a letter to the paper. He had never challenged him, he said, and had never knocked him out. Although they had boxed together a few times, it had been mainly for the purpose of working up a thirst for a glass of beer.

Mens Morbida in Corpore Sano

KEY WEST BECAME the Hemingways' permanent address in January 1930. For a while Pauline seemed content with rented places, but in the spring of 1931 she fell in love with a two-story white stone residence with a leaky roof and obsolete wiring on a fine corner lot on Whitehead Street, which her Uncle Gus purchased for eight thousand dollars and gave to her as a gift outright. Built shortly after the Civil War, it was one of the oldest structures on the island and had the imposing look of a courthouse, if one can imagine a courthouse with double porches and delicate wrought-iron railings around three sides. A tall iron fence and palm trees enclosed the once beautifully landscaped grounds.

Hemingway's way of life had now changed as dramatically as when he and Hadley had left Chicago for Paris. Change, however, was no guarantee of growth. He remained unable to transcend the past and forgive his mother. Financially, his treatment of her was above reproach. As he once told Fitzgerald with blistering candor, "The only thing in life I've ever had any luck being decent about is money so am very splendid and punctilious about that." With most of the royalties he had thus far earned from *A Farewell to Arms,* he set up a trust fund for Grace in 1931 which nicely supplemented the allowance he continued to pay her. Otherwise his relationship with her lacked any semblance of charity. In her letters to him, she couldn't keep from offering free advice or from philosophizing about touchy issues. "Poor Boy," she remarked of her late husband in a typical paragraph, "he worked so hard and got so little out of life. I could not wish him back for a minute. He earned his rest and peace and joy." Instead of overlooking such comments, Hemingway allowed them to make him angry, and his reactions bewildered and distressed her. She realized, she said contritely, that she had a talent for saying things that irritated him, but couldn't he try to be understanding?

Most definitely, he could not. During her first visit to Key West as a widow, in February 1931, he was not at all attentive to her, and not many months thereafter he abruptly stopped writing her letters, even though he knew she counted on them. "I won't bother you with any more letters after this," she told him on April 5, 1932, "as it will take you some time to answer the last six that I have written to you." Deeply hurt by his neglect but defiantly proud, she also abandoned her efforts to avoid confrontations with him. When he peremptorily commanded her in the midthirties to sell off the worthless Florida real estate that was eating her up with taxes, and threatened to cut off his financial aid to her unless she obeyed him, she responded in a steely voice, "Never threaten me with what to do. Your father tried that once when we were first married and he lived to regret it." To which Hemingway brutally replied, "My dear mother, I am a very different man from my father and I never threaten anyone. I only make promises. If I say that if you do not do certain sound things I will no longer contribute to your support it means factually and exactly that."

As one of Hemingway's closest friends in the early thirties, Dos Passos heard him inveigh against Grace so often that at the end of his life he would remark that Ernest was the only man he had ever known who really hated his mother. Even to people who were not his intimates he was willing to speak critically of her. "She had to rule everything," he burst out to Tillie Arnold, the wife of the photographer at Sun Valley, in 1939. And as the years passed, his feelings remained unaffected by the imminence of her death. Thus, in a ferocious letter to Charles Scribner in 1949—at which point Grace was in her late seventies—he said of their relations that "we never had any trouble. . . . Except that I will not see her and she knows that she can never come here [to Cuba]."

In regard to his father he was likewise caught in a web of unworked-out emotion. Nick Adams asserts in "Fathers and Sons" (1933) that his "passion" for hunting and fishing has "never slackened" and that now, at thirty-eight, "he was very grateful to his father for bringing him to know it." But in Hemingway's case that passion not only did not slacken in his thirties, it intensified, until it seemed like a madness. Whether he was reeling in thirty trout a day from the Clarks Fork branch of the Yellowstone River, or shooting quail as fast as he could reload in the bottomlands near Piggott, Arkansas, or stalking elk and deer in the Crazy Mountains wilderness area of western Montana, or trolling for kingfish off the Dry Tortugas, or battling giant marlin in the currents of the Gulf Stream, "Papa" Hemingway was frenziedly celebrating the attributes of his father that he had most admired as a small boy. Yet if he sought to imitate he also tried to surpass. Going after record-sized kills, as he habitually did, was a way of proving that he was more of a man than the mentor who had showed what a coward he was by killing himself.

Death in the Afternoon (1932), the first book he wrote in toto following his father's suicide, offers another measure of its imprisoning effect on him. Designed to introduce English and American readers to the modern Spanish bullfight, the book was grounded in Hemingway's experience as an aficionado, his friendship with a number of matadors—including most recently the pride of Brooklyn, New York, Sidney Franklin—and his alleged perusal of the 2,077 books and pamphlets on *tauromaquia* to which he makes reference in a bibliographical note. Nevertheless, he made room in this learned treatise for veiled references to a personal tragedy, apparently because he was incapable of screening them out. Thus, at the beginning the author gratuitously says that he had seen death before he saw his first bullfight, but had never been able to study it "as a man might, for instance, study the death of his father," and somewhat later he describes himself as "being much interested in suicides." The ghostly presence of Dr. Hemingway in *Death in the Afternoon* is not merely felt in these small ways, however. For he is lurkingly there in the obsession with death that runs through the whole volume.

2

Death in the Afternoon also testifies to the invasion of Hemingway's serious writing by his myth. The hero of the book is not a haunted Nick Adams, or a crippled Jake Barnes, or a hollowed-out Frederic Henry, but an overbearing know-it-all named Ernest Hemingway. While the side remarks he makes about the art of writing are indispensable to any reader interested in modern literature, his tauromachian erudition is a bore, his tough-guy posturing an embarrassment, and his cutting comments about fellow writers by and large unamusing. That Hemingway himself understood at least some of the shortcomings of *Death in the Afternoon* is certain. "Am just going over the just typed mss. of this last abortion," he wrote Dos Passos in some discouragement as he was preparing the book for submission to Max Perkins. "If it were all as bad as some of it it would be pretty bloody awful but if it were all as ok as some of it [it] would be pretty good. Am trying to excise the larger gobs of shyte."

Perkins's reactions, though, damped down his anxieties. "It's silly just to write you that it's a grand book—but it did do me great good just to read it," Max wrote him in February 1932. "The book piles upon you wonderfully, and becomes to one reading it—who at first thinks bullfighting only a small matter—immensely important." Three days later he added, "It gives the impression of having grown rather than of having been planned.—And that is the characteristic of a great book." After trying in vain to persuade Perkins to come fishing in the Dry Tortugas, Hemingway dickered with him by letter about the matter of illustrations. He himself wanted two hundred of them, but Perkins skillfully talked him into an amicable acceptance of sixty-four. The only point at which Hemingway blew up at his editor was when he started reading the galley proofs. Each page bore the caption, "Hemingway's Death," and he saw no humor in this. You should have known I was superstitious, he roared at Max; it was a "hell of a damn dirty business," he roared again, having to encounter that lousy heading every time he flipped a page. In his reply Perkins said that he hadn't noticed the heading. "If I had I would have known what to do with it," he assured his ruffled author, "because you cannot tell me anything about omens. I can see more than any man on the face of the earth, and once when things were bad and I was alone in the car and a black cat crossed the road I actually shot around the corner. When any of my family are in the car and that happens, I tell them not to be foolish."

The reviewers of *Death in the Afternoon* did not, by and large, agree with Perkins that it was grand. Robert Coates, writing in *The New Yorker,* began by describing the book as an "exhaustive treatise on bullfighting in all its aspects, from the breeding of the bulls to the moment of their dispatch in the ring, with a critical analysis of the technique of the various matadors besides; and I confess that a little of this goes a long way with me." Coates also did not care for Hemingway's "small-boy wickedness of vocabulary," or for his literary comments "in which his bitterness descends in petulance (as in his gibes at William Faulkner, who has done him no harm save to come under his influence, and at T. S. Eliot, Aldous Huxley, Jean Cocteau, and others, living and dead)." If there was anything he liked, it was the honesty with which the author had revealed, almost involuntarily, "the tremendous labor of simplification, the searching for the particularizing detail," that had gone into his stories over the years. In sum, Coates felt that *Death in the Afternoon* was "almost a suicidal book in its deliberate flouting of reader and critic alike, and I feel sure that because of it Mr. Hemingway has let himself in for some hard panning from those who have been most hysterical in praise of him." The book was, in fact, "suicidal" in more ways than one.

H. L. Mencken, who had never liked Hemingway's work, was offended by the book's "gross . . . cheapness." So long as the author confines himself to expounding the art and science of bullfighting, said Mencken, "he is unfailingly clear, colorful and interesting." Unfortunately, Mencken continued, he all too often turns aside from his theme in order "to prove fatuously that he is a naughty fellow, and when he does so he almost invariably falls into banality and worse. The reader he seems to keep in his mind's eye is a sort of common denominator of all the Ladies' Aid Societies of his native Oak Park, Illinois. The way to shock this innocent grandam, obviously, is to have at her with the ancient four-letter words. Mr. Hemingway does so with moral industry; he even drags her into the story as a character, to gloat over her horror."

But the harshest of all the reviews was the one in the June 7, 1933, *New Republic* by Max Eastman. "Bull in the Afternoon" he called the piece, because of the "unconscionable quantity of bull—to put it as decorously as possible—poured and plastered all over what he writes about bullfights." Hemingway's references to "ritual" and "tragedy" were "sentimental poppycock," of the sort dished out by "those Art nannies and pale-eyed professors of poetry whom [he] above all men despises." Why, then, asked Eastman, "does our iron advocate of straight talk about what things are, our full-sized man, our ferocious realist, go blind and wrap himself up in clouds of juvenile romanticism the moment he crosses the border on his way to a Spanish bullfight?" Eastman began his answer by cravenly hiding behind an unattributed opinion. "It is of course a commonplace that Hemingway lacks the serene confidence that he *is* a full-sized man." Thereafter, though, the reviewer made clear that he was speaking for himself.

> Most of us too delicately organized babies who grow up to be artists suffer at times from that small inward doubt. But some circumstance seems to have laid upon Hemingway a continual sense of the obligation to put forth evidences of red-blooded masculinity. It must be made obvious not only in the swing of the big shoulders and the clothes he puts on, but in the stride of his prose style and the emotions

he permits to come to the surface there. This trait of his character has
. . . begotten a veritable school of fiction-writers—a literary style,
you might say, of wearing false hair on his chest.

Having discounted Mencken's hostility in advance, Hemingway
wasn't notably bothered by his review, but in Paris he and Robert
Coates had been friends and consequently his attack took him off
guard. In a letter to Dos Passos, he denounced the review as a
"condescentious piece of phony intellectuality," and in a letter to
Coates, which *The New Yorker* printed without permission, he defended his wisecracks about Cocteau, Huxley, and Eliot and denied
that he had said anything derogatory about the author of *Sanctuary,*
even though he had. But at the end of the letter he retreated from
this untenable position and argued instead that the remarks he had
made about Faulkner were not a reflection of his overall opinion of
him. "I have plenty of respect for Faulkner and wish him all luck.
That does not mean that I would not joke about him. There are no
subjects that I would not jest about if the jest was funny enough
(just as, liking wing shooting, I would shoot my own mother if she
went in coveys and had a good strong flight)."

"Bull in the Afternoon" enraged him, and Archibald MacLeish
poured further fuel on the fire by mailing him a carbon of a letter he
had sent to the *New Republic* which the editor, Bruce Bliven, refused
to print. "By some psychoanalytic hocus-pocus," said MacLeish,
"the literary impotent" have come to believe that

> Mr. Hemingway's artistic virility . . . proceeds from the fact that
> Mr. Hemingway himself believes himself unvirile. . . . I do not
> know what constitutes confidence of virility in Mr. Max Eastman's
> mind. I do know that I have seen Mr. Hemingway in positions of
> considerable danger once at sea, once in the mountains and once on a
> Spanish street. . . . Of those more personal evidences of virility to
> which Mr. Eastman so daintily and indirectly refers I have no personal
> knowledge. I refer him however to the birth records of the cities of
> Paris [sic] and Kansas City where he can satisfy his curiosity in secret.

Picking up on MacLeish's protest, Hemingway himself wrote a
letter to the *New Republic* in which he, too, interpreted "Bull in the
Afternoon" as a slur against his potency. His instinct in this situation, not surprisingly, was to counterattack in kind, but since the
handsome Eastman's long-term success with the ladies was indisputable, he was reduced to making a sneering reference to his age
and to linking him with two other critics whose manhood it was

easier to impugn, the reputedly impotent Alexander Woollcott and the blatantly homosexual Stark Young.

> Sirs:
> Would it not be possible for you to have Mr. Max Eastman elaborate his nostalgic speculations on my sexual incapacity? Here it would be read (aloud) with much enjoyment. Our amusements are simple and I would be glad to furnish illustrations to brighten Mr. Eastman's prose if you consider this advisable. Mr. Alexander Woollcott and the middle aged Mr. Eastman having both published hopeful doubts as to my potency is it too much to expect that we might hear soon from Mr. Stark Young?

But these remarks did not relieve his anger, or his deepening depression. "I am tempted never to publish another damned thing," he bitterly wrote to Max Perkins.

> The swine aren't worth writing for. I swear to christ they're not. Every phase of the whole racket is so disgusting that it makes you feel like vomiting. Every word I wrote about the Spanish fighting bull was absolutely true and [the] result of long and careful and exhaustive observation. Then they pay Eastman, who knows nothing about it, to say I write sentimental nonsense. . . . And it is a commonplace that I lack confidence that I am a man—what shit. . . . They're a nice lot—the professional male beauties of other years—Max Eastman—a groper in sex (with the hands I mean), a traitor in politics [i.e., he had abandoned the Left] and—hell I won't waste it on them. . . . You see what they can't get over is (1) that I *am* a man (2) that I can beat the shit out of any of them (3) that I can write. The last hurts them the worst. But they don't like any of it. But Papa will make them like it.

In an effort to calm the storm he had stirred up, Eastman wrote a note to MacLeish vigorously disputing the interpretation that the poet had placed upon his review, sent a more humbly worded apology and denial to Hemingway and proclaimed in an open letter to the *New Republic* that he had had no intention of libeling Hemingway's "manhood, courage or what-not" and that in fact he admired his courage. When they had first met at the Genoa Conference, he recalled, Hemingway had just been blown out of a bathroom by a gas-heater explosion, yet he had walked away from the incident "with a smile on his face like a man on a toboggan." All he had meant to say about his recent book was that the real Hemingway was "gentle and sensitive" and that therefore his "roaring about whorehouses and bull's blood" was just "unreal interior bluster." But Hemingway was not mollified by these "kiss-ass" gestures,

as he called them, and four years later when he encountered Eastman
by chance in Max Perkins's office it took him only a few minutes to
become violently angry. Following some preliminary pleasantries,
he unbuttoned both his shirt and Eastman's, in order, he said with a
grin, to compare their chests. His own was "hairy enough for anybody," Perkins remembered, whereas Eastman's was "as bare as a
bald man's head." Both writers were laughing at this point and the
embarrassed Perkins was beginning to feel that the meeting was
going rather well, all things considered. Suddenly, Hemingway's
face reddened with rage. "What do you mean accusing me of impotence?" he yelled. Eastman glanced about as he tried to think of
the best way to reply. On the cluttered surface of Perkins's desk he
noticed a copy of his—Eastman's—collection of essays, *Art and the
Life of Action* (1934), in which "Bull in the Afternoon" was reprinted. Handing the book to Hemingway, he said, "Here. Read
what I *really* said." Hemingway began paging through it, muttering
profanities the while. Apparently, it was the actual sight of the review that caused him to lose the remainder of his control. Holding
the open book by the spine, he punched it into Eastman's face. The
infuriated Eastman grabbed Hemingway and they tussled one another to the floor. Perkins rushed forward to pull Hemingway off
his prostrate opponent before he killed him. To his amazement, the
editor discovered that Eastman was the man on top and that Hemingway, lying flat on his back beneath him, was grinning from ear
to ear. As in his showdown with Harold Loeb in Pamplona, his
mood had become benign in a matter of seconds. Eastman was
sixteen years older than he was and no physical match for him by
any stretch of the imagination. If he had wished to, he could have
really hurt him, but he hadn't wished to, despite the dire threats of
reprisal he had once voiced to Perkins.

In the stories that broke three days later in the New York morning
papers, most notably the *Herald Tribune,* Eastman was quoted as
saying that after being hit in the face he had wrestled with Hemingway and had thrown him across Perkins's desk, pinning him tightly
and allowing him up only when Perkins begged him to do so. Hemingway's countering version was that he had merely slapped Eastman because if he had hit him hard he might have knocked him
through the window out onto Fifth Avenue five floors below. Eastman "jumped at me like a woman, clawing . . . with his open
hands," but "I was laughing all the time," Hemingway assured the
reporters. "I said, 'Max, if you were ten years younger I'd knock
hell out of you.' " New York's numerous evening papers of that era
played up Eastman's version, by and large. One paper juxtaposed a

picture of a sullen-looking Hemingway with a smiling photograph of Eastman taken from the dust jacket of his book *Enjoyment of Laughter,* while another declared that Eastman was planning to write an essay called "Enjoyment of Thrashing Ernest."

Walter Winchell, O. O. McIntyre, Heywood Broun, and other columnists had a field day with the story. Damon Runyon claimed that six girls in Westchester County alone had broken their engagements upon learning that their fiancés had hairless chests; a ponderously humorous *New York Times* editorial referred to the antagonists as "Slogger" Hemingway and "Kid" Eastman; *The New Yorker's* "Talk of the Town" made ironical mention of the "embarrassments of the wise and the great"; and a cartoon in the same magazine showed a hairy-chested young man without his shirt on being examined by a doctor. "Writer?" the one-word caption asked.

The wiseacres of the press did their best to come up with witty comments about the fracas; overlooked was an odd passage in *Death in the Afternoon* in which Hemingway for the first and only time in his work employed the word "androgynous" and for the first and only time did not simply sneer at a man whom he considered "queer."

> Greco liked to paint religious pictures because he was very evidently religious and because his incomparable art was not then limited to accurate reproducing of the faces of the noblemen who were his sitters for portraits and he could go as far into his other world as he wanted and, consciously or unconsciously, paint saints, apostles, Christs and Virgins with the androgynous faces and forms that filled his imagination.
>
> One time in Paris I was talking to a girl who was writing a fictionalized life of El Greco and I said to her, "Do you make him a maricón?"
>
> "No," she said. "Why should I?"
>
> "Did you ever look at the pictures?"
>
> "Yes, of course."
>
> "Did you ever see more classic examples anywhere than he painted? Do you think that was all accident or do you think all those citizens were queer? The only saint I know who is universally represented as built that way is San Sebastian. Greco made them all that way. Look at the pictures. Don't take my word for it."
>
> "I hadn't thought of that."
>
> "Think it over," I said, "if you are writing a life of him."

On boyhood tours of the Art Institute in Chicago, Hemingway had come to know El Greco's fully formed "Assumption of the

Virgin." But in Spain he encountered the gaunt, extraordinary figures of El Greco's greatest work. Their attenuated features, elon-
gated hands, and flamelike forms apparently disturbed him. Instead
of interpreting these challengingly original emphases in the reli-
giously mystical terms favored by most critics of art in the twenties
and early thirties, he saw them as psychosexual emblems. It was an
interpretation that cast no light on El Greco's sensibility, but amidst
all the "unreal interior bluster" of *Death in the Afternoon* it endures as
a moment of truth about Hemingway's.

3

NINETEEN thirty-two, the year of *Death in the Afternoon,* also
marked the beginning of the end of Hemingway's second marriage.
Officially, the union would last until 1940, but long before then it
had lost all meaning.

The fatal trouble started in 1931, when Pauline informed him that
she was going to have another baby. It was a prospect that did not
please him. The only consolation was the hope that the baby would
prove to be a girl. At six o'clock in the evening on Armistice Day,
November 11, Pauline went into labor in the same Kansas City
hospital in which she had given birth to Patrick. Twelve hours later,
her doctor decided it would again be necessary for him to perform a
Caesarean section. The baby that was snatched from her womb was
a nine-pound boy with blue-black hair. His parents named him
Gregory Hancock, Gregory after any number of bad popes, the
baby's father bleakly wisecracked, and Hancock for his, Hemingway's, maternal grandmother, Caroline Hancock Hall.

The following April, he fled from the sound of a squalling infant,
as he had after the birth of Patrick. Accompanied by his Key West
crony, Joe Russell, the owner of Sloppy Joe's bar, he set off on the
latter's thirty-two-foot cruiser, *Anita,* for a two-week holiday in
Havana that ended up lasting two months. For two dollars a night
—and a half dollar more when Pauline came to stay with him, as she
did for a week on two separate occasions—he rented a corner room
on the fifth floor of the Hotel Ambos Mundos. To the north, he
could look out over the old cathedral to the entrance to the harbor
and the sea; to the east, he could see the Casablanca peninsula and
the width of the harbor. Most mornings, he and Russell went out
marlin fishing. His afternoons were generally devoted to the galley
proofs of *Death in the Afternoon* and the manuscript of a new short
story about Nick Adams. After nightfall many possibilities
beckoned: the Dance Academies at which wonderfully demure-

looking girls called *académicas* charged five cents a dance and variable rates for extra-curricular services; the betting pit in the jai-alai frontón where the odds were constantly fluctuating and the bookmakers accepted wagers on every point; and the Floridita, a seafood bar-restaurant with a golden frieze and formal drapes and a reputation for having invented the daiquiri. Mainly, though, Hemingway elected to spend his evenings in Jane Mason's company.

Jane was the twenty-two-year-old wife of G. Grant Mason, the head of Pan American Airways in Cuba and the owner of a beautifully situated estate in Jaimanitas, west of Havana. With her slender but curvy body and her strawberry blond hair, which she parted in the middle and pulled away from her oval face, she was the most beautiful woman whom Hemingway had ever gone after. A native of Tuxedo Park, New York, and a graduate of Briarcliff, she had made her debut in Washington, D. C., just before her impulsive marriage to Mason. Dancing, drinking, and deep-sea fishing were among her current enthusiasms, and so was pigeon shooting at the Club de Cazadores, a sport in which few other women engaged. At ease in the company of men, she wanted to be treated as though she were one of them, but the gallantry her beauty inspired made this difficult for her to achieve.

On finding that her husband bored her, she tried to lose herself in motherhood by adopting two little boys, but maternal responsibilities didn't enthrall her either and she very quickly turned the boys over to an English nanny. Renewing the interest in sculpture she had developed at Briarcliff was her next idea, and after that ran its course she invested in a craft shop specializing in the work of Cuban artisans.

Jane's fickleness could have been a consequence of her manic-depressive illness. Because the unsubtle man she had married wasn't interested in anything as tricky as mood swings, she became more alienated from him than ever. On the other hand, she felt grateful to the famous writer at the Ambos Mundos for the sympathy and encouragement he lavished upon her. Two months before arriving in Havana, Hemingway had learned that Zelda Fitzgerald had been admitted to the Phipps Clinic at the Johns Hopkins University Hospital in Baltimore. Conceivably, he came to think of Jane Mason as his very own Zelda, except that he proposed to make her well by giving her lessons in marlin fishing and by telling her over and over that she wasn't crazy, even as he had always responded to his own problems by publicly denying their existence. ("I know what I am doing and have never felt a 'malajust,' " he would assure one of his correspondents on August 9, 1932.) Thus, he entitled his new story about a nutty Nick Adams "A Way You'll Never Be," in order to inspire Jane to have confidence in herself.

Yet if he called on Jane to rise above her illness, he was irresistibly drawn to her because of it. "He says he's never been crazy," the head-battered and crazy Ad Francis remarks about the young Nick Adams. "He's got a lot coming to him," the crazy Bugs replies. Three years after writing "The Battler," Hemingway pulled a skylight down on his brow, and nine months later his distracted father killed himself with a shot to the brain. The connection between these two events was tenuous, yet they appeared to heighten vastly his fear that someday he might go out of his mind. Wherefore, as he had done many times before, he called on Nick Adams to be a stalking horse for exploring his anxieties. In "The Battler," Nick is clubbed on the head without ill effects. In "A Way You'll Never Be," he is a soldier in northern Italy who has suffered a traumatic head injury. That he is no longer the man he was is made explicit during a conversation he has with an Italian officer who keeps asking him how he is.

> "How are you really?"
> "I'm fine. I'm perfectly all right."
> "No. I mean really."
> "I'm all right. I can't sleep without a light of some sort. That's all I have now."
> "I said it should have been trepanned. I'm no doctor but I know that."
> "Well, they thought it was better to have it absorb, and that's what I got. What's the matter? I don't seem crazy to you, do I?"
> "You seem in top-hole shape."
> "It's a hell of a nuisance once they've had you certified as nutty," Nick said. "No one ever has any confidence in you again."

When Jane left Havana for New York in May 1932 and entered Doctors Hospital, it was for minor surgery, not psychotherapy, Hemingway was pleased to learn. After a brief convalescence at her mother's estate in Tuxedo Park, she alerted her fishing instructor to her impending return. ARRIVING SATURDAY MORNING. MAY I FISH SUNDAY. LOVE JANE. Once again, Hemingway was pleased.

Having sent Patrick and baby Gregory to their grandparents in Piggott in the care of a nurse named Ada Stern whom she had recently hired, Pauline had rejoined her husband in Havana and was still there when Jane arrived from New York. But shortly thereafter she herself departed for Arkansas, although there can be no doubt that she did so reluctantly. For the letters she sent back betrayed an alarmed awareness that she now had a rival to contend with who was fourteen years younger than she was and breathtakingly beautiful. On hearing from Ernest that he and Joe Russell and Jane had fought a huge marlin for more than two hours before losing it, she rushed to tell him, "Next year we'll go over and get enormous ones, you and me, and when you come here I'm not going to leave you again for a long, long time. . . . I miss you very much and all the time and will follow you around like a little dog and so will Patrick. Gregory looks too swell with his four teeth and his silky, curly hair. . . . Hurry, hurry, hurry, can't wait any longer than is possible. I think you'll like me." The last sentence referred to her latest hairstyle. As Hemingway would discover when he picked her up in Piggott en route to Wyoming, she now looked as androgynous as she had on the day of her marriage: dark hair trimmed severely short and combed forward over her forehead. In fact, ever since discovering in *A Farewell to Arms* that Frederic Henry's dream girl was a blonde, Pauline had been unsure of what to do with her hair, at the same time that she thoroughly understood that getting it right was of critical importance. In the summer of 1929, she became a blonde. During the early months of her second pregnancy, she similarly attempted to hold the interest of her husband by making tempting allusions to her new permanent wave. "I think you will like it," she wrote him. "Hurry up and grow yours and I will make braids or buckles in the back on rainy afternoons." Of the four women whom Hemingway married, Pauline was the only one who made hair a topic of correspondence.

Hemingway returned to Havana in the spring of 1933 for another extended visit—but once again he arrived without his wife. In rueful acknowledgment of her physical shortcomings, Pauline sent him a letter saying that she was going to have her "large nose, imperfect lips, protruding ears and warts and moles all taken off before coming to Cuba. Thought I better, Mrs. Mason and those Cuban women are so lovely." Bumby, however, provided her with an excuse to appear at the Ambos Mundos almost immediately. The boy had arrived in Key West for what had become his annual visit with his father, and even though he was nine years old and quite resourceful, Pauline insisted on escorting him to Havana. But because she wanted to oversee the landscaping work being done on the grounds of the Whitehead Street house she didn't remain in Cuba for long. Besides which, she hadn't been made to feel especially welcome there.

With both her husband and Hemingway in tow, Jane appeared at the Sans Souci on many a night that spring and danced with the novelist under the palms and gambled beside him at the roulette tables. During the day she drove Hemingway around Havana in her big Packard, went fishing with him on the *Anita,* and came to his room in the Ambos Mundos, although almost surely she didn't climb through the transom, as he later claimed.

At some point they apparently talked about getting married. But at the beginning of June their affair was violently interrupted when Jane jumped down into the hedge beneath the second-story balcony of her Jaimanitas home and broke her back. She had made halfhearted suicide attempts before, but without injuring herself, and her husband had scoffed at them as bids for attention. Her broken back, however, caused him to think twice. As soon as it was possible to do so, he put her on a ship to New York. The stateroom she occupied had bars on the portholes and a nurse in attendance around the clock. In New York she spent five months in a hospital, was fitted for a brace she had to wear for a year and embarked upon a course of psychotherapy with Dr. Lawrence Kubie.

4

ON a trip to New York without Pauline in January 1933 Hemingway met Thomas Wolfe at a lunch arranged by Max Perkins at Cherio's on Fifty-third Street. What struck Hemingway most forcibly about Wolfe was his childlike manner. As he observed to Perkins in a follow-up letter, geniuses of that particular kind were always like children and as such were a hell of a responsibility. Scott Fitzgerald was also in town at the time, more or less soused every waking moment, and he quarreled with both Edmund Wilson and Hemingway. This gave Hemingway another opportunity to speak condescendingly to Perkins about a Scribners author. Why does Scott refuse to grow up, he asked in a letter.

His own behavior while in the city had likewise been less than mature. A young man named John Gardner had come to his hotel to ask him as the masculine head of the Hemingway family for his permission to marry his youngest sister Carol, with whom Gardner had fallen in love during their days together as undergraduates at Rollins College in Winter Park, Florida. To Gardner's vast surprise, Hemingway was violently angered by his request and threatened to knock his teeth out if he didn't stop seeing Carol immediately.

Distress about the negative reviews of *Death in the Afternoon* probably had a lot to do with this ugly outburst against an innocent young man; another source of the pugnacity that he continued to display throughout the rest of the winter and into the spring of 1933

could have been the collection of stories he was assembling for fall
publication. For while he knew that *Winner Take Nothing* would
contain some stories that measured up to his earlier work, it would
nevertheless demonstrate that the crisis in his imaginative development was deepening.

The sensation it conveys of a man gone mad establishes "A Way
You'll Never Be" as another eerie Nick Adams masterpiece and the
outstanding story in the book. Night after night, Nick awakens
soaking wet, after dreaming of a yellow house outside of Fossalta
that he has never seen in actuality, and of the long stable beside it
and of a canal, and of the river much wider and stiller than it really
was. Because he is wearing an American uniform, he is allowed to
go about on his bike as he pleases, on the theory that the sight of his
uniform will boost the morale of the Italian troops, but he refuses to
keep his helmet on. "You know they're absolutely no damned
good," he says. "I remember when they were a comfort when we
first had them, but I've seen them full of brains too many times."
As superb as this portrait of Nick's madness is, "A Clean,
Well-Lighted Place" is almost as harrowing. With pity and awe,
Hemingway embodied his sense of his father's grapplings with age,
loneliness, and despair in a sketch of three Spaniards in a café, one
of them an old and deaf customer and the other two waiters, one
middle-aged and the other still young. The hour is late and the café
is quiet; yet its ambience offers the old man and the older waiter a
temporary refuge against the looming specter of nothingness. Another strong piece of work is the savagely angry and sardonic "God
Rest You Merry, Gentlemen," and so is the portrait of Clarence
Edmonds Hemingway in "Fathers and Sons."

These four stories, though, stand distinctly apart from the rest of
Winner Take Nothing. In "The Mother of a Queen," Hemingway
updated his quarrel with Grace by dealing symbolically with their
current financial relationship; unfortunately, its account of a young
homosexual who stops paying the rent on his mother's grave and
allows her remains to be dumped on a public bone-heap was nothing
but a revolting expression of a famous man's resentment at having
to send a woman he hated a monthly allowance. In "The Sea
Change," a tale largely made up of cutting exchanges in a Paris café
between a man and a woman who are breaking up because the
woman has taken another woman as her lover, the dialogue has
some of the pace and desperate energy of the talk in "Hills Like
White Elephants," but the setting is incomparably less memorable.
And in "The Light of the World" the emotionally fettered author
took yet another shot at his mother.

The title of the latter story derived from Holman Hunt's painting of the same name which Grace and her father had admired in an Oxford college chapel during their tour of Europe in the summer of 1896, following the collapse of her singing career. Upon her father's death, Grace presented a copy of the painting to her church, where it was hung in the sanctuary as a memorial to him. Looking up at the picture, as he did on countless Sunday mornings of his boyhood, Grandfather Hall's namesake could see the figure of Christ standing in the dead of night before a door. The hinges of the door were rusted, the doorway was overgrown with ivy, and a tangle of weeds lay before the threshold. Christ held a lantern in one hand, while his other hand was raised in the act of knocking. In the blasphemous literary version of this scene, a door is mentioned in the first sentence —a door to the barroom in a smelly Michigan town. Upon entering the bar, the youthful narrator and his friend Tom each drink a beer and Tom samples the free lunch of foul-tasting pig's feet. Later, the boys enter the door at the train station. Inside are five whores, four Indians, and six white men, one of whom is a homosexual. At three hundred and fifty pounds, the fattest of the whores might be described as a grander version of Grace, or perhaps of Gertrude Stein —for her name is Alice. Alice's dispute with another of the whores as to which of them had once had the privilege of servicing the famous boxer, Stanley Ketchel, whom they both refer to as Steve Ketchel, is not without lovely moments, and the story as a whole is not without moral complexity. Nevertheless, "The Light of the World" is markedly inferior to the boyhood tales in *In Our Time*. Despite his stout insistence that the story was a favorite of his, Hemingway was clearly coming to the bottom of the Michigan barrel.

"After the Storm" represented his first attempt to come to terms with Florida. But while the story contains some notable sequences of "motion and fact which made the emotion"—to quote from his definition in *Death in the Afternoon* of "the real thing" in writing— he summoned up Mango Key and Sou'west Key and the Rebecca Light in the same severely limited, puritanically restrained prose he had fashioned in wintry Paris a decade earlier. "Wine of Wyoming" is set in another region of the western hemisphere he had recently become familiar with, but the family in the story is French and the landscape is repeatedly likened to Spain; far from giving promise that the Rocky Mountain West would someday figure importantly in his fiction, "Wine of Wyoming" indicated that he didn't wish to cope with it, as did a tedious story called "The Gambler, the Nun, and the Radio," in which he drew on his experiences in St. Vincent's

Hospital in Billings, Montana, where he was a patient in November 1930 after running off the road in his car and seriously fracturing his right arm.

In "Homage to Switzerland," he trivialized his yearnings for Hadley in three vignettes that were supposed to be funny but weren't. In "A Day's Wait," he recalled a time in Piggott when Bumby had come down with a fever of 102° and the boy had become convinced that he was going to die, because he thought all thermometers were calibrated in centigrade; as T. S. Matthews would observe in the *New Republic,* "A Day's Wait" could be confidently recommended to admirers of Booth Tarkington's *Penrod and Sam.* "A Natural History of the Dead" was a part-fictional, part-factual disquisition on war that had already appeared in print in chapter twelve of *Death in the Afternoon.* "One Reader Writes," the shortest and poorest excuse for an entry in the collection, stemmed from the author's friendship with Dr. Logan Clendening, a Kansas City physician and syndicated columnist. On the assumption that a writer of fiction would be interested in the sort of letters he received from readers of his column, Clendening sent several samples to Key West. One was from a woman whose husband had contracted syphilis while stationed in Shanghai with the U.S. Marines. Would she ever again be able to have sexual intercourse with him without risking her health, the woman wanted to know. Hemingway made some minor editorial changes in the letter, tacked on a two-sentence introduction and a one-paragraph conclusion and published it. Poor Scott Fitzgerald had damaged his talent by writing stories for the *Saturday Evening Post,* Hemingway had become fond of saying. Nothing that Fitzgerald ever peddled to a slick-paper publication was shoddier than "One Reader Writes" or "A Day's Wait."

"It is among Mr. Hemingway's admirers that the suspicion is being most strongly created that the champion is losing, if he has not already lost, his hold," William Troy noted in *The Nation,* apropos of the critical responses to *Winner Take Nothing.* As for Troy's own opinion of the book, he bluntly stated that the collection included "the poorest and least interesting writing [the author] has ever placed on public view."

In a letter to Perkins—who himself found the reviews "absolutely enraging"—Hemingway called Henry Seidel Canby "a fool," waved off John Chamberlain's assessment as "shit" and replied to the rest of his tormentors by bragging that "*all the time* I can write better stories than anybody else writing." Yet if "those poor dumb pricks" who reviewed books for a living succeeded in upsetting him, it was Gertrude Stein who made him think about getting out his shotgun. For *The Autobiography of Alice B. Toklas,* after being serialized in the *Atlantic Monthly,* appeared between hard covers in the same season as *Winner Take Nothing.* He "looks like a modern and he smells of the museums" was Miss Stein's definitive word on Hemingway the writer. Of the quiverful of personal shafts she launched at him, the one that carried the most lethal poison in its tip was her statement that he was yellow, "just like the flat-boat men on the Mississippi river described by Mark Twain." Since his father's death, the cowardice issue had become Hemingway's hobgoblin; somehow, she had figured that out.

5

DESPITE the critics, *Winner Take Nothing* sold 12,500 copies in the first two months after its publication. The good news belatedly reached Hemingway in January 1934 in his bedroom at the New Stanley Hotel in Nairobi, Kenya, where he was recovering from the attack of amoebic dysentery that had forced him to interrupt the most lavish hunting expedition he had ever undertaken.

In an era of worldwide economic hardship, he was living on a grander scale than Fitzgerald had in the golden twenties, and his presence in East Africa was a particularly gaudy illustration of this fact. A proper safari, he had learned from reading the various pamphlets he had sent away for, cost in the neighborhood of twenty thousand dollars for two. The estimates hadn't fazed him. Gus Pfeiffer had offered to put up twenty-five thousand dollars toward such a trip, and Hemingway knew he could augment that sum if he had to by increasing his output of "Letters" for a glossy new magazine for men called *Esquire.* There had been a time when he had forsworn journalism, financially painful though it was to do so, because he believed it constituted a daily self-destruction for a serious creative writer. The days of that kind of artistic rigor were behind him, however. When Arnold Gingrich, the editor-in-chief of *Esquire,* announced his willingness to pay him $200 per contribution of 1,500 words (the amount would swell to $500 by 1936), he accepted the offer with enthusiasm.

Accompanied by their Key West friend Charles Thompson, Hemingway and Pauline arrived in Nairobi on December 10, 1933. Lying snugly against the Athi Plain at the foot of the rolling Kikuyu Hills, looking north toward Mount Kenya and south toward Kilimanjaro in Tanganyika, Nairobi was the gateway to a country that was still new. In less than thirty years, it had grown from a collection of corrugated iron shacks strung out along the tracks of the rickety

Uganda Railway into a confused mass of structures occupied by British, Boers, Indians, Somalis, Abyssinians, and other African natives. The British contingent was mostly made up of men of commerce, for Nairobi was a counting-house in a wilderness, but it also included a "white mischief" crowd of wealthy, rebellious, public-school types heavily involved in philandering, drinking, and horse racing. Still other Britishers lived lives of romantic adventure, and one of the most heroic of these figures was a woman, Beryl Markham, whom Hemingway found personally unpleasant but impressive. After apprenticing with her father as a trainer and breeder of horses, Markham had turned to aviation, carrying mail, passengers, and supplies in her small plane to far corners of the Sudan, Tanganyika, Kenya, and Rhodesia. In 1942 she would publish an elegantly crafted autobiography, *West With the Night*. "Did you read Beryl Markham's book, 'West With the Night'?" Hemingway would ask Max Perkins in astonishment.

> I knew her fairly well in Africa and never would have suspected that she could and would put pen to paper except to write in her flyer's log book. As it is, she has written so well, and marvelously well, that I was completely ashamed of myself as a writer. I felt that I was simply a carpenter with words, picking up whatever was furnished on the job and nailing them together and some times making an okay pig pen. But this girl . . . can write rings around all of us who consider ourselves as writers. . . . I wish you would get it and read it because it is really a bloody, wonderful book.

Through Tanganyika Guides, Ltd., the Hemingways met Baron Bror von Blixen, the director for Tanganyika (and the divorced husband of the writer Isak Dinesen), and the legendary Philip Percival, the director for Kenya. Percival, who had served Theodore Roosevelt as a white hunter a generation earlier, would be willing to act in a similar capacity for the Hemingways, he told them, if they would wait a week or so. In the meantime, they could stay at Percival's farm in the Mua Hills and hunt for gazelles and impala.

Young Alfred Vanderbilt, a friend of Grant and Jane Mason's, was also staying at Percival's farm, and if Hemingway had reached the farm a few days earlier he would have met another fabulously wealthy sportsman, Winston Guest, who would later become his good friend. Although Hemingway thought well of Vanderbilt and encouraged him to write some horseracing pieces for *Esquire,* the man who really interested him was Percival. As Chink Dorman-Smith had in World War I and Buck Lanham would in World War

II, this gray-haired hunter impressed him as being the complete professional. Percival, for his part, felt that Hemingway, with his big grin and amazing energy, was remarkably like ex-President Roosevelt.

Five days before Christmas, Percival and his new clients set off for the Serengeti Plain. A black driver, two black gunbearers, and a white assistant hunter traveled with them in a doorless, box-bodied motor car, while two trucks driven by blacks and loaded with camping equipment chugged along behind them. As the caravan neared the town of Arusha, where the five whites in the party would spend the night in a hotel, "Kilimanjaro kept appearing and disappearing high in the air like a Cheshire cat," Pauline recorded in her diary.

Their first view of the Serengeti was stunning. As far as the eye could see, the green landscape was black with wildebeests, three million of them, by the estimate of the Tanganyika Game Department. Following and living on the fringe of the herd were lions, spotted hyenas, and jackals. In two weeks and three days of shooting, Hemingway, Charles Thompson, and Pauline downed four lions, two big leopards, thirty-five hyenas, the limit all around on cheetah, a roan antelope, and numerous eland, waterbuck, and gazelles. Nothing that Hemingway had ever read in Roosevelt's *African Game Trails* or any other source had given him an adequate idea of the beauty of East Africa, or of the quantity of its game.

Yet if the trip was exceeding his expectations, it was not without its discouragements and annoyances. The most impressive kills were consistently achieved by Charles Thompson. The daily bloodletting began to offend Pauline. And the dysentery that Hemingway had contracted grew progressively worse. Finally, on January 14, the sufferer "became convinced"—so he later told the readers of *Esquire* —"that though an unbeliever I had been chosen as the one to bear our Lord Buddha when he should be born again on earth. While flattered at this, and wondering how much Buddha at that age would resemble Gertrude Stein, I found the imminence of the event made it difficult to take high incoming birds, and finally compromised by reclining against a tree and only accepting crossing shots." But although the bulging sensation he was experiencing made him think of himself as a woman having a baby, what it actually represented was the prolapse of his lower intestine.

Percival decided he would have to be flown to Arusha or possibly all the way to Nairobi for treatment. The assistant hunter, Ben Fourie, went off to the nearest telegraph station—on Lake Victoria, 115 miles away—to send a wire calling in a plane. "Ben will get there tonight," Pauline confidently wrote in her diary, "and the plane will be here in the morning." But the plane did not arrive in the morning, and the agonized waiting then began that Hemingway would recreate so brilliantly in "The Snows of Kilimanjaro." To conserve his energy, the invalid stayed in bed until evening, when he moved to a chair by the campfire. The following morning, he declared he was better, but after getting to his feet he couldn't walk, he was so weak. Pauline went off bird-shooting with Thompson, while Hemingway tried to amuse himself by reading English magazines. Not until the next morning did a pint-sized bush pilot with a pointed nose named "Fatty" Pearson finally touch down in a two-seater biplane. "Ernest went off very gay and handsome (partly due to extreme thinness) in a small silver plane with a tiny pilot belonging to the weasel family," Pauline noted in her diary shortly after they left. Pearson refueled the plane at Arusha and took off again for Nairobi. To the east, as they rose, he and his passenger could see the square top of Kilimanjaro, as wide as all the world, great, high, and unbelievably white in the sun.

"Your amoebic dysentery correspondent is in bed, fully injected with emetine," Hemingway wrote some days later in the first of his Tanganyika letters for *Esquire*. "Symptoms of a. d. run from weakly insidious through spectacular to phenomenal. I believe the record is held by a Mr. McDonald with 232 movements in the twenty-four hours although many old a. d. men claim the McDonald record has never been properly audited." While the joke was wonderfully good-humored, it fell far short of reflecting the full range of his mood. For the past couple of days, he knew, Percival had been showing Pauline and Thompson the spectacular country south of Ngorongoro Crater, whereas here he was, still languishing in bed in Nairobi. The contrast not only pointed up his humiliating failure to match his friend Thompson's exploits as a killer, but called attention to the superior durability of the much older Percival.

On rejoining the safari, Hemingway hunted for rhinos and kudus and spent nearly every evening in front of the campfire drinking whiskey and sodas with the fatherly white hunter, whom he would refer to as "Pop" in *Green Hills of Africa*. One of the many stories that Percival told him concerned a mountaineer named Reusch. In climbing the western side of Kilimanjaro in the fall of 1926, Reusch had found near the summit the dried and frozen carcass of a leopard. Hemingway found this inexplicable tale extraordinarily poetic. Perhaps he saw in the leopard a symbol of himself, foraging into strange habitats far beyond his birthplace and doomed to die before his time.

Apart from pressing Percival for details about the leopard, he also seemed interested in persuading him to pass judgment on the courage or cowardice of other clients he had worked for. In exchange, he offered some judgments of his own. His friend Dos Passos was as "brave as a damned buffalo," in contrast to his friend Fitzgerald, who was "a coward of great charm." Percival may well have been mystified by his questions and comments, but a canceled passage in the manuscript of *Green Hills of Africa* (1935) leaves little doubt about what was goading him into voicing them.

> My father was a coward. He shot himself without necessity. At least I thought so. I had gone through it myself until I figured it in my head. I knew what it was to be a coward and what it was to cease being a coward. Now, truly, in actual danger I felt a clean feeling as in a shower. Of course it was easy now. That was because I no longer cared what happened. I knew it was better to live it so that if you died you had done everything that you could do about your work and your enjoyment of life up to that minute, reconciling the two, which is very difficult.

In Africa, Hemingway set out to prove on a grander scale than ever before that he had more nerve than his father. Nevertheless, he, too, had a death wish. That being the case, the preservation of his manly reputation against the charge of cowardice, should he decide to end it all, would rest on his ability to die accidentally or at the hands of an enemy.

6

ON the first leg of their trip home, the Hemingways sailed from Mombasa to Villefranche aboard a luxurious Swedish ship, the *Gripsholm,* with Alfred Vanderbilt and Baron von Blixen as their companions. From Villefranche they traveled by car to Nice and by train from there to Paris, where Hemingway insisted on remaining for nine days so that he could renew friendships with those old friends whom he had not alienated. Janet Flanner tried to show that she still loved him, and so did Sylvia Beach, except that Sylvia made two bad mistakes. The first was to point out to him that the April 1934 issue of the English magazine *Life and Letters* contained an evaluation of his work by Wyndham Lewis. "The Dumb Ox" it was called, and there was scarcely a sentence in it that wasn't barbed.

> The sort of First-person-singular that Hemingway invariably invokes is a dull-witted, bovine, monosyllabic simpleton. This lethargic and stuttering dummy he conducts, or pushes from behind, through all the scenes that interest him. This burlesque First-person-singular be-

haves in them like a moronesque version of his brilliant author. He *Steins* up and down the world, with the big lustreless ruminatory orbs of a Picasso doll-woman (of the semi-classic type Picasso patented, with enormous hands and feet). It is, in short, the very dummy that is required for the literary mannerism of Miss Stein!

Hemingway was so infuriated by the piece that when he finished reading it he smashed one of Sylvia's vases of tulips with his fist and sent it crashing to the floor.

Her second mistake occurred on a cold, wet evening a few days later. She and Katherine Anne Porter were chatting when the door of Shakespeare and Company was abruptly thrown open and Hemingway dashed in, wearing an old raincoat and a floppy hat. Sylvia rushed forward to embrace him. Then, with an apostolic sweetness in her eyes, she took each of her distinguished guests by the hand, spoke each of their names in full and declared, "I want the two best modern American writers to know each other." Before she could say anything further, the phone rang and she flew off to answer it. "Hemingway and I stood and gazed unwinkingly at each other with poker faces for all of ten seconds, in silence," Porter would recall in a magazine article three years after his death. "Hemingway then turned in one wide swing and hurled himself into the rainy darkness as he had hurled himself out of it, and that was all. . . . All personal lack of sympathy aside, and they were real in us, it must have been galling to this most famous young man to have his name pronounced in the same breath as writer with someone he had never heard of, and a woman at that. I nearly felt sorry for him."

Quite a scene. Except that it may not have happened just that way. For when it came to telling stories, Katherine Anne Porter had long since acquired a justified reputation for unreliability and malice. To portray herself as having outstared the great Hemingway, as having caused him to turn and flee into the night, certainly fitted in with her lifelong dramatization of herself as a gutsy Texas gal. And to assert that Hemingway had never heard of her was a way of suggesting that with his roughneck sensibility he couldn't possibly have appreciated the subtlety of the sorts of stories she was writing. Yet "Flowering Judas," which had made her reputation, had first appeared in *Hound & Horn,* a magazine that Hemingway regularly read. And at the time of his death the library of his house in Cuba contained three books by Porter: *Pale Horse, Pale Rider; The Leaning Tower and Other Stories;* and *A Defense of Circe.* Thus, it is not unlikely that on that rainy evening at Shakespeare and Company Hemingway told her of his admiration for her work. If he left the shop before Sylvia got off the phone, it may have been because he had an appointment.

Possibly it was on the selfsame rainy night that he fought Robert McAlmon outside a Left Bank bar. For he had heard reports that McAlmon was at work on a book of reminiscences in which he planned to make some exceedingly nasty remarks about him, in response to his own biting sketch of McAlmon in *Death in the Afternoon*. Without giving his ex-publisher a chance either to confirm or deny these reports, Hemingway asked him to step outside, where he proceeded to beat him so badly that McAlmon had to go to the hospital for first-aid treatment.

Crossing the Atlantic on the *Ile de France* was much more pleasant than Old Home Week in Paris had proved to be, mainly because Marlene Dietrich was on board. The accidental way in which they met was later described by her in a ghost-written piece in *This Week* magazine. "I entered the dining salon to attend a dinner party," she recalled. "The men rose to offer me a chair, but I saw at once that I would make the thirteenth at table. I excused myself on the grounds of superstition, when my way was blocked by a large man who said he gladly would be the fourteenth. The man was Hemingway." Whether he had come to the dining salon by himself because Pauline was seasick or whether she was waiting for him at another table is unclear, but in any case he dined that night with Dietrich and afterwards walked around the deck with her while she recited a poem about suicide that had been written by her daughter Maria.

In the course of the next quarter of a century, he and Dietrich frequently talked on the long-distance telephone and usually got together for drinks or dinner whenever they were in the same city. She reminded him, he said more than once, of Catherine Barkley in *A Farewell to Arms,* which is an interesting remark, given Catherine's androgynous wish that she could look just like her lover. For if Dietrich projected more eroticism than any other female film star of her time, it was an ambiguous eroticism. "Your name begins with a caress and ends with the crack of a whip," Jean Cocteau once told her, while the film and drama critic Kenneth Tynan would contend that the essential quality of her silver-haired, high-cheekboned beauty was "sex without gender." In *Morocco* (1930), she not only made an appearance in white tie and tails, but kissed a woman full on the lips in a scene that she herself improvised. In *Blonde Venus* (1932), she once again wore tails, this time with a top hat, and appreciatively eyed a line of chorus girls, one of whom she chucked under the breast. When she made *The Ship of Lost Men* (1929), she threw herself with extraordinary panache into the role of a leather-

suited and begoggled American aviatrix who, after crashing near a
ship, is mistaken for a man by the men who rescue her, while off
camera she relaxed in a black, tailormade man's suit.

Hemingway made a joke out of the hard side of her image by
calling her "the Kraut." Buried within his humor, however, was a
profound attraction to her projection of ambivalence,* and the day
would come when he would incorporate her into one of the switch-
ing games in his fiction. In *Islands in the Stream,* Thomas Hudson
dreams he is in bed with his first wife. Although in most respects
she is Hadleyesque, she is also a movie star with "silvery" hair, high
cheekbones and hollows beneath them "that could always break
your heart." It is she who begins the game, for Hudson is the passive
partner:

> "Should I be you or you be me?"
> "You have first choice."
> "I'll be you."
> "I can't be you. But I can try."

A few days after the *Ile de France* docked in New York, Hemingway asked for and received a loan of $3,300 from Arnold Gingrich,
against his future contributions to *Esquire.* The money served as a
down payment on a sleek, thirty-eight-foot power boat with two
engines, twin screws, double rudders, and six bunks. In a seeming
tribute to Pauline, Hemingway named the boat the *Pilar,* although
Pauline would often be excluded from expeditions aboard her.

The *Pilar* was delivered to Miami in early May and from there her
new owner brought her down to Key West. For the next few weeks,
he spent his mornings working on the manuscript of *Green Hills of
Africa,* his afternoons fishing for sailfish up and down the Keys, and
his evenings entertaining seriatim the Murphys, Ada MacLeish, and,
among other writers, Dawn Powell and her husband and Dos Passos
and Katy. At the end of the month, he was due to pay his annual
visit to Piggott, but to his relief Pauline left for her parents' home
without him, taking Patrick with her as well, while three-year-old
Gigi, as Gregory was now called, went off with the nursemaid, Ada
Stern, to her home in Syracuse, New York. Although any infraction
of her numerous rules would cause the terrible-tempered Ada to
explode, Gigi clung to her skirts for dear life, for his mother showed

---

* That this projection was the expression of a very real ambivalence is suggested by the dancer
Vera Zorina's claim in her autobiography that Dietrich tried to seduce her, as well as by
persistent rumors about the nature of some of her friendships with other women. Cf. Vera
Zorina, *Zorina,* New York, 1986, 114–115.

almost no interest in him. "Ada, don't leave me, please don't leave me!" the little boy would scream. "All right, I'll stay, you little shitsky," Ada would yell in reply. "But if you misbehave one more time. . . ." Years later, Pauline explained to her younger son that she had let Ada raise him because "I can't *stand* horrid little children. . . . But I loved you, darling, I really did, though I guess I didn't always show it."

From Piggott, Pauline wrote Hemingway that her father had just given her $2,308 from a savings account he had set up for her as a child and had somehow forgotten about. "Have no end of this filthy money," she exclaimed. "Just leave me know [if you wish some] and don't get another woman, your loving Pauline." But this pathetic attempt to bribe him into loving her by reminding him of her family's wealth had no effect on him, except possibly to make him more callous than ever in his treatment of her, for the very idea of being a bird in a gilded cage was intolerable to him. Thus, it was only 3½ weeks after Pauline's return to Key West on June 21 that he said goodbye to her and set off in the *Pilar* for Cuba.

There were other reasons besides his annoyance with his wife's anxious attentions that caused him to flee. He was sick and tired, he wrote Arnold Gingrich the day before he left, of playing around with "chicken shit sailfish that I feel sorry for interrupting when I catch." Marlin fishing off Cuba would represent a big improvement, but the only thing he really wanted to do was to get out to Africa again with a gun in his hands. He was also fed up with Key West because of all the freeloaders around town who were living off government programs like the Federal Emergency Relief Administration. Why not take kids out to Africa, he raged, "and let them die or have fun rather than grow up in this F. E. R. A. Jew administered phony of a town." In fact, he said, broadening his assault, he didn't "give a godamn" any more about America in general. "Well good evening Mr. G.," he finished off by saying, his voice rising with the intensity of his depression, "and if you love America o.k. Pal but it doesn't move me and hasn't moved me for a long time and still I can be moved. It's like trying to imagine Sarah Bernhardt good because she was good once. I say the hell with it. I've been better places and [seen] better people (Spain). Here we have the flora and the finest trees and all that but I like the fauna and what the hell."

7

DURING the three months he spent in Cuba in 1934, Hemingway
saw far more of Jane Mason and her back brace than he did of his
wife, whom he tried to keep in Key West as much as possible.
Frantically, Pauline resorted to changing the color of her hair. One
weekend, she even canceled her reservation on a Pan Am flight to
Havana so that her hairdresser could remove some of the pink from
the dye he was using. "I would like it a little gold before showing it
off to friends in public demonstrations," she explained to her errant
husband.

He reappeared in Key West at the end of October and his mood
was foul. To begin with, his luck as a marlin fisherman had been
unremittingly bad. Despite efforts that had sometimes begun at
dawn and lasted until sunset, he had not once caught a specimen
worth mentioning. His Africa book was close to completion, which
was gratifying, but he was very nervous about its quality. Jane Mason's announcement of her intention to spend part of the forthcoming winter in East Africa gave another boost to his nervousness. For
he knew she would be staying in a cool, charming house overlooking Lake Manyara that belonged to an English friend of hers, Colonel Richard Cooper, and Colonel Cooper was highly attractive to
women, as Hemingway had had occasion to observe during his and
Pauline's brief encounter with him in February. Finally, there was
the matter of Gertrude Stein. Even though a year had passed since
the publication of *The Autobiography of Alice B. Toklas,* he was still
brooding about her insults. At times, she inspired an anger in him
that almost matched his murderous feelings about his mother.
"You'd never believe it and there's no evidence now to prove it, but
she was a damned pleasant woman before she had the menopause,"
he wrote Arnold Gingrich on November 16, "and it goes against
my digestion to take shots at anyone who's ever been a friend no
matter how lousey [sic] they get to be finally. Besides, I've got the
gun and it's loaded and I know where the vital spots are. . . ."

When John and Katy Dos Passos returned to Key West and rented
a bungalow for several months, Hemingway greeted them with
surly wisecracks about Dos Passos's recent work for Hollywood,
the point of the wisecracks being that for all his indignant talk about
capitalism's debasement of American values the author of *The 42nd
Parallel* was dollar-crazy himself. Having known Hemingway for
most of her life, Katy did not hesitate to kid him in return about his
superior airs, yet she never flung the most appropriate truth in his

face, which was that in condemning her husband for having sold out
to Hollywood he was really talking about his sense of his own
corruption.

In his memoir, *The Best Times,* Dos Passos would remember the
winter of 1934–1935 as a period when Hemingway had not only
been edgy but often sick, mainly from throat infections. After complaining repeatedly about whatever was bothering him, he would
retire to the master bedroom before supper and allow Pauline and
the Dos Passoses to wait on him. While they perched on chairs
around his bed and ate from trays, he reclined against the pillows
sipping drinks. "We called it the *lit royale,*" Dos Passos recalled. "I
never knew an athletic, vigorous man who spent as much time in
bed as Ernest did."

Dos Passos and Katy were also in Hemingway's company on
April 7, 1935, when he shot himself in both legs and was forced to
take to his bed for the better part of a week. With Mike Strater—
not Pauline—making the party a foursome, they had set out in the
Pilar that morning with the idea of getting acquainted with Bimini,
a narrow Bahamian island two hundred thirty miles northeast of
Key West on the eastern edge of the Gulf Stream. For months Hemingway had been eager to go after the giant tuna that could be taken
in those waters. About twenty miles out into the stream, Dos Passos
and Strater each hooked a dolphin and Hemingway a huge shark.
After bringing the shark alongside the boat, Hemingway picked up
a gaff with his left hand in order to hold the monster steady and
with his right hand he shot it in the top of the head with a .22-caliber
automatic pistol. As the shark went into a tremendous spiral convulsion, the gaff suddenly broke, striking his shooting hand and
destroying his aim just as he was about to fire again. Involuntarily,
he pulled the trigger several times, hitting among other objects the
brass rail of the boat, and fragments of the ricocheting bullets struck
him in the legs. The helmsman whom he had recently hired hastily
turned the *Pilar* around and headed back to Key West. Katy was so
mad at Hemingway that she barely spoke to him the whole way. As
far as she was concerned, he had handled the pistol in such a careless
fashion that he could easily have killed somebody.

8

IN the late spring of 1935, after recovering from his leg wounds,
Hemingway lived in Bimini harbor aboard the *Pilar.* Pauline and the
children would be flying in sometime during the first part of the
summer, he knew, for a month-long stay at the Compleat Angler

Hotel, but for the moment he was at loose ends. Out of loneliness, he wrote a letter to Jane Mason, urging her to come on over for a little fishing and conversation about her African trip and her Mr. Cooper, as he put it. "[Africa] was fine," she wrote back, "and I did love the whole trip. 'My Mr. Cooper' sent salutations and such." Although she finally did show up in Bimini a few weeks later, it was so clear from the start that her heart now belonged to another daddy that if Hemingway had any ideas about a renewed romance he abandoned them forthwith. "My sunburn hurts and Mr. Cooper is lovely," Jane told him in a note of thanks written in Miami on June 20. "He's off to Wyoming [to hunt and fish] so pl-ease keep your fingers crossed so that things will go well for him. *Erregardless of me* and what the 'future holds' he deserves a break."

Upon his return to Key West in August, Hemingway found in his mail a copy of an article entitled "Ernest Hemingway: The Tragedy of Craftsmanship." It was the work of Ivan Kashkin, a Soviet critic and translator who had also been born in 1899. The mirthlessness of Hemingway's spasmodic smile, Kashkin maintained, betrayed the tragic disharmony within him that had now brought him to the edge of disintegration. *Mens morbida in corpore sano,* he said in diagnostic summation. While on balance the article was very perceptive, its argument that Hemingway's psychic discord could be seen in his face was true of some pictures of him but not true of others, and especially not of those that were taken of him at Bimini in the summer of 1935. Whether he is serious or smiling, the man in those pictures has the look of a man at ease in Zion.

In one of the most impressive of the Bimini photos, his gaze is steady, his forearms are thick and he is wearing boxing gloves, as is the young black man beside him. For that was the summer in which he issued a blanket challenge to the island's male inhabitants. If any of them, no matter how big, could go three rounds with him wearing six-ounce gloves, Hemingway would pay him a hundred dollars. In the course of a month, four challengers tried—and failed—to win that purse. The Bimini beach was also the scene of a fight between Hemingway and a professional heavyweight named Tom Heeney who had once fought Gene Tunney. Although the amateur didn't win, neither did the pro, and in retelling the story of the fight to friends the amateur made it sound like a terrific struggle.

George Brown, the erstwhile trainer of Harry Greb and the proprietor for many years of a gymnasium in New York, knew Hemingway very well for a quarter of a century. While he considered him "one of the finest men I've ever known," Brown's opinion both of his ability and his ethics as a boxer was low. As he told Gregory

Hemingway in the 1970s, the Bimini blacks had probably known very little about boxing, so that Hemingway would have had no trouble knocking them out, even though he was slow of foot and didn't have good coordination or quick reflexes. As for the fight with Tom Heeney, Brown was sure that Heeney had carried Hemingway. "I knew Tom for years when he had a bar in Miami, and he was a nice guy," said Brown. What amazed Brown about his own experiences in the ring with Hemingway was the novelist's persistence in trying various dirty tricks on him, kneeing him in the groin or bringing his fist down on the top of his head during a clinch, even after Brown had punished him severely for that kind of behavior. One day, Brown recalled, Hemingway went into the steamroom in the gym carrying a newspaper. Through the doorway, Brown could see him folding up the paper the short way and pounding it into his fist. When Brown entered the room, Hemingway came up to him in a friendly way—and jabbed the newspaper into his side as hard as he could. The infuriated Brown promptly hit him with such force that when he fell his head smacked the tile on the floor.

First and last, the gym manager had a completely straightforward view of the novelist's psychology in these set-to's—he was out to win, any way he could. It never occurred to Brown to wonder whether his old friend's outrageous tricks might not have been a means of courting punishment as well as of dishing it out.

CHAPTER EIGHTEEN

The Big Out

GREEN HILLS OF AFRICA was published on October 25, 1935. It is "absolutely true autobiography," Hemingway had assured Max Perkins in a letter from Bimini in July, and in a prefatory note in the book he publicly repeated this statement. Perhaps he would not have felt obliged to insist so strongly on the book's truthfulness had he not been so aware of its disingenuousness.

Out of love for his niece, Gus Pfeiffer had made the Hemingways' safari financially possible, and the author of *Green Hills* discharged his sense of indebtedness to Gus by depicting Pauline as utterly adorable. Poor Old Mama, she is coyly called throughout the book, P.O.M. for short, and her presence makes her hero-husband feel complete, he claims, as no one else's could. "The only person I really cared about, except the children, was with me and I had no wish to share this life with any one who was not there." A reference to women as harmful to writers crops up, to be sure, during a discussion with an Austrian named Kandisky* of the hazards of the literary life, and P.O.M. questions Hemingway about this.

> "What was that about all these women?"
> "What women?"
> "When you were talking about women."

---

* Whose real-life counterpart, Hans Koritschoner, was an old East Africa hand whom Hemingway had met on safari.

"The hell with them," I said. "Those are the ones you get involved
with when you're drunk."
"So that's what you do."
"No."

Whether or not this flat denial of marital infidelity echoed an actual
protestation of innocence, Hemingway put it down on paper during
his three-month sojourn in Havana when he was sleeping with Jane
Mason and Pauline was back in Key West fine-tuning the color of
her hair. Yet if the portrait of her marriage in *Green Hills* could not
possibly have struck Pauline as "absolutely true autobiography," the
important question for Hemingway was whether other readers
would accept it, and there is evidence that they did. Thus, the reviewer for *Time* was deeply moved by Hemingway's candor about
his personal feelings and especially by the "delicacy of his love for
his wife."

The self-confidence exuded by Hemingway in his talk with Kandisky was likewise intended to deceive his readers. In the lofty tone
of voice of a man who is above the battle he is talking about, he
informs the Austrian that in America "We do not have great writers.
Something happens to our good writers at a certain age. I can explain
but it is quite long and may bore you." Not until Kandisky pleads
with him to continue does he consent to spell out what he means. It
is not an inner urgency, in other words, that compels him to speak.

We destroy [our writers] in many ways. First, economically. They
make money. It is only by hazard that a writer makes money although
good books always make money eventually. Then our writers when
they have made some money increase their standard of living and
they are caught. They have to write to keep up their establishments,
their wives, and so on, and they write slop. It is slop not on purpose
but because it is hurried. Because they write when there is nothing to
say or no water in the well. Because they are ambitious. Then, once
they have betrayed themselves, they justify it and you get more slop.
Or else they read the critics. If they believe the critics when they say
they are great then they must believe them when they say they are
rotten and they lose confidence. At present we have two good writers
who cannot write because they have lost confidence through reading
critics. If they wrote, sometimes it would be good and sometimes not
so good and sometimes it would be quite bad, but the good would
get out. But they have read the critics and they must write masterpieces. The masterpieces the critics said they wrote. They weren't
masterpieces, of course. They were just quite good books. So now
they cannot write at all. The critics have made them impotent.

Lest there be any doubt that this gloomy analysis does not apply to the career of Ernest Hemingway, the hero of *Green Hills* then allows Kandisky to ask him a few questions about his own life. Kandisky begins by wondering whether he, too, wants to make money. "I am interested in other things," Hemingway grandly says. "I have a good life but I must write because if I do not write a certain amount I do not enjoy the rest of my life." "Then you are happy?" Kandisky asks. "Except when I think of other people," is the condescending reply.

2

ALTHOUGH a good many reviewers across the country professed an admiration for *Green Hills of Africa,* almost all of the big guns attacked the book. The New York *Herald Tribune*'s Lewis Gannett dismissed it as "just another safari." T. S. Matthews, writing in the *New Republic,* said, "It used to be pretty exciting, sitting down to read a new book by Hemingway, but now it's damn near alarming. . . . He thinks he can write a piece about anything and get away with it. He probably can, too. But it isn't the hot stuff he says he knows it is." The trouble with this book, Bernard De Voto declared in the *Saturday Review of Literature,* "is that it has few fine and no extraordinary passages, and large parts of it are dull. . . . [The author] also appears to have been reading a prose translation of *The Odyssey* too closely, and something that sounds like a German translation of Hemingway. With the result that whereas the typical Hemingway sentence used to run three to a line it now runs three to a page." But it remained for Edmund Wilson to raise the question of whether Hemingway had not become imprisoned by his myth. Perhaps, Wilson speculated in the *New Republic,* "he is beginning to be imposed on by the American publicity legend which has been created about him and which, as Kashkeen [Ivan Kashkin] has pointed out, has very little to do with what one actually finds in his stories. But, in any case, among his creations, he is certainly his own worst-drawn character, and he is his own worst commentator. His very prose style goes to pot."

These drubbings not only angered Hemingway, but contributed to the serious depression he sank into in December. A dejected communication from Fitzgerald, complaining of lung trouble, heart trouble, and insomnia, gave him a chance to speak in turn about his own sleeplessness. "Have been haveing [*sic*] a big dose of it now lately too," he reported to his old friend a few days before Christmas. "No matter what time I go to sleep [I] wake and hear the clock strike either one or two then lie wide awake and hear three, four and five. But since I have stopped giving a good goddamn about anything in the past it doesn't bother much and I just lie there and keep perfectly still and rest through it and you seem to get almost as much repose as though you slept." In the period immediately after the holidays, his condition worsened. To Pauline's mother, whom he liked very much and addressed as "Dear Mother," he admitted on January 26, 1936, that for most of the past month he had been getting up at two or so every morning and working until daylight because his mind was racing and he couldn't sleep. After deciding that more exercise would help him to relax, he had started going out in the *Pilar* in any kind of weather, so now he was all right, he assured Mrs. Pfeiffer. "Had never had the real old melancholia before," he added, "and am glad to have had it so I know what people go through. It makes me more tolerant of what happened to my father." Although he denied ever having had "the real old melancholia," his depression was, in fact, chronic, and a letter he sent to Dos Passos on February 13 described what some of its components were. "I felt that gigantic bloody emptiness and nothingness like couldn't ever fuck, fight write and was all for death."

Sometime during the first ten days in January—at the very height of his crisis, that is to say—he came across the first of Fitzgerald's "Crack-Up" essays in the February *Esquire*. "Of course all life is a process of breaking down," the essay began, and it ended with a slight mis-quotation from Matthew 5:13: "Ye are the salt of the earth. But if the salt hath lost its savour, wherewith shall it be salted?" In between these observations was an appalling account of how, at the age of thirty-nine, Fitzgerald had "cracked like an old plate."

In the second essay, entitled "Pasting It Together" and published the following month, the broken-down novelist invoked his insomnia as a metaphor of his daily condition ("at three o'clock in the morning, a forgotten package has the same tragic importance as a death sentence . . . and in a real dark night of the soul it is always three o'clock in the morning, day after day") and in a spasm of anguish declared that, after years of feeding off the various strengths of Edmund Wilson, Ernest Hemingway, and other men he had no personality left that he could call his own. "So there was not an 'I' any more—not a basis on which I could organize my self-respect. . . . It was strange to have no self—to be like a little boy left alone in a big house, who knew that now he could do anything he wanted to do, but found that there was nothing that he wanted to do." The third essay, "Handle With Care," ran in the April *Es-*

quire and revolved around "the idea of the Big Out." In "Echoes of the Jazz Age," published five years before, he had already spoken of his consciousness of those friends of his who had disappeared into the dark maw of violence. "A classmate killed his wife and himself on Long Island, another tumbled 'accidentally' from a skyscraper in Philadelphia, another purposely from a skyscraper in New York. One was killed in a speak-easy in Chicago; another was beaten to death in a speak-easy in New York and crawled home to the Princeton Club to die; still another had his skull crushed by a maniac's axe in an insane asylum where he was confined." Since then, the maw had claimed Zelda's brother, Anthony, who jumped to his death in 1933 from the window of a hospital in Mobile after suffering a nervous breakdown, and Fitzgerald's society friend, Emily Vanderbilt, who shot herself to death on a Montana ranch in the summer of 1935. It was not, however, of these tragedies that he spoke in "Handle With Care," but rather of Dorothy Parker and Van Wyck Brooks. "I had stood by while one famous contemporary played with the idea of the Big Out for half a year; I watched when another, equally eminent, spent months in an asylum unable to endure any contact with his fellow men."

So as to avoid their fate, Fitzgerald said, he had decided that while he would continue to be a writer, he would "cease any attempts to be a person—to be kind, just or generous." He was working on a smile, he declared, that would "combine the best qualities of a hotel manager, an experienced old social weasel, a headmaster on visitors' day, a colored elevator man, a pansy pulling a profile, a producer getting stuff at half its market value, a trained nurse coming on a new job, a body-vender [*sic*] in her first rotogravure, a hopeful extra swept near the camera and a ballet dancer with an infected toe." With the help of a voice teacher, he hoped to perfect a larynx that "will show no ring of conviction except the conviction of the person I am talking to." The sign CAVE CANEM was going to be hung permanently above his door. But he would endeavor to be "a correct animal," he announced in conclusion, "and if you throw me a bone with enough meat on it I may even lick your hand."

First to John and Katy Dos Passos, then to Max Perkins, Hemingway expressed his horror at Fitzgerald's shamelessness in nakedly parading his defeat before the eyes of the world. "The Esquire pieces seem to me to be so miserable," he exclaimed to Perkins. "I always knew he couldn't think—he never could—but he had a marvellous talent and the thing is to use it—not whine in public. Good God, people go through that emptiness many times in life and come out and do work."

Hemingway knew whereof he spoke. After suffering through one of the worst sieges of depression in his life, he was now working very nearly as well as he ever had. By the time the remaining issues of the April *Esquire* had been taken off the shelves in the drugstores, he had finished writing "The Snows of Kilimanjaro" (which he had started writing the previous summer and then set aside) and had begun and finished "The Short Happy Life of Francis Macomber." Yet if these brilliant stories tacitly rebuked the failure of nerve exposed in "The Crack-Up," they nevertheless were saturated with "the idea of the Big Out." Along with another fine story he wrote in this period, "The Capital of the World," about an assistant waiter in a bullfighters' *pensión* in Madrid who bleeds to death from a wound he receives in his lower abdomen during a make-believe bullfight involving two heavy-bladed, razor-sharp meat knives tied fast to the legs of a chair, "Kilimanjaro" and "Macomber" signaled that a new phase in Hemingway's imaginative life had begun, in which the main character dies an untimely death, but not in a way that could be termed suicide. Although this development would eventually include several novel-length works, its most memorable representations were the brief masterpieces produced at its outset. In "Kilimanjaro" and "Macomber," an author who had appeared in *Green Hills of Africa* to be completely walled up inside a myth of himself was once again in touch with who he actually was.

3

ORIGINALLY, the dying writer in "Kilimanjaro" was named Henry Walden, even though Hemingway had never read Thoreau's book and had no plans to do so. But on reconsideration he decided to identify his protagonist with Henry James by calling him Harry, out of admiration for James's marvelously ironic examination in "The Lesson of the Master" of a famous writer's corruption.

Harry is dying of the same infection that Dr. Hemingway, on the day of his death, feared he was about to contract. A thorn scratch on his right leg has developed into gangrene. While waiting for the plane that will bear him away to a hospital, he has ample time to quarrel with Helen, his wife. All the negative feelings about Pauline that Hemingway suppressed in *Green Hills of Africa* are conveyed through Harry's utter boredom with Helen. Unlike "poor Scott Fitzgerald," who had considered the rich "a special glamorous race and when he found they weren't it wrecked him just as much as any other thing that wrecked him," Harry has always known that "the rich were dull and they drank too much, or they played too much backgammon," and he doesn't regard hard-drinking Helen as an exception. He doesn't love her and he never has, he cruelly informs her. "You bitch," he calls her at one point. "You rich bitch."

Harry's hatred of his wife seems unqualified, yet it is not his only sense of her. For Helen is totally concerned with his welfare. She offers to read to him, she tries to keep him from having a whiskey and soda because she knows that alcohol is very bad if you have gangrene, she goes off to shoot a Tommy ram so that the cook can make a nourishing broth that he might like. These gestures lead him to remember that while she wasn't pretty he liked her face, and that she was enormously well read and had a great talent and appreciation for the bed. "She *was* very good to him," he acknowledges to himself. "She was a fine woman, marvellous really." The person Harry really hates is himself. Once again, the story exposes feelings that had been left out of *Green Hills of Africa*.

To blame his wife for having destroyed his talent by leading him, with her "bloody money," into a life of self-indulgence is nonsense, Harry realizes. "He had destroyed his talent himself. . . . He had destroyed his talent by not using it, by betrayals of himself and what he believed in, by drinking so much that he blunted the edge of his perceptions, by laziness, by sloth, and by snobbery, by pride and by prejudice, by hook and by crook. . . . What was his talent anyway? It was a talent all right but instead of using it he had traded on it." Many factors in Hemingway's own life lay behind his protagonist's self-condemnation—his guilty sense of spending too much time playing instead of working, his fear of his drinking, his consciousness of how many of the new friendships he had formed were with millionaires, his pained awareness of the inadequacy of his recent books, his realization of the destructiveness of publicity. But perhaps the most significant of all the similarities between author and protagonist was symbolized by that phrase of Harry's about trading on his talent. For it echoed a word in the letter that Hemingway had been handed by his mother as she commanded him to leave Windemere —and that was still in his files in Key West. "Stop trading on your handsome face, to fool little gullible girls, and neglecting your duties to God and your Saviour Jesus Christ," Grace had admonished her son. In substantive essence as well as phrasing, that ancient criticism found its way into "Kilimanjaro." Harry has made his "bread and butter," he admits, by lying to his credulous wife; indeed, he has "sold vitality, in one form or another, all his life and when your affections are not too involved you give much better value for the money." In the dark night of his soul, Harry judges his record of behavior in the same way that his creator's had once been judged by his mother.

As Harry lies on his cot in the shade of a mimosa tree, looking out into the glare of the plain, he sees three huge birds squatting obscenely and a dozen more sailing above. These creatures are the horrid portents of his fate. Yet the presence of death is actually not a horror to him, for the horror has passed, he makes clear, now that he no longer feels pain. For years, he admits, death "had obsessed him." Now, however, "It was strange how easy being tired enough made it." When death finally comes for him, the sensation is akin to flying in a Puss Moth plane toward the highest mountain in Africa shining unbelievably white in the sun. In "The Snows of Kilimanjaro," the hero's death wish is fulfilled in a vision of beauty.

Which is not, however, the end of the story. Hemingway's own death had become so real an event in his mind that he could even imagine what it might be like for his wife to find his body, and he testified to this in "Kilimanjaro." Awakened by the cry of a hyena, Helen shines a flashlight on Harry's cot. The bulk of his body is lying under the mosquito bar, but his leg is hanging down alongside the cot. The dressings have all come down, exposing the flesh that has rotted halfway up his thigh. Outside the tent, the hyena makes the same strange noise that had awakened her. "But she did not hear him for the beating of her heart." The scene anticipated the ghastly moment a quarter of a century later when the terrified Mary Hemingway would come downstairs on a Sunday morning in Ketchum, Idaho, after being awakened by the sound of a shot, to discover her husband's crumpled form lying in a pool of blood and brain material on the linoleum tile floor of the front foyer of their house.

4

THIRTY-FIVE-YEAR-OLD Francis Macomber is tall, dark, and wealthy, and has publicly shown himself to be a coward shortly before the beginning of the story that bears his name by not standing up to the charge of a wounded lion out of the brush. That his cowardice is a part of a more encompassing problem involving sexual performance is brought out in the first scene through doubletalk. Macomber and his wife, Margot, and the English white hunter, Robert Wilson, are sitting at a table in the dining tent, preparing to have a drink before lunch.

"Will you have lime juice or lemon squash?" Macomber asked.
"I'll have a gimlet," Robert Wilson told him.

"I'll have a gimlet too. I need something," Macomber's wife said.

"I suppose it's the thing to do," Macomber agreed. "Tell him [the mess boy] to make three gimlets."

In ordering a gin drink named for a boring-tool, in response to Macomber's suggestion that he might like a lemon squash, Wilson calls attention to the difference between his virility and his rich employer's, and in quickly indicating which drink she herself prefers, Margot signals her readiness to share the white hunter's double cot that night.

Except for the fact that her hair is dark and that she is "well-kept" rather than young, the wonderfully handsome, perfectly oval-faced Margot is the spitting image of Jane Mason. In an essay called "The Art of the Short Story," written in Spain in "the dangerous summer" of 1959 but not published until 1981, Hemingway would affirm, without mentioning her name, that Jane had indeed been his model for Margot. "I invented her complete with handles from the worst bitch I knew (then) and when I first knew her she'd been lovely. Not my dish, not my pigeon, not my cup of tea, but lovely for what she was, and I was her all of the above, which is whatever you make of it." As for the white hunter, Robert Wilson, he based him on his idol, Philip Percival, Hemingway declared, albeit he slightly disguised him for family and business reasons.

The misleading statements about Jane Mason were the work of a drunken and demoralized man, desperately clinging to his myth. The prototype for Margot Macomber had not only been the author's dish at one time, but might have continued to be, had she not fallen in love with Colonel Cooper. The aging Hemingway, however, could not bring himself to admit this, and hence could not have further acknowledged that, in writing of Macomber's discovery in the middle of the night that Margot is not in the other cot in their tent, he was drawing on his own fund of jealousy. His further claim that the white hunter in "Macomber" was the fictional equivalent of Philip Percival was if anything an even more egregious lie, and Percival would surely have been insulted if he had lived long enough to read it. The interpretation of the ending of the story that Hemingway gave to an interviewer in 1953 is likewise not to be trusted. "Francis' wife hates him because he's a coward," Hemingway told the interviewer. "But when he gets his guts back, she fears him so much she has to kill him—shoots him in the back of the head."

Except for "Big Two-Hearted River," no other work of Hemingway's has been read so unrigorously so many times as "Macomber," and not merely because of the author's own comments about it.

Although a few doughty dissenters have also made themselves heard, critical opinion for almost half a century has overwhelmingly supported Edmund Wilson's contention in "Bourdon Gauge of Morale" that "the male [in "Macomber"] saves his soul at the last minute, and then is actually shot down by his woman, who does not want him to have a soul. Here Hemingway has at last got what [James] Thurber calls the war between men and women right out in the open and has written a terrific fable of the impossible civilized woman who despises the civilized man for his failure in initiative and nerve and then jealously tries to break him down as soon as he begins to exhibit any."

Wilson disliked the self-assured hero of *Green Hills of Africa* and had said so with brilliant acerbity. Nevertheless, that factitious figure coerced the critic's judgment of "Macomber." Starting from the assumption, apparently, that Hemingway of all writers would certainly sympathize with a man who knew about guns and was good at killing animals, Wilson seems to have further assumed that the white hunter in "Macomber" was speaking for the author; and since the white hunter accuses Margot of murdering her husband, Wilson concluded that she was guilty as charged. "The emotion which principally comes through in 'Francis Macomber,' " said Wilson, "is a growing antagonism to women." If he had trusted the tale, rather than his view of the author, he might have seen that that was too simple a formulation.

As they are drinking their gimlets before lunch, Margot makes a number of sarcastic remarks at Macomber's expense and then begins to cry and has to leave the table. When she returns twenty minutes later, her manner is coldly controlled and there is an edge to her comments that discomfits the white hunter as well as her husband. As she will make even clearer as the story proceeds, she has a genuine distaste for hunting. "Blowing things' heads off" is butchery masquerading as sport, the odds are brutally stacked against the animals, and Macomber—whom she loves in spite of his failure to meet her needs—is making an ass of himself in pursuing a barbaric pastime to which he is unsuited and may well endanger his life by doing so. "I've dropped the whole thing," she says, sitting down at the table. "What importance is there to whether Francis is any good at killing lions? That's not his trade. That's Mr. Wilson's trade. Mr. Wilson is really very impressive killing anything. You do kill anything, don't you?" Resentfully, Wilson thinks to himself, "They are . . . the hardest in the world; the hardest, the cruelest, the most predatory and the most attractive and their men have softened or gone to pieces nervously as they have hardened. . . . She is away for twenty minutes and she is back, simply enamelled in that American female cruelty. They are the damnedest women. Really the damnedest." These comments of Wilson's have an energy in them that cannot be denied. Yet they have to be set in the context of Margot's scornful opinion of him and of what the story reveals in other ways about the sort of man he is.

The Englishman's face is red; indeed, it is very red; indeed, it is baked red. The emphasis hints at his bloodymindedness—at his British colonial bloodymindedness, for in the thirties cartographers were still coloring the British Empire red. "Flat, blue, machine-gunner's eyes" and a smile that is only pleasant "if you do not notice how his eyes showed when he was hurt" are further indications of Wilson's coarse and unappetizing nature, and they are confirmed beyond doubt by his reaction to the mess boy who looks at the humiliated Macomber in a way that the white hunter deems disrespectful. For he threatens the boy with fifteen lashes, even though whipping black servants is illegal. But "they prefer it to . . . fines," Wilson callously explains to Macomber.

On the morning of the lion hunt, a flashback reveals, Wilson had armed himself with a "short, ugly, shockingly big-bored .505 Gibbs." It is another instance of his brutality. As Philip Percival would later emphasize in an unpublished autobiography, a Gibbs rifle is so powerful as to render its use on safaris unsportsmanlike, which is why he himself had never carried one. In "Macomber," however, the awful roar of the Gibbs—"*ca-ra-wong! . . . carawong!*" —is heard both on the lion hunt and again the next day when the hunters go after buffalo.

Three huge, tanklike bulls moving at a gallop across the edge of an open prairie; the hunters' wild pursuit of them in a car going forty-five miles an hour; the excellent marksmanship demonstrated by both Wilson and Macomber as they tumble out of the car and start firing: these are the main components of one of the most exciting action sequences that Hemingway ever produced. After all three bulls have supposedly been dispatched, a white-faced, admittedly frightened Margot, sitting in the car, can't help expressing admiration for her husband's performance. "You were marvellous, darling," she says. "What a ride," she adds. Yet as soon as she has calmed her nerves with a slug of whiskey, her distaste for the whole enterprise returns. "It seemed very unfair to me," she remarks to Wilson, "chasing those big helpless things in a motor car."

"Did it?" said Wilson.
"What would happen if they heard about it in Nairobi?"

"I'd lose my licence for one thing. Other unpleasantnesses," Wilson said, taking a drink from the flask. "I'd be out of business."

"Really?"

"Yes, really."

"Well," said Macomber, and he smiled for the first time all day. "Now she has something on you."

"You have such a pretty way of putting things, Francis," Margot Macomber said.

At this ugly juncture, a gun-bearer approaches them and says that one of the bulls isn't dead and has got up and gone into the brush. The test of courage that Macomber had failed against the wounded lion can therefore be repeated against a wounded buffalo if he wishes. Not only is he ready for the test, he is eager for it. Margot, for her part, goes white in the face once again and looks ill. As for Wilson, his thoughts move toward the sexual implications of his client's transformation. "The great American boy-men. Damned strange people. But he liked this Macomber now. Damned strange fellow. Probably meant the end of cuckoldry too. Well, that would be a damned good thing."

As Macomber and Wilson get ready to head for the brush, Margot speaks quite contemptuously to her husband about how awfully brave he has suddenly become, "but her contempt was not secure. She was very afraid of something." Macomber laughs a very natural hearty laugh and admits that he really has become brave. Margot bitterly asks him whether it isn't sort of late for that. It is the last remark she will ever address to her husband, and Hemingway lifts the veil a little on the state of mind that has prompted it. "Because she had done the best she could for many years back and the way they were together now was no one person's fault." For all of her frustration-born bitchiness, she finally doesn't make her husband the scapegoat for the unhappy life they have had together. Her bitterness proceeds out of a tragic view of their marriage, not out of a petty wish to assign blame.

From the car, Margot sees the bull burst out of the brush and charge straight toward Wilson and her husband. Both men keep firing, but the bull keeps coming. Aiming carefully, even though the bull is almost on him, the unflinching Macomber shoots again. Whereupon he feels "a sudden white-hot, blinding flash explode inside his head and that was all he ever felt." Margot, firing a 6.5 Mannlicher from the car, "had hit her husband two inches up and a little to one side of the base of his skull."

Wilson instantly leaps to the conclusion that Margot has deliberately shot Macomber, and he thinks he understands why. She was deathly afraid that her husband's newfound manliness might mean that he now had the courage to leave her, and so she killed him. "He *would* have left you too," Wilson says to her, as she sits crying in the corner of the car. What makes agreeing with Wilson—or with Edmund Wilson—an impossibility for the careful reader is that the story specifically states that Margot intended to kill the buffalo. "Mrs. Macomber, in the car, had shot at the buffalo with the 6.5 Mannlicher as it seemed about to gore Macomber." She fired in an effort to save her husband's life, not end it. From where she stood, it had looked as if the bull was about to smash into Macomber and kill him; if she had really wanted Macomber to die, her impulse surely would have been to do nothing. In piling an accusation of murder atop Margot's bereavement, Wilson has merely proved once again that he is a brute—and has found a perfect protection, moreover, against the threat of her reporting him in Nairobi for unsportsmanlike conduct. Edmund Wilson to the contrary, "Macomber" is not a fable about a soul-destroying bitch.

Rather, it is a fable about the perils of self-overcoming. It is not wifely malevolence that brings Macomber down, but his own dangerous aspiration to be recognized as intensely masculine. Two contrasting aspects of the author are split down the middle in the story. Brutish Robert Wilson, with his double cot and his big rifle, incarnates the Hemingway of the myth, while the doubt-haunted Macomber represents the Hemingway for whom the dark had always been peopled and always would be. Near the end of the fable, the doubter succeeds in winning the approval of the brute. He becomes, in short, the sort of man he is not, and he pays for it with his life. Just as the wife in "Kilimanjaro" is finally relieved of blame by her husband for the tragic waste of his talent, so a critically important narrative detail absolves Margot of responsibility for Macomber's tragedy. In making clear her lack of culpability, Hemingway demonstrated that his ability to portray real women with real problems and to respond to their unhappiness with an overarching sympathy had not vanished with the completion of "Cat in the Rain." Yet when he talked to an interviewer about "Macomber" a decade and a half after he wrote it, he was again hiding behind the Hemingway of myth and thus gave the story a misogynistic gloss.

5

WHILE working on both the African stories, Hemingway was cheered by a visit from his sister Ursula, who at once fell in love with Key West. Late one afternoon, however, she came back to the house in tears. At a cocktail party, Wallace Stevens had forcefully informed her that her famous brother was a sap and not really very much of a man. On hearing this, Hemingway set off with Ursula into the rainy twilight and encountered Stevens just as he was leaving the party. The six-foot-two, 225-pound poet was a muscular fellow who fancied himself a fighter, but after the two men squared off, Stevens missed with his Sunday punch and Hemingway put him down in a puddle of water in the street. Following two more knockdowns, Stevens connected with a blow to the jaw—and broke his hand in two places. At which point, Hemingway knocked him down again. Several days later, Stevens called at the Hemingway home and apologized to Ursula and made peace with his erstwhile opponent. Hemingway promised not to tell anybody about what had happened so as not to damage the credibility of Stevens's official story that he had injured his face and hand falling downstairs. But no sooner had Stevens left town than Hemingway recapitulated the fight story in detail in a gleeful letter to Sara Murphy. "Nice dear good Mr. Stevens," he sneered. "I hope he doesn't brood about this and take up archery or machine gunnery."

His wish to humiliate fellow writers flared up again the following September in a contretemps with Fitzgerald. In the course of reading "The Snows of Kilimanjaro" in the August *Esquire,* Fitzgerald had come upon the dying hero's disdainful reference to poor Scott Fitzgerald's romantic awe of the rich. From Asheville, North Carolina, where Zelda had recently been admitted to Highland Hospital and he himself was battling depression, the offended novelist wrote Hemingway a dignified note asking that he lay off him in print. "If I choose to write *de profundis* sometimes," he said apropos of "The Crack-Up," "it doesn't mean I want friends praying aloud over my corpse." Hemingway's response was apparently destroyed by Fitzgerald, but not before he showed it to Arnold Gingrich, who described it many years later as having been written in language that "you'd hesitate to use on a yellow dog." To Max Perkins, Fitzgerald simply reported that he had received a "crazy letter" from Hemingway, "telling me about what a great Writer he was and how much he loved his children," but to a recently cast-off mistress, Beatrice Dance, he spoke more caustically. "[Hemingway] is quite as nervously broken down as I am but it manifests itself in different ways. His inclination is toward megalomania and mine toward melancholy."

Hemingway in turn wrote Perkins about Fitzgerald's letter. Considering "those awful things about himself" that he'd said in *Esquire,*

his old friend's huffy reaction to the crack about him in "Kilimanjaro" was damned curious, in his opinion. As for what he had said
to Fitzgerald in reply, he maintained that he had simply made clear
to him that for five years he hadn't written about people he knew
because he felt sorry for them, but that from here on he was going
to be a novelist, not a gentleman. As Perkins undoubtedly had no
trouble recognizing, this threatening statement was a nasty paraphrase of Fitzgerald's description in "The Crack-Up" of his own
resolve to be less kind.

Not wishing to alienate Hemingway, Perkins carefully concealed
from him, and from most people, his massive disgust with his vanity
and cruelty. With Elizabeth Lemmon, however, the lovely Virginia
aristocrat with whom he had been conducting an agonizingly platonic love affair since 1922, he shared at least some of his negative
feelings about the most famous writer on his list. In the magazine
version of "Kilimanjaro," Hemingway had had Harry remember
that "poor Scott Fitzgerald . . . had started a story once [it was "The
Rich Boy"] that began, 'The very rich are different from you and
me,' " and that "someone" had wisecracked, " 'Yes, they have
more money.' " However, Perkins confided to Elizabeth, he himself
had been present when that wisecrack had been made, and Hemingway had been the butt of it, not the author. Over lunch in a New
York restaurant, said Perkins, Hemingway had told him and the
Irish writer Mary Colum that he was "getting to know the rich."
Perhaps it was the sound of self-satisfaction in his voice that inspired
Mary Colum to rejoin, "The only difference between the rich and
other people is that the rich have more money."

PART FIVE

1936–1945

CHAPTER NINETEEN

The Spanish Tragedy

FROM THE NORDQUIST RANCH near Cody, Wyoming, Hemingway wrote to Max Perkins on September 26, 1936, to say that ever since the outbreak of war in Spain two months before he had hated not being on the scene "worse than anything in the world," but that he hoped to get there very soon. The letter was also full of enthusiasm about the three grizzly bears he had shot in the last six days, and so was the letter he wrote the same day to Archibald MacLeish—except that halfway through his mood suddenly switched. "Me I like life very much. So much it will be a big disgust when have to shoot myself. Maybe pretty soon I guess although will arrange to be shot in order not to have bad effect on kids."

If only the carnage in Spain would continue until somebody invited him to cover it, he could arrange to be shot if he wanted to with no questions asked. But that was only one of the reasons why the war attracted him. Exposing himself to its dangers might furnish him with new materials for fiction, as his African safari had, and it might assuage his guilt for living a gilded life in the midst of a worldwide depression. Furthermore, it would constitute a perfect excuse for getting away from Pauline. Thus when John Wheeler, the general manager of the news service known as the North American Newspaper Alliance, wrote to him in late November to inquire if he had any interest in becoming a war correspondent once again, there was no doubt as to what his answer would be.

All told, he would pay four visits to the war-stricken country, in the spring and fall of 1937 and the spring and fall of 1938. From his reports from the front and his other activities in behalf of the Loyalist cause, as well as from his preachment of social solidarity in a new novel, *To Have and Have Not* (1937), he would emerge in the eyes of the world as a man of strong leftist sympathies. And this public drama would unfold simultaneously with a private drama. Not only would the war offer him refuge from Pauline, but he would find in Martha Gellhorn a woman to share it with. In pursuit of the danger and excitement of being under fire, he would become the willing object of her pursuit, even as Pauline had chased him while he was still married to Hadley. Ultimately, the adulterous relationship with Gellhorn would lead to marriage. But in both the marriage and the romance with left-wing politics, Hemingway would discover himself to have been sadly deceived.

2

THE Popular Front alliance which assumed power in Spain in February 1936 had the backing of less than 50 percent of the voters. Besides being regarded with fear or contempt by the millions of Spaniards who had voted for the rightist National Front, the new government could not control the militants of the Left, and the nation descended into chaos in a matter of months. By mid-June, 160 churches had been burned to the ground, 269 political murders had occurred, 69 political centers had been wrecked, 10 newspaper offices had been sacked, 113 general strikes and 228 partial strikes had been called, armed peasants had occupied many large estates and divided up the land, and gun warfare between the two vast trade unions of Spain, the CNT and UGT, was raging. Most of the random violence perpetrated by the Left was the work of Anarchists, Syndicalists, adherents of the newly organized revolutionary Marxist party, POUM (Partido Obrero de Unificación Marxista), street gangs affiliated with the Communist-Socialist Youth Movement, and members of the Republican riot police, the Guardia de Asalto, whose official mission was to help keep the peace. Gangs affiliated with the leading youth organization on the Right, the Juventudes de Acción Popular, were meanwhile busy with provocations and atrocities of their own, including some of the church burnings for which the Left was blamed. The final blow to civil order was struck during the second week in July when the arch-conservative parliamentary leader, Calvo Sotelo, was murdered by Assault Guards in reprisal for the killing of two Guards by a rightist gang. On July 17, the cunning and ambitious General Francisco Franco led an Army mutiny in Morocco, and within two days the uprising spread to the mainland.

Not only had a civil war between Loyalists and Nationalists begun, but a proxy world war, as Franco's forces immediately received the support of Mussolini's Italy and Hitler's Germany, while the Popular Front was backed by the Soviet Union, Mexico, and the foreign volunteers of the International Brigades, most of whom were Communists. On the Loyalist side, moreover, there was a war within a war. Barcelona in the spring of 1937 was the scene of bitter fighting between the Communists and an Anarchist-POUM alliance, the quelling of which required the intervention of the navy and four thousand Assault Guards. The subsequent refusal of the revolutionary Socialist Prime Minister, Francisco Largo Caballero, to dissolve the POUM was then used as an excuse by the Communists to force him from office. His successor was Juan Negrín, a moderate Socialist, but the Communists' old enemy, Angel Galarza, was removed as Minister of Interior and Reds took over the under-secretaryships in the Ministry, as well as key police posts in numerous cities and towns.

The ouster of Caballero and the chess moves by the Communists thereafter were reminiscent of Stalin's Byzantine machinations in the Soviet Union, while other political developments inside Loyalist Spain also bore the Kremlin leader's trademark. Thus, the Communist-controlled Madrid police conspired with two members of Franco's Falange whom they had captured and intimidated to manufacture a phony plan calling for an uprising in the city by a Nationalist "Fifth Column," and to forge on the back of the plan a letter to Franco bearing the signature of the POUM leader, Andrés Nin. With this "evidence" in hand, the Communists were able to order the arrest and torture of Nin and his principal associates. (Because Nin didn't buckle under the torture, apparent plans for a show trial along the lines of the Moscow trials of Soviet "traitors" had to be abandoned.) By the end of the war, countless other non-Communist leftists had either been tortured to death or executed after drumhead trials in Communist-controlled prisons. One of the earliest and most distinguished of these victims was José Robles, a lecturer on Spanish literature at Johns Hopkins University, who had been Dos Passos's friend for years and the translator of his work. In all likelihood, Robles was liquidated because he had served as the interpreter for General Jan Antonovich Berzin, the head of the Russian military mission in Spain, and consequently knew too much about the relations between the Spanish war ministry and the Kremlin to suit the taste of the Spanish section of the Russian secret police, the NKVD.

Rudyard Kipling, who died in 1936, once slightingly referred to "brittle intellectuals who crack beneath the strain"; at no time was this remark more justified than in the year of his death. From a thousand pulpits, anti-Fascist intellectuals who could not stand the strain of facing up to the complexities of the Spanish tragedy romanticized the Loyalist cause into a thrillingly united struggle by democracy-loving have-nots for political freedom and social justice, thereby ignoring on the one hand the appalling disarray within the non-Communist Left and refusing on the other hand to face up to the fact that the anti-Fascist propaganda being generated by the Comintern's cleverest liars, Willi Muenzenberg and Otto Katz (both later liquidated on Stalin's orders), was a rhetorical cover for the imperialistic designs of a system no less ruthless than Hitler's and infinitely more so than the repressive régime that Franco would establish.

An incapacity to stand up to strain was not Hemingway's problem, however. If he was fatally susceptible to the temper of the times, it was mainly because of his lack of political sophistication. Only at rare moments in his life had he taken an interest in politics, yet he proposed to make his way through the Spanish labyrinth. The results were foreordained. Although he presented himself to his readers as an unfoolable "Papa," he in fact was easily fooled, and the Communists were well served by him until the outcome of the war was no longer in doubt.

At no point during his visits to Spain did he consider reporting the conflict from the Nationalist as well as the Loyalist side. For as he indicated in a letter to Pauline's parents a few weeks before his first trip, he had already decided what the war was about. To placate Mrs. Pfeiffer's Catholic sensibilities, he began by saying that "the Reds may be as bad as they say," but then added emphatically that "they are the people of the country," and that the war was a struggle between them and "the absentee landlords, the moors, the italians and the Germans." Another indication that his mind was fully made up before he left the States was his decision to spend most of the month of January 1937 working in New York City with the young novelist Prudencio de Pereda on a pro-Loyalist propaganda film *Spain in Flames;* still another indication was that on a second visit to New York in February he joined Dos Passos, MacLeish, and Lillian Hellman in founding Contemporary Historians, Inc., for the purpose of funding and producing a documentary film on the war that the Dutch movie director Joris Ivens had in mind and for which Hemingway would write the narration. MacLeish, a sentimental liberal, had a benign view of Stalin's foreign-policy intentions that would last into the late forties and early fifties. Despite a persona of fierce integrity, Lillian Hellman consistently followed the Soviet line. Ivens had been a card-carrying Communist from 1928 to 1930 and was still a Party sympathizer. Alone of the four, the anarchist-oriented Dos Passos was capable of making independent-minded political judgments from which Hemingway might have learned something. But it was with Dos Passos, alas, that he would very soon quarrel.

Ivens and his young Dutch cameraman, John Fernhout (called Ferno), were frequently joined by Hemingway on their expeditions into the battle zones around Madrid in the spring of 1937. In between stretches of filming the fighting, Ivens reinforced his new friend's home-grown notions about the war with Marxist explanations delivered in flawless English. Once the film was in the can and named *The Spanish Earth,* Ivens asked for help in reworking his statement of its theme, and Hemingway obliged with three sentences that perfectly complemented the pitch of the Comintern's agitprop department. "We gained the right to cultivate our land by democratic elections. Now the military cliques and absentee landlords attack to take our land from us again. But we fight for the right to irrigate and cultivate this Spanish Earth which the nobles kept idle for their own amusement."

In the dispatches he filed as a NANA correspondent, Hemingway created the impression that enemy aircraft and artillery bombardments, along with curtains of machine-gun and automatic-rifle fire, were constantly threatening his life. Even when he went to bed he was in danger, for his suite in the Hotel Florida in Madrid was on the front side of the building, facing squarely toward the Nationalists' big guns two miles away, he explained to his readers. As had been the case in 1918, there were important elements of truth in his mythmaking. That his life was indeed in jeopardy many times, there can be no doubt. Nor is there much question that he behaved admirably under fire, for numerous witnesses have testified to this. And *The New York Times*'s Herbert Matthews has described how Hemingway saved his life:

> It was during the Ebro battle in 1938; we had to take a rowboat to get over from the west to the east bank because the bridges had been bombed down. The current was swift and there were some nasty rapids a few hundred yards down the river, so the boat was being partly pulled across by a rope, which snapped. We started drifting swiftly toward the rapids. Hemingway quickly took the oars . . . and

by an extraordinary exhibition of strength . . . got us safely across. He was a good man in a pinch.

Yet he was not suicidally brave, nor was he willing to allow his companions to take foolish risks. Inasmuch as he was sharing that suite in the Florida with a fellow correspondent, Martha Gellhorn, he most certainly would not have gone on living there if it had been as exposed to artillery bombardment as he implied. In such places, moreover, as "The Old Homestead," a top-floor roost in a shell-smashed apartment building overlooking the fighting in the Casa del Campo, his conduct was mainly marked by caution. Ivens and Matthews and the other observers who also took advantage of this splendid position were constantly being warned by him that the slightest reflection from a pair of binoculars would give away their position to Franco's Moorish artillery spotters and provoke a burst of fire. "If you wanted to be properly sniped," he later wrote in the short story "Night Before Battle," "all you had to do was use a pair of [field] glasses without shading them adequately. They [the Moors] could shoot, too, and they . . . kept my mouth dry all day." The author of "Kilimanjaro" and "Macomber" didn't put his obsession with early death behind him in Spain—far from it. On the other hand, he still loved life, and being in his favorite country in Europe served to remind him of how much. The Russian writer Ilya Ehrenburg's impression of Hemingway in this period was that he was basically a cheerful man who was firmly attached to the land of living, albeit "attracted to danger, death, great deeds." Ehrenburg further believed that the heroic defenders of Madrid had a potent effect on Hemingway. Because of their refusal to surrender, "he was revived and rejuvenated." Perhaps at this time Hemingway exemplified Nietzsche's belief that suicide is a great consolation, because by means of it one successfully gets through many a bad night.

After the first phase of the historic fighting on the Guadalajara front, Hemingway reported that he had spent several days going over the ground with the commanders who directed it and the officers and men under them, checking the positions and following the tank trails. It was the first but not the last instance in which he would publicly hint that he knew so much more about warfare than mere journalists like Herbert Matthews and Sefton Delmer that the Loyalist commanders viewed him as a consultant. The military Munchausenism to which he was given in private was even more outrageous. Following his second visit to Spain, for instance, he was upset by an article in *Time* which seemed to him to imply that Matthews had been the only correspondent at the battle of Teruel.

In an incoherent letter to Hadley, who now was married to Paul Mowrer, he said,

> Tell Paul I'd like to tell him about Teruel some time. After I took Mathews [sic] and Delmer on my own responsability [sic] when they'd been refused passes, had the censor so she was prepared to lose her job to let our stuff through (they were only allowed to send the communique) got the first story of the battle to N. Y. ten hours ahead of Mathews even, went back, made the whole attack with the infantry, entered town behind one company dinamiters [sic] and three of infantry, filed that, went back and had most godwonderful housetohouse fighting story ready to put on wire when Nana [NANA] cabled they didn't want any more. Too expensive I guess.

At how many points this letter departed from truth is hard to say, but what is indisputable is that the man who wrote it was not a good reporter. Far from being superior to Herbert Matthews, he often was reduced to duplicating his stuff, and after his third visit to Spain John Wheeler did not renew his contract with NANA.

The officer who guided him around the Guadalajara front was an ex-Prussian Colonel turned Communist, named Hans Kahle. Because Kahle was the commander of the XIth International Brigade, Hemingway was frequently invited to visit it, and he came to know the officers and men of the XIIth and XIVth Brigades as well, especially the political commissar of the XIIth, the heroically handsome German Communist writer, Gustave Regler, and the commander of the XIVth, the Polish General "Walter," whose scarred, shaved head made him heroically ugly. If there was any high-ranking Communist officer whom he took an aversion to, it was the Frenchman André Marty, who he thought was crazy. The commander of the International Brigade base at Albacete, Marty owed his position not to military achievement, but to an unswerving loyalty to Bolshevism that went back to 1919, when as a seaman-machinist he had led the mutiny of the French Black Sea Fleet against orders from Paris to support the White Russian armies.

At Gaylord's, the Madrid hotel that the Russians had taken over, the ready availability of good food and the heady air of power and intrigue drew Hemingway like a moth to the flame. Here he met four Communist commanders whose toughness and professional savvy stirred him just as Philip Percival's had in East Africa. Enrique Lister, an ex-quarryman from Galicia who had gone on from organizing bloodshed and revolution in La Coruña to the command of a division, was the most ruthless of these men. The most intelligent was Juan Modesto, an ex-woodcutter who had served as a sergeant in the Spanish Foreign Legion under Franco and who spoke fluent Russian, as did Lister, for after participating in the abortive uprising among the miners of Asturias in 1934 they both had escaped to the Soviet Union and studied at the Frunze military school. The third member of the foursome was a bearded and talkative giant named Valentín González but known professionally as El Campesino (the peasant) because the Communist wanted him to attract more peasants into the Party, and the fourth was an engaging and able Hungarian whose nom de guerre was Emilio Kléber.

Gaylord's also brought Hemingway into the orbit of three other notable Communists: Mikhail Koltsov, the young and very brainy correspondent for *Pravda;* Dolores Ibarruri, known as La Pasionaria, who always dressed in black and was known for her violent, theatrical speeches over Madrid radio, especially for the one that ended with the slogan, "It is better to die on your feet than live on your knees! *No pasarán!*"; and Pepe Quintanilla, the sinister "Executioner of Madrid" and brother of Hemingway's longtime friend, the Socialist painter Luis Quintanilla. In gossiping with these political insiders, NANA's innocent abroad gained a false sense of knowing what the score was himself. Thus, when Dos Passos became worried about the continued detention of his old friend José Robles and began asking pointed questions of the authorities, Hemingway patronizingly assured him that Pepe Quintanilla had given him his word that Robles would receive a fair trial for whatever crimes he was charged with. He also urged his friend Josie Herbst, who had recently arrived in Madrid, to tell Dos Passos to "lay off making inquiries" which were sure to get "everybody into trouble if he persisted" and might hamper the completion of *The Spanish Earth.* Herbst stingingly replied that a "reliable source" in Valencia had just told her that Robles would never come to trial because he was dead, and that Popular Front officials hoped to keep this news from Dos Passos for as long as possible, lest he denounce their cause. She herself, Herbst declared, could not violate the confidence of her informant by telling Dos Passos what had happened, but Hemingway could and should. Hemingway, gaping and sputtering, said in response that if Robles was dead he must have been a spy. He agreed, however, to convey the news to Dos Passos.

With sadistic nicety, he chose to do so on a public occasion. During a festive luncheon honoring the reconstitution of the XVth International Brigade, he offhandedly informed Dos Passos that Robles had been executed. He also let Dos Passos know by the manner in which he spoke that in his politically sophisticated judgment Robles had got what he deserved. Apropos of Hemingway as a political judge, Herbst would later observe that his mind had been ill-equipped to deal with the "new realms of experience" that he had attempted to annex in Spain, and that Dos Passos "was absolutely right" in refusing to believe his translator to be guilty of treason. Dos Passos for his part was deeply offended by the callous way in which Hemingway had given him the bad news and by his condescending treatment of him as though he were a shrinking violet and a simpleton. In Dos Passos's view, it was Hemingway who was the simpleton for having allowed himself to be politically exploited. Once a target of leftist abuse for not dealing in his fiction with the great issues of the day, Hemingway was now the Left's "fair-haired boy," of whom much was expected, Dos Passos reflected.

3

WHEN the Spanish war's most famous correspondent reached New York aboard the *Normandie* on May 18, 1937, he was instantly surrounded on the dock by a gaggle of reporters and a photographer for *Life* magazine. All his old friends in Madrid were still alive and in good health, he beamingly assured the press, and he predicted that Franco would never take the Spanish capital and that the Loyalists would win the war.

Following two weeks of fishing in Bimini, he flew back to New York. Scott Fitzgerald was also in the city, and the two men had a brief but cordial meeting. "It was fine to see you so well and full of life, Ernest," Fitzgerald wrote him that night on a train traveling south. The main purpose, however, of Hemingway's return to New York was to address the Second American Writers' Congress at Carnegie Hall on the night of June 4.

Sponsored by the Communist-dominated League of American Writers, whose next president would be the covertly card-carrying Donald Ogden Stewart, the Congress essentially represented an effort on the part of the Communists to enlist liberals under a Popular Front banner for the purpose of manipulating them. That malleable man of good will, Archibald MacLeish, served as master of ceremonies on the evening that Hemingway spoke, and the two other featured speakers on the program were Earl Browder, the Secretary of the Communist Party, U.S.A., and Joris Ivens, who intended to show the audience *The Spanish Earth,* even though the film did not as yet have a sound track.

Fighting a case of the jitters and fogged-up spectacles—for the jampacked hall was hot that night—Hemingway launched into a

stumbling delivery of his remarks before the waves of applause for
him had subsided. After about a minute, though, he "warmed up
eloquently," according to the account in *Time*. Writers have a special
stake in fighting fascism, he proclaimed, because it is the only form
of government that will not allow them to tell the truth, thereby
implying that the Soviet Union was a free society and hence unwittingly helping it to reduce the propaganda losses it would suffer as a
result of the events of precisely one week later. For on June 11, in a
renewal of the Great Terror initiated by Stalin the year before, the
Soviet army commander, Marshal Tukhachevsky, and seven other
senior generals were shot as German collaborators. (By the time the
Terror had engorged its last victim, about a million Communist
Party members in Russia would be dead and thirty thousand army
officers, approximately half the total.) Having indirectly performed
this service for Stalin, Hemingway then directly served himself by
calling the audience's attention to the difference between writers
who were willing to pursue the truth about war at the risk of their
lives and intellectuals who stuck to their armchairs.

> Whether the truth is worth some risk to come by, the writers must
> decide themselves. Certainly it is more comfortable to spend their
> time disputing learnedly on points of doctrine. And there will always
> be new schisms and new fallings-off and marvelous exotic doctrines
> and romantic lost leaders, for those who do not want to work at what
> they profess to believe in, but only to discuss and maintain positions
> —skillfully chosen positions to be held by the typewriter and consol-
> idated with the fountain pen. But there is now, and there will be from
> now on for a long time, war for any writer to go to who wants to
> study it.

The audience ate it up.

Two weeks later, he again returned to New York, this time for
the purpose of revising his script for *The Spanish Earth*. Although he
flared up at Ivens's criticism of his commentary as too wordy, he
soon settled down and agreed that the film required a more econom-
ical text. But according to Orson Welles, a more serious confrontation occurred between him and Hemingway. The trouble began
when Archibald MacLeish, on behalf of Contemporary Historians,
Incorporated, gave Welles a copy of the final draft of the script and
asked him to record it. Ivens may have been satisfied that Hemingway's revisions had made it terse enough, but Welles regarded some
of the lines as needlessly complicated or downright pompous and he
said so. This opinion didn't sit well with Hemingway, Welles would
recall in 1966 in *Cahiers du Cinéma*,

and, since I had, a short time before, just directed the Mercury Theatre, which was a sort of avant-garde theatre, he thought I was some
kind of faggot and said, "You —— effeminate boys of the theatre,
what do you know about real war?"

Taking the bull by the horns, I began to make effeminate gestures
and I said to him, "Mr. Hemingway, how strong you are and how
big you are!" That enraged him and he picked up a chair; I picked up
another and, right there, in front of the images of the Spanish Civil
War, as they marched across the screen, we had a terrible scuffle. It
was something marvellous: two guys like us in front of these images
representing people in the act of struggling and dying . . . We ended
by toasting each other over a bottle of whiskey.

MacLeish and Ivens were both pleased with Welles's polished delivery of the script, but Lillian Hellman and her friend, actor Fredric
March, found his mellifluous voice unsuited for the harsh reality of
a war film. Bowing to their theatrical expertise, Ivens then asked
Hemingway to read the words he had written. As the son of a
singer, Hemingway replied that he had never been given training in
proper breathing and therefore couldn't accept the assignment.
Eventually, though, he was persuaded to do so, and Ivens was
pleased with the results. Because of poor recording techniques,
Hemingway's voice sounded flat, in the Dutchman's opinion, but
there was a naturalness in his tone that made the narrative compel-
lingly believable. When Ivens informed Welles that his own recording was going to be junked, Welles was miffed, especially since he
had waived his right to a fee.

In July, Hemingway and Ivens journeyed to Los Angeles to drum
up financial support for Spanish—i.e., Loyalist Spanish—war relief
from Hollywood moguls and movie stars. At a meeting arranged by
Fredric March and his wife Florence Eldridge, Ivens ran off the film
and Hemingway read a speech about the suffering of the soldiers
and the bombing of innocent civilians. Fitzgerald was among those
present, and Hemingway's vibrancy enthralled him as of old. "Ernest came like a whirlwind," he wrote Max Perkins, and "put Ernst
Lubitsch the great director in his place by refusing to have his picture
prettied up and remade for him à la Hollywood at various cocktail
parties. I feel he was in a state of nervous tensity, that there was
something almost religious about it. He raised $1000 bills won by
Miriam Hopkins fresh from the gaming table, the rumor is $14,000
in one night." To Hemingway himself, Fitzgerald sent an admiring
telegram: THE PICTURE WAS BEYOND PRAISE AND SO WAS YOUR ATTI-
TUDE.

Lillian Hellman was also on hand that evening, and when the

party broke up—so she claimed in *An Unfinished Woman* (1969)—
she and Hemingway and Fitzgerald and a few other people were
invited by Dorothy Parker to come back to her house for a nightcap,
despite the fact, she said, that Dottie and Ernest really didn't like
each other. (That statement was, of course, untrue, at least as far as
Parker was concerned.) Fitzgerald, Hellman continued, invited her
to ride with him, which did. Apparently, he was afraid of driving, for he went no faster than ten or twelve miles an hour and his
hands kept trembling as they gripped the wheel, even after Hellman
placed her hands over his as a steadying gesture. Upon reaching
Parker's house, he announced that he didn't want to go in. He was
on the wagon, he explained, and "I'm afraid of Ernest, I guess,
scared of being sober when . . ." "Don't be," Hellman interjected.
"He [Hemingway] could never like a good writer, certainly not a
better one. Come. You'll have a good time."

They entered the house just in time to see Hemingway throw a
highball glass against the stone fireplace in the living room. Fitzgerald turned to bolt, but Hellman held his arm and pulled him into the
kitchen, where she whispered to her great and good friend, Dashiell
Hammett, "Please help Mr. Fitzgerald. He's frightened of Ernest
and the glass throwing didn't help." In a splendid non-sequitur,
Hammett replied, "Ernest has never been able to write a woman.
He only puts them in books to admire him." The rest of the evening
was quiet, according to Hellman. Why Hemingway threw the glass
she did not bother to explain, nor did she say why Fitzgerald had
gone to Dottie Parker's in the first place if he didn't intend to go in
and was afraid to be at the wheel of a car, nor why her rendition of
the remarks she allegedly addressed to Hammett makes her sound
like Myrna Loy in the movie version of Hammett's *The Thin Man*.

Her opinion of Hemingway, however, in this episode and others
in a memoir sprinkled with encounters that have been called into
question, is clear enough. He was a second-rate writer and a drunken
lout. Nevertheless, "I liked Ernest," she comments at one point.
Perhaps she liked him in 1937 and 1938, when he was a darling of
the Stalinists at home and abroad, but after he said farewell to the
Comintern in *For Whom the Bell Tolls* (1940), she no longer cared for
him. After knocking him in private conversation for a quarter of a
century, she did her inventive best to finish him off in *An Unfinished
Woman*.

Shortly before leaving the States for his second visit to Spain in
the fall of 1937, Hemingway attended a dinner in New York staged
by David Smart, the publisher of *Esquire,* who wanted to publicize
Ken, the new magazine that he planned to launch in early 1938 under

Arnold Gingrich's editorship. As Smart conceived of it, *Ken* would be sumptuously packaged and avowedly leftist, albeit anti-Communist, and it was Gingrich's desire that it be an "insider's magazine" that would tell people what was really going on in world politics. To the surprise and delight of both men, Hemingway asked if he could be one of the editors, and in the advance announcements of the magazine he was listed as such. In the first issue, however, this claim was retracted. "Ernest Hemingway has been in Spain since *Ken* was first projected. Although announced as an editor, he has taken no part in the editing of the magazine or in the formation of its policies. If he sees eye to eye with us on *Ken* we would like to have him as an editor. If not he will remain as a contributor until he is fired or quits." This was a polite way of saying that on learning that the magazine would not be extending the hand of comradeship to Communism, Hemingway had changed his mind about having his name on the masthead. While he wrote for *Ken* for a solid year, he never did become reconciled to its brand of leftism. Two anti-Communist cartoons in the first issue were especially offensive to him, and in a piece that appeared in the magazine the following June he explained why. There could be "no anti-fascist magazine which does not maintain a popular front against fascism," he argued, and any leftist editor who engages in Red-baiting must be "either a fool or a knave."

The aspect of *Ken* that Hemingway found most congenial was its knowing tone. In his own contributions, he repeatedly dramatized himself as a possessor of information not available to other commentators on Spain. Without mentioning Dos Passos by name, he made condescending reference in a piece called "Treachery in Aragon" to a fellow writer's "good hearted naivete" and "typical American liberal attitude." There was treachery afoot among the politicians in the Popular Front government, he darkly hinted in two other pieces, but it would be a while before he could break this story that no one else had. And in a late piece called "Fresh Air on an Inside Story," he once more ridiculed Dos Passos without naming him, this time for believing that a political terror was under way in Madrid. Hemingway knew better. He had "friends in Seguridad" whom he had "known from the old days and could trust," and he could assure the readers of *Ken* that Madrid was as "free from any terror as any capital in Europe."

4

BIASED reporting, script writing, and speechifying were not the only means by which Hemingway established credentials with the Left. His burgeoning political fan club was also pleased by the direction a book of his took. Published on October 15, 1937, *To Have and Have Not* was characterized by Scribners as a novel, although it actually consisted of three short stories, two of which had been previously published, in the April 1934 *Cosmopolitan* and the February 1936 *Esquire*.

"One Trip Across," the first story, is a first-person account of the travails of Harry Morgan, the owner of a cabin cruiser, temporarily working out of Havana as a fishing guide. In every tough-talking word, the narrative promotes a myth about the author, to the point where it even glories in the details of a sadistic murder. For when Harry becomes involved with a double-crossing Chinese crook named Mr. Sing, he solves the problem of "the Chink's" duplicitousness by forcibly taking away his money and then killing him with his bare hands: "I got him forward onto his knees and had both thumbs well in behind his talk-box, and I bent the whole thing back until she cracked. Don't think you can't hear it crack, either."

"The Tradesman's Return," the second story, evolved out of a journalistic piece about the "hurricane of the century" that swept over the Florida Keys on Labor Day, 1935, destroying among other things a CCC work camp and killing a number of its inmates, most of them army veterans. Because the Civilian Conservation Corps was widely considered to be one of Franklin Roosevelt's most successful achievements as President, the Communist editors of the *New Masses* in New York were anxious to discredit its operation, and by treating the deaths of the veterans as a symbol of capitalistic callousness they believed they could do so. One of the editors, Joseph North, wondered whether Hemingway might be willing to write a piece that would prove useful in this regard. For in an advance copy of *Green Hills of Africa,* due out in October, North had come across a passage in which the garrulous hero, sounding like an Oak Park Republican gone sour on reform, had inveighed against the New Deal as "Some sort of Y.M.C.A. show. Starry eyed bastards spending money that somebody will have to pay. Everybody in our town quit work to go on relief. Fishermen all turned carpenters. Reverse of the Bible." Perhaps a scoffer at the New Deal could serve as a Communist helpmeet, North reasoned, and the piece he shortly received from Hemingway proved him exactly right.

"Who Murdered the Vets?" demanded to know why the veterans had been sent to work for a measly forty-five dollars a month in a CCC camp in hurricane season and why no precautions had been taken to ensure their safety. While Hemingway confessed that he had no specific answers to these questions, his ignorance did not keep him from laying down an indictment of the rich and the powerful. "Wealthy people, yachtsmen, fishermen such as President Hoover and President Roosevelt," avoided the Keys during the hurricane season so that their boats and other valuable property would not be damaged. "But veterans, especially the bonus-marching variety of veterans, are not property. They are only human beings; unsuccessful human beings, and all they have to lose is their lives." As for the government bureaucrats in Washington who actually ordered the veterans into the Keys, Hemingway said in effect that they were guilty of manslaughter.

In "The Tradesman's Return," written three months after "Who Murdered the Vets?", he resumed his attack on the alphabet agencies of the Roosevelt administration by satirizing the self-importance of an official who decides to deprive Harry Morgan of his livelihood. Even though Prohibition has been repealed, Harry and a "nigger" named Wesley are working as bootleggers between Cuba and the Keys. Apprehended before the story begins by American customs agents, they somehow manage to get away, but both are shot in the process. As the story opens, the wounded bootleggers are approaching the channel off Woman Key, where Harry starts dumping sacks of liquor into the water so that the customs people will have no proof of their crime. Unfortunately for them, his actions are observed by two men in a charter boat. One of them is Frederick Harrison, by his own description "one of the three most important men in the United States" and in the words of the other man, named Willis, "one of the biggest men in the administration." Convinced that Harry is a crook, Harrison orders Willis to take down the number of his boat. The captain of the charter boat protests that Harry has a wife and two daughters to feed. "Who the hell do you eat off of," the captain indignantly asks, "with people working here in Key West for the government for six dollars and a half a week?" The big cheese from Washington is adamant, however, and the story ends with the certainty that Harry will soon be in trouble with the law.

An inconsequential plot, crude characterizations, an absence of exciting action, and heavy-handed dialogue are the principal characteristics of "A Tradesman's Return." Hemingway, though, professed to be delighted with it and immediately began writing a third Harry Morgan story, only to put it aside when a downward shift in mood overwhelmed him. But in the fall of 1936 at the Nordquist Ranch he resumed work on the story, and by the time he left for Spain the manuscript of *To Have and Have Not* was essentially complete. Upon his return he made stabs at revising it, in between trips to New York to speak at the Writers' Congress and to work with Ivens on the narrative of *The Spanish Earth*.

On the first of these trips, he stopped off to see Perkins at his home. Max's wife, Louise, was offended by the way he barged in and took over. "Ernest Hemingway came in here," she would recall, "hardly looking at Max and barked, 'Where's the telephone? I have to talk to Scott [Fitzgerald]. He's the only person in America worth talking to.' " But in private conversation with Max, his manner became more tentative. He had doubts about his new novel, he confessed. On the theory that it would be helped by not having to stand alone, he suggested filling out the volume with three aces, "Macomber," "Kilimanjaro," and "The Capital of the World," the tragic tale of Paco, the boy waiter in Madrid.

Flying home, he had another idea. Under the blanket title, *To Have and Have Not* (or maybe *The Various Arms,* he alternatively suggested, or *Return to the Wars*), the volume could include the novel, which he would probably call *Harry Morgan,* the three short stories he had previously mentioned, the *New Masses* piece about the murder of the vets, one of his news dispatches from Madrid and the text of his Writers' Congress speech. Such an anthology would make a "major work," he asserted, and Perkins could plug it accordingly.

With some difficulty, Perkins obtained a copy of the speech. Muffling his low opinion of it as best he could, he wrote Hemingway that he wasn't sure about the advisability of reprinting it in an omnibus book. "I do think that bringing in a speech just because it is one, does tend to make the book seem too miscellaneous, perhaps."

Upon reading *Harry Morgan,* which he shortly did, he pronounced it "very good, very moving," and it doubtless called up vivid memories for him of the life of the Keys and the Gulf Stream, for he had gone down there to fish with Hemingway almost every year since 1929. But to his old Harvard friend, Waldo Peirce, he voiced a fundamental misgiving about the book by constantly referring to Harry Morgan as a "type," not as an individual. There was no use passing on this assessment to the author, however. For at this point, Perkins sensed, Hemingway was not in any shape to accept anything but the mildest of criticisms. Instead of zeroing in on the novel's shortcomings, Perkins concentrated on disposing of the idea of enclosing it in an omnibus volume. By the end of July 1937 he had succeeded in persuading Hemingway to publish the novel on its own, under the title *To Have and Have Not*. Only after the book was in print did he dare to criticize it, on a day when Hemingway came to his brownstone house for a drink and appeared in the editor's estimation to be relaxed. To his dismay, Perkins discovered that he had misread the signals. Even as he was explaining that he hoped his adverse remarks would be of help to Hemingway in the future, Hemingway slammed his hand down on the coffee table and exclaimed, "Hell, let Tom Wolfe write it for you then!"

One suspects that if the novelist had encouraged his editor to speak the unvarnished truth, Perkins would have concentrated his fire on the third section of the book. For as bad as the first two sections are, the last is the most lamentable, first of all because of the comic-book simplicity of its sexual sociology. As a result of the gunshot wound he suffered while getting away from the customs agents, Harry has had to have his right arm amputated, and thanks to the testimony of Frederick Harrison, his boat has been impounded. Yet as he himself says, he still has his cojones, and no one knows this better than his wife, Marie. In a conversation in bed with him as well as in a couple of Molly Bloom–like monologues, she makes plain her belief that no other man in the world is built the way her husband is—and Harry thinks she is awfully sexy, too, in her overweight way. The novel's rich people, by contrast, have horrendous sex problems, for example the Bradleys, whom Hemingway modeled so closely on Grant and Jane Mason that the lawyers at Scribners forced him to include a disclaimer at the front of the book stating that "there are no real people in this volume." Tommy Bradley is impotent; Helène Bradley is a nymphomaniac; and Tommy doesn't care who his wife calls on to ease her hunger just so long as he gets to watch from time to time. But when he makes a smiling appearance in the doorway of her bedroom while she is being made love to by the writer Richard Gordon, Gordon becomes so agitated that he loses his erection. Helène, trembling with desire and shaking with frustration, slaps her lover with such force that it "lighted flashes of light in his eyeballs."

Gordon is a vicious caricature of Dos Passos, and the question is what had the novelist done to incite it. The Robles affair was not, and indeed could not have been, the irritant. For Hemingway created Gordon well before he quarreled with Dos Passos in Spain. But if politics wasn't the irritant, what was? Jealousy, in a word. Dos Passos ran afoul of Hemingway for the same reason the dead Fitzgerald would—he was achieving a degree of literary success that Hemingway did not expect and could not abide. In the early thirties, no one had given Dos Passos more helpful encouragement about his

work than good old Hem—but the encouragement had always been
delivered *de haut en bas*. Thus, your new book is "bloody splendid,"
Hemingway informed him in early 1932, just after he finished reading *1919,* the second volume of the projected trilogy that Dos Passos
intended to call *U. S. A.*

> It's 4 times the book the 42nd [Parallel] was—and that was damned
> good. It comes off all the time and you can write so damned well it
> spooks me that something might happen to you—wash and peel all
> the fruit you eat. Now watch one thing. In the 3rd volume don't let
> yourself slip and get any perfect characters in—no Stephen Daede-
> luses [*sic*]—remember it was Bloom and Mrs. Bloom saved Joyce—
> that is the only thing could ruin the bastard from being a great piece
> of literature. If you get a noble communist remember the bastard
> probably masturbates and is jallous [jealous] as a cat. Keep them
> people, people, people, and don't let them get to be symbols.

Yet when the longest and most ambitious volume in the trilogy was
finally completed, Hemingway's benevolent attitude toward its author began to change.

The trouble started in May 1936. The Dos Passoses plus Sara
Murphy, who was still grieving over the death of her son, Baoth,
agreed to join Hemingway for a holiday in Havana, centering
around some fishing aboard the *Pilar*. Dos Passos, however, brought
the galley proofs with him of the British edition of *The Big Money,*
which was scheduled to appear in September, one month after the
American edition. Hemingway complained at the time and complained again later that he had hardly seen Dos Passos in Havana
because he had been buried in proofs the whole time. The camara-
derie of earlier years, when he had been able to summon Dos and
other cronies "to cavort in the deep with him," had proved unrecap-
turable. Sara's sadness had also cast a damper on the party, and to
top everything off the fishing had been poor. On his return to New
York, Dos Passos tried to make amends by sending Hemingway a
case of champagne and a somewhat apologetic letter. "Gosh Hem it
was a tough proposition for you, bringing all the women folk to
Havana, but the trip really did Sara a great deal of good."

Hemingway had asked Dos Passos to leave a spare set of the
proofs with him, and after he had gone through them he sent the
author his reaction: "You must have had hell with that to proofread
—it's as long as the Bible but I can see why you couldn't cut it more.
The shorter those years [the twenties] seemed, the longer it takes to
write them." The absence of compliments for his book must have

struck Dos Passos like a blow in the face, and he could not have been mollified very much by Hemingway's apology for his prima-donna behavior in Havana which closed out the letter. "Will make a good trip soon with lots of exercise and no proof and no bellyaching by old Hem. . . . Would like to have a chance to not mistreat my friends sometime."

The acclaim from reviewers that greeted the publication of *The Big Money* was of a sort that Hemingway had not received for any of his books since *A Farewell to Arms*. The August 10 issue of *Time* made matters worse, for a photograph of Dos Passos, without his glasses, smoking a cigar and looking rugged, graced the cover. Underneath the picture was the writer's full name, John Roderigo Dos Passos, and an arresting phrase: "Writes to be damned not saved." Four older American novelists had previously made the cover of *Time*, Sinclair Lewis in 1927, Willa Cather in 1931, Gertrude Stein in 1933, and Upton Sinclair in 1934, but no novelist of Hemingway's generation had. That the honor of being first should have gone to Dos Passos rather than himself was galling.* A countering denigration was in order, and Hemingway found the vehicle for it in a series of new chapters in *To Have and Have Not*.

The difference between Harry Morgan, who really *is* rugged, and the tanned, sandy-haired, well-built Gordon, who merely looks as if he is, is established in chapters eighteen and nineteen, the first of which is devoted to Harry and the second far briefer one to Gordon. Chapter eighteen begins with Harry in temporary possession of two promising items: another boat and a verbal agreement with four Cuban revolutionaries to put them ashore in their native land for two hundred dollars. But when the revolutionaries rob a Key West bank, kill Harry's deckhand and storm aboard with drawn guns, Harry knows that once he has taken them across the water, the biggest of the Cubans, a brute named Roberto, will try to kill him.

Out in the Gulf Stream, the hours pass and the sky grows dark. Sitting at the wheel of the boat, Harry listens to Emilio, the youngest and most attractive of the revolutionaries, talk about the bank robbery and about his association with men like Roberto. "We just raise money now for the fight," the boy earnestly explains. "To do that we have to use means that later we would never use. Also we have to use people we would not employ later. But the end is worth the means. They had to do the same thing in Russia. Stalin was a sort of brigand for many years before the revolution." Harry's pri-

* Hemingway's first appearance on the cover of *Time* occurred in the fall of 1937, following the publication of *To Have and Have Not*.

vate opinion of this little speech is "F— his revolution," and when he makes a sudden bid to save his neck by seizing the Thompson submachine gun he has hidden beneath the hatch, he kills the boy idealist without a qualm. Once he has disposed of all four of the revolutionaries—or so he thinks—he stands up to shut the hatch and is promptly shot in the belly by Roberto, who has merely been wounded. In an animal-like convulsion, the desperately injured Harry kills the big Cuban with an answering burst of fire. His revenge is not complete, however, until he acts out a head-wound ritual that casts light on his creator's gathering obsession with such injuries. Placing the machine gun against the dead Roberto's head, he touches the trigger. ". . . the gun made a noise like hitting a pumpkin with a club." Whereupon Harry turns the blood-spattered boat about and heads for home.

Chapter nineteen takes place the next morning in Key West. As Richard Gordon is bicycling home after a visit to Freddy's Bar, he spots a heavyset woman with tear-reddened eyes and bleached-blond hair. Although Gordon doesn't know it, the woman is Harry Morgan's wife, and she has been crying because she still doesn't know whether her husband is dead or alive. Dos Passos's sublime confidence in his ability to size up people on seeing them just once, his panoramic mode of storytelling and his burning commitment to social justice are all held up to scorn in Hemingway's description of the uses to which Gordon puts his fleeting glimpse of Marie. Sitting down in the front room of the bungalow that he and his wife Helen have rented, he addresses himself to the novel he is writing about a strike in a textile factory.

> In today's chapter he was going to use the big woman with the tear-reddened eyes he had just seen on the way home. Her husband when he came home at night hated her, hated the way she had coarsened and grown heavy, was repelled by her bleached hair, her too big breasts, her lack of sympathy with his work as an organizer. He would compare her to the young, firm-breasted, full-lipped little Jewess that had spoken at the meeting that evening. It was good. It was, it could be easily, terrific, and it was true. He had seen, in a flash of perception, the whole inner life of that type of woman.

Viciousness, though, did not overtake Hemingway's caricature of Dos Passos until he examined Gordon's sex life in chapter twenty-one. Not only does the writer experience erectile failure atop the exigent Mrs. Bradley, but his sexual lordship over his wife comes to an end. Revolted by his attentions to "that dirty rich bitch of a

Bradley woman," Helen allows another man to kiss her, and when Gordon objects, she tells him she is sick of him. That Hemingway chose to focus the bulk of their quarrel on Gordon's insistence on keeping their marriage childless has to be ranked as one of the supremely shameful acts of his career, for as he surely must have known, Dos Passos wanted very much to be a father.* Katy, however, was apparently incapable of bearing children, so that it was not until after Dos Passos married Elizabeth Holdrige in 1949 (Katy having died in a car accident two years before) that his dream of parenthood was at last fulfilled.

We could have had children and I certainly wanted them, but we could never afford them, Helen Gordon reminds her husband. "But we could afford to go to the Cap d'Antibes to swim and to Switzerland to ski. We can afford to come down here to Key West." All her married life, she realizes, she has been giving up what she wanted most out of love for Gordon. "Love was the greatest thing, wasn't it?" she says.

> And you were a genius and I was your whole life. I was your partner and your little black flower. Slop. Love is just another dirty lie. Love is ergoapiol pills to make me come around because you were afraid to have a baby. Love is quinine and quinine and quinine until I'm deaf with it. Love is that dirty aborting horror that you took me to. Love is my insides all messed up. It's half catheters and half whirling douches. I know about our love. Love always hangs up behind the bathroom door. It smells like lysol. To hell with love. Love is you making me happy and then going off to sleep with your mouth open while I lie awake all night afraid to say my prayers even because I know I have no right to any more. Love is all the dirty tricks you taught me that you probably got out of some book. All right. I'm through with you and I'm through with love. Your kind of picknose love. You writer.

In a novel in which most of the conversations between men and women are dramatically unconvincing, the emotional authenticity of Helen's speech is conspicuous. Hemingway may have used the quarrel between the Gordons as a means of sneering at the manhood of *Time* magazine's rugged-looking cover boy, but he did not model Helen on Dos Passos's wife. Unlike the agnostic Katy, Helen is a Catholic who is still upset because Gordon wouldn't marry her in the church. "It broke my poor mother's heart as you well know,"

---

* The assiduity with which Hemingway later spread the rumor that Dos Passos had Negro blood was another sign of his determination to hurt him by striking low blows.

she reproachfully reminds him. Her Catholic conscience also lies behind the abhorrence with which she speaks of birth-control devices and abortion. The name that Hemingway bestowed upon Pauline's alter ego in "Kilimanjaro" was Helen; he had the same identification in mind when he used the name in *To Have and Have Not*.

Following the Caesarean delivery of Gregory, Pauline's doctor had warned her that she must not become pregnant again. A decade and a half later, Hemingway told Gregory that it was the necessity to practice coitus interruptus that had broken up his marriage to Pauline. "But any fool, and certainly a doctor's son," Gregory would remark in *Papa: A Personal Memoir* (1976), "knew there are some periods of the month when one can have satisfying intercourse without fear of pregnancy." Apparently, it did not occur to Gregory to wonder whether his father—despite his talk of coitus interruptus —had not compelled his mother to violate her Catholic scruples and resort to the practices so bitterly alluded to in *To Have and Have Not*.

Whatever the truth of this matter, *To Have and Have Not* represented yet another instance of Hemingway's ability to abandon a masculine point of view in his fiction and vigorously identify with a woman whose real-life counterpart was a person with whom he was quarreling. His second marriage was close to collapse in the fall of 1936; as soon as he found a plausible successor to Pauline, he would begin thinking about walking out on her. Yet in the manuscript of the novel he was working on, he sided with a wife who walks out on her husband, and with a withering epithet on her lips in the bargain: "You writer."

The final words of the mortally wounded Harry Morgan, gasped out to the captain and mate of the Coast Guard cutter that is towing his boat to the Key West pier, were intended to be read allegorically. "No matter how a man alone ain't got no bloody fucking chance." Early and late, homicidal Harry has acted out a psychopathological view of life that Hemingway had never once identified as a sickness. Instead, he had bathed it in a heroic light, and at the end he put a twist on his tale that turned a murderer into a political philosopher. Implicit in Harry's valedictory to the world is the realization that young Emilio had been right in arguing that revolutionary idealists have to ally themselves with brutes like Roberto and brigands like Stalin because solidarity is necessary to victory and the end always justifies the means.

The most cogent review of the book was Bernard De Voto's in the *Saturday Review of Literature*: "[*To Have and Have Not*'s] social assertions and findings are so naive, fragmentary and casual that they cannot be offered as criticism of the established order: beside them, the simplest of the blue-jeans-and-solidarity Cinderella stories that the *New Masses* was praising three or four years ago would seem profound," De Voto caustically observed. He also was distressed by Hemingway's celebration of animalism. When Marie Morgan praises her husband's body movements, De Voto pointed out, she compares them to an animal's, and beauty in the novel is embodied in the long curve of a shark diving for gouts of blood. Mr. Hemingway is certainly entitled to fall in love with sharks if he wants to, De Voto conceded; yet it is hard to see, he felt forced to add, what reference anthropophobia has to the problems man is working with in the modern world. "And it will be interesting to see how the literary left, which temporarily regards Mr. Hemingway as an ally, will adapt his conclusions when adopting them. The cult of blood-consciousness and holy violence, as well as the clean beauty of the shark, has so far been the property of their political opponents [i.e., Hitler]."

The Left was not, it turned out, totally devoid of reviewers who found the novel dreadful. In the *Southern Review* Delmore Schwartz dismissed it as "a stupid and foolish book, a disgrace to a good writer, a book which should never have been printed," and Louis Kronenberger described it to the readers of *The Nation* as "a book with neither poise nor integration, and with shocking lapses from professional skill." Yet in spite of these negative comments Edmund Wilson was not exaggerating when he disgustedly remarked two years after the book was published that "the Left . . . received his least credible piece of fiction as the delivery of a new revelation."

The *New Republic*'s Malcolm Cowley, who had recently found proof of guilt in the confessions of the defendants in the Moscow trials, likewise saw what he wanted to see in *To Have and Have Not*. Admittedly, the novel lacked "unity and sureness of effect," yet it also contained "some of the best writing" Hemingway had ever done. "There are scenes that are superb technical achievements and other scenes that carry him into new registers of emotion." As for the scene in which Harry gasped out his realization that one man alone didn't have a chance, it was "beautifully done." Harry's words, said Cowley, might be Hemingway's "own free translation of Marx and Engels: 'Workers of the world unite, you have nothing to lose. . . .' " For some years now, Cowley concluded, "the literary hyenas have been saying that Hemingway was done for, but their noses have betrayed them into finding the scent of decay where none existed. From the evidence of this book, I should say that he is just beginning a new career." Among the many judges who agreed

was the twenty-two-year-old wunderkind of the New York reviewing world, Alfred Kazin, who trumpeted his pleasure in the New
York *Herald Tribune* that *To Have and Have Not* had shown him
something new about Hemingway. For here was an author who
could "get angry and snarl with his heart open" and whose hatred
of the rich was wonderful to behold. Although the book as a whole
was "hardly up to snuff," Kazin granted, it nevertheless was the
work of "a genuine artist who has worked his way out of a cult of
tiresome defeatism."

5

IF Hemingway had wanted to share his adventures in Spain with a
woman not his wife, he found the companion he was looking for in
Sloppy Joe's Bar in Key West, in December 1936, two months before his first journey to the war. Just as he was paying his bill and
getting ready to go home, three tourists walked in, an older woman,
a young man, and a young woman whose beautiful mane of tawny-
gold shoulder-length hair, high cheekbones, and full-lipped mouth
caused him to do a double take. His eyes followed the simple lines
of her black cotton dress down to her long and shapely golden-
brown legs. The young woman spoke to her companions, he further
noted, in a low, husky, eastern-seaboard-accented voice. The next
afternoon, he was again in the bar when the trio walked in. It was
an easy matter to introduce himself and to work his magic upon
them. The young woman said her name was Martha Gellhorn. The
older woman was her mother and the young man was her younger
brother, Alfred, who was on vacation from medical school.

The black bartender at Sloppy Joe's, a man named Skinner, said
later that the sight of Miss Gellhorn and Hemingway talking together that afternoon reminded him of beauty and the beast. The
comparison more aptly applied to Hemingway, in his odoriferous
Basque shorts tied around his middle with a piece of rope, than it
did to her. For while she gave a split-second impression of being a
blonde bombshell, she had an overly prominent nose and double
chin. Another Jane Mason she was not. Martha was quick on the
uptake and very intelligent, though, and only twenty-eight years old
(to Pauline's forty-one and Hemingway's thirty-seven). Her home
town was St. Louis, she told him, which may have made him think
of Hadley. There was another echo. Her late father had been a doctor; so had his.

As darkness fell, the lights in the bar were lit. Yet Hemingway
still showed no signs of wishing to take leave of his newfound

friends. He told them something about the history of Key West and offered to take them on a tour of the island and show them where the swimming was good. On Whitehead Street, meanwhile, Pauline was holding their crayfish dinner and having another drink with their guests, Charles and Lorine Thompson. Finally, she asked Charles to go to Sloppy Joe's and find out what was delaying her husband. At the bar, Hemingway told him to tell Pauline that he wouldn't be home for dinner, but would meet her later at Penna's Garden of Roses. When Thompson reported back to Pauline, she at once wanted to know what Miss Gellhorn looked like, and was distressed to learn that she was young and blond.

6

ANOTHER resemblance to Hadley was that Martha had attended Bryn Mawr College but hadn't graduated. For at the end of her junior year she had been offered a temporary job on the *New Republic* and had decided not to pass it up. After a brief stint there, she briefly wrote for a newspaper in upstate New York. By the end of 1929, her address was Paris, where she successively worked for *Vogue,* the United Press and the St. Louis *Post-Dispatch.* During the summer of 1933 she went to Capri and wrote a novel about three young American women who drop out of college in order to find themselves. *What Mad Pursuit* was the Keatsian title and the epigraph was borrowed from Hemingway: "Nothing ever happens to the brave."

In the autumn of 1934 she returned to the States, her liaison of several years with a French journalist, the Marquis Bertrand de Jouvenel, having ended. An introduction provided by her friend Marquis Childs, the Washington correspondent for the St. Louis *Post-Dispatch,* enabled her to get into Harry Hopkins's White House office, where she proposed that he hire her as an investigator for the Federal Emergency Relief Administration. She wanted to determine by means of interviews how acute the problems of the unemployed really were. Hopkins sent her all over the country, and the reports she sent back of suffering and despair were so moving that he introduced her to Eleanor Roosevelt. Mrs. Roosevelt, Hopkins knew, had been extremely interested in the reports of another FERA investigator, Lorena Hickok. Martha's Bryn Mawr manner impressed Mrs. Roosevelt, as did her reporting. A correspondence sprang up between them, which quickly ripened into what would prove to be a lasting friendship.

Through the First Lady, Martha met the President. On another White House occasion, she was introduced to H. G. Wells, who was

touring the States in connection with some articles on the New Deal
that he was planning to write for *Collier's*. Although Wells was still
very much involved with Moura Budberg, his last great love,
Moura was in Estonia at the moment and he found the young Miss
Gellhorn charming. Subsequently, Wells contributed an appreciative
preface to *The Trouble I've Seen*, a collection of stories based on her
FERA interviews, and recommended it to the English publisher,
Putnam, who brought out a British edition even before Morrow
published the American edition.

Mrs. Roosevelt, who was sent an advance copy of the book,
included glowing references to Martha in three of her "My Day"
columns during the week of August 5, 1936. "The American edition
of *The Trouble I've Seen*," she wrote in her longest tribute,

> will come out on the 23rd of this month. I cannot tell you how Martha
> Gellhorn, young, pretty, college graduate [*sic*], good home, more or
> less Junior League background, with a touch of exquisite Paris clothes
> and "esprit" thrown in, can write as she does. She has an understand-
> ing of many people and many situations and she can make them live
> for us. Let us be thankful she can, for we badly need her interpretation
> to help us understand each other.

The reviews were equally favorable and prominently featured.
Dorothy Thompson in the New York *Herald Tribune* was full of
praise. The *Saturday Review of Literature* ran a photograph of the
author on the cover and an enthusiastic estimate of her book inside.
Lewis Gannett, in his syndicated column, compared her work to
Hemingway's. ("Who is this Martha Gellhorn?" he asked. "Her
writing burns. . . . Hemingway does not write more authentic
American speech. Nor can Ernest Hemingway teach Martha
Gellhorn anything about economy of language.")

Fame brought her several invitations to speak—plus an invitation
to lunch with the Roosevelts at Hyde Park on November 1—and by
December she was ready for a vacation. Since Christmas was going
to be a difficult time for her family without her father, who had died
early in the year, she proposed to her mother and brother that they
spend it in Miami. Upon finding the city not to their taste, they
moved on by bus to Key West, where Martha quickly spotted the
bar called Sloppy Joe's. Conceivably, that first afternoon, she also
spotted Hemingway.

In the course of driving the Gellhorns around the island one day,
Hemingway saw Pauline walking along the street and stopped the
car. Even though she readily accepted his invitation to get in and

meet his new friends, she was "very grumpy," Martha recalled years afterward, and Hemingway was "very sharp." Yet it "never occurred to me," Martha insisted, that "she could be jealous." This protestation of innocence does not compel belief, however, nor is it likely that her desire to do some more swimming and sunbathing was the real reason why she elected to stay on in Key West for a week after her mother and brother left.

Except for one evening when Pauline entertained her at Whitehead Street, she saw Hemingway away from his home. She herself had already decided to cover the war in Spain if she possibly could. Consequently, the question of how to get into the country came up often in their conversations, along with other problems that related to their writing. For on the surface at least their relationship at this point was largely professional. He was a world-famous writer, while she was becoming better-known every day. Gellhorn was a familiar name to the readers of *Harper's Bazaar* and other magazines, and the syndicated book columnist Harry Hansen had just hailed the author of *The Trouble I've Seen* as the literary discovery of the year.

Martha left Key West on or about January 10, headed for St. Louis. The next day, Hemingway told Pauline he had to go to New York on urgent business. In Miami, he overtook Martha and suggested dinner at a steak house with his boxer friend Tom Heeney. Afterwards they caught the same train north. A telegram from Arnold Gingrich to Hemingway had meantime reached Key West. Gingrich had heard a rumor that he had fallen ill and was anxious to learn the truth of the matter. Pauline answered the wire with gallows humor. SECONDHAND REPORT ABSOLUTELY BASELESS ERNEST IN MIAMI ENROUTE TO NEW YORK IN SHALL WE SAY PERFECT HEALTH THANKS FOR SOLICITUDE.

7

FROM St. Louis, Martha wrote Pauline a friendly letter that was reminiscent of nothing so much as the friendly letters that Pauline had once written to Hadley. Freezing rain was falling in Missouri, she reported, but reading the collected works of "Ernestino," as she was currently doing, was one source of pleasure at least. Memories of the occasion on which Pauline had received her at Whitehead Street were also a comfort to her. ". . . if I kept a diary it would be full of fine words about you."

Even before Pauline received this suspicious letter she was so wrought up with anxiety and bitterness about her marriage that she couldn't sleep unless she wore herself out playing tennis and swim-

ming. Telegrams addressed to her husband from the chairmen of
various committees to aid the Spanish Loyalists made his intentions
plainer with every passing day. He was going to go off to the war
and leave her behind. Try as she would, she couldn't keep her desolate feelings out of the letters she sent to him in New York. "Would
love to be with you instead of being here with nobody and the sea.
And all those telegrams about Spain and ambulances bring my situation of impending doom pretty near the front door where I am
only used to the wolf and the stork. . . . So goodbye big-shot-in-
the-pants, good luck and why not start keeping me informed?"

Upon his return to Key West, she proposed that she accompany
him to Spain, but he vetoed this idea at once. Yet at the same time
he went out of his way to thank her parents in a belated Christmas
letter for having given him Pauline, "who's made me happier than
I've ever been."

Reading Martha's steadfastly cheerful letters was much more entertaining, he found, than talking to his disconsolate wife, but on
February 15, 1937, in the last letter he would receive from her before
he left for Europe, Martha gave way to nervousness about the non-
intervention pact that France and Britain had signed in regard to the
Spanish Civil War. Perhaps the pact would make it impossible for
her to enter Spain from France. "Angel, I have much to tell you,"
she jumpily exclaimed, "but suddenly I find that there is no time
even to think straight." In case she did not get to New York until
after he had sailed, she wanted him to know of her hope that he
would leave word in Paris of where he was staying. "Please don't
disappear," she begged. "Are or are we not members of the same
union? Hemingstein, I am very fond of you."

She arrived in New York two weeks later, to find that Hemingway had indeed departed for Spain by way of France several days
before, accompanied by Evan Shipman and the Brooklyn bullfighter
Sidney Franklin. He had also left Paris by the time she got there, but
thanks to Kyle Crichton of *Collier's,* who had given her a letter
identifying her as a special correspondent for the magazine even
though she wasn't, she was able to persuade the French authorities
to give her the papers she would need to get past the military guards
at the Spanish border. On the next to last day of March, having
traveled circuitously to Madrid via Barcelona and Valencia, she finally caught up with Hemingway in the sub-basement dining room
of the Hotel Gran Vía, the designated eating place for foreign correspondents. "I knew you'd get here, daughter," he boomed, as he
stood up to give her a bear hug, "because I fixed it so you could."

In his megalomania, he wasn't joking. Martha was astonished and —momentarily—furious.

That Hemingway now had a mistress became obvious to everyone in the Hotel Florida on the night that a Nationalist shell struck the hotel's hot-water tank and escaping steam began to fill the upper floors. "All kinds of liaisons were revealed," Sefton Delmer remembered, "as people poured from their bedrooms to seek shelter in the basement, among them Ernest and Martha." During the day, Martha sometimes tagged along with Hemingway on his filmmaking expeditions with Ivens. Yet she also was interested, as he definitely was not, in visiting the wounded in the city's hospitals. Her wish to spend time learning Spanish was another factor that led them to split up after breakfast. In the evenings, though, the lovers came together again over drinks of barrel Scotch or yellow gin at Chicote's Bar.

At the end of April, they went off with a driver on a weeklong tour of the four central fighting fronts. If they were sometimes too far from Madrid to warrant an overnight return to the Florida, they either slept on cots in the headquarters of field commanders or in the car. Under enemy fire, Martha behaved extremely well, mainly because she was determined to do so. Yet her cool deportment was also a tribute to Hemingway's didactic skills. He taught her to recognize the different sounds of gunfire and when it was imperative to take cover, and he constantly reassured her that she not only was the bravest woman he had ever met, but braver than most men. In addition, he kept telling her to take her credentials from *Collier's* seriously, until finally she sat down and wrote a piece for the magazine called "Only the Shells Whine." His ultimate purpose in all this may have been to make her more like himself. But whether it was or not, he indubitably helped her to become a competent war correspondent—which was an achievement he would live to regret.

8

SPENDING money was one of Pauline's principal stratagems for holding on to her man. During her husband's absence in the spring of 1937, she had a high wall constructed around the Whitehead Street property for the sake of his privacy and a saltwater swimming pool installed, a luxury previously unheard of south of Miami. In the course of what she devoutly hoped would be a tranquil summer, perhaps Ernest would rework the manuscript of *To Have and Have Not,* relax in his swimming pool and come back to her.

Her plans weren't even given a chance to succeed. When he got back in May, he went off straight away to Bimini, and then his junkets to New York began. Moreover, Martha Gellhorn also had plans for him. At lunch with Mrs. Roosevelt at the White House on May 28, she suggested that the First Lady invite Hemingway, Joris Ivens, and herself to show *The Spanish Earth* to the President. "Martha Gellhorn seems to have come back with a deep conviction," Mrs. Roosevelt told the readers of her column the next day, "that the Spanish people are a glorious people and something is happening in Spain which may mean much to the rest of the world." Deeper than that deep conviction, however, was Martha's belief in herself as a winner.

On July 8, she met Hemingway and Ivens in Manhattan. From there they took a taxi to the Newark airport to catch an afternoon flight to Washington. Knowing how bad the food could be in the Roosevelt White House, Martha ate three sandwiches before takeoff, but Hemingway thought she was crazy and Ivens could not be persuaded to take any precautions, either. Unfortunately for hungry men, she wasn't crazy. Almost a month later, Hemingway was still talking about the worst meal he had ever eaten. "We had a rainwater soup followed by rubber squab, a nice wilted salad and a cake some admirer had sent in," he told Pauline's mother in a wonderfully observant letter. Mrs. Roosevelt impressed him as being "enormously tall, very charming, and almost stone deaf. She hears practically nothing that is said to her but is so charming that most people do not notice it." Alert as always to hints of androgyny, Hemingway described the President as "very Harvard charming and sexless and womanly, seems like a great Woman Secretary of Labor, say. . . ." (Although Hemingway was certainly not aware of this, FDR's formidable mother had kept him in girlish skirts and long blond curls until he was nearly six.)

Mrs. Pfeiffer's correspondent also made casual mention of Martha Gellhorn, identifying her as "the girl who fixed it up" for him and Ivens to be asked to the White House. At considerably greater length, Hemingway filled his mother-in-law in on family news. "Pauline and the children are fine. She looks lovely; is really much prettier than ever. The children are delightful which as you know is something pretty difficult for children to be in hot weather. Gregory will go with Ada [the foul-tempered nursemaid] to Syracuse when they leave Key West and Pauline is taking the other two boys to a ranch." As for himself, it was time to return to Spain. He was aware, of course, that Mrs. Pfeiffer strenuously objected to the idea, on the grounds that it was his duty to remain in Key West and look after his boys. While granting that her objection was "very sound," he said he couldn't go back on his promise to his friends in Spain that he would rejoin them. Besides, he added, he probably would not be able to teach his boys much if he did stay at home.

His praise of Pauline did not represent pure and simple hypocrisy. The closer he came to deciding to end his second marriage, the more conscious he became of the advantages of hanging on to it. Pauline had always given him excellent advice about his writing, and she had always tried her hardest to make him happy. Her life had been his life. Furthermore, he was full of doubts about Martha. Since she was as fastidious in her personal habits as he was slovenly, they had made an odd couple in their suite of rooms at the Florida. There was something scary, too, about her ambition. A dozen years earlier, he had aired his misgivings about marrying Pauline in *The Torrents of Spring*. During lulls in the fighting around Madrid in the fall of 1937, at the very moment when Martha was once again sharing his bed in the Florida, he wrote a three-act play in which he worked his way through to the realization that he was probably about to make another marital mistake.

The Fifth Column was published by Scribners a year later in *The Fifth Column and the First Forty-Nine Stories*. Following long and troubled tryouts in Philadelphia, Boston, and Baltimore, a Theatre Guild production of the play, financially backed by Billy Rose, liberally adapted for the stage by a Hollywood scriptwriter named Benjamin F. Glazer and starring Franchot Tone (as Philip Rawlings), Katherine Locke (as Dorothy Bridges), Lenore Ulric, Lee J. Cobb, and Arnold Moss, finally reached Broadway in March 1940. The reviews were mixed. "Although *The Fifth Column* is an uneven play that never recovers in the second act the grim candor of the beginning," Brooks Atkinson wrote in *The New York Times,* "it manages to make a statement that is always impressive and sometimes significant or shattering." The New York *Post*'s John Mason Brown felt that while the script was "excellently acted in most cases and holds the attention fairly well, its virtues are mainly deceptive because of the lack of distinction and genuine relevance in its writing." *Commonweal*'s reviewer, Grenville Vernon, set the play in the context of the whole Hemingway oeuvre and found its failings characteristic. "There is . . . a love story concerning the newspaper man and an American girl, but it is a very weak and trite story indeed and proves that Mr. Hemingway has not yet learned how to write love scenes."

Philip Rawlings has a big body, a hearty laugh, a walk like a gorilla, and a love of sandwiches with lots of onions in them and of the barrel Scotch at Chicote's Bar. His suitemate in the Hotel Florida is Dorothy Bridges, a tall, handsome blonde from Vassar with good legs, an upper-class voice, a silver fox cape, and a passion for making rooms homelike and keeping them neat and tidy. As soon as her grasp of the war improves, she is going to finish an article for *Cosmopolitan,* but unfortunately she understands—by her own admission—only "a little bit" about University City, while the Casa del Campo is "a complete puzzle" and Usera and Carabanchel are simply "dreadful."

In the second act, a Moorish tart named Anita (sultrily played on Broadway by Lenore Ulric) undertakes to warn Philip about Dorothy. "Listen, you don't want make mistake now with that big blonde." Ruefully, Philip admits that that's just the trouble. "I'm afraid I do," he says. "I want to make an absolutely colossal mistake." That big blonde, Anita steadfastly rejoins, "is not like you. Is a different breed of people." Philip objects to these remarks, but not without revealing more of his ambivalence. "You're unjust to her, Anita. Granted she's lazy and spoiled, and rather stupid, and enormously on the make. Still she's very beautiful, very friendly, and very charming and rather innocent—and quite brave." In the third act, Philip's Spanish friend, Comrade Max, asks him about Dorothy's background, and by this time he can think of almost nothing favorable to say.

> She has the same background all American girls have that come to Europe with a certain amount of money. They're all the same. Camps, college, money in family, now more or less than it was, usually less now, men, affairs, abortions, ambitions, and finally marry and settle down or don't marry and settle down. They open shops, or work in shops, some write, others play instruments, some go on the stage, some into films. They have something called the Junior League I believe that the virgins work at. All for the public good. This one writes. Quite well too, when she's not too lazy. Ask her about it all if you like. It's very dull though, I tell you.

The speech prepares us for the decision Philip makes at the end of the play to break off with Dorothy. She has been useful to him in bed, he concedes, but "that's a commodity you shouldn't pay too high a price for." Stunned by his rejection but not at a loss for words, Dorothy tells him to get out and calls him a commodity, too. As her fury mounts, her Junior League fastidiousness comes surging to the fore. "You're a perfectly vicious commodity," she cries. "Never home. Out all night. Dirty, muddy, disorderly. You're a *terrible* commodity."

The Fifth Column, it can be argued, ought to have been a clear warning to Martha Gellhorn that the odds against her finding lasting happiness in a marriage to Hemingway would be very long. There was a considerable discrepancy, though, between his actual treatment of her in Spain and his fictional treatment, so perhaps she can be pardoned for thinking that the real Hemingway was not shadowed forth in Philip Rawlings. Furthermore, the play is not exclusively devoted to a love affair that doesn't pan out. Philip Rawlings's brilliant work as a counterspy for the Seguridad must have made it even easier for Martha to conclude that The Fifth Column was a work of the imagination that need not concern her personally.

The first scene of the play's second act takes place in a starkly furnished room with shuttered windows in Seguridad headquarters. As the curtain rises, Philip is talking to "a short man with a very thin-lipped, hawk-nosed, ascetic-looking face." His name is Antonio, but as Dos Passos and other knowledgeable readers and playgoers had no difficulty in recognizing, his physical description matches that of Pepe Quintanilla, the Communist counterespionage chief. The meaning of Philip's association with Antonio is triumphantly revealed in the third act. Philip and Comrade Max clear out an artillery post manned by half a dozen Fascists—Edmund Wilson would rightly describe the scene as "in the nature of a small boy's fantasy, and would probably be considered extravagant by most writers of books for boys"—and nab a Fifth Columnist whom Antonio is eager to deal with for his crimes against the Republic. Alas, the play never alludes to Pepe Quintanilla's own crimes against the Republic, not even to the part he played in the disappearance of Andrés Nin and the destruction of the POUM leadership, despite the fact that many people in Spain and elsewhere had begun asking "Where is Nin?" well before Hemingway set down the first word of The Fifth Column. As a study of love, Hemingway's play represented a painful exercise in self-discovery; as a study of politics, it was self-indulgent and self-deceiving.

9

IN December 1937, having finished writing The Fifth Column, Hemingway had Christmas dinner with Martha in the atmospheric Hotel Majestic in Barcelona, where he always stayed when he was in the city. Following which he put her on the train for Paris. From there she went on to Le Havre and sailed for home. That he still was not prepared to ask her to marry him was evident from the reserved tone of the letter she wrote to him from aboard the *Normandie*. "I hope all is well with you and that the yuletide season is the yuletide season. See you sometime, greetings, Marty."

Once he reached Paris himself, he discovered that Pauline was in town, ensconced in a top-floor suite at the Hotel Elysée-Park. Having spent the fall secretly growing her hair long in a Gellhornesque bob, she had come to Europe with the intention of rejoining her husband in Spain unannounced. Instead, she had run into visa problems. The couple's reunion at the Elysée-Park was appalling. Pauline raged at Hemingway for his continuing infidelity, swore that someday she would get even and threatened to jump off the balcony of her suite, à la Jane Mason. He, in turn, was in acute pain from a liver malady, and on seeking out a physician for his ailment, was given Chophytol and Drainochol and warned that he must give up drinking completely if he expected to get well. The long, eventually horrifying decline into illness of a man who exulted in his physical powers had now begun.

CHAPTER TWENTY

"Book Selling Like Frozen Daiquiris in Hell"

ALL THROUGH 1938, Hemingway left Pauline twisting in the wind. Twice more he took up residence in Madrid, both times with Martha in tow. Unable to bear Key West without him, Pauline rented an apartment in New York for two months that fall, so she could be near her sister Jinny. During the week Jinny saw to it that her sister had lots of lunches and openings to attend and on the weekends took her up to Connecticut to visit their Pfeiffer aunts. When the two sisters were alone, practically the only topic of conversation was Hemingway. Jinny, who had long since turned against him, was of the opinion that if he asked for a divorce Pauline should demand a financial settlement, rather than allowing him to go scot-free, and the more Jinny talked the deeper Pauline's sense of grievance became.

During the Christmas season in Key West that year, Hemingway and Pauline put up a front of being happily married for the sake of their boys. A month and a half later, they went into their act again when Hemingway's mother appeared, for the first time in seven years. Ostensibly, what had brought her to Florida was her youngest daughter, Carol, who was living in Lake Wales with her husband and children. Yet it was also true that Grace was dying to see her grandson Gregory, whom she had never laid eyes on, and that she had never completely abandoned hope of renewing loving relations with Ernest. So she swallowed her pride and wrote to him in December, asking if she could come to Key West. Although he at once wrote back and said of course she could, he rented a room for her in the Casa Marina on the other side of the island, rather than inviting her to stay at Whitehead Street.

At sixty-six, Grace was still an imposing figure, and made more so by the long chiffon gowns of an earlier era that she still wore. "It was like royalty arriving, when she entered a room," a woman who was introduced to her at this time would distinctly recall forty years later. "She spoke eloquently, often in metaphysical terms . . . [and] radiated such zest and enthusiasm that for me it was as if some exotic bird of paradise had flown into our midst and we were all brown sparrows by comparison." Young Patrick Hemingway, however, got the idea that his grandmother was a liar, because she described the small penknife she gave him one day as having belonged to her father. At age ten, Patrick was old enough to realize that the knife must have been purchased quite recently in a five-and-ten, but not old enough to consider that a lonely old woman was trying to get him to love her.

Presumably, Grace repeated to Ernest some of the things she had told him in her Christmas letter. The looming defeat of the Spanish Loyalists had saddened her, if only because she knew how much their cause had meant to her son. Even though she didn't have much of an income, she had been making donations to agencies that were caring for Spanish war orphans. And while she was immensely grateful to Ernest for the large check he had recently sent her, his love meant far more to her than money; if only he would come back to Windemere for a visit, how pleased she would be.

His answers to these overtures must have been fairly hard-hearted, for after her departure she did not write to him with any regularity or with any great show of warmth. Fifteen months later, indeed, she sent him a note saying that she had heard he was working on a new novel and that she hoped it would say "something constructive" for once. The iciness of his reply indicated that for all his fame she had hurt him yet again, and when *For Whom the Bell Tolls* was published the following fall it proved to contain a paragraph that bared his feelings. At the end of a long memory of his grandfather's Smith & Wesson revolver and of his father's use of it to kill himself, Robert Jordan devotes a couple of thoughts to his mother. My father, he thinks, "was just a coward and that was the worst luck any man could have. Because if he wasn't a coward he would have stood up to that woman and not let her bully him. I wonder what I would have been like if he had married a different woman? That's something you'll never know, he thought, and grinned. Maybe the bully in her helped to supply what was missing in the other."

2

AS soon as his mother left Key West, Hemingway abandoned his uxorious pretenses and crossed to Cuba aboard the *Pilar* without Pauline. Just before leaving he sent Perkins a letter about his writing plans. He was thinking of bringing out a new collection of his short stories, comprising three stories about the war in Spain that had recently appeared in *Esquire,* "The Denunciation," "The Butterfly and the Tank," and "Night Before Battle," and a fourth story, "Nobody Ever Dies!", that would be coming out in the next issue of *Cosmopolitan.* He also wanted the collection to include two very long stories about the war that he hadn't written yet, one about the battle of Teruel and the other about the storming of a mountain pass by Polish lancers, and another projected story about an old commercial fisherman who fights a swordfish all alone in his skiff for four days and four nights, only to lose it to sharks after he has brought it alongside. (Neither the Teruel nor the Polish lancers story would ever get written, but a dozen years later he would recount the saga of the old fisherman in *The Old Man and the Sea.*) He also was eager, he said, to get to work on a novel about the war. Having disclosed his plans, he finished off the letter with an interesting confession. He had been having bad dreams every night about a military retreat. "Really awful ones in the greatest detail. It is strange because I never had any *ever* in Spain about anything that [actually] happened. . . . Last night I was caught in this retreat again in the goddamndest detail. I really must have a hell of an imagination. That's why [I] should *always* make up stories—*not* try to remember what happened."

In Havana, in a small second-floor room of the Ambos Mundos filled with his fishing gear and other baggage and littered with magazines and newspapers, he turned out in two weeks a war story called "Under the Ridge." From his NANA dispatches to *The Fifth Column,* Hemingway had exalted the discipline of the Communists. "Under the Ridge" was an indication that he no longer wished to make a distinction between their discipline and their brutality. This was not a sign, however, of an emerging political realism on his part, but rather of a reemerging disgust with politics in any form. As defeat was engulfing the Loyalist cause, a bitterly disappointed author was looking for political scapegoats and he did not care what color they came in.

On March 1, 1939—a date he would always remember—he started writing his novel about the Spanish Civil War. Three weeks later, he had fifteen thousand words in hand, at which point he returned to Key West to see Bumby, who at 15 weighed 165 pounds and played on the football team at his school. By mid-April, he was back in Havana and hard at work once again. If he played tennis or swam in the late afternoons, it was just to keep his bowels moving, he said, and in the evenings he tried to hold down his drinking to three Scotches before dinner.

When Martha came to join him, she expected to be told that he had found a house for them to share. But the squalor of his room at the Ambos Mundos had been of no concern to him and he hadn't even looked for a nicer place. ("I am really not abnormally clean," Martha would protest many years later. "I'm simply as clean as any normal person. . . . But Ernest was extremely dirty, one of the most unfastidious men I've ever known.") Taking charge of the house-hunting herself, she came across a newspaper listing of a fifteen-acre estate called Finca Vigía, or Lookout Farm, on a hilltop overlooking the village of San Francisco de Paula, fifteen miles from downtown Havana. The one-story farmhouse, a sprawling, Spanish-style structure with a sixty-foot living room, had most decidedly seen better days, and the furnishings were hideous. Furthermore, the outdoor swimming pool was filled with suspiciously green water and huge weeds had obliterated the surface of the fenced-in tennis court. Although Hemingway thought the joint was a hopeless mess and not worth the bargain rent of one hundred dollars a month, its very dilapidation appealed to Martha's imagination. Drawing on her own funds at first, she hired a painter, a carpenter, and two gardeners and began the process of bringing the Finca back to life.*

A special workroom would ultimately be prepared for Hemingway, but he always preferred to write in his capacious bedroom, with its white walls, yellow-tiled floor, and windows facing south and east that let in oceans of light and lovely breezes. In these pleasant surroundings the words poured out of him at the rate of six to seven thousand a week, and new characters and new episodes kept multiplying in astonishing fashion. Although he was quite sure in May that he would finish in late July, July came and went and the end of the story was nowhere in sight.

The only way for him to stop writing, it seemed, was to take a vacation. After staying in Key West just long enough to pick up his black Buick convertible—for Pauline was traveling in Europe with friends and there was no one in the Whitehead Street house except a

---

* Hemingway finally bought the Finca Vigía on December 28, 1940, for $18,500.

caretaker—he drove Martha to St. Louis to visit her mother. In the last days of August, he then continued on alone to Wyoming, where he had arranged a rendezvous with all three of his sons at the Nordquist Ranch. En route, he called on Hadley and Paul Mowrer, who were enjoying a fishing vacation at a ranch near Cody. Some weeks earlier he had written to Hadley from Cuba about the suicidal feelings that were besetting him, for as his marriage to his second wife approached the breaking point he wanted comfort from his first. "Life is quite complicated," he had confessed. "Important thing for me to do is not get discouraged and take easy way out like your and my noted ancestors. Because very bad example to children."

From Europe, Pauline had written him determinedly cheerful letters, as if nothing were amiss between them. On landing in New York, she telephoned him at the Nordquists' spread to announce that she wanted to fly out and make the family reunion complete. Unfortunately, she caught a cold on the plane and was feverish by the time she reached the ranch. Hemingway took care of her in an utterly impersonal manner, bringing her light meals and replenishing the rock and rye in her glass, but allowing the responsibility of comforting her to be borne by Patrick, her favorite child. Sick and distraught, she finally got out of bed to unpack her clothes. The "knock-out punch"—as Patrick later phrased it—started with her discovery that the wax buttons on one of her favorite suits had melted and run into the fabric. She began to cry, and once the tears started to come they didn't stop. Nothing that Patrick could do for her was of any avail. With the sound of her racking sobs driving him to distraction, Hemingway at last made the decision to leave her once and for all. After making arrangements for Pauline and the boys to be driven back east, he phoned Martha in St. Louis and asked her to meet him at the airport in Billings, Montana.

3

THE lodge at Sun Valley, Idaho, was their destination as he and Martha headed west out of Billings. Since 1936, Averell Harriman had been engaged in developing Sun Valley into a year-round resort as a means of increasing the passenger business of his family's oldest major holding, the Union Pacific Railroad. Steve Hannagan, Harriman's publicist, had come up with the idea that the lodge could acquire quick glamour if a number of movie stars and other celebrities, including Hemingway, could be lured into making use of the facilities. Consequently, when Hemingway phoned to say that he and Martha would be arriving, they were allotted a luxurious corner suite on the second floor with fireplaces in both bedrooms and beautiful views of the mountains, for which, he knew, they would not be billed.

Martha had no previous familiarity with guns and would never become a blood-sport enthusiast. Like Pauline and Hadley before her, however, she was expected to share her lover's recreational interests, and the Sun Valley floor supported a population of partridges, mallard ducks, and mourning doves that made it a hunter's paradise. Guided by Hemingway's tactful teaching, she made excellent progress as a marksman.

Her happiness was apparently unbounded. Nevertheless, she announced that come November she would be leaving Sun Valley to cover the Russo-Finnish War for *Collier's*. As the day approached for her departure, Hemingway began complaining to all and sundry that he was being abandoned. "What old Indian likes to lose his squaw with a hard winter coming on?" he asked Tillie Arnold, the wife of the Sun Valley photographer. The night before Martha left, though, he rose above his resentment and held a farewell dinner for her, at which he toasted her courage. "Keep your eye on this big clown," Martha told Tillie, as she was preparing to leave. ". . . see that he's shaved and cleaned up when you go out on the town." While the injunction was superficially affectionate, it actually was a sign of tension, for Hemingway's lack of cleanliness was rapidly becoming a serious problem for Martha. "The Pig" was the rather edgy term of endearment she had fastened on him.

After she was gone, he dubbed their suite in the lodge "Hemingstein's Mixed Vicing and Dicing Establishment," but nightly poker and crap games with the boys were not much of a consolation to him, and he also failed to persuade Max Perkins—who was caught up in tax problems relating to Thomas Wolfe's estate—to join him for a week or so. After leaving Hadley, he had missed Pauline so much during her trip to America that it was like an abortion. Having left Pauline, he missed Martha just as keenly. In a letter to Pauline's mother, he spoke of the "very lonely time" he was having, although he made no mention of Martha's absence as the cause. Instead, he told Mrs. Pfeiffer that vicious rumors spread by her daughter Jinny had been responsible for the breakup of his marriage to Pauline. "Virginia's version of my life and conduct is a very fantastic one," he assured her. "But she spread it sufficiently and at the right time to break up my home." In reply, Mrs. Pfeiffer simply said, "This is the saddest Christmas I have ever known. A broken family is a tragic thing, particularly so when there are children."

On his return to Cuba, he sent Perkins the first eight pages of the new novel, plus another thirty from the middle of the story. The editor's cabled reply was all that he could have wished. EXTREMELY IMPRESSED STOP OPENING PAGES BEAUTIFUL AND CHAPTER 8 TREMENDOUS WILL SEND CONTRACT.

When Martha rejoined him, he was overjoyed to see her—and full of reproaches. On January 19, 1940, he drew up a mock contract for her to sign that revealed precisely how he felt. At the same time that he was deeply dependent upon her, he wanted to control her.

> I, the undersigned Mrs. Martha, or Mrs. fathouse Pig . . . hereby guarantee and promise never to brutalize my present and future husband in any way whatsoever. . . . I recognize that a very fine and sensitive writer cannot be left alone two months and sixteen days during which time many trying and unlikely things are put upon him voluntarily and involuntarily, and that I . . . was a great cause for his uneasiness of mind during this long period of solitude. . . . I also state for witnesses that far from putting him out of business, he and his business are what matter to me in this life. . . . I am deeply sorry therefore and shall attempt . . . to make up to him for the wretchedness he has gone through and shall also attempt to protect him against same wretchedness in the future. This statement is given of my own free will and in my rightest mind and with love. Martha Gellhorn. Witnesses: Judge R. R. Rabbitt, Judge P. O. [Pissed Off] Pig.

A measure of sexual incompatibility also figured among the problems they had to contend with. As Martha would admit years later to Bernice Kert, the author of *The Hemingway Women,* one of the great bonds between two people in love—"with my body I thee worship"—was always lacking for her.

Starting in February, Hemingway began to let his hair grow. The explanation he offered to friends was that he had resolved not to cut it until he had finished his novel, in order not to break the spell of his creative surge. Actually, he grew it long because he wished to conceal its increasing thinness. In addition, he may have been looking for a way to disconcert Martha, who was always so anxious for him to be well barbered. For in the early months of 1940 she continued to manifest a degree of independence for which two decades of living with utterly complaisant wives had not prepared him. About politics, for example, they differed considerably, mainly because she found the subject absorbing, as he did not. Twice a day on the average, she became eloquently indignant about taxation or some other topic. When Hemingway told her in effect to knock it off and salted his instruction with profanities, she walked out in a huff and took a plane to New York.

A month later, she came back, bringing her mother with her, and another contretemps ensued. Edna Gellhorn, by common consent, had a lovely spirit. T. S. Matthews, Martha's next and ultimately unsatisfactory husband, would say of his ex-mother-in-law in a memoir published in 1985 that "if there are any angels at all, she's one." Although Hemingway loved Edna too, he forgot one day that he had made plans to go somewhere with her and Martha and instead went to the Floridita and had a few drinks with some tourists. When he failed to show up at the agreed-on meeting place, Martha was certain she knew where she could find him. Storming into the Floridita, she bawled him out for his thoughtlessness and demanded that he apologize to Edna. "You can stand me up," she told him, "but you can't do that to my mother." Abashed by her fervor, he humbly followed her out of the bar.

4

ON April 21, 1940, in a letter accompanying the first 512 pages of his new manuscript, Hemingway offered Max Perkins an interesting suggestion for a title:

For Whom the Bell Tolls
A Novel
By Ernest Hemingway

No man is an *Iland,* intire of itselfe; every man is a peece of the *Continent,* a part of the *maine;* if a *Clod* bee washed away by the *Sea, Europe* is the lesse, as well as if a *Promontorie* were, as well as if a *Mannor* of thy *friends,* or of *thine owne* were; any mans *death* diminishes me, because I am involved in *Mankinde;* And therefore never send to know for whom the *bell* tolls; It tolls for *thee.*

John Donne

It has the magic that a title has to have, he added, and Perkins agreed by cable. ALL KNOCKED OUT. THINK [BOOK] ABSOLUTELY MAGNIFICENT AND NEW . . . TITLE BEAUTIFUL. CONGRATULATIONS.

Three months later, the book was done. On July 13, while still working to get the ending right, he informed Perkins that he himself would bring the manuscript to New York in about a week. He also couldn't keep from telling his editor that the last chapter was the most exciting in the book. "It's almost unbearably exciting during and after the bridge is blown. I finished the part where—what the hell—will not tell you—you can read it. I was as limp and dead as though it had all happened to me. Anyhow it is a hell of a book."

All the way north from Miami, he proofread the typescript in a poorly lit and un-air-conditioned parlor car. As he toiled up the steps of Penn Station in New York City, he felt like "a blind sardine in a processing factory." After settling into a suite with twin beds in the Hotel Barclay, he started sending batches of typescript to Scribners by messenger service as fast as he could correct them. The process took a couple of days longer than it might have because of his wish to spend time talking to Gustavo Durán, whom he had invited to move in with him. He had first made Durán's acquaintance in the twenties, shortly after the young Spaniard arrived in Paris to finish his music studies and begin his career as a composer, but it was not until they met again in Madrid in 1937 that Durán became a "God damn hero" to Hemingway. For with the outbreak of the war it was discovered that the composer had military talent; starting out as a second lieutenant in the reserves, he rose quickly to the command of the 69th Division. Just before Franco's final triumph he fled to London and thence to the United States, following his marriage to an American heiress, Bonte Crompton. From the vantage point of the other twin bed in the Barclay, Durán observed through half-shut eyes that Hemingway got up very early, that he walked around the suite barefoot and on tiptoes so as not to disturb his guest, and that he breakfasted on a fog-cutting mixture of tea and gin. Partly because Hemingway wanted Durán to check his English renditions of Spanish, but mainly because he was eager to have his opinion of the story, he asked him to read the typescript. Although Durán was made uneasy by the dialogue and found some of the episodes in the story unbelievable, on the whole he approved of the novel.

Some of the galley proofs were read at the Finca at the end of August, the rest in Sun Valley in early September. All three of Hemingway's sons as well as Martha and himself were the nonpaying guests of Averell Harriman on this occasion, and some of the charges run up by nine-year-old Gregory alone—for private skeet-shooting lessons, for private ice-skating lessons, for suppers of steak or frogs' legs or guinea hen under glass—made the lodge bookkeeper wince. When Dorothy Parker and her husband and Gary Cooper and his wife also appeared at the lodge, the usually sociable Hemingway felt that he had almost too much company to cope with, even though he was very much taken with Cooper. The Hollywood star had played Frederic Henry in the film version of *A Farewell to Arms* produced by Paramount in 1932 (with Helen Hayes as Catherine Barkley), and Hemingway told him he thought he would make an excellent Robert Jordan, should a Hollywood studio decide to make *For Whom the Bell Tolls* into a motion picture.

While he had hoped to be married again by mid-October, the final settlement with Pauline took longer to hammer out than he had expected, largely because of her surprising intransigence. All year he had been complaining that she was trying to put him out of business with her demands; indeed, he had even grumbled about having to send her monthly checks for the support of their boys, for as he saw it she didn't need the money. To Pauline, however, the payments represented an admission on his part of how atrociously he had behaved and of how much she had suffered. After seeking advice from her Uncle Gus, she finally proposed as a basis for the settlement that if she were ever to sell the Key West house the money from the sale should be divided with Hemingway sixty-forty. Inasmuch as Uncle Gus had bought the house to begin with and Pfeiffer funds had paid for most of the improvements, this proposition was quite generous. But while Hemingway finally agreed to it, he resented it and began telling friends that besides driving a hard bargain Pauline had also forced him to part with some valuable real estate he owned in Ketchum, Idaho (which in fact he did not), and a large share of his earnings from his books (which was another lie).

On November 4, two weeks to the day after the publication of *For Whom the Bell Tolls,* with its dedication to Martha Gellhorn, Pauline was granted a divorce in Miami, on the grounds of desertion. Two and a half weeks later, Hemingway and Martha were married before a justice of the peace in Cheyenne, Wyoming.

5

THE black dust jacket was printed in red, white, blue, and gray, and a photograph of Hemingway, taken by Lloyd Arnold at Sun Valley, appeared on the back cover. The initial printing, over and above the Book-of-the-Month Club printing of 135,000 copies, was 75,000 copies. By the end of December, booksellers had disposed of 189,000 copies and by the first of April 1941, 491,000. As Hemingway telegraphically phrased it in a letter to Hadley, "Book selling like frozen Daiquiris in hell." At the end of 1943 the cumulative sales figures stood at 785,000, plus another 100,000 in England, thus making the novel the biggest seller in American fiction since *Gone With the Wind*. And all through the latter half of 1943 and into early 1944, Paramount's film version of the novel, a multiethnic collaboration starring Gary Cooper as Robert Jordan, Ingrid Bergman as Maria, Katina Paxinou as Pilar and Akim Tamiroff as Pablo, was a box-office smash.

The initial reviews of the novel certainly helped to sell it. J. Donald Adams in a front-page salute in *The New York Times Book Review* called it the best, the fullest, the deepest, the truest book that Hemingway had ever written. The love scenes between Robert Jordan and Maria were not only superior to the comparable scenes in *A Farewell to Arms,* said Adams, but were the best in American fiction, period. The playwright Robert Sherwood, writing in the *Atlantic Monthly,* also loved the love scenes. They are "complete," he raved. "Complete love scenes are rare in modern literature. Any writer with knowledge of his craft can write skillfully about sex, but it takes an artist to write thus beautifully and truly about love." In the professorial opinion of Howard Mumford Jones, the *Saturday Review of Literature*'s reviewer, *For Whom the Bell Tolls* was "the finest and richest novel Mr. Hemingway has written . . . [Maria] is tenderly presented—a new Haidee for a relatively chaste and very republican Don Juan. . . . In the rich and Falstaffian figure of La Pilar, wife of Pablo, disillusioned chieftain of the guerrillas, Hemingway has created a character like a mountain. . . . In the descriptive and narrative portions [he] achieves a wider variety of effects than, I think, in any other story . . . I think it at least possible that *For Whom the Bell Tolls* may be the *Vanity Fair,* or the *Uncle Tom's Cabin* of the Spanish War." And in a memorably phrased assessment in the *New Republic* Edmund Wilson asserted, "The big game hunter, the waterside superman, the Hotel Florida Stalinist, with their constrained and fevered attitudes, have evaporated like the fantasies of alcohol. Hemingway the artist is with us again; and it is like having an old friend back." Following an especially eloquent tribute to the book's "sense of terrain," Wilson then spoke of its weaknesses. Its shape was "sometimes slack and sometimes bulging," and the love affair between Jordan and Maria lacked "the true desperate emotion of the love affairs in some of Hemingway's other stories." In his final paragraph, though, Wilson could hardly have been more affirmative. "That [Hemingway] should thus go back to his art, after a period of artistic demoralization, and give it a larger scope, that, in an era of general perplexity and panic, he should dramatize the events of the immediate past in terms, not of partisan journalism, but of the common human instincts that make men both fraternal and combative, is a reassuring evidence of the soundness of our intellectual life."

Today, what is most interesting about these reviews is that not one of them called attention to the curiousness of the love story, or to the book's obsession with the idea of self-destruction. Hemingway the artist may have returned in *For Whom the Bell Tolls,* but the Hemingway myth was still blinding readers to the very darkest impulses that informed his work.

6

MEETING a nurse named María had been the most significant feature of a trip that Hemingway made in April 1938 to the coastal town of Mataró north of Barcelona. His intention had been to spend an hour or so in a hospital there cheering up a friend of his named Fred Keller, who was recuperating from a hip wound he had suffered while fighting with the Abraham Lincoln Brigade; talking to María, however, proved more interesting. A quiet and hardworking young woman, she was the "soul of serenity," despite her ghastly memory of having been gang-raped by a bunch of Nationalist soldiers early in the war. Something of her submissive personality, as well as her traumatic experience, were recalled by Hemingway in his character-ization of Maria in *For Whom the Bell Tolls.* Basically, though, Maria was conceived by him as the antitype, except in appearance, of the woman to whom he would dedicate the novel.

Her legs slant long and clean from the open cuffs of her trousers. Her teeth are white and her skin and eyes are the same golden tawny brown. She has high cheekbones, merry eyes, a straight mouth with full lips, and hair the color of "the golden brown of a grain field that has been burned dark in the sun." The only important difference between Maria's looks and Martha Gellhorn's is that Maria's hair is "cut short all over her head so that it was but little longer than the hair on a beaver pelt." After she was seized by the Fascists in Valla-dolid, she says, in explanation of her boyish appearance, her head had been forcibly shaved, and in the three months since then it has only partially grown out. Its peltlike quality is a fitting complement to her animal-like devotion to Robert Jordan, which in turn comple-ments the pet name of "Rabbit" that he pins on her.*

A college teacher of Spanish from Montana, Jordan has a reputa-tion among Loyalist commanders for his knowledge of explosives and his consecration to his work. The job whose dimensions he is just reconnoitering as the novel begins is to blow a steel bridge over a gorge in a section of the Sierra of Segovia controlled by a band of Loyalist guerrillas and to coordinate the demolition with a surprise attack by Loyalist troops under the command of his friend General Golz (whose shaved head marks him as the fictional counterpart of

---

* "Rabbit" is also one of the more vulgar Spanish terms for a woman's sex organ—as Hem-ingway carefully did not explain to Max Perkins.

Hemingway's friend General "Walter"). A dangerous job in the best of circumstances, it has become even more dangerous as a result of the bitter opposition to it of the cowardly guerrilla leader, Pablo, and of the enemy's treacherously obtained knowledge of where and when Golz's attack will take place. All of these worrisome complexities must somehow be dealt with in a time span of not quite three days and three nights. Every night, nevertheless, and sometimes during the day as well, Jordan occupies himself with Maria, for reasons that begin with sex but go beyond it.

To get around the certainty of censorship by his editor, Hemingway substituted sensations of swelling and feelings of thickness in Jordan's throat for what happens to his member when he strokes Maria's hair.

> "*Qué va*," Robert Jordan said and reaching over, he ran his hand over the top of her head. He had been wanting to do that all day and now he did it, he could feel his throat swelling. She moved her head under his hand and smiled up at him and he felt the thick but silky roughness of the cropped head rippling between his fingers. Then his hand was on her neck and then he dropped it.
> "Do it again," she said. "I wanted you to do that all day."
> "Later," Robert Jordan said and his voice was thick.

And in his sleeping robe under the stars at a much later point in the novel:

> "I have thought about thy hair," he said. "And what we can do about it. You see it grows now all over thy head the same length like the fur of an animal and it is lovely to feel and I love it very much and it is beautiful and it flattens and rises like a wheatfield in the wind when I pass my hand over it."
> "Pass thy hand over it."
> He did and left his hand there and went on talking to her throat, as he felt his own throat swell. "But in Madrid I thought we could go together to the coiffeur's and they could cut it neatly on the sides and in the back as they cut mine and that way it would look better in the town while it is growing out."
> "I would look like thee," she said and held him close to her. "And then I never would want to change it."

In point of fact, the short-haired Maria and the shaggy Jordan ("I don't like to have my hair cut," he explains) already resemble one another. As Pilar observes of them very early, "You could be brother and sister by the look," to which Maria replies, "Now I

know why I have felt as I have. Now it is clear." Jordan, too, likes
to think that he and Maria are related. "Maria is my true love and
my wife. I never had a true love. I never had a wife. She is also my
sister, and I never had a sister, and my daughter, and I never will
have a daughter." In their nights of lovemaking in his sleeping robe,
these lookalike, siblinglike lovers feel so much a part of one another
that it is as if they have merged ("I am thee and thou art me and all
of one is the other") and could switch identities if they wished ("if
thou should ever wish to change I would be glad to change").★

Some kind of incompatibility may have marred Hemingway's sex
life with Martha, but in the dream world of his novel erotic compat-
ibility reigns. Even when Maria cannot allow Jordan to enter her on
their last night together before the blowing of the bridge, because of
the great soreness that is the memento of the Fascists' abuse of her,
he only briefly has to kid himself about the virtues of continence,
for her wish to please him in some other way finally leads to a
"delight of acceptance."

Yet if sexual fulfillment heightens the lovers' fantasy that they are
the flesh of one another's flesh and the blood of one another's blood,
so does a tragic similarity in their family backgrounds. "My father
was a republican all his life," Maria tells Jordan, as he sits in the
guerrillas' cave watching her help Pilar wash and dry the dishes after
supper the first night. "It was for that they shot him," she adds.
"My father was also a republican all his life," Jordan replies, but the
difference is that "[my father] shot himself." When Pilar inquires
whether he took his life to avoid being tortured, Jordan echoes her
words. "To avoid being tortured." Not comprehending the black
humor of his response, Maria looks at him with tears in her eyes and
says, "My father could not obtain a weapon. Oh, I am very glad
that your father had the good fortune to obtain a weapon." "Yes. It
was pretty lucky," Jordan says in another burst of black humor.
"Then you and me we are the same," says Maria.

That Maria has spent many hours thinking about suicide becomes
more evident the next day. If Jordan will teach her to shoot his
pistol, she says, then "either one of us could shoot the other and
himself, or herself, if one were wounded and it were necessary to
avoid capture." Of her own volition, she also shows him the single-
edged, Gem-type razor blade that she carries in a leather holder in

---

★ A further instance of the endless influence of Hemingway's peculiar childhood upon his
literary imagination occurs in the scene in which Pablo, who is drunk, discovers that Robert
Jordan is from the United States. "Is it there that the men wear skirts as do the women?" asks
Pablo. Even though Jordan assures him that he must be thinking of Scotland, Pablo insists
that "it is well known that you wear skirts."

her breast pocket. "I keep this always," she affirms. "Pilar says you must make the cut here just below the ear and draw it toward here," she says, showing him with her finger. "She says there is a big artery there and that in drawing the blade from there you cannot miss it. Also, she says there is no pain and you must simply press firmly below the ear and draw it downward. She says it is nothing and that they cannot stop it if it is done." And in the course of her last rendezvous with Jordan in the sleeping robe she admits that some months earlier she had been positively eager to die; on the day of her father's execution, her mother, too, had been shot by the Fascists and Maria had hoped they would shoot her as well.

With his heroine, Hemingway gave his death fantasies free rein. But in dealing with his obviously autobiographical hero he held himself in rather close check and only gradually loosened his grip in the final third of the story. The novel establishes quite early, to be sure, that Jordan is brooding about his father's suicide, and Jordan later sheds more light on his feelings in an interior monologue: "Any one has a right to do it, he thought. But it isn't a good thing to do. I understand it, but I do not approve of it. *Lache* [cowardly] was the word. But you *do* understand it? Sure, I understand it but. Yes, but. You have to be awfully preoccupied with yourself to do a thing like that. . . . I'll never forget how sick it made me the first time I knew he was a *cobarde*. Go on, say it in English. Coward." But for all its honesty, the passage only begins to suggest that Jordan is using the death of his father as a vehicle for carrying on a debate with himself about suicide. A similar self-concealment obtains in his conversations with Maria. Thus, when she finishes demonstrating that killing herself by cutting her carotid artery is something she knows how to do, Jordan's reaction to her chilling words is minimal. "So she goes around with that all the time, he thought, as a definitely accepted and properly organized possibility." But what is most striking is the way he responds—or rather, doesn't respond—to Pilar's story of the Loyalist massacre of the Fascist leadership of a mountain town. In several respects, Pilar is a gypsy version of Grace Hemingway, especially in her domination of her husband, Pablo, her attraction to the sexually ambiguous Maria, which is so strong she feels impelled to deny that it is rooted in sexual perversion, and her operatic way of speaking.

Twenty men, Pilar recalls, had been forced to run a gauntlet between a double line of men with flails, who beat them to death and threw their bodies off the top of a cliff into the river far below. Don Benito Garcia, the mayor, was the first victim. A Loyalist sympathizer whose face was working and who was biting his lips and whose hands were white on the flail "smashed a blow at Don Benito that hit him on the side of the head and Don Benito looked at him and the man struck again and shouted, 'That for you, *Cabron,*' and the blow hit Don Benito in the face and he raised his hands to his face and they beat him until he fell. . . ." Don Federico González, the owner of a mill and feed store, was the second victim. Tall and thin, with his hair brushed over the top of his head to cover a baldness (à la Ernest Hemingway?), he was so frightened that his legs wouldn't propel him through the gauntlet and he just stood there, his eyes turned up to heaven and his hands reaching up as though they would grasp the sky. A peasant wielding a club "hit him a great blow alongside the head," and Don Federico "dropped his hands and put them over the top of his head where the bald place was and with his head bent and covered by his hands, the thin long hairs that covered the bald place escaping through his fingers, . . . ran fast through the double line with the flails falling on his back and shoulders until he fell and those at the end of the line picked him up and swung him over the cliff." And thus it had gone, until all twenty of the Fascists were dead.

The massacre chapter in *For Whom the Bell Tolls* is a recreation of a real massacre, which occurred in Ronda. Yet the stunning power of Pilar's account derives not from any historical record, but from Hemingway's preoccupation with head wounds. If, however, Robert Jordan shares that preoccupation it is carefully concealed. The one thought of his that we are made privy to, after Pilar has finished talking, is of a literary nature: "If that woman could only write. He would try to write it and if he had luck and could remember it perhaps he could get it down as she told it. God, how she could tell a story."

Not until the climactic phase of the novel is the hero permitted to debate the question that had been hounding Hemingway for years. If one is ready to die, is it not better to contrive to be killed than to commit suicide? After the bridge has been blown, Jordan and the guerrillas are making what appears to be a successful escape from the advancing Fascists until the big gray horse that he has been riding rolls over on him and snaps his left thighbone. The guerrillas, including Maria, must go on without him. As he lies alone in the forest, a submachine gun cradled in the crook of his left arm, he comes close to passing out from pain. If he does pass out, he realizes, the Fascists will capture him and interrogate him about the whereabouts of the guerrilla band, possibly using torture as a means of making him talk. Hence it becomes relevant for him to consider killing himself. The only respectable alternative is to remain conscious somehow until the Fascist cavalry appears; by engaging them with gunfire, he can force them to kill him.

Jordan's luck, Hemingway affirms, is very good. No sooner does he tilt toward the alternative of trying to hang on to consciousness until the cavalry appears than some troopers ride out of the timber, led by a lieutenant. Jordan feels "completely integrated" now. He takes a good long look at the big white clouds in the sky and touches the palm of his hand against the pine needles around him and the bark of the pine trunk he is lying behind. He will hold his fire until the lieutenant has reached the sunlit place where the first trees of the pine forest join the green slope of the meadow. "He could feel his heart beating against the pine needle floor of the forest."

7

THE Communist reviewers were furious about the book, and not only because of the massacre chapter, which portrayed Fascists as victims. The *Daily Worker*'s literary hatchetman, Mike Gold, aware that the word "mutilated" had always been important to Hemingway, gave it a Marxist spin: the author of *For Whom the Bell Tolls* had been "mutilated" by class egotism. The novel simply proved, Gold continued, that a writer without principles had joined the Loyalist cause in order to exploit it for personal advantage. Once the cause seemed lost, he had deserted it, as Frederic Henry had done in *A Farewell to Arms,* "leaving a trail of alibis, whines and slanders." The novelist Alvah Bessie, who remembered with gratitude that on a spring day in 1938 on the eastern bank of the Ebro River Hemingway had handed him a pack of Lucky Strikes, paid tribute in *New Masses* to his participation in the war, but called his novel about it "his finest achievement only in the sense that he has now perfected his extraordinary technical facility and touched some moments of action with a fictional suspense that is almost unbearable." Both in depth of understanding and breadth of conception, Bessie found the book woefully deficient, owing to the author's self-absorption. "He has yet to expand his personality as a novelist to embrace the truths of other people everywhere; he has yet to dive deep into the lives of others, and thus to find his own." Bessie was also the author of an open letter to Hemingway, signed by three high officials of the Veterans of the Abraham Lincoln Brigade and published in the *Daily Worker,* that denounced him for having "mutilated" the cause of democracy by maligning La Pasionaria, slandering André Marty, falsifying the attitude of the Soviet Union toward the Spanish Republic, and obscuring the meaning of the war by failing to link it with the continuing worldwide struggle against Fascism.

The agent of Robert Jordan's disillusionment with the Communists is a journalist named Karkov. "Wearing black riding boots, gray breeches, and a gray tunic, with tiny hands and feet, puffily fragile of face and body, with a spitting way of talking through his bad teeth, he looked comic when Robert Jordan first saw him. But he had more brains and more inner dignity and outer insolence and humor than any man he had ever known." Karkov's real-life prototype was the *Pravda* correspondent, Mikhail Koltsov, whose murder was ordered by Stalin at the very end of the Great Terror in late 1938. Although Hemingway made no anticipatory reference to the murder in *For Whom the Bell Tolls,* which is set in the spring of 1937, his portrait of Koltsov was clearly affected by his awareness of the circumstances in which the journalist had died. For Karkov is a cynic, and his mocking repetitions of the Comintern line, voiced in the course of the nightly partying at Gaylord's Hotel, make him seem like a grinning ghost at a banquet. Mike Gold, Alvah Bessie, and company must have been almost apoplectic at Hemingway's willingness to give a "traitor" so much talking room.

"We do not believe in acts of terrorism by individuals," Karkov smilingly remarks to Jordan. "Not of course," he adds,

> by criminal terrorist and counter-revolutionary organizations. We detest with horror the duplicity and villainy of the murderous hyenas of Bukharinite wreckers and such dregs of humanity as Zinoviev, Kamenev, Rykov and their henchmen. We hate and loathe these veritable fiends," he smiled again. "But I still believe that political assassination can be said to be practised very extensively."
>
> "You mean—"
>
> "I mean nothing. But certainly we execute and destroy such veritable fiends and dregs of humanity and the treacherous dogs of generals and the revolting spectacle of admirals unfaithful to their trust. These are destroyed. They are not assassinated. You see the difference?"
>
> "I see," Robert Jordan said.

Karkov's responses to Robert Jordan's questions about the fighting in Barcelona between the Communists and their far-left allies, the Anarchists and the semi-Trotskyist Marxist party, the POUM, echo the scorn for the quixotism of the latter two forces that Hemingway had long since developed. But Karkov's discourses also illustrate the determination of a resurgently antipolitical novelist not to spare the Communists, either, for their persecution of the POUM after the fighting in Barcelona had ceased, for their cynical justification of their ruthlessness on the grounds that the POUM was being subsidized by Franco, and for their disgusting lies about the fate of Andrés Nin.

If Karkov's comments got Hemingway in trouble with Communist reviewers, they also aroused the ire of romantic revolutionaries like Dwight Macdonald. In a bitter assault on *For Whom the Bell Tolls* in *Partisan Review,* Macdonald seized on Hemingway's "vindictive picture" of the Anarchists as proof that at heart he was still a Stalinist. It was a ridiculous accusation and could only have heightened Hemingway's contempt for armchair radicals.

"Dolores [Ibarruri, La Pasionaria] made me vomit, always," Hemingway told a newspaper friend, Jay Allen, in April 1940. He spelled out that sentiment in chapter thirty-two of his novel, in which Dolores becomes a subject of dispute between Karkov and a correspondent for *Izvestia* whose gray, heavy, sagging face, puffed eye pouches, and pendulous under-lip bespeak his spiritual condition. This man is thrilled by the news—the falsified news—that the Fascists have been fighting among themselves near Segovia, putting down mutinies with machine-gun fire and bombing their own troops with airplanes. "Dolores brought the news herself," he tells Karkov. "She was here with the news and was in such a state of radiant exultation as I have never seen. The truth of the news shone from her face. That great face—"

> "That great face," Karkov said with no tone in his voice at all.
> "If you could have heard her," the puffy-eyed man said. "The news itself shone from her with a light that was not of this world. In her voice you could tell the truth of what she said. I am putting it in an article for *Izvestia.* It was one of the greatest moments of the war for me when I heard the report in that great voice where pity, compassion and truth are blended. Goodness and truth shine from her as from a true saint of the people. Not for nothing is she called La Pasionaria."
> "Not for nothing," Karkov said in a dull voice.

While the passage is somewhat heavy-handed, the influence it has exerted is impressive. Among historians of the Spanish Civil War, only Communist apologists have not been swayed by Hemingway's ironies about a phony saint.

Well before the war was lost he had been equally appalled by André Marty and he duly made him appalling in the novel. "His face," he wrote in another assessment that historians of the war have found unforgettable, "looked as though it were modeled from the waste material you find under the claws of a very old lion." A monster of paranoia, the Marty of *For Whom the Bell Tolls* has purged the Brigades of so many suspected deviationists of so many different nationalities that, in the words of a corporal who serves under him, "*Purifica más que el Salvarsán.* He purifies more than Salvarsan." Because the portrait of Marty threatened his thesis that *For Whom the Bell Tolls* was the product of a Stalinist imagination, Dwight Macdonald argued that Hemingway had presented him as an eccentric individual, rather than as a symbol of a system. Once again, Macdonald was confused. Marty in the novel was a symbol, all right; he simply wasn't the kind of symbol that Macdonald wanted him to be. To Hemingway, the politicization of the war against Franco was the essence of what had been wrong with it from the start: political generals, political leaders, and political intrigue, of whatever persuasion, had been the curse and the downfall of the Loyalist cause. That this judgment was crude is not surprising; in 1936, Hemingway had been an innocent about politics and by the middle of 1939 at the latest he had turned his back on the subject once again. (One looks in vain, for instance, for references in his correspondence to the sordid Nazi-Soviet deal of August 1939, which divided Poland and freed the Germans for their next move.) But was his judgment any cruder, finally, than the contention of the supposedly sophisticated Macdonald that he was still a Stalinist?

Lionel Trilling, in an estimate of *For Whom the Bell Tolls* that appeared in the same issue of *Partisan Review* as Dwight Macdonald's, called the depiction of André Marty "brilliant." Nevertheless, he felt that the novel had not managed to convey Spain's political tragedy. By "some failure of mind or of seriousness," Hemingway had not permitted the shabby vice of the Russian politicos, the moral fraudulence of La Pasionaria, the psychopathology of André Marty, and other tragic facts "to become integral with the book by entering importantly into the mind of the hero," with the result that "the novel itself fails, not absolutely but relatively to its possibility and implied intention." Robert Jordan's story is "at best cinematic," said Trilling. He can "experience" all the political badness, "but he cannot deal with it, dare not judge it."

In 1949, two years after Trilling's novel of ideas, *The Middle of the Journey,* appeared, Hemingway asserted, "You could put Lionel Trilling, Saul Bellow, Truman Capote, Jean Stafford . . . and Robert Lowry into one cage and jack them up good and you would find that you have nothing." One can pardon him if he also had a low opinion of Trilling's claim that Robert Jordan dares not judge the politics of the Loyalists.

Like the fisherman in "Big Two-Hearted River," Jordan wants to suppress troubling thoughts. "My mind is in suspension until we win the war," he tells Karkov. But in fact he is unable to shut off the apparatus. Thus, while he tries to tell himself in chapter eight that the Fascists can't know about his friend General Golz's plan of attack, "something in him said, why can't they? They've known about all the others." Suspicions of treachery within the Loyalist military ineluctably lead him on to dark conclusions about Loyalist politicians. The government of that passionate but ineffective liberal, Santiago Casares Quiroga, which collapsed like a house of cards at the news of Franco's uprising, is derided—although not specifically identified—by Jordan as "that bunch of horse thieves that brought [the Republic] to the pass it was in when the rebellion started."

In another phase of what Jordan refers to as his education, he listens to Karkov's analysis of the consequences of the craven decision of Largo Caballero to move the seat of government from beleaguered Madrid to Valencia. "I have just come back from Valencia where I have seen many people," says Karkov. "The cowards who fled from Madrid still govern there. They have settled happily into the sloth and bureaucracy of governing. . . . Their obsession now is the weakening of the commissariat for war." As for Barcelona, where the red and black flag of the Anarchists had once flown, "It is all still comic opera," Karkov assures Jordan. "First it was the paradise of the crackpots and the romantic revolutionists. Now it is the paradise of the fake soldier. The soldiers who like to wear uniforms, who like to strut and swagger and wear red-and-black scarves. Who like everything about war except to fight. Valencia makes you sick and Barcelona makes you laugh."

The upshot of the hero's education is the disgusted realization that the entire leadership of the Republic is corrupt, like virtually all Spanish governments before it. "Oh . . . muck this whole treacherous muck-faced mucking country," Jordan thinks to himself as he lies in the sleeping robe with Maria on the last night of his life.

Muck them to hell together. Largo, Prieto, Asensio, Miaja, Rojo, all of them. Muck every one of them to death to hell. Muck the whole treachery-ridden country. Muck their egotism and their selfishness and their selfishness and their egotism and their conceit and their treachery. Muck them to hell and always. Muck them before we die for them. Muck them after we die for them. Muck them to death and

hell. . . . God pity the Spanish people. . . . Muck all the insane, egotistical treacherous swine that have always governed Spain and ruled
her armies. Muck everybody but the people and then be damned
careful what they turn into when they have power.

Apparently, Lionel Trilling found this wholesale indictment so
intolerable that he could not even remember it. The Columbia professor's own favorite commentator on the Spanish war was George
Orwell. The author of *Homage to Catalonia* (1938) also believed, to
be sure, that all the forces within the Popular Front had acted perfid-
iously. But whereas Hemingway did not care to measure relative
culpabilities, Orwell placed the lion's share of the blame for politically sabotaging the possibility of a united fight against Fascism
upon the Communists. As a judge of war-making errors, moreover,
Orwell was similarly inclined to let the Anarchists and the POUM
off lightly. Although Hemingway knew for a fact that the far-left
militias had not as a rule been militarily effective units, Orwell asserted that they had. And he repeatedly stated that in the ranks of
the POUM militia, in which he had served, he had breathed the air
of political equality and comradeship. "There was no military rank
in the ordinary sense; no titles, no badges, no heel-clicking and no
saluting." The author of *Homage to Catalonia* may have had no illusions about the Communists, but he still clung to a utopian dream
of universal brotherhood. The same could not be said of Hemingway, despite his "No man is an *Iland*" epigraph. Robert Jordan's
love for Maria has no political implication, nor does his affection for
the old man, Anselmo, who helps him to blow the bridge. *Homage
to Utopia* would have been a more appropriate title for Orwell's
book, even as *Homage to Death* could have served as Hemingway's.

8

OUT of who knows what combination of competitiveness and kind-
liness, Hemingway sent a copy of the novel to Fitzgerald, inscribed
"To Scott with affection and esteem." On November 8, 1940, Fitzgerald wrote to thank him and to offer his opinion of the book. "It's
a fine novel, better than anybody else writing could do. . . . I read
it with intense interest, participating in a lot of the writing problems
as they came along and often quite unable to discover how you
brought off some of the effects, but you always did. The massacre
was magnificent and also the fight on the mountain and the actual
dynamiting scene. . . . I'm going to read the whole thing again."
But he never did, because six weeks later he suffered a fatal heart
attack.

Presumably, the highly cinematic episodes that Fitzgerald liked best were also admired by the officials at Paramount Pictures who agreed to pay Hemingway a hundred thousand dollars for the film rights. But if the moguls were right in thinking that a movie version of the novel would do big business at the box office, artistically it would not endure. For while the novel's most memorable action scenes had the immediacy and fluidity of a motion picture, they also were suffused with the magic of Hemingway's language, which the camera eye could not even begin to duplicate. Furthermore, Dudley Nichols's script was sentimentally anti-Fascist, rather than politically nauseated, while the love scenes in the sleeping robe—which had to be played within severe restraints so that the production could receive the seal of approval of the all-powerful Hays Office—contained next to nothing of the relationship that the novel had described. After reading Max Perkins's report on the movie, Hemingway expressed the hope that he would never be forced to see it.

CHAPTER TWENTY-ONE

Combined Operations

AT THE PINNACLE OF FAME he did not forget the friends of yesteryear. On a visit to New York City in January 1941, Hemingway had a drink with Solita Solano in her Washington Square apartment. Solita had left Paris in 1940 after the fall of France to the Nazis, but Margaret Anderson, she reported, had elected to stay behind and take care of her onetime lover, Georgette Leblanc, who was ill with cancer. Now that Georgette was dead, Solita added, Margaret was desperately short of funds and had very few friends in the French capital to whom she could turn. Almost immediately after this disturbing talk, Hemingway came down with a bad case of grippe and had to take to his bed in the Lombardy Hotel. Nevertheless, he wrote out a check to Margaret Anderson for four hundred dollars and sent it to Solita, along with a note that concluded, "Much love Solita and take care of yourself and don't ever worry because as long as any of us have money we all have money." In 1941, four hundred dollars was no mean sum, but *The Little Review* had once been important to him and he wanted to help its old editor any way he could, even as he would do his best for Ezra Pound some years later.

As the sales of *For Whom the Bell Tolls* continued to soar, he even tried to be an accommodating husband by accompanying Martha on a trip to the Far East, where she planned to write a series of articles for *Collier's* about the China-Japan War and the flow of American military supplies to the Chiang Kai-shek government. Martha's idea of fun, he tolerantly observed, was to finish out their honeymoon on the Burma Road, by which he meant to suggest that Asia held very little interest for him. Yet as Martha would reveal long afterwards in her account of the trip in *Travels With Myself and Another* (1978), he took to Hong Kong with utter ease, collecting almost overnight an entourage ranging from a local policeman to fat Chinese millionaires of the crook type and had much less trouble than she did in adjusting to the primitive facilities of the one and only hotel in the muddy city of Shaokwan. While she wondered aloud how two people could possibly manage to wash with the one bowl of water that was allotted to them, he said that they shouldn't wash at all and that if Martha was dreaming of brushing her teeth she was a nut case. "Cheer up," she remembered him cheerfully saying. "Who wanted to come to China?" After an arduous flight to Chungking, where they lunched alone with Chiang Kai-shek and his calculating wife and had a clandestine meeting with Chou En-lai, they went on to Rangoon, at which point they parted. For by this time Hemingway was eager to get back to Cuba, whereas Martha was more interested in inspecting the military and naval defenses of Singapore and the Dutch East Indies.

En route home, he spent a few days in Key West with his two younger sons, Pauline being in San Francisco at the time. The reunion earned him no credits with her, however. Despite her own spotty record as a parent, she rebuked her ex-husband by letter on July 16 for shirking his fatherly responsibilities. In his unconvincing defense of himself, he emphasized financial considerations. The Internal Revenue Service would be after him for extra tax payments unless he stayed outside the United States for six months of every year, so it was incumbent upon him to hang around the Finca and make long visits to places like China. He also reminded Pauline with more acerbity than accuracy that the $6,000 he was forced to give her every year for the sake of the boys was the residue of $21,000 in pretax earnings.

In the fall, though, he managed to please everybody by once again arranging to have all three of his sons join him and Martha at Sun Valley Lodge.* Under the guidance of "Beartracks" Williams, a Kentucky Colonel in the employ of the Lodge, the four Hemingway men did some antelope hunting on horseback in the high, rolling country near the Middle Fork of the Salmon River. During the first two days, they saw whole herds of antelope, but only at a distance,

---

* The photographer Robert Capa, whom Hemingway had come to know during the Spanish Civil War, was also with them for a time.

for the animals ran off at an amazing speed as soon as their sentinels signaled danger. Then at the end of the third day they came upon a herd feeding in a bottle-necked valley. Hemingway jumped off his horse, grabbed a Springfield .30-06 from the gun sling behind the saddle, ran as fast as he could for a hundred yards to a wide hump of land over which the fleeing antelope would have to pass, flung himself down, swung his rifle out before him and fired. At a distance of 275 yards, his single shot broke the neck of the largest buck. "That's rifle shooting, if you ask me," was Colonel Williams's drawling comment.

In setting a well-nigh godlike example to his sons as a hunter, Hemingway was reenacting the role that Dr. Hemingway had assumed in his eyes as a child. At the same time, there was a strong oppositional streak in his attitude toward Hemingway family values. Whatever his parents had been in favor of, he was more likely than not to be against and vice versa. Thus, in the spring of 1943 he decided that Bumby, who had come to stay with him at the Finca following his first year at Dartmouth College, needed to lose his virginity if he had not already done so. "Bum, have you ever been laid?" he asked him. "No, Papa," was Bumby's lying response. "Would you like to be?" "Yes, Papa," Bumby sincerely replied. It then became apparent that Hemingway had already engaged the services of a prostitute named Olga and had arranged with his friend Winston Guest to have the assignation take place in Guest's apartment. Upon meeting Olga, Bumby burst out laughing, as did she. The night before, it seemed, they had encountered one another in a bar and had subsequently spent a pleasant hour in bed together. Since she already knew him, so to speak, Olga felt free to tell him that his father had asked her to furnish him with a full report on his performance. Just before she and Bumby parted the next morning, she telephoned the Finca. "*Sí, señor,*" she assured Hemingway. "*Sí, como un toro!*"

In the summers of 1942 and 1943, when Patrick and Gregory also came to the Finca for extended stays, they were allowed to drink hard liquor whenever they wanted to, and Gregory—who was ten in the first of those summers—took repeated advantage of his father's permissiveness. As a result, he sometimes had a hangover in the morning that not even a prolonged immersion in the swimming pool could fix. On coming back to the house around ten, there would be his father, a Scotch and soda in hand, bidding him a cheerful good morning and asking him how he was. Gregory would then confess that he felt sick, but this information never inspired his father to read him the riot act, let alone give him a moral lecture.

Instead he would say, "I'll fix you a bloody mary. You've just got a hangover." The closest he ever came to talking about setting some rules was to ask Giggy whether he shouldn't cut down on his drinking, on the grounds that "we can't send you back to Mother at the end of the summer with the D. T.'s."

Although Hemingway still held to his habit of arising at first light in order to write, he got very little work done during either of the summers before he went off to war again. For one thing, he loved spending a lot of time with his boys, playing tennis or baseball, or shooting live pigeons at the Club de Cazadores, or fishing off the *Pilar*. In the evenings, he liked to escort them to the jai alai matches, where the boys' pleasure was increased by the realization that their father not only knew all the players personally, but had had most of them out to the Finca for drinks and a swim. After the matches were over, the proud father and his sons would eat supper at the Floridita as a rule, although sometimes they went to a fifth-floor Chinese restaurant called El Pacifico that was two floors above a whorehouse and had a fine view of the city.

A polio epidemic struck Havana in the summer of 1942, so that when Gregory began to complain of aches in his legs and developed a sore throat and a fever, it was feared that he had suffered an attack. The Cuban doctors who came to the Finca twice a day hit his knees with soft rubber hammers, prescribed worthless medicines, and were so noncommittal on the question of whether he would ever get well that the boy was filled with fear. At his best, as always, in a frightening situation, Hemingway assumed complete charge of caring for his son, taking his temperature every four hours and bringing his meals to his room. And at night he would lie beside him on his cot, "telling wonderful stories," Gregory would remember,

> about his life up in Michigan as a boy, how he'd caught his first trout and how beautiful the virgin forests were before the loggers came. He told me about the times he'd been scared as a boy, how he used to dream about a furry monster who would grow taller and taller every night and then, just as it was about to eat him, would jump over the fence. He said fear was perfectly natural and nothing to be ashamed of. The trick to mastering it was controlling your imagination; but he said he knew how hard that was for a boy.

After the crisis passed and Gregory got well, Hemingway talked about his recovery in a way which suggested that he believed he himself had been responsible for it. Not long afterwards, though, he may indeed have saved Gregory's life. The episode occurred on one of the days he took Patrick and Gregory spearfishing. Anchoring the *Pilar* off a deepwater reef on the edge of the Gulf Stream, Hemingway dropped into the water wearing goggles and carrying a spear, and the boys followed suit. As they fanned out along the reef, they were looking for yellowtail, snapper, and grunts. Whenever they impaled a fish, they returned to the dinghy where Gregorio Fuentes, the Cuban mate and cook of the *Pilar,* was waiting to remove it. Finding this routine somewhat exhausting, young Gregory hit on another scheme for storing the grunts he was catching. He unbuckled his belt, passed one end into the mouth of the fish and out through the gills and then buckled up again. Soon, the scent of blood in the water attracted unwelcome company, in the form of three hammerhead sharks. At the sight of their high, triangular fins coming toward him in leisurely S-shaped curves, the boy screamed uncontrollably, again and again. Despite the roar of the waves breaking over the reef, his father heard him, forty yards away. "Okay, pal," he called, "take it easy, throw something at them to get their attention, and swim toward me." Gregory took the grunts off his belt, tossed them at the sharks and swam to his father. Hemingway hoisted him on his shoulders and took off for the dinghy, swimming sidestroke in long, powerful thrusts. Across the reef Gregory could see a disturbance in the water where the sharks were devouring the grunts.

Gregory later guessed that any man would have tried to rescue a child. Even so, he never felt more like Hemingway's son than he did that day. Underneath the boisterous exterior, his papa was a reserved man, somewhat incapable of expressing paternal affection in conventional ways, so that Gregory hadn't realized how deeply he was loved until Hemingway swept him up on his massive shoulders and swam back across the reef with most of his own body still exposed under the surface of the water to deadly attack.

2

CAPTAIN Mario Ramírez Delgado was the only Cuban national to be credited with sinking a German U-boat during World War II. Years later, Delgado characterized the skipper of the *Pilar* as "a playboy who hunted submarines off the Cuban coast as a whim."

Hemingway's first idea for getting involved in World War II without leaving Cuba was to set up a counterintelligence group that would ferret out Nazi spies in Havana. He had formed a similar network of covert operatives in Madrid five years before, he assured his friend Robert Joyce at the American Embassy. Through Joyce he got the chance to explain his plan to the new American Ambassador, Spruille Braden, and through Braden he received authorization from the Cuban government to recruit a bunch of intrepid men and set them loose. Just as Theodore Roosevelt's Rough Riders in Cuba half a century earlier had been a mix of cowboys and Ivy League graduates, so Hemingway's Crook Factory, as he called it, was for the most part composed of fishermen and jai alai players on the one hand and refugee noblemen from Spain on the other—plus a Catholic priest who had once manned a machine gun in the fight against Franco. Beginning in May 1942 the Factory's collective reports were collated and typed up by Hemingway at the Finca and hand carried by him to Robert Joyce's office at the Embassy.

That it took him no longer than three weeks to find this routine insufficiently engaging is evident from the new proposal that he put to Spruille Braden at the end of May. In addition to keeping on with the Crook Factory, he wanted to stock the *Pilar* with government-issue bazookas, hand grenades, .50-caliber machine guns and radio equipment. Disguised as a vessel belonging to the American Museum of Natural History and carrying a crew of eight, the *Pilar* would keep cruising along the north coast of the island, Hemingway explained, until halted by a German sub. As soon as a boarding party had gathered on the deck of the sub, the men of the *Pilar* would open up with machine-gun fire and then attempt to destroy the sub itself with their bazookas and their hand grenades. Probably because this half-baked plan was the product of Hemingway's brain, Ambassador Braden gave his blessing to it.

The large-bodied millionaire sportsman, Winston Guest, whom Hemingway called Wolfie, a Basque sailor named Francisco Paxtchi Ibarlucia and the *Pilar's* mate Gregorio Fuentes were among the men whom the quixotic sub-hunter picked to accompany him. Such was the mesmerizing power of his enthusiasm that the men all seemed to take their work seriously, even though they must have known from the outset that their weaponry was murderously outclassed by the cannon with which the U-boats were armed. But as the months passed and no German sub commander evinced the slightest interest in Hemingway and company, the cruises of the *Pilar* turned into fishing trips (courtesy of government-issue gasoline) and grenades were hurled into the sea in drunken sport. By adding his sons Patrick and Gregory to the crew, Hemingway tacitly acknowledged that his sub-hunting had turned into a charade, but he never admitted this straightforwardly. To the contrary, he insisted some years later to his young friend A. E. Hotchner that "we were able to send in good information on U-boat locations and were credited by Naval Intelligence with locating several Nazi subs which were later bombed out by Navy depth charges and presumed sunk." Furthermore, he said, piling fantasy atop fantasy, "our capture attack plan would have worked."

Martha, on the other hand, was openly contemptuous of his expeditions right from the start and could not understand why he wasn't as eager as she was to get to Britain to be on hand for the cross-Channel invasion of Hitler's Festung Europa whenever it should occur. From London she wrote to him on November 6, 1943, and once again tried to persuade him to give up his "shaming and silly life" in Cuba by telling him that he was a hero to everyone she had met since arriving in the city. "I think people like me because you chose me and so put on me the mark of superior approval." Yet it may have been precisely because he was a hero to so many people that he was so reluctant to accede to Martha's urgings. In 1918 he had behaved admirably on the battlefield. Not content with the credit that was his due, he had enveloped himself in a myth—and had done so again in Spain in the thirties. By 1943 he was its prisoner. Extraordinary gallantry under fire would now be expected of him as a matter of course if he got involved in the fight for Europe. But while he was still an exceptionally courageous man, as well as exceptionally knowledgeable about war, age, physical problems and alcohol had taken their toll, and his awareness of these factors could well have placed a strain on his nerves. As a young man in post–World War I Chicago, he had produced a fantasy about a young soldier named Orpen who hadn't wished to fight any longer with the heroes in Valhalla. Upon returning home, he had found to his relief that his mother had been willing to grant him this wish. Forever afterwards, she had assured him, he would be able to devote himself to his art. Conceivably, the third wife of Ernest Hemingway could have given her blessing to the same idea. Instead, she did her utmost to make her man return to combat. Perhaps that was one of the reasons why he began to treat her so viciously.

3

WHEN Martha left the Finca in the early fall of 1943, it was not only because the editors of *Collier's* wanted her to survey the scene in Britain, but because she could no longer tolerate being abused. Shortly before her departure, she encountered Dr. José Luis Herrera Sotolongo, the personal physician of the Hemingways. "I'm saying goodbye to you, Doctor," she told him. "I'm leaving for Europe and I won't come back to the *beast*." ("She's from St. Louis, Missouri," Hemingway cryptically replied when Dr. Herrera asked him to explain the meaning of Martha's words.)

Yet she missed him as soon as she left and wrote him long letters in which she allowed herself to dream of the wonderful times that lay in store for them in the future. ". . . we'll write books and see the autumns together and walk around the corn fields waiting for the pheasants." After not hearing from him for quite a while, four letters reached her on December 13, "so it is a national holiday," she declared. In all four of them, however, he gave the back of his hand to her reiterated pleas that he leave Cuba and join her. Trying as hard as she could to rise above her disappointment, she promised him, "I won't urge you to come any more. . . . I think you will regret it and it will be a great general loss for all the people who need and love to read . . . but I will not speak of it again." Yet as far as she was concerned, she emphatically added, "I would give anything to be part of the invasion and see Paris right at the beginning and watch the peace. . . . I have to live my way as well as yours or there wouldn't be any me to love you with. You really wouldn't want me if I built a fine big stone wall around the Finca and sat inside it."

He did not care for the implication that staying put at the Finca was like being in prison, nor did he care for her Christmas letter, for although she began by saying, "You are real and my own," she went on to admit that everything else about Cuba, "the good boring loving people, and the life, is remote, somehow awful, and I dread it. Please forgive me. When I think of it, it is like being strangled by those beautiful tropical flowers that can swallow cows!" Nevertheless, in March 1944, after a whirlwind inspection of the Italian front and a touch-down in North Africa, she flew home, for the simple reason that she was still in love with her husband. Much to her distress, he at once began to rave at her. "He woke me when I was trying to sleep," she remembered, "to bully, snarl, mock—my crime really was to have been at war when he had not, but that was not how he put it. I was supposedly insane, I only wanted excitement and danger. I had no responsibility to anyone, I was selfish beyond belief . . . it never stopped and believe me, it was fierce and ugly."

In the midst of one of his tirades, he announced that he had changed his mind about not getting involved in the invasion of Europe. Wherefore, he told her with malicious satisfaction, he would be covering it for *Collier's*. Of all the news organizations that were clamoring for his byline, he had deliberately chosen the one she worked for, thus destroying her chances of obtaining official credentials to cover the fighting in France, for by press-corps rules magazines were permitted to have only one correspondent at the front.

In April, the unhappy couple flew to New York, where Hemingway's "hideous and insane reviling" of Martha resumed. He was going to get killed, he told her, and when he was, he hoped that she'd be satisfied with what she had done. So saying, he took further revenge upon her by refusing to use his influence to get her aboard the Pan Am flight on which he had managed to wangle a seat for himself. "Oh no," he said. "I couldn't do that. They only fly men." Following a circuitous and hazardous trip across the Atlantic on a cargo ship laden with dynamite, Martha learned that her husband had had female companionship on his flight to London after all. In addition to carrying a bunch of naval officers, the plane had been graced by the presence of the actress Gertrude Lawrence.

4

THE hair on his head was receding and thinning faster than ever, and he was upset about it. In Cuba, he had responded to the crisis by growing a huge beard, his excuse being that constant exposure to the sun during sub-hunting forays was making his face too sensitive to shave. A wish to look more military would cause him to discard the beard before joining the fighting in France, but he was still wearing it on the unseasonably warm day in London in late May 1944 when he decided to have lunch at the White Tower in Soho.

As he was wading through the crowd toward the rear of the restaurant, he caught sight of young Irwin Shaw seated at a table for two opposite a cute but not pretty woman in her mid-thirties whose curly honey-brown hair was cut boyishly short and whose sweater called attention to her bosom. Shaw had been romantically involved for some months with his companion, but four years later in *The Young Lions* he would recall her with less than complete fondness in the character of Louise M'Kimber. Blessed with bright hair and a small, elegant body, Louise "seemed to know every bigwig in the British Isles. She had a deft, tricky way with men, and was always being invited to week-ends at famous country houses. . . ." Hemingway shook Shaw's hand, eyed his lady, and asked the writer to introduce them. Shaw obliged. Her name was Mary Welsh, he said, and she worked in the London bureau of *Time*. From Shaw's manner it was clear that he was having an affair with her, which set off an echo, perhaps, in the mind of the anti-Semitic Hemingway of another Jew who liked goy blondes, Harold Loeb. In any case, he proceeded to ask Mary if she would have lunch at the White Tower with him someday. This bold muscling-in infuriated Shaw (who would later repay Hemingway for it by depicting him in *The Young Lions* as a short, fat correspondent for *Collier's* with a round face heavily mottled with much drinking), but it made Mary study him more closely. "Above the great, bushy, brindled beard, his eyes were beautiful," she noted. Having lunch with him would suit her fine, she indicated.

Yet as far as she was concerned their first date was not memorable. For the twice-married Mary had dated a lot of men in wartime London, and Hemingway maintained such a serious demeanor throughout the meal (he was probably depressed) that he made her miss the raillery of her other escorts. The next time she saw him, though, at a party in the Dorchester Hotel where they both were staying, things were different. He trailed her back to her room, jovially greeted her startled roommate, Connie Ernst, and Connie's friend Michael Foot, made himself at home beside Mary's diminutive form on the twin bed on which she had stretched out to rest, and as the long English twilight lingered in the sky spilled out an account of his Oak Park boyhood. When he had finished telling about his overbearing mother, his affected older sister Marcelline, whom he had been forced to take to proms, and his younger sister Ursula who was pretty and quick and bright, he abruptly made a remarkable confession. "I don't know you, Mary," he said softly. "But I want to marry you." Mary assumed that he wasn't serious— until he solemnly repeated what he had said. She reminded him that they both were married and had only recently met. "This war may keep us apart," he resolutely continued. "But we must begin our Combined Operations." Hemingway had not broken with either of his first two wives until their replacements were waiting in the wings; now he was scrambling to line up wife number four before having a final showdown with number three.

His reaching out to Mary was a revealing choice. Born in 1908, she had grown up in Bemidji, Minnesota, as the only child of Adeline and Tom Welsh, both of whom came from socially humble families. Rugged Tom Welsh worked for a logging company, but added to his income by operating a Mississippi riverboat during the warm-weather months, taking tourists and local people on daylong excursions. Summer after summer, little Mary lived for three months with her father and his deckhands aboard the boat, leaving her primly religious mother behind in Bemidji. Although her parents did not talk of divorce, they were clearly incompatible, not least in their ideas about raising their daughter, and Mary so preferred her father's man-to-man way of treating her that she sometimes wished she had been born a boy.

After college at Northwestern, she set out to make a career in journalism. For a time she worked as a society reporter on the Chicago *Daily News* (where young Leicester Hemingway eventually joined the staff and Paul Mowrer was the managing editor), but what she really wanted was to work in Europe, and an offer from the London *Daily Express* gave her a chance to do so. Since 1940 she had been employed by *Time,* with mixed results. Her colleague Lael Tucker Wertenbaker admired her "absolute guts" in any sort of stressful situation, but another colleague, William Walton, was of the opinion that she had no feeling for the deeper significance of events.

As for her romantic history, it was checkered. In 1929, she married a student at Northwestern, Lawrence Cook, only to divorce him two years later. In 1938, she married Noel Monks, an Australian newspaperman, but by 1944 this marriage, too, was on the rocks. Monks had found himself another woman, while Mary's life, in Bill Walton's words, was "full of lovers," some of whom Hemingway would later accuse her of having cuddled up to in order to obtain information that might prove useful to her as a reporter.

The third meeting between Hemingway and Mary occurred a day or so after a party that he attended but she did not at Robert Capa's apartment in Belgravia on May 24. Among the celebrated *Life* photographer's mob of guests that night were Hemingway's brother Leicester, who had come to England with a documentary film unit, the dashing Bill Walton, who was getting ready to jump into France with the paratroopers of the 82nd Airborne, and an English doctor named Peter Gorer and his German-refugee wife. Around three in the morning, the Gorers offered to drive Hemingway back to the Dorchester. Because of the blackout, the streets were dark, while the Gorers were somewhat the worse for alcoholic wear. When their car collided with a steel water tank, Hemingway's head went forward into the windshield and his knees banged hard against the dashboard. At St. George's Hospital at Hyde Park Corner, it took the doctors two and a half hours and fifty-seven stitches to close the wound in his scalp. The swelling in his knees made walking painful and the throbbing headaches caused by his concussion were almost incessant, he found. On the day that Mary Welsh popped in to see him at St. George's, she found him lying in a big, bare, dusty room with his head swathed in a turban of bandages. "I'll be back at the Dorch in a day or two," he said. "Come and see me." Mary smiled. "I will," she promised.

Another visitor to that dusty room was Martha. She had heard from reporters about her husband's accident on the day her ship docked in Liverpool. After settling in at the Dorchester, in a room that Hemingway had reserved for her adjacent to his, she went round to the hospital. Despite a grave warning from the doctors that he must abstain from alcohol, a profusion of bottles lay beneath his bed, Martha at once discovered to her disgust. Their ensuing conversation was not only not pleasant, but much more decisive than Hemingway had bargained on. For while he taunted Martha by saying that he had been in England for almost two weeks and as yet hadn't had a WAC shot out from under him, he was not quite prepared at this point to tell her that they were finished. Consequently, Martha's reply came as a shock to him. In a setting that must have reminded him of the American Hospital in Milan and— by a further process of association—of being jilted by Agnes, Martha informed him that while crossing the Atlantic she had had plenty of time to think about his "ceaseless, crazy bullying" of her in Cuba and New York and his disgraceful "play-acting" aboard the *Pilar*. She was through with him, she announced, and on that note she stalked out of the room, returned to the Dorchester and took a room on a higher floor.

5

WEARING a bandage to protect his head wound and limping perceptibly from the swelling in his knees, Hemingway forced himself to board the attack transport *Dorothea L. Dix* on the night before D-Day. The dawn light of the following morning, June 6, 1944, found him seated in the stern of an LCVP jampacked with helmeted troops. The mission of the landing craft's commander, Lieutenant Robert Anderson of Roanoke, Virginia, was to put the troops ashore in the Fox Green Beach sector of Omaha Beach. Having done so, Anderson gunned his boat back to the *Dix,* where his civilian passenger was hoisted to the deck in a bosun's chair. By evening, Hemingway was at work in the Dorchester on an account for *Collier's* of "how we took Fox Green Beach."

"Voyage to Victory" not only gave the impression that the author had gone ashore with the troops, but strongly suggested that Lieutenant Anderson and his men would have had a great deal of difficulty in locating the beach had it not been for the help of "Mr. Hemingway," who had memorized all the pertinent maps so well that he was able to recognize such landmarks as the church tower of the town of Colleville with much greater assurance than they could muster. World War II, it was clear, was going to be another vehicle for the Hemingway myth—and as had been the case a quarter of a century before, even the tallest of the tales that Hemingway dreamed up would be eagerly disseminated by ingenuous admirers. Thus, *True,* the self-styled "Man's Magazine," ran an article in the early sixties entitled "Hemingway's Longest Day," in which an unidentified veteran of D-Day was quoted as saying that."this Hemingway guy" had assumed command of a combat team that was pinned down on the sand by a murderous enfilade from German pillboxes and had led it to safety in the lee of a hill, whereupon he had crawled back toward the water in order to convey his estimate of the battle to the beach commander. The men whose lives he had just saved were convinced he was going to be killed and could not understand why he wasn't. The author of this gripping tale was a former naval officer, William Van Dusen, but the source of the story was not an unidentified veteran, as he implied, it was Hemingway himself. For Van Dusen had been one of Hemingway's companions on that Pan Am flight across the Atlantic in May 1944 and had fallen so completely under his spell that he never thereafter doubted anything the novelist told him. Leicester Hemingway also believed in his brother's Fox Green Beach exploits and dutifully described them in his memoir about him.

Not for a good month and a half after the June 6 landings was Hemingway in any kind of physical shape to join the ground fighting in Normandy. In the interim, he went aloft several times with the RAF and squired Mary Welsh about town. And one afternoon he accompanied the critic Cyril Connolly to tea in the huge suite in the Dorchester occupied by Emerald Cunard, the redoubtable mother of Nancy, whom Hemingway remembered so well from Paris. The young novelist Frederic Prokosch had also called on Lady Cunard that day, and he later published his fanciful impressions of what ensued when she tried to put Hemingway down.

She began by inquiring how he liked London. He did not care for it, he allowed, especially not the houses, which all looked alike. "Look at Eaton Square, for instance. The houses are all identical. It makes for monotony." Lady Cunard saw her first opening and took it. "That does," she agree. "There is doubtless a certain monotony. Staring into her teacup, she pensively added, Yes, monotony. It's a dreadful failing, isn't it, Mr. Hemingway? I've been reading *The Iliad.* There are moments of monotony....Have you read *The Iliad,* Mr. Hemingway?"

He had read it in college, he grunted. Lady Cunard confessed that she herself had never been to college. There was nothing wrong,

Hemingway replied, with being a self-taught man. "But that's the dreadful thing," Lady Cundard said quickly. "I am not a man, as luck would have it. It is so harrowing to be a lady. We suffer from such inadequacies. You as a man, and a brave one, do not suffer from these inadequacies." So swiftly and delicately were these rapier thrusts delivered, Prokosch recalled, that one scarcely noticed the cruelty.

"Inadequacy in a man," Lady Cunard went on, "is more visible than in a woman. It can measured, as it were. The length, the depth, depth, the immediacy. When one sees an inadequate man one is instantly aware of it. With a woman it is more difficult. There are no commodious measurements. One has to rely on intuition, but intuition can be deceiving. Do you rely on your intuitions about women, Mr. Hemingway?" "My intuitions aren't as clever as yours, I guess," said Hemingway, grinning. With this exchange, Prokosch felt, something in the atmosphere altered imperceptibly; he had a sense of fluctuations, changing odds, weakening weapons, as in the critical phase of a tennis match.

The literary dilettante Desmond McCarthy, who had been sleeping in a chair in the corner of the room, was now awake. "There is always Tolstoy on the horizon," he said. "He strides it like a colossus. A colossus with a beard." Lady Cunard took the cue. "Beards," she said, "are the *sine qua non* for a novelist. Charles Dickens had a beard. George Meredith had a beard. . . . I admire your beard, Mr. Hemingway." "*Chacun à son gout,*" Hemingway replied. The riposte caused Prokosch to look more closely at Hemingway's massive jaws, shaggy beard, sullen smile, and glinting eyes. "There was a sheen of animal stealth and of carnivorous stupidity, but even the stupidity was part of his charm." At the same time, there was something wrong with the great man, Prokosch decided, although he couldn't define what it was. It simply "hovered in mid-air, like a stench in the jungle." Suddenly, Prokosch recalled the long-ago day in Sylvia Beach's bookshop when he had picked up a volume of Hemingway's early stories. In going through them he had been struck by the "glint of animal fear and animal violence" they gave out.

Lady Cunard next brought up the subject of Russia. What do you think of that puzzling country, she asked. There was a pro and a con about Russia, Hemingway muttered, and he wasn't sure either, about Patagonia. Lady Cunard exclaimed that she would adore to go to Patagonia with him. "What a delicious time we'd have!" Hemingway broke into a smile. It was a beautiful white smile, Prokosch saw, a smile of victory and glory.

After Hemingway took his leave, Cyril Connolly whispered in Prokosch's ear that the first round had been Emerald's but that after that "it was all Hemingway." Lady Cunard divined in a glance what Connolly had said. Prokosch detected in her eyes the smolder of defeat. It was quickly followed, however, by a flashing look of triumph. "I was startled," Lady Cunard said softly. Not a bit of what I expected. You may think it bizarre of me but he struck me as androgynous." Connolly replied that that was a very peculiar word to apply to Hemingway. "I am sure that it is," she said. "It is not the *mot juste,* perhaps. But that's how he struck me. Distinctly emasculated."

Whatever Hemingway's opinion of Lady Cunard was, he kept it to himself, possibly because of his excitement at the prospect of being able at last to join one of George S. Patton's armored divisions in Normandy. Tank warfare, however, proved too confusing for him, and he took up instead with the Fourth Infantry Division of the First Army. "We have a very jolly and gay life, full of deads, German loot, much shooting, much fighting," he exultantly wrote Mary Welsh on August 1. Four days later his mood was bleak. He had been knocked down by a tank shell and had again hurt his head, he reported to Mary, while riding in the sidecar of a captured German motorcycle in the vicinity of the village of St-Pois.

What had actually happened is that the driver of the motorcycle, Pfc. Archie Pelkey of the Fourth Division's motor pool, went around a downhill curve between hedgerows at very high speed and would have run right into a German antitank gun if he had not jammed on the brakes as hard as he could. Pelkey and Hemingway took headers into the ditch on one side of the road and Robert Capa, who had been sitting behind Pelkey, dived into the ditch on the other side. A machine-gunner in the antitank crew began firing at the motorcycle. For the next two hours, two German soldiers equipped with machine pistols remained on the alert for any sign of movement from the ditches. When the Germans were finally convinced that the Americans were dead, they withdrew. Pelkey and Capa came through the harrowing incident unscathed, but in landing on the rock-covered bottom of the ditch Hemingway had hurt one of his kidneys and again banged his head.

The consequences of this second head injury were dire. Dr. Herrera later told him in Havana that in the aftermath of the concussion in London the doctors should have opened up his head and drained the hemorrhage, and Herrera deplored the fact that Hemingway had concealed from the doctors the gravity of his headaches in order to get out of the hospital in time for D-Day. Thus the second concussion in Normandy, Herrera continued, had compounded damage that had not yet been undone, and the proof of this was the symptoms from which Hemingway had at once begun to suffer and several of which dogged him for months: double vision, slowness of speech, loss of verbal memory, a tendency to write backhand and backwards, dull headaches, ringing in the ears, and sexual impotence. Finally, Herrera was appalled that despite all these difficulties Hemingway had not taken leave of the war for longer than a two-day holiday at Mont-St-Michel.

Around the 20th of August, he bade goodbye to the Fourth Division. Having assembled, with the blessing of Colonel David Bruce of the OSS, a private maquis, he began doing reconnaissance work in the neighborhood of the village of Rambouillet, thirty miles from Paris. Stanford professor Albert J. Guerard would recall in 1985 that Hemingway had "outraged fellow correspondents by playing soldier and intelligence scout," and the humorist Andy Rooney would also remember the antipathy of the correspondents to this showboating celebrity, although Rooney conceded that he probably "knew more about German gun and tank placements than any of the military assigned to the task."

As soon as he heard that the honor of liberating Paris had been conferred upon General Jacques Leclerc and the Second French Armored Division, he tried to get through to the general the intelligence he had gathered, but was ordered to "buzz off," he told the readers of *Collier's,* and an officious French lieutenant subsequently warned him and his "guerrilla rabble" to stay put until all of Leclerc's troops had passed by. Undaunted and ever resourceful, the correspondent for *Collier's* "took evasive action at this point and waded down the road to a bar." His thirst quenched, he rejoined his men, sped down a side road and caught up with the tanks at the forefront of Leclerc's advance. "Paris was going to be taken," correspondent Hemingway proclaimed in a voice fairly vibrating with self-dramatization. "I had a funny choke in my throat and I had to clean my glasses," he confessed, "because there now, below us, gray and always beautiful, was spread the city I love best in all the world."

In private, he would later boast that he had "entered Paris with very first troops." But except for a passing assertion in *Collier's* that "I took cover in all the street fighting—the solidest cover available —and with someone covering the stairs behind me after we were in houses or the entrances to apartment houses," he did not publish any description of his activities in the city on the day of its liberation. He didn't have to, however, for that job was carried out for him by other writers. "Task Force Hemingway," it seemed, was already mopping up elements of the German rearguard around the Arc de Triomphe at a time when most of the Second French Armored was still fighting skirmishes on the south bank of the Seine. When the careful Leclerc at last entered the capital, he allegedly noticed a sign hanging from the door of a church, "Property of Ernest Hemingway." And then, of course, there was the well-known fact that Hemingway liberated the Ritz Hotel. As Robert Capa averred in his memoir, *Slightly Out of Focus* (1947), he himself arrived at the hotel on the night of the liberation and was met by Hemingway's French driver, who said, "Papa took good hotel. Plenty stuff in cellar. You go up quick." But the truth of the matter is that other men in Allied uniforms got to the hotel well before Papa, for he had been diverted into helping to clear a few German soldiers out of an apartment building near the Bois de Boulogne, after which he paused for a champagne toast at the Travellers' Club on the Champs-Elysées. As for the intelligence-gathering achievements of "Captain" Hemingway and his maquis around Rambouillet, they do not rate even a footnote in the Office of the Chief of (U.S.) Military History's authoritative *Breakout and Pursuit* (1961). In the tactfully worded private judgment of David Bruce, Hemingway and his men "were active and fearless, sometimes purveyors of valuable intelligence, but the best intelligence was that furnished by the natives of villages and of the countryside between Rambouillet and Paris."

6

UNTIL the end of August, he remained at the Ritz, awash in whiskey, champagne, and endless streams of visitors, including the youthful J. D. Salinger, who came to pay him homage, and André Malraux, with whom he engaged in a sneering match.★

Mary Welsh also appeared at the Ritz within a day of its liberation, having persuaded Walter Graebner, her boss at *Time,* to allow her to cover the victory march of the Second French Armored down the Champs-Élysées. "Papa, there's a dame here," Pfc. Pelkey called, after answering her ring at the door of Hemingway's room. Hem-

★ In 1935, Hemingway had said of Malraux's *La Condition humaine* that it was "the best book I have read in ten years." But after an abrasive meeting with him in Barcelona in the spring of 1938, he began to refer to the Frenchman as a prick and a faker who had pulled out of Spain in February 1937, in order to write a "gigantic masterpiss" about the war before the war had really started. Their encounter at the Ritz in 1944 did nothing to soften his hostility. Typical of his later remarks about Malraux was an observation he made to Bernard Berenson in January 1953: "How you can tell a man who has killed men (armed) is that usually his eyes do not blink at all. A liar's eyes blink all the time. Meet Malraux sometime."

ingway came out into the hallway, spun her off her feet in "a welcoming merry-go-round bear hug," escorted her inside and introduced her to two roughly dressed members of his maquis who were sitting on the bare floor cleaning their rifles and quaffing champagne. That evening, he took Mary to dinner in a Left Bank restaurant, after which they walked all the way back to the hotel in the soft night air. "Could you be my Pickle? Sour but pungent?" he gently asked her as they strolled along. "Dill pickle," Mary replied. "And since you are Hemingstein, kosher." Although she herself had taken a room at the Ritz, she followed Hemingway to Room 31 and in her underwear promptly slid into his bed and "plunged into sleep." (The other bed in the room, she remembered, "was entirely occupied with Garand M-1 army rifles, hand grenades and other metal objects.") Rather early the next morning, the pop of a champagne cork awakened her. "You snored all night. You snore very well," Hemingway cheerfully announced, handing her a glass of Perrier-Jouët, brut. Not until after she had tossed off the glass and rung the bell for coffee did she notice Archie Pelkey quietly brewing a potful on a little GI stove in the empty fireplace.

All too quickly, she was catapulted into what she herself called "the role of a whipping boy." Hemingway had foreseen a bad end to his marriages to both Pauline and Martha before he married them, and now the rockiness of his relations with Mary made him unhappily aware that another marital disaster was in the making. Unable to love her wholeheartedly and at the same time unable to give her up, he repeatedly denounced her—"You goddamn smirking, useless female war correspondent," he called her on one occasion—and then did his best to make amends by introducing her to wonderful people like Sylvia Beach or by showing her his old haunts in Montparnasse.

If there had been something panic-stricken in the way he had raged to friends in London about Martha's cruel neglect of him, there was something desperate about his courtship of Mary in Paris. And in his attitude toward his personal safety he began to reveal even more disturbing psychological signs. On the first of September, he impulsively decided to make a trip that was at once so dangerous and so nonsensical as to raise the question of whether he was deliberately trying to get himself killed or was losing his sanity. What triggered the trip was a written message from Colonel Charles T. (Buck) Lanham, the colorfully profane, bantam-roosterish commander of the Fourth Infantry Division's 22nd Regiment, who in the course of the Normandy breakout had earned Hemingway's admiration and affection.

Born in Washington, D.C., in 1902, Lanham was a graduate of

West Point (1924), the Infantry School (1932) and the Command and General Staff School (1939). During the thirties, he had helped to edit the *Infantry Journal* and, as war was approaching, had gone to Hollywood, where he wrote and supervised the production of a widely used series of training films. A poet and short-story writer as well as a professional soldier, he was very proud of the fact that *Harper's* magazine had published several of his sonnets. The seventeen decorations he would hold by the time of his retirement from the military in 1954 backed up Hemingway's hero-worshiping tribute to him as "the finest and bravest and most intelligent regimental commander I have ever known."

In late August 1944, a fast-moving American task force, including Lanham's troops, had pursued the Germans northward across the Aisne and the Oise toward the Belgian frontier. Near the town of Landrecies, the 22nd Regiment took two thousand prisoners in a notable action. "Go hang yourself, brave Hemingstein. We have fought at Landrecies and you were not there," Lanham informed his friend at the Ritz, not reckoning on the effect that his good-humored taunt would have on him. On the morning of September 2, less than twenty-four hours after receiving Lanham's note, Hemingway took off for Landrecies in a jeep driven by Jean Décan, a thirty-three-year-old anti-Nazi fanatic who had been with him at Rambouillet. After an arduous day and a half of driving, they caught up with the astounded Lanham in the village of Pommereuil. Inasmuch as no further fighting in the area was anticipated, Hemingway and Décan headed back to Paris almost immediately. Going and coming, though, they traversed territory that was crawling with outflanked but heavily armed detachments of German soldiers, any one of which could have made short work of two men in American uniforms traveling in a jeep. In Buck Lanham's opinion, Hemingway was damned lucky to have survived that crazy adventure.

Two days after returning to the Ritz, he and Décan again left the city, this time in the hope of linking up with the Fourth Division in its assault on the Germans' fearsomely fortified Siegfried Line. When the American artist John Groth encountered Hemingway in late September, he was commanding a bunch of irregulars and living in a farmhouse he called "Schloss Hemingway" (alternatively, "Schloss Hemingstein") that had no Allied troops between it and the Germans. The novelist's unearthly calmness under fire was best illustrated, in Groth's view, by what happened one evening at the officers' mess in Colonel Lanham's headquarters. During the meal a shell landed directly outside, breaking the windows and knocking out the lights. Although every officer at once hit the floor, Hemingway imperturbably continued to cut and eat his meat in the darkness. After a candle was lit, the officers returned to the table wearing their helmets and were amazed that Hemingway refused to follow their prudent example. In another version of this story, Colonel Lanham remembered that as soon as the shell exploded he and his fellow officers headed for the potato cellar, but that when Hemingway did not heed his command to "get his ass out of there and into the cellar," Lanham rejoined him at the table. At the sound of a second explosion, the Colonel told Hemingway to put on his goddamned tin hat, only to be ignored again. At which point, Lanham removed his. Because Lanham admired Hemingway so much, he found nothing suicidal in his behavior; in his eyes, sangfroid sufficed to explain it. Groth, on the other hand, found it both impressive and insane.

His letters to Mary in this period, addressed to "Dearest Pickle," "Dearest Small Friend," and "My Beloved," were brimming with love and longing for her. Yet after he got back to the Ritz at the end of September he lavished the bulk of his attentions on Marlene Dietrich, who had also settled in at the hotel and loved being in Hemingway's company. "Marlene used to wander down to Ernest's room to sit on his bathtub and sing to him while he shaved," Mary would recall in her autobiography, whereas a "serious spat" she herself had with him immediately upon his return was but the prelude to other quarrels. Thus when three or four of the 22nd Regiment's battalion commanders came to dinner one night, Hemingway was loud in his approval of the way Marlene treated them, but accused Mary of having been insulting. "All evening . . . you insulted my friends," he coldly informed her when they were finally alone in her room. "You could not have behaved more horribly," he added for good measure. For a moment, Mary held back her fury—but only for a moment. "Your friends are drunks and slobs," she said. "They threw up all over my bathroom. . . . They drove Marlene away. They may be heroes in Germany, but they stink, stink, stink here. But I DID NOT INSULT THEM, your boorish friends." The phrase "may be heroes," she later decided, was the straw that broke the camel's back. Hemingway stepped forward and gave her a slap on the jaw. It was the first physical attack Mary had endured since her mother had spanked her with the back of a hairbrush. She fell onto the bed, a hand on her smarting skin. "You poor coward," she hissed. "You poor, fat, featherheaded coward. You woman-hitter." Hemingway sat down next to her. She pushed him flat, straddled his hips and pounded his chest with her fists. "You big bully. You fly-blown ego," she cried. To her astonishment, Hemingway looked up at her with a grin and genially remarked that she looked pretty when she was mad.

That night they slept in their separate rooms. In the morning, Mary woke up still angry and quite determined to pursue her life apart from this terrible man. A succession of emissaries, including two of the battalion commanders and Marlene, arrived at her door in the next few hours. Their message was that Papa was sorry and that he really loved her. About noontime the doorbell rang again. It was Hemingway, Mary discovered, looking positively ebullient. "Pickle," he said, "I finally discovered what was wrong last night. Please listen." With a show of impatience, Mary allowed him to continue. "You had your hair done yesterday, didn't you?" he asked. Yes, she said; her friend the coiffeuse at the Ritz did it every week. "Something she did to your hair made you look mean and malicious," Hemingway eagerly explained. "She really changed the expression of your face. I didn't know what it was last night. But that was it." Despite her instantaneous response that he was talking nonsense, she soon forgave him.

7

ON the complaint of several reporters that he had been violating the Geneva Convention governing the conduct of newsmen in war, Hemingway was summoned to a hearing in early October at the headquarters in Nancy of the Inspector General Third Army. The specific charges against him were that in Rambouillet he had removed the correspondent's insignia from his uniform, had assumed command of Free French partisans who addressed him as Captain or Colonel, had helped to defend the town and had persistently conducted patrols in the area. The reporters who had turned him in further testified that they had seen hand grenades, land mines, bazookas, rifles, and small arms in his room, that he had set up and maintained a map room and that a full colonel had in effect served as his chief of staff. Inasmuch as these allegations were true, they ought to have resulted in his expulsion from France.

Under oath, Hemingway artfully set about to dig himself out of trouble. He had taken off his tunic and insignia on occasion because the August weather had been hot and humid. Although he had offered advice to resistance groups, he had repeatedly spurned their pleas to assume command of them. Major James W. Thornton had likewise sought his advice about disposing his troops around the edges of the town, but with that exception he had played no role in its defense. If some of the partisans had addressed him as Captain or Colonel, they had done so out of affection, even as the inhabitants of New England towns were wont to call dory skippers Captain. Weapons and ammunition had been stacked in his room because storage space in Rambouillet was in short supply. He went out on patrols in his capacity as a newspaperman looking for a good story. While it was true that he owned maps, they were for his personal and professional use. As for the colonel who had allegedly been his chief of staff, the fact was that Hemingway had worked for him as a translator, for the colonel's French was so poor that he had needed help in communicating with the partisans. On October 8, he triumphantly informed Buck Lanham that he had beaten the rap.

For the next five weeks, he roughed it with Mary at the Ritz, his main goal being to regain command of Mr. Scrooby, as he called his sexual potency. Yet for all of her experience and skill, the aftereffects of his second concussion continued to inhibit his ability to perform.

In this time of sexual anxiety he somehow learned that Martha had arrived in Paris from Italy and was at the Hotel Lincoln. When he finally reached her by phone, he insisted that she have dinner with him. On the theory that it was high time for them to start talking about a divorce, she agreed to do so. But unfortunately, she bitterly recalled, he brought along "a band of his young soldier pals from 'his' regiment and in front of them insulted and mocked me throughout the dinner. They were miserable and slowly left and when I could, I got up from the banquette where I'd been hemmed in and fled." Filled with morning-after remorse, he sent her a note of apology in which he likened his treatment of her to spitting upon the Holy Grail. Hyperbole cut no ice with her, however, and from the Netherlands she wrote him on November 3 that the time for definitive action had come. "We are honest people, Bug," she said cajolingly, "and this is a no-good silly arrangement. It is not our style. . . . I think it would be best for you to get this finished with me."

As if he were strongly tempted to finish off more than a marriage, he flung himself in mid-November into one of the most savage campaigns of the whole war in the West, the battle of Hürtgen Forest. Bill Walton, who was his bunkmate during the hellish days and nights that the battle lasted, was struck by the fact that in the intervals of quiet he kept reverting to the subject of his mother. One of the reasons for his contempt for her, he wanted Walton to know, was the way she accepted money from him, money he had earned from books of which she disapproved on moral grounds. This was unforgivable, he said with feeling.

After two and a half weeks of being haunted by the sound of shells ricocheting off trees, Hemingway returned to Paris by jeep and collapsed into bed with a fever, a sore throat, and a temper that was variable, as Mary found out the hard way. Dressed in civilian clothes because she had been invited to a spiffy party, she stopped by his room with a bottle of cognac that she hoped would cheer him up. Jean-Paul Sartre and Simone de Beauvoir had been in to see him, he told her. "Did they have anything interesting to say?" she offhandedly inquired, for her mind was on her pretty black dress. "Did you know you look like a spider poised there?" he angrily asked. Without deigning to answer him, Mary took off like a shot. In her diary she later wondered whether she and Hemingway were really meant for each other. He knew nothing of affection, she sadly observed, and she wondered why other women had tried to hang on to him, inasmuch as he drove them to bitchery.

The doctors that the Ritz management sent up to examine him were of the opinion that he had developed pneumonia, and Hemingway's younger brother could believe it. On the two or three occasions he was with him, Leicester was shocked by the paleness of his complexion and by the unsteady way he walked as he headed back to his bed after sieges of vomiting in the bathroom. Nevertheless, Leicester's idol answered the call of battle one more time. What came to be called the Battle of the Bulge began on December 16 with a thrust by von Runstedt's forces against the American First Army's stretched-out line in Luxembourg. On the morning of the seventeenth, the sweating, feverish Hemingway set out for Luxembourg, having managed to secure the services of a jeep and a driver. As soon as Buck Lanham saw the shape he was in, he handed him over to the regimental doctor, who made him get into bed and gobble some sulfa pills. By the twenty-second he was up and about again, but the Germans' drive had been blunted in the meantime.

Around noon on the twenty-fourth Martha appeared in Luxembourg and at once got in touch with her husband. After all her shows of resolve that their marriage must end, she seemed to be offering him a last-minute chance to save it. They went to a Christmas party that evening and then spent the night together in Buck Lanham's billet in Rodenbourg. The next day, though, as they were touring some command posts in a jeep, he began to disparage her abilities as a correspondent and they parted in anger. A week later, he seized another opportunity to degrade her. Shortly after checking into the hotel in Luxembourg where all the American reporters were staying, Bill Walton happened to meet Martha in the lobby and invited her to have dinner with him that night. Later in the day, Walton encountered Hemingway and told him that he was about to have a New Year's Eve date with his wife. "I'll come along, too," Hemingway said with a big grin.

The dinner was a nightmare. Hemingway called Martha all sorts of insulting names and she thought of some that applied to him. At one point, Walton told Hemingway that he could not sit idly by and listen to such insulting language being addressed to a woman, but the maddened novelist shrugged off the rebuke by saying that he couldn't hunt an elephant with a bow and arrow. After their return to their hotel, he went after his wife in a different fashion. In Walton's room, he stripped down to his long underwear and grabbed a mop and bucket from the utility closet. With the bucket on his head and the mop clutched like a lance, he began trying to batter down Martha's securely locked door. "Go away, you drunk," she furiously called, and to Walton's immense relief as well as hers he finally did.

Thereafter he seemed to accept the fact that his marriage to Martha was indeed over, for his spirits markedly improved, as Mary noted upon his return to Paris in mid-January. Bill Walton was living at the Ritz at the time and he, too, remarked upon his friend's good-tempered friskiness. Mr. Scrooby was operational once again, said Hemingway, and he was grateful to Mary for making him feel like a man. "He talked about it a lot," Walton remembered, "and he was proud of [Mary], this cute little girl on his arm as he swept into the Ritz dining room." She did not play up to him as a man of letters, Walton added. "Instead, she treated him as the hotshot warrior, macho man, great in bed."

Flushed with her sexual success, Mary seemed prepared to believe that for all his moodiness Hemingway would make her happy— even though she shortly received another warning to the contrary. Buck Lanham brought him a present of two German pistols in a velvet-lined case, together with suitable ammunition. With drunken delight, Hemingway promptly loaded one of them and began prancing around the room, aiming through the French windows now and again at imaginary enemies in the back garden of the Ministry of Justice. As he was on the point of firing into the fireplace, Lanham restrained him. Hemingway next spied a photograph of Mary and her second husband that he had asked her to lend him. Picking it up, he danced into the bathroom, pursued by Mary. "Don't be a bloody fool," she muttered. In hypnotized revulsion, she watched him set the picture in the toilet bowl and fire into it six times. Not only the picture, but the toilet bowl and some of the hotel's plumbing were destroyed by the barrage of bullets. Members of the hotel staff came running and Mary departed for "the sanity and order" of her own room.

During the first week in March 1945, Hemingway surprised Martha by coming to see her at the Dorchester, as he was passing through London en route home to Cuba. "Though he had previously refused even to talk of divorce," Martha would recall, "he then came to say Yes, he would get the divorce in Cuba as I wanted. . . . I was intensely eager for the divorce so I could get my passport changed back to Gellhorn. I wanted above all to be free of him and his name; and step out of the whole picture fast." Because she was in bed with flu when he showed up, he stayed only long enough to promise that he would look after her interests, both during and after the divorce proceedings, as though they were his own.

As he boarded the Army Air Forces bomber that would bear him back to the States, he was full of hope and high resolve. Mary would be following by ship, and after a visit to Chicago to break the news to her parents of her intention to divorce Noel Monks in order to marry Ernest Hemingway, she would be joining him at the Finca. Their time apart would be difficult for him, but he would take advantage of it to regain his health. He would swim in his pool every day, build some much-needed bookshelves and postpone his first drink until noon. It was a time for wary optimism. He had survived his third major war, acquitting himself with a bravery that bordered on the lunatic; he had cast off his unsuitable third wife and was about to take another who might more closely correspond to his fantasies. Just before leaving Paris, he had written Mary a note, addressing her as "Dearest Pickle" and signing himself "Your loveing husband, Mountain." He would, he swore, love her always. But would their marriage mark a new beginning, or the mere repetition of old patterns and the beginning of the end? There was yet another war to fight—the climactic one with himself.

PART SIX

1945–1961

CHAPTER TWENTY-TWO

~~

Horrors

IN THE SIXTEEN YEARS OF LIFE that were left to him, it was easy for Hemingway to cut back on his drinking; he did it often. And in the words of Mario Menocal, Jr., the American-educated son of a Cuban sugar-mill owner who was one of his drinking companions in the postwar years, "[Hemingway's] capacity for recuperation was incredible. He would be drinking quite heavily; one day he would stop drinking heavily, and drink normally. The next day he was just as well, just as strong, just as normal as he could be. . . ." Besides remarkable recuperative powers, he also had the ability to appear completely or at least relatively sober when in fact he was partly or utterly drunk. It was a talent that would enable him to fool Lillian Ross, A. E. Hotchner, and many another observer.

Miss Ross met Hemingway for the first time on the day before Christmas in 1947, in Ketchum, Idaho. She had come to interview him in connection with the "Profile" she was working on for *The New Yorker* about his bullfighter friend Sidney Franklin. He was waiting for her in front of his tourist cabin, she remembered,

> standing on hard-packed snow, in dry cold of ten degrees below zero, wearing bedroom slippers, no socks, Western trousers with an Indian belt that had a silver buckle, and a lightweight Western-style sports shirt open at the collar and with button-down pockets. He had a graying mustache but had not yet started to wear the patriarchal-

looking beard that was eventually to give him an air of saintliness and
innocence—an air that somehow or other never seemed to be at odds
with his ruggedness. That morning he looked rugged and burly and
eager and friendly and kind. I was wearing a heavy coat, but I was
absolutely freezing. However, Hemingway, when I asked him, said
he wasn't a bit cold. He seemed to have a tremendous built-in
warmth.

Was the built-in warmth some kind of antifreeze? Apparently, Miss
Ross did not ask herself that question.

In the spring of 1948, Aaron Edward (A. E.) Hotchner, an Air
Forces veteran in his middle twenties from St. Louis, who adored
Hemingway's work and had aspirations of his own as a writer, went
to Havana to interview him for an article on "The Future of Literature" for *Cosmopolitan,* his current employer. By telephone, the two
men agreed to meet at the Floridita around five in the afternoon.
Hotchner arrived first. While waiting at the massive, burnished mahogany bar, he ordered a Papa Doble. As the name implied, the
Papa Doble had been named for Hemingway. The recipe called for
two and a half jiggers of Bacardi White Label Rum, the juice of half
a grapefruit, and six drops of maraschino to be placed in an electric
mixer, vigorously whirled and served foaming in a goblet. When
Hemingway finally arrived, Hotchner observed that he was

wearing khaki pants held up by a wide old leather belt with a huge
buckle inscribed GOTT MIT UNS, a white linen sport shirt that hung
loose, and brown leather loafers without socks. His hair was dark
with gray highlights, flecked white at the temples, and he had a heavy
mustache that ran past the corners of his mouth, but no beard. He
was massive. Not in height, for he was only an inch over six feet, nor
in weight, but in impact. Most of his two hundred pounds was concentrated above his waist: he had square heavy shoulders, long hugely
muscled arms (the left one jaggedly scarred and a bit misshapen at the
elbow), a deep chest, a belly-rise but no hips or thighs. Something
played off him—he was intense, electrokinetic, but in control, a race
horse reined in. He stopped to talk to one of the musicians in fluent
Spanish and something about him hit me—*enjoyment:* God, I thought,
how he's *enjoying* himself! I had never seen anyone with such an aura
of fun and well-being. He radiated it and everyone in the place responded.

As he came toward the bar, Hotchner further noticed that he had a
large oblong welt on his forehead. "Hotchner," said the novelist,
shaking hands, "welcome to the Cub Room." The bartender placed

two frozen daiquiris in front of them; they were in vaselike glasses and twice the size of Hotchner's previous drink. "Here we have the ultimate achievement of the daiquiri-maker's art," Hemingway said. "Made a run of sixteen here one night." The bartender, who had been listening, said that sixteen was the house record. Hemingway without delay sampled his drink, Hotchner recalled, by taking a large mouthful, holding it a long moment, then swallowing it in several installments.

For the next three hours, the double Dobles kept coming, as the two men discussed Robert Flaherty's films, the batting of Ted Williams, the Book-of-the-Month Club, Lena Horne, Proust, swordfish recipes, aphrodisiacs, and Indians. At eight o'clock, Hemingway left for the Finca, sitting in the front seat of a station wagon next to his chauffeur, Juan, and carefully holding a drink for the road—his eighth, by Hotchner's enthusiastic count—while Hotchner headed back to his hotel, where he somehow managed to make some notes on their conversation despite the "rum-mist" in his head.

Hotchner's physical description of Hemingway added an inch to his height and his scorekeeping on the daiquiris the two of them consumed may likewise have been exaggerated. Nevertheless, his anecdote added up to an alcoholic understatement, for he gave no sign of understanding—even in retrospect—that the aura of fun hanging about Hemingway as he entered the bar had been induced by the booze he had been tapping into in all likelihood since dawn and that the drink he took for the road was but the prelude to the wine he would drink at dinner and the nightcaps afterwards.

Eight years before, Hemingway himself had boasted in a "regular Sunday hangover letter" to Max Perkins that the previous night he had started out on absinthe, had drunk a bottle of red wine with dinner, had shifted to vodka in town before the pelota game, and had "battened it down with whiskys and soda until 3 a.m." After the war, in a perfect illustration of the proposition that increased tolerance accompanies increased drinking, he was able to consume considerably more without passing out. Buck Lanham's impression during a visit to the Finca in 1949 was that he was drinking "gallons of hard liquor—mostly Martinis mixed at the rate of fifteen-to-one. . . . Although he takes handfuls of sleeping pills, he always wakes up around four-thirty o'clock in the morning. He usually starts drinking right away and writes standing up, with a pencil in one hand and a drink in the other."

Thus while he appeared to be cold sober on the rainy morning of June 20, 1945, when Mary was scheduled to fly back to Chicago to arrange the legal finalities of a divorce from her second husband, his reactions were more than likely slowed down by alcohol. Ordering Juan, the chauffeur, to sit in the back, he got behind the wheel himself for the drive to the airport. At the Club de Cazadores he turned off the main road to Havana and took a shortcut. Trucks had been hauling clay and leaking hunks of it onto the road's high-crowned surface, and the rain had made the clay as slippery as soap. As the car started to skid, Hemingway warned Mary, who was sitting beside him, "This is bad, Pickle. We have to go off." At an accelerating rate of speed, they slammed into a high bank of earth. Hemingway's forehead was bloodied by the rearview mirror, four of his ribs were cracked by the steering wheel and his left knee was damaged by the dashboard. Mary went through the windshield and would have borne disfiguring scars on her face for the rest of her days had it not been for the ministrations of a clever plastic surgeon.

Heavy drinking was also the drill on board the *Pilar,* and in the summer of 1950 the percentages caught up with Hemingway when he slipped on the wet deck while relieving his mate at the wheel. As he described the accident to Chink Dorman-Smith, "Had one leg over the guard rail and my weight on my right (worse) leg when he swung her broadside to enter the channel. Drew a five inch cut (incised) that reached into the bone and severed some artery whose name I never caught. . . . Also a concussion of about force 5 (Beaufort scale)." It was his third concussion in six years and the fourth or fifth of his life—but not his last.

2

TOWARD the end of the summer of 1947, he began to hear a strange buzzing and humming inside his head like the sound of telephone wires along country roadsides. He had a tendency to hypertension, but the amount of drinking he was doing vastly increased his susceptibility. Upon consulting Dr. Herrera, he discovered that his blood pressure was 215 over 125 and that he tipped the scales at 256 pounds. By watching his diet, cutting back on his drinking, and taking anti-hypertension pills, he lost 28 pounds by the end of the year and reduced his blood pressure to 150 over 104. A return to heavy drinking, however, soon washed away this triumph.

Edema first struck him in September 1950, causing severe pains in his right leg and right foot. His foot, he said, felt as cold as ice, and was swollen like "an elefant in the circus." Within a few years, the edema could be seen in the puffiness of his eyelids, as Madrid's Dr. Juan Madinaveitia noted in November 1956 when Hemingway came to see him for a physical checkup following several weeks of nonstop drinking. Dr. Madinaveitia also found that his blood pressure was 210 over 105, that his cholesterol count stood at 380 and that he was afflicted with liver disease, arteriosclerosis (a signal oftentimes of diabetes), and inflammation in the area around the aorta. At the airport later that day, Hemingway gave the bad news to Aaron Hotchner, who by this time had become his most intimate confidant. "I flunked all the tests," he announced. "[Madinaveitia] put me on a strict food diet with no more than one glass of wine per meal and five ounces of whisky per day, and no, repeat, no screwing. Would you say that's a bulletin designed to resurrect a former cheerful?" By disciplining himself severely, he was able by early 1957 to get his weight down to two hundred pounds and to improve his blood pressure and cholesterol level appreciably. But this triumph didn't last either.

The risk of cirrhosis, that deadly ailment that alters liver architecture and impairs liver function, increases in anyone who consumes four ounces or more of 86 proof liquor a day. During the late summer of 1953, which Hemingway spent in East Africa, he was drinking two or three bottles of liquor a day, as well as wine with meals. Denis Zaphiro, a ranger with the Kenya Game Department, has testified that "he was drunk the whole time," although he seldom showed it. "Just became merrier, more lovable, more bull-shitty. Without drink he was morose, silent and depressed." That his liver was in trouble had been rudely brought to Hemingway's attention by the terrible attack of cirrhotic pain he suffered in Paris in January 1938 and liver-related problems plagued him throughout the final phase of his life. "The protagonist" in Ernest's current depression, Mary Hemingway wrote Bernard Berenson in 1957, is "his poor, long-suffering liver." And George Plimpton has recalled from his meetings with Hemingway in the fifties, "His liver was bad. You could see the bulge of it stand out from his body like a long fat leech."

Even the concussion of the brain, the ruptured liver, spleen and right kidney, the temporary loss of vision in his left eye, the loss of hearing in his left ear, the crushed vertebra, the sprained right arm and shoulder, the sprained left leg, the temporary paralysis of his sphincter, and the first-degree burns on his face, arms and head that he suffered in the second of two plane crashes in Africa in January 1954 did not serve to wean him from the bottle, with the result that seemingly minor stresses on his system were thereafter apt to result in shocking collapses. One of the worst of these collapses began on November 17, 1955, when he was forced to sit for two hours under the TV lights at a decoration ceremony in the badly ventilated Sports

Palace in Havana, while waiting to receive the Order of San Cristobal. As he wrote Wallace Meyer of Scribners some three weeks later,

> Sweated through all my clothes so that at the end you could wring water out of the coat of the dark suit I was wearing. I changed shirt and coat in one of the unheated dressing rooms but had thoughtlessly brought no alcohol to rub down with nor any reserve trousers. So ended up catching a bad cold in the right kidney which ruptured in the air crash. It cut out on me and then the other kidney and the liver were affected. The first I knew it was bad was when my right foot swelled like a football and the pressure brought blood out at the base of the toe-nails. This was rather impressive. . . . The foot swelling occurred on Nov. 19 and the doctor has had me in bed since Nov. 20. I was not able to get him until late that night. He and two other doctors were very spooked by the analyses (will not bother you with details) but for 3 days now the analyses are excellent.

All told, he spent forty days in bed recovering.

In the summer of 1959 he was treated by Dr. George Saviers, a Sun Valley friend, for a kidney disorder which had developed out of his uncontrolled drinking during a recent visit to Pamplona. Twelve months later, a Cuban doctor informed him that he had hemochromatosis, a rare disease characterized by widespread deposits throughout the body, particularly in the liver and pancreas, of hemosiderin, a breakdown substance containing iron. Seen almost exclusively in men over fifty, hemochromatosis is defined in approximately three-quarters of all cases by a combination of cirrhosis of the liver, bronzed skin, and diabetes. The sufferer's liver generally is enlarged, firm and nodular; his diabetes tends to become severe; testicular atrophy is frequent; and myocardial fibrosis is not uncommon. During the winter following the Cuban doctor's diagnosis, Hemingway was diagnosed at the Mayo Clinic as having a dangerous case of hypertension, liver and kidney disease, edema of the ankles, high blood urea, high prothrombin (clotting) time, and mild diabetes mellitus, the main symptoms of which are excessive urination, excessive thirst, and dryness of the skin. It was also the opinion of the Clinic's specialist in liver disease, Dr. Hugh R. Butt, that he "might possibly" have hemochromatosis as well.

Recurrent muscle cramps and chronic sleeplessness, episodes of sexual impotence and premature aging: these, too, were among the calamities that were visited upon Hemingway by his alcoholism, and because of his diminished immunity to disease he developed hellishly uncomfortable and ultimately disfiguring skin problems.

The skin problems began with an infection from a dust particle which got into his left eye in Cortina d'Ampezzo in March 1949 and developed into erysipelas, an acute streptococcal infection of the skin usually accompanied by chills and fever and sometimes by nausea. In Hemingway's case, the infection covered his entire face including his eyelids and was so severe that the doctors feared it would inflame the meninges in his brain and culminate in blindness. Treatment with penicillin in a hospital in Padua cleared up most of the "crut," as Hemingway called it, but at the Finca later in the year Buck Lanham noted that his skin disease was still so bad that he could not shave. On his return to Cortina in February 1950 he came down with another skin infection. Although a million units of penicillin a day, supplemented by aureomycin and frequent applications of ichthyol ointment, eventually subdued it, he continued to be susceptible to rashes, as well as to the disfigurements produced by a benign skin cancer. By 1960, the Spanish journalist José Castillo-Puche remembers in his book on Hemingway in Spain, a chronically bright red patch extended from the bridge of the novelist's nose almost down to his mouth and up to his eyes and was constantly peeling off in scaly white flakes.

But the damage that strong drink did to his psyche was probably even more serious than its effects on his bodily functions. Over a period of time, many scientists now believe, alcohol abuse alters brain-cell function, promotes nerve damage, shrinks the cerebral cortex, and so imbalances the hormonal system that it induces the body to shut off production of natural euphoriants, thereby robbing the alcoholic, as soon as his high wears off, of any normal feeling of well-being. In Hemingway's case, the blockage of such feeling was the tragically ironic consequence of his need to drink in order to lift his spirits—and that longtime need became infinitely more urgent in his later years as a result of his pill-taking. For his antihypertension pills were depressants, as were the sleeping pills he gobbled by the handful every night. In washing down those pills with slugs of Gordon's gin or glasses of wine, Hemingway was playing a psychological version of Russian roulette.

In the spring of 1945, however, the litany of ailments that would require ever crueler tests of his bravery—and offer further proofs of his impulse toward self-destruction—had not yet been disclosed. On the surface at least, there seemed no reason to doubt that the wounded warrior who returned to Cuba to await the arrival of the woman who would become his fourth wife still remained at the peak of his physical and literary powers.

3

"MISS Mary is durable," he confided to the readers of *Look* magazine in 1956. "She is also brave, charming, witty, exciting to look
at, a pleasure to be with and a good wife. She is also an excellent
fisherwoman, a fair wing shot, a strong swimmer, a really good
cook, a good judge of wine, an excellent gardener, an amateur as-
tronomer, a student of art, political economy, Swahili, French and
Italian and can run a boat or a household in Spanish." Mary was
durable, all right. She had to be, to survive a decade and a half of
marriage to a man who, in the latter-day judgment of Martha Gellhorn, grew "progressively more insane every year."

Most mornings, Mary says in her autobiography, Hemingway
"awoke cheerful and with budding plans." But breakfasts of Scotch,
gin, or champagne could turn Dr. Jekyll into Mr. Hyde with a speed
that could take Mary's breath away, as the events of her wedding
day, March 14, 1946, served to remind her. The Cuban marriage
contract, it was explained to her that morning by a somber lawyer
in a somber office full of old-fashioned canebacked Cuban furniture,
required that any gift made by one party to the other had to be
returned if the marriage was dissolved. "Even my engagement
ring?" the astonished Mary wanted to know. "Of course,"
her husband-to-be interjected. "I can't take you for anything?" Mary
asked in mock despair. "Just for everything I'll ever have, my Kitten," Hemingway replied, suddenly bristling.* As he and Mary, his
two younger sons, and Winston Guest prepared to adjourn for lunch
at the Floridita, Hemingway muttered, "Let's take the cup of hemlock now." Stung, Mary burst out, "You bastard. The condemned
man will drink a hearty lunch." Her rebuke failed to shame him.
"The bride wore a dark scowl," he mockingly rejoined. "I feel more
like a middle-aged sparring partner than a bride," Mary shot back.
Following a second session in the lawyer's office, during which the
marriage contract was formally signed, the supposedly happy couple
and two dozen friends assembled for champagne and caviar in a
Havana apartment. For a few "increasingly spirited" hours, Mary
remembered, she and Hemingway enjoyed themselves, but on the
way home her sense of contentment was swallowed up in "a small,
furious earthquake of incrimination and abuse." On arriving at the

---

* Under Cuban law it was also true that if you won a divorce on the grounds of desertion,
you had a right to everything belonging to your ex-partner. Hemingway invoked this law to
hold on to many items belonging to Martha Gellhorn, including $500 in a bank account, her
car, her shotgun, her typewriter, her tennis racket, and her long underwear.

Finca, Hemingway "retired with apparent ease into smooth sleep," while Mary furiously dug some luggage out of closets and started packing her clothes. In the morning, Hemingway was "refreshed and cheerful as always" and Mary decided not to leave him after all.

At the end of the fifties, when she was once again on the brink of leaving him, she spoke openly for the first time about her lack of a sex life. Just how long or how often she had been putting up with this disappointment she did not say. But both in private and in public, Hemingway himself insisted that his sex life with Mary was great. In East Africa, for instance, on the morning of December 20, 1953, he picked up the diary she was keeping about their trip and in a couple of the sentences of the long entry he inscribed he recalled the lovemaking they had enjoyed at Torcello in 1948. During the late fall and a small portion of the ensuing winter, they had lived at the Locanda Cipriani and had "burnt the Beech logs in the fireplace and made love at least every morning, noon and night and had the loveliest time Papa ever knew of."

But what makes that diary entry moving is certainly not the notation of the frequency of their lovemaking, but the helpless fascination it reveals with androgyny and sexual transposition. In Hemingway's life with Mary, the fantasies that had found muted expression in his creation of Catherine Barkley and Maria had become reality.

> She has always wanted to be a boy and thinks as a boy without ever losing any femininity. If you should become confused on this you should retire. She loves me to be her girls [sic], which I love to be, not being absolutely stupid. . . . In return she makes me awards and at night we do every sort of thing which pleases her and which pleases me. . . . Mary has never had one lesbian impulse but has always wanted to be a boy. Since I have never cared for any man and dislike any tactile contact with men except the normal Spanish abrazo . . . , I loved feeling the embrace of Mary which came to me as something quite new and outside all tribal law. On the night of December 19th we worked out these things and I have never been happier.

4

WHATEVER Mary's awards may have been, Hemingway did not repay her with the shows of fidelity she craved. Throughout their married life, he flirted outrageously with other women. In the late forties, the movie director Howard Hawks's beautiful blond wife Slim, who had once been a model (and later became Lady Keith), was one of his "admired and admiring girlfriends," according to

Mary, and so was the curly-lashed and vivacious Jigee Viertel, the wife of the novelist and screenwriter Peter Viertel. (Ensconced in her old wartime room in the Paris Ritz, Mary jealously observed in her notebooks a few minutes before midnight on December 1, 1949, "It is now one hour and a half since I left Jigee Viertel's room . . . and Ernest said, 'I'll come in a minute.' ") The likelihood, though, is that there was far less infidelity involved in these relationships than appearances often implied, for appearances seemed to be what mattered most to him. Even when he summoned an eighteen-year-old Havana whore, whom he nicknamed Xenophobia, to have dinner with him at the Finca, Mary being in Chicago at the time, he was probably motivated by a wish to boast about his dinner partner to accomplished womanizers like Mario Menocal and Winston Guest, rather than by any serious intention of taking Xenophobia to bed. Play acting also marked his courtship of Adriana Ivancich.

They met on a rainy day in December 1948. An Italian sportsman, Barone Nanyuki Franchetti, had invited Hemingway to join him at a shooting lodge he owned on the Tagliamento River, twenty-five miles north of Fossalta di Piave. The only woman among Franchetti's guests was Adriana. At the end of a long afternoon of shooting, Hemingway came upon her as she was drying her beautiful black hair before an open fire in the kitchen of the lodge. On learning that she had forgotten to bring a comb with her, he fished out his own from his jacket pocket, broke it neatly in two and handed her half. It was a talismanic gesture on the part of a man who needed a woman in order to feel whole.

She was just about to have her nineteenth birthday, precisely the same age he had been on the night he was wounded at Fossalta, so that it was only natural that in *Across the River and Into the Trees* he would have Colonel Cantwell talk in detail about battlefield matters with his youthful Italian mistress, Renata—whose name was also a reflection of the novelist's fantasy that Adriana was himself reborn. Another link with her that he wished to believe in began with the fact that her father was dead. The owner of a substantial house on the Calle de Rimedio in Venice, as well as an estate at San Michele al Tagliamento, Carlo Ivancich had planned to run for mayor of Venice after the war, but was murdered by his political enemies in the spring of 1945. Consequently, when Hemingway began calling Adriana "Daughter" it had a special significance. Marlene Dietrich and many other mature women to whom he was attracted may also have been "Daughter" to him, but in the fatherless Adriana's case, there really was a generational difference between them, so that the appellation added an incestuous twist to his longing for her.

After recovering in a Padua hospital from an attack of erysipelas, Hemingway returned to Venice in April 1949 and invited Adriana and her older brother Gianfranco to have lunch with him at the Gritti Palace Hotel. They wrote letters back and forth for the next half year while he was working on *Across the River* and they had several well-chaperoned reunions in Italy and France during the winter and spring of 1950. Accompanied by her mother and her brother Gianfranco, she arrived at the Finca the following October and remained until February 1951.

In his letters to Adriana he spoke in a voice throbbing with unrequited passion. He missed her "rapier wit and lovely mind, body and spirit," he cried; he wanted to hold her in his arms, he told her, even though he knew he was not permitted to do so; and he repeatedly addressed her as "Hemingstein" and signed himself "A. Ivancich" in an effort to persuade her that they were so close they could exchange identities. Whenever they were together, he would stroke her hand for minutes on end and always remembered to praise her wretched poetry and abominable drawings, and when she had the audacity to submit jacket designs to Scribners for *Across the River* and *The Old Man and the Sea* the foolish fond author pressured his publisher into accepting them.*

"Perhaps if Adriana had had the slightest spark of feeling for him as a man, they would have had an affair," Mario Menocal, Jr., later said of her relationship with Hemingway. "She accepted his hospitality, kindness, generosity towards herself and her family—and gave nothing in return." To put it another way, Adriana was prepared to marry Hemingway as a means of restoring her family's declining fortunes and of fulfilling her dream of hobnobbing with glamorous people, but she was not physically attracted to him. Hemingway, in sum, could have her only if she was Mrs. Hemingway. Such was the intensity of his belief that she was smarter, lovelier, and infinitely better bred than Mary that he might eventually have been tempted to pay the price she had set on herself, had not Mary come down on him hard after a particularly ugly scene in front of the Ivanciches at the Finca.

According to Mary's rather self-serving autobiography, the scene had developed without the slightest warning that foul weather was brewing. At dinner one night, she offered to help Gianfranco Ivancich fill out an application for a visa to visit the United States, and after they finished their dessert, she brought her portable typewriter

---

* According to the advertising and promotion director of Scribners at the time, "The jacket drawings for both of these books as executed by 'A' were so bad that we had to have them skillfully redrawn."

out to a table in the living room. As she and Gianfranco were working, Hemingway entered the room and instantly became violently
angry. Picking up her typewriter, he hurled it to the floor. Later in
the evening, while the Ivanciches, Dr. Herrera, and their hosts were
in the sitting room sipping wine, some incautious word of Mary's
set Hemingway off once again. This time he threw his wine in
Mary's face. "You must endear yourself to our guests, throwing
things," said Mary, as she headed to her room.

After thinking out her position very carefully, she interrupted
Hemingway at his typewriter one morning and asked him to join
her in the living room—which he did, docilely enough. As she
reconstructed it in her autobiography, the ensuing showdown went
like this:

> "I will be brief, but you listen carefully," I said, looking straight
> into his gloomy brown eyes.
> "I think I understand about your feeling for this girl." (I had edited
> out the word "infatuation.")
> "As I told you long ago you have my sympathy." (I held back such
> words as "juvenile" and "fool.")
> "Your insults and insolences to me hurt me, as you surely know.
> "But in spite of them I love you, and I love this place, and I love
> *Pilar* and our life as we have it here normally.
> "So, try as you may to goad me to leave it and you, you're not
> going to succeed. Are you hearing me? Because I think it would be
> bad and disorienting for you as well as me."
> Ernest nodded. He was hearing me.
> "Okay, that's it. No matter what you say or do—short of killing
> me, which would be messy—I'm going to stay here and run your
> house and your Finca until the day when you come here, sober, in the
> morning, and tell me truthfully and straight that you want me to
> leave.
> "I hope you've heard me."
> Ernest stood there a moment, his legs showing goose pimples
> below his khaki shorts, his face thoughtful. It was a chilly morning.
> "Yes, I heard you," he said and went out.
> He never asked me to leave.

He never asked her to leave, but a month and a half after being
faced down by her he called her a slut, grabbed an ashtray she had
bought in Venice, and threw it out the door, where it broke into
pieces on the red-tile terrace. And he continued to make a fool of
himself over Adriana, both in letters and in person. At their final
meeting in April 1954 when he was recuperating in Venice from his

two plane crashes in Africa, his yearning for the youth she symbolized became so strong that he broke down and wept. He wanted to
live just so he could see her again, for he still was in love with her,
he said; leaving her was like having an amputation, he wildly added.
And as the tears started to come he cried piteously, "Look, daughter,
look. Now you can tell everybody that you have seen Ernest Hemingway cry."★

5

THE way to make up for the fact that by 1950 he would have published nothing worth mentioning for a decade, Hemingway decided,
was to embark upon big projects. His decision, however, tragically
dovetailed with his diminishing self-discipline and resulted in spectacularly unmanageable work.

Off and on between 1945 and 1947, he turned out 1,195 pages of
manuscript of a story called "The Sea When Young," the first section of a projected three-part yarn about the sea that would eventually serve, he hoped, as the introductory volume of a massive
Land, Sea and Air trilogy. Around the first of December 1950 he
started writing section two, "The Sea When Absent," and the day
before Christmas he announced he had "finished" it. After dashing
off in only six weeks an untitled novella about an old man's battle in
the Gulf Stream with an enormous fish, he started writing section
three, "The Sea in Being," on March 5, 1951. Three and a half
months later, he summed up his labors in a letter to Charles Scribner. At present, he said, he was engaged in revising section one of
his sea book, which he had not looked at since 1947. In a month of
hard effort, he had "completely rewritten it" and cut 179 pages, but
a lot of cutting remained to be done, for he wanted to hold the story
to a maximum of a hundred fifty thousand words. The letter to
Scribner also indicated that it was now his intention to include as a
fourth part of his sea book the untitled novella about the old man
and the fish. Finally, he wanted his publisher to know,

> My chances of living to complete the book are excellent according to
> my doctor. However, I have worked so hard in the last six months

★ Not content with having told this story many times to friends, Adriana repeated it in 1980
in her memoir, *La Torre Bianca* (the title referred to a tower that Hemingway and Mary had
added to the Finca). Although Adriana had high hopes for her book, neither the critics nor the
public cared for its narcissism. After all the other sorrows that had marked her life—two
disastrous marriages, alienation from her sons, heavy drinking and a series of nervous illnesses
—she found herself unable to cope with the failure of her literary ambitions as well. In March
1983 she hanged herself from a tree on her farm at Orbetello, northwest of Rome.

that I know I need a rest and a change of climate. You can whip your blood pressure, as I have, by training and abstemiousness and then work so hard that you can be worn down so anything can hit you. I do not think there are many writers who ever averaged over 1000 words a day for over four months, at a stretch, of the sort of writing you read when you were down here. Maybe there were. But I can tell you I never did. Now I want to get the same tempo in the first part. And please, because I say that, do not think I think the first part is inferior.

His brave assurance to Scribner that the first part was up to snuff masked a despairing fear that it wasn't—and that the second and third parts were not much better. For the story about the old man and the fish was the only sea manuscript that he finally was willing to put his name on in print. Nine years after his death, however, his widow in collaboration with Charles Scribner, Jr., cut and edited all the unpublished sea manuscripts that he hadn't destroyed and brought them out as *Islands in the Stream,* "A Novel by Ernest Hemingway."

Niched in this ruin of a book are passages which show that the older Hemingway could still write like the young Hemingway. Beginning with its sunlit, sea-sprayed opening pages and continuing through its gripping description of an hours-long losing attempt by one of Thomas Hudson's sons to best a giant fish, the "Bimini" section of *Islands* beautifully testifies to the author's inexhaustible responsiveness to everything in this world connected with nature. Yet the "Bimini" section also shows that Hemingway had no will to purge his prose of self-pity, that he could not think of a convincing way to account for the references, both oblique and direct, to suicide, and that his decision to "twin" himself by pairing a writer named Davis with the painter Hudson simply resulted in a loss of narrative focus. In the rest of the novel, the evidences of a runaway machoism are everywhere. The second section, "Cuba," featuring a scene in the Floridita in which Hudson converses with a group of barflies including a whore named Honest Lil, is both boring and embarrassing, while the third section, "At Sea," a romantic replay of the author's sub-hunting experiences, is a meaninglessly violent adventure story of the sort that a Hemingway imitator might have turned out for a men's magazine.

The most powerfully mounted critiques of the novel, following its appearance in print on October 6, 1970, came from Jonathan Yardley in the *New Republic,* Irving Howe in *Harper's,* John Updike in the *New Statesman,* Stephen Donadio in *Commentary* and Christopher Ricks in the *New York Review of Books,* and their verdicts cannot be quarreled with. "[*Islands*] contains just enough flickering reminders of [Hemingway's] wasted genius," said Yardley, "to make reading it a frustrating and saddening experience." The "crippling limitation" of Thomas Hudson, Howe contended, "is that he deeply reflects his creator yet isn't a deeply created figure. One looks through him toward the Hemingway psyche, but not into him, as a man interesting in his own right." In Hemingway's earlier work, Updike observed, "his harsh obsessions seem honorable and necessary; an entire generation of American men learned to speak in the accents of [his] stoicism. But here, the tension of art has been snapped and the line between sensitive vision and psychopathy has been crossed." The last section clearly gave Hemingway the greatest difficulty, Donadio asserted, "but there is a quality of insomnia about the novel as a whole, an edge of desperation reminiscent of a man driving himself beyond exhaustion. The resulting combination of determination and distractedness probably accounts for the book's uneven momentum: the narrative often seems slightly out of control, as if it had begun growing with a life of its own, bulging out in strange and unexpected blossoms which are then cut back, only to reappear after a time like the heads of the Hydra." To Ricks, *Islands in the Stream* was like "the Father Brown story where there are too disconcertingly many murder weapons," by which he meant that the awesome list of Hudson's afflictions—the failure of his marriages, the deaths of his sons, the threats posed by drink and indiscipline to the quality of his work as a painter—constituted a circumvention of the problem of what is really the matter with him. As a result, Ricks concluded, "the novel resembles *Hamlet* as it seemed to T. S. Eliot. Eliot sought an objective correlative, 'a set of objects, a situation, a chain of events which shall be the formula of that *particular* emotion'; what he found was pathology and failure."

An invocation of the problem of Hamlet as analyzed by Eliot was surely a brilliant way of getting at the problem of Thomas Hudson, even though there is a sense in which their problems are mirror opposites. For Hudson, unlike Hamlet, has nothing to say about his disgust with his mother.

6

THE writer who was about to marry a woman who had wanted to be a boy was also demanding to be heard. Wherefore in January 1946

Hemingway embarked on a novel in which he proposed to dramatize in more arresting terms than he ever had before that male and female were ambiguous conditions.

The original manuscript of *The Garden of Eden* was suffused with memories of both of the author's first two wives, although their fictional representatives are younger than their husbands. At the outset, the focus was on the honeymoon of a successful writer named David Bourne and his bride, Catherine, in Le Grau-du-Roi, the fishing village at the foot of the Rhône estuary where Hemingway and Pauline had gone after their wedding in 1927. In the next sequence of chapters, the author "twinned" himself, as he had in *Islands in the Stream,* by introducing a second hero, the young painter Nick Sheldon, whose Indian-black hair is thick and long and who lives with his redheaded wife, Barbara, in a Paris flat very like the apartment that was home for Hemingway and Hadley in 1922 and 1923. Eventually the two couples meet. Lines of reciprocal sexual attraction make the relationship between the two women tingle. Lesbian longings, however, are merely a function of a larger deviationism. Within their marriages, each Eve shares with her Adam a mesmerized interest in a statue of Metamorphosis in the Rodin Museum in Paris, of which "there are no photographs . . . and of which no reproductions are sold." And the point of their interest is that the statue symbolizes the cross-sexual experimentalism that dominates their lives and haunts their thoughts.

Hemingway's speed in turning out pages was that of a man possessed. By mid-February 1946 he had four hundred in hand; by the end of April, seven hundred; by mid-July, one thousand. To Buck Lanham he confessed to being driven by a premonition that he would die within the year. Yet in early 1947 he acknowledged that only a hundred of these pages had been ground through the typewriter, and not long thereafter he put the manuscript in his files. A year later, though, he showed that he was still thinking about it when he came up with a statement of its theme: "the happiness of the Garden that a man must lose." Further attempts to clarify the manuscript occupied the author off and on at the beginning of the fifties, but it was not until the spring of 1958 that he finally undertook a systematic revision of the entire story. As of the end of June of that year, twenty-eight chapters had been reworked. The ensuing month came to a close on a note of high confidence; within three weeks, Hemingway boisterously declared, he would be finished. In mid-September, he again made mention of being "close to the end." Yet by the end of the year he had ceased to speak of the book.

Another ambitious project—amounting to more than two hundred thousand words—had ended in fiasco.

No other piece of his fiction, not even the picaresque novel about Nick Adams and his sister Littless, which he also worked on in the fifties and also failed to complete, reveals as much about Hemingway's sexual duality as does *The Garden of Eden*. Perhaps one of the factors that caused him to withhold the book from publication was a feeling that its audacity was more than public taste at the time could cope with. Surely, though, he gave up on the manuscript mainly out of a helpless awareness that it was a mess. Driven by a manic need to unburden himself of his thoughts, he had initially turned out a thousand pages in six months; but in the end he could not remedy the awkwardness of much of the descriptive writing, or the zigzag incoherence of the plot, or the pathological repetitiveness of the dialogue.

Yet if the novel's enormous flaws deterred him from publishing it, they did not, in the long run, deter his publishers. In the spring of 1986, after brilliant, drastic editing by the writer and editor Tom Jenks, Scribners put out a cut-down version of the David and Catherine part of the story, plus an interpolated yarn, supposedly the work of David, about a father and son hunting elephant on safari in Africa.* The first printing of one hundred thousand copies was sold out in a week. The book was also taken by the Book-of-the-Month Club and excerpts from it appeared in *The New York Times Book Review, Sports Illustrated,* and *Life.*

At Le Grau-du-Roi, the twenty-eight-year-old Oklahoman, David Bourne, finds himself being pressured by a strong-willed madwoman into pretending, on occasion, to be a girl. The madwoman in question is not his mother, but his twenty-one-year-old bride, whose height and tawny-blond hair mirror Martha Gellhorn's, but whose behavior with him in bed recalls the author's diaristic account on safari of his and Mary's. The further the story proceeds, the more diabolical Catherine's craziness becomes (not for nothing does David nickname her "Devil"), and when she is in the full grip of her mania she denounces his stories about his adolescence as "worthless," promotes a ménage à trois as a further means of undermining him, and finally destroys his manuscripts by dousing

---

* The Africa story bears a striking resemblance to Beryl Markham's account in *West With the Night* of her hunting experiences as a girl in Kenya. Given Hemingway's enormous admiration for Markham's book, it seems fairly certain that he borrowed from its imagery and drama. That he could project his hero into Markham's girlhood is thus another instance of the sexual transmutations that characterize *The Garden of Eden*.

them with gasoline and setting them afire. (In conjuring up that last act of madness, Hemingway combined Hadley's loss of his manuscripts in Paris—for which he had "never forgiven her," in Buck Lanham's opinion—with his mother's penchant for burning things.)

Initially, though, the honeymooners are happy in their sunbaked "Garden." Like Hemingway and Pauline in 1927, they wear fishermen's shirts and shorts and are very tan and their hair is streaked and faded by the sun and the sea. "Most people thought they were brother and sister until they said they were married. Some did not believe they were married and that pleased the girl very much."

After making love one day after lunch, Catherine tells David that she is "going to be changed." He protests, even though he doesn't understand what she means, but she is adamant—and not merely for her sake, she contends. "It's for you," she says. "It's for me too. I won't pretend it's not. But it will do something to you." Upon her return from a mysterious bike trip to Aigues Mortes, he gets his first inkling of what she has in mind. Her hair has been cropped like a boy's, with the sides cut uncompromisingly short and the ears clear and the line on top close to the head and smooth. "That's the surprise," she tells him. "I'm a girl. But now I'm a boy too and I can do anything and anything and anything."

That night in bed, she asks him to take his hands off her breasts ("they're just my dowry") and feel how short her hair is. "Feel my cheeks and the back of my neck," she urges. "Oh it feels so wonderful and good and clean and new." Lying beneath the long, light weight of her, he feels her take hold of him and then search lower, and he helps the guidance with his own hands. Although the room is dark, David shuts his eyes anyway; all he is conscious of is "the weight and the strangeness inside." When she asks, "Now you can't tell who is who can you?" he has to admit that he can't. "You are changing," she exclaims. "Oh you are. You are. Yes you are and you're my girl Catherine. Will you change and be my girl and let me take you?" He reminds her that she is Catherine, but she denies it. "No," she says. "I'm Peter. You're my wonderful Catherine. You're my beautiful Catherine. You were so good to change. Oh thank you, Catherine, so much." The eroticism of the scene is more powerful than that of any other in all of Hemingway's work.

The next day David is worried about what will become of them as a result of things having gone so wildly and dangerously and fast. But there is no stopping Catherine, now that she has started. Thus when they move from Le Grau-du-Roi to Hendaye, she goes off to Biarritz and gets another haircut. "I told the coiffeur that I wanted it all brushed forward," she subsequently explains to David, "and he brushed it and it came down to my nose and I could hardly see through it and I said I wanted it cut like a boy when he would first go to public school. . . . So after he was finished and I looked like the most attractive girl who ever went to Eton I just had him keep on shortening it until Eton was all gone and then I had him keep on shortening it. Then he said very severely that is *not* an Eton crop, Mademoiselle. . . . So then I had him shorten it some more and then I kept him shortening it. . . ."

After a trip to Spain, they return to the Riviera, where they rent three rooms at the end of a long, low, rose-colored hotel set amongst the pines on the Esterel side of La Napoule. David's idea is that he will write every morning, but the plan lasts only a little more than a month, as his personal life becomes too complicated for him to concentrate on his work. At the shop in Cannes of Monsieur Jean, the coiffeur, Catherine orders another masculine cut for herself and has the color of her hair changed to silver, so as to set off her incredibly dark suntan.* David, too, decides to get a haircut, and Catherine wants it to be just like hers. "But shorter," David says. "Please just the same," Catherine says—and her will prevails. At first, David is also opposed to having the color of his hair lightened, but then he looks in the mirror (*The Garden of Eden* is full of mirrors) and sees that the resemblance between him and his wife is already very striking. His face is as brown as hers, and his haircut is "her haircut." Sensing his indecision, Catherine makes up his mind for him. "Go ahead and do it," she instructs the coiffeur.**

A short, darkly handsome young woman named Marita now enters their lives and before too long has sex with each of them, for as Catherine observes, Marita is "a girl and a boy both." Inasmuch as making love to a woman is what Catherine has wanted to do for years, seducing her is no problem for Marita. Seducing David, however, not only requires forward behavior on her part, but blatant efforts by Catherine to throw them together. "Go and talk with her David," Catherine urges him at one point. "And if you want to fuck her then fuck her good for me." The adulterous arrangement that Hemingway had maintained with Hadley and Pauline at Juan-les-Pins in the summer of 1926 is thus recreated at La Napoule, except that the Pauline figure is the wife, who corruptly blesses her husband's infidelities and is herself the part-time lover of her rival. As

---

* Cf. Hemingway's evocation in *A Moveable Feast* of the deep Riviera suntans acquired in the summer of 1924 by Scott and Zelda Fitzgerald and Edouard Jozan.
** In early 1947, Hemingway urged Mary to have her hair bleached silver and gave his own a henna rinse. To the servants at the Finca he explained the change in his appearance by saying he had doused his hair with what he thought was a bottle of shampoo left behind by Martha.

for the nude swimming in which the threesome indulges, did it represent a disturbed recollection of the nocturnal skinny-dipping of Hemingway and his sisters at Walloon Lake?

Work, too, is a realm of corruption in *The Garden of Eden*. Despite David's boast at the beginning of the book that he never drinks before or while writing, he drinks more and more as the story unfolds. The fact that Catherine and Marita (whom David calls Heiress) are both wealthy is emphasized time and again, and the proposition that money can destroy a writer is implicit in the references to it. (After informing David that Marita has just bought him a case of Bollinger Brut 1915, Catherine says, "Isn't it lucky Heiress and I are rich so you'll never have anything to worry about?")

Publicity is yet another threat to David's integrity. Thus when it is asserted rather late in the story that David writes "from an inner core which could not be split nor even marked nor scratched," the statement comes across as bravado, and in the next-to-last chapter the reader's disbelief in his unscathed sensibility is confirmed by David's harrowing discovery that after writing a first simple declarative sentence he cannot get the next sentence down on paper, even though he keeps trying for hours. Only in the dreamlike last chapter, when he is tenderly beginning his life again with Marita, is he able to resume writing without any sign that "it would ever cease returning to him intact."

Because David is happy with Marita (Little Mary) at the end of the book, some reviewers of *The Garden of Eden* felt that it was finally meant to reflect Hemingway's peace of mind in 1946, the year in which he married Mary Welsh. David, however, is not the only character in whom Hemingway took up his stand. Just as it is Catherine, not David, who takes the initiative in acting out the author's erotic fantasies, so she speaks for him when she confesses to a sense of failure in living up to the demands of the sexual identity she was born with. "You aren't really a woman at all," Marita says rather scornfully, and Catherine can only agree. "I know it," she says. "I broke myself in pieces in Madrid to be a girl and all it did was break me in pieces." These connections between Catherine and Hemingway are of critical importance, as is her fearful consciousness of her craziness, her determination nevertheless that she will be heard, her inability to find happiness in the marriage she has just made, and her blindly angry destruction of it. Is it any wonder that she is the most vivid character in the book? Her creator had invested in her the bulk of his imaginative capital.

Pauline, who bore Hemingway two more sons, succeeded in domesticating her restless husband for a time in Key West in the early 1930s.

The stone house in Key West that Pauline's wealthy uncle, Gus Pfeiffer, bought for her and Hemingway in 1931. The swimming pool was added by Pauline in 1937 in a vain effort to persuade her husband to spend more of his time with her.

24

Hemingway posed proudly with his latest conquest as a big game hunter on safari in East Africa in January 1934. Out of such experiences would come one of his least successful books, Green Hills of Africa (1935), and two of his most memorable short stories, "The Snows of Kilimanjaro" and "The Short Happy Life of Francis Macomber," both published in 1936.

Hemingway's frequent trips to Cuba and his affair with the beautiful but emotionally unstable Jane Mason signaled his growing estrangement from Pauline. Here Jane is standing by his side aboard Pilar, Hemingway's deep-sea fishing boat, in Havana harbor in the summer of 1934.

25

26
Hemingway made four trips to Spain in 1937 and 1938 to report the Spanish Civil War. Always eager to prove himself, he bore arms in battle, although it was illegal for reporters to do so. (Teruel, Spain, December 1937)

27

At work on his novel of the Spanish Civil War, For Whom the Bell Tolls (1940), in Sun Valley, Idaho, December 1939.

Hemingway met Martha Gellhorn in Key West in 1936 and not long afterward they began an affair that finally led to their marriage in 1940. Here the newlyweds arrive in Hawaii en route to China in February 1941.

29 *Like his own father, Hemingway shared his love of the outdoors with his sons: (left to right) Gregory, John ("Bumby") and Patrick, here setting off with their father and new stepmother on a bird hunt in Idaho, in the fall of 1941.*

30

During a pause in the hunt, Gregory pours his father a drink. From the time he was eleven, Gregory likewise drank hard liquor—with his father's approval.

Sporting a bushy gray beard, Hemingway reported his initial impressions of his third major war in the early summer of 1944 from a room in London's Dorchester Hotel.

Hemingway and his great friend, Colonel Charles T. "Buck" Lanham, standing near a captured gun on the Siegfried Line, September 1944. A month earlier, or so he claimed, he had personally "liberated" the Ritz Hotel in Paris.

Hemingway became estranged from his third wife and courted his fourth, Mary Welsh, in wartime London. Here he is with Mary (left) and the Gary Coopers in Sun Valley, Idaho, November 1946. Cooper portrayed Robert Jordan in the film adaptation of For Whom the Bell Tolls.

Hemingway's pleasant days of duck-hunting in Torcello, Italy, in November 1948 would inspire the opening scene of Across the River and Into the Trees *(1950). Superb as that first chapter was, the novel was received with critical scorn.*

Adriana Ivancich (right) was the model for Renata, the beautiful Italian countess in Across the River and Into the Trees. *Mary (left) tolerated her husband's passionate but physically chaste relationship with Adriana, who, after a life of many sorrows, committed suicide in 1983. (Torcello, December 1948)*

En route from Italy to Cuba aboard the SS Jagiello *in May 1949. Hemingway had recently recovered from a serious skin infection contracted in Cortina d'Ampezzo. Although he was only fifty, his health problems were mounting.*

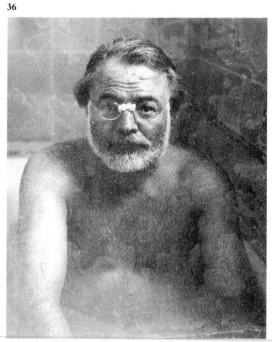

Hemingway, shown here with the celebrated white hunter Philip Percival (left) and a young game warden, Denis Zaphiro (right), returned to East Africa in August 1953. The trip turned into a nightmare of near-fatal accidents and an almost eerie re-creation of the death-haunted atmosphere of "The Snows of Kilimanjaro."

After the enormous popular success of The Old Man and the Sea *(1952) and with the Nobel Prize for Literature (1954) in hand, Hemingway's life with Mary at the Finca Vigía in Havana was outwardly secure and serene. But he refused to moderate his drinking, and thoughts of failure and suicide obsessed him.*

The house in Ketchum, Idaho, that Hemingway purchased as a second home in 1959 seemed to reflect his own sense of barren isolation.

With a cat for company in Ketchum in the winter of 1959.

Although he wrote compulsively, often standing up, Hemingway in his last years was unable to complete to his satisfaction another book-length work. A memoir of Paris in the twenties, A Moveable Feast, *and two artistically flawed but intensely revealing novels,* Islands in the Stream *and* The Garden of Eden, *would be published posthumously, in 1964, 1970, and 1986 respectively.*

In a desperate effort to recapture an earlier source of inspiration, Hemingway returned to Spain in the summer of 1959 on a trip that became a drunken debacle. The "mess" he created in his account of the trip, entitled "The Dangerous Summer" and published in Life magazine in 1960, made him feel "ashamed and sick."

43   *On a walk in the woods near his home in Ketchum in the final winter of his life. Suffering severe bouts of depression and paranoia and no longer able to sustain the art that had given his life meaning, Hemingway committed suicide on July 2, 1961.*

CHAPTER TWENTY-THREE

"How Do You Like It Now, Gentlemen?"

FROM THE LATE FORTIES ONWARD, the media exploited him —and he exploited the media—as never before. In the "People" section of *Time* alone, items of Hemingwayana appeared nine different times between 1945 and 1948, and four of those times the magazine ran accompanying photographs of him. Anyone who believed what was published in *Time* could be sure that the novelist was having "the time of his life" shooting and fishing with "Poloist Winston Guest," that he was partial to a drink known as "Death in the Gulf Stream," consisting of a dash of bitters, the juice of one lime and a tall glass of Holland gin, and that a panel of magazine illustrators had announced that he had one of the six "most startling and exciting heads in the world."

On the occasion of his divorce from Martha, an article in the *New York Sunday Mirror Magazine* recapitulated his history of broken marriages under the title, "Bell Tolls for Three of Ernest's Wives." Not to be outdone in its coverage of Hemingway and sex, Hearst's *American Weekly* proclaimed a year later in a piece called "Hemingway Sets the Style" that he had a "short hair" ideal of feminine beauty which he had tried to impose on all his women, while a female reporter who interviewed him for the *New York Post Weekend Magazine* came away saying that "Papa" looks "virile enough to make bobby-soxers swoon by the droves."

In "The Great Blue River," published in *Holiday* in 1949 and embellished with photographs of him fishing barechested aboard the

Pilar, Hemingway himself helped to keep his name before the public by elaborating upon the wonderful life he was leading in Cuba, where cockfighting was legal, eighteen varieties of mango grew on the long slope up to his house, every morning was cool and fresh even in the hottest months and "you can plug the bell in the party-line telephone with paper so that you won't have to answer, and . . . you work as well there in those cool early mornings as you ever have worked anywhere in the world."

On the other hand, there were moments when he had the sickening feeling that "too damned much" had been written about him. At such times, he tried to avoid publicity, but was rarely successful. His attempt to ward off Malcolm Cowley was a case in point. In 1948, after being commissioned by *Life* magazine, the single most powerful engine of publicity in the world, to write a nine-thousand-word "Portrait of Mr. Papa," Cowley asked for permission to come to the Finca. Although Hemingway tried for a while to put him off, he apparently was swayed by Cowley's plea that the fee he would earn from *Life* would enable him to send his son to Exeter. For the upshot was that the critic spent close to two weeks with him.

"Portrait of Mr. Papa" was not seen by Hemingway until it appeared in print on January 10, 1949. His verdict was that it was "OK" but "not awfully accurate." Some years later, Cowley stoutly defended his reportorial reliability by pointing out that the only specific objection that Hemingway had ever raised was about the anecdote of his carrying canteens of gin and vermouth at his belt during combat in World War II. In the first place, Hemingway had scoffed, good vermouth hadn't been available, and in the second place he would never have wasted a whole canteen on the stuff, no matter what. But unfortunately the canteen story was far from being the only flaw in the bauble. For the critic whose Introduction to the *Portable Hemingway* five years before had not even got the novelist's birth year right was simply incapable of getting the facts straight about Ernest Hemingway. On boozy days and nights at the Finca, the lord of the manor had undoubtedly grown expansive, and Cowley seems never to have wondered whether his host's fascinating yarns could be trusted. "A Portrait of Mr. Papa" not only took Hemingway's sub-hunting activities far too seriously, but grossly exaggerated the significance of his war service in France. While Cowley had quietly abandoned the notion that Hemingway had served with the Arditi in World War I, he compensated for the loss of this tidbit by reaffirming Dorothy Parker's claim that an aluminum kneecap was one of the novelist's mementoes of Fossalta di

Piave. He also reported that at the tender age of fourteen Hemingway had taken boxing lessons in a Chicago gym from a pro named Young A'Hearn, that he had had his nose broken in a match but had returned to the ring the next day and that after graduation from high school he had talked himself into a job on the Kansas City *Star*. (So much for *your* help, Uncle Tyler!) But Cowley's amazing credulousness was most fully revealed in his assertion, culled from who knows where, that *For Whom the Bell Tolls* had been used by Stalin's armies in World War II as a textbook of guerrilla fighting, whereas in fact the novel was anathema to Stalin and was not even translated into Russian until after his death.

Following Cowley's visit, Hemingway sent him a letter saying that their talks about his life had destroyed his ability to write for an entire week. But that was just the first of the negative consequences of "A Portrait of Mr. Papa." Because he was writing for a mass audience, Cowley paid next to no attention to Hemingway's work; indeed, he seemed anxious to demonstrate that the novelist was a man of action, not a writer. Published at a time when Hemingway's literary stature was being questioned even more severely than in the thirties, largely because of his long silence, the Cowley piece furnished ammunition to critics like Dwight Macdonald who wished to disparage his whole achievement as the work of a man with a false attitude toward life. Hemingway himself admitted as much in the aftermath of the critics' wholesale abuse of *Across the River and Into the Trees* when he told an editor at Rinehart, Thomas Bledsoe, that "It was a very bad thing for me that Malcolm Cowley's article was published in LIFE." Showing a capacity for forgiveness which some people believed he didn't possess, he then told Bledsoe "that . . . it was not Malcolm's fault and everything he did was well intentioned." Forgiveness, however, did not imply respect. Thus in a letter to Hotchner on March 9, 1949, he said with some bitterness,

> The Life piece made me sort of sick. Sure is a lot of difference between Life and life. Not to mention liberty. . . . But I don't think Cowley knows anything about whatever material people like me are made of. I felt all the time, reading it, as though I were being formed in his image. Well the hell with it. I had a nice private life before with a lot of undeclared and unpublished pride and now I feel like somebody had shit in it and wiped themselves on slick paper and left it there.

And two years later he admonished the young critic Charles Fenton, who was gathering materials for *The Apprenticeship of Ernest Hemingway,* to "think of poor old Cowley who has staked out my whole life of which he knows practically fuck-all nothing."

2

ANOTHER writer who prevailed upon Hemingway's good nature
was *The New Yorker*'s Lillian Ross. Having got along famously at
their meeting in Idaho in 1947, they had begun writing letters to one
another and as a result had become good friends. In his letters he
affectionately called her "Daughter" and praised her for the meticu-
lousness of her journalism. "His compliments were straight and
honest," she warmly recalled after his death, "and they were designed to make you feel good. He might call you reliable and compare you to Joe Page and Hugh Casey, and you wouldn't have to be
an archivist of baseball to realize you were being praised. The way
he wrote in his letters . . . in itself made me feel good—it was so
fresh and wonderful."

Having scored a success with her "Profile" of Sidney Franklin,
she and *The New Yorker*'s editor, Harold Ross, decided that she
should write one on Hemingway as well, if he agreed to cooperate.
Which he did by allowing her to spend two days with him in mid-
November 1949, when he came to New York with Mary after a
long stint of work on *Across the River and Into the Trees* that had
brought the manuscript close to completion. It was a "sympathetic
piece," she later said of it, in which she "tried to describe as precisely
as possible how Hemingway, who had the nerve to be like nobody
else on earth, looked and sounded when he was in action, talking,
between work periods—to give a picture of the man as he was, in
his uniqueness and with his vitality and enormous spirit of fun intact." As soon as she received galley proofs of the "Profile," she had
The New Yorker send duplicates to Hemingway and Mary, and they
returned them marked with minor corrections. In an accompanying
letter, Hemingway proposed only one deletion and told her that
otherwise he found the piece funny and good. It appeared in the
May 13, 1950, issue of the magazine under the title, "How Do You
Like It Now, Gentlemen?" It marked the first time that a journalist
had succeeded in peeking behind the curtain of promotion and self-
promotion that concealed the man.

By prearrangement, Miss Ross began, she met the novelist at a
gate at Idlewild airport. He was looking around for Mary, who had
gone to pick up their luggage. His hair was long in back and gray,
except at the temples, where it was white; his mustache, too, was
white, and he had a ragged, half-inch, full white beard. Under one
arm he was hugging a battered briefcase containing the unfinished
manuscript of *Across the River* and the other was wrapped tightly

around a little man named Myers, whom he had met on the flight
and who had agreed to read a portion of his new book right then
and there. "Book too much for him," Hemingway said. "Book start
slow, then increase in pace till it becomes impossible to stand. I bring
emotion up to where you can't stand it, then we level off, so we
won't have to provide oxygen tents for the readers. Book is like
engine. We have to slack off gradually." When Mary appeared with
a porter who was pushing a cart with fourteen pieces of luggage
heaped upon it, Hemingway carefully checked to see if anything was
missing.

Although Mary seemed eager to get into town, her husband had
another idea. "Let's not crowd, honey. Order of the day is to have
a drink." Standing at the bar in the airport cocktail lounge, he
knocked off three double bourbons. "First thing we do, Mary, as
soon as we hit the hotel," he told his wife between swallows, "is call
up the Kraut." "The Kraut" was Marlene Dietrich, he explained to
Miss Ross, raising the back of his fist to his face as he did so, as if he
were warding off a blow, and yet laughing the while.

The Hemingways were stopping at the Sherry-Netherland Hotel.
The living room of their suite was furnished with imitation-
Chippendale chairs and tables. "Guess they call this the Chinese-
Gothic Room," said Hemingway. After shedding his necktie and
jacket and unbuttoning his collar, he called Miss Dietrich at the Plaza
Hotel and left a message and then asked room service to send up
some caviar and a couple of bottles of Perrier-Jouët, brut. Having
completed his phoning, he seemed uncertain about what to do next.
Miss Ross told him that among literary critics there was a huge
interest in his work. Hemingway made clear that his opinion of
literary critics was low.

The first of his striking mood swings occurred as he sat down on
the couch to drink a glass of champagne. In a voice that was suddenly very angry he said, "I can remember feeling so awful about
the first war that I couldn't write about it for ten years." After
referring to a recent war writer as a man who apparently thought of
himself as another Tolstoy, he added, "I started out very quiet and I
beat Mr. Turgenev. Then I trained hard and I beat Mr. de Maupassant. I've fought two draws with Mr. Stendhal, and I think I had an
edge in the last one. But nobody's going to get me in any ring with
Mr. Tolstoy unless I'm crazy or I keep getting better."

His new book, he said, had started out as a short story, which was
true of all his novels. He had written *The Sun Also Rises* in six weeks
and had spent five months revising it because the first version had
been lousy. Knowing this about him would encourage young writ-

ers, he hoped, to stay away from psychoanalysts. An analyst, he remembered, had once written him to ask what he had learned from psychoanalysts, and he had replied, very little. "You never saw a counter-puncher who was punchy," he explained to Miss Ross. "Never lead against a hitter unless you can outhit him. Crowd a boxer, and take everything he has, to get inside. Duck a swing. Block a hook. And counter a jab with everything you own." Miss Ross wanted to know whether his new book was different from the others, and he gave her a long, reproachful look. Touching his brief-case, he said that he thought he had *A Farewell to Arms* beaten in this one, since it didn't have the youth and the ignorance. "How do you like it now, gentlemen?" he said wearily.

Miss Dietrich arrived. Mary Hemingway came out of the bed-room where she had been unpacking and greeted her warmly, as did Hemingway. "The Kraut's the best that ever came into the ring," he announced, as he poured her a glass of champagne and refilled the other glasses. Miss Dietrich passed around snapshots of her eighteen-month-old grandson and told about doing a lot of babysit-ting and household chores in her daughter's apartment on Third Avenue. "Daughter, you're hitting them with the bases loaded," Hemingway said.

When Miss Ross arrived at the Hemingways' suite the following morning, she found the novelist wearing an orange plaid bathrobe and sipping a glass of champagne. He told her that he had been up since six and had done a lot of cutting in his manuscript. Two champagne coolers were on the table near the couch. After deter-mining that the bottle in one of them was empty, Hemingway un-corked the other bottle. As he refilled his glass, he sang the "Song of the Third Infantry Division." He loved all music, even opera, he said, but he had no talent for it and couldn't sing. Although Miss Ross did not know this, his next statement conflated a portion of his sister Marcelline's past with his own. His mother had taken him out of school one year, he said, and made him play the cello. He had wanted to be outside playing football in the fresh air, but his mother had wanted the sound of chamber music in the house.

He sat down on the couch, nodded his head a couple of times to catch Miss Ross's attention and observed that it was harder to have heroes as you got older, but was still necessary. He had a cat named Boise who wanted to be a human being, he said, his voice lowering into a kind of grumble. The result was that Boise ate everything that human beings eat. He chewed Vitamin B Complex capsules, even though they were as bitter as aloes, and thought that Hemingway was holding out on him when he refused to give him any of his blood-pressure tablets and let him go to sleep without Seconal. Hemingway abruptly laughed. "How do you like it now, gentlemen?" he asked.

Mary came into the room. She was going out to do errands and she suggested that Hemingway get dressed and do some himself. He said it was lunchtime. Mary said she would arrange for lunch in the room while he got dressed. Hemingway finished his drink and went into the bedroom. By the time he came out, the waiter had set up the table. Hemingway said that they couldn't have lunch without a bottle of Tavel. They waited until the waiter brought it. Hemingway began his meal with oysters, chewing each one many times. "Eat good and digest good," he said. When Mary finished eating, she quickly finished her wine. Hemingway slowly finished his. Miss Ross looked at her wristwatch and saw that it was almost three o'clock. They all got up. Hemingway looked sadly at the bottle of champagne, which wasn't empty. "The half bottle of champagne is the enemy of man," he said. They all sat down again.

The remaining scenes in the "Profile" take place at Abercrombie & Fitch, where Hemingway buys a topcoat and a pair of slippers and runs into Winston Guest; at the Sherry-Netherland the following morning, where Hemingway tells Miss Ross in the presence of his son Patrick, a Harvard sophomore, that Dr. Hemingway had shot himself when he, Ernest, had been a boy; at the Metropolitan Museum of Art, where Hemingway takes swigs from a silver flask, argues the merits of various paintings with Patrick and talks about his love of El Greco's "View of Toledo" and about how much he had learned as a writer from Cézanne's landscapes; and finally at the Sherry-Netherland once again, where the Hemingways greet Charles Scribner, who has been invited to have lunch with them, and Patrick sits quietly in a corner and watches his father.

Miss Ross was fascinated by Hemingway's every word and gesture, and thanks to her mimetic skills she made him come alive on the printed page. But precisely because of its lifelikeness, "How Do You Like It Now, Gentlemen?" offers a glimpse or two of hidden horror beneath its evocation of a big-city fling. A quarter of a century before it was written, Hemingway had obliquely suggested in "The Battler" that young Nick Adams's future might be mirrored in the pathetic figure of Ad Francis, the punch-crazed fighter. "You never saw a counter-puncher who was punchy," Hemingway insisted to Miss Ross, by way of repudiating the notion that he himself was going crazy. But his choice of a boxing metaphor in which to proclaim his mental health suggests how fearful he was that "The Battler" was proving to be prophetic. "I am a strange old man," he remarked to Miss Ross in a rare moment when his guard was completely down. At the time, he was a scant four months past his fiftieth birthday.

3

MOST readers, Miss Ross would always insist, took the "Profile" the way she meant it. However,

> a certain number of readers reacted violently, and in a very complicated fashion. Among these were people who objected strongly to Hemingway's personality, assumed I did the same, and admired the piece for the wrong reasons; that is, they thought that in describing that personality accurately I was.ridiculing or attacking it. Other people simply didn't like the way Hemingway talked (they even objected to the playful way he sometimes dropped his articles and spoke a kind of joke Indian language); they didn't like his freedom; they didn't like his not taking himself seriously; they didn't like his wasting his time on going to boxing matches, going to the zoo, talking to friends, going fishing, enjoying people, celebrating his approach to the finish of a book by splurging on caviar and champagne; they didn't like this and they didn't like that. In fact, they didn't like Hemingway. They wanted him to be somebody else—probably themselves.

Dwight Macdonald proclaimed that the "Profile" illustrated how completely Hemingway had accepted the public personality that had been built up by the press and how much he gloried in being a "grotesque (but virile) Philistine." Morton Dauwen Zabel said that after pondering Miss Ross's portrait of the artist "one was left wondering what could survive for the serious business of art and writing." Joseph Warren Beach was pained to find that "a serious artist, in the fulness of maturity and fame, can be such a boyish—and bearish—show-off," that "an experienced man of the world should be willing to expose to the world so many intimate personal secrets," and that "a man who has seen so much and thought so much about life should be so shamelessly self-confident and self-absorbed." And James Thurber observed to a friend in a letter that "One of our present day wits is John McNulty [a *New Yorker* writer], who had this to say about Lillian Ross's profile of Hemingway: 'It was like the Eddie Waitkus affair—she loved him so much she shot him.'"

Once Hemingway got wind of remarks like these, he advised his flustered profilist not to worry about them; it was just that readers were apt to get things mixed up. In later letters he again sought to comfort her. "Some people," she paraphrased him as saying in one of them, "couldn't understand his enjoying himself and his not being really spooky; they couldn't understand his being a serious writer without being pompous." In communications with other correspondents, however, he soon began to claim that when he had read the proofs of the "Profile" he had been horrified. And while he would forever disagree with those critics who viewed Lillian Ross as a journalistic Delilah—"she was not writing in malice," he affirmed to Thomas Bledsoe—he belatedly defended himself against some of the implications in her piece. Although "she had a right to make me seem that way if she wished," he told Bledsoe, "I did not believe that I talked like a half-breed choctaw nor that it gave a very sound impression of some one who gets up at first light and works at writing most of the days of his life. But I had just finished a book and when you have done that you do not really give a damn for a few weeks. So I did not mind it although I knew it was harmful to me just as the Life piece [by Cowley] was. There was no harm intended and much received. But I am still fond of Lillian."

Of all the remarks about the "Profile," the one which probably would have upset this proud man the most, if he had known about it, was set forth in a private letter to a friend by his ancient enemy, Alice B. Toklas. For her comment revealed an appreciation of the tragic nature of Lillian Ross's portrayal. "It has strange revelations and exposures by himself and his wife which were partially explained by Janet Flanner's telling me that he was mortally ill. It is painful to know the present situation and the horror it must hold for him."

4

THROUGH the first eight months of 1950, Hemingway reverted several times to the subject of suicide, most notably in a letter in August to Lillian Ross, in which he told of a deep dive he had recently taken off the deck of the *Pilar*. He had gone way down, he claimed, in water that was a mile and a half deep, at which point he had let all the air out of his lungs. If he had not suddenly thought of what a bad example he was setting for his sons, he would not have tried to kick back to the surface.

The step-up in tempo of this kind of talk from him was partly the consequence of extreme nervousness about the forthcoming publication—on September 7, 1950—of *Across the River*. Not only would the novel mark his first new fictional statement in a decade, but he had composed it without the presiding encouragement and advice of the editor on whom he had counted for these things for more than twenty years.

In a late afternoon in January 1946, Max Perkins had gone out for a drive in his car through the countryside near his home in New Canaan, Connecticut. Very soon it grew dark. "It was too dark a night to see much," he later wrote Hemingway, "and after a while I thought I would come back and do some work, and so I was driving too fast, I guess. Anyhow—I came around an easy curve and after a minute saw the shadow of a truck ahead. I don't think there was a tail light. I thought of skidding around it but a man might have got out. It stood right in the middle of the road. I did everything I could with the brake, but I must have hit the truck hard because it certainly wrecked my car, all the front of it. I got right out and felt all right except that to my surprise my nose bled." Despite painfully cracked ribs that required him to wear a corset, he returned to work almost immediately. The following summer, Charles Scribner confidentially reported to Hemingway that Max needed a rest badly but refused to take a vacation. "There does not seem to be anything he wants to do except work," Scribner added. "I wish you could lure him away, but for heaven's sake don't tell him that I suggested such an idea." Although Hemingway did his best to talk Perkins into joining him in Sun Valley, he failed, and in fact when the editor—a proud man himself—heard by the grapevine that Hemingway was concerned about him, he worked straight through the fall without any letup whatsoever just to prove he was all right. By December, his colleagues at Scribners were terribly concerned about him. He looked tired and frail, his hands trembled, and he had a persistent cough.

An immense sadness about life had long ago enveloped the editor, but this feeling became more marked in him than ever in the first months of 1947, for reasons which included a sense of defeat about his most famous author. He had been aware for some time that Hemingway was working very hard on the manuscript of a new novel—it was *The Garden of Eden*—but then in early 1947 he learned that the work had ceased. Perkins was deeply discouraged by the news. One day in the spring he told his wife, "Hemingway is through." A couple of months later, he collapsed. At a hospital in Stamford, Connecticut, it was discovered that he had an advanced case of pleurisy and pneumonia. At five o'clock in the morning on June 17, 1947, he died. When Hemingway heard of his death, he was shaken. Max was a great, great editor and a wise, loyal friend, he disconsolately wrote to Charles Scribner.

Had Perkins still been alive in 1950, would he have tried to persuade his touchiest author to distill the best parts of *Across the River* into a short story? The question is tantalizing. For, as the Canadian critic Northrop Frye discerned,

> The theme of *Across the River and Into the Trees* is death in Venice, with Colonel Cantwell . . . as a military counterpart of [Thomas] Mann's beat-up old novelist. The colonel is a lonely man. Around him is an impersonal hatred directed, like a salute, at his uniform; behind him is the wreck of a marriage and of the career of a good professional soldier; in front of him is his next and last heart attack. . . . It is a great theme, and in the hands of someone competent to deal with it—say Ernest Hemingway—it might have been a long short story of overwhelming power.

With its icy intimations of mortality and its beautifully sustained awareness of the frozen grasses in a shallow lagoon and of ducks dropping down, their wings set to brake, from a gray dim sky, the hunting scene at the beginning of the book is magical. The curt description of the colonel's death at the end of the story also bears the touch of the master. There is a moving moment too in chapter seven, wherein the author voices through Cantwell his pained awareness of how inordinately difficult to live with he has become. In a book dedicated "To Mary With Love," the author's alter ego asks himself,

> Why am I always a bastard and why can I not suspend this trade of arms and be a kind and good man as I would have wished to be. I try always to be just, but I am brusque and I am brutal, and it is not that I have erected the defense against brown-nosing my superiors and brown-nosing the world. I should be a better man with less wild boar blood in the small time which remains. We will try it out tonight, he thought. With whom, he thought, and where, and God help me not to be bad.

Unfortunately, these and other bits of a potentially marvelous short story lie strewn across the weary length of a novel, and in the waste spaces between them the garrulous colonel goes on and on and on about the stupidity of various World War II commanders, the loveliness of his young mistress's hair and the quality of the food at the Gritti Palace and how well he chews it and how intimately he knows the headwaiter.

Hemingway had spoken in *The Garden of Eden* of a writer's inner core which could not be split nor even marked nor scratched. But in fact his own core had become so flooded with media images that he could no longer create a fictional warrior without superimposing his public persona upon him. The result was self-parody, and *The New Yorker*'s E. B. White promptly piled another parody atop it. The opening paragraphs of "Across the Street and Into the Grill" are particularly delicious:

> This is my last and best and true and only meal, thought Mr. Perley as he descended at noon and swung east on the beat-up sidewalk of Forty-fifth Street. Just ahead of him was the girl from the reception desk. I am a little fleshed up around the crook of the elbow, thought Perley, but I commute good.
>
> He quickened his step to overtake her and felt the pain again. What a stinking trade it is, he thought. But after what I've done to other assistant treasurers, I can't hate anybody. Sixteen deads, and I don't know how many possibles.
>
> The girl was near enough now so he could smell her fresh receptiveness, and the lint in her hair. Her skin was light blue, like the sides of horses.
>
> "I love you," he said, "and we are going to lunch together for the first and only time, and I love you very much."
>
> "Hello, Mr. Perley," she said, overtaken. "Let's not think of anything."
>
> A pair of fantails flew over from the sad old Guaranty Trust Company, their wings set for a landing. A lovely double, thought Perley, as he pulled. "Shall we go to the Hotel Biltmore, on Vanderbilt Avenue, which is merely a feeder lane for the great streets, or shall we go to Schrafft's, where my old friend Botticelli is captain of the girls and where they have the mayonnaise in fiascos?"
>
> "Let's go to Schrafft's," said the girl, low. "But first I must phone Mummy." She stepped into a public booth and dialled true and well, using her finger. Then she telephoned.

The novelist John O'Hara, meanwhile, had sensed that the reviewers of *Across the River* were going to run roughshod over a writer whom he himself had revered from afar for many years and with whom he had had an amiable dinner at Tim Costello's restaurant on Third Avenue in New York in early 1944, just before Hemingway flew off to the war in Europe. O'Hara therefore tried to protect him in the estimate of the novel he was asked to write for *The New York Times Book Review*. Alas, he only succeeded in making matters worse by speaking of Hemingway's entire achievement in unconscionable hyperbole and by couching his qualified praise of *Across the River* in the parlance of an unillusioned Hemingway tough guy. "The most important author living today," O'Hara asserted, "the outstanding author since the death of Shakespeare," he added, raising the ante, "has brought out a new novel." Of course, he said, that author is Ernest Hemingway, "the most important, the outstanding author out of the millions of writers who have lived since 1616. . . . To use his own favorite metaphor, he may not be able to go the full distance, but he can still hurt you. Always dangerous. Always in there with that right cocked. Real class." ("Naturally," Hemingway groaned in a letter to Charles Scribner, "the thing about Shakespeare, the undisputed champion, is ridiculous. . . . Why did he have to say such a thing?")

The gang instincts of literary intellectuals are notorious. In the case of *Across the River,* they smelled blood in the water and instantly swarmed around it like so many killer sharks. Yet the very savagery of their assault generated a contempt for them in certain quarters. Prompted by a favorable notice of the novel in the *Atlantic Monthly* by the editor Edward Weeks, the novelist Raymond Chandler wrote a letter to his old friend Charles Morton, who also worked for the magazine, asking him to congratulate Weeks

on belonging to that very small minority of critics who did not find it necessary to put Hemingway in his place over his last book. Just what do the boys resent so much? Do they sense that the old wolf has been wounded and that this is a good time to pull him down? I have been reading the book. Candidly, it's not the best thing he's done, but it's still a hell of a sight better than anything his detractors could do. There's not much story in it, not much happens, hardly any scenes. And just for that reason, I suppose, the mannerisms sort of stick out. You can't expect charity from knife throwers naturally; knife throwing is their business. But you would think some of them might have asked themselves just what he was trying to do. Obviously he was not trying to write a masterpiece; but in a character not too unlike his own trying to sum up the attitude of a man who is finished and knows it, and is bitter and angry about it. Apparently Hemingway had been very sick and he was not sure that he was going to get well and he put down on paper in a rather cursory way how that made him feel [toward] the things in life he had most valued. I suppose these primping second-guessers who call themselves critics think he shouldn't have written the book at all. Most men wouldn't have. Feeling the way that he felt, they wouldn't have had the guts to write anything. I'm damn sure I wouldn't.

A very different writer, Evelyn Waugh, chose a public forum for his views of the critics. "They have been smug, condescending and derisive," he wrote in *Commonweal,*

[and they] all are agreed that there is a great failure to celebrate. . . .
Why do they all hate [Hemingway] so? I believe the truth is that they
have detected in him something they find quite unforgivable—Decent
Feeling. Behind all the bluster and cursing and fisticuffs he has an
elementary sense of chivalry—respect for women, pity for the weak,
love of honor—which keeps breaking in. There is a form of high
supercilious caddishness which is all the rage nowadays in literary
circles. That is what the critics seek in vain in this book, and that is
why their complaints are so loud and confident.

As for Hemingway's own response to the reviews, he was beside
himself with rage—and angry to boot at his publisher. "[Where] the
hell you been, boy?" he fairly yelled at Charles Scribner on September 9. "Did you read the Time review and take off for the wilds of
Jersey to launch your counter-attack from there? Well everybody
has their own way of doing things. But isn't it sort of customary to
inform an author about how things go and what people say when a
book comes out that he has bet his shirt on and worked his heart out
on nor missed a deadline nor failed to keep a promise?"

His jealousy of other writers also soared, not that it hadn't already
reached a high level in the years immediately beforehand because of
his frustration about the various books he had started writing but
couldn't finish. In 1949, for instance, he had jeeringly characterized
Thomas Wolfe as the overbloated Li'l Abner of literature and John
O'Hara as an alcoholic has-been with an inferiority complex about
being Irish, and when Arthur Mizener asked him in early 1950 for
some reminiscences about Scott Fitzgerald, he had come up with
nothing but poisonous anecdotes. But it was not until the reviewers
trashed *Across the River* that his comments about other writers went
beyond the bounds of decency, most notably in regard to James
Jones.

From Here to Eternity was published in early 1951 by Scribners. On
the front flap of the jacket, the publishers proclaimed their belief that
"the appearance of this novel is of comparable importance to the
publication of *This Side of Paradise* or *Look Homeward, Angel*. For
like the first novels of Fitzgerald and Wolfe, *From Here to Eternity*
introduces a writer who will take a commanding place in American
literature." Not only had Hemingway's own house praised another
novelist to the skies, but it had done so by comparing *From Here to
Eternity* to *This Side of Paradise* and *Look Homeward, Angel,* rather
than to the appearance in 1926 of both *The Torrents of Spring* and
The Sun Also Rises. Furthermore, virtually every reviewer proceeded
to praise the novel for its military authenticity. Private Prewitt,

Sergeant Warden, Sergeant Stark, and the other men who lived in Schofield Barracks in the months before Pearl Harbor—these were real people in a real situation, the reviewers enthusiastically agreed, even as they had agreed that *Across the River* was full of fakery. The more Hemingway thought about *From Here to Eternity,* the closer to the edge of psychopathy he came, and when Charles Scribner was foolish enough to ask him whether he didn't think that Jones was a great writer, he lapsed into it—although there were undeniable insights in his ravings.

> . . . To me he is an enormously skillful fuck-up and his book will do great damage to our country. Probably I should re-read it again to give you a truer answer. But I do not have to eat an entire bowl of scabs to know they are scabs; nor suck a boil to know it is a boil; nor swim through a river of snot to know it is snot. I hope he kills himself as soon as it does not damage his or your sales. If you give him a literary tea you might ask him to drain a bucket of snot and then suck the puss [*sic*] out of a dead nigger's ear. Then present him with one of those women he is asking for and let him show her his portrait and his clippings. How did they ever get a picture of a wide-eared jerk (un-damaged ears) to look that screaming tough. I am glad he makes you money and I would never laugh him off. I would just give him a bigger bucket on the snot detail. He has the psycho's urge to kill himself and he will do it.

5

GRACE Hemingway had been plagued by blood-circulation problems for years, and in the late fall of 1950, at the age of seventy-eight, she was forced to quit her home on Keystone Avenue in River Forest, Illinois, where she was being cared for by Ruth Arnold, and enter Oak Park Hospital. Around the first of the year, an attendant tipped over her wheelchair and she sustained a head injury which severely impaired her memory and quickly led to senile dementia. The most recent of her battles with her world-famous son had taken place in the summer of 1949, but now there would be no more of them.

That final battle had started when Ernest learned that a woman writer at *McCall's* was trying to get in touch with his mother in the hope of setting up an interview. In the hands of a clever reporter, an aged and talkative woman might be easily led into remembrances of her son as a very young child. Hemingway moved swiftly to block the interview.

In a letter from the Finca on August 27, he directed Charles Scrib-

ner to ask his secretary to "write to the woman from McCall's and
tell her that I support my mother and I will cut off her support if she
gives out any repeat *any* interview or contributes information to any
article about me." As if aware that his publisher must be wondering
why he seemed so anxious, he went on to say that "My mother is
very old, her memory is more than spotty and she is addicted to
fantastic statements." With a hatred exacerbated by fear, he added
that because she now was so old he had lately "played the role of a
devoted son," although actually he still "hate[d] her guts" for having
"forced my father to suicide."

For all the intensity of these opening sentences, he was just getting
started. "[Where] does that miserable McCall's woman get the
idea," he demanded to know, "that she can write about our family
and how I differ from less talented bros. [*sic*] and sisters such as my
bitch sister Marcelline, my lovely sister Ura and my kid sister Sunny
(nicknames) who pitched on the school team (boys) and plays the
harp like an angel? . . ." The longer he foamed, the more profane
he became. "Do such bitches think I want publicity?" he asked near
the end of his tirade. "I know you have to have some, and I go
through with it, but it is as pleasant to eat as cat shit."

At the same time that he wrote to Scribner, he seems to have
written to someone in Key West, requesting that some boxes of
personal effects which he had left at Whitehead Street be sent to him,
for one of them contained his mother's multivolume compilation of
photographs and other materials relating to his childhood and adolescence. Once these albums reached the Finca, he hid them, out of
the paranoid fear that if Mary saw them she would sell the photographs to a magazine. And the next step he took was to write his
mother a letter.

> It made me so happy the other day to receive the books that you made
> for all of us children. They have been in storage in Key West and I
> have not seen them for many years. Please let me congratulate you on
> [your] diligence and your lovingness for all of us kids when we were
> young and must have been great nuisances to you. Your hand writing
> in the book was lovely to see and the photos that my father took were
> almost uniformly excellent. I hope you are getting along well and that
> everything goes well with you and with Ruth Arnold, to whom I
> send my best love.

His tone was warm. Perhaps looking at the albums had made him
feel close to his mother in spite of himself, or perhaps he was simply
relieved to have them back in his control. In the next paragraph,

though, his tone turned hard, and it left no doubt that his main purpose in writing had been to threaten his mother.

> Scribner's have written me that some woman from McCall's magazine, I believe, was contacting them to get in touch with you to write a piece about me when I was a boy. I do not care for this type of publicity and will not permit it. I told Scribners to write the woman, who was a very pushing, and vicious and, I thought, rather a detestable type of journalist, that I contributed to your support and that I would withdraw this contribution in case they published any such article without my consent. Hope this handled the matter.

After her head accident in Oak Park Hospital, Grace lived the last months of her life with Sunny and her family in Memphis. Unable to identify Sunny as her daughter, she often hid from her like a frightened child. Finally it became apparent that she would have to be hospitalized again. As if aware that it was goodbye, she sat down at the piano on her last evening in her daughter's house and played for a time with something like her old vivacity. Death came in a Memphis hospital on June 28, 1951.

On the evening that Sunny's cablegram brought this news to the Finca, Hemingway's wartime friend Bill Walton was on hand. Walton remembers that after a while Hemingway dug Grace's albums about his early life out of their hiding place in a bottom bureau drawer. Together, the two men studied a number of the pictures in considerable detail and laughed at some of Grace's inscriptions. But Walton was not shown any of the photographs of Ernest dressed as a girl.

Two days later, Hemingway wrote to Carlos Baker that his mother's passing had called up memories in his mind of how beautiful she had been when she was young before "everything went to hell in the family" and how happy her children had been before it all broke up.

6

WHILE staying with Pauline in Key West in the spring of 1947, Patrick and Gregory were involved in a car accident and Patrick bumped his head. Although a series of bad headaches ensued, he did not appear to have been seriously injured, so that his mother had no objection when he resumed playing tennis, or when he went through with his plan to visit his father in Cuba. At the Finca, however, he abruptly lapsed into a violent delirium, during which, as Hemingway related in a letter to Lillian Ross, he kept "defying Satan and all fiends and all local devils"—and one of the biggest devils was his father. Nevertheless, Hemingway insisted on personally caring for his son, bringing him food and helping him eat and sleeping outside his room in case he needed help in the night, until finally, after three months, Patrick recovered.

Hemingway's relations thereafter with his middle son seemed cordial enough. But on at least one occasion in his maturity Pauline's favorite child would react with cold anger and refuse to comment when asked if it was fair to say that he had got along well with his father. Perhaps it was in his delirious conjuration of his father as a devil that Patrick had expressed his deepest filial feelings. As to Bumby, on the other hand, it is unarguable that he always rejoiced in his father's company; indeed, in the spring of 1986 he would speak very emotionally at a ceremony at the John F. Kennedy Library in Boston about what a wonderful father he had had, and he would make bitter reference to the failure of Hemingway's biographers to bring this out. In regard to Gregory, Hemingway's brainiest son, the nature of the father-son relationship is also clear. The intimacy that had once obtained began to deteriorate with the boy's unceremonial departure in the spring of 1950 from St. John's College in Annapolis, Maryland. And the terrible events that followed led inexorably to estrangement.

Having completed his freshman year, Gregory found the idea of continuing in college unbearable and enrolled instead in a dianetics cult. By the summer of 1951, he was living in southern California with the first of his three wives, an ex-Powers model named Jane, and working in an aircraft factory. But toward the end of September he got into drug-related difficulty and was arrested. Pauline, who was in San Francisco at the time, flew down to see what she could do to help him. From her sister Jinny's home in Los Angeles, she phoned the Finca around nine o'clock on the night of the thirtieth to give Hemingway the latest news. According to Jinny, his sarcastic comments to his ex-wife soon had her shouting and sobbing uncontrollably. After putting down the phone, the distraught Pauline went straight to bed, but was awakened at one in the morning by a ghastly abdominal pain. Three hours later, she died on an operating table in a hospital. Hemingway's letter to Charles Scribner on October 2 was as full of feeling as his letter to Carlos Baker three months before about his mother's death. "The wave of remembering has finally risen so that it has broken over the jetty that I built to protect the open roadstead of my heart and I have the full sorrow of Pauline's death with all the harbour scum of what caused it. I loved her very much for many years and the hell with her faults." He did not, however, consider that their emotional conversation on the phone had somehow contributed to her sudden death.

Some months after Pauline's funeral, Gregory, Jane, and their baby girl showed up at the Finca. The visit went well for a time, and Gregory relaxed to the point where he felt able to bring up the subject of his arrest. "It wasn't so bad, really, papa," he said. His father's response blindsided him. "No? Well, it killed Mother." At the airport not long afterwards, Hemingway tried a witticism by way of farewell. "Well, don't take any wooden trust funds." Gregory smiled. It was the last view of him that his father would ever have.

The remaining years of the fifties were hell for Gregory. He drank too much, he couldn't hold a job, he got divorced from Jane, he squandered his inheritance on African safaris (on one of which he frenziedly killed eighteen elephants in a single month), and he submitted to electric shock treatments in order to short-circuit his depression. From time to time he also wrote foamingly angry letters to his father, deriding him as an alcoholic has-been, threatening to sock him, and letting him know that *The Old Man and the Sea* "was as sickly a bucket of sentimental slop as was ever scrubbed off the bar-room floor."

Yet in spite of his inner turmoil, Gregory managed to get through college—at UCLA—and to gain admission in 1960 to the University of Miami Medical School. One of his first acts after being admitted was to write the California hospital where his mother had died, requesting an autopsy report. She had died, he was told, of pheochromocytoma, an unusual form of tumor of the adrenal gland— unusual, he learned from reference works, because it secretes abnormally large amounts of adrenalin, which send the blood pressure rising to unbelievable heights. Some of the tumors of this sort, he further learned, secrete adrenalin constantly, others intermittently. Gregory guessed that his mother's had been of the latter type. In a letter he composed forthwith, he triumphantly pointed out to his father that it was clearly not his own drug troubles that had upset his mother, but the brutal phone conversation she had had with good old Ernesto eight hours before she died. "The tumor had become necrotic or rotten and when it fired off that night, it sent her blood pressure skyrocketing; a medium-sized blood vessel, within or adjacent to the rotten area, had ruptured. Then the tumor stopped discharging adrenaline, her blood pressure dropped from about 300 to zero, and she died of shock on the operating table."

Hemingway phoned Gregory when he got the letter—to congratulate him on being admitted to medical school. Having done so, he reminded Gregory that his grandfather had been a doctor, but that he had killed himself. At this point there was a pause in the flow of his words. Then he added in a flat, bitter voice that earlier that day he had been to see a doctor in Havana who had told him he had a rare disease (i.e., hemochromatosis) that would make him blind and permanently impotent. Gregory tried to comfort him by saying that Cuban doctors weren't any good and that he should go to New York for a second opinion. Hemingway said that he had already made some calls to New York and would be going up there soon.

Suddenly his voice changed. He wanted Gregory to remember an experience that they had once shared. "Remember that painting by Bosch of the end of the world? All the devils were rounding up the sinners and I pointed out one man robed like a gentleman who was rising from his table indignantly and drawing his sword. Remember? I pointed him out to you, out of all those grotesque figures, and said, see, see him there, he thinks he can handle death with a sword? And you seemed to understand so well what I was saying."

CHAPTER TWENTY-FOUR

"The Country Is Beautiful Around Here"

HE HAD BET HIS SAGGING REPUTATION ON *Across the River* and he had lost, badly. He bet it again on *The Old Man and the Sea,* and the critics loved it. "I believe this is the best story Hemingway has ever written." (Cyril Connolly, London *Sunday Times.*) "It is a tale superbly told." (Robert Gorham Davis, *The New York Times Book Review.*) "Mr. Hemingway is once again 'the champ.' " (Arthur Calder-Marshall, *The Listener.*) "His best." (William Faulkner, *Shenandoah.*) On and on the accolades rolled, until it became an inevitability that the book would at last bring Hemingway the Pulitzer Prize and a probability that he would soon be awarded the Nobel. Among the scattering of harsh comments, the most authoritative voice was John Aldridge's. "I confess that I am unable to share in the prevailing wild enthusiasm for . . . *The Old Man and the Sea,*" he wrote in the *Virginia Quarterly Review.* As far as he was concerned, the story was "distinctly minor Hemingway fiction." In a reconsideration of it a dozen years later in the *New York Herald Tribune Book Week,* Aldridge was even more severe. "The action of the novel is . . . to my mind, a façade, a classic parable in stone, terribly picturesque and *meaningful,* but quite dead. One must question the vitality of a story that becomes a myth too quickly, that is accepted as universal before it has been felt as particular."

As astonishing as the book's succès d'estime was its succès populaire. A week before its publication by Scribners on September 8,

1952, *Life* ran the full 27,000-word text in a single issue and sold 5,300,000 copies of it in two days, most of them, apparently, within eight hours of their appearance on the newsstands. The Book-of-the-Month Club picked the novel as a main selection and ordered a first printing of 153,000 copies. The trade edition quickly climbed on to the best-seller lists and remained there for twenty-six weeks.

Today, there is only one question worth asking about *The Old Man*. How could a book that lapses repeatedly into lachrymose sentimentality and is relentlessly pseudo-Biblical, that mixes cute talk about baseball ("I fear both the Tigers of Detroit and the Indians of Cleveland") with crucifixion symbolism of the most appalling crudity ("he slept face down on the newspapers with his arms out straight and the palms of his hands up"), have evoked such a storm of applause from highbrows and middlebrows alike—and in such overwhelming numbers?

The short answer is that people give up on their heroes reluctantly. As Delmore Schwartz argued in the November 1952 issue of *Partisan Review,* the ovation which greeted *The Old Man* consisted in the main of "a desire to continue to admire a great writer." There has been "a note of insistence in the praise and a note of relief," Schwartz shrewdly observed, the note of relief because *Across the River* had been "extremely bad in an ominous way," and the note of insistence because "this new work is not so much good in itself as a virtuoso performance which reminds one of Hemingway at his best." But larger historical circumstances also figured in the response the novel aroused. For while *The Old Man* was a profoundly personal statement on the part of an author who was deathly afraid that he wasn't any good any more, it expressed a collective mood of disillusionment no less surely than had *The Sun Also Rises*.

In the autumn weeks in which everyone in the United States, it seemed, was reading and talking about *The Old Man and the Sea,* Dwight D. Eisenhower forged into an overwhelming lead over Adlai Stevenson in the Presidential race. One of the main reasons for this was that the electorate held the Democrats responsible for the interminable fighting in Korea. Seven years before, America's enemies had surrendered unconditionally, but in the case of the Korean conflict dreams of achieving that goal had been abandoned. Ending the war honorably was the sum total of what the nation now wanted, and it believed in the ability of Eisenhower, the fatherly compromiser, to find a way.

Behind the reassuring figure of "Ike" there loomed a considerably older general whose poignant story was an even better key to the nation's vanished sense of illimitable power. When the massed ar-

mies of North Korea came pouring down across the 38th parallel
into South Korea on June 25, 1950, General Douglas MacArthur
was dispatched to the scene by President Truman to take command
of a United Nations force. On September 15, in a flanking move of
classic brilliance that took advantage of America's command of the
sea, MacArthur landed a force at Inchon near the 38th parallel. With
their lifeline cut, the invading Communist armies shattered into
fragments, and MacArthur sent his troops racing into North Korea.
It was grand, it was glorious, it was World War II all over again, in
miniature. Intervention by the Chinese, however, suddenly punc-
tured the prospect of victory. MacArthur asked for permission to
use his air power to strike at the enemy's privileged sanctuaries
beyond the North Korean border. Fearing the possibility of Russian
involvement and atomic apocalypse, Truman turned down
MacArthur's request, and when MacArthur publicly protested, Truman fired him.

A Gallup poll revealed that more than two-thirds of the American
people sympathized with the humiliated general. Moreover, the parade that was staged for him upon his return to New York produced
a turnout twice the size of the crowd which had lined the streets for
Eisenhower after V-E Day, while his address to a joint session of
Congress, culminating in the haunting line, "Old soldiers never die,
they just fade away," generated an extraordinary surge of emotional
comment nationwide.

But these tributes represented a farewell salute to something more
than just a remarkable career. Although MacArthur had registered a
stunning triumph at Inchon, in the end it had turned to ashes in his
mouth. Except for a minority of diehard believers in a MacArthur
Presidency, the citizens who cheered him on curbsides in 1951 and
who named boulevards, causeways, and high schools in his honor
knew that he stood for an outdated philosophy of international conduct. The great general was a has-been.

Whether by deliberate design or unconscious groping, the Korean
War and all its implications were quickly reflected in various ways
in popular art. Indeed, such was the power of America's chastened
consciousness of its new situation that the mass audience could find
symbols for it even in works whose genesis had to do with other
matters altogether. The most fascinating instance involved a famous
movie script by Carl Foreman. A longtime Soviet sympathizer,
Foreman was outraged that Congressional investigators should have
become concerned with the loyalty of workers in the movie industry. But when he called on his leftist friends to form a united front
of uncooperative witnesses, he found himself deserted by them,

leaving him to fight on—as he saw it, at least—more or less alone. Overcome with disgust for his friends and with contempt for governmental authority, he transposed his feelings into a drama of conscience set in the Old West. Moviegoers, however, would never have become interested in the film that was made of Foreman's script if they had believed it to be the sort of political parable that he had in mind. They flocked to see *High Noon* because it reflected their feelings, not Foreman's.

The film starred the legendary Gary Cooper, who knew just as well as Douglas MacArthur how humiliating it was to be considered a has-been. When he and Hemingway had first become friends at Sun Valley in 1940, the novelist had found him tremendously attractive. He is a fine man, he enthusiastically told Max Perkins, "as honest and straight and friendly and unspoiled as he looks." Those looks and that manner had made Cooper a box-office draw since the twenties. In the midforties, however, his appeal to audiences began to falter, and in 1951—the year of his fiftieth birthday—the *Motion Picture Herald* dropped him from its list of the top ten box-office performers. Age had etched lines on his forehead and cut deep creases on either side of his mouth, but the haunted look in his always moist eyes and the tight way he walked were signs of his intense suffering from ulcers. Thus, his appearance in *High Noon* represented an attempt to salvage his career by turning physical deterioration into an advantage. As it turned out, the performance he gave won him an Academy Award.

Will Kane, the retiring marshal of Hadleyville, marries a young Quaker woman (Grace Kelly) and then leaves with her for another town, where he expects to earn his living running a general store. Shortly before his departure, though, he is told that an outlaw whom he had helped to put behind bars five years before has been let out of jail and is headed back to Hadleyville to take his revenge on the marshal with the help of three other violent men. While en route to his new home, Kane decides that he can't just run away from these ruffians and turns around and goes back to Hadleyville, despite the protestations of his pacifist wife. To his consternation, he discovers that his fellow townsmen are unwilling to take a stand alongside him. Having known peace for half a decade, they have no stomach for another fight, and some of them, furthermore, seem not to have much respect for Kane. Bereft of their support, the grave-faced marshal is assailed by doubts. The challenge he will be facing in the dusty streets appears overwhelming.

In the hallowed tradition of the Western, the hero triumphs after all. But when the townspeople gather around to acclaim him, he coldly rebuffs them, contemptuously throws his badge on the ground and strides away. A conscientious return ending in alienation and departure, a victory with a taste as sour as defeat: here was a Western with a difference, and it spoke to an America which had learned to appreciate such ironies.

High Noon had its premiere in New York on July 30, 1952, and was still packing in the customers in hundreds of movie houses when Hemingway's own attempt at a comeback appeared in *Life* five weeks later. Santiago the fisherman is considerably more marked by age than Gary Cooper's marshal ("the old man was thin and gaunt with deep wrinkles in the back of his neck"). Some of his neighbors have not only lost their respect for him, but regard him as something of a joke ("many of the fishermen made fun of the old man"). After having gone eighty-four days without taking a fish, he desperately needs to have a successful expedition. In search of real-life examples to inspire him, Santiago thinks of a veteran baseball player who had been disabled for some time by a painful bone spur in his heel. Recently, however, the player had recovered and "the great Di Maggio is himself again." Just as Will Kane has to do, Santiago sets out alone to do battle, against an adversary that turns out to be the most formidable of his career. And once again like Kane, he both wins and loses, for the flesh of his record-breaking marlin is totally devoured by sharks. The skeleton of the great fish proclaims a most ironic victory as the fisherman comes into port. Inasmuch as he has fought so bravely, one might say that in the end Santiago is vindicated; nevertheless, the little boy who is his friend is crying.

In the period following the MacArthur dismissal, the period that marked the beginning of the inconclusive, financially draining, and sometimes bloody struggle against its enemies in which the United States is still engaged, the American hero was perceived to have changed. Somehow he had lost something. Exactly what was hard to put a finger on. It wasn't his prowess. It wasn't his resourcefulness. And by and large it wasn't his belief in himself, although the pangs of self-doubt were not unfamiliar to him. Mainly his problems had to do with his situation. He was experienced, but older now. Going on fighting was a demanding business, and made more so by a climate of skepticism in which it was questioned whether his skills were adequate and whether they even represented the right approach. Worst of all, there was no longer any common agreement about what the meaning of winning was, so that no victory ever brought unalloyed satisfaction.

The Old Man and the Sea was a thinly veiled fictionalization of Hemingway's struggles with himself as a writer and as a man. It also fitted into a larger configuration of symbols.

2

THE news that *The Old Man* had been awarded the Pulitzer Prize reached him via radio on a fine spring afternoon in May 1953 as he and Mary were fishing off Pinar del Río. Although he at once began making light of it by referring to it as the IgNoble Prize, he was in fact terribly—almost pathetically—pleased, and he derived further pleasure from casually signing over the check that came with it to Bumby.

The gesture was one which he could easily afford. For under the terms of the contract he had just signed with Leland Hayward he would receive twenty-five thousand dollars for the movie rights to *The Old Man,* plus an additional twenty-five thousand dollars for serving as a consultant on the filming of the fishing scenes. And ten days after hearing about the Pulitzer more money poured in upon him when the publisher of *Look* magazine sent a delegation of editors to Cuba to offer him a five-figure sum for a series of articles about East Africa, to which he would be returning with Mary in August.

A touching reunion with Philip Percival in Mombasa, followed by a visit to the old white hunter's lovely farm in the Mua Hills near Machakos, made for a splendid beginning to the trip, but thereafter it was marred by Hemingway's acts of self-degradation. One day he was so drunk that he fell out of a fast-moving Land Rover and cut his face rather badly and sprained a shoulder. His drinking also made for an embarrassing inconsistency in his shooting, which he attempted to minimize by taking credit for kills that were patently the work of his dead-eye companion from Cuba, Mario Menocal. After one particularly bad show, he started excusing himself, only to be cut off by Philip Percival's disgusted exclamation, "Oh, Ernest, don't give me that nonsense. The whole thing has been a disgrace!"

The fear that his masculinity was being called into question by such episodes drove him to other extremes of behavior. He shaved his head, explaining that he wanted to go native, and he elaborated upon this charade by going hunting with a spear, dyeing his clothes a rusty Masai color, and courting a Wakamba girl named Debba who lived on a farm near the village of Laitokitok. The game warden Denis Zaphiro regarded Debba as "an evil-smelling bit of camp trash," and Mary, too, was of the opinion that she could have used a bath, but to hear Hemingway tell it, she was an African Prudy

Boulton. My girl is "black and very beautiful," he assured his pen pal, Harvey Breit of *The New York Times*. She is also "completely impudent," he continued, "but absolutely loving and delicate rough. I better quit writing about it because I wanted to write it really and I mustn't spoil it. Anyway it gives me too bad a hardon."

Only in the quiet time after Menocal and Percival and Percival's assistant Roy Home had departed and he had only Zaphiro and Mary for company did he know any peace of mind. Instead of shooting any more animals, he simply had his driver take him out to look at them, and whenever there was nothing of interest to see he pulled out a book and started reading. "He loved Africa," Zaphiro told Hemingway biographer Jeffrey Meyers in 1983. "He loved to sit in it and watch it. He had a natural knowledge of what animals would do and where they would be. . . . [And] he was always reading, reading. Carried soft covers and papers and magazines in his pockets all the time."

In order to view his beloved East Africa from another perspective, Hemingway hired a pilot named Roy Marsh to take him and Mary up in a Cessna 180 for a series of flights over such marvelous spots as the Ngorongoro Crater, the Mountains of the Moon in Ruanda-Urundi and the Murchison Falls in Uganda, where the Nile descends in various levels, rather than abruptly plunging down like Niagara. As Marsh circled over the Falls for the third time, he saw a flight of ibis in front of the plane and dove sharply under them. The plane's propeller and tail assembly struck a telegraph wire suspended above the gorge and Marsh was forced to crash-land in heavy bush. Mary suffered two broken ribs and Hemingway another shoulder sprain, but Marsh was unhurt.

After dozing the night away in front of a fire that Hemingway built, they were able to flag down a passing riverboat, which took them to Butiaba on the eastern shore of Lake Albert. In the course of their journey, Hemingway discovered that the boat had figured prominently in the movie *The African Queen,* starring Katharine Hepburn, "who has my great admiration," he later wrote, and Humphrey Bogart, "whom I have never yet seen at bat in real life."

At Butiaba, they found two men waiting for them on the dock, a policeman named Williams and a bush pilot who introduced himself as Captain Reginald Cartwright. Williams and Cartwright had spent most of the day in the air searching for their bodies, for in flying across Murchison Falls a BOAC pilot had seen the wreckage of the Cessna but no sign of survivors. The report of Hemingway's death had already gone out on the wire services, and on Monday morning, January 25, 1954, the New York *Herald Tribune* would be one of many papers that ran a full obituary. Cartwright and Williams expressed their pleasure at finding that the news of his death had been exaggerated. Cartwright also said that his ancient but capacious twin-engine de Havilland was at Hemingway's disposal. Let me fly you and your party to Entebbe, he urged.

The air strip at Butiaba was subsequently compared by Hemingway to the red hills of South Dakota, since its large ridges had the same sort of washboard look. The de Havilland sped down the strip, "leaping from crag to crag and precipice to precipice in the manner of the wild goat." Suddenly, the starboard engine and the right-wing fuel tank exploded in flame. Due to the head wind, the flames roared toward the rear of the aircraft. Roy Marsh kicked out one of the windows with his feet and he and Mary squirmed through and ran. Meanwhile, Hemingway had discovered that the door of the aircraft was jammed shut by bent metal. Instead of using his feet to smash it open—which presumably he could have done—he butted it with his head, like a bull. All of his contradictory wishes to live and die seem contained in the terrible, all-out lunges with which he inflicted another concussion upon himself and made his way to freedom. Cartwright was the last person to leave the plane, which he did by kicking open another window.

Mary was limping from the pain of a blow to her knee. Hemingway's scalp was bleeding, brain liquid was leaking out of his skull, the crushed vertebrae in his lower back felt like a red-hot poker and he couldn't stop vomiting. In what seemed like the longest ride of his life, he and Mary were driven to the Railway Hotel in Masindi, fifty miles away. The next day another motorcar took them a hundred miles further to Entebbe, where they were given a corner room in the Lake Victoria Hotel. Even though he was seeing double and could hear only intermittently out of one ear, Hemingway agreed to meet with a group of reporters, none of whom had any idea that the injuries to his liver, spleen, and one of his kidneys, not to mention his head, were serious enough to kill him. According to the almost totally apocryphal account which went out on the United Press wire—in New York, the story was displayed with the greatest prominence in the *Times,* the *Post,* and the *Mirror*—and which cropped up again in the "People" section of *Time,* he arrived at the clamorous press conference clutching a bottle of gin and a bunch of bananas and defiantly proclaiming that his luck was running good. The story caught the eye of Ogden Nash and "A Bunch of Bananas" was the poetic result, which was then set to music and recorded by José Ferrer and Rosemary Clooney: "A bunch of bananas and a bottle of jeen,/Keeps the hunger out and the happiness een,/I got a bunch of bananas and a bottle of jeen—/My luck she is running very good.''

Having somehow got through the press conference without throwing up, Hemingway stumbled back to his room, where he and Mary were joined for dinner by the South African novelist Stuart Cloete. His principal memory of the evening was that in his eyes Cloete had looked like twins.

3

NOT to be outdone by *Time* in the apocrypha department, *Newsweek* reported on February 15 that after the second crash the indestructible "Papa," in defiance of his doctors' orders that he take a complete rest, had climbed Mount Kilimanjaro. The true story of his indomitability was less impressive but heartrending. During the course of a brief stay in Nairobi, he dictated a fifteen-thousand-word account for *Look* of what had happened to him and then flew to a beach camp on the Kenyan coast, where he had been scheduled to do some fishing with his son Patrick and Philip Percival but was in too much pain to go out on the water more than two or three times. Nevertheless, when a serious brushfire broke out near the camp he tried to demonstrate that he was still a good man to have around in a crisis. Although the other firefighters pleaded with him not to exert himself, he insisted on lending a hand, only to lose his balance and fall into the flames. In the burning plane at Butiaba he had taken two breaths of fire ("which is something that never really helped anybody except of course Joan of Arc," he wrote Harvey Breit), but now he suffered even more searing damage. Before the firefighters could pull him free, he sustained second-degree burns on his lips, chest, stomach, and legs and third-degree burns on his left hand and right arm.

In Venice, the next stop on his journey back to Cuba, he spent the better part of the month of April in bed at the Gritti Palace. Photographers repeatedly tried to invade his room, but he wouldn't let them in. "It's not legal," he protested, "to surprise a defeated man." The friends whom he did admit noted that his hair had gone suddenly white, that he had lost twenty pounds, and that he seemed somehow diminished—"I don't mean physically diminished," said Aaron Hotchner, "but some of the aura of massiveness seemed to have gone out of him."

The following summer at the Finca, he discovered to his despair that he could write only letters, and he filled them with dispraise of other writers. Scott Fitzgerald had all the smugness of a drunk com-

bined with the self-abasement of an Irish drunk, he told Harvey
Breit, who was also apprised, as were Buck Lanham and Lillian
Ross, of his low opinion of Faulkner's latest novel, *A Fable*. All a
man needed in order to do five thousand words a day of that kind of
stuff, he announced, was a quart of whiskey, a barn loft, and a lack
of interest in syntax.

When the rumors began to circulate that he was going to be
awarded the Nobel Prize that fall, he was obviously pleased, but also
leery of it; as he observed to Buck Lanham, no one who had ever
won had ever written anything worth reading afterwards. On October 28, the day the rumors were proved correct, a crowd of reporters and well-wishers showed up at the Finca and he made a
statement in which he surprised his audience by speaking in praise
of Carl Sandburg, Isak Dinesen, and Bernard Berenson. To Buck
Lanham he later explained,

> You know I know more or less what category of writer I am but
> that's no reason to act swelled headed. Or tell anybody. . . . Between
> us I was thinking like this: Sandburg is an old man and he will appre-
> ciate it. (He did.) Blickie's wife (Dinesen) is a damn sight better writer
> than any Swede they ever gave it to and Blickie (Baron Bror Von
> Blixen-Finecke) is in hell and he would be pleased if I spoke well of
> his wife. Berenson I thought deserved it (no more than me) but I
> would have been happy to see him get it. Or any of the three.

The official citation from the Nobel Committee grated on him.
Although it paid tribute to his "powerful, style-making mastery of
the art of modern narration," it characterized his early writings—
i.e., his best work—as "brutal, cynical, and callous." Once again,
the Hemingway myth had interfered with the perception of supposedly careful readers.

Uncertain health served him as an excuse not to go to Stockholm
and give a speech—a form of exercise which he hated—so the U.S.
Ambassador to Sweden, John Cabot, accepted the prize in his behalf.
He did, however, send a statement to the Swedish Academy which
was read aloud at the ceremonial banquet. Without making direct
reference to the official citation, he nevertheless rebuked it, in one of
the most suggestive sentences he ever composed about his work.
"Things may not be immediately discernible in what a man writes,
and in this sometimes he is fortunate; but eventually they are quite
clear and by these and the degree of alchemy that he possesses he
will endure or be forgotten." Having said that, he went on to talk
about the daily lot of the writer. Once again, his words were admi-

rably honest, but also full of dignity, so that even though he was speaking in personal terms he spared his listeners all but a glimpse or two of the tragedy that was consuming him.

> Writing, at its best, is a lonely life. Organizations for writers palliate the writer's loneliness but I doubt if they improve his writing. He grows in public stature as he sheds his loneliness and often his work deteriorates. For he does his work alone and if he is a good enough writer he must face eternity, or the lack of it, each day.

His alarmed awareness of his failing powers was mounting even as this statement was being read to the Swedish Academy. Following a frighteningly sterile summer, he had begun work that fall on a fictionalized diary of his disastrous safari, and the more he wrote the less it pleased him. After more than a year and a half of sporadic effort, "African Journal" consisted of two hundred thousand undisciplined words, at which point the dissatisfied author wrapped the manuscript in cellophane and consigned it to a bank vault. Perhaps when he got back from Peru, where he was supposed to offer advice on the filming of the fishing scenes in *The Old Man and the Sea,* he would finally be able to whip the journal into shape.

But upon his return to the Finca in the late spring of 1956, he found it impossible to resume work on the Africa book and instead began writing short stories at a feverish pace. Only two of them were deemed worthy by him of publication, "Get a Seeing-Eyed Dog" and "A Man of the World," both of which appeared in the hundredth anniversary number of the *Atlantic Monthly* in November 1957 under the general heading, "Two Tales of Darkness." The former portrayed an American writer gone blind in Venice, the latter a bum named Blackie who is blinded in a brawl in a Wyoming saloon. Had Hemingway's name not been attached to them, these unsatisfactorily developed stories would surely have been rejected by the *Atlantic.* Yet if they are of no moment, literarily speaking, they throw a bar of light into the author's anxieties. Ever since his bout with erysipelas in 1949 Hemingway had been afraid that someday he might lose his eyesight.

4

AT the Ritz in Paris in the late fall of 1956 one of the older porters who brought the Hemingways' luggage to their suite made mention of two small trunks of his which had been gathering dust in the basement of the hotel for years. On opening them, Hemingway to his surprise found all sorts of mementoes of his life in Paris in the twenties. As George Plimpton has recalled, a number of Hemingway's friends had remarked in the aftermath of his traumatic plane crashes that they had had the effect of making him turn inward and backward, that reminiscences came more easily to his lips than ever before. But the discovery of the forgotten trunks prompted more than talk; they inspired him to recapture the most storied part of his past in a memoir.

He got off to a brisk start on *A Moveable Feast* in 1957 and worked on it off and on for a year, but then set it aside in favor of trying to fix up *The Garden of Eden*. In the winter of 1958–1959, in the old mining town of Ketchum, Idaho, where he and Mary rented a couple of furnished houses in quick succession before buying—for fifty thousand dollars—a place of their own from the millionaire playboy, Bob Topping, he tinkered once again with the memoir, and when he and Mary left for Spain in the spring of 1959 the manuscript went with him. A multitude of distractions, however, kept him from devoting much time to it.

5

THEY sailed for Spain aboard the S.S. *Constitution*. The professional reason for their going was that Scribners had decided to reissue *Death in the Afternoon* and Hemingway felt the need to update it; by following a full season of bullfights all over the country and also by taking in the dangerously demanding mano a mano duels—involving only two matadors with six bulls rather than the usual complement of three—that a promoter had set up between Antonio Ordóñez and Luis Miguel Dominguín, he would acquire enough fresh material, he hoped, to augment the new edition with an epilogue of several thousand words.

When the Hemingways landed at Algeciras in late April, they were greeted on the dock by an American expatriate whom Hemingway had previously met on a brief trip to Mexico, Nathan (Bill) Davis. The son of a wealthy Californian with business interests in Spain, Davis was the brother-in-law of the literary critic Cyril Connolly and a collector of literary lions whom he delighted in entertaining at La Consula, his beautiful estate near Málaga. Having Hemingway as his house guest represented the fulfillment of Davis's fondest social dream, and he considered it a privilege to wait on him personally.

On Sunday, May 10, Davis drove the Hemingways in a rented

pink Ford to Málaga to take in a novillada. Both the matadors and the bulls proved to be of such poor quality, however, that the disappointed visitors drank "an extra martini," as Mary gently put it, before their 11 P.M. dinner and "too much wine" in the course of it. The evening was a portent of overindulgences to come.

The next event on the Hemingways' itinerary was the fiesta of San Isidro in Madrid. For eleven days, their life resounded with the roars of the crowd at the barrera and the multilingual chatter of the clusters of people with whom they had lunch and were apt to see again at festive dinners that lasted until two in the morning. And in the hours immediately preceding dinner, Hemingway and Mary either went out for drinks and tapas with friends or invited them to receptions in their suite at the new Hotel Suecia.

They were almost never alone and only rarely was there a letup in the pace of the "circus," as Mary called it. After Madrid came Cordoba, and then Seville. After Seville, Mary was too exhausted to do anything but return to La Consula to rest, but Bill Davis and Hemingway went on to Aranjuez, where they witnessed the first of the two severe gorings that Ordóñez suffered that year. Spending time with the injured matador and his numerous friends and hangers-on in his room in a Madrid hospital became the next order of business for Hemingway, and when he and Davis finally got back to La Consula a new round of parties at once began. "Darling, you're so thin and beautiful," Slim Hayward exclaimed to the guest of honor as she floated into lunch one day with a Hollywood friend in tow. "You're even bigger than I imagined," cooed Lauren Bacall.★ As Hemingway puffed up his chest like a pouter pigeon, Mary seethed at being ignored by these "man-capturing" females. Lunch was served at 3:30 and lasted for three hours.

The pursuit of bullfights in the pink Ford resumed. Sometimes Mary went along, sometimes she did not, but either way it didn't seem to matter to her husband, for the number of people around him was constantly swelling. Hotchner showed up at the end of June, and when a dark-haired, nineteen-year-old Irish girl named Valerie Danby-Smith arranged a meeting with Hemingway at the Hotel Suecia (her excuse being that the Belgian news agency for which she worked as a stringer wanted her to interview him), he promptly hired her as his secretary at two hundred fifty dollars a

★ In 1944, Bacall had costarred with Humphrey Bogart in the movie version of *To Have and Have Not*. Although William Faulkner wrote much of the dialogue, Bacall's most famous line, addressed to Bogart, was dreamed up by the movie's director, Howard Hawks: "You know how to whistle, don't you? You just put your lips together and blow."

month. José Luis Castillo-Puche, a Spanish journalist who also attached himself to the Hemingway cortege, later remarked in his book, *Hemingway in Spain,* that whereas the novelist was so cold and distant and indifferent to Mary that it was as though "he were a stranger living at her side," he "couldn't keep himself from casting covert glances at the affectionate little Irish girl with the unkempt hair, or touching her."

In Pamplona, where the cortege came to include the writer Peter Buckley and his bride, Dr. George Saviers of the Sun Valley Hospital and his wife, and two pretty American girls, Teddy Jo Paulson and Mary Schoonmaker, Hemingway played up to Valerie and froze out Mary with the same blatancy with which he had cozied up to Duff Twysden right in front of Hadley in the self-same cafés. On a trip out from Pamplona to the Irati River for swimming and a picnic, Valerie rode in the front seat of the Ford between Davis and Hemingway, while Mary sat in the rear. But that was just the beginning of the humiliation she would endure that day. While clambering over rocks toward water deep enough to swim in, she fell and broke the third toe of her right foot in two places. Although her pain was intense, Hemingway showed no concern about her. "I'm sorry you broke your toe," he remarked with chilling formality.

For the rest of the Pamplona fiesta, the unhappy Mary was not only less mobile because of her injury, but increasingly offended and bored by "the dirty tables, the sour smell of spilled wine, the stupid chitchat with strangers who moved in for autographs and free drinks, and Ernest's endlessly repeated aphorisms." Her husband, by contrast, appeared to revel in the attention to him, reducing his sleep to three or four hours a night in order to soak up more of it and stepping up his consumption of vodka and wine to keep going. Not surprisingly, he developed a new kidney disorder, for which Dr. Saviers had to treat him.

That he also was suffering from a mental disorder became apparent to Buck Lanham on the evening of July 20, the night before Hemingway's sixtieth birthday, at a dinner-dance in the Hotel Miramar in Málaga. Having danced with Mrs. David Bruce, Lanham passed behind Hemingway's chair on the way back to his seat, and as he did so his left arm brushed the back of Hemingway's head. Hemingway reacted as though Lanham had slugged him. In a loud, belligerent voice, he warned him that nobody was allowed to touch his head. Too angry to speak, his old comrade walked away without a word. Later, Hemingway came up to him, his eyes filled with tears. He apologized by piteously explaining that he had combed his hair forward in a bang to hide his baldness and that the movement of Lanham's arm had disrupted the arrangement. If Lanham would forgive him, he would go to a barber in the morning and have his hair cut just as short as his. While Lanham did not understand that that promise had a long history behind it, he did realize that something was awfully wrong with his old friend and gruffly told him to stop talking like a jackass.

Valencia on July 30 was the scene of the first mano a mano between Ordóñez and Dominguín, and the promoters of the duel made much of the fact that Hemingway had been in attendance. Even before this burst of publicity, the editors of *Life* had become aware of the literary motives behind his presence in Spain and they now dispatched a man named Will Lang from their Paris bureau to talk to him. Would he be interested, Lang was authorized to ask, in allowing *Life* to publish the piece on bullfighting he was planning to write before it appeared in hard covers, just as he had given the magazine first crack at *The Old Man and the Sea*. Most certainly he would, said Hemingway.

Committing himself to *Life,* however, meant that he had to stick with his itinerary of corridas, even though he was beginning to have his fill of back-and-forth journeys across Europe's second most mountainous country. From Madrid to Cuenca to Alicante; from Murcia back to Alicante, and then back to Murcia; from Ronda to Seville and then north to Mérida and then north again to Béjar: on and on the pink Ford rolled, and the more tired of the road Hemingway became the more brutally he ignored his wife. She had become "inaudible" to him, she felt.

From Paris, Mary flew home on October 4 without him. Ostensibly, her only reason for doing so was to ready the houses in Cuba and Idaho for a visit by Ordóñez and his beautiful wife Carmen, who was Dominguín's sister. But after a few days of hard work at the Finca she wrote Hemingway a single-spaced letter of three and a half pages recapitulating his recent treatment of her. She was going to rent a small apartment in New York, she finished by informing him, and would establish herself there just as soon as she finished opening the house in Ketchum.

Hemingway cabled his reply. THANKS LETTERS AND TREMENDOUS WORK DONE. SORRY CAN'T AGREE ITEMS AND CONCLUSIONS PERSONAL LETTER BUT RESPECT YOUR VIEWS ALTHOUGH DISAGREE PROFOUNDLY. . . . SORRY SO MUCH WORK AND NUISANCE. . . . STILL LOVE YOU. It was an awfully small meal for an awfully hungry woman, but it sufficed and she didn't leave him after all.

6

HAVING written five thousand words of his piece for *Life,* Hemingway sailed for New York on the *Liberté.* On the last day of the crossing, he had a drink in the first-class bar with the future biographer of Scott Fitzgerald, Andrew Turnbull. A tortured, sensitive man whose own life would end in suicide, Turnbull was struck by the "sad mask" of Hemingway's face, the "delicacy" of his features above the "froth" of his beard, and the look of "grazing diffidence" in his red-veined eyes.

The vacation that the reunited Hemingways spent in Ketchum with Carmen and Antonio Ordóñez was a disappointment to all concerned. To make matters worse, Mary fell while out hunting one day and shattered her left elbow. Thus it was with considerable relief that Hemingway and Mary returned in January 1960 to the Finca, where he resumed work on his account of the Ordóñez-Dominguín duels. In February, he reported to Hotchner by long-distance telephone that he already had written more than seventeen thousand words. A month later, he again phoned Hotchner. The piece was expanding unexpectedly, he confessed. His latest estimate was that when completed it would run to thirty thousand words. Would Hotchner please call up Ed Thompson, the managing editor of *Life,* he asked, and say that he was aiming for an April 7 deadline.

The next time Hemingway called, Hotchner thought his voice sounded tired and tense. The word count of the *Life* article now stood at 63,562. There was no chance that he would make the April deadline. Perhaps he could finish by the end of May—if his eyes held up, he added. A Cuban doctor had told him, he explained, that he was suffering from "a rap called *keratitis sicca,*" and that as a result, the "only book in the joint with type big enough for me to read is *Tom Sawyer.*"★

On May 4, Hotchner was awakened sometime after midnight by another call from Hemingway. "The Dangerous Summer," as he was calling the piece, was 92,453 words long and climbing. Three weeks later, he announced to Hotchner that he had 108,746 words in hand, but that the story he had wanted to tell was at last complete —except for a coda that would require another trip to Spain. His immediate problem, though, was to cut seventy thousand words

★ *Keratitis sicca* occurs more commonly in adult women than men. It initially reduces tear production, which leads to burning and irritation. In advanced cases, ulceration, vascularization, and scarring of the cornea may lead to severe visual disability.

from the manuscript, so as to bring it down to what he regarded as the proper length for *Life*.

During the next month he phoned Hotchner a dozen times, with mounting anxiety in his voice. Despite three and a half weeks of work from early morning all through the day, he finally admitted, he had been able to cut only 530 words. Since *Life* had already advertised the piece, he couldn't just forget about it, he said. And yet, "I just can't go over it again, Hotch; it all seems locked-in to me and I can't use my eyes any more." A writer who had often ridiculed Thomas Wolfe for his verbal diarrhea, who had scorned him for needing Max Perkins's help in shaping his work and making it publishable, now found himself in the same situation. At Hemingway's urgent request, Hotchner flew to Havana on June 27.

In short order, Hotchner composed a list of eight suggested cuts in the first hundred pages (out of 688 all told) of the typed manuscript and submitted it to Hemingway. The following morning, the two men conferred in Hemingway's bedroom. Hotchner noticed two things right off: an array of seven different-colored pills that Hemingway proceeded to swallow one by one with siphon water, and a lined pad of paper on which he had written his reasons for rejecting all of Hotchner's proposed cuts. The reasons, Hotchner was further startled to discover, were badly phrased and in some cases incomprehensible.

For the next three days, Hotchner continued to propose cuts and Hemingway continued to reject them. Thereafter, Hemingway gradually gave way, until 54,916 words had been excised. At which point he couldn't consider any further cuts because his eyes gave out and he couldn't see the words on a page for more than ten or twelve minutes. "I'll tell you, Hotch," he burst out, "it is like being in a Kafka nightmare. I act cheerful like always but am not. I'm bone tired and very beat up emotionally."

Hotchner carried the abridged version back to New York and gave it to Ed Thompson. The *Life* editor was appalled. Even the abridgement was more than twice the length he had bargained on. Nevertheless, he agreed to buy a selection of it for ninety thousand dollars, plus ten thousand dollars for reprint rights in the Spanish language edition of the magazine.

Hemingway flew back to Spain on August 4. Bill Davis was staggered by the psychological changes that had taken place in his friend in less than a year. He couldn't sleep, in spite of the pills he gulped, and everything worried him—including the idea that Bill was plotting to kill him by wrecking the automobile in which he drove him about. Feelings of loneliness, guilt, and remorse swept over him in enormous waves, along with a terrible frustration whenever his memory failed him. There had been a time when he had expressed utter contempt for Scott Fitzgerald's "crack-up" confessions, but now he used that very word himself, not only in paranoiac whispers to friends about Bill's automobile plot, but in haunted letters to Mary about his physical and mental condition.

Life's condensation of "The Dangerous Summer" appeared in three installments, the first of them on September 5, 1960.★ A color picture of the author—with a smile on his face and looking surprisingly healthy—appeared on the cover. For Hemingway, though, there was no satisfaction in this event. The magazine "made me sick," he cried to Mary, and the face on the cover was "horrible." As for the writing and the photographic layout inside, he felt "ashamed and sick to have done such a job."

Hotchner joined him at the Hotel Suecia in Madrid one afternoon in early October. The following morning, Hemingway came to his room and they had breakfast together. The novelist complained that his bad kidney had kept him up all night. As he raised his teacup to his lips, his hand was unsteady. The two men then talked about a projected movie version of *Across the River,* and Hotchner suggested Sophia Loren for the part of Renata. Hemingway had never heard of her. "I lead a very sheltered life," he explained. "You've got a lot coming to you," Hotchner replied in a roguish tone. Hemingway's eyes snapped with anger. "That's out of 'The Battler,' " he said in a hard voice. "Did you realize that?" Inadvertently, Hotchner had indeed quoted a line from the part of the story in which crazy Ad introduces Nick Adams to Bugs.

> "Glad to meet you," Bugs said. "Where you say you're from?"
> "Chicago," Nick said.
> "That's a fine town," the negro said. "I didn't catch your name."
> "Adams. Nick Adams."
> "He says he's never been crazy, Bugs," Ad said.
> "He's got a lot coming to him," the negro said.

7

IN Hemingway's last years at the Finca, according to Dr. Herrera, he talked a lot about killing himself; indeed, on more than one occasion he actually acted out a suicide scenario in front of an audience. "Look, this is how I'm going to do it," he would say. Whereupon,

★ A more substantial percentage of Hemingway's manuscript was published by Scribners in 1985, with an introduction by James A. Michener.

Herrera remembers, he would "sit in his chair, barefoot, and place the butt of his Mannlicher .256 on the fiber rug of the living room between his legs. Then, leaning forward, he would rest the mouth of the gun barrel against the roof of his mouth. He would press the trigger with his big toe and we would hear the click of the gun." Raising his head smiling, he would conclude the demonstration by saying, "This is the technique of harakiri with a gun. . . . The palate is the softest part of the head."

Guns also figured in a nasty way in his relationship with Mary, says Dr. Herrera. "It got so bad," the physician recalls, "that I had to intervene and he and I came to blows. I left the farm around four in the morning after I decided that the worst was over and they were no longer in danger, for they had threatened each other with guns. I had to take away their guns and put them in my car. As a matter of fact, I removed all of their arms and took them to my house."

At Ketchum in the fall of 1960, the sickness unto death that was Hemingway's life became more hellish than ever. To Hotchner and Mary and everyone else within earshot, he proclaimed that the FBI was after him. He was fearful as well that the Castro government in Cuba would no longer allow him to live at the Finca, that he did not have enough money to pay his income taxes, that the local sheriff was going to arrest him any day for nicking another car while backing out of a parking lot, and that his inability to complete the manuscript of *A Moveable Feast* meant that he would never again be able to write. Allusions to suicide were constantly on his lips, and just before Thanksgiving his erratically fluctuating blood pressure measured 250/125.

Dr. Saviers, over the course of the fall, was gradually able to convince him that specialists in the treatment of "worries" could help him. But when Saviers proposed the name of a world-famous psychiatric hospital in Topeka, Kansas, Hemingway would not hear of it. "They'll say I'm losing my marbles," he said, apparently thinking of the ways in which the news of his incarceration in the Menninger Clinic would affect his public image. Furthermore, psychoanalysts spooked him, he said; not a one of the ones he had met had possessed a sense of humor. The analyst he had relied on was his "portable Corona number three." To enter upon a Freudian modality of treatment at the Menninger at the age of sixty, to talk about his early childhood★ and peel back all the encrusted layers of

---

★ Because Mary Hemingway was in poor health for several years before her death in November 1986, discussions with students of Hemingway's life about the extent of her knowledge of

cover-up, would therefore have been extremely painful for him—if he had taken it seriously, which in all probability he would not have. The Mayo Clinic, however, which Dr. Saviers also mentioned, was an entirely different kettle of fish. People went there for all sorts of reasons. When the news got out, as it inevitably would, that he was there, it could be explained that he was being treated for hypertension. And indeed that was the only therapy he had in mind initially.

On November 30, in the company of Dr. Saviers, he flew to Rochester, Minnesota, the home of the Mayo, and registered under Saviers's name at St. Mary's Hospital. After a number of consultations with the novelist, Dr. Howard P. Rome of the Section of Psychiatry recommended a full course of electroshock treatments. Inasmuch as it represented a mechanistic approach to his problems, Hemingway agreed to it.

ECT

Invented by two Italian doctors in 1938, electroconvulsive therapy (ECT) came to the United States two years later. A course of eight to twelve treatments was found to produce a rapid remission of symptoms among patients suffering from major depression or delusional depression. It was also found that electroshock patients generally incurred memory deficits. Some psychiatrists claimed that the deficits merely involved events that had happened in the six months before treatment and two months after and that in time they disappeared, while others spoke of profound memory loss and physically damaged brains. Critics of the therapy further asserted that after a while the patient's depression returned.

Despite the lack of agreement about the efficacy of ECT, Dr. Rome had little choice but to recommend it to Hemingway. The modern-day armamentarium of neuroleptic drugs like Thorazine and tricyclic anti-depressants like Elavil was not available. Hemingway had been deeply depressed for so long that it was obvious that he was now incapable of recovering on his own, as he had done so many times in the past. And for this patient, talk therapy was virtually out of the question. What other option besides ECT was left?

Hemingway returned to Idaho on January 22, 1961. Despite Mary's angry claim that "the psychiatrist decided the cure was complete," the continued sequestration of Hemingway's hospital records leaves it far from clear whether Dr. Rome really believed that, or whether he considered his patient's remarkably buoyant spirits the manifes-

---

her husband's peculiar upbringing were out of the question. When Martha Gellhorn was asked in 1985 whether Hemingway had told her about his and Marcelline's twinhood, she replied flatly, "No."

tation of a "flight into health" that was more seeming than real. What is clear, however, is that Hemingway was eager to get out, that Mary made no attempt to persuade him to stay, and that Dr. Rome had no power to keep him there against his will.

As soon as he reached Ketchum, he got out the manuscript of *A Moveable Feast*. "Working hard again," he cabled his son Patrick at his Tanganyikan farm three days later. A more detailed communication would have conveyed this information: Each morning he arose at seven, started work at eight-thirty and kept at it until one. After lunch he took a nap. In the midafternoon, schoolchildren returning home in a yellow schoolbus could count on getting the white-bearded man in the checked cap, light jacket, and heavy boots to respond to their waves as he walked along Route 93. At dinnertime he ate moderately and drank a glass of claret.

A letter addressed to L. H. Brague, Jr., of the Scribners trade department on February 6 described what he had been up to in regard to the memoir. He had gone over the material and arranged it into chapters. He was also working on a title out of "my usual long list." Most important of all, he was writing another chapter, number nineteen, which he termed "the last one."★

Once again, it seemed, he had beaten his disabilities and his furies, exorcising them in the act of writing and in therapeutic recall of the streets, the cafés, the good food and wine, the friends, the wife, and the long hours of work that made Paris in the years between 1921 and 1926 a symbol for him of the man he once was. "If you are lucky enough to have lived in Paris as a young man," he had declared to a friend in 1950, in a poignant statement from which Mary would eventually take the title for the book, "then wherever you go for the rest of your life, it stays with you, for Paris is a moveable feast."

8

SELECTED passages from *A Moveable Feast* appeared in the April 10, 1964, issue of *Life*. The entire manuscript, edited by Mary,★★ was published by Scribners 3½ weeks later, in a first printing of 85,000 copies, plus 204,000 copies for the Book-of-the-Month Club. From

★ The evidence of the manuscript suggests that the chapter dealt with the matter of Fitzgerald's alleged anxiety about his sexual equipment. In the published version of the memoir, however, "A Matter of Measurements" appears as the second last chapter.
★★ Cutting and rearranging passages, mixing elements of various drafts and rearranging the order of the chapters were among the editorial responsibilities that Mary elected to assume, albeit she did not refer to them in her prefatory note to the published text. Rather, she disingenuously declared that her husband had finished the book in 1960 in Cuba.

May 24 to December 6, the book maintained a position on *The New York Times Book Review*'s best-seller list and was in first place for nineteen weeks. By and large, the reviewers were extraordinarily complimentary. Stanley Kauffmann in the *New Republic* called the memoir "a small diamond mine" and Frank Kermode in the *New York Review of Books* said that "in some ways [it is] Hemingway's best book since the 1920s." But it remained for Marvin Mudrick in the *Hudson Review* to come right out and say what so many of the reviewers had merely implied. That Hemingway could have written *A Moveable Feast,* he proclaimed, "is the proof of the health he died in." George Plimpton, however, could not accept this view, possibly because his memories of Hemingway's disintegration in the fifties were so vivid. "But for all the cataloguing of meals, of wines, of Paris streets . . . and even pervading the fine humor of the sketches," he wrote in the *New York Herald Tribune Book Week,* "there is a note of impending chaos and death." It was a judgment that has endured.

The first chapter of the memoir leads the reader into a dream. Like Frederic Henry and Catherine Barkley, Hemingway and Hadley are insulated from reality by an all-sufficient love. Despite their poverty, they look down on the rich, for they have each other and are warm together in the night.

That the superlatively healthy and happy hero is nevertheless suffering from some sort of malaise is first suggested at the end of the chapter called "A False Spring," after he and Hadley have had a fine dinner at Michaud's and then made love in the dark of their bedroom. Despite these pleasurable satiations, a hunger of an indeterminate nature has not been quieted in him, and when he awakes in the night and looks out the window at the light on the roofs of the tall houses, it is still there. Pulling his face away from the moonlight and into the shadow, he tries to think out what is bothering him, but is "too stupid" to do so. Life had seemed simple that morning, he reflects. But Paris was a very old city and nothing was simple there, the memoirist then remarks in an older, more bitter voice.

A grimmer intrusion of dark feelings occurs at the end of the chapter in which Hemingway remembers a drink he had at the Dôme one evening with the painter Jules Pascin, whom he liked very much for his sense of humor as well as for his paintings, and two young models, one of them a blonde, the other a cropped-headed brunette, who claimed to be sisters. The anecdote begins with Pascin asking Hemingway if he wants to bang the dark sister. Hemingway replies, "You probably banged her enough today." The sexual banter continues, until the blonde exclaims, "I'm tired of this talk." As Hemingway gets up to go, he glances at Pascin. With his hat on the back of his head and a big grin on his face, the Frenchman looked like a Broadway character out of the nineties. ". . . and afterwards when he had hanged himself, I liked to remember him as he was that night at the Dôme," the memoirist adds, by way of introducing a surreptitious comment about himself. "They say the seeds of what we will do are in all of us, but it always seemed to me that in those who make jokes in life the seeds are covered with better soil and with a higher grade of manure."

On the second page of the next chapter, a free association of thought occurs which once again goes beyond the ostensible time frame of the memoir. The memoirist has been talking about the dislike he had acquired as a young man for the paintings of Picabia and Wyndham Lewis versus Ezra Pound's enthusiasm for them.

> We never argued about these things because I kept my mouth shut about the things I did not like. If a man liked his friends' painting or writing, I thought it was probably like those people who like their families, and it was not polite to criticize them. Sometimes you can go quite a long time before you criticize families, your own or those by marriage, but it is easier with bad painters because they do not do terrible things and make intimate harm as families can do. With bad painters all you need to do is not look at them. But even when you have learned not to look at families nor listen to them and have learned not to answer letters, families have many ways of being dangerous.

Because his mother had taken up painting in the twenties, it was but an easy leap for Hemingway to shift from talking about painters to talking about families, and from there the leap to talking about letters that you finally learned not to answer was easier still. Although Grace had been dead for years when he wrote those words, the author of *A Moveable Feast* was still fighting with her.

The red thread of death-wish is unwound in the later chapters mainly through a choice—whether conscious or unconscious—of metaphors, such as the description of the transformation of Scott Fitzgerald's face into a death's head after one sip of champagne too many in the Dingo bar. But it is in the chapter called "The Man Who Was Marked for Death," which is about Ernest Walsh, that he talks most revealingly about Ernest Hemingway.

Dark, intense, and tubercular, Walsh is a con man who makes his living out of his death, as the memoirist says in a wicked phrase. Walsh's con, in other words, is his consumption, on which he trades for sexual favors, economic subsidies, and the sympathy of fellow writers. His purpose in buying Hemingway an expensive lunch is to manipulate him into contributing to the magazine he coedits and into seeing it through the printers whenever he himself has to be out of Paris. Walsh makes his first move by pulling his patented marked-for-death look and then telling Hemingway that there is nothing wrong with *him*. "You mean I am not marked for death?" Hemingway asks. "No. You're marked for Life," Walsh says. "Give me time," Hemingway says, in a sentence that somehow seems to echo "The Battler."

The last chapter in the book, as Mary decided to present it, is devoted to Hadley, and an aching longing for her can be felt in every line. So, however, can a longing for death.

There were no ski lifts from Schruns in the old days, Hemingway says, and no funiculars either, and you climbed for hours and hours on seal skins attached to the bottoms of your skis. For it was the belief of Walther Lent, the head of the ski school, that the fun of skiing was to get up into the highest mountain country, even though there was the constant threat of avalanches when the snow fell late on still warm slopes.

"I remember. . . ." In five different paragraphs this incantation appears, as the memoirist watches Hadley and his youthful self move across orchards and fields, up through beech and pine woods, and finally up into the high mountains above the tree line, where Hemingway sees a fox with a forefoot raised and is startled by the clutter of a ptarmigan bursting out of the snow. A "strange world," the memoirist calls it, but to the reader of his fiction the place is reminiscent of the snowy Swiss refuge in which Frederic and the pregnant Catherine spend their happiest hours together and of a mountaintop shining white in the African sun. Wrapped in their Vorarlberg cocoon, the Hemingways ski all winter long. In March, the conditions are finally right for a climactic plunge. ". . . towards spring there was the great glacier run, smooth and straight, forever straight if our legs could hold it, our ankles locked, we running so low, leaning into the speed, dropping forever and forever in the silent hiss of the crisp powder." *Forever and forever.* As the death-haunted author of those words looked out the window at the snow-covered peaks of the Sawtooth Mountains after his return from the Mayo Clinic, he may have imagined Hadley and himself skiing together into eternity.

The following winter was a "nightmare," the memoirist suddenly bursts out in violent anger. Unable to take responsibility himself for any of his failed marriages, Hemingway pinned the blame for the failure of the first on four people he did not identify by name, but whose identity is obvious: Gerald and Sara Murphy, John Dos Passos, Pauline Pfeiffer. A rich couple led by a "pilot fish" of bastard origin taught a trusting young man to believe that every day should be a fiesta, while a young woman who was also rich became the temporary best friend of the trusting young man's trusting wife and then relentlessly set out to take the young man away from her.

If the young man himself did anything wrong, it lay in his decision to stop in Paris on his way back to Schruns from a quick trip to New York so that he could spend time with the rich young woman. At last, though, he boarded the train for Austria, and when he glimpsed his wife standing by the piled logs at the train station with her hair red gold in the sun, grown out all winter awkwardly and beautifully, "I wished I had died before I loved anyone but her."

9

THE remission of depression produced by the shock treatments did not last very long, and Hemingway set aside *A Moveable Feast* forever because he had lost the capacity to write. On or about February 20, 1961, according to Mary, he tried to compose a few sentences for a volume of handwritten tributes that a woman in Washington was compiling in honor of the newly inaugurated President, John F. Kennedy. Although he worked for hours, none of the dozens of attempts he made came close to satisfying him. A smell of desperation filled the room, Mary remembered. The next thing that happened was that Dr. Saviers arrived to take his patient's blood pressure. Sitting on the couch with his sleeve rolled up, Hemingway broke down and wept. That one gift which had meant everything had now deserted him. Nothing could better describe his definitive despair than four of the lines that Milton gives to Samson Agonistes:

> *My hopes all flat: Nature within me seems*
> *In all her functions weary of herself;*
> *My race of glory run, and race of shame,*
> *And I shall shortly be with them that rest.*

During March, he became more and more silent; the staring, vacant look in his eyes recalled certain photographs of his father. One night, Mary tuned in their TV set to a production of *Macbeth,* which she found wonderful. But Hemingway said that the play was terrifying, that he couldn't stand to watch it, and flicked off the set. On April 21, Mary came downstairs and found him standing in the front vestibule of the sitting room holding one of his favorite shotguns.

Attempt at suicide

Two shells were resting on the windowsill in front of him. Mary kept up a mainly one-sided conversation until Saviers arrived to take his blood pressure. With the help of another doctor, whom Mary phoned, Saviers persuaded him to go to a nearby hospital, where he was placed under sedation.

A few days later, Hemingway insisted on returning to the house —to pick up something he needed, he said. A nurse and a husky fellow named Don Anderson brought him back. The instant the car stopped, he raced inside the house in front of the others and before they could catch him jammed a shell into the breech of a shotgun and swung the muzzle under his chin. In a silent, desperate struggle, Anderson at last managed to break the breech open, whereupon the nurse took out the shell. Silent and sullen, Hemingway returned with them to the hospital, where his clothes were taken from him and locked in a closet.

To Ursula, the sister he loved most, Mary sent a brief message saying, "He is immoveably [sic] convinced that he cannot be healed." Nevertheless, he made no protest when Dr. Saviers immediately arranged for him to be readmitted to the Mayo Clinic. En route to Rochester, the pilot of the Piper Comanche he was traveling in put down at Rapid City, South Dakota, to refuel. With Don Anderson following him like a shadow, Hemingway got out to stretch his legs. In a nearby hangar, he pawed through some tool chests, apparently looking for a gun, and then started walking very rapidly toward the propellers of a taxiing plane, but abruptly stopped when the pilot cut his engines. As soon as the Piper Comanche was airborne once more, he perked up and talked cheerfully for the remainder of the flight.

He was placed in the "suicide watch" section of St. Mary's with the nurses on duty and the nuns who ran the hospital forever looking in on him and bringing him things and asking how he was today. The mothering these women gave him was probably one of the reasons why his spirits appeared to improve, as the rainy days at the end of April gave way to beautiful weather in early May and May ended in turn in a heat wave that lasted until mid-June, when the days became cool and lovely again and the nights wonderful for sleeping.

As a consequence of the new series of electroshock treatments he received, his sex drive was reawakened, and when he complained to Dr. Rome about being horny, Rome phoned Mary and asked her to come to Rochester. While she was only too glad to do so, the night she spent in her husband's room was not, in her laconic words, "entirely satisfactory to either of us."

It was only a night or two later that Dr. Rome telephoned Mary at her room in the Kahler Hotel in Rochester and asked her to come to his office the next morning at eight-thirty. He had some good news to tell her, he said, or so she later said he said. Upon her punctual arrival, she was astonished and distressed to see Hemingway there, dressed in street clothes and grinning like a Cheshire cat.

In the long years of her widowhood, Mary would be loud in her complaints about the Mayo's Section of Psychiatry. Hemingway had "charmed and deceived Dr. Rome to the conclusion that he was sane," she would write in her autobiography. And Martha Gellhorn would echo her sentiments by saying, "The Mayo made terrible mistakes with Hemingway." Maybe it did and maybe it didn't.

One of life's ironies is that the rich, the famous and the powerful frequently receive less rigorous medical care than ordinary mortals because their doctors are in awe of them. Hemingway was not only a Nobel laureate, but known worldwide for his resiliency and courage. When he came to Dr. Rome's office and told him—as it must be presumed he did—that he wanted to go home, it would have been a difficult assignment for any doctor to stand up to him. It is possible that Hemingway bullied him and threatened to inform the media he was being held against his will, until at last Dr. Rome caved in and let him go. It is also possible that Hemingway *did* deceive his doctor; he had been deceiving people all his life, after all. Only by opening the Hemingway file to public inspection can the Mayo hope to settle all the rumors and questions about his release. But one must respect the Clinic for continuing to maintain the confidentiality of the doctor-patient relationship in the face of enormous pressure over the years to violate it.

Bright and early on the morning of June 26, Hemingway left Rochester with his old sparring partner, George Brown, at the wheel of a rented Buick and Mary in the back seat. Hemingway couldn't stop worrying that they might not be able to find a place to spend the night, so they frequently put up at motels at two or three in the afternoon. Not until the evening of June 30 was the seventeen-hundred-mile journey completed.

On Saturday evening, July 1, Mary and George Brown persuaded Hemingway to go out to dinner at a local restaurant. His behavior there was markedly paranoid. As the three of them were sitting down at the table in the corner of the room that he considered the least vulnerable to attack, he noticed a couple of strange men at another table. Suzie, the waitress, was summoned and asked if she had any idea who they were. Probably salesmen from Twin Falls, Suzie volunteered. "They're FBI," said Hemingway. That night, as

Mary was undressing for bed, she began singing an old Italian folk-
song. Its theme was hair, as the title suggested—"Tutti Mi Chia-
mano Bionda" ("They All Call Me Blonde"). From his room,
Hemingway heard her and joined in. When the song was done he
called, "Good night, my kitten."

Although all the guns in the house had been locked in a storeroom
in the basement, the key had been left in plain view on a windowsill
in the kitchen. While Mary had thought of hiding it, she had finally
decided that "no one had a right to deny a man access to his posses-
sions." Around seven o'clock on Sunday morning, Hemingway
arose from his bed, went to the kitchen, got the key, opened the
storeroom, selected a twelve-gauge, double-barreled English shotgun he had bought at Abercrombie & Fitch, pushed two shells into
it, walked upstairs to the foyer, turned the gun against himself and
fired. The explosion blew away his entire cranial vault. Whether he
had placed the gun barrels in his mouth or pressed them to his
forehead is impossible to say.

The funeral was delayed until July 5 to allow Patrick time to fly in
from Africa. At the gravesite, Mary and Hemingway's three sons
stood on one side and his brother Leicester and three of his sisters,
Marcelline, Ursula, and Sunny (Carol did not attend), lined up on
the other, while an amiable but somewhat feckless Catholic priest,
Father Robert Waldman, conducted the service. At the request of
Jack, Patrick, and Gregory, the priest had agreed to read the "sun
also rises" passage from *Ecclesiastes,* but in fact he read only the first
line from a Bible that was not the King James version.

Both before and after the ceremony, Valerie Danby-Smith, who
had come out to cover the funeral for *Newsweek,* was given the cold
shoulder by Mary, but found Gregory Hemingway quite attentive.
(They later married.) Ursula seemed very withdrawn and did not
say much to anybody. Sunny exclaimed that while praying in church
she had seen a perfect outline of Ernest's head on the carpeting
leading up to the altar and that his sad eyes seemed to be pleading
with her. Marcelline busied herself taking notes in preparation for
the book she was writing on growing up in the Hemingway family.
Ill will was in her voice when she remarked to Sunny that suicides
didn't go to heaven. It was virtually the same remark with which
her famous brother had offended her at the time of their father's
funeral.

The grave lay between two pines facing the Sawtooth Mountains.
For the remains of Ernest Hemingway, the location seemed right.
Just a couple of weeks before his death, he had written a letter from
the Mayo Clinic to Dr. Saviers's nine-year-old son Fritz, who had

been hospitalized in Denver with the viral heart disease that would kill him six years later. "The country is beautiful around here," Hemingway had said, "and I've had a chance to see some wonderful country along the Mississippi where they used to drive the logs in the old lumbering days and the trails where the pioneers came north. Saw some good bass jump in the river. I never knew anything about the upper Mississippi before and it is really a very beautiful country and there are plenty of pheasants and ducks in the fall." Even though he was crazy to die, he could still take delight in the things of this world—and could still feel impelled to try to restore the hopes of someone else in trouble. As always, his meaning and power lay in his contradictoriness.

The man who was buried beneath the pine trees had not been felled in battle, nor in any other physical test of strength and courage. The battle he finally lost was with himself. With all the odds against him, it is amazing that he survived anywhere near as long as he did. " . . . how much better to die in all the happy period of undisillusioned youth, to go out in a blaze of light, than to have your body worn out and old and illusions shattered," he exclaimed at age nineteen in Milan. But because the youth was able to hold his death longings at bay, he had time to make his greatness—to create a style that came to dominate storytelling long and short and to invent characters and situations through which his thoughts and experiences could pass and an essence of truth could emerge. Once he was dispossessed by age and illness of the capacity to write, once he was overwhelmed by demoralizing fears that he was no longer capable of living up to the image he had created for himself, the end he had long debated probably became inevitable. In a blood-drenched century, his death in all its bloody ghastliness remains unforgettable. Nevertheless, his legacy to the world, as to the boy in the Denver hospital, included the gift of hope. Through the enormous curiosity and gusto with which he pursued new adventures and the valorous dedication he brought to his art, he affirmed the possibilities of life in this tough world.

ACKNOWLEDGMENTS

At the conclusion of a long task, I am conscious of many debts. Without the help of other books on Hemingway, most notably Carlos Baker's *Ernest Hemingway: A Life Story;* Michael Reynolds's *Hemingway's First War, Hemingway's Reading,* and *The Young Hemingway;* and Bernice Kert's *The Hemingway Women,* my own would have been much the poorer. The biographical studies by Scott Donaldson, Jeffrey Meyers, Peter Griffin, and the late Charles Fenton have also been of assistance to me. And while the extraordinary exfoliation of Hemingway scholarship in the past twenty-five years precludes specific mention of all the authors from whose articles I have benefited, there are five whom I simply must thank by name: Millicent Bell, James Hinkle, Robert W. Lewis, Kenneth G. Johnston, and Paul Smith. Professor Smith also read my manuscript and preserved me from blunders, as well as offering me sensible advice about certain matters of expression. Even though we have never met, Michael Reynolds was likewise very kind to me, patiently answering the many questions I put to him and sending me an advance copy, in page proofs, of *The Young Hemingway.* I owe thanks too to Mildred Marmur, the former president and publisher of Charles Scribner's Sons, for generously supplying me with an advance copy of *The Garden of Eden.*

The professional skill and dedication of my literary agent, Lois Wallace, have sustained me at every stage of the project, from before it was actually begun until its completion. At Simon and Schuster, I owe thanks to Donald Hutter for mixing much-needed encouragement and tactful criticism in his comments on early drafts of the early chapters, to Herman Gollob for his keen-minded review of a late draft of the entire manuscript, to Eric Rayman for his reassuringly detailed advice on a whole host of legal questions, and above all to Frederic W. Hills and Burton Beals for contributions that are not easily summarized. Right from the start of our association, Mr. Hills displayed a superbly clear perception of the many changes that I needed to make in the narrative in order to maximize its effectiveness, uncommonly good judgment about all sorts of ancillary issues, and an iron commitment to high standards which I found exhilarating, while Mr. Beals's sensitive, unfailingly resourceful, unflaggingly scrupulous attention to the manuscript represented the sort of editing which I did not believe existed any more; whatever the merits of what I have accomplished, they have been mightily enhanced by these two men.

To Neal Kozodoy of *Commentary* I am grateful for helping me to begin to clarify my ideas about Hemingway in a lengthy essay for the magazine in 1981. On the basis of that essay, my colleague at Johns Hopkins, Louis Galambos, urged me to undertake a book on Hemingway; if the result, half a decade later, bulks larger than the "short" work he envisioned, my thanks to him have increased proportionately. Another Hopkins colleague, William W. Freehling, likewise took an interest in the book and offered fruitful suggestions about it. And the chairman of the Johns Hopkins History Department, John Russell-Wood, was a consistent supporter of my endeavors. But my largest debt at Hopkins is to two younger scholars, Wilfred McClay and Peter Kafer, with whom I have had many conversations that improved my understanding of Hemingway's life and work. Furthermore, Mr. McClay carefully read my manuscript —portions of it several times over—and shared his characteristically incisive reactions with me.

Among other readers of portions of the manuscript, I should mention especially Thomas C. Wallace and Joseph Epstein. I am also grateful to Mr. Epstein and his wife Barbara for hospitality during a visit my wife and I paid to Oak Park and Chicago. For providing me with conveniently situated launchpads for my forays into the Hemingway Room at the John F. Kennedy Library in Boston, I thank Roderick and Joan Nordell, Gerald and Miriam Berlin, and Virginia Lewisohn Kahn and Dr. Ernest Kahn; for other forms of hospitality I thank Dr. Ingrid Gifford and Dr. Sanford Gifford.

For special insights into Hemingway and his world, I am grateful for the cooperation of Edward Wagenknecht, Martha Gellhorn, William Walton, Prentiss Taylor, John H. N. Hemingway, Patrick Hemingway and Clare Boothe Luce. For medical and/or psychiatric instruction, I thank Dr. Arnall Patz, Dr. Douglas A. Jabs, Dr. Charles G. Rob, Dr. Sanford Gifford, and Dr. John W. R.-Love. For heightening my awareness of the Korean War's effect on American movies, I thank Thomas H. Pauly. For deepening my appreciation of Van Wyck Brooks, I thank James Hoopes.

Jo Hills and her successor, Joan O'Connor, were marvelously helpful to me in my delvings into the riches in the Hemingway Room at the Kennedy Library. Cathy Henderson likewise aided my examination of the Hemingway collection in the Harry Ransom Humanities Research Center at the University of Texas. I am grateful in addition to the staffs of the Manuscript Division of the Library of Congress, the Bettmann Archive in New York City, the Firestone Library at Princeton University, the Beinecke Rare Book Library at Yale University, the Alderman Library at the University of Virginia, the McKeldin Library at the University of Maryland, the Oak Park, Illinois, Public Library, and the library of the Villa I Tatti in Florence. I owe a debt too to Margaret Christman of the National Portrait Gallery in Washington, D.C., for sharing with me her knowledge of sources of information about children's costumes and hairstyles at the turn of the century.

Finally there is my family: Andrew, Elisabeth, and Sophia Lynn have played a larger part than they know in the making of this book; Ernest Lynn told me fascinating stories about newspaper life in the 1920s; and my wife, Valerie, with her understanding of people, her editorial judgment, her good spirits, patience, and devotion, offered indispensable strengths.

NOTES

In most instances, each section of the Notes begins with selected references to sources that lend support to the narrative and then goes on to the identification of quotations. The following abbreviations have been used throughout:

ABT	Alice B. Toklas
AFTA	Hemingway, *A Farewell to Arms* (1969 edition)
AMF	Hemingway, *A Moveable Feast*
ARIT	Hemingway, *Across the River and Into the Trees*
ATH	Marcelline Hemingway, *At the Hemingways*
CEH	Clarence Edmonds Hemingway
DIA	Hemingway, *Death in the Afternoon* (1960 edition)
EH	Ernest Hemingway
EH	Baker, *Ernest Hemingway: A Life Story*
EP	Ezra Pound
EW	Edmund Wilson
FSF	F. Scott Fitzgerald
FWTBT	Hemingway, *For Whom the Bell Tolls*
GHH	Grace Hall Hemingway
GHOA	Hemingway, *Green Hills of Africa* (1954 edition)
GS	Gertrude Stein
HIW	Mary Hemingway, *How It Was*
HR	Hadley Richardson Hemingway
HR	Hemingway, *The Hemingway Reader*
HRC	Harry Ransom Humanities Research Center
HW	Kert, *The Hemingway Women*
IS	Hemingway, *Islands in the Stream*
JDP	John Dos Passos

JFK	John F. Kennedy Library
MP	Maxwell Perkins
MWW	Hemingway, *Men Without Women*
OMATS	Hemingway, *The Old Man and the Sea*
PP	Pauline Pfeiffer Hemingway
SAR	Hemingway, *The Sun Also Rises*
SL	Hemingway, *Selected Letters*
SSEH	Hemingway, *Short Stories of Ernest Hemingway* (1966 edition)
THAHN	Hemingway, *To Have and Have Not*
TNAS	Hemingway, *The Nick Adams Stories*
VPH	Hemingway, *The Viking Portable Hemingway*
YH	Reynolds, *The Young Hemingway*

PREFACE

Page
10   "We are all bitched": EH to FSF, May 28, 1934; *SL,* 408.
11   "Things may not be": EH, Statement to the Swedish Academy; JFK.
11   "If people bring": *AFTA,* 249.

"I HAD A WONDERFUL NOVEL TO WRITE ABOUT OAK PARK"

1

ATH, 38, 125. *EH,* 9. *YH,* 228–30. Horowitz, *Culture & the City,* passim. Goodwin, *Oak Park Strategy,* 1, 29–35. In re GHH's cultural ambitions: letter from Edward Wagenknecht to the author, January 30, 1983.

2

Goodwin, *Oak Park Strategy,* 32. Eaton, *Two Chicago Architects,* 229, passim. Sprague, *Guide to Frank Lloyd Wright,* 5, 7, 49. Larkin, *Art and Life in America,* 344. *ATH,* 103–5.
18   "Prose is architecture": *DIA,* 191.
18   "If I started to write": *AMF,* 12.

3

Goodwin, *Oak Park Strategy,* 32–33. St. John, *This Was My World,* 15. Edward Wagenknecht to the author, January 30, 1983. *ATH,* 14–15, 18–19, 39, 148. Leicester Hemingway, *My Brother,* 19. *HW,* 22, 42. *EH,* 2, 16, 18. Barton, *The Gospel of the Autumn Leaf,* 14.
21   "I am not raising": *YH,* 3.
21   "a God without wrath": Niebuhr, *The Kingdom of God,* 193.

22   "My conduct at Church": EH to CEH, May 11, 1913; JFK.
22   "the First Congregational Church": *ATH*, 148.

4

Reynolds, *Hemingway's Reading*, 16–17, 27, 40–41. Schleden and Rawls, eds., *Ernest Hemingway as Recalled*, 12. *HW*, 22. *ATH*, 133, 136–38. *EH*, 29.
25   "deeper things": Lloyd Harter to EH, June 14, 1917; JFK.

5

YH, 9–10, 12–13, 28, 107, 160, 230.

6

26   "a mind of great subtlety": Tate, "Random Thoughts on the Twenties," 56.
26   I had a wonderful novel": EH to Charles Fenton, June 18, 1952; *SL*, 764.
27   "cease and desist": Ibid.
27   "none of the letters": *SL*, xxiii.
27   "From my earliest days": *HW*, 21.

A PECULIAR IDEA

1

HW, 22–23, 25, 79. *ATH*, 54, 55–57. Ovesey., *Homosexuality and Pseudo-homosexuality*, 76, 85. Leicester Hemingway, *My Brother*, 19. Griffin, *Along With Youth*, 3–5, 30, 229. In re the possibility of a connection between scarlet fever and visual impairment: Dr. Douglas A. Jabs of Johns Hopkins Medical School to Dr. Arnall Patz of Johns Hopkins Medical School, June 19, 1985, and Dr. Arnall Patz to the author, July 29, 1985.
28   "Come quick": *ATH*, 53.
30   "during his term": Griffin, *Along With Youth*, 53.
30   "the finest purest noblest": GHH to EH, February 9, 1920; JFK.
30   "was a woman" et seq.: GHH, "Heritage" ms.; Fuentes, *Hemingway in Cuba*, 323.

2

HW, 24, 34. *ATH*, 27–30, 31–33, 36, 56–60. *SSEH*, 489, 496. Griffin, *Along With Youth*, 6. *YH*, 106.
33   "I'm sorry to hear": GHH to EH, February 20, 1927; JFK.
35   "saw as a big-horn ram": *SSEH*, 489.

35   "Daddy could make": *ATH*, 32.
35   "My father's dimpled cheeks": Ibid., 31.

3

HW, 26. Leicester Hemingway, *My Brother*, 22. *ATH*, 65. *SL*, 243.
37   "both cruel and abused": *SSEH*, 489.

4

ATH, 61–64, 125–26, 141. The research on turn-of-the-century dress and hairstyles for little boys was conducted by the author and Valerie R. Lynn.
40–41   "plump and perfect," "his Mama's," "summer girl": GHH scrapbooks;
        JFK.
41   "to feel like twins": *ATH*, 62.
42   "I submitted to the bleaching": *HIW*, 170.
42   "boy-fashion": *ATH*, 109–11.

5

HW, 27. *EH*, 4, 5–6, 460.
43   "He is contented to sleep": GHH scrapbooks; JFK.
44   "He loves to sew": Ibid.
44   "I not a Dutch dolly": *EH*, 5.
44   "Two sturdy little chaps": GHH scrapbooks; JFK.
44   "a sort of compromise": *ATH*, 61.
45   "Ernest Miller at 2 years": GHH scrapbooks; JFK.
45   "Such a man" et seq.: GHH scrapbooks; JFK.
45   "When asked what he is afraid of": *EH*, 5.
45   "he was quite fearful": GHH scrapbooks; JFK.
45   "I think maybe Jesus": *EH*, 5.
46   "My darling": GHH scrapbooks; JFK.
46   'As to Ernest": FSF, *The Crack-Up*, 174.
46   "He was always": *TNAS*, 13–14.
47   "we moved away": *SSEH*, 365.
47   "my mother was always": Ibid.
47   "What's this?": Ibid., 366.
48   "there were only": Ibid.

A LAND OF MAGIC

1

ATH, 113. GHH scrapbooks; JFK.
49   "my mother died": EH, "My First Sea Vouge" ms.; JFK.
50   "arbiter": *EH*, 13.

2

TNAS, 34–35, 266. *EH*, 16, 26. GHH scrapbooks; JFK.
51   "And when I look": EH, *By-Line*, 188.
52   "pleasured"; *HIW*, 102.
52   "threshing around": *TNAS*, 32.
52   "In the morning": Ibid., 33.
52   "All his bachelor friends": GHH scrapbooks; JFK.
52   "Ernest and Marcelline": Ibid.

3

ATH, 75. Fraiberg, *The Magic Years*, 132. *EH*, 5, 19–20. Madelaine Hemingway Miller, *Ernie*, 51–53. Leicester Hemingway, *My Brother*, 36–38. Death of Ursula Hemingway Jepson, *New York Times*, November 1, 1966, 3. GHH scrapbooks; JFK.
53   "Something within him": Callaghan, *That Summer*, 124.
54   "saved the family": *HIW*, 95.
54   "a great baseball player": Ibid., 226–27.
54   "Secret Society": *ATH*, 75.
55   "I thought them burglars": GHH to CEH, July 30, 1915; JFK.
55   "Lady, I've learned a lesson": *EH*, 21.
56   "You killed what they took": *TNAS*, 74.
56   "eleven or twelve": Ibid., 95.
57   "There was only one person": Ibid., 265–66.
57   "[Littless] and Nick loved each other": Ibid., 71.
57   "I want to be your common-law wife," "We'll have a couple": Ibid., 121–22.
57   "She turned and looked": Ibid., 112.
58   "my sister Ura": EH to Arthur Mizener, June 2, 1950; *SL*, 697.

4

EH, 11, 19, 22, 31. *ATH*, 127–28, 133. Coffey, "They Still Remember 'Ernie,' " 3–4. Madelaine Hemingway Miller, *Ernie*, 17. Meyers, *Hemingway*, 48, 110–16.
59   "You know how he was": *EH*, 49.
59   "We girls watched": *ATH*, 137.
60   "flying to destruction": "Dare Girls Rescued," *Oak Leaves*, February 3, 1917.
61   "We tended to buy": Sarason, *Hemingway and "The Sun" Set*, 164, 172.
61   "When I was your age": EH, "Letter to a Young Man," 19.
61   "It's fine": *SSEH*, 118.
61   " 'Tisn't life": Walpole, *Fortitude*, 3.
62   "It gave him pleasure": Ibid., 105.
62   "He . . . crossed to her": Ibid., 107.
62   "Make of me": Ibid., 490.

62   "His father came back": *SSEH*, 496.
64   "the way he looks": GHH scrapbooks; JFK.
64   "Thinking of his mother's": Meyers, *Hemingway*, 8.

THE CHAMPIONSHIP GAME

1

Steele, *Hugh Walpole*, 55–56. Walpole, *The Dark Forest*, 32, 33, 34, 147ff., 245, 267.
67   "had really happened": *VPH*, 145.

2

EH, 28–30, 35, 570. Fenton, *The Apprenticeship*, 31ff. Interview, EH and Paul W. Fisher, Kansas City *Times*, November 26, 1940, 1. Dance, *The World of Count Basie*, 12. EH, "Mix War, Art and Dancing," 1.
67   "his father had kissed": *FWTBT*, 405–6.
68   "Wellington was a stern disciplinarian": Fenton, *The Apprenticeship*, 35–36.
68   "began to learn": MP, "Ernest Hemingway," 4.
69   "I never thought Chicago": EH, *Hemingway At Auction*, 167.
69   "Moise was the guy": *EH*, 570.
69   "Lionel Moise was a great": Sketch of Lionel Moise; JFK.
70   "lodgings," "dago red," "Sometimes I think": Brumback, "With Hemingway before *A Farewell to Arms*," in EH, *Ernest Hemingway: Cub Reporter*, 4, 5.
70   "Now dry those tears": EH to GHH, January 16, 1918; *SL*, 3–4.
72   "I've prayed and done everything," "awful lust," "It is wrong": *SSEH*, 394.
72   "the day, the very anniversary": Ibid., 395.
72   "prevailing, continual": Miller, *Jonathan Edwards*, 272.

3

ATH, 52, 156–57. Fenton, *The Apprenticeship*, 47–49.
72   "one more good summer": EH to his family, November 15, 1917; *SL*, 3.
73   "We all have that bad eye": *ATH*, 156–57.
73   "preyed upon his mind": Brumback, "With Hemingway," 7.
74   "camouflaged 1st Lieuts": EH to his family, May 14, 1918; *SL*, 6–7.
74   "a fine look at Woodrow": EH to his family, May 17, 1918; JFK.
74   "Miss Marsh no kidding": EH to Dale Wilson, May 19, 1918; *SL*, 8.
74   "We are so eager to hear": GHH to EH, May 16, 1918; JFK.
75   "only yesterday": GHH to EH, May 18, 1918; JFK.
75   CHEER UP: telegram from EH to CEH, May 19, 1918; JFK.
75   "My! but wouldn't the folks": GHH to EH, May 20, 1918; JFK.

4

EH, *The Hemingway Manuscripts*, 11. *EH*, 41–43. Ludington, *John Dos Passos*, 159. JDP, *The Fourteenth Chronicle*, 187–88. "Hemingway's War Days Recalled by a Friend," North American Newspaper Alliance, December 19, 1936.

75 "pitched, rolled": EH to his family, c. May 27, 1918; *SL*, 9.
76 "where those shells": Brumback, "With Hemingway," 9.
76 "Regarding the sex": *DIA*, 135–37.
78 "There's nothing here": Brumback, "With Hemingway," 9.
78 "Each aft and morning": EH to Ruth Morrison, c. June 22, 1918; *SL*, 11.
78 "wore a uniform": *AFTA*, 7.
79 "Sometimes I think": Ibid., 65–66.
79 "I heard a cough": Ibid., 54.
80 "I'd rather wait": Ibid., 58.
80 "Multiple superficial wounds": Ibid., 59.

5

"Hemingway Speaks to High School," *The Trapeze*, March 21, 1919, 1. *YH*, 16–19, 55–57. In re World War I machine guns: Dr. Charles G. Rob to the author, August 26, 1986.

80 "a trench mortar bomb": telegram from American Red Cross to CEH and GHH; JFK.
80 WOUNDED IN LEG: cablegram from EH to CEH and GHH; JFK.
80 "E. M. Hemingway was wounded": *Report of the Department of Military Affairs*, 14, 15, 16.
80 "Ernest Miller Hemingway of Illinois Park": *Motivazione Della Medaglia*, in Lewis, "Hemingway in Italy," 223–24.
81 "I have just come": Ted Brumback to CEH, July 14, 1918; JFK.
82 "entered newspaper work": GHH scrapbooks; JFK.
82 "you were a mighty welcome": GHH to EH, July 21, 1918; JFK.
82 "I'm the first American": EH to his family, July 21, 1918; *SL*, 12.
83 "The machine gun bullet": EH to his family, August 18, 1918; *SL*, 14.
84 "They want to get you": *AFTA*, 63.
84 "I showed them the papers": *SSEH*, 269–70.
85 "A distaste": Ibid., 145–46.
86 "groped for": *EH*, 45.
86 "where the copper-jacketed": Ibid., 50.
86 "fiction": *YH*, 21.
86 "served for a time": *VPH*, xii.

6

HW, 50–53, 54, 63. *EH*, 50–56. Hanneman, *Ernest Hemingway*, 6. Oldsey, *Ernest Hemingway, The Papers of a Writer*, 27–28. YH, 32.

87   *"like a good mother"*: Elsie Macdonald to EH, December 14, 1926; JFK.
87   "a broken doll": Elsie Macdonald to EH, October 20, 1929; JFK.
88   "I really honestly": EH to Bill Smith, December 13, 1918; *SL*, 20.
89   "except from a bedroom window": *EH*, 56.
89   "My idea": *HW*, 63–64.
90   "had been badly wounded": *EH*, 53.
91   "clear and noble": EH to EP, August 5, 1923; *SL*, 91.
91   "It was a frightfully": *SSEH*, 113.
91   "after being severely wounded": EH, *Men at War*, x–xi.
92   "It does give you": EH to his family, October 18, 1918; *SL*, 19.
92   "When a mother brings a son": Ibid.

REJECTION SLIPS

1

YH, 18–19.
96   "started over the parapet": New York *Sun*, January 22, 1919, 8.
96   "Marcelline feels very close": GHH to EH, July 30, 1918; JFK.
96   "I do not write to you": GHH to EH, April 13, 1920; JFK.
97   "under the knife": EH to Marcelline Hemingway, May 20, 1921; *SL*, 49–50.
97   "played out": GHH to EH, August 7, 1921; JFK.
97   "from when I first knew her": EH to Madelaine Hemingway Mainland, c. August 15, 1949; *SL*, 663.

2

EH, 57, 59. *ATH*, 178–89, 193–98. Michael S. Reynolds, "Looking Backward," in Reynolds, ed., *Critical Essays*, 2–5. *YH*, 69–70, 79, 80, 81, 129–33.
97   "You know I don't": Agnes von Kurowsky to EH, February 15, 1919; JFK.
97   "I'm not [at] all the perfect being": Agnes von Kurowsky to EH, March 1, 1919; JFK.
98   "theirs had been only": *SSEH*, 141–42.
98   "I set out to cauterize": EH to Howell Jenkins, June 16, 1919; *SL*, 25.
98   "15 martinis": Ibid.
98   "Poor damned kid": Ibid.
99   "I had a nervous breakdown": GHH to CEH [spring 1919]; *YH*, 70.
100   "I love you all": *HW*, 73.
100   "How I wish I cd": Ruth Arnold to GHH, June 25, 1920; HRC.
100   "Wished you were here": Ruth Arnold to GHH and Marcelline Hemingway, June 8, 1909; HRC.
100   "It is 9 P.M.": Ruth Arnold to GHH, September 1, 1919; HRC.
100   "malicious story": GHH to Marjorie Andree and Clara Harell, July 10, 1934; HRC.
100   "dear faithful Ruth": *YH*, 80.
101   "It is hard enough": Ruth Arnold to GHH, September 1, 1919; HRC.
101   "insane on the subject": *YH*, 81.
101   "Ernest is very like me": *ATH*, 198.

3

Dwight Macdonald, "Ernest Hemingway," *Encounter,* January 1962, 115–18, 120–21.

102   "I lost one": EH to Howell Jenkins, c. September 15, 1919; *SL,* 29.
102   "trying to do the country": EH to GS and ABT, August 15, 1924; *SL,* 122.
102   "He watched them": *SSEH,* 209.
102   "Ahead of him": Ibid., 211.
102   "burned-over country," "the far blue hills": Ibid., 209, 211.
102   "He felt he had left": Ibid., 210.
103   "homelike," "he was settled": Ibid., 215.
103   "starting to work," "choke it": Ibid., 218.
103   "a little sick": Ibid., 226.
103   "There were plenty of days": Ibid., 232.
104   "In the swamp": Ibid., 231.
104   "a touch of panic": EW, *The Portable Edmund Wilson,* 399.
105   "Malcolm thot": EH to Harvey Breit, July 23, 1956; *SL,* 867.
105   "are most of them continued": *VPH,* ix.
105   "a somewhat different attitude": Ibid., x.
106   "ported a *Portable Hemingway*": Young, *Ernest Hemingway,* 5.
106   "sick man": Ibid., 47.
106   "Nothing more important": Schorer, "Ernest Hemingway," 675.
106   "coming back": *AMF,* 76.
107   "I was hurt bad": Cowley, "Hemingway's Wound," 229–30.
107   "a story about a boy": EH to Charles Poore, January 23, 1953; *SL,* 798.
107   "the most difficult death": Mailer, "The Big Bite," 134.
107   "It is not likely": Mailer, "Punching Papa," 13.

4

EH, 62–64, 574. Montgomery, *Hemingway in Michigan,* 172–73. EH to JDP, April 22, 1925; Alderman Library, U. of Virginia.

109   "short and dark," "so jolly": *SSEH,* 81.
109   "The two main characters": *ATH,* 216.
109   "Then she": *SSEH,* 86.
109   "It is a state of *conscious*": D. H. Lawrence, review of *In Our Time, Calendar of Modern Letters,* reprinted in Meyers, ed., *The Critical Heritage,* 73.
110   "The boards were hard": *SSEH,* 85.

5

Stevenson, *Babbitts and Bohemians,* 91–92. *EH,* 65–67, 69. EH, *By-Line,* 3–15. Paul Smith, "The Tenth Indian and the Thing Left Out," in Nagel, ed., *Ernest Hemingway: The Writer in Context,* 67–74.

111   "and I should say, offhand": Stevens, *Letters of Wallace Stevens,* 411–12.

111   "the Café Cambrinus," "a sudden silence," "But one time": "The Mercenaries—A Story," in Griffin, *Along With Youth,* 104–5.

112   "must have got mixed up": *SSEH,* 289.

112   "He was about the same size": Ibid., 280.

112   "In their tight overcoats": Ibid., 285.

112   "You talk too much": Ibid.

114   "this Toronto thing": EH to Howell Jenkins, December 20, 1919; *SL,* 30.

114   "His favorite escapade": Meyers, *Hemingway,* 50.

114   "large, rather heavy": Ibid., 51–52.

6

115   "Mother is a good deal better": CEH to EH, March 18, 1920; JFK.

115   "I rejoice *so*": GHH to EH, April 13, 1920; JFK.

115   "Do hope dear Ernest": CEH to EH, June 4, 1920; JFK.

116   "moron literature": *YH,* 135.

116   "Ernest called me": Ibid., 136.

117   "My Dear Son Ernest": GHH to EH, July 24, 1920, but personally presented
on July 27; HRC.

118   "Mother was glad": EH to Grace Quinlan, August 8, 1920; *SL,* 37.

119   "Ernest's last letter": CEH to GHH, July 30, 1920; JFK.

119   "Mother's part": CEH to GHH, September 2, 1920; JFK.

119   "I am wondering": CEH to EH, September 18, 1920; JFK.

119   "I was sorry": GHH to EH, October 4, 1920; JFK.

120   "Dearest Mother": EH to GHH, December 22, 1920; *SL,* 42.

120   "Well, Merry Christmas": Ibid., 43.

7

EH to Owen Wister, March 11, 1929; Library of Congress. Yardley,
Ring, 215. Asinof, *Eight Men Out,* passim. Fieve, *Moodswing,* 58. Carr, *Dos Passos,*
457.

120   "By 1920": Leuchtenburg, *Perils of Prosperity,* 84.

121   "There's going to be": EH to Grace Quinlan, January 1, 1920; *SL,* 31.

121   "fixed the World Series": FSF, *The Great Gatsby,* 74.

121   "a great and overpowering": EH to Grace Quinlan, September 30, 1920;
SL, 41.

121   "What'll we drink to?": *TNAS,* 212.

122   "Hemingway's heavy drinking": Fieve, *Moodswing,* 58.

122   "Trouble was all my life": Meyers, *Hemingway,* 351.

122   "prayed for all": EH to Grace Quinlan, September 30, 1920; *SL,* 41.

123n   "Everybody seemed much older": Carr, *Dos Passos,* 457.

"THE WORLD'S A JAIL AND WE'RE GOING TO BREAK IT TOGETHER"

1

EH, 73–74. Leicester Hemingway, *My Brother,* 70, 117. *HW,* 83.

2

Sokoloff, *Hadley,* 2–12. Griffin, *Along With Youth,* 143.
125   "a woman of strong personality": Sokoloff, *Hadley,* 2.
126   "marriage was a trap," "throw over everything": HR to EH, April 3, 1921; JFK.

3

HW, 87–93. Leicester Hemingway, *My Brother,* 71. Ludington, *Dos Passos,* 265. Sokoloff, *Hadley,* 19–21. *YH,* 154–55.
127   "hulky, bulky": HR to EH, January 9, 1921; JFK.
127   "an intense feeling": Leicester Hemingway, *My Brother,* 71.
128   "I still cherish": HR to EH, November 11, 1920 (letter #1); JFK.
128   "Connable is a strangerish creature": Ibid.
128   "I understand": HR to EH, November 11, 1920 (letter #2); JFK.
128   "poor old Odgar": *TNAS,* 228.
128   "pitiful," "twice operated," "fried-fish": Ibid., 217–18.
128   "Was I bad, Wemedge?": Ibid., 227.
129   "kill himself": Ibid., 218.
129   "a little while at least": *EH,* 77.
129   "Do you mean": HR to EH, January 1, 1921; JFK.
129   "needed *so much*": HR to EH, December 13, 1920; JFK.
130   "The world's a jail": HR to EH, June 4, 1921; JFK.

4

Fenton, *The Apprenticeship,* 97. *EH,* 69, 77, 79–80. Sokoloff, *Hadley,* 32–33. Griffin, *Along With Youth,* 222–24. *YH,* 144, 155, 156, 184.
130   "play the role": EH to GHH, December 22, 1920; *SL,* 43.
131   "That's so sweet my dear" et seq.: Story of Orpen ms.; JFK.
133   "It was a history": *SSEH,* 148.
133   "some other Wop killer": EH to CEH, April 15, 1921; *SL,* 46.
133   "Aggravatin' papa": Hinkle, "Note on Two-Timing at Zelli's," 3–4.
133   "Guy loves": EH to Bill Smith, April 28, 1921; *SL,* 48.
134   "as white as the belly": *ARIT,* 50.
134   *"Half a million":* EH, *88 Poems,* 28.
135   *"Desire and":* Ibid., 35.

135 *"It is cool"*: Ibid., 30.
136 "Suppose you want": EH to Grace Quinlan, July 21, 1921; *SL*, 51.
136 *"Cover my eyes": EH, 88 Poems*, 36.

5

Howe, *Sherwood Anderson*, 47–48, 95. Sutton, *The Road to Winesburg*, 36, 192–95, 275. Anderson, *Sherwood Anderson's Memoirs*, 339–41. *GHOA*, 19. Fitch, *Sylvia Beach*, 82–84.

137 "acted queerly," "I feel as though": Sutton, *Road to Winesburg*, 186–87.
137 "did a lot of woman chasing": Ibid., 177.
138 "Why do the children cry": Ibid., 554–56.
139 "wasn't my own face": Sherwood Anderson, "The Man Who Became a Woman," in Anderson, *The Portable Anderson*, 381.
139 "Jes' you lie still": Ibid., 390.
139 "got hold of the cheeks": Ibid., 394.
139 "burned all that": Ibid., 395.
139 "When in speaking": Anderson, *Letters of Sherwood Anderson*, 53.
139–40 "wrote some stories": EH to Owen Wister, March 11, 1929; Library of Congress.
140 "Once she startled": Anderson, *Winesburg, Ohio*, 45.
140 "I believe he wrote": Anderson, *Letters of Sherwood Anderson*, 33.
141 "kitchen of words": Anderson, *Sherwood Anderson's Notebooks*, 48–49.
141 "a young fellow": Anderson, *Letters of Sherwood Anderson*, 82.
141 "instinctively in touch": Ibid., 85.

6

HW, 102, 104. *EH*, 79–80, 81, 82–83. Anderson, *Memoirs of Sherwood Anderson*, 473. *YH*, 207, 237–40.

142 "wonderful times," "I wish I could," "Remember how": *HW*, 98.
143 "being very suggestible": Ibid., 96.
143 "I need you": Ibid., 99.
144 "It was a long row": *TNAS*, 232.
144 "She kissed him back": Ibid.
144 "as she liked to do": *IS*, 343–44.
145 "collect the residue": EH to Y. K. Smith, October 1, 1921; *SL*, 55.
145 "You can readily understand": Y. K. Smith to EH, c. October 2, 1921; *SL*, 56.

AMERICANS IN PARIS

1

Johnson, *Modern Times*, 138–42. Wickes, *Americans in Paris*, 150.
148 "the Restaurant of the Pre aux Clercs": EH to Sherwood Anderson, c. December 23, 1921; *SL*, 59.

148 "good Pinard": EH to Howell Jenkins, December 26, 1921; *SL*, 60.
148 "a famous London house": EH to Howell Jenkins, January 8, 1922; *SL*, 61.
149 "the horse-cabs": *VPH*, 14.

2

EH, 84. Sokoloff, *Hadley*, 44–46. *VPH*, 7, 11.
151 "the smell of dirty bodies": *AMF*, 3.
151 "how Paris was": Ibid., 211.
152 "all the things": EH to Katy Smith, February 16, 1922; Alderman Library, U. of Virginia.
152 "genuwind 7 year old": EH to Howell Jenkins, January 8, 1922; *SL*, 61.
152 "a wild, cold, blowing day": *AMF*, 5.

3

Fitch, *Sylvia Beach*, 42–43, 115, 116, 119, 121, 138–40. Lewis, *Time and Western Man*, 54. Flanner, *Paris Was Yesterday*, vii–viii. Beach, *Shakespeare and Company*, 78–79.
153 "brushed back": *AMF*, 35.
154 "Ernest's chair": *EH*, 138.
154 "I . . . learned that he had spent": Beach, *Shakespeare and Company*, 78–79.
154 "Feather Cat," "an attractive," "delightfully jolly": Fitch, *Sylvia Beach*, 116.
154 "If he comes in": *AMF*, 36.
154 "No one that I ever knew": *AMF*, 35.

4

HW, 108–9.
156 "unfurled": Fitch, *Sylvia Beach*, 14.
156 "a stout sled": EH, *By-Line*, 20–21.
156 "Suisse is a wonderful country": EH to Katy Smith, February 16, 1922; Alderman Library, U. of Virginia.
157 "The beer was very cold": *AMF*, 72–73.
157 "coldly beaded": *VPH*, 240.
157 "one of the best": Ibid., 242.
158 "deer and wild boar": EH to CEH, May 2, 1922; *SL*, 66–67.

5

Levin, *Contexts of Criticism*, 140–67. *AMF*, 38, 53, 61, 64. *AFTA*, 184–85.
158 "write one true sentence": *AMF*, 12.
159 "Plump and sweet-fleshed": Ibid., 43.

159 "a natural quick linguist": *EH*, 138.
159 "It was gambling": *AMF*, 61.
160 "avocation": Ibid., 59.
160 "The scum of Greenwich Village": EH, *By-Line*, 23.
160 "left an emptiness": *AMF*, 62.

6

Fitch, *Sylvia Beach*, 121, 171. Jacqueline Tavernier-Courbin, "Ernest Hemingway and Ezra Pound," in Nagel, ed., *Ernest Hemingway: The Writer in Context*, 179–200. *EH*, 86, 90–91, 258. EP, *Gaudier-Brzeska*, 100–103. EP, *Selected Poems*, 35, 61, 62, 64. Stock, *The Life of Ezra Pound*, 221, 230, 232. Torrey, *The Roots of Treason*, 132–33, 196–97.
161 "Joyce has a most": EH to Sherwood Anderson, March 9, 1922; *SL*, 62.
161 "the greatest writer," "letting [me] in": Callaghan, *That Summer*, 27–29.
161 "The weakness of Joyce": *TNAS*, 238.
161 "a big powerful peasant": Ellmann, *James Joyce*, 695.
161 "We would go out to drink": Ibid., 695*n*.
162 "such a tough fellow": Beach, *Shakespeare and Company*, 78.
162 "he and all his family": EH to Sherwood Anderson, March 9, 1922; *SL*, 62.
162 "worship": *EH*, 258.
163 "When I last saw him": EH to Allen Tate, August 31, 1943; *SL*, 550.
163 "Mr. Squirmy": Torrey, *Roots of Treason*, 186.
163 "totem de tribu": Ibid., 141.
164 "la copulation": Stock, *Life of Ezra Pound*, 242.
164 "So far, we have Pound": EH, "Homage to Ezra," 221–25.
165 "fine bitter tongue": EH to Sherwood Anderson, March 9, 1922; *SL*, 62.
165 "I've been teaching": Ibid.
165 "I'm boxing regular": EH to Howell Jenkins, March 20, 1922; *SL*, 65.
166 "I think you are more intelligent": EP to EH, January 25, 1927; JFK.
166 *"The apparition"*: EP, "In a Station of the Metro," in *Selected Poems*, 35.
166 "I have stood": "Paris, 1922" ms.; JFK.
167 "This is a good story": EP to EH, December 21, 1926; JFK.

7

Mary Berenson, *A Self Portrait from Her Letters & Diaries*, 160. GS, *Everybody's Autobiography*, 76–77.
167 "one of the best rooms": *AMF*, 13.
168 "reflection": Mellow, *Charmed Circle*, 29.
168 "When I first knew her": Ibid., 28.
168 "plenty of brains": Mary Berenson, *A Self Portrait*, 103.
168 "fat unwieldy person": Ibid.
168 "we saw on the hill": Ibid., 130.
169 "[today] we had": Ibid., 146.
169 "was very big but not tall": *AMF*, 14.

169 "I think about ten pounds": Sokoloff, *Hadley*, 50.
169 "put up in the same way": *AMF*, 14.
169 "I liked her better": EH to W. G. Rogers, July 29, 1948; *SL*, 650.
169 "Gertrude Stein and me": EH to Sherwood Anderson, March 9, 1922; *SL*, 62.
169 "all women who are truly famous": Simon, *Biography of Alice B. Toklas*, 50.
169 "the woman who attracts": Ibid.
170 "What a book": GS, *Autobiography of Alice B. Toklas*, 265–66.
170 "seemed to like us": *AMF*, 14–15.
170 "direct, Kiplingesque": GS, *Autobiography of Alice B. Toklas*, 261.
170 "You can either buy clothes": *AMF*, 15–16.
171 "general principles": GS, *Autobiography of Alice B. Toklas*, 271.
171 "weakness": Ibid., 271.
171 "Care for me": Simon, *Biography of Alice B. Toklas*, 70.
172 "Gertrude's fear": Ibid., 116.
172 "dark luminous eyes," "flashing smile," "made him look like an Italian": Ibid.
172 "on account of Hemingway": Ibid., 118.
172 "You know, I made Gertrude": Ibid., 121.

DRAGONS' TEETH

1

Slocombe, *The Tumult and the Shouting*, 156. Eastman, *Great Companions*, 42. Johnson, *Modern Times*, 235. EH, *The Wild Years*, 176. *EH*, 89. EH, *By-Line*, 180–181. EH, *88 Poems*, 45.
173 "You mustn't let": Scott Donaldson, "Hemingway of *The Star*," in Oldsey, ed., *Ernest Hemingway. The Papers of a Writer*, 91.
173 "This goddam newspaper stuff": EH to Sherwood Anderson, March 9, 1922; *SL*, 62.
174 "who looks like a tuba player": EH, *By-Line*, 32.
174 "fresh faces": Ibid.
175 "The North Italian Red": Ibid., 28.
175 "a brood of dragons' teeth" et seq.: Ibid., 27–28.
176 "We Americans": Steffens, *The Letters of Lincoln Steffens*, 519.
176 "*Workingmen believed*": EH, "Roosevelt," *Poetry. A Magazine of Verse*, January 1923, 193–95.

2

SL, 66, 68. EH, *By-Line*, 33. EH, 91, 124. EH, *The Wild Years*, 186–88.
177 "induced me to wear": *HW*, 119.
177 "I was a human blister": Ibid., 120.
177 "Mrs. Hemingway's feet": EH to GS and ABT, June 11, 1922; *SL*, 69.

3

Sokoloff, *Hadley*, 56–57. *HW*, 123–25.
179   "The ground began to flatten": EH, *By-Line*, 42–43.
179   "It was then in a kind of way": Simon, *Biography of Alice B. Toklas*, 119, 122
179   "Even though I kissed you": EH to Dorothy Butler, 1924; JFK.
179   "It was just awful": *HW*, 123.
179   "practising [the piano]": HR to GHH, October 5, 1922; JFK.
180   "In those days": *SSEH*, 392.
180   "alone in Constantinople": Ibid., 64–65.

4

EH, 10, 579. EH, *By-Line*, 51, 56–57, 59. *HW*, 26.
181   "That was the day": *SSEH*, 65.
182   "silent, ghastly procession": EH, *By-Line*, 51.
182   "the slow, rain soaked": Ibid., 59.
182   "There was a woman": *SSEH*, 97.

5

Steffens, *Autobiography of Lincoln Steffens*, 834–35. *EH*, 100. EH, *By-Line*,
221–22, 225–26. Smith, *Mussolini*, 36.
183   "more beautiful than ever": EH to William D. Horne, July 17–18, 1923;
       SL, 86.
184   "I've been crazy": EH to HR, November 22, 1922; *SL*, 73.
184   "running a twenty-four hour": Donaldson, "Hemingway of *The Star*,"
       94–96.
185   "I say, is the Imperial Buggah in?": EH, *By-Line*, 226.
185   "Mussolini sat": Ibid., 64.
185   "Mussolini came out": Ibid., 65.
186   "the headquarters of the party" et seq.: *SSEH*, 157–58.
187   "Very bitter," "Lots of nail holes": *AFTA*, 280.

6

SL, 105. EH, "They All Made Peace—What Is Peace?", *Little Review*, Spring
1923, 20–21.
188   "Hadley had made": EH to EP, January 23, 1923; *SL*, 77.
188   "what I did": *AMF*, 74.
188   "nigger eyes": EH, "They All Made Peace—What Is Peace?", 20.
188–89 "like an old clothes man," "a man without a weakness," "until he was
       twelve," "The boy who was kept": EH, *By-Line*, 66–69.

7

189   "the Roosians": EH to Isabel Simmons, c. December 1, 1922; *SL*, 76.
189   "far from her family": *HW*, 132.
189   "So then the letter": *SSEH*, 66.
190   "After I recovered": *HW*, 129–31.
190   "this high altitude": EH to EP, January 29, 1923; *SL*, 79.
191   "[Hemingway] and his wife": GS, *Autobiography of Alice B. Toklas*, 262.
191   "Will you go back": *SSEH*, 187.

SPORTS

1

Ford, *Published in Paris*, 34–35, 40–41, 43–44, 95 et seq. EP, *The Letters of Ezra Pound*, 183–84. Smoller, *Adrift Among Geniuses*, 7, 37.
193   "inquest": *EH*, 101.
193   "Even as a little boy": Smoller, *Adrift Among Geniuses*, 13.
194   "He had an ideal": Williams, *Autobiography of William Carlos Williams*, 175–76.
194   "he attracted people": Beach, *Shakespeare and Company*, 25.
194   "one overmastering passion": Bryher, *The Heart to Artemis*, 182.
194   "a young American writer": Ibid., 201.
195   "the most honest and authentically American": Ford, *Published in Paris*, 34.
195   "whom America . . . finds it hard": Ibid., 47.

2

SL, 79. GS, *Autobiography of Alice B. Toklas*, 262. Michael S. Reynolds, "Two Hemingway Sources for *in our time*," in Reynolds, ed., *Critical Essays*, 32–33.
196   "deliberately hard-boiled": McAlmon, *Being Geniuses Together*, 175–76.
197   "If you keep on doing": GS, *Autobiography of Alice B. Toklas*, 262.
197   "working hard": EH to GS, c. February 18, 1923; *SL*, 79.
197   "taken out on a stretcher": Reynolds, "Two Hemingway Sources," 32–33.
198   "They shot": *SSEH*, 127.

3

EH, 108–9, 118–19. *SL*, 81. Kenneth G. Johnston, "Hemingway's 'Out of Season' and the Psychology of Errors," in Reynolds, ed., *Critical Essays*, 227–34. McComas, "The Geography of Hemingway's 'Out of Season,' " 46–49. *HW*, 136. Smith, "Hemingway's Early Manuscripts," 268–88. Paul Smith, "Some Misconceptions of 'Out of Season,' " in Reynolds, ed., *Critical Essays*, 235–51.

199 "and I did not think": *AMF,* 74.

199 "as a curiosity": Ibid.

199 "Angina": EH to EP, March 10, 1923; *SL,* 80.

200 "they look each other": EH, *The Wild Years,* 140–43.

201 "and as that was the last job": EH to FSF, December 24, 1925; *SL,* 181.

201 "right off on the typewriter": Ibid., 180.

201 "and I wanted": Ibid., 181.

201 "This was omitted": *AMF,* 75.

202 "the sun coming out" et seq.: *SSEH,* 173.

202 "I'm sorry you feel so rotten": Ibid., 175.

203 "Of course you haven't": Ibid., 176.

203 "You're cold": Ibid., 177.

203 "Part of the time": Ibid., 176.

203 "the doctors, nurses, hospitals": *HW,* 136.

204 "uncomfortable and afraid": *SSEH,* 177.

204 "relieved": Ibid., 178.

204 "I may not be going": Ibid., 179.

4

SL, 82. EH, *The Wild Years,* 221–22, 225–26. Smoller, *Adrift Among Geniuses,* 93, 178, 179, 180. *EH,* 111. McAlmon, *McAlmon and the Lost Generation,* 225–40.

205 "made me feel": EH to Edward J. O'Brien, May 21, 1923; *SL,* 82.

205–6 "Hemingway's self-hardening," "My reactions," et seq.: McAlmon, *Being Geniuses Together,* 178–79.

206 "absolutely unbelievable": EH, *By-Line,* 94.

206 "X. Y., 27 years old": *DIA,* 496.

208 "You know": *EH,* 227.

208 "Children of my experience": Smoller, *Adrift Among Geniuses,* 91.

5

EH, *The Wild Years,* 229–31.

209 "stalwart": EH to Isabel Simmons, June 24, 1923; *SL,* 84.

210 "By God they have bullfights": EH to William D. Horne, July 17–18, 1923; *SL,* 88.

210 "absolutely unbelievable": EH, *By-Line,* 106–7.

210 "I thought of prize fighters": Ibid., 107.

210 "Era muy hombre": *DIA,* 82.

6

EH, 113.

211 "straight ahead brilliantly": *SSEH,* 139.

212 "not a sport": EH, *By-Line,* 95.

213 "He felt warm and sticky": *SSEH,* 207.

7

213 "all hook up": EH to EP, c. August 5, 1923; *SL,* 91.

214 "The bulls start": Ibid., 91–92.

214 "Hemingway gave a slow": Cowley, *Exile's Return,* 120.

214 "long been patronized": Ibid., 164.

214 "duly ponderous, fairly slow": McAlmon, *Being Geniuses Together,* 42.

214 "And there in the café": "The Snows of Kilimanjaro" ms.; HRC.

215 "twirp": EH to JDP, May 30, 1932; *SL,* 360.

215 "fool": EH to JDP, October 14, 1932; *SL,* 375.

215 "that American poet": *SSEH,* 66.

215 "very good and clean": EH to Robert McAlmon, August 5, 1923; *SL,* 90.

8

216 "young feller," "Hadley hasn't been sick": EH to William D. Horne, July 17–18, 1923; *SL,* 88.

216 "the only thing": Ibid., 87.

216 "Most wives": *EH,* 114.

"NICK IN THE STORIES WAS NEVER HIMSELF"

1

Harkness, *J. E. Atkinson,* 164. Callaghan, *That Summer,* 22–24. Fenton, *The Apprenticeship,* 244–56.

219 "corking": EH to GS and ABT, October 11, 1923; *SL,* 94.

219 "the fistulated asshole": EH to EP, October 13, 1923; *SL,* 95.

219 "If anybody pulls": EH to EP, c. September 6, 1923; *SL,* 92.

220 "All the time" et seq.: EH to GS and ABT, October 11, 1923; *SL,* 94.

220 "fatigue and strain": *EH,* 117.

220 "utter contempt": EH to EP, October 13, 1923; *SL,* 96.

220 "Shot from nervous fatigue": Ibid.

220 "diseased oyster": Ibid.

220 "understood for the first time": EH to GS and ABT, October 11, 1923; *SL,* 94.

221 "The Baby has taken": EH to CEH, November 7, 1923; *SL,* 99.

2

EH, 118. EW, *The Shores of Light,* 115–22.

221 "amusing stuff": Burton Rascoe, "A Bookman's Day Book," New York *Herald Tribune,* June 15, 1924, Book Section, 20.

221 "Dear Mr. Wilson": EH to EW, November 11, 1923; *SL,* 102–3.

221   "Three stories and ten poems": GS, review of *Three Stories & Ten Poems*, Chicago *Tribune* [Paris edition], November 27, 1923.
222   "I am very glad you liked" et seq.: EH to EW, November 25, 1923; *SL*, 104–5.
223   "You can get from it": EH to EW, November 25, 1923; *SL*, 105.
223   "the first distinction": EW, "Mr. Hemingway's Dry Points," *The Dial*, October 1924, 340–41.
223   "has only to publish": Harry Esty Dounce, review of *The Sun Also Rises*, *The New Yorker*, November 20, 1926, 88, 90.

3

SL, 107. *EH*, 117. *HW*, 142.
223   "the first big mistake": HR to Sylvia Beach, November 27, 1923; JFK.
223   "Our hearts are heavy, heavy": HR to Isabel Simmons, October 12, 1923; JFK.
223   "He seemed to feel": Callaghan, *That Summer*, 27–29.
224   "the best country": EH to CEH, November 7, 1923; *SL*, 100.
225   "I cannot tell you": GHH to EH, December 26, 1923; JFK.
225   "filth": *ATH*, 219.

4

EH, 119. *HW*, 144. Cohen, *J. B. Watson*, 258.
226   "tremendous reaction" et seq.: EH to EP, February 10, 1924; *SL*, 110–11.
227   "They were all interested": *AMF*, 82.
227   "and I watched how well": Ibid.
227   "Oh, Daddy": *SSEH*, 92.
228   "exalted and talkative": Ibid., 94.
228   "Why did he kill himself, Daddy?": Ibid., 95.
228   "In the early morning": Ibid.
228   "Nick in the stories": *TNAS*, 238.

5

Edel, *Henry James. 1901–1916. The Master*, 40. MacShane, *The Life and Work of Ford Madox Ford*, 75–79, 163. Poli, *Ford Madox Ford and the "Transatlantic Review,"* 17–19. Bowen, *Drawn from Life*, 117. EH, *The Torrents of Spring*, in *HR*, 57.
230   "He's an experienced journalist": Ford, *It Was the Nightingale*, 295.
230   "You should have seen": Ford Madox Ford, "Introduction" to *AFTA*, New York, 1932, xii–xiv.
231   "The Leviathan": Gorman, "Ford Madox Ford," 6.
231   "listen to the onetime": Putnam, *Paris Was Our Mistress*, 71.
231   "turn off the light": *HR*, 51.

6

SL, 111, 127. Poli, *Ford Madox Ford,* 56, 61, 71, 81–83, 102–6, 107, 110, 116. GS, *Selected Writings,* 178. Josephson, *Life Among the Surrealists,* 75.

232 "He is so goddam involved": EH to EP, March 17, 1924; *SL,* 113.
232 "I object" et seq.: Poli, *Ford Madox Ford,* 54–55.
232 "What stands out": Ibid., 61.
232 "bled too white": Ibid.
233 "Ford's running": EH to EP, c. May 2, 1924; *SL,* 116.
233 "sick of Ford": EH to GS and ABT, September 14, 1924; *SL,* 125.
233 "Hemingway came in then": GS, *Autobiography of Alice B. Toklas,* 264.
234 "some other story": Ibid., 265.
234 "he got so excited": Poli, *Ford Madox Ford,* 81.
234 "paragraph by paragraph": Loeb, *The Way It Was,* 193.
235 "During our absence": Poli, *Ford Madox Ford,* 106.

7

SL, 114, 120, 125. Wescott, "A Sentimental Contribution," 523. *EH,* 127. Fielding, *Emerald and Nancy,* 6. Wickes, *The Amazon of Letters,* 18–20. Joost, *Ernest Hemingway and the Little Magazines,* 135–37.

236 "and after ½ hour": EH to Robert McAlmon, November 20, 1924; *SL,* 135.
236 "A saggy bending": Eliot, *Collected Poems,* 47.
236–37 "You heard of course": EH to EP, July 19, 1924; *SL,* 120.
237 "Abe Linc Steffens": EH to EP, c. May 2, 1924; *SL,* 114.
237 "fake," "fundamentally unsound": EH to Louis and Mary Bromfield, c. March 8, 1926; *SL,* 195.
237 "He was from New York": *VPH,* 21.
238 "Ernest's game," "like blasting hell": Loeb, *The Way It Was,* 194, 207, 216.
239 "I'm about broke": EH to Edward J. O'Brien, May 2, 1924; *SL,* 117.
239 "he paid them off": Levant, *The Memoirs of an American,* 224.
239 "Hem . . . had an evangelistic": JDP, *The Best Times,* 143.
239 "used to get himself up": Ibid., 142.
240 "sorry for himself": Ibid., 143.
241 *"They say Ezra is the shit"*: EH, "Part One of The Soul of Spain with McAlmon and Bird the Publishers," *Der Querschnitt* Autumn 1924.

8

Hoopes, *Van Wyck Brooks,* 158, 185.
242 "E. E. Cummings": EH to EP, May 2, 1924; *SL,* 114.
242 "For every writer": Joost, *Ernest Hemingway and the Little Magazines,* 88–89.
243 "the book of a sick man": Hoopes, *Van Wyck Brooks,* 163.
243 "great luminous": Brooks, *Days of the Phoenix,* 187.
243 "When Eleanor": Hoopes, *Van Wyck Brooks,* 177.

9

In re Chard Powers Smith: author's interview with Prentiss Taylor, August 9, 1984. Poli, *Ford Madox Ford*, 82.
244 "tried very hard": *SSEH*, 161.
244 "big medieval bed": Ibid., 164.
244 "all quite happy": Ibid.
245 "My dear Smith": EH to Chard Powers Smith, c. January 21, 1927; *SL*, 242.
246 "pretending to confuse him": *AMF*, 111.
246 "by grinding": EH, *By-Line*, 133.
247 "college nymphomaniac," "couldn't have a baby": EH, *88 Poems*, 77.
247 "the progress of an artist": Eliot, *Selected Essays*, 7.
247 "an invalid": Eliot, *The Waste Land*, ed. Valerie Eliot, xix.
247 "an aboulie": Ibid., xxiii.
248n "In my musings": *DIA*, 139.

"WE HAVE MORE FUN TOGETHER ALL THE TIME"

1

HW, 144. *EH*, 123, 584. Sokoloff, *Hadley*, 173. Loeb, *The Way It Was*, 207.
249 "naturally cried": Williams, *Autobiography of William Carlos Williams*, 227.
250 "Hemingway *père*": Beach, *Shakespeare and Company*, 82.
250 "We have more fun": EH to Howell Jenkins, November 9, 1924; *SL*, 132.
250 "Hem was hard" et seq.: JDP, *The Best Times*, 143.
251 "a bad example": *EH*, 124.
251 "in a sort of imitation": *VPH*, 45.
251 "bastard," "To see whether I was buying": Sarason, *Hemingway and "The Sun" Set*, 148–50.

2

251 "wonderfully bad": Sarason, *Hemingway and "The Sun" Set*, 148–50.
252 "I'm going down": *SSEH*, 167.
252 "Don't you think": Ibid., 169–70.
253 "terribly low" et seq.: Sarason, *Hemingway and "The Sun" Set*, 148–50.

3

253 "an offensive bludy ass": EH to Bill Smith, December 6, 1924; *SL*, 136.
253 "almost everything worth a damn": Ibid., 136–37.
253 "have had and have a damn good time": Ibid., 137.
254 "It is just about morning": EH to Robert McAlmon, c. November 15, 1924; *SL*, 133.

255 "There's going to be a moon tonight" et seq.: *SSEH*, 110–11.
255 "You were very wise" et seq.: Ibid., 122–24.

4

256 "I have read your article": CEH to EH, March 8, 1925; JFK.
256 "Thanks for your fine letter": EH to CEH, March 20, 1925; *SL*, 153.
256 "If you call me Doc once again": *SSEH*, 101.
256 "her Bible" et seq.: Ibid., 102–3.
257 "the quality of humiliation": FSF, "How To Waste Material," 262–65.

5

258 "his best sister," "We're playing indoor": *SSEH*, 149–50.
259 "I hadn't thought about it" et seq.: Ibid., 151–52.
259 "feel all right about it," "He wanted his life": Ibid., 153.

6

HW, 149. *EH*, 129. JDP, *The Best Times*, 156–57. McAlmon, *Being Geniuses Together*, 275–76. Raeburn, *Fame Became of Him*, 13, 24–25.
260 "I've never seen a man": Archibald MacLeish, comments on Hemingway; Patrick Hynan, ed., "Hemingway—A Portrait in Sound," Canadian Broadcasting Company, 1970, Sides One and Two.
260 "The godamdest": EH to Howell Jenkins, November 9, 1924; *SL*, 131.
261 "the bull did not swerve" et seq.: Stewart, *By a Stroke of Luck!*, 132.
261 BULL GORES 2 YANKS: *Chicago Tribune*, July 29, 1924, 1.
262 "the worst shot-up man": WORST SHOT-UP MAN IN U. S. ON WAY HOME, *Chicago American*, January 22, 1919, 3.
262 "an annoyed toro": I. M. P., "Turns With a Bookworm," *New York Herald Tribune Books*, March 30, 1927, 23.
262 "Author Hemingway": review of *Men Without Women*, *Time*, October 24, 1927, 38.
262 "a semiprofessional": "A Bookman's Notes," *Bookman*, February 1929, xxiii.
263 "tremendous physical presence": MacLeish, comments on Hemingway; Hynan, ed., "Hemingway—A Portrait in Sound."

HAROLD AND HORACE, SCOTT AND ZELDA

1

EH, 130. *VPH*, 115. Carr, *Dos Passos*, 202.
264 "the wildest damn country": EH to Howell Jenkins, November 9, 1924; *SL*, 130.
264 "He was never the hiker": Carr, *Dos Passos*, 202.

2

EW, *The Shores of Light*, 119–23. *EH*, 138, 139, 143. Williams, *H. L. Mencken*, 93. Loeb, *The Way It Was*, 216–19, 225–27. *SSEH*, 249.

265   "to give the picture": EH to EW, October 18, 1924; *SL*, 128.
266   "Mr. Doran felt": EH to Harold Loeb, January 5, 1925; *SL*, 143.
266   "The sort of brave, bold stuff": H. L. Mencken, "Check List of New Books" column, *American Mercury*, August 1925, xxxviii.
267   "Did you see": EH to EP, October 22, 1924; Beinecke Library, Yale University.
268   "I am inclined to think that": EW, "Mr. Hemingway's Dry Points," 340–41.
268   "cool and clear minded": EH to EW, October 18, 1924; *SL*, 129.
268   "curious defect" et seq.: EW, "Mr. Hemingway's Dry Points," 340–41.
268   "The veteran Manolo": *SSEH*, 249.

3

EH, 137, 139, 188–90. Swanberg, *Dreiser*, 193–204, 222–73. Loeb, *The Way It Was*, 220.

269   "good crucifixes": EH to Harold Loeb, December 29, 1924; *SL*, 141.
270   "if you don't come": Ibid.
270   "What a lousy business": EH to Harold Loeb, January 5, 1925; *SL*, 142.
270   "with the terrible industry": H. L. Mencken, "The Dreiser Bugaboo," in Mencken, *The Young Mencken*, 556–57.
270–71   "I do not know of any young woman": Swanberg, *Dreiser*, 273.
271   "Jesus it was cold": EH to Harold Loeb, February 27, 1925; *SL*, 151.
271   "The new story makes": EH to Horace Liveright, March 31, 1925; *SL*, 155.
271   "that lousy crut of a brakeman": *SSEH*, 308.
272   "His nose was sunken": Ibid., 131.
272   "What made him crazy?" et seq.: Ibid., 136–37.
272   "she was an awful good-looking woman": Ibid., 137.
273   "little man," "looked childish": Ibid., 132, 138.
273   "You'll feel better": Ibid., 138.
273   "He says he's never been crazy": Ibid., 133.

4

273   DELIGHTED ACCEPT: *EH*, 141.
274   "I hope this is so": Berg, *Max Perkins*, 88.
274   "a young man named Ernest Hemmingway" et seq.: FSF, *The Letters of F. Scott Fitzgerald*, 167.
274   "[The book] accumulates": Berg, *Max Perkins*, 87.
274   "we could have seen": Ibid.

275   "I cannot tell you how pleased" et seq.: EH to MP, April 15, 1925; *SL*, 156.
275   "What rotten luck": Berg, *Max Perkins*, 88.

5

Mellow, *Invented Lives*, 201–4. Le Vot, *F. Scott Fitzgerald*, 196.
276   "out of the pit of my stomach": Le Vot, *F. Scott Fitzgerald*, 252.
276   "women didn't like": FSF and MP, *Dear Scott/Dear Max*, 99.
276   SALES SITUATION DOUBTFUL: Mellow, *Invented Lives*, 231.
276   "depressed": FSF and MP, *Dear Scott/Dear Max*, 101.

6

Bruccoli, *Some Sort of Epic Grandeur*, 227–28n. SL, 162–63. Mellow, *Invented Lives*, 23–24. Glenway Wescott, "The Moral of Scott Fitzgerald," in FSF, *The Crack-Up*, 324–25.
277   "I wonder what your idea": EH to FSF, July 1, 1925; *SL*, 165.
278   "When I like men": FSF, *Notebooks*, no. 938.
278   "one true genius," "It simply had not occurred": Wescott, "The Moral of Scott Fitzgerald," 324, 325.
279   "He was romantic": EH to Arthur Mizener, April 22, 1950; *SL*, 690.
279   "Scott was a man then": *AMF*, 149.
279   "extraordinarily nice": Ibid.
280   "he had very short legs," "fitted him well," "I thought I ought to tell him": Ibid., 150.
280   "cynical and funny": Ibid., 153.
280   "it was late spring": Ibid., 154.
281   "you could not be angry": Ibid., 154–55.
281   "Try and make Monsieur": Ibid., 162.
281   "I am not sure": Ibid., 163.
282   "I was getting tired": Ibid., 165.
282   "it was wonderful": Ibid., 175.
282   "Know you will be glad": EH to FSF, c. December 24, 1925; *SL*, 182.
282   "We had a great trip together": EH to MP, June 9, 1925; *SL*, 162–63.
282   "Hemingway and I", *The Letters of F. Scott Fitzgerald*, 484.

7

AMF, 191. Le Vot, *F. Scott Fitzgerald*, 236. FSF, *The Crack-Up*, 76. Mellow, *Invented Lives*, 82, 119–20.
283   "what was then called": *AMF*, 189.
283   "never slept with anyone": Ibid., 190.
283   "perfectly fine": Ibid.
283   "It is not basically a question": Ibid., 191.

283   "astonishing incident": Le Vot, *F. Scott Fitzgerald*, 236.
284   "no end to our delight": Mellow, *Invented Lives*, 82.

8

285   "something tragic," "to know and understand": *AMF*, 172–73.
285   "taut and drawn," "tired": Ibid., 180.
285   "had been ruined" et seq.: Ibid., 179.
285   "Ernest, don't you think": Ibid., 186.
285   "she was making": Ibid., 181.
286   "bogus": Donnelly, *Sara & Gerald*, 21.
286   "phony as a rubber check": Mayfield, *Exiles*, 112.
286   "as male as all that": Donnelly, *Sara & Gerald*, 21.
286   "No more, baby": Mellow, *Invented Lives*, 359.
286   "We came back to the Rue Palatine": FSF, *The Correspondence of F. Scott Fitzgerald*, 241.
287   "vague despondency": Mellow, *Invented Lives*, 68.
287   "told us to be married": Ibid.
287   "We're twins": FSF, *The Beautiful and Damned*, 131.
287   "as though he": *AMF*, 179.
288   "Zelda would begin complaining": Ibid., 181.
288   "meant she knew": Ibid., 180.

BETRAYALS

1

Callaghan, *That Summer*, 127. *HW*, 156–65. *VPH*, 22 et seq.
290   "go to bed": *SSEH*, 118.
291   "like the hull," "brushed back": *VPH*, 22.

2

EH, 148. *HW*, 156–65.
291   "When she laughed": *HW*, 158.
291   "liquid quality": Loeb, *The Way It Was*, 249.
291   "I think . . . that you see": *HW*, 159.
292   "Pamplona's going to be": EH to Harold Loeb, June 21, 1925; *SL*, 164.
292   "I'm miserable without you": Loeb, *The Way It Was*, 280.
292   "It will be a great joy to see you": Ibid., 282.

3

HW, 161–65.
293   "Made me feel sick": EH to CEH, August 20, 1925; *SL*, 168.

293   "The Garden of Eden": *EH,* 150.

293   "devil, sex": Ibid.

293   "Pat broke the spell": Loeb, *The Way It Was,* 284.

293   "wild about Ernest": *EH,* 150.

294   "saying she had fallen," "You lay off," "I don't want to hit you": Loeb, *The Way It Was,* 292–97.

294   "I was terribly tight": EH to Harold Loeb, July 12, 1925; *SL,* 166.

295   "He knocked me cold": Mills, "Ernest Hemingway and Nathan Asch," 51.

295   "I'm sorry, Jake": *VPH,* 189.

295   "hard, Jewish, stubborn streak": Ibid., 12.

295   "like a bloody steer": Ibid., 138.

296   "I liked to see," "I wished": Ibid., 144.

296   "He can be damn nice": Ibid., 98.

296   "I hate him, myself": Ibid., 178.

296   "Somehow I feel": Ibid., 44.

4

DIA, 89. *EH,* 146–56.

296   "He did everything": EH to GS and ABT, July 15, 1925; *SL,* 167.

297   "She had been turning": *SAR,* ms.; JFK.

297   "Scott Fitzgerald": Ibid.

298   "I'm terribly glad": EH to Barklie Henry, August 12, 1925; JFK.

298   "Toward the last": EH to Bernard Berenson, October 14, 1952; *SL,* 792.

299   "Ernest my dear": *EH,* 156.

5

HW, 155–56, 171–72. JDP, *The Best Times,* 144. Meyers, *Hemingway,* 346.

301   "I was talking": *EH,* 144.

301   "I'd like to": Ibid., 142.

302   "I said perfectly calmly": EH to PP, November 12, 1926; *SL,* 222.

6

Peter Quennell, review of *The Torrents of Spring, New Statesman and Nation,* February 18, 1933, 196.

303   "Ah, there was a woman!": *HR,* 74–75.

303   "detestable": *EH,* 159.

303   "quite good enough": JDP, *The Best Times,* 158.

303   "About the best comic book": FSF, *The Correspondence of F. Scott Fitzgerald,* 183.

304   "a small masterpiece": Allen Tate, review of *The Torrents of Spring, The Nation,* July 28, 1926, 89–90.

304   "The Best by Test": *HR*, 35.
304   "A field of golden daffodils": Ibid., 50.
304   "picturesque," "strange": Ibid.
304   "relief waitress," "buxom": Ibid., 48.
305   "no better than a slut": Ibid., 54.
305   "She knew it was over": Ibid., 81.
305   "You are my woman": Ibid.
305   "It grows late": Ibid., 84.

7

Herschel Brickell, review of *In Our Time, Literary Review of the New York Evening Post*, October 17, 1925, 3. *SL*, 173–80, 799.

306   "lyricism, aliveness": Paul Rosenfeld, review of *In Our Time, New Republic*, November 25, 1925, 22–23.
306   "at once," "all those blurbs": EH to Horace Liveright, December 7, 1925; *SL*, 173–74.
307   "To hear him talk": Berg, *Max Perkins*, 93.
307   "easy for me to write": EH to FSF, c. December 24, 1925; *SL*, 180.
307   "What do you think about?": *SSEH*, 305.
308   "I'm going to need a lot" et seq.: Ibid., 300–301.
308   "some sort of a Dane," "What do you call yourself": Ibid., 321.
309   "they don't take any": Ibid., 311.
309   "I'll get twenty-five thousand": Ibid., 313.
309   "fine bunch": Ibid., 311.
309   "This Lardner": Ibid., 304–5.
309–10 "unerring," "He discards": Dorothy Parker, review of *MWW, The New Yorker*, October 29, 1927, 94.
310   "Come on and fight": *SSEH*, 324.
310   "Then he swung the left": Ibid., 325.
310   "dangerous influence": Parker, review of *MWW*, 94.

8

310   "pretty good": EH to Archibald MacLeish, December 20, 1925; *SL*, 179.
311   "The first impression": Ernest Walsh, review of *In Our Time, This Quarter*, Autumn-Winter 1925–1926, 319–21.
311   "swell," "Oh Christ": EH to Ernest Walsh, January 2, 1926; *SL*, 187.
311   "a son of a bitch": EH to FSF, c. December 24, 1925; *SL*, 181.
311   "He also wrote": EH to Ernest Walsh, January 2, 1926; *SL*, 188.
312   "sons of bitching": EH to FSF, c. December 24, 1925; *SL*, 181.
312   "Christ nose" et seq.: Ibid.
312   "with plenty of insomnia": EH to FSF, c. September 7, 1926; *SL*, 217.
312   "I've never gotten": *VPH*, 204–5.
313   "I was a little ashamed": Ibid., 93.
313   "Listen, Jake": Ibid., 120.

9

AMF, 210. REJECTING: *EH*, 162.

314 "So, I'm loose": Ibid.

314 "might rock the country": *SL*, 184.

314 "I am not going to Double Cross": EH to FSF, December 31, 1925–January 1, 1926; *SL*, 184.

315 "six week lapse": Ibid., 185.

315 "Oh, my soul": *HW*, 173.

315 "hells own amount": EH to Louis and Mary Bromfield, c. March 8, 1926; *SL*, 195.

315 "full of a strange misty light": Wolfe, *You Can't Go Home Again*, 442–43.

315 "grand": *EH*, 164.

316 "very damned nice," "awfully swell": EH to Louis and Mary Bromfield, c. March 8, 1926; *SL*, 195.

316 "cockeyed": EH to Isabel Simmons Godolphin, February 25, 1926; *SL*, 193.

DOUBLE MEANINGS

1

SL, 196, 200. JDP, *The Best Times*, 153–54.

317 "too damn clumsy": Carr, *Dos Passos*, 217.

318 "slept like dormice," "last unalloyed": Ibid.

2

Wiser, *The Crazy Years*, 74, 111–15. Le Vot, *F. Scott Fitzgerald*, 188–90, 230. Hulme, *Undiscovered Country*, 100. Fitch, *Sylvia Beach*, 136. Field, *Djuna*, 15–17, 136–46. Meyers, *The Critical Heritage*, 89, 92, 96. EH on Djuna Barnes, ms.; JFK. EH on Aldo Lombardo, ms.; JFK. EH on young woman who gets a haircut, ms.; JFK.

319 "Popess of Lesbos": Le Vot, *F. Scott Fitzgerald*, 188.

320 "crowd of young men": *VPH*, 20.

320 "Georgette Mangeuse": EH to EP, c. May 2, 1924; *SL*, 115.

320 "I wish to present": *VPH*, 18.

322 "heard someone speaking": *AMF*, 118.

322 "Barnes!": *VPH*, 17.

323 "I've promised": Ibid., 23.

323 "What's the matter": Ibid., 54–55.

325 "Promiscuity no solution": EH to Archibald MacLeish, c. May 5, 1943; *SL*, 545.

3

Svoboda, *Hemingway & "The Sun Also Rises,"* 34–36. Donaldson, "Irony and Pity—Anatole France Got It Up," 31–34. Edel, *Henry James. The Untried Years,* 173–76. Adeline R. Tintner, "Ernest and Henry: Hemingway's Lover's Quarrel with James," in Nagel, ed., *Ernest Hemingway: The Writer in Context,* 165–78. Edel, *Henry James. The Master,* 74, 77. Hinkle, "What's Funny in *The Sun Also Rises,"* 31–41.

325   "After a while": *VPH,* 89.
325   "the falsity or tragedy": EW, "The Sportsman's Tragedy," 103.
326   "a lot of cheap, prurient": Berg, *Max Perkins,* 97.
326   "with irony and pity and a consuming passion": Donaldson, "Irony and Pity," 31–34.
326   "could not have been better": *AMF,* 154.
326   "Work for the good of all": *VPH,* 109.
327   "You know what's the trouble": Ibid., 110–11.
327   "hot spot": Berg, *Max Perkins,* 98.
327   "shabby conflagration" et seq.: James, *Notes of a Son and Brother,* 296–99.
328   "Henry James; expatriation and castration": Wescott, "A Sentimental Contribution," 523–24.
328   "non-sequitor": EH to MP, June 5, 1926; *SL,* 209.
328   "turn out to be": EH to HR, November 25, 1943; *SL,* 556.
328   "in the wake of H. J.": Reynolds, *Hemingway's Reading,* 22.
328   "Listen, Jake": *VPH,* 12.
329   "Live all you can": James, *The Ambassadors,* 454.
329   "Pauline has been fine": EH to Waldo Peirce, December 13, 1927; *SL,* 266.
329   "For your information": EH to Charles Scribner, September 6 and 7, 1949; *SL,* 673.
330   "First the egg" et seq.: VPH, 117–18.

4

Toy, "Ecclesiastes," 849–50. Hinkle, "What's Funny in *The Sun Also Rises,"* 31–41.
330   "a clairvoyant's crystal": EW, "The Sportsman's Tragedy," 103.
330   "a quite extraordinary" et seq.: Conrad Aiken, review of *SAR,* in *New York Herald Tribune Books,* October 31, 1926, 4.
331   "Mr. Hemingway has produced": Allen Tate, review of *SAR,* in *The Nation,* December 15, 1926, 642–44.
332   "to see someone": EH to MP, November 19, 1926; *SL,* 229.
332   "to show the superiority": EH to Paul Romaine, August 9, 1932; *SL,* 365.
333   "C'est une génération": *EH,* 155.
333   "all of you young people": *AMF,* 29–31.
333   "a hollow or bitter satire": EH to MP, November 19, 1926; *SL,* 229.
334   "Brett's not a sadist": *VPH,* 162.
334   "had the old thing": Ibid., 164.
334   "badly cogido" et seq.: Ibid., 193–94.

335 "left both ear": Ibid., 195.
335 "Brett wants to see": Ibid., 172.
335 "I could not make" et seq.: Ibid., 236–37.
335 "I'd have lived": Ibid., 239.
335 "He wanted to marry": Ibid., 238.
336 "I'm thirty-four": Ibid., 239.
336 "You know it makes one feel": Ibid., 241.
336 "Oh, Jake": Ibid., 243.
336n "I believe it was Ernest Hemingway": FSF, *The Letters of F. Scott Fitzgerald*, 363.

5

336 "learned it by heart": Barrett, "Babes in the Bois," 724.
336 "So many young men": *VPH*, 41.
336 "were modelling themselves": Cowley, *Exile's Return*, 225–26.
337 "The point of the book": EH to MP, November 19, 1926; *SL*, 229.
337 "expressed the romantic disillusion": EW, *The Portable Edmund Wilson*, 401.
337 "My life was more or less": EH to Owen Wister, March 11, 1929; Library of Congress.

"I LOVED HER FINE"

1

EH, 168–69. *SL*, 199.
341 "330 typewritten": EH to MP, April 1, 1926; *SL*, 198.
341 "Is Ernest any way": *HW*, 178.
341 "thing," "What he seemed": Ibid., 178–79.
342 "Ja, I loved her": *SSEH*, 348.
342 "I have tried to follow": EH to FSF, c. April 20, 1926; *SL*, 200–201.
343 "Grace under pressure": Ibid., 200.

2

343 "I tell you, he was": *SSEH*, 358.
343 "must get to you," "weight starts to pull": Ibid., 357–58.
344 "You see I feel": EH to Sherwood Anderson, May 21, 1926; *SL*, 205–6.

3

Mellow, *Invented Lives*, 267–71.
345 "Here it was": *HW*, 180–81.
345 "sophomoric": Tomkins, *Living Well*, 125.

345   "You can't expect anyone": FSF, *The Correspondence of F. Scott Fitzgerald,* 196.
345   *"You ought to know"*: Ibid., 197.
345   "sneers" et seq.: Ibid., 193–95.

4

346   "Next year": *EH,* 172.
346–47   "all the time bitterly unhappy": *HW,* 182.
347   "I'm going to get a bicycle": Ibid.
347   "We were returning to Paris": *SSEH,* 142.

5

349   "And how does she": *HW,* 186.
349   "very much on the bright side": Ibid.
349   "a madhouse depression": Ibid., 187.
349   "You got your terrible hell": Ibid.

6

350   "typed up by the well known": EH to MP, August 21, 1926; *SL,* 214.
350   *"re*-present them": McAgy, "Gerald Murphy," 3–4.
350   " 'the thing itself' ": MacLeish, *Riders,* 126.
351   "All I can think": EH to PP, November 12, 1926; *SL,* 220.
351   "All day long": Ibid., 221.
351   "all I want is you": Ibid., 222.
351   "[missing you] doesn't take": EH to PP, December 3, 1926; *SL,* 234.
351   "when two people love": Ibid.
351   "I want you to tell me": Keats, *You Might As Well Live,* 296.
352   *"O thou who"*: EH, *88 Poems,* 87.
353   *"Thou hast committed"*: Eliot, *Collected Poems,* 18.
353   "In the fall": *SSEH,* 267.
354   "Very interesting," "You have confidence?" "No": Ibid., 268.
354   "idiotic," "He said I was," "and he was a fool": Ibid., 271.
354   "What will you do": Ibid.
355   "It is very difficult": Ibid., 272.

7

355   "I took you originally": *HW,* 189.
355   "My dearest Hadley": EH to HR, November 18, 1926; *SL,* 226.
355   "all royalties" et seq.: Ibid., 227–28.

8

SL, 240, 243–44. *EH,* 180.

356 "Think the family": EH to Isabel Simmons Godolphin, December 3, 1925; *SL,* 172.

356 "many compliments" et seq.: CEH to EH, December 9, 1925; JFK.

357 "Congratulations": EH to GHH, December 14, 1925; *SL,* 174.

357 "My mother sent me": EH to Archibald MacLeish, December 20, 1925; *SL,* 178.

357 "You surely are now": CEH to EH, December 13, 1926; JFK.

357 "cooling off of affection" et seq.: GHH to EH, December 4, 1926; JFK.

358 "Did the family tell you": GHH to EH, January 31, 1927; JFK.

358 "as I could not help": EH to GHH, February 5, 1927; *SL,* 243.

358 "the good ladies" et seq.: Ibid., 243–44.

359 "Your statement that": GHH to EH, February 20, 1927; JFK.

9

Hanneman, *Ernest Hemingway: A Comprehensive Bibliography,* 14–15, 20. *HW,* 200–201, 203, 204.

360 "The Sun has risen": *EH,* 182.

360 "Italian tour": *HW,* 200.

361 "He adores you": *SSEH,* 294.

361 "Certainly": Ibid.

361 "Bananas are all right": Ibid., 295.

362 "why everybody you use": *EH,* 595.

363 "The hills across": *SSEH,* 273.

363 "I know you wouldn't mind" et seq.: Ibid., 275–78.

364 "Mss for Pauline": "Hills Like White Elephants" ms.; JFK.

A HOLLOW MAN

1

366 "a grand town": EH to Barklie Henry, c. August 15, 1927; *SL,* 255.

2

367 "Had you answered": CEH to EH, August 8, 1927; JFK.

367 "split up" et seq.: EH to CEH, September 14, 1927; *SL,* 257–58.

367 "I know you don't like": Ibid., 258–59.

368 "I love you very much": Ibid., 259–60.

3

EH, 187–89, 596. *SL*, 273–74. Hanneman, *Ernest Hemingway: A Comprehensive Bibliography*, 20.

369 "The softening feminine" et seq.: Virginia Woolf, review of *MWW*, in *New York Herald Tribune Books*, October 9, 1927, 1, 8.

369 "a blend of Gertrude Stein's": Cyril Connolly, review of *MWW*, in *The New Statesman*, November 26, 1927, 208.

369 "have made huge successes": H. L. Mencken, review of *MWW*, in *The American Mercury*, May 1928, 127.

370 "the art of the reporter": Percy Hutchison, review of *MWW*, in *New York Times Book Review*, October 16, 1927, 9, 27.

370 "probably the best": William Curtis, review of *MWW*, in *Town & Country*, December 15, 1927, 59.

370 "a truly magnificent": Dorothy Parker, review of *MWW*, in *The New Yorker*, October 29, 1927, 92–94.

370 "has, in a very short time": EW, "The Sportsman's Tragedy," 102–3.

370 "our outstanding": N. L. Rothman, review of *MWW*, in *The Dial*, April 1, 1928, 336–38.

4

370 "Haow the hellsufferin": *EH*, 190.
370 "You poor dear old thing!": Ibid.
371 "the clean way": *HW*, 199.

5

EH, 191, 192. *A Guide to Key West*, 13–76. Windhorn and Langley, *Yesterday's Key West*, 7–23. *HW*, 202, 206, 208. Carr, *Dos Passos*, 231, 253, 257, 282. Reynolds, *Hemingway's First War*, 20.

373 "the biggest tarpon": EH to MP, April 21, 1928; *SL*, 277.
373 "going very well": Ibid., 276.
373 "radiant with enthusiasm": 1928 news clipping; JFK.
375 "lesbian enclave": Carr, *Dos Passos*, 282.
375 "Glimpse of her": EW, *The Thirties*, 257.
375n "When he invited": Madelaine Hemingway Miller, *Ernie*, 113.

6

Reynolds, *Hemingway's First War*, 24–25.

376 "[My wife] had a very": EH to MP, July 23, 1928; *SL*, 280.
376 "bughouse": *EH*, 195.
376 "monumental opus": EH to Guy Hickok, c. July 27, 1928; *SL*, 281.

377 "With you away": *HW*, 211.

377 "Hurry up": Ibid.

377 "Jinny was cutting out": Ibid., 212.

377 "This is a cockeyed" et seq.: EH to Waldo Peirce, c. August 23, 1928; *SL*, 284.

377 "I've never felt better": EH to MP, September 28, 1928; *SL*, 286.

7

YH, 221.

379 "It opened, and in the darkened room": Leicester Hemingway, *The Sound of the Trumpet*, 182–83.

379 "I will take care of it": GHH to EH, March 24, 1929; JFK.

379 "worry a moment": GHH to EH, December 22, 1928; JFK.

379 "What makes me feel": EH to MP, December 16, 1928; *SL, 291.*

380 "I've had hell's own time": EH to Owen Wister, February 20, 1929; Library of Congress.

380 "more or less": Ibid.

380 "I have my bloody book": EH to JDP, 1928; Alderman Library, U. of Virginia.

8

Oldsey, *Hemingway's Hidden Craft,* 58, 72. Reynolds, *Hemingway's First War,* 26–27, 36–37, 45–46, 50, 67–68, 71, 72–73, 76–77. *AFTA,* 330, 332. Berg, *Max Perkins,* 141–43.

380 "My legs hurt so": Reynolds, *Hemingway's First War,* 36–37.

380 "When I was awake": *AFTA,* 107.

381 "The baby is alive": Reynolds, *Hemingway's First War,* 45.

381 "Take the baby": Ibid., 46.

382 "certain words" et seq.: Ibid., 67.

382 "who has always been good": Ibid., 71.

383 "frame my enthusiasm": Ibid., 76.

383 "[My] first point relates": MP to EH, May 24, 1929; Princeton University Library.

9

Reynolds, *Hemingway's First War,* 18–19, 36–37, 41, 126. *EH,* 190, 217, 598. *HW,* 235, 237, 247–50. Oldsey, *Hemingway's Hidden Craft,* 71–72. EH to Owen Wister, July 26, 1929; Library of Congress. GHH to EH, October 5, 1929; JFK. Plimpton, "Ernest Hemingway. An Interview," 66–67. Baker, ed., *Critiques of Four Major Novels,* 75. Millicent Bell, "*A Farewell to Arms:* Pseudoautobiography and Personal Metaphor," in Nagel, ed., *Ernest Hemingway: The Writer in Context,* 107–28.

384   "in conscious imitation": Ross, *Reporting*, 218.
384   "In the late summer": *AFTA*, 3–4.
384   "a filthy place": Ibid., 242.
385   "There isn't always": Ibid., 18.
385   "[The war] did not have": Ibid., 37.
385   "I was always embarrassed": Ibid., 184–85.
385   "the fate of a generation": Wohl, *The Generation of 1914*, 106–7.
386   "we quarrelled so much": *AFTA*, 304.
386   "Oughf": Ibid., 11.
386   "had written to his father," "it was what I had wanted," "I . . . could not understand": Ibid., 13.
386   "sometimes a dispute": Ibid.
386   "Between the idea": Eliot, *Collected Poems*, 104.
386   "chess game": *AFTA*, 26.
386   "I did not care": Ibid., 30.
386   "rotten game," "But I do love you": Ibid., 31.
387   "Hello, darling" et seq.: Ibid., 91.
387   "You're seeing him": FSF, *The Correspondence of F. Scott Fitzgerald*, 225–28.
387   "lovely temperature," "a little boy": *AFTA*, 103, 104.
387   "I would take out the pins" et seq.: Ibid., 114–16.
388   "Darling, why don't you let": Ibid., 299.
389   "I want us to be all mixed up": Ibid., 300.
389   "We had a fine life": Ibid., 306.
389   "who has always loved God" et seq.: Reynolds, *Hemingway's First War*, 40–41.
390   "But . . . it wasn't any good": *AFTA*, 332.
390   "I wished the hell": Ibid., 327.

10

Raeburn, *Fame Became of Him*, 27–31.
391   "like hell and through it," "He has the most profound," "grace under pressure": Parker, "The Artist's Reward," 28–31.
392   "the romantic and false": Raeburn, *Fame Became of Him*, 27.
392   "a vivid fragment": Ibid.
392   "enlist and leave": Reynolds, *Hemingway's First War*, 7–8.
392   "a brutally masculine": Meyers, *The Critical Heritage*, 136.
392   "a beautiful tenderness": Ibid., 137.
393   "He, the male": Ibid., 139.
393   "a legend very important": Callaghan, *That Summer*, 240.

MENS MORBIDA IN CORPORE SANO

1

A Guide to Key West, 92–93. Samuelson, *With Hemingway*, 9. GHH to EH, February 6, 1930; JFK. GHH to EH, March 9, 1930; JFK. JDP, "Young Hemingway: A Panel," *Fitzgerald/Hemingway Annual,* 1972, 136. *SL,* 360. Hotchner, *Papa Hemingway,* 139.

394 "The only thing in life": EH to FSF, c. November 24, 1926; *SL,* 232.
394 "Poor Boy": GHH to EH, September 24, 1929; JFK.
395 "I won't bother you": GHH to EH, April 5, 1932; JFK.
395 "Never threaten me": quoted in EH to Charles Scribner, August 27, 1949; *SL,* 670.
395 "My dear mother": Ibid.
395 "She had to rule everything": *HW,* 335.
395 "we never had any trouble": EH to Charles Scribner, August 27, 1949; *SL,* 670.
395 "passion": *SSEH,* 490.
395 "he was very grateful": Ibid.
396 "as a man might": *DIA,* 3.
396 "being much interested": Ibid., 20.

2

396–97 "Am just going over": EH to JDP, January 1932; Alderman Library, U. of Virginia.
397 "It's silly just to write": Berg, *Max Perkins,* 194.
397 "It gives the impression": Ibid.
397 "hell of a damn dirty business": Ibid., 196.
397 "If I had I would have known": Ibid.
397–98 "exhaustive treatise," "small-boy wickedness," "in which his bitterness," "the tremendous labor," "almost a suicidal book": Robert Coates, review of *DIA,* in *The New Yorker,* October 1, 1932, 61–63.
398 "gross," "he is unfailingly," "to prove fatuously": H. L. Mencken, review of *DIA,* in *The American Mercury,* December 1932, 506–7.
398 "unconscionable quantity" et seq.: Eastman, "Bull in the Afternoon," 94–97.
399 "condescentious piece": EH to JDP, October 14, 1932; *SL,* 374.
399 "I have plenty of respect": EH to Robert M. Coates, October 5, 1932; *SL,* 368–69.
399 "By some psychoanalytic": MacLeish, *The Letters of Archibald MacLeish,* 261.
400 "Sirs" et seq.: EH to editors of the *New Republic; New Republic,* June 12, 1933; JFK.
400 "I am tempted": EH to MP, June 13, 1933; *SL,* 394–95.
400 "manhood, courage" et seq.: Max Eastman, "Red Blood and Hemingway," *New Republic,* June 28, 1933, 184.
400 "kiss-ass": *EH,* 242.
401 "hairy enough" et seq.: *EH,* 317.
401 "jumped at me": *The New York Times,* August 14, 1937, 15.
402 "Enjoyment of Thrashing Ernest": Eastman, *Great Companions,* 65.
402 "Slogger," "Kid," "Writer?": Raeburn, *Fame Became of Him,* 96.
402 "Greco liked to paint": *DIA,* 204.

3

HW, 237, 240, 241, 242, 248–49. *SL,* 343. Fuentes, *Hemingway in Cuba,* 8, 9, 10. Mellow, *Invented Lives,* 394–95. *EH,* 222, 228.

404 "I know what I am doing": EH to Paul Romaine, August 9, 1932; *SL,* 366.
405 "He says he's never been crazy": *SSEH,* 133.
405 "How are you really?": Ibid., 407.
405 ARRIVING: *HW,* 243.
406 "Next year": Ibid.
406 "I think you will like it": Ibid., 233.
406 "large nose": Ibid., 247.

4

Berg, *Max Perkins,* 215. Meyers, *Hemingway,* 236. Bruccoli, *Some Sort of Epic Grandeur,* 348. *SSEH,* 383. *DIA,* 192. *EH,* 197, 227, 236, 246. T. S. Matthews, review of *Winner Take Nothing,* in *New Republic,* November 15, 1933, 24. Arthur Power, *Conversations with James Joyce,* Dublin, 1974, 107. *YH,* 104–5.

408 "You know": *SSEH,* 413.
409 "motion and fact": *DIA,* 2.
410 "It is among": William Troy, review of *Winner Take Nothing,* in *The Nation,* November 15, 1933, 570.
410 "absolutely enraging": Berg, *Max Perkins,* 218.
410 "a fool," "shit," *"all the time,"* "those poor dumb pricks": EH to MP, November 16, 1933; *SL,* 400–401.
411 "looks like a modern": GS, *Autobiography of Alice B. Toklas,* 265–66.

5

EH, 225–26, 249, 251, 252, 253. Raeburn, *Fame Became of Him,* 45. Gingrich, *Nothing But People,* 80–81. Markham, *West With the Night,* 6.

412 "Did you read": EH to MP, August 27, 1942; *SL,* 541.
413 "Kilimanjaro kept": *HW,* 256.
413 "became convinced": EH, *By-Line,* 159.
413 "Ben will get there": *HW,* 257.
414 "Ernest went off": *HW,* 258.
414 "Your amoebic": EH, *By-Line,* 159.
415 "brave as a damned," "coward": *EH,* 609.
415 "My father was a coward": Ibid.

6

Raeburn, *Fame Became of Him,* 58, 153–54. EH, "Introduction" to *AFTA,* New York, 1948, vii–xi.

415 "The sort of First-person": Lewis, "The Dumb Ox," 33–45.

416   "I want the two": Fitch, *Sylvia Beach*, 344.
416   "Hemingway and I": Porter, "Paris: A Little Incident," 54–55.
417   "I entered": Dietrich, "The Most Fascinating Man I Know," 8–9.
417   "Your name begins," "sex without gender": Higham, *Marlene*, 11, 13.
418   "silvery," "that could always": *IS*, 306.
418   "Should I be": Ibid., 344.
419   "Ada, don't leave me": Gregory Hemingway, *Papa*, 39.
419   "I can't *stand*": *HW*, 263.
419   "Have no end": Ibid.
419   "chicken shit" et seq.: EH to Arnold Gingrich, July 15, 1934; *SL*, 410.

7

HW, 260, 265, 269–70. *EH*, 268. JDP, *The Best Times*, 210, 215, 219. EH,
By-Line, 199, 201.
420   "I would like it": *HW*, 264.
420   "You'd never believe it": EH to Arnold Gingrich, November 16, 1934; *SL*,
      411.
421   "We called it the *lit royale*": JDP, *The Best Times*, 219.

8

SL, 417, 421. Kashkin, "Ernest Hemingway," 72–90.
422   "[Africa] was fine": *HW*, 270.
422   "My sunburn hurts": Ibid.
422   "one of the finest": Gregory Hemingway, *Papa*, 58.
423   "I knew Tom": Ibid., 57.

THE BIG OUT

1

GHOA, n. p., 17, 23, 47, 51.
424   "absolutely true": *EH*, 275.
424   "The only person": *GHOA*, 40.
424   "What was that": Ibid., 24.
425   "delicacy of his love": review of *GHOA*, in *Time*, November 4, 1935, 81.
425   "We do not have great": *GHOA*, 17.
426   "I am interested": Ibid., 21.

2

C. G. Poore, review of *GHOA*, in *New York Times Book Review*, October
27, 1935, 3, 27. Edward Weeks, review of *GHOA*, in *Atlantic Monthly*, November
1935, 30. *SL*, 433, 437–38. Mellow, *Invented Lives*, 441–42.

426 "just another safari": Lewis Gannett, review of *GHOA*, in *New York Herald Tribune*, October 25, 1935, 17.

426 "It used to be pretty exciting": T. S. Matthews, review of *GHOA*, in *New Republic*, November 27, 1935, 79–80.

426 "is that it has few fine": Bernard De Voto, review of *GHOA*, in *Saturday Review of Literature*, October 26, 1935, 5.

426 "he is beginning": EW, "Letter to the Russians," 135–36.

426 "Have been haveing": EH to FSF, December 21, 1935; *SL*, 428.

427 "Had never had": EH to Mrs. Paul Pfeiffer, January 26, 1936; Ibid., 436.

427 "I felt that gigantic": EH to JDP, February 11, 1936; Alderman Library, U. of Virginia.

427 "Of course all life," "Ye are the salt": FSF, *The Crack-Up*, 69, 74.

427 "at three o'clock," "So there was not": Ibid., 75, 79.

428 "the idea of the Big Out": Ibid., 81.

428 "A classmate killed": Ibid., 20.

428 "I had stood by" et seq.: Ibid., 81–84.

428 "The Esquire pieces": EH to MP, February 7, 1936; *SL*, 437–38.

3

EH, 290. *GHOA*, 18.

429 "poor Scott Fitzgerald": "Snows of Kilimanjaro" ms.; HRC.

429 "a special glamorous race": *SSEH*, 72.

429 "the rich were dull": Ibid.

430 "You bitch": Ibid., 58.

430 "She *was* very good": Ibid., 64.

430 "bloody money": Ibid., 54.

430 "He had destroyed": Ibid., 60.

430 "bread and butter": Ibid., 58.

430 "sold vitality": Ibid., 61.

431 "had obsessed him": Ibid., 54.

431 "But she did not hear": Ibid., 77.

4

SL, 403. *EH*, 284–85.

431 "Will you have lime juice": *SSEH*, 3.

432 "well-kept": Ibid., 4.

432 "I invented her": EH, "The Art of the Short Story," 92–93.

432 "Francis' wife hates him": Jackson Burke, "Ernest Hemingway—Muy Hombre!", *Bluebook*, July 1953, 7.

433 "the male [in "Macomber"]": EW, *The Portable Edmund Wilson*, 416.

433 "The emotion which principally": Ibid., 414.

433 "Blowing things' ": *SSEH*, 9.

433 "I've dropped" et seq.: Ibid., 8–9.

434 "they prefer it": Ibid., 6.

434 "short, ugly": Ibid., 13.

434   "*ca-ra-wong!*": Ibid., 20.
434   "You were marvellous": Ibid., 29.
435   "The great American boy-men" et seq.: Ibid., 33–36.

                                    5

437   "Nice dear good": EH to Sara Murphy, c. February 27, 1936; *SL*, 440.
437   "If I choose to write": FSF, *The Letters of F. Scott Fitzgerald*, 311.
437   "you'd hesitate to use": Arnold Gingrich, "Coming to Terms with Scott and Ernest," 55.
437   "crazy letter": FSF, *The Letters of F. Scott Fitzgerald*, 267.
437   "[Hemingway] is quite": Ibid., 543.
437   "those awful things": *EH*, 290.
438   "getting to know the rich": Berg, *Max Perkins*, 305.

THE SPANISH TRAGEDY

                                    1

EH, 293, 296.
441   "worse than anything": EH to MP, September 26, 1936; *SL*, 455.
441   "Me I like life": EH to Archibald MacLeish, September 26, 1936; *SL*, 453.

                                    2

Madariaga, *Spain: A Modern History*, 455. Johnson, *Modern Times*, 321–40. *EH*, 299, 303, 304, 306, 308–9, 313, 328, 329. *SL*, 458, 462. North, *No Men Are Strangers*, 142. JDP, *Journeys Between the Wars*, 367–68. Matthews, *Two Wars and More to Come*, 282–84. *FWTBT*, 230. Raeburn, *Fame Became of Him*, 87. Thomas, *The Spanish Civil War*, 4–6, 111, 128, 242, 324, 326.
444   "the Reds may be as bad": EH to the Pfeiffer family, February 9, 1937; *SL*, 458.
445   "We gained the right": *EH*, 313.
445   "It was during": Matthews, *A World in Revolution*, 24–25.
446   "If you wanted to be": EH, *The Fifth Column and Four Stories*, 110.
446   "attracted to danger": Ehrenburg, "Hemingway," 22–26.
447   "Tell Paul": EH to HR, January 31, 1938; *SL*, 462.
448   "lay off making inquiries" et seq.: Herbst, "The Starched Blue Sky of Spain," 93, 96, 97, 108.
449   "new realms," "was absolutely right": Ibid., 93.
449   "fair-haired boy": Carr, *Dos Passos*, 368.

3

Raeburn, *Fame Became of Him*, 91, 92. FSF, *The Letters of F. Scott Fitzgerald*, 274. Johnson, *Modern Times*, 301. Hart, ed., *The Writer in a Changing World*, 69–73. Meyers, *Hemingway*, 312–13. Ivens, *Mémoire d'un regard*, 144, 146.

449   "It was fine": FSF, *The Letters of F. Scott Fitzgerald*, 311.
450   "warmed up eloquently": *Time*, June 21, 1937, 80.
450   "Whether the truth": EH, "Fascism Is a Lie," 4.
451   "and, since I had": Welles, "A Trip to Quixoteland," 42.
451   "Ernest came like a whirlwind": FSF, *The Letters of F. Scott Fitzgerald*, 274.
451   THE PICTURE: FSF, *The Correspondence of F. Scott Fitzgerald*, 475.
452   "I'm afraid of Ernest," "Please help," "Ernest has never," "I liked Ernest": Hellman, *An Unfinished Woman*, 67–69, 76.
453   "insider's magazine": Gingrich, *Nothing But People*, 133.
453   "Ernest Hemingway has been in Spain": *Ken*, April 7, 1938, 37.
453   "no anti-fascist magazine," "either a fool": EH, "United We Fall Upon Ken," 38.
453   "good hearted," "typical American": EH, "Treachery in Aragon," 26.
453   "friends" et seq.: EH, *By-Line*, 295.

4

EH, 314. Carr, *Dos Passos*, 348–49, 452, 476, 489. Raeburn, *Fame Became of Him*, 98.

454   "I got him forward": THAHN, 53–54.
454   "Some sort of Y.M.C.A.": GHOA, 130.
455   "Wealthy people" et seq.: EH, "Who Murdered the Vets?", 9.
455   "one of the three most" et seq.: THAHN, 80, 81.
456   "Ernest Hemingway came in here": Berg, *Max Perkins*, 323.
456   "major work" et seq.: Ibid., 324–25.
457   "lighted flashes of light": THAHN, 190.
458   "bloody splendid" et seq.: EH to JDP, March 26, 1932; SL, 354.
458   "to cavort in the deep": Carr, *Dos Passos*, 348.
458   "Gosh Hem": Ibid.
458   "You must have had hell" et seq.: Ibid.
459   "We just raise money," "To do that": THAHN, 166.
460   "F— his revolution": Ibid., 168.
460   ". . . the gun made a noise": Ibid., 172–73.
460   "In today's chapter": Ibid., 177.
460   "that dirty rich bitch": Ibid., 186.
461   "But we could afford": Ibid., 183.
461   "Love was the greatest" et seq.: Ibid., 185–86.
461   "It broke my poor mother's heart": Ibid., 185.
462   "But any fool": Gregory Hemingway, *Papa*, 125.
462   "No matter how": Ibid., 225.
462   "[*To Have and Have Not*'s] social assertions": Bernard De Voto, review of THAHN, in *Saturday Review of Literature*, October 16, 1937, 8.

463 "a stupid and foolish book": Delmore Schwartz, review of *THAHN*, in *Southern Review*, Spring 1938, 769–82.

463 "a book with neither": Louis Kronenberger, review of *THAHN*, in *The Nation*, October 23, 1937, 439–40.

463 "the Left . . . received": EW, *The Portable Edmund Wilson*, 409.

463 "unity and sureness of effect" et seq.: Malcolm Cowley, review of *THAHN*, in *New Republic*, October 20, 1937, 305–6.

464 "get angry and snarl" et seq.: Alfred Kazin, review of *THAHN*, in *New York Herald Tribune Books*, October 17, 1937, 3.

5

McLendon, *Papa: Hemingway in Key West*, 163–64. HW, 281–91. EH, 297.

6

HW, 285–87, 290. Faber, *The Life of Lorena Hickok*, 137–99. G. P. Wells, *H. G. Wells in Love*, 193. EH, 304. SL, 461.

466 "The American edition of": *HW*, 289.

466 "Who is this Martha Gellhorn?": Ibid.

467 "very grumpy" et seq.: Ibid., 290.

467 SECONDHAND REPORT: *EH*, 299.

7

467 "if I kept": *HW*, 292.

468 "Would love to be": Ibid.

468 "who's made me happier": EH to the Pfeiffer family, February 9, 1937; *SL*, 458.

468 "Angel" et seq.: *HW*, 294.

468 "I knew you'd get here": *EH*, 304.

469 "All kinds of liaisons": Ibid., 309.

8

SL, 464. EW, *The Portable Edmund Wilson*, 411.

470 "Martha Gellhorn seems to have": *HW*, 302.

470 "We had a rainwater soup" et seq.: EH to Mrs. Paul Pfeiffer, August 2, 1937; *SL*, 460.

470 "the girl who fixed it up," "Pauline and the children," "very sound": Ibid.

471 "Although *The Fifth Column*": Brooks Atkinson, review of *The Fifth Column*, in *The New York Times*, March 7, 1940, 18.

471 "excellently acted": John Mason Brown, review of *The Fifth Column*, in the New York *Post*, March 7, 1940, 10.

471   "There is . . . a love story": Grenville Vernon, review of *The Fifth Column*, in *Commonweal*, March 22, 1940, 475–76.

472   "a little bit," "complete puzzle," "dreadful": EH, *The Fifth Column and Four Stories of the Spanish Civil War*, 5.

472   "Listen, you don't want," "I'm afraid," "is not like you," "You're unjust": Ibid., 42–44.

472   "She has the same": Ibid., 66.

472   "that's a commodity," "You're a perfectly vicious": Ibid., 83–84.

473   "a short man": Ibid., 34.

473   "in the nature of a small boy's": EW, *The Portable Edmund Wilson*, 411.

9

EH, 320–21, 323–24.
474   "I hope all is well": *HW*, 311–12.

"BOOK SELLING LIKE FROZEN DAIQUIRIS IN HELL"

1

EH, 338. EH to GHH, c. May 12, 1940; JFK.
476   "It was like royalty": *HW*, 323.
476   "something constructive": *EH*, 349.
476   "was just a coward": *FWTBT*, 339.

2

SL, 479, 484–85, 493, 501. EH, *The Fifth Column and Four Stories*, 140–51.
Plimpton, "Ernest Hemingway," 62.
477   "Really awful ones": EH to MP, February 7, 1939; *SL*, 479.
478   "I am really not": *HW*, 325.
479   "Life is quite complicated": EH to HR, July 26, 1939; *SL*, 493.
479   "knock-out punch": *HW*, 329.

3

Arnold, *High on the Wild with Hemingway*, 70, 71.
480   "What old Indian": *HW*, 331.
480   "Keep your eye": Ibid., 332.
480   "The Pig": *EH*, 345.
480   "Hemingstein's": Ibid., 344.
480   "very lonely time," "Virginia's version," "But she spread it": EH to Mrs. Paul Pfeiffer, December 12, 1939; *SL*, 499.
480   "This is the saddest": *SL*, 500.
481   EXTREMELY: Berg, *Max Perkins*, 377.

481   "I, the undersigned": *HW*, 338–39.
481   "with my body": Ibid., 382.
482   "if there are any angels": Matthews, *Angels Unawares*, 265.
482   "You can stand me up": *HW*, 343.

4

SL, 518. *EH*, 235, 309, 352, 355, 629. Gregory Hemingway, *Papa*, 64–65. *HW*, 344–45, 347–48.
482   "For Whom the Bell Tolls": EH to MP, April 21, 1940; *SL*, 504.
482   ALL KNOCKED OUT: Berg, *Max Perkins*, 378.
482   "It's almost unbearably": EH to MP, July 13, 1940; *SL*, 506.
483   "a blind sardine": *EH*, 350.

5

Hanneman, *Ernest Hemingway: A Comprehensive Bibliography*, 51–52. *EH*, 359, 383, 385, 630.
484   "Book selling": EH to HR, January 26, 1941; *SL*, 521.
485   "Complete love scenes": Robert Sherwood, review of *FWTBT*, in *Atlantic Monthly*, November 1940, front section.
485   "the finest and richest": Howard Mumford Jones, review of *FWTBT*, in *Saturday Review of Literature*, October 26, 1940, 5, 19.
485   "The big game hunter" et seq.: EW, review of *FWTBT*, in *New Republic*, October 28, 1940, 591–92.

6

SL, 513–14.
486   "soul of serenity": *EH*, 328.
486   "the golden brown," "cut short": *FWTBT*, 22.
487   "*Qué va*": Ibid., 67.
487   "I have thought about thy hair": Ibid., 345.
487   "I don't like": Ibid., 172.
487   "You could be brother and sister": Ibid., 67.
487–88   "Now I know": Ibid.
488   "Maria is my true love": Ibid., 381.
488   "I am thee": Ibid., 262.
488   "if thou should ever": Ibid., 263.
488n   "Is it there," "it is well known": Ibid., 206.
488   "delight of acceptance": Ibid., 342.
488   "My father was a republican," "My father was also": Ibid., 66.
488   "To avoid being tortured": Ibid.
488   "My father could not": Ibid., 67.
488   "Yes," "Then you and me": Ibid.
488   "either one of us" et seq.: Ibid., 170–71.

489   "Any one": Ibid., 338.
489   "So she goes": Ibid., 171.
490   "smashed a blow" et seq.: Ibid., 108–10.
490   "If that woman": Ibid., 134.
491   "completely integrated," "He could feel": Ibid., 471.

7

Thomas, *The Spanish Civil War*, 455. *EH*, 327, 356. Orwell, *Homage to Catalonia*, 3–4. Zwerdling, *Orwell*, 77–78.
491   "mutilated": Michael Gold, review of *FWTBT*, in *Sunday Worker*, December 8, 1940.
491   "his finest achievement": Alvah Bessie, review of *FWTBT*, in *New Masses*, November 5, 1940, 25–29.
491   "mutilated": Open letter to Ernest Hemingway, *Daily Worker*, November 20, 1940.
492   "Wearing black riding boots": *FWTBT*, 231.
492   "We do not believe": Ibid., 245.
493   "vindictive picture": Dwight Macdonald, review of *FWTBT*, in *Partisan Review*, January–February 1941, 24–28.
493   "Dolores made me vomit": *EH*, 347.
493   "Dolores brought": *FWTBT*, 357–58.
493   "His face": Ibid., 417.
494   *"Purifica"*: Ibid., 419.
494   "brilliant" et seq.: Lionel Trilling, "An American in Spain," *Partisan Review*, January–February 1941, 63–67.
494   "You could put": EH to Malcolm Cowley, October 11, 1949; *SL*, 681.
495   "My mind is in suspension": *FWTBT*, 245.
495   "something in him": Ibid., 77.
495   "that bunch of horse thieves": Ibid., 163.
495   "I have just come" et seq.: Ibid., 246–47.
495   "Oh . . . muck": Ibid., 369–70.
496   "There was no military": Crick, *George Orwell*, 214.

8

EH, 383.
496   "It's a fine novel": FSF, *The Letters of F. Scott Fitzgerald*, 312.

COMBINED OPERATIONS

1

Jack Hemingway, *Misadventures of a Fly Fisherman*, 94–95. *EH*, 355, 358, 365–66, 368. *SL*, 522. Gregory Hemingway, *Papa*, 74, 75, 76, 77, 95, 96. Gellhorn, *Travels With Myself and Another*, 23–24, 31–32.

498   "Much love": EH to Solita Solano, January 26, 1941; *SL*, 522.
499   "Cheer up": Gellhorn, *Travels With Myself and Another*, 23–24, 31–32.
500   "That's rifle shooting": *EH*, 368.
500   "Bum, have you ever been laid?" et seq.: Jack Hemingway, *Misadventures of a Fly Fisherman*, 94–95.
501   "I'll fix you": Gregory Hemingway, *Papa*, 75.
501   "we can't send you back": Ibid.
501   "telling wonderful stories": Ibid., 91–92.
502   "Okay, pal": Ibid., 95.

2

Fuentes, *Hemingway in Cuba*, 193. *EH*, 372–73, 374–75. *HW*, 385–86.
502   "playboy who hunted": Fuentes, *Hemingway in Cuba*, 191.
503   "we were able": Hotchner, *Papa Hemingway*, 10–11.
504   "shaming and silly life": *HW*, 385.
504   "I think people": Ibid., 386.

3

Gregory Hemingway, *Papa*, 25, 123, 124–25. *EH*, 389.
504   "I'm saying goodbye": Fuentes, *Hemingway in Cuba*, 22.
505   "She's from St. Louis": Ibid.
505   "we'll write books": *HW*, 384.
505   "so it is a national": Ibid., 388.
505   "I won't urge you": Ibid.
505   "You are real": Ibid., 390.
505   "He woke me": Ibid., 391–92.
506   "hideous and insane" et seq.: Ibid., 392.

4

506   "seemed to know": Shaw, *The Young Lions*, 382.
507   "Above the great, bushy": *HIW*, 94.
507   "I don't know you": Ibid., 95.
507   "This war may keep us apart": Ibid., 96.
508   "absolute guts": Meyers, *Hemingway*, 393.
508   "full of lovers": *HW*, 403.
508   "I'll be back": *HIW*, 99.
508   "I will": Ibid.
509   "ceaseless, crazy," "play-acting": *HW*, 398.

5

EH, 393–95, 403, 405, 415–17, 419–421. Raeburn, *Fame Became of Him*, 112–19. EH, *By-Line*, 340–55, 364–83. Leicester Hemingway, *My Brother*, 219–20.

Cowley, "Portrait of Mr. Papa," 88–89. Marshall, "How Papa Liberated Paris," 99. Prokosch, "Voices: A Memoir," 24–25.

509   "how we took": EH, *By-Line,* 340.
510   "this Hemingway guy": Van Dusen, "Hemingway's Longest Day," 55, 62.
510   "Look at Eaton Square" et seq.: Prokosch, "Voices: A Memoir," 24–25.
512   "We have a very jolly": EH to Mary Welsh, August 1 and 6, 1944; *SL,* 562.
513   "outraged fellow correspondents": Guerard, "Hemingway at Stanford," 92.
513   "knew more about": Rooney, "One Eye on the War, One Eye on Paris."
513   "buzz off," "guerrilla rabble," "took evasive," "I had a funny": EH, *By-Line,* 374, 378, 383.
513   "entered Paris with very first troops": EH to MP, October 15, 1944; *SL,* 574.
513   "I took cover": EH, *By-Line,* 381.
514   "Property of Ernest Hemingway": Marshall, "How Papa Liberated Paris," 99.
514   "Papa took": Capa, *Slightly Out of Focus,* 167–71.
514   "were active and fearless": *EH,* 411.

6

HIW, 116–17, 128–33. *EH,* 393, 427. Groth, *Studio Europe,* 204, 205–9, 214.
514n   "the best book": EH to Ivan Kashkin, August 19, 1935; *SL,* 420.
514n   "gigantic masterpiss": EH to MP, May 5, 1938; *SL,* 467.
514n   "How you can tell": EH to Bernard Berenson, January 24, 1953; *SL,* 802.
514   "Papa, there's a dame," "welcoming": *HIW,* 109.
515   "Could you be my Pickle?" et seq.: Ibid., 112–16.
516   "the finest and bravest": Charles T. Lanham obituary, *The New York Times,* July 22, 1978, 22.
516   "Go hang yourself": *EH,* 420.
517   "get his ass": Ibid., 427.
517   "Marlene used to wander": *HIW,* 128.
517   "serious spat": Ibid., 129.
517   "All evening . . . you insulted" et seq.: Ibid., 131.
518   "Pickle" et seq.: Ibid., 132.

7

EH, 428–29, 439, 441, 445, 642–43. *HIW,* 135, 142–43, 147. *HW,* 410–11, 414–16, 417.
519   "a band of his": *HW,* 411.
519   "We are honest": Ibid.
520   "Did they have": *HIW,* 143.
520   "Did you know": Ibid.
521   "I'll come along": *HW,* 415.
521   "Go away": Ibid., 416.
521   "He talked about it": Ibid.
521   "Don't be a bloody": *HIW,* 147.

522   "the sanity and order": Ibid.
522   "Though he had previously": *HW*, 417.
522   "Dearest Pickle," "Your loveing": EH to Mary Welsh, c. March 6, 1945;
      SL, 578.

HORRORS

1

EH, 447–48. *HIW*, 154.
525   "[Hemingway's] capacity": Meyers, *Hemingway*, 331.
525   "standing on hard-packed snow": Ross, *Reporting*, 188.
526   "wearing khaki pants" et seq.: Hotchner, *Papa Hemingway*, 6–9.
527   "regular Sunday hangover letter": EH to MP, c. February 4 or 11, 1940; *SL*,
      500.
527   "gallons of hard liquor": Sulzberger, *Long Row of Candles*, 612.
528   "This is bad": *HIW*, 166.
528   "Had one leg": EH to E. E. Dorman-O'Gowan [Dorman-Smith], c. July 27,
      1950; *SL*, 708.

2

Franks, "A New Attack on Alcoholism," 47–48, 50, 61–65, 69. Meyers,
Hemingway, 426, 505, 508, 512, 539–40. Charles E. Lyght, M.D., ed., *The Merck
Manual of Diagnosis and Therapy*, Rahway, N.J., 1970, passim. *EH*, 462–63.
Castillo-Puche, *Hemingway in Spain*, 36, 169.
528   "an elefant in the circus": *EH*, 486.
529   "I flunked all the tests": Hotchner, *Papa Hemingway*, 189.
529   "he was drunk": Meyers, *Hemingway*, 508.
529   "The protagonist . . . his poor, long-suffering": *EH*, 537.
529   "His liver was bad": Macdonald, *Against the American Grain*, 183.
530   "Sweated through all my clothes": EH to Wallace Meyer, December 5, 1955;
      SL, 851–52.
530   "might possibly": *EH*, 556.
531   "crut": Ibid., 471.

3

HIW, 136. *HW*, 422–23. *EH*, 475, 524.
532   "Miss Mary is durable": EH, *By-Line*, 473.
532   "progressively more insane": Meyers, *Hemingway*, 414.
532   "awoke cheerful": *HIW*, 136.
532   "Even my engagement ring?" et seq.: Ibid., 183–84.
533   "burnt the Beech": Ibid., 369.
533   "She has always wanted": Ibid., 369–70.

4

Meyers, *Hemingway,* 424, 440, 441. *HW,* 470.
533   "admired and admiring": *HIW,* 182.
534   "It is now one hour": Ibid., 249.
535   "rapier wit": Ivancich, *La Torre Bianca,* 207.
535   "Hemingstein," "A. Ivancich": Meyers, *Hemingway,* 443.
535n "The jacket drawings": Ibid., 445.
535   "Perhaps if Adriana": Ibid., 446.
536   "You must endear": *HIW,* 280.
536   "I will be brief": Ibid., 280–81.
537   "Look, daughter": Ivancich, *La Torre Bianca,* 324.

5

537   "finished": *EH,* 488.
537   "completely rewritten": EH to Charles Scribner, July 20, 1951; *SL,* 731.
537   "My chances": Ibid.
539   "[*Islands*] contains": Jonathan Yardley, "How Papa Grew," *New Republic,* October 10, 1970, 26.
539   "crippling limitation": Irving Howe, "Great Man Going Down," *Harper's,* October 1970, 120–25.
539   "his harsh obsessions": John Updike, "Papa's Sad Testament," *The New Statesman and Nation,* October 16, 1970, 489.
539   "but there is a quality": Stephen Donadio, "Hemingway," *Commentary,* November 1970, 93–99.
539   "the Father Brown story": Christopher Ricks, "At Sea with Ernest Hemingway," *New York Review of Books,* October 8, 1970, 17–19.

6

EH, 477, 540.
540   "there are no photographs": *The Garden of Eden* ms.; JFK.
540   "the happiness of the Garden": *EH,* 460.
540   "close to the end": Ibid., 540.
541   "worthless": EH, *The Garden of Eden,* 228.
542   "never forgiven her": *HW,* 409.
542   "Most people": EH, *The Garden of Eden,*, 6.
542   "going to be changed": Ibid., 12.
542   "It's for you": Ibid.
542   "That's the surprise": Ibid., 15.
542   "they're just my dowry" et seq.: Ibid., 17–18.
542   "I told the coiffeur": Ibid., 47–48.
543   "But shorter": Ibid., 83.
543   "Please just": Ibid., 84.
543   "her haircut": Ibid.

543 "a girl and a boy": Ibid., 200.
543 "Go and talk": Ibid., 155.
544 "Isn't it lucky": Ibid., 125.
544 "from an inner": Ibid., 191.
544 "it would ever cease": Ibid., 258.
544 "You aren't really": Ibid., 200.

"HOW DO YOU LIKE IT NOW, GENTLEMEN?"

1

Raeburn, *Fame Became of Him,* 130, 131.
545 "the time of his life": Raeburn, *Fame Became of Him,* 120–21.
545 "Death in the Gulf Stream": Ibid., 121.
545 "most startling": Ibid., 120.
545 "Bell Tolls" et seq.: Ibid., 121.
546 "you can plug the bell": EH, *By-Line,* 404.
546 "too damned much": EH to Thomas Bledsoe, December 9, 1951; *SL,* 744.
546 "OK": *EH,* 470.
547 "It was a very bad thing": EH to Thomas Bledsoe, December 9, 1951; *SL,* 744.
547 "The Life piece": EH to A. E. Hotchner, March 9, 1949; JFK.
547 "think of poor old Cowley": EH to Charles Fenton, January 12, 1951; *SL,* 719.

2

548 "His compliments": Ross, *Reporting,* 189.
548 "sympathetic piece": Ibid.
549 "Book too much": Ibid., 195.
549 "Let's not crowd": Ibid., 196.
549 "First thing we do": Ibid., 198.
549 "Guess they call": Ibid., 200.
549 "I can remember" et seq.: Ibid., 202–5.
550 "How do you like it" et seq.: Ibid., 209–11.
551 "I am a strange": Ibid., 209.

3

Raeburn, *Fame Became of Him,* 137.
552 "a certain number": Ross, *Reporting,* 190.
552 "grotesque": Macdonald, *Against the American Grain,* 172.
552 "one was left": Morton Dauwen Zabel, "A Good Day for Mr. Tolstoy," *The Nation,* September 9, 1950, 230.
552 "a serious artist": Joseph Warren Beach, "How Do You Like It Now, Gentlemen?", *Sewanee Review,* Spring 1951, 311.

552   "One of our present day": Thurber, *Selected Letters of James Thurber*, 87.
553   "Some people": Ross, *Reporting,* 190.
553   "she was not writing": EH to Thomas Bledsoe, December 9, 1951; *SL*, 744.
553   "It has strange revelations": ABT, *Staying on Alone*, 194.

4

554   "It was too dark": Berg, *Max Perkins*, 438.
554   "There does not seem": Ibid., 439.
554   "Hemingway is through": Ibid., 447.
555   "The theme": Northrop Frye, review of *ARIT*, in *Hudson Review*, Winter 1951, 611–12.
555   "Why am I always": *ARIT,* 65.
556   "This is my last": White, "Across the Street," 28.
556   "The most important": John O'Hara, review of *ARIT*, in *The New York Times Book Review*, September 10, 1950, 1, 30–31.
557   "Naturally": EH to Charles Scribner, September 9, 1950; *SL*, 713.
557   "on belonging": Chandler, *Selected Letters of Raymond Chandler*, 229.
557   "They have been smug": Evelyn Waugh, "The Case of Mr. Hemingway," *Commonweal,* November 3, 1950, 97–98.
558   "[Where] the hell": EH to Charles Scribner, September 9, 1950; *SL,* 712.
559   ". . . To me he is": EH to Charles Scribner, March 5, 1951; *SL,* 721.

5

EH, 237, 239. *HW,* 425–26, 462–63. William Walton to the author, October 18, 1985.
560   "write to the woman": EH to Charles Scribner, August 27, 1940; *SL*, 670.
560   "[Where] does that": Ibid., 671.
560   "It made me so happy": EH to GHH, September 17, 1949; *SL,* 675.
561   "Scribner's": Ibid.
561   "everything went to hell": *EH,* 493.

6

Gregory Hemingway, *Papa,* 25–27, 31–32. Patrick Hemingway to the author, July 21, 1986.
562   "defying Satan": EH to Lillian Ross, July 2, 1948; *SL,* 645.
562   "The wave of remembering": EH to Charles Scribner, October 2, 1951; *SL,* 737.
563   "It wasn't so bad": Gregory Hemingway, *Papa,* 27.
563   "Well, don't take any": Ibid.
563   "was as sickly": Meyers, *Hemingway,* 481.
563   "The tumor had become necrotic": Gregory Hemingway, *Papa,* 30.
564   "Remember that painting": Ibid., 34.

"THE COUNTRY IS BEAUTIFUL AROUND HERE"

1

SL, 518.

565 "I believe this is": Cyril Connolly, review of *OMATS,* in *London Sunday Times,* September 7, 1952, 5.

565 "It is a tale": Robert Gorham Davis, review of *OMATS,* in *The New York Times Book Review,* September 7, 1952, 1, 20.

565 "Mr. Hemingway is once again": Arthur Calder-Marshall, review of *OMATS,* in *The Listener,* September 18, 1952, 477.

565 "His best": William Faulkner, review of *OMATS,* in *Shenandoah,* Autumn 1952, 55.

565 "I confess": John W. Aldridge, review of *OMATS,* in *Virginia Quarterly Review,* Spring 1953, 311–20.

565 "The action of the novel": John W. Aldridge, "Two Poor Fish on One Line," *The New York Herald Tribune Book Week,* June 20, 1965, 16, 19.

566 "I fear both": *OMATS,* 17.

566 "he slept face down": Ibid., 122.

566 "a desire to continue": Delmore Schwartz, review of *OMATS,* in *Partisan Review,* November 1952, 702–3.

568 "as honest": EH to MP, c. October 12, 1940; *SL,* 518.

569 "the old man": *OMATS,* 9.

569 "many of the fishermen": Ibid., 11.

569 "the great Di Maggio": Ibid., 21.

2

EH, *By-Line,* 425–69. *EH,* 521.

570 "Oh, Ernest, don't give me": Meyers, *Hemingway,* 501.

570 "an evil-smelling": Ibid., 502.

571 "black and very beautiful": EH to Harvey Breit, January 3, 1954; *SL,* 826.

571 "completely impudent" et seq.: Ibid., 827.

571 "He loved Africa": Meyers, *Hemingway,* 502.

571 "who has my great": EH, *By-Line,* 437.

572 "leaping from crag": Ibid., 444.

572 "A bunch of bananas": Raeburn, *Fame Became of Him,* 146.

3

Raeburn, *Fame Became of Him,* 147. Hotchner, *Papa Hemingway,* 83. EH, "A Man of the World," 64–66. EH, "Get a Seeing-Eyed Dog," 66–68. Official Citation of the Nobel Committee and EH's statement to the Swedish Academy; JFK.

573 "which is something": EH to Harvey Breit, February 4, 1954; *SL,* 829.

573 "It's not legal": Meyers, *Hemingway,* 508.

573 "I don't mean physically": Hotchner, *Papa Hemingway,* 83.

574 "You know I know": EH to Charles T. Lanham, November 10, 1954; *SL*, 839.
574 "powerful, style-making mastery": *EH*, 528.
574 "Things may not be": Ibid.
575 "Writing, at its best": Ibid., 528–29.

4

EH, 548.

5

Meyers, *Hemingway*, 527–28. *HIW*, 461, 477. Castillo-Puche, *Hemingway in Spain*, 48, 66, 134, 191, 346, 347.
577 "an extra martini": *HIW*, 463.
577 "circus": Ibid., 473.
577 "Darling, you're so thin" et seq.: Ibid., 466.
578 "he were a stranger": Castillo-Puche, *Hemingway in Spain*, 66.
578 "couldn't keep himself": Ibid., 191.
578 "I'm sorry": *HIW*, 471.
578 "the dirty tables": Ibid.
579 "inaudible": Ibid., 475.
579 THANKS LETTERS: Ibid., 477.

6

Hotchner, *Papa Hemingway*, 236–42. *HIW*, 489, 490.
580 "sad mask," "delicacy," "grazing diffidence": Turnbull, "Perkins's Three Generals," 26.
580 "a rap called": Hotchner, *Papa Hemingway*, 238.
581 "I just can't": Ibid., 240.
581 "I'll tell you, Hotch": Ibid., 242.
582 "made me sick," "horrible," "ashamed": *HIW*, 490.
582 "I lead" et seq.: Hotchner, *Papa Hemingway*, 258.
582 "Glad to meet you" et seq.: *SSEH*, 133.

7

Fuentes, *Hemingway in Cuba*, 66. O'Connor, "Electroshock: Again!", 12–13, 18–22. *HIW*, 493–94, 495.
582 "Look, this is how" et seq.: Fuentes, *Hemingway in Cuba*, 68.
583 "It got so bad": Ibid., 63.
583 "worries": *HIW*, 493.
583 "They'll say": Ibid.
583 "portable Corona": Hotchner, *Papa Hemingway*, 139.

584   "the psychiatrist decided": *HIW*, 495.

585   "Working hard again": *EH*, 558.

585   "my usual long list": EH to L. H. Brague, Jr., February 6, 1961; *SL*, 916.

585   "If you are lucky enough": *AMF*, title page.

8

586   "a small diamond mine": Stanley Kauffmann, review of *AMF*, in *New Republic*, May 9, 1964, 17–18, 20–21, 23–24.

586   "in some ways": Frank Kermode, review of *AMF*, in *New York Review of Books*, June 11, 1964, 4–6.

586   "is the proof": Marvin Mudrick, review of *AMF*, in *Hudson Review*, Winter 1964–1965, 572–79.

586   "But for all": George Plimpton, review of *AMF*, in *New York Herald Tribune Book Week*, May 3, 1964, 1, 12–13.

586   "too stupid": *AMF*, 57.

586   "You probably banged": Ibid., 102.

586   "I'm tired": Ibid., 104.

587   ". . . and afterwards": Ibid.

587   "We never argued": Ibid., 107–8.

588   "You mean I am not": Ibid., 127.

588   "I remember" et seq.: Ibid., 202, 206.

589   "I wished I had died": Ibid., 210.

9

    HIW, 495, 503. Meyer, *Hemingway*, 561–63.

589   "My hopes all flat": John Milton, *Paradise Regained. The Minor Poems. Samson Agonistes*, New York, 1937, 568–69.

590   "He is immoveably": *HIW*, 498.

590   "entirely satisfactory": Ibid., 500.

591   "charmed and deceived": Ibid.

591   "The Mayo made": Meyers, *Hemingway*, 546.

591   "They're FBI" et seq.: *HIW*, 502.

592   "no one had a right": Meyers, *Hemingway*, 560.

593   "The country is beautiful": EH to Frederick G. Saviers, June 15, 1961; *SL*, 921.

BIBLIOGRAPHY

I. LIBRARY COLLECTIONS

Alderman Library, University of Virginia, Charlottesville: Ernest Hemingway letters to John Dos Passos and Katy Smith.

Beinecke Rare Book and Manuscript Library, Yale University, New Haven, Conn.: Ernest Hemingway letters to Grace Quinlan, Edmund Wilson, Ezra Pound, Gertrude Stein; typescript of original ending of "Big Two-Hearted River."

Bettmann Archive, New York City: illustrative documentation of the dress and hairstyles of little boys at the turn of the century.

Firestone Library, Princeton University, Princeton, N.J.: Ernest Hemingway letters to Sylvia Beach, Maxwell Perkins, Harold Loeb, F. Scott Fitzgerald, Henry Strater, Charles T. Lanham, Charles Scribner, et al.; carbon typescript of *The Torrents of Spring,* inscribed "To Scott and Zelda with love from Ernest"; archive of Scribners correspondence.

Harry Ransom Humanities Research Center, University of Texas, Austin: Ernest Hemingway letters to Adriana Ivancich, W. G. Rogers, et al.; Hemingway family correspondence; ms. of the original version of "The Snows of Kilimanjaro."

Hemingway Room, John F. Kennedy Library, Boston, Mass.: *the* great assembly of Ernest Hemingway correspondence, Ernest Hemingway manuscripts, Hemingway family correspondence, scrapbooks, and photographs.

Manuscript Division, Library of Congress, Washington, D.C.: Ernest Hemingway letters to Owen Wister and Archibald MacLeish.

McKeldin Library, University of Maryland, College Park: Ernest Hemingway letters to Arthur Mizener.

Oak Park Public Library, Oak Park, Ill.: documents relating to Oak Park's history.

Villa I Tatti, Florence, Italy: Ernest Hemingway letters to Bernard Berenson; Martha Gellhorn letters to Bernard Berenson.

II. NEWSPAPERS AND MAGAZINES

Atlantic Monthly
Chicago Daily News
Chicago Tribune
Collier's
Cooperative Commonwealth
Cosmopolitan
Esquire
Exile
Holiday
Ken
Life
Little Review
London Daily Express
Look
New Masses
New Republic
New York Times
PM
Poetry, A Magazine of Verse
Scribner's Magazine
This Quarter
Time
Toronto Daily Star
Toronto Star Weekly
Trapeze
True

III. BOOKS AND ARTICLES BY ERNEST HEMINGWAY

Across the River and Into the Trees. New York, 1950.
"Art of the Short Story, The." *Paris Review,* Spring 1981, 85–102.
By-Line: Ernest Hemingway. Selected Articles and Dispatches of Four Decades. Ed. William White. New York, 1967.
Dangerous Summer, The. Intro. by James Michener. New York, 1985.
Death in the Afternoon. New York, 1932.
Death in the Afternoon. New York, 1960.
88 Poems. Ed. Nicholas Gerogiannis. New York, 1979.
Ernest Hemingway: Cub Reporter. Ed. Matthew J. Bruccoli. Pittsburgh, 1970.
Ernest Hemingway: Selected Letters, 1917–1961. Ed. Carlos Baker. New York, 1981.
Ernest Hemingway's Apprenticeship. Ed. Matthew J. Bruccoli. Washington, D.C., 1971.
Farewell to Arms, A. New York, 1929.
Farewell to Arms, A. Intro. by Ford Madox Ford. New York, 1932.
Farewell to Arms, A. Intro. by Ernest Hemingway. New York, 1948.

Farewell to Arms, A. Intro. by Robert Penn Warren. New York, 1949.

Farewell to Arms, A. New York, 1969.

"Fascism is a Lie." *New Masses*, June 22, 1937, 4.

Fifth Column and the First Forty-Nine Stories, The. New York, 1938.

Fifth Column and Four Stories of the Spanish Civil War, The. New York, 1972.

For Whom the Bell Tolls. New York, 1940.

Garden of Eden, The. New York, 1986.

"Get a Seeing-Eyed Dog." *Atlantic Monthly*, November 1957, 66–68.

Green Hills of Africa. New York, 1935.

Green Hills of Africa. New York, 1954.

Hemingway. The Viking Portable Library. Ed. and intro. by Malcolm Cowley. New York, 1944.

Hemingway At Auction. Eds. Matthew J. Bruccoli and C. E. Frazer Clark, Jr. Detroit, 1973.

Hemingway Manuscripts, The. Eds. Philip Young and Charles W. Mann. University Park, Pa., 1969.

Hemingway Reader, The. Foreword and twelve Brief Prefaces by Charles Poore. New York, 1953.

"Hemingway Speaks to High School." *The Trapeze*, March 21, 1919, 1.

Hemingway: The Wild Years. Ed. and intro. by Gene Z. Hanrahan. New York, 1962.

"Homage to Ezra." *This Quarter*, May 1925, 221–25.

in our time. Paris, 1924.

In Our Time. New York, 1925.

In Our Time. Intro. by Edmund Wilson. New York, 1930.

Islands in the Stream. New York, 1970.

"Letter to a Young Man." *Mark Twain Journal*, Summer 1962, 19.

"Man of the World, A." *Atlantic Monthly*, November 1957, 64–66.

Men at War. Ed. and intro. by Ernest Hemingway. New York, 1942.

Men Without Women. New York, 1927.

"Mix War, Art and Dancing." Kansas City *Star*, April 21, 1918, 1.

Moveable Feast, A. New York, 1964.

Nick Adams Stories, The. Preface by Philip Young. New York, 1972.

Old Man and the Sea, The. New York, 1952.

Short Stories of Ernest Hemingway, The. New York, 1966.

Spanish Earth, The. Intro. by Jasper Wood. Cleveland, 1938.

Sun Also Rises, The. New York, 1926.

Three Stories & Ten Poems. Paris, 1923.

To Have and Have Not. New York, 1937.

Torrents of Spring, The. New York, 1926.

"Treachery in Aragon." *Ken*, June 30, 1938, 26.

"United We Fall Upon *Ken*." *Ken*, June 2, 1938, 38.

"Who Murdered the Vets?" *New Masses*, September 17, 1935, 9–10.

Winner Take Nothing. New York, 1933.

IV. BOOKS AND ARTICLES ABOUT ERNEST HEMING-WAY

Algren, Nelson. *Notes from a Sea Diary: Hemingway All the Way*. New York, 1965.

Arnold, Lloyd R. *High on the Wild with Hemingway*. Caldwell, Idaho, 1968.

Asselineau, Roger, ed. *The Literary Reputation of Hemingway in Europe*. New York, 1965.

Atkins, John. *The Art of Ernest Hemingway*. London, 1952.

Baker, Carlos. *Ernest Hemingway. A Life Story*. New York, 1969.

––––––. *Ernest Hemingway: Critiques of Four Major Novels*. New York, 1962.

––––––. *Hemingway: The Writer as Artist*. Princeton, 1972.

Barrett, Richmond. "Babes in the Bois." *Harper's*, May 1928, 724.

Beck, Warren. "The Shorter Happy Life of Mrs. Macomber." *Modern Fiction Studies*, November 1955, 28–37.

Benson, Jackson J. *Hemingway: The Writer's Art of Self-Defense*. Minneapolis, 1969.

Brasch, James D. *Hemingway's Library*. New York, 1981.

Brian, Denis. "The Importance of Knowing Ernest." *Esquire*, February 1972, 98–101, 164–66, 168–70.

Bruccoli, Matthew J. *Scott and Ernest*. New York, 1978.

Buckley, Peter. *Ernest*. New York, 1978.

Burgess, Anthony. *Ernest Hemingway and His World*. New York, 1978.

Castillo-Puche, José Luis. *Hemingway in Spain*. Garden City, N.Y., 1974.

Cecchin, Giovanni. "Peduzzi Prototype." *The Hemingway Review*, Spring 1985, 54.

Coffey, Raymond R. "They Still Remember 'Ernie.' " *Chicago Daily News,* April 29, 1969, 3–4.

Cohn, Louis H. *A Bibliography of the Works of Ernest Hemingway*. New York, 1973.

Cowley, Malcolm. "Hemingway's Wound—And Its Consequences for American Literature." *The Georgia Review*, Summer 1984, 223–39.

––––––. "A Portrait of Mr. Papa." *Life*, January 10, 1949, 86–101.

DeFalco, Joseph. *The Hero in Hemingway's Short Stories*. Pittsburgh, 1963.

Dietrich, Marlene. "The Most Fascinating Man I Know." *This Week*, February 13, 1955, 8–9.

Donaldson, Scott. *By Force of Will*. New York, 1977.

––––––. "Irony and Pity—Anatole France Got It Up." *Fitzgerald/Hemingway Annual*, Detroit, 1978, 31–34.

Eastman, Max. "Bull in the Afternoon." *New Republic,* June 7, 1933, 94–97.

Ehrenburg, Ilya. "Hemingway." *Soviet Review*, October 1962, 22–26.

Farrington, S. Kip, Jr. *Fishing with Hemingway and Glassell*. New York, 1971.

Fenton, Charles A. *The Apprenticeship of Ernest Hemingway*. New York, 1954.

Friedrich, Otto. "Ernest Hemingway: Joy Through Strength." *The American Scholar*, Autumn 1957, 470, 518–30.

Fuentes, Norberto. *Hemingway in Cuba*. Secaucus, N.J., 1984.

Gellhorn, Martha. *Travels With Myself and Another*. New York, 1978.

Gingrich, Arnold. "Coming to Terms with Scott and Ernest." *Esquire,* June 1983, 55.

Grebstein, Sheldon N. *Hemingway's Craft.* Carbondale, Ill., 1973.

Griffin, Peter. *Along With Youth.* New York, 1985.

Guerard, Albert J. "Hemingway at Stanford." *California Magazine,* September 1985.

Gurko, Leo. *Ernest Hemingway and the Pursuit of Heroism.* New York, 1968.

Hanneman, Audre. *Ernest Hemingway: A Comprehensive Bibliography.* Princeton, 1967.

————. *Supplement to Ernest Hemingway: A Comprehensive Bibliography.* Princeton, 1975.

Harrington, Mary. "They Call Him Papa." *New York Post Weekend Magazine,* December 28, 1946, 3.

Hemingway, Gregory H. *Papa.* Boston, 1976.

Hemingway, Jack. *Misadventures of a Fly Fisherman.* Dallas, 1986.

Hemingway, Leicester. *My Brother, Ernest Hemingway.* Cleveland and New York, 1962.

Hemingway, Mary Welsh. *How It Was.* New York, 1976.

Hinkle, James. "Note on Two-Timing at Zelli's." *The Hemingway Newsletter,* July 1982, 3–4.

————. "Re Query on Passage from *SAR*." *The Hemingway Newsletter,* January 1984, 4.

————. "What's Funny in *The Sun Also Rises.*" *The Hemingway Review,* Spring 1985, 31–41.

Hotchner, A. E. *Papa Hemingway.* New York, 1966.

Hovey, Richard B. *Hemingway: The Inward Terrain.* Seattle, 1968.

Hynan, Patrick, ed. "Hemingway—A Portrait in Sound," sides one and two. Canadian Broadcasting Company, 1970.

Ivancich, Adriana. *La Torre Bianca.* Milan, 1980.

Joost, Nicholas. *Ernest Hemingway and the Little Magazines.* Barre, Mass., 1968.

Josephs, Allen. "In Papa's Garden." *Boston Review,* June 1986, 20–21.

Kashkin, Ivan. "Ernest Hemingway: The Tragedy of Craftsmanship." *International Literature,* May 1935, 72–90.

Kert, Bernice. *The Hemingway Women.* New York, 1983.

Kiley, Jed. *Hemingway: An Old Friend Remembers.* New York, 1965.

Klimo, Vernon. *Hemingway and Jake.* New York, 1972.

Latham, Aaron. "A Farewell to Machismo." *New York Times Magazine,* October 16, 1977, 51–55, 80–82, 90–99.

Laurence, Frank M. *Hemingway and the Movies.* Jackson, Miss., 1981.

Lewis, Robert W. "Hemingway in Italy: Making It Up." *Journal of Modern Literature,* May 1982, 209–27.

————. *Hemingway on Love.* New York, 1973.

Lewis, Wyndham. "The Dumb Ox: A Study of Ernest Hemingway." *Life and Letters,* April 1934, 33–45.

McCaffery, John K. M., ed. *Ernest Hemingway: The Man and His Work.* New York, 1969.

McComas, Dix. "The Geography of Hemingway's 'Out of Season.' " *The Hemingway Review,* Spring 1984, 46–49.

Macdonald, Dwight. "Ernest Hemingway." *Encounter,* January 1962, 115, 118, 120–21.

McLendon, James. *Papa Hemingway in Key West.* Miami, Fla., 1972.

Mailer, Norman. *Advertisements for Myself.* New York, 1959.

———. "The Big Bite." *Esquire,* November 1962, 134.

———. "Punching Papa." *New York Review of Books,* August 1963, 13.

Mann, Charles W., ed. "Young Hemingway: A Panel." *Fitzgerald/Hemingway Annual,* 1972, 113–44.

Marshall, S. L. A. "How Papa Liberated Paris." *American Heritage,* April 1962, 5–7, 92–101.

Meyers, Jeffrey. *Hemingway. A Biography.* New York, 1985.

———, ed. *Hemingway. The Critical Heritage.* London, 1982.

Miller, Madelaine Hemingway. *Ernie.* New York, 1985.

Mills, Eva B. "Ernest Hemingway and Nathan Asch: An Ambivalent Relationship." *The Hemingway Review,* Spring 1983, 48–51.

Montgomery, Constance Cappel. *Hemingway in Michigan.* New York, 1966.

Nagel, James, ed. *Ernest Hemingway: The Writer in Context.* Madison, 1984.

Nahal, Chaman. *The Narrative Pattern in Ernest Hemingway's Fiction.* Rutherford, N.J., 1971.

Noble, Donald R., ed. *Hemingway: A Revaluation.* Troy, N.Y., 1983.

Oldsey, Bernard S., ed. *Ernest Hemingway. The Papers of a Writer.* New York, 1981.

———. *Hemingway's Hidden Craft.* University Park, Pa., 1979.

Parker, Dorothy. "The Artist's Reward." *The New Yorker,* November 30, 1929, 28–31.

Perkins, Max. "Hemingway." *Book-of-the-Month Club News,* October 1940.

Plimpton, George. "Ernest Hemingway. An Interview." *The Paris Review,* Spring 1958, 61–89.

Porter, Katherine Anne. "Paris: A Little Incident in the Rue de l'Odéon." *Ladies' Home Journal,* August 1964, 54–55.

Prokosch, Frederic. "Voices: A Memoir." *The New Criterion,* March 1983, 24–25.

Raeburn, John. *Fame Became of Him.* Bloomington, 1984.

Rama Rao, P. G. *Ernest Hemingway.* New Delhi, 1980.

Reynolds, Michael S., ed. *Critical Essays on Ernest Hemingway's "In Our Time."* Boston, 1983.

———. *Hemingway's First War.* Princeton, 1976.

———. *Hemingway's Reading. 1910–1940. An Inventory.* Princeton, 1981.

———. *The Young Hemingway.* Oxford, 1986.

Ross, Lillian. *Portrait of Hemingway.* New York, 1961.

Samuelson, Arnold. *With Hemingway.* New York, 1984.

Sanford, Marcelline Hemingway. *At the Hemingways.* Boston, 1962.

Sarason, Bertram D., ed. *Hemingway and "The Sun" Set.* Washington, D.C., 1972.

Schleden, Ina Mae, and Marion Rawls Herzog, eds. *Ernest Hemingway as Recalled by his High School Contemporaries.* Oak Park, Ill., 1973.

Schorer, Mark. "Ernest Hemingway," in Perry Miller, gen. ed., *Major Writers of America,* 2 vols. New York, 1962. II, 675–77, 679–82.

Seward, William W. *My Friend Ernest Hemingway*. South Brunswick, 1969.

Smith, Paul. "Hemingway's Early Manuscripts: The Theory and Practice of Omission." *Journal of Modern Literature*, June 1983, 268–88.

Sokoloff, Alice Hunt. *Hadley*. New York, 1973.

Stephens, Robert O. *Hemingway's Non-Fiction*. Chapel Hill, 1968.

Stone, John A. "Hemingway Sets the Style." *American Weekly*, September 8, 1946, 6–7.

Sutherland, Fraser. *The Style of Innocence*. Toronto, 1972.

Svoboda, Frederic Joseph. *Hemingway & "The Sun Also Rises."* Lawrence, Kan., 1983.

Tate, Allen. "Random Thoughts on the Twenties." *Minnesota Review*, Fall 1960, 46–56.

Turnbull, Andrew. "Perkins's Three Generals." *The New York Times Book Review*, July 16, 1967, 26.

Updike, John. "The Sinister Sex." *The New Yorker*, June 30, 1986, 85–88.

Van Dusen, William. "Hemingway's Longest Day." *True*, February 1963, 55, 62.

Wagner, Linda W. *Ernest Hemingway*. East Lansing, 1974.

Waldhorn, Arthur. *Ernest Hemingway*. New York, 1973.

———. *A Reader's Guide to Ernest Hemingway*. New York, 1975.

Watts, Emily S. *Ernest Hemingway and the Arts*. Urbana, Ill., 1971.

Weeks, Robert P., ed. *Hemingway: A Collection of Critical Essays*. Englewood Cliffs, N.J., 1962.

White, E. B. "Across the Street and Into the Grill." *The New Yorker*, October 14, 1950, 28–29.

Wilson, Edmund. "Ernest Hemingway: Bourdon Gauge of Morale." *Atlantic Monthly*, July 1939. Reprinted with an addendum in Edmund Wilson, *The Portable Edmund Wilson*, ed. Lewis M. Dabney. New York, 1983, 396–418.

———. "Letter to the Russians About Hemingway." *New Republic*, December 11, 1935, 135–36.

———. "Emergence of Ernest Hemingway," in *The Shores of Light. A Literary Chronicle of the Twenties and Thirties*. London, 1952, 115–24.

———. "The Sportsman's Tragedy." *New Republic*, December 14, 1927, 102–3.

Wylder, Delbert E. *Hemingway's Heroes*. Albuquerque, 1969.

Young, Philip. *Ernest Hemingway*. New York, 1952.

———. *Ernest Hemingway*. Minneapolis, 1959.

———. *Ernest Hemingway. A Reconsideration*. University Park, Pa., 1966.

V. OTHER BOOKS AND ARTICLES

Anon. *A Guide to Key West*. New York, 1941.

———. *Report of the Department of Military Affairs. January to July, 1918*. Rome, 1919.

Aldridge, John W. *After the Lost Generation: A Critical Study of the Writers of Two Wars*. New York, 1951.

Anderson, Margaret C. *My Thirty Years' War: An Autobiography*. New York, 1930.

Anderson, Sherwood. *Letters of Sherwood Anderson.* Eds. Howard Mumford Jones and Walter B. Rideout. Boston, 1953.

———. *Memoirs of Sherwood Anderson.* New York, 1942.

———. *The Portable Sherwood Anderson.* Ed. Horace Gregory. New York, 1977.

———. *Sherwood Anderson's Memoirs.* Ed. Ray Lewis White. Chapel Hill, 1969.

———. *Sherwood Anderson's Notebooks.* New York, 1926.

———. *Winesburg, Ohio. Text and Criticism.* Ed. John H. Ferres. New York, 1966.

Armstrong, Hamilton Fish. *Peace and Counterpeace: From Wilson to Hitler.* New York, 1971.

Asinof, Eliot. *Eight Men Out.* New York, 1963.

Bakewell, Charles M. *The Story of the American Red Cross in Italy.* New York, 1920.

Barea, Arturo. *The Forge.* London, 1941.

Barton, Bruce. *The Man Nobody Knows.* New York, 1940.

Barton, William E. *The Autobiography of William E. Barton.* Indianapolis, 1932.

———. *The Gospel of the Autumn Leaf.* Oak Park, Ill., 1900.

Beach, Sylvia. *Shakespeare and Company.* New York, 1959.

Berenson, Mary. *A Self Portrait from Her Letters & Diaries.* Eds. Barbara Strachey and Jayne Samuels. New York, 1983.

Berg, A. Scott. *Max Perkins. Editor of Genius.* New York, 1978.

Bessie, Alvah. *Men in Battle.* New York, 1939.

Bowen, Stella. *Drawn from Life.* London, 1940.

Bowers, Claude G. *My Mission to Spain.* New York, 1954.

Braden, Spruille. *Diplomats and Demagogues.* New Rochelle, 1971.

Bridgman, Richard. *The Colloquial Style in America.* New York, 1966.

Briggs, Ellis O. *Shots Heard Round the World: An Ambassador's Adventures on Four Continents.* New York, 1957.

Brinnin, John Malcolm. *The Third Rose: Gertrude Stein and Her World.* Boston, 1959.

Brooks, H. Allen. *The Prairie School. Frank Lloyd Wright and his Midwest Contemporaries.* Toronto, 1972.

Brooks, Van Wyck. *Days of the Phoenix.* New York, 1957.

Bruccoli, Matthew J. *Some Sort of Epic Grandeur.* New York, 1981.

Bryher. *The Heart to Artemis.* New York, 1962.

Callaghan, Morley. *That Summer in Paris.* New York, 1963.

Capa, Robert. *Slightly Out of Focus.* New York, 1947.

Carr, Virginia Spencer. *Dos Passos. A Life.* New York, 1984.

Carter, Paul A. *Another Part of the Twenties.* New York, 1977.

Chandler, Raymond. *The Selected Letters of Raymond Chandler.* Ed. Frank MacShane. New York, 1981.

Charters, James. *This Must Be the Place: Memoirs of Montparnasse.* London, 1934.

Cloete, Stuart. *The African Giant: The Story of a Journey.* Boston, 1955.

Cohen, David. *J. B. Watson. The Founder of Behaviourism.* London, 1979.

Collins, Larry, and Dominique Lapierre. *Is Paris Burning?* New York, 1965.

Cowley, Malcolm. *Exile's Return,* rev. ed. New York, 1956.

Cranston, J. Herbert. *Ink on My Fingers.* Toronto, 1953.

Crick, Bernard. *George Orwell: A Life.* Boston, 1980.

Crosby, Caresse. *The Passionate Years.* London, 1955.

Cunard, Nancy. *These Were the Hours.* Carbondale, Ill., 1969.

Dance, Stanley. *The World of Count Basie.* New York, 1980.

De Voto, Bernard. *The Literary Fallacy.* Boston, 1944.

Donnelly, Honoria, with Richard N. Billings. *Sara & Gerald.* New York, 1982.

Dos Passos, John. *The Best Times.* New York, 1966.

———. *The Fourteenth Chronicle. Letters and Diaries of John Dos Passos.* Ed. Townsend Ludington. Boston, 1973.

———. *Journeys Between the Wars.* New York, 1938.

Eastman, Max. "Bull in the Afternoon." *New Republic,* June 7, 1933, 94–97.

———. *Great Companions.* New York, 1959.

Eaton, Leonard K. *Two Chicago Architects and Their Clients.* Cambridge, Mass., 1969.

Edel, Leon. *Henry James: The Master. 1901–1916.* Philadelphia and New York, 1972.

———. *Henry James. The Untried Years.* Philadelphia and New York, 1953.

Eliot, T. S. *Collected Poems.* New York, 1936.

———. *Selected Essays. 1917–1932.* New York, 1932.

———. *The Waste Land.* Ed. and intro. by Valerie Eliot. New York, 1971.

Ellis, Havelock. *Erotic Symbolism.* Philadelphia, 1914.

Ellmann, Richard. *James Joyce.* New York, 1982.

Faber, Doris. *The Life of Lorena Hickok. E. R.'s Friend.* New York, 1980.

Farr, Finis. *Frank Lloyd Wright. A Biography.* New York, 1961.

Field, Andrew. *Djuna.* New York, 1983.

Fielding, Daphne. *Emerald and Nancy.* London, 1968.

Fieve, Ronald R. *Moodswing.* New York, 1975.

Fitch, Noel Riley. *Sylvia Beach and the Lost Generation.* New York, 1983.

Fitzgerald, F. Scott. *The Beautiful and Damned.* New York, 1922.

———. *The Correspondence of F. Scott Fitzgerald.* Eds. Matthew J. Bruccoli and Margaret Duggan. New York, 1980.

———. *The Crack-Up.* Ed. Edmund Wilson. New York, 1956.

———. *F. Scott Fitzgerald's Ledger. A Facsimile.* Washington, D.C., 1972.

———. *The Great Gatsby.* New York, 1953.

———. *The Letters of F. Scott Fitzgerald.* Ed. Andrew Turnbull. New York, 1963.

———. *The Notebooks of F. Scott Fitzgerald.* Ed. Matthew J. Bruccoli. New York, 1980.

——— and Max Perkins. *Dear Scott/Dear Max.* Eds. John Kuehl and Jackson R. Bryer. New York, 1971.

Fitzgerald, Zelda. *Save Me the Waltz.* Carbondale, Ill., 1967.

Flanner, Janet. *Paris Was Yesterday.* New York, 1972.

Ford, Ford Madox. *The Good Soldier.* New York, 1951.

———. *It Was the Nightingale.* New York, 1975.

Ford, Hugh, ed. *The Left Bank Revisited.* University Park, Pa., 1972.

———. *Published in Paris.* New York, 1975.

Fraiberg, Selma H. *The Magic Years*. New York, 1959.

Franklin, Sidney. *Bullfighter from Brooklyn*. New York, 1952.

Franks, Lucinda. "A New Attack on Alcoholism." *The New York Times Magazine,* October 20, 1985, 47–48, 50, 61–65, 69.

Frost, Robert. *The Selected Letters of Robert Frost*. Ed. Lawrance Thompson. New York, 1964.

Gilmer, Walker. *Horace Liveright: Publisher of the Twenties*. New York, 1970.

Gingrich, Arnold. *Nothing But People*. New York, 1971.

———. *The Well-Tempered Angler*. New York, 1965.

Glassco, John. *Memoirs of Montparnasse*. Toronto and New York, 1970.

Goodman, Paul. *Speaking and Language: Defense of Poetry*. New York, 1971.

Goodwin, Carole. *The Oak Park Strategy*. Chicago, 1979.

Gorman, Herbert. "Ford Madox Ford—A Portrait in Impressions." *The Bookman,* March 1928, 56.

Graham, Sheilah. *The Garden of Allah*. New York, 1970.

Groth, John. *Studio Europe*. New York, 1945.

Hapgood, Hutchins. *A Victorian in the Modern World*. New York, 1939.

Harkness, Ross. *J. E. Atkinson of "The Star."* Toronto, 1963.

Harrison, Gilbert A. *The Enthusiast. A Life of Thornton Wilder*. New Haven and New York, 1983.

Hart, Henry, ed. *The Writer in a Changing World*. New York, 1937.

Hasbrouck, Wilbert R., and Paul E. Sprague. *A Survey of Historic Architecture of the Village of Oak Park*. Oak Park, Ill., 1974.

Hellman, Lillian. *An Unfinished Woman*. Boston, 1969.

Hemingway, Leicester. *The Sound of the Trumpet*. New York, 1953.

Herbst, Josephine. "The Starched Blue Sky of Spain." *Noble Savage,* February 1960, 76–117.

Higham, Charles. *Marlene*. New York, 1977.

Hoopes, James. *Van Wyck Brooks*. Amherst, 1977.

Horowitz, Helen Lefkowitz. *Culture & the City*. Lexington, Ky., 1976.

Howe, Irving. *Sherwood Anderson*. New York, 1951.

———. *A World More Attractive*. New York, 1963.

Huddleston, Sisley. *Back to Montparnasse*. Philadelphia, 1931.

Hulme, Kathryn. *Undiscovered Country: A Spiritual Adventure*. Boston, 1966.

Ivens, Joris. *Mémoire d'un regard*. Paris, 1982.

James, Henry. *The Ambassadors*. New York, 1969.

———. *Notes of a Son and Brother*. New York, 1914.

Johnson, Paul. *Modern Times*. New York, 1983.

Josephson, Matthew. *Life Among the Surrealists*. New York, 1967.

Keats, John. *You Might As Well Live*. New York, 1970.

Kinney, Arthur F. *Dorothy Parker*. Boston, 1978.

Laney, Al. *Paris Herald*. New York, 1947.

Larkin, Oliver W. *Art and Life in America*. New York, 1949.

Lash, Joseph P. *Eleanor and Franklin*. New York, 1971.

Leuchtenburg, William E. *The Perils of Prosperity*. Chicago, 1958.

Levant, Oscar. *The Memoirs of an American*. New York, 1965.

Levin, Harry. *Contexts of Criticism*. Cambridge, Mass., 1957.

Le Vot, André. *F. Scott Fitzgerald*. Garden City, N.Y., 1983.

Lewis, Wyndham. *Time and Western Man*. Boston, 1957.

Loeb, Harold. *The Way It Was*. New York, 1959.

Ludington, Townsend. *John Dos Passos. A Twentieth Century Odyssey*. New York, 1980.

MacAgy, Douglas. "Gerald Murphy: 'New Realist' of the Twenties." *Art in America,* April 1963, 3–4.

McAlmon, Robert. *Being Geniuses Together*. Revised by Kay Boyle. Garden City, N.Y., 1968.

————. *McAlmon and the Lost Generation*. Ed. Robert E. Knoll. Lincoln, 1962.

Macdonald, Dwight. *Against the American Grain*. New York, 1962.

MacLeish, Archibald. *The Letters of Archibald MacLeish*. Ed. R. H. Winnick. Boston, 1983.

————. *Riders on the Earth: Essays and Recollections*. Boston, 1978.

MacShane, Frank. *The Life and Work of Ford Madox Ford*. London, 1965.

Madariaga, Salvador de. *Spain: A Modern History*. London, 1961.

Markham, Beryl. *West With the Night*. San Francisco, 1983.

Matthews, Herbert. *Two Wars and More to Come*. New York, 1938.

————. *A World in Revolution*. New York, 1971.

Matthews, T. S. *Angels Unawares. Twentieth-Century Portraits*. New York, 1985.

Mayfield, Sara. *Exiles from Paradise*. New York, 1971.

Mellow, James R. *Charmed Circle. Gertrude Stein & Company*. New York, 1982.

————. *Invented Lives*. Boston, 1984.

Mencken, H. L. *The Young Mencken*. Ed. Carl Bode. New York, 1973.

Milford, Nancy. *Zelda*. New York, 1971.

Miller, Perry. *Jonathan Edwards*. New York, 1949.

Morris, Edmund. *The Rise of Theodore Roosevelt*. New York, 1979.

Niebuhr, H. Richard. *The Kingdom of God in America*. New York, 1937.

North, Joseph. *No Men Are Strangers*. New York, 1958.

O'Connor, Eileen. "Electroshock Again!" *The Washington Post Magazine,* December 1, 1985, 12–13, 18–22.

O'Faolain, Sean. *The Vanishing Hero: Studies in the Novelists of the Twenties*. Boston, 1957.

O'Hara, John. *Sweet and Sour*. New York, 1954.

Orwell, George. *Homage to Catalonia*. New York, 1980.

Ovesey, Lionel. *Homosexuality and Pseudohomosexuality*. New York, 1969.

Poli, Bernard J. *Ford Madox Ford and the "Transatlantic Review."* Syracuse, 1967.

Porges, Irwin. *Edgar Rice Burroughs*. Provo, Utah, 1975.

Pound, Ezra. *Gaudier-Brzeska*. London, 1916.

————. *The Letters of Ezra Pound*. New York, 1950.

————. *Selected Poems*. New York, 1949.

Power, Arthur. *Conversations with James Joyce*. Dublin, 1974.

Putnam, Samuel. *Paris Was Our Mistress*. New York, 1947.

Rascoe, Burton. *We Were Interrupted*. Garden City, N.Y., 1947.

Ray, Man. *Self Portrait*. Boston, 1963.

Regler, Gustav. *The Owl of Minerva*. London, 1959.

Rochester, Stuart I. *American Liberal Disillusionment in the Wake of World War I*. University Park, Pa., 1977.

Rooney, Andy. "One Eye on the War, One Eye on Paris." *Overseas Press Bulletin,* August 1964.

Ross, Lillian. *Reporting.* New York, 1969.

St. John, Robert. *This Was My World.* Garden City, N.Y., 1953.

Sevareid, Eric. *This Is Eric Sevareid.* New York, 1964.

Shaw, Irwin. *The Young Lions.* New York, 1948.

Sheean, Vincent. *Not Peace But a Sword.* New York, 1939.

Simon, Linda. *The Biography of Alice B. Toklas.* New York, 1977.

Slocombe, George. *The Tumult and the Shouting.* London, 1936.

Smith, Denis Mack. *Mussolini.* New York, 1982.

Smoller, Sanford J. *Adrift Among Geniuses.* University Park, Pa., 1974.

Spender, Stephen. *World Within World.* New York, 1951.

Sprague, Paul E. *Guide to Frank Lloyd Wright and the Prairie School of Architecture in Oak Park.* Foreword by H. Allen Brooks. Oak Park, Ill., 1979.

Stearns, Harold E. *The Street I Know.* New York, 1935.

Steele, Elizabeth. *Hugh Walpole.* New York, 1972.

Steffens, Lincoln. *The Autobiography of Lincoln Steffens.* New York, 1931.

————. *The Letters of Lincoln Steffens.* Eds. Ella Winter and Granville Hicks. 2 vols. New York, 1938.

Stein, Gertrude. *The Autobiography of Alice B. Toklas.* New York, 1933.

————. *The Flowers of Friendship: Letters Written to Gertrude Stein.* Ed. Donald C. Gallup. New York, 1953.

————. *Everybody's Autobiography.* New York, 1937.

————. *Selected Writings of Gertrude Stein.* Ed. Carl Van Vechten. New York, 1946.

Stevens, Wallace. *Letters.* Ed. Holly Stevens. London, 1966.

Stevenson, Elizabeth. *Babbitts and Bohemians.* New York, 1967.

Stewart, Donald Ogden. *By a Stroke of Luck!* New York, 1975.

Stock, Noel. *The Life of Ezra Pound.* New York, 1970.

Sulzberger, C. L. *Long Row of Candles.* New York, 1969.

Sutton, William A. *The Road to Winesburg.* Metuchen, N.J., 1972.

Swanberg, W. A. *Dreiser.* New York, 1961.

Thomas, Hugh. *The Spanish Civil War.* New York, 1961.

Thurber, James. *The Selected Letters of James Thurber.* Eds. Helen Thurber and Edward Weeks. Boston, 1981.

Toklas, Alice B. *Staying on Alone. Letters of Alice B. Toklas.* Ed. Edward Burns. New York, 1973.

Tomkins, Calvin. *Living Well is the Best Revenge.* New York, 1982.

Torrey, E. Fuller. *The Roots of Treason.* New York, 1984.

Toy, Crawford Howell. "Ecclesiastes," in *The Encyclopaedia Britannica,* eleventh ed. New York, 1910.

Turnbull, Andrew. *Scott Fitzgerald.* New York, 1962.

Walpole, Hugh. *The Dark Forest.* New York, 1916.

————. *Fortitude.* London, 1913.

Welles, Orson. "A Trip to Quixoteland." *Cahiers du Cinéma,* November 1966, 42.

Wells, G. P. *H. G. Wells in Love.* New York, 1984.

Wescott, Glenway. "A Sentimental Contribution." *Hound & Horn,* April-June 1934, 523–34.

Wickes, George. *The Amazon of Letters*. New York, 1976.

————. *Americans in Paris*. New York, 1969.

Wiebe, Robert. *The Search for Order, 1877–1920*. New York, 1960.

Williams, W. H. A. *H. L. Mencken*. Boston, 1977.

Williams, William Carlos. *The Autobiography of William Carlos Williams*. New York, 1951.

Wilson, Edmund. *The Shores of Light*. London, 1952.

————. *The Thirties*. Ed. Leon Edel. New York, 1980.

Windhorn, Stan, and Wright Langley. *Yesterday's Key West*. Miami, Fla., 1973.

Wiser, William. *The Crazy Years*. New York, 1983.

Wohl, Richard. *The Generation of 1914*. Cambridge, Mass., 1979.

Wolfe, Thomas. *You Can't Go Home Again*. New York, 1940.

Yardley, Jonathan. *Ring*. New York, 1977.

Zwerdling, Alex. *Orwell and the Left*. New Haven, 1974.

INDEX

Kenneth S. Lynn is Arthur O. Lovejoy Professor of History at the Johns Hopkins University and the author of numerous books and articles on American history and literature, including *Mark Twain and Southwestern Humor* and *William Dean Howells: An American Life*. A native of Cleveland, Ohio, he did both his undergraduate and graduate work at Harvard and was for some years a member of the Harvard English Department and chairman of the university's graduate program in American Civilization. He lives with his wife in Washington, D.C., and is the father of three children.

PICTURE CREDITS